ALLIES

OTHER BOOKS BY RICHARD J. BARNET

RICHARD J. BARNET

ALLIES

America · Europe · Japan
Since the War

JONATHAN CAPE
THIRTY BEDFORD SQUARE · LONDON

First published in Great Britain 1984

Jonathan Cape Ltd, 30 Bedford Square, London WC1

British Library Cataloguing in Publication Data

Barnet, Richard J.
Allies: America, Europe and Japan since the war.
1. World politics—1945–
I. Title
327'.09171'3   D843

ISBN 0-224-02127-3

*Originally published in the United States of America in 1983
by Simon and Schuster, New York, New York*

PRINTED IN THE UNITED STATES OF AMERICA

ACKNOWLEDGMENTS

I am indebted to many people for assistance in the preparation of this book. Peter Kornbluh was a brilliant research assistant, and Carol Benke, Susan Coyle, and Marian Myszkowski worked devotedly on the manuscript at different stages. The following were generous with information, advice, or criticism: Ulrich Albrecht, Janice Alderman, Glenn C. Alex, William Arkin, Egon Bahr, Arnulf Baring, Ann Barnet, Julie Barnet, Robert Barnett, C. Fred Bergsten, Norman Birnbaum, Wilhelm Bittorf, Philip Brenner, Margaret Brooks, Zbigniew Brzezinski, David Calleo, Jonathan Dean, Dieter Dettke, Klaas G. De Vries, Marion Dönhoff, Ariel Dorfman, Hans Magnus Enzensberger, Elizabeth Eudey, Jens Fischer, Raoul Fontanez, Wilhelm Grewe, Fred Halliday, Hermann Hatzfeldt, Denis Healey, Seymour Hersh, Mark Hertsgaard, Martin J. Hillenbrand, Christopher Hitchens, Diana Johnstone, Mary Kaldor, Gordon Kingsley, Gabriel Kolko, Walter Lafeber, Saul Landau, David Leech, Klaus Liedtke, Andrew Mack, Michael MccGwire, Michael Moffitt, Albrecht Müller, David Owen, Glenn Oztemel, Christian Potthoff-Sewing, Gwen Prins, Karl Pütz, Marcus Raskin, Rustum Roy, Hiroharu Seki, William Shawcross, Theo Sommer, Ronald Steel, Walter Stüzle, James Sutterlin, Michele A. Ward, Joseph Wargo, Paul Warnke, Steven Warnke, David Watts, Roger Wilkins, Uwe Zimmer.

William Shawn encouraged me from the beginning, as did my editor Alice Mayhew. Without the support of my colleagues at the Institute for Policy Studies and especially its director Robert Borosage, this book could not have been completed.

FOR FRIENDS AND COLLEAGUES
OF TWENTY YEARS
AT THE INSTITUTE FOR POLICY STUDIES

CONTENTS

10   CONTENTS

PREFACE

This book is the story of a small circle of politicians, diplomats, industrialists, bankers, and generals on three continents who created and shaped the postwar world by building an alliance of North America, Europe, and Japan. This association of industrialized capitalist nations which has already endured longer than the Holy Alliance of the last century, has been the vehicle by which the defeated nations of World War II, Germany and Japan, were transformed from America's enemies into protectorates and ultimately into formidable commercial rivals. The web of political, economic, and cultural relationships which the United States took the lead in creating at the end of World War II, surely one of the most ingenious political inventions of our century, has over two generations not only produced dramatic changes in the relationships of three continents, but has also exerted strong influence in the domestic life of every member country.

The stated purpose of the alliance is the security of its members and while the relationship has served a variety of other functions as well, it rests on a military arrangement. The North Atlantic Treaty Organization (NATO) has been organized as a multinational fighting force permanently mobilized for a war beyond experience and imagination, a war few politicians have thought was coming and fewer have believed that their countries could survive. It is commonly asserted that had the United States *not* organized the recovery of Europe, had West Germany *not* been integrated into the West, had rearmament *not* occurred, World War III would have already happened. But history cannot be replayed. All one can say is that in the years since the birth of NATO and the conclusion of the Japanese Peace Treaty neither a nuclear nor conventional war has occurred on the European continent (aside from brief bloody repression in the eastern half), and Japan has been the most pacific of the industrialized nations. Following in the wake of two terrible world wars triggered in Europe, this is an extraordinary achievement, especially when one considers that beyond the territories of the Allies more than twenty-five million people have died in violent conflicts since 1945.

The history of the postwar transformation of the industrial world begins in rubble. Never before had political dreamers had such a chance to create a global order as the American president seemingly had at the end of World War II. Unlike the other belligerents, the United States had escaped devastation. The collapse of the old empires of the victorious Allies, Britain, France, and Holland, the sudden death of Hitler's upstart order and the eerie conquest of Japan with two atomic bombs, had left America richer than ever and supreme among nations. The new president, a Missouri politician of hitherto modest accomplishments, and the lawyers, bankers, and generals who advised him, proceeded to make the key decisions to put into place the political, economic, and military structures that have defined the postwar world. For the first time in more than a thousand years hegemonic power on the Continent of Europe (except for a substantial eastern slice taken by the Soviet Union) passed into the hands of a non-European nation. The successor to Napoleon's France, Victorian England, and Hitler's Germany was Truman's America. But America's moment of global supremacy turned out to be puzzlingly brief. Even as the alliance that symbolized American might grew, the extraordinary power of the United States was slipping away.

The waning of Pax Americana is traceable as much to the actions and policies of America's friends and allies as to its adversaries. Though number one among nations, as her presidents liked to proclaim, the United States always had to accommodate its protectorates. Even as American officials held the power of life and death in occupied Germany and Japan, Konrad Adenauer and Shigeru Yoshida, two acerbic septuagenarians, so mastered the diplomacy of weakness that they were able to create the conditions for their nations' spectacular recovery. The leaders of the United States seemingly held all the cards, but they could not always get their way. More often, as we shall see, America found her influence diminished because her leaders, unaware of the surprises lurking in their most beguiling dreams, had their wishes granted.

Over the four decades since the United States struck its original bargain with Europe and Japan, the world capitalist order has been transformed. The political, military, economic, cultural, and ideological climate of today bears little resemblance to the period of the Berlin Blockade and the Korean War when the alliance was forged. Trade wars within the aging alliance are growing more intense. American, European, and Japanese outlooks on a variety of world problems are increasingly diverging. The common defense is becoming more problematical. Domestic consensus for the alliance in the member countries is eroding. Twilight is descending on the familiar postwar world. This book is a history of how that world was created and how it is coming apart.

PART I

CREATION

ONE

RITES OF PASSAGE:

Herr Adenauer Disarms the Conquerors

1

Stiff as ever, the old man with the craggy face, looking more like an ancient Apache warrior than a German politician, gazed at the row upon row of white crosses and sobbed. Nineteen times the sound of guns boomed across the gentle slope. The U.S Army band struck up the "Deutschlandlied," and the first chancellor of the Federal Republic of Germany stepped forward, tears in his eyes, to place a wreath on the grave of an American unknown soldier who had died fighting Germany. For any visiting dignitary the ceremony at Arlington National Cemetery is a special honor, but for Konrad Adenauer in early April 1953 it was a rite of passage. "The turning point in history," he called it and "the greatest moment" in a very long life.

Eight years earlier Hitler's Reich had collapsed. Eisenhower, the conqueror of Germany, became the occupier, and one of his first acts was to ban the swaggering anthem with the famous Haydn tune; for years thereafter the song the Americans remembered from old war movies as "Deutschland über Alles" was heard only at clandestine neo-Nazi gatherings. Even Adenauer himself, who once ordered it played as an act of defiance, had been publicly rebuked by occupation authorities for his "bad taste." But now the conqueror of Germany was in the White House and the chancellor was his honored guest.

For Adenauer the long journey to Arlington began in Cologne. He outlived Adolf Hitler by more than twenty years, but he was born a dozen years before. Like *Der Führer*, he was the son of a minor official in a provincial city far from the center of power in Bismarck's Prussian Reich. The family were devout Rhineland Catholics, and the captivating force in Konrad's personal and political life was Catholicism. As a young lawyer he joined the Zentrum, a party

15

dedicated to protecting the rights and privileges of Roman Catholics against the Protestant Prussians. That was no small mission; in Bismarck's time it was not uncommon to imprison bishops. "The Zentrum had no parallel in any other European country," A. J. P. Taylor notes in his history of Germany. "It was prepared to be German or anti-German; liberal or anti-liberal; free trade or protectionist; pacific or bellicose; a party of expediency as unscrupulous as Bismarck himself." Thanks to the support of the Zentrum, Adenauer became Oberbürgermeister (lord mayor) of Cologne in 1917 and served continuously until the spring of 1933, when Hitler assumed power.

Adenauer's sixteen-year service in Cologne was marked at each end by political violence. As the First World War ended, the German fleet at Kiel mutinied and sparked an insurrection which spilled into the Rhineland. The revolutionary brigades of the Soldiers and Sailors' Council took over Cologne City Hall and demanded the ouster of the conservative Oberbürgermeister. The Socialists who assumed power in the city after the Armistice, fearing the revolutionaries more than the right-wing Catholics, saved Adenauer's job for fifteen years.

On February 17, 1933, Hitler paid his first visit to Cologne as chancellor. Adenauer had ordered all swastikas removed from public property and sent an underling to meet the Reichschancellor's plane. Furious, Hitler jumped into his car and sped off. Less than a month later Adenauer learned that Gestapo thugs were coming the next morning to throw him from his office window, and he slipped out of Cologne before dawn. As he fled, Adenauer, now fifty-seven, took the key to the city hall with him. All through the nightmare years he was determined to return.

After three years of living as a refugee inside Germany, some of Adenauer's banking friends came to his aid and persuaded the Nazi regime to give the former Oberbürgermeister a pension. Returning to the Rhineland in 1936, he spent most of the Hitler period in discreet retirement, building a villa on the Rhine, tending roses, and collecting clocks. He refused to participate in the July 20 plot against Hitler, but he was taken to a concentration camp anyway. The commandant pleaded with Adenauer not to commit suicide because it would reflect badly on the administration of the camp. "Your life is finished anyway." A few months before the end of the war Adenauer, then nearing seventy, managed to escape.

One day in mid-March 1945, a jeep drew up to Adenauer's villa in the Zennisweg in Honnef and two American officers jumped out. "We wish to know, sir, whether you are willing to take over the administration of Cologne. If so we should propose to appoint you Oberbürgermeister with the full approval of the Allied Military Command." Adenauer's conspicuous anti-Nazism, his persecution—only by feigning a heart seizure while in the hands of the Gestapo did he escape being sent to Buchenwald—and his long experience made him number one on the "White List," the select band of untainted Germans urgently needed to carry out the orders of the occupation.

A quarter hour later Konrad Adenauer was on his way back to his old city. The city hall was rubble, as indeed were more than half of all public buildings and private houses. Of Cologne's 750,000 inhabitants, about 32,000 were to be found, and most of these were in hiding in air raid shelters amidst the wreckage. Only 300 houses in the whole city were undamaged. The sewage, gas, and water mains had been severed, and the danger of epidemic mounted as the shell-shocked citizens crept back. Adenauer sent city buses to Buchenwald, Dachau, and Theresienstadt to pick up survivors and bring them home. As he wandered through the rubble he came upon the old Gestapo office and helped himself to a bronze candlestick which he took home "as a constant reminder of all that happened."

2

For the army engineer it was the biggest project of his career. The great-grandnephew of Henry Clay and the son of a three-term senator from Georgia, Lucius Clay was no stranger to politics. Moving easily in Georgia society, he was hardly the typical peacetime West Pointer. As a schoolboy he had served as a page in the Senate. As a young man he had steeped himself in reconstruction lore. Years later he would say that he wanted to bring to Germany the victor's peace without malice Lincoln had wanted for the South.

But the task he had been given was staggering. To be chief of Military Government for a fragment of Hitler's Reich and at the same time to be a negotiator for the future of all of Germany with three wartime Allies, each with its own agenda, would have been a challenge in itself. But to make matters worse, among Clay's superiors in Washington there was from the first a profound ambivalence about Germany's fate.

Clay began his assignment completely unaware of the secret policy directive for Germany then being prepared in Washington. JCS 1067, which was approved by President Harry Truman six days after Germany surrendered, called in Clay's words for a "Carthaginian peace." It was a set of broad guidelines for implementing the Morgenthau Plan, the ideas of Franklin Roosevelt's secretary of the treasury, Henry Morgenthau, Jr., for reducing Germany to a "pastoral" state to keep her from making war a third time. JCS 1067 "specifically prohibited us from taking any steps to rehabilitate or maintain the German economy except to maximize agricultural production," Clay wrote in his memoirs. "The German economy was to be controlled only to the extent necessary to meet the needs of the occupation forces or to produce the goods which might prevent disease and unrest, which might endanger the occupying forces." The only guidance he received from Franklin Roosevelt when he called on the president just before taking up his duties was that he ought to do something about "developing a more inquisitive mind in German youth." (FDR had gone to school in Germany and thought the Germans "arrogant and provincial.") Perhaps, the president added, a European version of the TVA

[Tennessee Valley Authority] could solve Europe's need for power and encourage international cooperation. Twelve days later the president was dead.

For four years Clay's top State Department adviser in running occupied Germany was Robert Murphy, who in 1940 had been plucked from the obscurity of a conventional diplomatic career to become FDR's secret agent in North Africa. For him JCS 1067 presented "overwhelming difficulties," in no small measure because it forbade "any personal relations with the people we had defeated." Dwight D. Eisenhower spent his brief time as military governor successfully avoiding any contact with the natives. When Harry Truman came to Potsdam in July 1945, he showed no interest in meeting any Germans. Jim Crow toilets for German employees in the Military Government office buildings were mandatory. Years later when the housing compound at the U.S. embassy at Bad Godesberg was dedicated, the architect pointed out its most impressive feature: Diplomats could shop and do their laundry in the embassy complex without ever having to come into contact with a single German.

JCS 1067 was a schizophrenic document. It asked the conquering bureaucrats to do irreconcilable things: restore a stable economy to stave off starvation, disease, and social unrest, and dismantle German industry all at the same time; get the utilities, railroads, and factories working but hire no one with a Nazi past; stamp out inflation but impose no financial controls. For five months the existence of the directive was top secret. By October when it was published it became clear that the contradictory policies Lucius Clay had been pursuing since V-E Day were more than the product of random confusion. The proponents of two quite different priorities for dealing with Germany in Washington —one favoring punishment and the other recovery—had masked their differences in bureaucratic prose so vague and so bland that the brisk but courtly engineer from Marietta, Georgia, and his assistants from Wall Street, William H. Draper, Jr., and Lewis H. Douglas, had considerable room to improvise.

By the time the victors gathered at Yalta in February 1945, the long-term U.S. objective for Germany had been agreed upon. A "reformed, peaceful, and economically non-aggressive Germany" would eventually be integrated "into a liberal system of world trade." But first Germany would have to be purged, its cartels broken, its Nazis punished, and its youth reeducated for democracy. The U.S. military governor General Lucius Clay had five thousand administrators to do the job. (The British had five times the number to run their more populous but geographically somewhat smaller zone.)

No one writing directives in Washington could have imagined the hell that was Hitler's legacy. The advancing Allied armies had rounded up 6.5 million displaced persons, most of whom had been brought into Germany in cattle cars to do forced labor. The round-the-clock bombing by U.S. and British Air Forces had destroyed between 30 and 40 percent of all factories, but in the American zone the level of destruction was worse. Only about 10 percent of the 12,000 factories in the area were even in limited production at the end of the war. Fifty percent of the locomotives and 30 percent of the freight cars were destroyed along with 2341 railway bridges. (The rail system had been transporting 75 percent of domestic goods.) What the Allies had inadvertently spared, Hitler himself sought to destroy. "If the war is lost," Hitler told Albert Speer, his minister for armaments and war production, as the final days approached, "the nation will also perish."

This fate is inevitable. There is no necessity to take into consideration the basis which the people will need to continue a most primitive existence. On the contrary, it will be better to destroy these things ourselves because the nation will have been proved to be the weaker one. . . . Besides those who remain after the battle are only the inferior ones, the good ones have been killed.

Hitler ordered everything destroyed—"all industrial plants, all important electrical facilities, water works, gas works, all stocks of food and clothing . . ." Speer refused to carry out these orders, but Hitler prolonged the resistance until his own bunker was in range of Russian mortars. By the time of the surrender the Allied armies had managed to make Hitler's *Gotterdämmerung* fantasies real. Essen, the site of the Krupp armaments complex, had only 13 percent of its prewar housing still standing. The town fathers of Kassel, population 181,000, with their customary thoroughness, calculated that they had 9,321,500 cubic meters of rubble, 51 cubic meters per person. In Berlin the rubble was piled so high that the British government estimated it would take thirty years to clear it all away.

Germans were cold and hungry. (So, of course, were the French, the Dutch, and other victims of Nazi aggression. Indeed, the French began to ration bread in December 1945.) But the food situation in occupied Germany was becoming desperate. Accustomed to a prewar diet of 3000 calories, the inhabitants of the American zone were put on a daily ration of 1550 calories. The next winter, the most severe in a century, the ration in the Ruhr fell to 600 to 700 calories a day. For those with a little property left, a trip to the surrounding countryside with a suitcase filled with china, crystal, or furs might yield a few eggs, a kilo or two of potatoes, or even a bit of meat. For those without property, the prospects were grim. In Hamburg alone there were 100,000 cases of edema due to acute malnutrition in the first postwar year; in Cologne only 12 percent of the children surveyed were of normal weight. In the British zone the death rate rose 50 percent; 260,000 people developed tuberculosis. Coal production dropped to a fourth of what it was before the war, and of this 25 percent was shipped abroad as reparations to Allied countries. Respectable *bürger* became scavengers; families roamed the rail yards looking for coal cars to pilfer, so many, in fact, that Joseph Cardinal Frings, archbishop of Cologne, declared that stealing coal was no longer a sin. Even the newly appointed Oberbürgermeister of Cologne was cold. "I slept in an unheated room, lying in bed in my suit and coat, shaking with cold like most Germans. . . ." Adenauer recalls. His driver slept in a hospital bathtub because he could not get a room, but "he was very pleased because the bathroom was reasonably warm."

For a world that had just encountered the living corpses of Auschwitz and Buchenwald, the gas chambers, the mass graves, and the corrupt remnants of Nazism, there was little sympathy to waste on the Germans. "We come as conquerors," General Dwight D. Eisenhower had declared in his Proclamation No. 1 to the people of Germany. From the first, Lucius Clay would be caught between his business friends for whom Germany was too strategic to be allowed to stagnate, much less starve, and an angry band of civil libertarians, trustbusters, left-wingers, and grieving Jews for whom the enormity of Nazi evil blotted out all other considerations.

With his suicide Hitler's spell was broken. The Bavarian redoubt where the faithful were supposed to gather for resistance to the death turned out to be the last great lie of the Nazi period. The rush was on to shed swastikas, iron crosses, dog-eared copies of *Mein Kampf*, and especially personal histories of Nazi service. A "state of intoxication," Golo Mann, the historian, had called the Third Reich, a "machine for the manufacture of power" that depended on an individual and a moment that were gone forever.

Physical resistance was over, but psychological resistance was strong in the early occupation days. "Hitler was right when he promised us a 1000-year Reich," so went a typical wry comment of the time. "That's what we have today: 12 years of nazification under Hitler and 988 years of denazification under the Americans." Dangerous jokes of this sort were elaborately filed and cataloged by the occupation authorities. A few pamphlets issued by the "Free Corps of Adolf Hitler" threatened women who "go with U.S. soldiers" or officials who collaborated with the occupation authorities. "We're coming again and soon. The penalty for treason is death." But the only weapon most Germans had to use against the Americans was contempt. "Germans talk only about food!" so went a typical bit of Bavarian humor. "Americans talk about music, culture, and art. I guess everyone talks about what they don't have." Some of the émigrés coming back from America reinforced the anti-American stereotypes. "A country in which we don't belong, that has nothing to give us, from which we have nothing to learn, and to which we have nothing to say . . . A country without tradition, without culture," pronounced Carl Zuckmayer, German playwright, on returning from wartime refuge in America.

Yet from the first, the bitterness of defeat was mixed with grudging admiration for the victors. These strange conquerors—gigantic black men who sat in *Gasthäuser* guzzling beer and reading Mickey Mouse, gum-chewing Southern boys with blond crew cuts who would go out of their way to help an old woman across the street and hand her a chocolate bar when she was safely on the sidewalk—seemed untouched by hate. Americans helped themselves to the best houses still standing and played the conqueror's role to the hilt, but they showed little impulse to demean the conquered so obvious in some of the French troops. It was as if the Americans had wandered in halfway through the play as, indeed, they had. This remarkable army did not march to the familiar martial rhythms of Hitler's army but shuffled and slouched to the strange captivating beat of music long forbidden. Hit tunes blared across Germany through the Armed Forces Radio and the cultural tastes of a generation were formed. "I knew why the Americans had won the war," Hans Magnus Enzensberger, one of the intellectual leaders of the 1968 student revolt recalls, "when I saw my first K ration." Here in a little package was soup, meat, a little stove to heat it, even a condom. "I was sixteen at the time, and I marveled at the thought and sophistication that had gone into that technological wonder."

The official military government *Handbook* carried by American soldiers in their knapsack reflected the supreme confidence of the conquerors in their ability to remake a nation. In its 300 pages it listed over 1250 separate and distinct areas of Allied supervision and control of German civilian life. "No steps toward economic rehabilitation would be taken . . . Germany will always be treated as a defeated country and not as a liberated country."

The German people were to be indoctrinated in the values of democracy and peace, but the dominant psychological mood that prevailed in 1945 was hardly encouraging. "A sickening docility," Drew Middleton concluded in a report on postsurrender Germany in *The New York Times Magazine,* coexisted with barely concealed fury. It's the fault of "those English," an old lady in Aachen bursts into tears, "who wouldn't surrender in 1940." The wife of a German officer living in shattered elegance in Wiesbaden complains about the sloppiness and drunkenness of the occupation forces: "You are not fit to govern the German people." In the years 1945 to 1948, Lewis Coser, the young American academic, observed in *Commonweal* magazine, Germany was a land ruled not "by reason, libido, [or] economics, but by calories." The American professor made his point with a sampling of items from the German press. The Berlin Zoo's sole surviving elephant, Siam, dies and an attendant at the Berlin Zoo is charged with selling a twenty-pound slice at an exorbitant price. Asked what was the most beautiful day of her life, a twelve-year-old schoolgirl in Nuremberg answers: "February 17, 1947, when my brother died and I inherited his overcoat, his shoes, and his woolen jacket."

Lucius Clay's orders set four explicit goals for the occupation; the three-quarters of the Reich that remained German was to be demilitarized, denazified, democratized, and most importantly deindustrialized. At the Potsdam Conference in July 1945, the Big Three decided that the vanquished country would be administered as a single unit, but would be divided into four autonomous zones, each run by one of the occupying powers. France was excluded from the Potsdam Conference, but was given an occupation zone at the insistence of the Americans. At Yalta, Roosevelt had agreed at Stalin's insistence to consider reparations, possibly as high as $20 billion, but the reparations question could not be settled until the machinery for quadripartite economic control of Germany was in place.

That would never happen for reasons that now seem obvious. Each of the four occupying powers had very different views about what should happen to Germany, different memories of the German past, and different strategies for using the shattered shell of the thousand-year Reich to serve its own interests.

What ultimate fate the Russians had in mind for their zone in the early postwar months is not clear. In 1945 Stalin had told the Yugoslav comrade Milovan Djilas that each nation would impose its social system on every bit of territory occupied by its armies. "It cannot be otherwise," he said. But the Soviets did nothing to interrupt four-power relations in 1946. "Whatever secret cynicisms they may maintain," Robert Murphy wrote his superiors in Washington, "it has not been manifest in their negotiations or official action." So far at least they had been "meticulous" in their observance "of the several principles of the Potsdam Agreement . . ." He noted that the Soviets were suspicious of "the British and French lack of faith in their four-power cooperation management of Germany" and that indeed "there is foundation for the Soviet suspicion and distrust in this particular instance."

In the first few months after the war the Russians set about dismantling and shipping back to the Soviet Union anything of value. Special units from Moscow arrived to supervise the looting of German factories. Local occupation authorities stepped in to restrain the carnival of plunder, but the dismantling continued until the spring of 1948. In all, more than 1300 factories were dismantled and 4500 miles of railroad track torn up. The Russians took immediate control of the political process, introduced moderate land reform, allowed workers' councils to run the factories, and nationalized the coal industry. Robert Murphy reported to the secretary of state in November 1945, that "eastern Germany is now experiencing the beginning of a social revolution. Perhaps the most important change so far is psychological. Radical workers, supported by Soviet MG . . . are taking possession of economic instruments of power." In some respects, particularly the treatment of workers in critical industries, the Soviet authorities ruled with a lighter touch than did the American authorities—and were rewarded for it. Coal output in the East remained 98 percent of the 1936 level compared with 53 percent in the West. Industrial output was 50 percent of the prewar level, but in the Anglo-American zones it was only 34 percent. The Russians helped themselves to one-half the output, about a billion dollars a year for three years. While they dismissed 400,000 people from their jobs, the Russians tried to make it clear that they wished to win over, not reform the Germans who had fallen into their power.

At Potsdam the wary Allies had haggled over the spoils of victory and agreed to divide them. Harry Truman had come armed with State Department briefing books that contained a warning: to turn the remnants of the Reich into separate zones run by countries with different social systems would lead inevitably to the partition of Germany. The new president chose to ignore the warnings because something else worried him more. If the Allies were to agree on a specific figure for exacting reparations, in the end the United States would be paying the bill. The ghost of World War I hovered over Potsdam. The United States had ended up lending the Weimar Republic the money to pay their wartime reparations. In October 1924, 1100 U.S. banks subscribed to a loan to Germany to pay off France. The American bondholders, as John Foster Dulles, their principal lawyer never forgot, got little of their money back. In

1945, no one knew what sort of reparations Germany could now afford. Would it not be better to trade machinery from the West for Soviet-zone food and coal in amounts to be determined by the rate of recovery?

Once the Cold War was under way everyone in the West held the Soviet Union responsible for the partition of Germany. But that was not Lucius Clay's opinion in late 1945. At a State Department meeting Clay made his views clear:

> The entire record of the Control Council showed that the USSR was willing to cooperate with the other powers in operating Germany as a single political and economic unit. The USSR had blocked no more than one or two papers in the Control Council, which is more than can be said for the other members.

"French unwillingness to enter into agreements relative to governing Germany as a whole makes it difficult to place blame on Soviets," Clay wrote General Joseph T. McNarney, commander of U.S. forces in Europe, later in the year. The French were adamant in their insistence upon the detachment of the industrial Saarland from Germany and its subjection to international control—without the Russians participating. "The French Government," Murphy noted in an exasperated cable April 3, 1946, "has done everything it could to sabotage the Agreements. Clay points out, and rightly so, that apart from an active interest in reparations, restitution, and intelligence matters, the French have thus far not contributed one single solitary constructive idea or effort in the entire quadripartite management of Germany."

As the war ended, France had two paramount ambitions with respect to Germany. One was to see that Germany would never rise again as a formidable military power. The other was to use her minority shareholder position in the councils of victory to force recognition of her grandeur. Despite years of defeat and humiliation, General Charles de Gaulle was determined to make the world see the true France. As far as Americans were concerned, his triumphal march down the Champs Elysées in August 1944 was purchased with a generous gift of tens of thousands of American and British casualties. Most French, on the other hand, as Alfred Grosser points out, believe that the capital was actually liberated by the joint action of the population and French troops, "without American help, and perhaps even in spite of it, and this notion has been reinforced by the creation of later legends in books, films, and on television."

In short, the French calculated the credits of sacrifice quite differently from the Americans. Had not Roosevelt turned a deaf ear to Premier Paul Reynaud's pathetic plea for "clouds of airplanes" to stave off defeat in 1940? "I am a drowning man" he had cabled the president. Had not the United States ignored the monumental sacrifice of French lives in World War I in its relentless demands for repayment of the war debt? (In August 1914 alone, more than 300,000 Frenchmen died.) The United States, so many in France believed, was not fighting the same Great War in common cause against the enemies of civilization. The American Expeditionary Force was a last-minute affair to secure American profits and prestige. "What an injustice if now, after the money to clothe our soldiers has been lent us, we should be asked to repay the price plus interest for every single coat in which they died?'' French school-children were aware, as their American counterparts most certainly were not, that Congress had refused to settle its debts to the king of France after the Revolutionary War.

De Gaulle had much fresher grievances to feed his anger toward the Americans. Roosevelt's cardinal sin was not to see De Gaulle as he saw himself: the personification of France. FDR was concerned about seeming to impose a leader on liberated France, especially one whose haughty manners and pontifical style suggested a dictatorial bent. Roosevelt never understood the determination of the French Resistance to break with the decadence of the Third Republic or how much the brilliant, self-important brigadier symbolized the hopes for a new France. In his *War Memoirs* De Gaulle describes the exasperating ally with customary hauteur: "The United States brings to great affairs elementary feelings and a complicated policy." The towering French general was enraged when he was told two days before the Normandy invasion that it would take place. He was handed a manuscript for a speech to read over the radio and shown a specimen of the francs already printed by the Anglo-Saxons for use in liberated France. The Americans had thought of everything. On the bills were familiar inscriptions: "Liberté, Egalité, Fraternité" and even "Imprimé en France." On D day only one Free French company of 180 men under direct American control was allowed to land with the Allied forces storming the Normandy beachheads.

De Gaulle's principal grievance, however, was his exclusion from the major conferences, Yalta and Potsdam, in which the contours of the postwar world were fashioned. *Yalta, or the Partition of the World* was a best-seller in Gaullist France of the mid-1960s. The Yalta myth, that a dying president had sold out his Allies to Stalin in a corrupt and foolish bargain to establish American and Soviet hegemony, was the cornerstone of General De Gaulle's world view.

In dealing with the Americans De Gaulle played for high stakes. In January 1945, during the Battle of the Bulge, he deliberately disobeyed Eisenhower's orders to evacuate Strasbourg, swearing that he would sabotage the communications network of the American army if the supreme commander carried out his threat to cut off French supplies. His ploy probably saved the population of Strasbourg from Nazi reprisals but it did nothing for U.S.–French relations. Four months later, De Gaulle ordered General de Lattre de Tassigny to occupy Stuttgart, again in defiance of Eisenhower's orders. The city was to be used as a bargaining chip in the negotiations over the dimensions of the French zone. "Don't rush things," Winston Churchill had told him in 1942 in a lesson on how to deal with Roosevelt. "Look at the way I yield and rise up again, turn and turn about." De Gaulle had replied, "You can, because you are seated on a solid state, an assembled nation, a united Empire, large armies. But I? Where are my resources? And yet I, as you know, am responsible for the interests and destiny of France. It is too heavy a burden, and I am too poor to be able to bow." To the Free French in London, he had cabled in

August 1941: "Our greatness and our weakness lies solely in our inflexibility concerning the rights of France. We will need that inflexibility until we are on the far side of the Rhine."

The British too were skeptical of four-power control of Germany and suspicious of American naïveté in the face of the Russians. For Clement Attlee, the Labour party prime minister elected in the midst of the Potsdam Conference, as for Winston Churchill, his Conservative predecessor, Germany was primarily important as an instrument for forging a new relationship with the United States on which it now seemed the very survival of Britain hung. "Everything depends on the extent the Americans are willing to cooperate," the British National Union of Manufacturers declared at the end of the war. Britain had liquidated $5 billion of overseas property and incurred $12 billion in debt to fight the war. (To comprehend the true magnitude of Britain's financial disaster, the numbers translated into current dollars should be multiplied ten times.)

The ironies of victory became apparent almost immediately. On August 21, 1945, President Truman abruptly suspended all Lend-Lease shipments to Britain and tough negotiations for a $3.75 billion loan began. The negotiation, as we shall see, was a key American instrument for inducing Churchill's successors to do what the old Tory had grandly forsworn: preside over the liquidation of His Majesty's Empire. At the same time a $2 billion U.S. subsidy began pouring into the U.S. Zone in Germany. In 1946 German production was rising, but by the end of 1947 the British found that their separate zone was costing them more than £80 million a year. The only solution was to have the United States bear the burden. This fitted neatly with two emerging American objectives, a desire for a U.S. role in the industrial Ruhr and for the Germans to take more initiative to become self-supporting. In a speech at the Stuttgart Opera House on September 6, 1946, the secretary of state, James F. Byrnes, announced the end of the purely punitive phase of occupation. A good part of the Ruhr and industrial north Germany was now merged with the largely agricultural areas of the American Zone, and the Germans were given a greater role in day-to-day administration and in the development of economic policy. The new bureaucratic creation was given the inevitable name of Bizonia.

Besides finding ways to cut their financial losses, the British were concerned about the French. They opposed French claims for the internationalization of the Ruhr. Too close a French-German collaboration in the development of the industrial heartland of Europe was not a prospect to delight a seriously weakened Britain. It was these concerns that brought the British into immediate conflict with Konrad Adenauer. In June 1945, Cologne had passed from American administration to British. On October 6, the British military commander called Adenauer to his headquarters, dismissed him from office, commanded him to desist from all political activity, and even ordered him out of the city. (It was not the first brush Adenauer had had with British authorities. Forty years after the event, Adenauer bitterly describes how the

British officers moving into Cologne after the First World War dropped ashes on his rug and ordered the Oberbürgermeister's constituents to doff their hats at the approach of a British officer.) The official reason for his dismissal was that he had been too slow in clearing the streets and repairing the buildings. Adenauer's own interpretation was that he was too conservative for the British Labour party which preferred to work with Social Democrats.

But clearly there were other considerations. On one level Adenauer was a nuisance. The British began cutting down his beloved "Green Belt" around the city for firewood and the Oberbürgermeister howled. The Secret Service was worried about more serious matters. Files from the World War I occupation revealed that Adenauer had "separatist tendencies." As he himself puts it in his autobiography, "I advocated a plan for an organized integration of the French, Belgian, and German economies for the safeguarding of a durable peace." On December 1, 1923, Adenauer had told a Paris newspaper that the Rhineland might have to break away from Prussia in the interest of peace; French and German industry could then work together. Years later Franz von Papen, a fellow member of the Zentrum, recalled with disgust how Adenauer, though serving as president of the Prussian State Council "advocated the establishment of a new Rhineland republic with its capital in Cologne." For Von Papen, a former Reichschancellor who served Hitler well, the idea was "treason."

The day before his dismissal, Adenauer had told two correspondents that the Allies should set up a federal state linking the three Western occupation zones and forget about working with East Germany or the Russians. He repeated his idea of a generation before about linking up German, French, and Belgian industry. During the weeks just before his dismissal, according to British intelligence officers who had been tapping Adenauer's private phone, the Secret Service received reports that the Oberbürgermeister himself or possibly an agent was meeting with De Gaulle's agents at the Abbey of Maria Laach inside the French Zone. Whether true or not, the suspicion that the most vocal politician in occupied Germany was secretly acquiescing in De Gaulle's ambitions to annex the Saar and "internationalize" the Ruhr and the Rhineland was enough to prompt the British military to get rid of him. In so doing they made an enemy with a long memory.

3

In August 1947, the City Council of Essen decreed that streetcar conductors could now wear shoulder straps similar in style to those lately worn by German army officers. "A touch of military insignia might help to restore good order and public discipline," the *Frankfurter Rundschau* reported. So far had the pendulum swung against *militarismus* that the reintroduction of military symbols for any purpose was news. Hitler himself had achieved the first of the occupation objectives for his conquerors. By V-E Day Germany was already effectively demilitarized. Two and a half million German soldiers were prisoners of war, 2.1 million were dead, and another 2.9 million were missing in action. The dive bombers, the tanks, and the mammoth artillery pieces that had scourged all of Europe were either in Allied hands or their twisted remains were sitting by the roadside as grotesque memorials to the derailed Nazi war machine.

In the French and Soviet zones German POWs were put to work as slave labor without a note of apology. At the end of the war 470,000 German soldiers were working in French factories. This repayment for years of Nazi coerced labor in occupied France and the conquered provinces of Russia was regarded in Paris and Moscow as a form of reparations. In England the government sought a "middle course between the requirements of the Geneva Convention and the demands of the British economy." To send the German POWs home too quickly, a minister reported to the House of Lords, "would imperil the harvesting" of the 1946 crop.

The United States had no need for battalions of bean pickers, but for General George S. Patton, it seemed a terrible waste not to rearm one or two German crack Waffen-SS divisions and incorporate them into his Third Army. "What do you care what those goddam bolshies think?" he demanded of General Joseph T. McNarney, after he had passed on a complaint from the Soviet commander, Marshal Georgi Zhukov that Patton was a bit slow in disbanding the German units in Bavaria. "We're going to have to fight them sooner or later. Why not now while our army is intact and we can kick the Red Army back into Russia? We can do it with my Germans. . . . they hate those red bastards." "[W]ith a gleam in his eye," Robert Murphy recalls, Patton inquired "whether there was any chance of going on to Moscow, which he said he could reach in thirty days. . . ."

In 1945 Patton's views of the Russians were as unconventional among the U.S. military as his views of the Germans. Shortly after his conversation with Murphy he was dismissed as military governor of Bavaria for suggesting that Nazis joined Hitler's party "about the same way that Americans become Republicans or Democrats." More mainstream in 1945 were the views of the man who called to tell him he was fired, General Walter Bedell Smith. Eisenhower's chief of staff had flared at the British intelligence chief not long after the British government removed its intelligence operations from U.S. command. Britain was "through"; the Soviet Union was "the country of the future" and America's natural ally.

It would take almost ten years before West Germany would rearm and join an anti-Soviet alliance. But some forms of military cooperation began even as Hitler's divisions were being rounded up in U.S. Army compounds. A group of German generals was brought to a secret installation at Oberursel in the Taunus hills not far from Frankfurt. In relatively luxurious surroundings considering the ruin all around them, high officers of Hitler's army were interrogated on matters of particular interest to the Americans—rocketry, advanced weapons development, and especially, intelligence concerning the Russians.

The more cooperative the generals were prepared to be, the smoother their path to reunion with their families and an honorable retirement. (The Soviets took a more direct approach. Any scientists of potential military interests were taken into custody as "war criminals.") Germans known to have been high Nazi officials were recruited by U.S. Army Intelligence in Germany to report on missing Nazis and to supply information about Soviet forces. One notorious case came to light almost forty years later. Klaus Barbie, the head of the Gestapo in Lyons, France, during the war who, according to the Resistance, had 4000 people killed and another 7500 deported, was hired by U.S. Intelligence at $1700 a month and shielded for many years from prosecution by the French.

As the war was coming to an end, Reinhard Gehlen, Hitler's intelligence chief who had specialized in behind-the-lines espionage operations in Russia, was determined to make a deal with the Americans. With resistance collapsing all around him, he looked for someone to whom he could surrender who would understand what a catch he was. It was he who had managed Andrey Vlasov's "Liberation Army," which fought Stalin's armies in the Ukraine after the Soviet general's capture and defection. Although a number of rival intelligence agents were competing with the master spy to sell their services to the Allies, Gehlen knew more about Soviet military operations and intelligence than anyone in the West. On August 22, 1945, disguised as an American general, he was put aboard a U.S. Air Force transport and taken to America. After months of interrogation and shrewd negotiation with American intelligence officials who were in the process of organizing what later became the Central Intelligence Agency, Hitler's former Russian expert returned to Germany to become head of a secret, largely autonomous organization for conducting espionage operations against the Soviet Union on behalf of the Americans. In 1949, the Gehlen organization which had been set up with U.S. funds in a former SS housing development in Pullach, was integrated into the new CIA. His secret organization did the initial planning for a new German army, and he himself became head of West German Intelligence once the occupation was over. Thus even as the mandate for demilitarization was being carried out, military assets of the Hitler era were being used to lay the foundations of German rearmament. In the next few years Gehlen's operatives successfully infiltrated the East German government and maintained radio contact with "White armies" that were continuing the fight against the Communists in the Ukraine years after the war had ended.

In 1948, Frank Wisner, a dashing wartime OSS operative who, according to his former collaborator and secret adversary, master Soviet spy Kim Philby, was now "balding and running self-importantly to fat," returned to intelligence work in Germany under cover of an assignment as "deputy assistant secretary of state for occupied territories." A primary task was to re-create the network of White Russian anti-Soviet activists who had collaborated with the Nazi SS in the wake of Hitler's invasion in setting up a puppet regime in parts of the Soviet Union. These White Russians had intimate knowledge of Soviet vulnerabilities, but they also were particularly barbarous war criminals. Some of these intelligence "assets" had been members of SS *Einsatzgruppen* that had slaughtered Jews at the rate of five thousand a day. To keep them out of Soviet hands, hundreds of Nazi collaborators were smuggled into the United States without the knowledge of the White House. Radislaw Ostrowsky, the president of the puppet regime, Franz Kushel, a police commander who executed forty thousand Jews, and others, were secretly given American citizenship.

4

Denazification was a much harder task than demilitarization; dismantling weapons is easier than exorcising ideas. The commitment to "eradicate Nazism" was embodied in Law 38 of the Allied Control Council, but each ally was free to do it in its own way. "We French take the point of view that every German was or still is a Nazi, and if you don't want to kill off all the Germans, then you have to work with these Nazis," General Perrin-Pelletier, the deputy French military governor, told a press conference in 1946. "In the Saar we did not make the idiotic mistake of denazification." There were 17,000 denazification proceedings in the French Zone, but the former Nazi managers of the Saar steel mills and coal mines were kept on the job to produce the fuel and materials France needed. To be sure, French troops enjoyed the opportunity to repay Germans in kind for the long humiliation of their countrymen but French national policy always put reparations ahead of vengeance.

For the British, punishment was important, but they were quite skeptical of using denazification for reform. Judicial proceedings were for criminals, and their attention was concentrated on the criminal organizations of the Reich as defined by the International Military Tribunal at Nuremberg. With a larger population under their control than the Americans, they conducted a fraction of the trials that took place in the U.S. zone (22,296 compared with 169,282). Only about 10 percent of the population was involved in any way; in the U.S. Zone the figure was three times greater.

The Russians used denazification to liquidate class enemies. "Particular emphasis was placed on the owners of businesses, public officials and persons in important private positions," an early postwar U.S. military government report noted. Nazis who joined the officially sanctioned Socialist Unity Party (SED) were eligible for immediate rehabilitation. Scientists, engineers, or especially talented managers willing to cooperate were exempt. "As we Russians are unlikely to be affected politically, we use the brains of the Nazis as much as possible." Although the Russians may have taken as much as $25 billion in reparations from East Germany, unlike Americans, they were more interested in helping themselves than in punishing wickedness. As Brigadier General Frank Howley, the American commandant in Berlin, noted in his diary, "The Russians also from the start freely recognized the Germans as liberated, whereas we have considered them a conquered people." Once an East German government was in place, any former Nazi official or army officer not guilty of a war crime was restored to full citizenship. Indeed, many became part of the new Communist elite.

The Americans had more radical ambitions. The official objective of the program was to eradicate the sources of Nazism in the German character, education, economy, and political structures. According to the Denazification Policy Board, the U.S. mission in Germany was to change "basic German attitudes." Political and economic power had to be shifted "from the ruling groups in German society during the Nazi regime to other groups in whom we may justifiably have greater confidence." In short the military bureaucrats had as their assignment the making of "a political and social revolution."

A professor of criminology at the University of California, Orlando Wilson, was put in charge of denazification. Occasionally the Americans went at their task with an excess of zeal. One intelligence officer, Robert Murphy recollects, operated "a Nazi torture camp, equipped with devices to extort confessions." He was impressed "how effectively Nazi devices persuaded Nazis to confess their own misdeeds." The usual technique, however, was to invite self-incrimination. In the American and British zones every German was ordered to complete a *Fragebogen,* a detailed questionnaire outlining one's Nazi past. Since Nazi party documents were in American hands—they had been rescued from a Munich paper mill just as they were about to be pulped— it was risky to lie. Anyone making a false statement or refusing to give information to Allied authorities could face a life sentence under American occupation law. Thirteen million completed questionnaires came back to U.S. authorities and 3.6 million Germans were indicted. Before the Americans turned over the denazification program to the Germans on June 1, 1946, 80 percent of the schoolteachers and 50 percent of the doctors in the U.S. Zone had lost their jobs because of their party membership.

When the administration of the programs was turned over to the Germans, their officials moved slowly in carrying out the process of self-purgation that had been laid upon them, so slowly, in fact, that Clay complained: "We are sorely disappointed with the results and we have yet to find the political will and determination to punish those who deserve to be punished. . . . I do not see how you can demonstrate your ability for self-government nor your will for democracy if you are going to evade or shirk the first unpleasant and difficult task that falls upon you." But the contradictions in the program proved overwhelming. Virtually all civil servants, administrators, and industrial managers were in one or another of the four categories of crimes described in the law of the conquerors. "I cannot operate these banks," General Patton fumed, "with the charwomen who are about the only non-Nazis I can find." True, "hell on wheels," as the press called him to his delight, had a reputation for being "soft" on Nazis, but Patton's exasperation was increasingly shared by others. After a tour in the spring of 1947 encouraged by Clay's staff to build political support for putting a brake on the denazification program, Lewis H. Brown, chairman of the Johns-Manville Corporation, issued a scathing denunciation of "the extreme to which denazification has gone":

The brains of Germany are today, by and large, no longer in places where they can be any use to German recovery, which is, today, world recovery. The majority, if allowed to work at all, are doing work that requires a strong back and no brains. A highly trained mining engineer passes bricks one by one from the rubble of the ruins to be loaded on a wheelbarrow to a chemist who knows how to make dyes that will not run, and the vehicle is trundled off by a man who used to design electrical generators. On a park bench close by sits a dejected former executive who once coordinated the work of 5,000 men into a perfect working machine. He can't get work at all. . . . These men of brains, skill, and competence who made Germany great before the war are among the world's greatest human assets for recovery. We are plowing them under and the economic waste will ultimately be footed as usual by the patient American taxpayer.

The injunction placed upon the Germans to punish themselves for what not so long ago had been a moment of glory inevitably produced bizarre results. Erich Teich, a cowherder drafted into an army unit later incorporated into the Waffen-SS, gets a three-year prison term, has 10 percent of his personal assets confiscated, is barred for five years from any but menial employment, and is forbidden to drive an automobile. Franz Halder, Hitler's army chief of staff, is acquitted. The SS General Karol Baron von Eberstein, former Munich chief of police, is a "minor offender." In 1948, 40 percent of higher civil service positions and 30 percent of the ownership of German private industry were still in the hands of former Nazis. By 1950, 65 percent of the top jobs in the Bremen judicial system were held by former Nazis and two-thirds of the teachers throughout Germany had more than trivial Nazi past. According to Joseph F. Napoli, chief of the Denazification Division in Bremen, the United States had acquiesced in the "spectacular renazification" of Germany. Writing in 1950, Napoli concluded "Denazification is a failure . . . the program was an impossibility from the very start."

Among the first to realize this impossibility were the political parties. First the parties of the right made political capital out of the long, ineffectual program, and the parties of the left (notably the Social Democratic Party) have been saddled with it. A genuine liberal element which insisted on a thorough denazification in the early days either has been discredited or has become discouraged. Politicians were unanimous in agreement that any connection with denazification or the trial tribunals meant political suicide. Leaders of the Social Democratic Party were most unhappy about being associated with denazification, and in their way often gave covert support to those forces which have wrecked the program.

Expediency—the need to make Germany self-sufficient and to convert the conquered provinces into an ally—had caused both Americans and Germans to become conveniently forgetful. "We are experienced *Russen kämpfer*" became a familiar taunt as the Cold War dawned. Five years after the war, Napoli recalled sadly, "the evidence of bones piled on bones by the ton . . . the nauseatingly sweet smell of the dead Jews, gypsies, and foreign slave laborers in Germany" no longer seemed to matter.

Denazification thus satisfied nobody. To dispense justice to a whole nation strained the capacities of the most conscientious bureaucratic reformers, and these were soon outmaneuvered by American politicians more interested in

Germany's future than her past and by German politicians whose personal future depended upon being rid of the albatross. Within two years of the liberation of Auschwitz to be identified with the denazification process was more of a stigma than to be identified with Nazism. "Can't you think of something positive you did for the Nazi Party during the war . . . ?" Edwin Hartrich of the *International Herald Tribune* recalls hearing one man say to another on a Frankfurt streetcar. "That shows you made a mistake . . . You pay a small fine, but after that, you can still live with your neighbors because you are just like them."

Almost forty years after the end of the war Germans still have trouble coming to terms with what is decorously called "the weight of the past." The denazification program clearly failed in its explicit purpose. Many Nazi criminals escaped. Even as late as 1978 a minister-president of Baden Württemberg was forced to resign after it was discovered that as a military judge right after V-E Day he had condemned a sailor to death for stealing chocolates. Nonetheless, some Germans agree, the American effort implanted a healthy consciousness of guilt which otherwise might not have developed. Unlike the twenties no "stab in the back" legend was invented to evade responsibility for the war. But many young people believe that the American program helped their parents to avoid confronting their own complicity. It was so easy to dismiss the well-meaning, overly ambitious American experiment in judicial retribution as just another humiliation of defeat. Indeed, they point out, it took an American TV series, *Holocaust,* to spark the first real mass confrontation with the evil of Nazism, thirty-three years after Hitler's death.

The occupation authorities were under orders not only to get rid of bad ideas but to instill good ones. American soldiers were to be missionaries of democracy. This was especially difficult, since for the first few months fraternization of any kind was forbidden, and, the missionaries set themselves up in compounds surrounded by ten-foot-high barbed-wire fences. The principal compound was the old headquarters building of I.G. Farben-industrie. There planning for German democracy went on behind closed doors. Despite the pressure of army wives who arrived to take up residence in the compounds and soon grew accustomed to imperial luxuries like live-in maids and "denazified" china, the fraternization rules were gradually relaxed. All a German girl had to do to receive passes to army social events was to present a note from her doctor certifying freedom from venereal disease—a serious problem in the early occupation years—a certificate of good character from her pastor, and a clean bill of health from the local police station.

The only spontaneous democratic movement in Germany in 1945 was the workers' councils that sprang up in factories where Social Democrats or Communists were in control. For Clay they were much too radical and he banned them until April 1946, by which time the workers' movement had lost most of its steam. The liberals in the military government argued that a strong labor movement was crucial for building democracy. Clay and his conservative economic advisers were not enthusiastic, particularly since the stronger the labor movement, the stronger Adenauer's political opponents would be. But Clay's choices were limited: either a rebirth of a national labor movement under the old Social Democratic leaders who had survived or a risky experiment with a grass-roots movement. Thus the Military Government decided to help build German unionism. But for the first year and a half unions were restricted to plant-wide organization and their rights of bargaining were severely restricted, as indeed they were in the French and British zones as well.

Radical home-grown expressions of democracy were forbidden, but American models of democracy were vigorously promoted. In late 1948 the military government detachment in Baden Württemberg staged a New England town meeting, one of many held throughout the U.S. zone. Germans were encouraged to speak out against the local authorities. When someone did, he was fined by the German local government for abusing public officials, and that finished off the program. Newspapers were licensed and required to stay within the main lines of American policy, but there was no real effort to affect mass culture. Instead a mass athletic program was chosen as the vehicle for ideological purification— The program was the "best thing we ever did," Brigadier General Frank Howley observed, "to sell young Germany on American ideas of democracy and fair play."

The Americans tried their hand at reforming the authoritarian German universities which had long been incubators of rightist movements. The student organizations that had agitated in behalf of Hitler were in a long tradition. But little endured of the American effort at university reform. Indeed, about a quarter of a century later the radical student movement in Germany was calling for some of the very changes that the Americans had intended to introduce.

Education at every level was difficult in the occupation years because there was very little motivation to learn. Indeed, faced with a world in pieces the human reaction was to hold on to old traditions. In August 1948, the *British Zone Review* offered a shrewd assessment of the Allied failure.

In any event, political education is difficult in Germany today. Democracy is not taught in a sunny schoolroom but in a gray ruin. Napoleon sought to impose democracy on Germany and the German people; but instead merely intensified their nationalism. In the days of the Weimar Republic democracy came again, after a lost war, as an imposed blessing, and was rejected. Today for the third time, the victor nations bring the opportunity of democracy to the German people, but synchronized with its arrival come hunger and distress.

5

Deindustrialization was the centerpiece of the Carthaginian peace originally envisioned in JCS 1067. "Dangerous concentrations of economic power" were to be broken up. Under Hitler the entire German economy had been in the hands of seventy cartels and six banks; fewer than one hundred men controlled two-thirds of German industry. To implement the promises made at Potsdam "to eliminate or to control all German industry that could be used for military production" required massive industrial dismantling, for almost any factory could be converted to war production. But to pay reparations, another principle agreed upon at Potsdam, Germany had to produce enough of a surplus to compensate its victims, not easy for a country that at the end of the war was bankrupt.

By October 1947 the dismantling program was for the most part finished, although some dismantling continued even after the Federal Republic was established. But now workers whose jobs were threatened by the plant closings were engaging in wildcat strikes. Riots broke out in March 1950 at the former Hermann Göring Works in the British Zone, and the British High Commissioner had to send in troops to disperse the workers so that their machines could be melted down. Of the original list of 1546 industrial plants slated for destruction only 683 were actually destroyed, and of these, 336 were war plants. Ironically, one consequence of the dismantling program and the wartime bombardment which preceded it was to improve the competitive position of German industry. On the ashes of old factories the postwar industrialists built modern efficient plants that put to shame the obsolescent steel mills and run-down factories of their conquerors.

A variety of interests joined forces to derail the watered-down Morgenthau Plan embodied in JCS 1067. Some Americans had warned against a peace of vengeance. Henry Stimson, the retiring secretary of war, told Clay in July 1945 that he "could see no purpose in the deliberate destruction of the German economy because he was convinced that its reconstruction was essential to create an atmosphere in which it might be possible to develop the true spirit of democracy." Others had less ideological reasons for wanting to preserve German industry. To the French who intended to annex the Saar, there was hardly any reason to cripple its economy. In the meantime, as a French military government report for 1947 put it, "the German population has been put to work in the principal centers of production, especially those which are necessary for the recovery of the French economy." The British who ran the Ruhr had similar interests. The original notion of the Morgenthau Plan to close down the coal mines seemed absurd when the victors were freezing. Critics reiterated what had now become the classic argument for abandonment of denazification and decartelization and the promotion of reindustrialization. German industry was being destroyed in the name of reform and the result was chaos that affected the victors as much as the vanquished. "To keep the German people permanently in chains," Hector McNeil, under secretary in the British Foreign Office, had put it, "means to keep ourselves permanently in rags." It soon became clear to the Americans that the taxpayer was paying heavily for the wrecking of the German economy. It was costing about $700 million a year to prevent mass starvation; to keep the Germans from growing their own food or earning the money to buy it made no sense. The architects of the Morgenthau Plan had failed to recognize the dependence of other West European economies, particularly the Low Countries, on the German economy. To raise up Germany's victims and to keep Germany down at the same time was an impossible task.

Then, too, by May 1946 it had become clear that the French would not permit Germany to be run as a single economic unit, and influential Americans were having second thoughts about it. The Russians, the State Department Soviet specialist, George Kennan, noted in early March 1946, "see in central agencies a possibly indispensable device for entering at an appropriate moment into the other three zones and facilitating there accomplishment of Soviet political program." The Soviets had pared their demands for reparations from the West German zones to about $2.5 billion, but negotiations had stalled on the details of implementation. To give the Soviets as reparations German assets the United States would end up having to replace was a beneficence unsuited to the times. In the gathering state of tension with the Soviets, the economy of West Germany was an indispensable asset. "If economic unity proves impossible," Clay cabled on May 25, 1946, "only those plants in the U.S. zone which were designed solely for the production of war munitions should be removed." A little over a year later JCS 1067 was quietly replaced with JCS 1779, based on the proposition that "an orderly and prosperous Europe requires the economic contribution of a stable and productive Germany."

With the end of the New Deal and the election in 1946 of the Republican Eightieth Congress, American business interests began to exert increasing influence on U.S. economic policy for Germany. Leading U.S. firms owned plants in Germany and did not want them dismantled. As the occupation went on, James Stewart Martin, chief of the Decartelization Branch of the Military Government charged:

[W]e saw more than a scattering of plants revived and put into full production, not because their product proved necessary to the orderly development of the economy and the best use of scarce materials, but because the plants happened to belong to the Singer Sewing Machine Company, the International Harvester Company, the Chicago Pneumatic Tool Company, or General Motors; or because Swedish SKF, or Dutch AKU or British Unilever, or American Bosch, claimed an interest in the German Company; or because an American, Belgian, or British company had a prewar arrangement that made it desirable to get military government to reopen a particular line of German production.

Nor did influential business leaders in the United States wish to see decartelization carried very far.

For a variety of New Dealers, left wingers, reformers, a few isolationist Republicans, and civil libertarians, however, the resurgence of Fascism in Germany was a greater threat to the United States than Soviet influence over Germany. They believed that the world war had its origins in the shameful marriage of business and Hitlerism. To keep peace in Europe required extirpating the roots of Fascism, and these were economic no less political. A few of Germany's leading industrialists, such as Fritz Thyssen, Germany's largest steel producer, Gustav Krupp, a member of the famous arms cartel and chairman of the National Association of German Industries, Erich Fickler, chairman of the bituminous coal cartel, and Carl Bechstein, the piano manufacturer, had made early contributions to Hitler. However, most of his early support came from lesser tycoons. Indeed some of the most powerful industrialists tried to stop Hitler on the eve of his accession to power, but they were too vulnerable to blackmail to eliminate the fanatical paper hanger. The Nazis effectively neutralized their efforts by threatening to expose their own corrupt political dealings during the Weimar Republic.

Big business in Germany became a weapon of war. Cartel arrangements between U.S. and German firms effectively restricted American output of critical war materials. Rohm & Haas of Philadelphia, Du Pont, I. G. Farben-industrie and Rohm & Haas of Darmstadt had an agreement to restrict production of transparent plastic sheets essential for the production of bomber noses. Bendix, Zenith, and Siemens had a patent agreement that made it impossible for the British to expand their production of aircraft carburetors. Less than a year after the evacuation of Dunkirk, the low point in British fortunes in the war, Zenith U.S. wrote its British affiliate explaining why it intended to adhere to its agreements with the Germans:

You know that we have got to win the war if we are going to survive and it is because we know we shall win and survive that we are anxious that post-war business should not be complicated by departing from the conditions of the contract in the meantime and under the excuse of war conditions. . . .

A few months before the end of the war U.S. Attorney General Francis Biddle testified before a Senate committee about German cartels:

These firms in reality operated as departments of the German Government. They evaded and violated the peace treaties in order to build up Germany's military strength. It was the theory of the German Government that operating under the guise of ordinary commercial arrangements, these firms could be used to weaken Europe and America so that when the military war was resumed, we would lose. Through the techniques of industrial penetration, they hoped to be able to cripple American production, to gain from us technical know-how, to conduct espionage upon us, and to establish centers of propaganda throughout the world.

At the Nuremberg war crimes trials nauseating documentation of the complicity of German big business in Nazi atrocities rekindled the zeal of the decartelizers. Joseph Borkin had been an investigator for the 1934 hearings headed by Senator Gerald P. Nye on the role of munitions makers such as Basil Zaharoff, the Krupps and other "merchants of death" in promoting the First World War, and he later had served as head of the Patent and Cartel Section of the Justice Department under the trustbuster Thurman Arnold. While the war against Hitler was on he developed the strategy for fighting I. G. Farben-industrie and kept at the fight for forty-four years. I. G. Farben, he wrote shortly before his death, was his Moby Dick. During the war, Farben ran a rubber installation and a gasoline plant at Auschwitz. Degesh (German corporation for pest control), the company that owned the patent for making

Zyklon-B, was a subsidiary. It was reasonably clear that the managing director of Degesh knew what the gas was being used for, since Kurt Gerstein, "chief disinfection officer" of the SS, had filled him in on the details of the Final Solution. Degesh profits for 1942, 1943, and 1944 were double those of the preceding years and attributable in large measure to the huge orders of Zyklon-B. The SS ordered the gas to be delivered in canisters without the warning of a special odor required by German law for all pesticides. Degesh officials complied only reluctantly because they had a patent on the warning odor and were afraid that they were jeopardizing their monopoly control of the product by releasing the gas in huge quantities without the telltale smell. Earlier company officials had complained in the Farben-Auschwitz Weekly *Report* that the SS did not understand "the working methods . . . of free enterprise."

For James Stewart Martin, "international finance" was a reality, and the primary task of postwar reconstruction was to shrink the octopus and cut off its tentacles. Martin, like Borkin, an antitrust lawyer and a New Dealer, believed that decartelization required a frontal attack. Any corporation employing more than three thousand persons that turned out 25 percent or more of the total production in its industrial sector was presumed to be an "excessive concentration of economic power" and a prime candidate for being chopped up.

The reformers in the Decartelization Branch had more in mind than punishment of the German industrialists who helped Hitler. The system of interlocking directorates, control over patents, and secret market agreements, they believed, had produced two wars. The legal structure that had allowed the Krupps, the mammoth German munitions combine, to collect £6 million from the British firm Vickers, a sum representing royalties for every fuse in every hand grenade used by the victorious British army in World War I and had allowed U.S. firms to put their German connections ahead of the American national interest had to be changed. The "centrally controlled and planned industrial economy," as Martin called it, needed to be transformed if Fascism and militarism were to be expunged from the German political scene. The reformers saw decartelization as one essential part of the "political and social revolution" called for by the Denazification Policy Board that also included "land reforms, intensive agriculture, the rebalancing of heavy and light industry, political decentralization, re-education. . . ."

General Clay considered that "the decartelization group was composed of extremists, sincere but determined to break up German industry into small units regardless of their economic efficiency." Martin, as far as he was concerned, was "a very liberal Wallace supporter," which in 1950, when Clay's memoirs were published, was a bit like calling someone a Communist. Not long afterward Elizabeth Bentley, a former high U.S. Communist party official, agreed with Senator James Eastland when she appeared before a Senate Committee that the Morgenthau Plan was a "Communist plot to destroy Germany and weaken her to where she could not help us." The liberal reformers in Germany had become casualties of McCarthyism.

Clay's principal economic adviser was Brigadier General William H. Draper, on loan from Dillon, Read, the prominent investment firm. To no small extent some of the German giants were creations of the great New York banking house which in the mid-twenties had floated a huge bond issue in behalf of Fritz Thyssen's Vereinigte Stahlwerke. ("The largest industrial unit in Europe," the Dillon, Read prospectus had proclaimed.) Within eighteen months of the collapse of Nazism, Draper was arguing vigorously that denazification and decartelization were hindering German recovery. In the campaign against the "trustbusters," as the reformers were called, Draper had powerful allies. Not the least important was the former president of Dillon, Read, then serving as secretary of the navy and soon to be the nation's first secretary of defense, James Forrestal.

In addition to such strategically placed government officials more interested in the financial future of German industrial giants than in their moral history were American industrialists eager to reassert their interests in the German economy. A vice-president of International Telephone and Telegraph (ITT), Gordon Kern, succeeded in having the firm's German subsidiary, the third largest electrical combine in Germany, make repeater tubes for the Signal Corps despite the ban on the manufacture of electronic equipment contained in the Potsdam Agreement. Switching Germany from heavy to light industry, Clay told Forrestal in 1946, was not so easy because certain U.S. companies, Eastman Kodak, for one, feared future German competition. In 1947, Herbert Hoover toured Europe for President Truman and reported that recovery required making concessions to the old-line financiers and industrialists to enlist their managerial experience. The War Department appointed fourteen American businessmen to make their own report which was released exactly two years after V-E Day. The American businessmen attacked decartelization on the very grounds the reformers justified it. It "represented economic principles quite new to the German mind and to the past industrial development of the country."

At the end of 1946 the secretary of war, Robert Patterson, first proposed using the economic leverage of the Western Zones of Germany to combat Soviet influence over East Germany. Since "the Russians have need for Ruhr steel," Eisenhower agreed, reindustrialization could serve as a "great political weapon." The decartelization program continued all during the years 1945–48, but its activities were rendered almost quixotic by the economic buildup already under way.

Decartelization was probably more difficult to accomplish than the reformers would admit, but much more could have been done to transform the German economy into a system of decentralized, competitive firms and to encourage a new class of entrepreneurs untainted by monopoly capitalism and a Nazi past had these been priorities of the occupying powers. Some of the seemingly far-reaching changes in the industrial sector that were actually made had less substance than it appeared. For example, Friedrich Flick, a key Hitler supporter, had to sell his coal and steel empire but was allowed to put his money into what would soon become another corporate giant—Mercedes-Benz. "The Mercedes is the Volkswagen of the Ruhr" chroniclers of the *Wirtschaftswunder* would marvel as the 1950s boom got under way. Flick had bought up 37.5 percent of the company for $20 million; in 1975 his heirs sold off a little less than 80 percent of his holdings for $800 million. The hated name of I. G. Farben was extinguished by decree, but each of the three successor companies—Bayer-Leverkusen, Farbwerke Hoechst, and BASF—is considerably larger than I. G. Farben ever was.

On July 31, 1948, the International Military Tribunal at Nuremberg ordered Alfried Krupp, the heir to the four-hundred-year-old munitions dynasty to "forfeit all your property, both real and personal," and to spend twelve years in prison. But three years later John J. McCloy, the U.S. high commissioner, released him and restored all his property because, he said, confiscation of property was "repugnant to our American concepts of justice."

6

The most remarkable journey the Germans of the West made in the early postwar years was the six-year passage from the Lucky Strike economy to the *Wirtschaftswunder*. Considerable mythology has grown up around the extraordinary phenomenon; considerable energy has been expended in analyzing what Yale professor Henry Wallich, who served as an economic adviser in the occupation calls "the mainsprings of German revival." Conservatives have celebrated the miraculous German recovery as the triumph of Adam Smith over statism, bureaucracy, and muddleheaded liberalism. German nationalists have attributed it all to the Teutonic addiction to hard work. "We got back on our feet because we worked hard," a chemical manufacturer explained to a *U.S. News & World Report* interviewer in 1959. "This was a German miracle," a Ruhr steel industrialist agreed. American officials, watching the colossal German export machine develop in the 1970s, emphasized the $4 billion of Marshall Plan aid that had been pumped into the wounded industrial heartland of Europe twenty years before.

At crucial stages the Americans acted as midwife for the new German economy. For five years occupation authorities set the framework within which German politicians, industrialists, and consumers were forced to act. Eisenhower's armies had brought with them millions of occupation reichsmarks (RMs) printed in the United States. The Russians had by agreement been given a set of plates too. In the United States the occupation currency could be redeemed for 10 cents each, but the Russians could use theirs only to buy goods; thus Russian soldiers would willingly pay 5000 marks printed in Russia for a $15 wristwatch from the PX. With the worthless occupation currency the Soviets managed within a few weeks to exact a $500 million transfer from the American zone and $300 million from the British. In July 1945 the Americans and British announced without warning that Soviet marks—identifiable by a little dash in front of the serial numbers—would no longer be redeemed in the West. This was the beginning of the currency dispute with the Soviets, one of the principal issues that in three years would lead to the Berlin blockade and the irrevocable sundering of the two halves of Hitler's Reich.

But the black market in Germany continued to flourish. The Americans stopped paying the troops in marks, substituting scrip that was redeemable only on military posts. The cigarette quickly became the reserve currency. An American soldier could buy a dollar carton of Lucky Strikes, for some reason the favorite brand in war-ravaged Germany, and sell it for 1000 Reichsmarks worth of merchandise. (The average weekly take-home pay of a semiskilled German worker was then about 80 RMs.) Cartons of cigarettes became the accepted unit of capital. The publication *Europa-Archiv* was started with ten cartons of cigarettes supplied by the Frankfurt bureau of the *International Herald Tribune*. The U.S Army set up a "Barter Mart" in Frankfurt and Berlin to regulate the black-market activities of the occupation personnel, hiring appraisers to establish a value for the silver, jewels, rugs, and porcelain German civilians eagerly sought to trade for American cigarettes, tins of coffee, or Christmas delicacies. On June 19, 1948, Lucky Strikes reached an all-time high, $2300 a carton at the official exchange rate. Lucius Clay was asked by a persistent German reporter whether there was any substance to the rumor that the U.S. government was about to stabilize the economy with a loan of fifty million cartons of Lucky Strikes.

Although the inflation rate in postwar Germany was one-half that in the United States in the first two and a half years of the occupation, the economy was plainly stalled and misery was growing. Goods disappeared from the stores and ration cards for food, clothing, shoes, and household necessities were often not honored. Clay's answer to the deteriorating German economy was the lightning swift execution of Operation Bird Dog, a monetary reform that had been under secret preparation for two years in Washington by two Treasury economists and a Detroit banker, Joseph Dodge. It was clear to the authors of the daring proposal that it meant the permanent partition of Germany, for the outlawing of the old reichsmark and its replacement with an initial shipment of 500 tons of deutsche marks (DMs) printed in Washington sealed off the Western Zones of Germany into a watertight economic compartment. But by June 20, 1948, the date Operation Bird Dog was sprung, four-power talks with the Russians had broken down. As early as May 1946, Clay had warned the Soviets that unless they modified their demands for reparations and for a share in control over the industrial Ruhr, the United States would choose the ". . . inevitable alternative of treating West Germany as [an] economic unit and integrating this unit closely with West European economy." Although the Soviets had made a number of proposals in 1946 and 1947 for renegotiating reparations and instituting four-power political machinery, the United States was much too suspicious of Soviet intentions and too conscious of the political vulnerability of the German provinces under its control to the rising tide of leftism in Europe even to consider serious negotiations with the

Soviets on the future of Germany in the first two years after the war. The last meeting of the Allied Control Council took place on March 20, 1948. "I see no sense in continuing this meeting," Marshal Vassily Sokolovsky had said as he stalked out of the room. Eleven days later he issued the first of a series of orders curtailing the access to Berlin, which would culminate in a total blockade four days after Operation Bird Dog went into effect.

The currency reform was, as the British MP Aiden Crawley called it, "one of the harshest acts of confiscation imposed on a people by their conquerors." With a stroke of a pen General Clay had abolished about 93 percent of the paper wealth of the German people. Ten near worthless reichsmarks could be exchanged for 1 deutsche mark but only 40 to a person. Then two months later another 20 deutsche marks could be acquired. In a few weeks 6.1 billion deutsche marks were exchanged and in the process hundreds of billions of stocks, bonds, mortgages, and bank accounts denominated in RMs were wiped out.

The reform hit those with small savings the hardest; they were left with virtually nothing. Hoarders of goods, black marketeers, and holders of real estate did well. (Some entrepreneurs had such an uncanny sense of timing that many Germans suspect that Operation Bird Dog was not a universal secret. One German builder who was in the midst of putting up a Methodist church was paid in dollars one day before the currency reform went into effect.) In 1948 hoarding was clearly the most profitable enterprise in occupied Germany, netting billions of new DMs in a few months. For the majority of Germans, however, particularly workers, the reform amounted to an extravagant dose of austerity, a harbinger of the sort of medicine that would be administered a generation later to Third World governments struggling to make ends meet. The monetary reform was designed to encourage the accumulation of investment capital and to get goods back in the stores. By these criteria it succeeded brilliantly. As Henry Wallich, who helped administer the currency reform, puts it:

. . . [it] transformed the German scene from one day to the next. One June 21, 1948 goods reappeared in the stores, money resumed its normal function, the black and grey markets reverted to a minor role. . . . The spirit of the country changed overnight. The grey, hungry and dead-looking figures wandering about the streets in their ever-lasting search for food came to life as, pocketing their 40 D-marks, they went on their first spending spree.

The currency reform provided the indispensable framework for the recovery of Germany. Confidence in the mark rose; black market traders on the day of the reform exacted 45 DMs for a dollar, but within six months the exchange rate was stabilized at 6 to the dollar. Yet the most important function of the American reform was to build a hospitable climate to test the economic policies of Ludwig Erhard.

A fat and comfortable man, Erhard had a religious faith in the iron laws of the market and a strong inclination to help nature along. He found himself the economics minister for Bavaria at the end of the war for much the same reason Adenauer found himself the mayor of Cologne. He had spent the Nazi time doing market research in Nuremberg, having been barred from teaching economics at the university for his refusal to join the Nazi professional association. His ideological opposition to the Nazis, which commended him to his captors, went beyond conventional distaste for the brutalities of Hitlerism. He was convinced that the bureaucratic regimentation, the centrally administered economy, and the inefficient and burdensome planning associated with the Nazi behemoth led inevitably to totalitarianism. A disciple of the Freiburg school, Germany's version of Chicago economics, he was determined to put into practice the free-market theories of Walther Eucken and Wilhelm Röpke. (After Erhard became economics minister in Adenauer's government he would check his ideas with Röpke, who was the source of most of them. Röpke had emigrated to Geneva and now qualified as a prestigious foreign authority.) Erhard had great faith in the currency reform imposed by the conquerors because it stimulated the free market.

Various liberalizing measures have recently been announced in the field of capital and consumer goods. The welcome given to these measures shows that our people are tired of administrative tutelage and set much store by their right of free choice as consumers. If we had taken a single step further in the wrong direction it would have meant a death blow to democracy, the negation of our people's democratic rights. Only when every German . . . can freely decide what goods he will consume, will our people be able to play an active part in the political life of their country.

All through 1946 and 1947 Erhard pushed his heresies: The answer to the food shortage was to abolish rationing. The cure for inflation was to end wage and price controls. The American authorities resisted. Strong free-enterprisers though they were, Clay's advisers from Dillon, Read; Sears Roebuck; and the Detroit National Bank were sensitive to the political realities of postwar Europe.

The right-wing parties of prewar Europe had been discredited. From Norway to Italy the resistance movements had stood for more than the expulsion of the foreign enemy. They had demanded an end to social injustice and the cynical use of the nation by the old rich who under the Nazi yoke had so often sold out workers and shopkeepers to save a few of their own comforts. As Alfred Grosser puts it:

Everywhere, in France, Denmark, Italy, Germany, and Belgium, a push toward the Left was taking place. To be "Left" meant to demand social change which would be brought about by having the national community take charge of the economy. To the extent socialism can be defined, the Europe of 1945–46 was certainly right to call itself socialist.

In war-ravaged France, Italy, and in bankrupt Britain extensive social security programs were passed. The British Labour government favored the nationalization of the coal mines of the Ruhr which Clay strongly opposed. In 1946 the military governor had called upon his superiors in Washington for a policy statement on socialism. "It seems to me that we must either accept or reject socialization now . . ." and his own recommendation was not in doubt. The official position in Washington was that if the Germans voted for Socialism they could have it. But Clay kept pressing for an ideological commitment to free enterprise which he saw as a necessary weapon in the growing propaganda war with the Russians and as a sound principle for getting the German economy working again. Even though parts of Adenauer's Christian Democratic party at the end of the war favored socialization of monopolies and mines, Clay used his authority to the limit in the fight against leftist tendencies in Germany. The voters in the state of Hesse had approved by a 71 percent majority a constitutional provision calling for the socialization of industry. Clay declared it inoperative. He opposed a law authorizing Socialism in Berlin. He drastically cut the authority of the Executive Committee for Economics in early 1947 when a Socialist, Victor Agartz, was elected to head it, and restored it when Erhard took over. Fear of Socialism was the principal reason for proceeding with the decartelization program, Clay told his skeptical adviser, General Draper.

In the spring of 1948 more immediate challenges to the American occupation were building. Johannes Semler, a Christian Democrat who had replaced Agartz as executive director of economics, openly attacked the Americans and British at a party meeting in Bavaria for robbing Germany of foreign exchange by setting the export price of coal and scrap iron lower than the world market price and by outlawing shipbuilding and other industries on which the German economy was absolutely dependent. He charged the Americans with sending only "chicken feed" when the Germans were starving. If the American taxpayer expected thanks, Semler declared, he should be set straight. Semler was promptly dismissed.

Anger in Germany was mounting. The winter of 1946–47 had been the most severe in more than a century. Miners in the Ruhr went on strike in early 1948 to protest the dwindling food rations. Herbert Hoover, who had gone on an investigative mission at Clay's request to dramatize Germany's plight, called on Americans to make substantial private donations to supplement the hundreds of millions of dollars pouring in from the Treasury. Subsisting on 1500 calories a day if they were lucky, Germans could summon little gratitude for American generosity or even for Hoover's public relations effort in their behalf.

In the wake of the terrible winter of 1947 there was a noticeable shift of mood in Germany. Eisenhower's troops had rolled into German towns in 1945 expecting to be shot at from behind every house, only to find a puzzlingly submissive population. Now after billions of dollars spent, months of effort at reconstruction, widespread "fraternization" among GIs and fräuleins and even a few friendships, the typical German posture toward the conqueror seemed to be an upturned lip, an outstretched palm, or a whimpering look. For two years the Americans had been having their first postwar experience in trying to figure out another nation for which they had accepted "responsibilities," and they were baffled by the strange contradictory psychological crosscurrents that blew across the Rhineland and Bavaria. Germany had a "deformed conscience," William Harlan Hale, who had served for five months with the occupation forces, concluded in the January 1946 *Harper's,* citing a collection of contradictory and mystifying vignettes: In the last days of the war a famous Panzer general surrenders and asks to broadcast an appeal to the troops to tear "the badge of dishonor" from their tunics—only to replace the swastika with the Iron Cross, "the symbol of the last five wars of Prussian militarism"; the rector of the University of Marburg tells his interrogators that "the rule of an authoritarian regime, which assumed all responsibility, relieved the German people of all blame for whatever took place"; a young man in Erfurt blurts out that he is so ashamed of all the crimes that his country had committed that he hoped "there will never be a Germany again"; others echo Goebbels, "important is not what is right but what wins"—Germany was now the responsibility of others; Robert Ley, a top Nazi, commits suicide and leaves an anguished confession and plea to his countrymen to make restitution to the Jews. The parade of articles dissecting "the German mind," whether written by visiting professors of sociology or veteran newspaper correspondents, all came to the same general conclusion: The Nazi legacy was a generation of shameless, self-pitying, rather mystical folk quite capable of making a lot more trouble in the future.

Thus Erhard's Draconian policies carried grave risks. At a time when the German people were asking for more, he proposed to give them less. The danger was all the greater because for two years Europe appeared to be "slithering to the left," as Churchill had put it. (In 1946 the Communist party had received almost 11 percent of the vote in local elections in Hesse and 14 percent in North Rhine–Westphalia.) Nonetheless, Erhard was allowed by Clay and Sir Brian Robertson, the British military governor, to enact an emergency law which abolished most of the economic controls of the occupation. "Into the wastebasket in one fell swoop," Erhard explained, went hundreds of decrees for regulating economic behavior. The politicians in power in most of Europe were committed to a "full employment" economy—the United States made a milder commitment in the same direction in the Employment Act of 1946—but, as Andrew Shonfield in his study *Modern Capitalism* points out, the idea of government policies to promote employment "hardly figured at all in Germany."

By February 1950, there were 2.2 million unemployed, up from 450,000 at the time of the currency reform. The price of eggs tripled in a month. On November 12, 1948, there was a one-day general strike in the Ruhr. But the new economics czar pressed relentlessly ahead. Erhard reduced tariffs to force manufacturers to confront international competition. He persuaded a reluctant General Clay to approve a thoroughly regressive income tax with large exemptions for industrial investment and specially favored industries such as shipbuilding. How could he justify such tax breaks for Germans to the American taxpayer, Clay asked, when the profits were being made on Marshall Plan millions? But Erhard's argument that the incentives would raise production carried the day. The tax burden on workers rose and real wages fell.

Erhard's tight money policy had led to what Clay estimated was a $100 to $200 million annual flight of capital. Meanwhile the Americans outmaneuvered the British in their plans to nationalize the heavy industry of the Ruhr, and over French opposition issued Law 75, which vested authority in twelve German businessmen as "trustees" under the leadership of Heinrich Dinkelbach, a prominent businessman of the Nazi era. The trustees could become owners if the German people opted for capitalism over socialism. By the onset of the Berlin Blockade and the Marshall Plan that looked like a good prospect indeed.

But despite the inequities involved, Erhard's economic policies succeeded in raising productivity dramatically. The production index in 1946 was 33 percent of the 1936 figure. By 1949 it was 90 percent. Between 1949 and 1959 industrial production rose 126 percent, exceeding the production for the last prewar years. By 1952 the new Bundesrepublik had a favorable balance of trade and the Landtag of North Rhine–Westphalia was ordering new seats to accommodate the more ample bottoms of the newly well-fed deputies. Payrolls were trimmed, productivity rose. Absenteeism declined. Germans began to work hard again as overtime pay was virtually tax-free. German industrialists were required to turn over 3.5 percent of their profits to a special development bank, and by 1953 the steel industry was financing most of its own development with reinvested profits. Tax-exempt savings deposited in the *Bausparkassen*, special home construction banks, financed over 55 percent of the huge construction program that got under way in 1949. The unemployment rolls began to fall and by the end of the 1950s virtual full employment had been achieved. Erhard's *Wirtschaftswunder* became a conservative fable. In 1953, *The Wall Street Journal* exulted that West Germany's recovery was made possible by

. . . ignoring the prescriptions of the "new economics" and by following some very old and quaintly orthodox economic principles. . . . Instead of trying to manage its inflation it stopped inflation—the country was given a hard currency even though at first this hardness hurt. It eliminated wage and price controls. It progressively returned more and more industry to private management and relaxed its foreign trade and exchange controls. The government got a tight grasp on its budget. . . . It's all rather baffling to the prophets of managed economy. But at least the West Germans don't find it a matter of embarrassment.

The German economic experience was so extraordinary that economists and politicians of various persuasions drew quite different lessons from it. Against the conservative fable celebrating hard work and healthy greed as the keys to success, liberals and Socialists preferred to emphasize the billions in U.S. aid, the German freedom from heavy defense expenditures that still weighed down the recovery efforts of the victors, and the bonanza of the Korean War. (The war scare over Korea a year after Erhard's reform was under way initially caused a sharp rise in raw materials prices and a financial crisis from which Germany was rescued by the European Payments Union, but thereafter the tremendous market for merchant shipping, steel, and heavy machinery produced a boom.)

Some German economists argued that in a curious way Nazism and the war deserve considerable credit for the *Wirtschaftswunder*. At the most the Allied bombing destroyed little more than one-third of industrial plant and equipment; some put the figure at less than 15 to 20 percent. In important sectors of heavy industry, capacity was actually rising as the war ended. By crushing the labor movement the Nazis kept wages artificially low for twelve years. This left a legacy of labor discipline and demoralization that carried over into the immediate postwar years. The cheapness of labor, aided in no small degree by the flood of refugees from the east looking for jobs in the industrial cities of the west, helped to account for the spectacular profits on which the rebuilding of the West German economy was based. Luck of course was also a factor. The mild winter of 1948 made it possible to divert hundreds of thousands of tons of coal from home heating to industry. But Erhard's government, contrary to the later myth, intervened directly in the economy to help the miracle along. The government took strong measures to encourage capital formation and to steer investment into those enterprises such as the railroads, considered crucial to the growth of the economy as a whole.

7

On June 24, 1948, the day the new D marks were to become legal tender in the western sectors of Berlin, the Soviet military commander in Berlin cut the rail traffic, leaving the 2.5 million people living there with food stocks to last thirty-six days. "How long do you plan to keep it up?" General Clay inquired of Marshal Sokolovsky. "Until you drop your plans for a West German Government" was the reply.

The Berlin Blockade was one of those symbolic events that light up the world in a new way. Stalin's brutal act gave definition to a new nation. The machinery to produce a separate German state had already begun to grind, but that tentative process now seemed inevitable. Overnight the conquerors became saviors, and a bond was formed. "From then on," Alfred Grosser has written, "no foreign policy was acceptable to the West Germans except on the basis of meriting the Americans' confidence so that they would continue to extend their protection over Berlin and West Germany." Within twenty-four hours, one hundred C-47 transport planes delivered 250 tons of supplies at Tempelhof Airdrome. Before the blockade was lifted almost a year later, U.S. planes were bringing in 13,000 tons a day. Although the blockade had its *opéra bouffe* aspects, to use Clay's description—two days after the blockade began Marshal Sokolovsky was caught speeding in the U.S. sector and overzealous GIs dragged him from the backseat at gunpoint—the United States had shown itself willing to face down the Russians to preserve its position in Germany, and in the process rescue the conquered population in its charge.

Municipal and state elections had been held in the various *Länder* ("states") of the three Western occupation zones beginning in 1946. But a week after the Berlin Blockade began, the military governors invited the presiding ministers *(Ministerpräsident)* of the eleven *Länder* to draft a constitution for a federal state that would include them all. German sovereignty would not yet be restored, but the Germans could effectively run their own affairs if they did not contravene the conquerors' directives banning military production, regulating the level of industry, and promoting decartelization. A Parliamentary Council met for eight months in Bonn and produced the Basic Law, a constitution for a state without sovereignty within a territory that was declared half a nation. The Basic Law would become "invalid" on the day the German people (on both sides of the Elbe River) would choose a constitution for a reunified nation. For almost twenty years, long after German sovereignty was restored in 1955, the United States and its allies reserved the right to exercise emergency powers in Germany.

Politics in Germany revived as soon as the few surviving politicians with anti-Nazi credentials had gathered the physical strength to resume the struggles of the pre-Hitler era. Two figures, each heir to a long tradition, overshadowed all the rest.

Kurt Schumacher emerged from the war with a political history that was almost a perfect counterpoint to Adenauer's. The son of a prosperous businessman in a small Prussian town on the Vistula not more than twenty miles from the western borders of Czarist Russia, he was a Protestant by family tradition, an atheist by conviction. Within a few weeks of the outbreak of the First World War, he was crippled for life at age eighteen by a burst of machine-gun fire. Discharged with the Iron Cross, Second Class but without even a stump of a right arm, he joined the Social Democratic party (SPD). Banned by Bismarck for twelve years for "subverting the political and social order," by the eve of the Great War the Social Democrats were to choose kaiser and flag over proletarian internationalism, and German workers went dutifully to the trenches to kill French workers. In the revolution of November 1918, Schumacher was a member of the Soldiers and Sailors' Council of Berlin, part of the same radical movement Adenauer, with the support of the local SPD, successfully outmaneuvered in Cologne.

Schumacher soon became a stormy SPD activist in Stuttgart, lashing out at the Versailles Treaty, at the push for rearmament, and particularly at the rise of the Nazis. In 1924 he became local head of the *Reichsbanner,* the SPD paramilitary organization, and fought both Nazis and Communists in the streets. A remote figure, without a discernible personal life, he was a political gladiator with a gift for the withering insult: Hitler's propagandist, Goebbels, was a dwarf too big for his breeches, Nazism an appeal to the "schweinehund" in the ordinary man, and Communism nothing but Nazism "varnished red." His forensic style, his energy, and his dedication guaranteed him an impressive array of enemies to the end of his life. "Heads will roll, bones will be broken," the Nazi *gauleiter* of Stuttgart crowed at a victory celebration a few weeks after Hitler came to power. Schumacher, one of the minority of his party who called for resistance to Hitler's bid for dictatorial powers, was a prime target, and by the following July he was in the concentration camp at Heuberg.

Advised by a guard on his arrival to hang himself, Schumacher said that his captors would have to perform the act of liquidation themselves. His determination to survive Hitler was fierce. His personal courage—he would go out of his way to give a forbidden word of encouragement to Jewish prisoners and would stand up defiantly to old Nazi enemies who would come to the camp to taunt him—became a legend in postwar Germany. In Dachau, where he spent almost ten years, he had time to reflect on the beliefs that had landed him a short train ride from the gas chambers.

He was convinced that the big bankers and industrialists had sold out the German workers to Hitler. These "pseudopatriots," who for the sake of profits were prepared to confuse Hitler's imperialist dreams with the destiny of the nation, would have to be fought after the collapse. Marxism was "an indispensable analytical method in the fight for the liberation of the workers." There could be no German labor movement that was not based on the class struggle. But Marxism offered little prescriptive help in formulating a political strategy. Certainly the Soviet experience was instructive of only what to avoid.

On his release his health was broken but his determination to build a new Germany was greater than ever. For a brief moment he thought that the forced "proletarianization" brought on by the Allied air forces—two-thirds of what had been the middle class now had a standard of living no better than that of workers—had created a revolutionary moment. But his pragmatic sense triumphed over his hopes, and he quickly recognized that Socialism could not come to Germany without the support of the middle class. The dominant political mood in postwar Germany was disillusionment with politics of all sorts. After the first general election for the Bundestag in 1949, a majority of those questioned said that "political parties and their spokesmen in parliament were concerned far more with satisfying their own selfish interests than with doing anything for the voters of the country." Nazism, according to a series of public opinion surveys, was "a good idea badly executed." Economic security was far more to be prized than free elections, free speech, free press, or freedom of religion. About one-half of the respondents in the U.S. Zone in November 1947 favored socialization of heavy industry and barely one-quarter opposed it, but apathy and a yearning for economic security rather than proletarian fervor defined the public mood.

Convinced that the SPD must become a reform party with a much broader appeal to the middle class than before the war, Schumacher reorganized the party around some very broad principles—"a new Germany, not a reconstruction of the old." The choice was either a socialist democracy—without the huge capitalist enterprises which "bitter experience" had shown were incompatible with democracy—or no democracy. But his brand of Marxism was without rigid ideological content. "This is a time to survive, not philosophize," he would say.

On the destiny of the German nation in the world he had clearer ideas more vociferously stated. "This sad beggar's role in which we find our people," he wrote a friend in 1946, must be quickly ended; "patriotism must be enlisted in the struggle for socialism." The Allied occupiers were the obvious foil for a campaign of patriotic resurgence. His own legitimacy as a leader was based on his ranking membership in the anti-Nazi counterelite. The party must establish itself as the rallying movement of the untainted; "naive idealistic admirers" of Hitler would be courted, but the enemy was the bankrupt establishment that had made Hitler possible. The Christian Democrats under Adenauer were betraying the hopes of the German people, he would thunder, by bringing back Nazi collaborators in key positions and by acceding to the sinister plans of the Allies to dismember Germany forever. "[F]riends and pathmakers of the Third Reich, who have fought all their lives against democracy," he charged, "find a home in the Christian Democratic Union" supported by "foreign propertied elements allied to it by social bonds and material interests" and, of course, "the direct support of the Roman Catholic Church. . ." The Americans, British, and French were all practicing "the politics of moralizing property acquisition, justified in the name of sanctimonious morality." Military governments, he told the party congress at Düsseldorf in 1948 with his customary sarcasm, "cannot be exactly admired as the ultimate and most perfect form of democracy." The task of the party would be to undo the work of the American "re-educators" who were communicating the message, as surely as if they meant to, that "democracy and national decline go hand in hand."

"[T]he world is very well able to survive without a unified Germany," Schumacher had warned within weeks of emerging from the concentration camp in 1945. Both the Western Allies and the Soviet Union for which he reserved his bitterest invective were actively uninterested in the reunification of Germany. "We cannot regard as a friend of the German people," he declared in one of the first sessions of the Bundestag in September 1949, "anyone whose political actions deny or hinder German unity." After taunting Adenauer as "the Chancellor of the Allies," he was expelled from the chamber for twenty days.

Schumacher's role as the spokesman for a reunified Germany belonging neither to East or West earned him considerable attention. For *Time,* in an article a few weeks before his death in 1952, Schumacher was "one of the most important men in Europe," but clearly "the Man in the Way." For *Pravda* he was "an eager warmonger" and an "unscrupulous demagogue." "The most dynamic and independent of German politicians," Drew Middleton, chief correspondent of *The New York Times,* concluded, Schumacher was "difficult not to admire but equally difficult to like." Some of Clay's advisers thought that the uncompromising Socialist had the makings of another Hitler. For Dean Acheson, Truman's secretary of state, Schumacher was a "bitter and violent man." After meeting the new German chancellor, Konrad Adenauer, for the first time in November 1949, "in a small private room in a very Victorian Bonn hotel, where we drank the delicious wines of the Rhineland," Acheson was taken to meet the crippled SPD leader. Schumacher immediately launched into "an unrestrained" attack on Adenauer. "Breaking off this futile interview as soon as politeness permitted," Acheson recalls, "I went on to a reception which the Chancellor was giving for me."

Clay saw the Socialist leader only a few times and increasingly came to see him as a threat to American interests. For Schumacher, Americans were motivated by a mixture of misplaced reformist zeal, shrewd power politics, and plain greed. Food shipments in 1946, he said, were a way of reaping huge U.S. farm profits from German starvation, and Marshall Plan aid two years later was a blunt instrument of American capitalism. Germany's conquerors, Schumacher believed, were bunglers, bent on "managing and exploiting" the country, living luxuriously on the German economy with the hungry Germans paying the bills. (Like most of his countrymen he mistakenly believed that the conquerors were extracting the full cost of the occupation.) Only "legitimate" national leaders, meaning himself, could establish democracy, certainly not the suspect reformers from four thousand miles across the sea.

As the Allies proceeded with their plans for a separate West German state, Schumacher stepped up his resistance. From the start he had been for a strong central state. Rhineland, Bavaria, Hanover, and Hesse were "not ends in themselves. . . . They can only be component parts of a future Germany; they should only serve as stepping stones toward the reorganization of the Reich." After the currency reform which he believed would greatly strengthen SPD prospects because of its crushing impact on workers, he became bolder in opposing Clay's plans for a separate West German federal state with a weak central government. On April 20, 1949, he suddenly announced that the Social Democrats would refuse to endorse the Basic Law unless it was amended to give the federal government supreme authority in financial matters and to curb the powers of the *Länder* authorities in the Bundestag. Three days later the military governors gave him his way. Almost fifty-five years old, his left leg recently amputated, Schumacher confidently expected to become the first federal chancellor and to exercise the broad powers for which he had fought.

The man in his way was Konrad Adenauer. On August 14, 1949, contrary to general expectations, the CDU/CSU polled about 400,000 more votes than the SPD, giving Adenauer's party eight more seats in the Bundestag than the Socialists, but not a majority. The balance of power, as has been the case almost ever since, was in the hand of the Free Democratic party (FDP), originally a party of small businessmen and professionals of a nineteenth-century liberal stripe. Adenauer, now seventy-three, became the first Bundeskanzler, heading a coalition committed to creating the "social market economy." His personal physician, he informed party leaders, had told him that he could carry on for two years. He would stay fourteen.

The two founding leaders of the major postwar German parties were both domineering, powerful men, each with enormous energy despite the age of one and the frailty of the other, each determined to have his way because he had earned it. For Adenauer, the paterfamilias of the rose garden, with his high-pitched drone, his piety and hidebound morality, his Rhenish vision of a small

Germany in a big Europe, his banker friends, clerical connections, and classical economic conservatism, Schumacher, the atheistic, Prussian socialist, the loner, the shrieker, the agitator, the strident nationalist, represented the dark side of the German soul.

Adenauer read the Nazi era completely differently from his antagonist. The essence of Hitlerism was government. Big business was not in control. The machinery of the state had been captured by men without principles. The solution was to keep the role of the state small and to put men of principles into positions of authority. "Only a great party with its roots in Christian-Western thinking and ethics could educate the German people for their resurgence, and build a strong dike against the atheistic dictatorship of communism." The party would be Catholic but, unlike its spiritual ancestor, the Zentrum, not exclusively so.

For many decades the German people suffered from a wrong attitude to the state, to power, to the relationship between the individual and the state. They made an idol of the state and set it upon an altar; the individual's worth and dignity had been sacrificed to this idol.

Nazi planning and Socialist planning, according to Adenauer, were indistinguishable. The activist state threatened the liberty of the individual. "National Socialism was simply the last logical development—pushed to criminal lengths—of that worship of power and that scorn for the individual which naturally arises from a materialist ideology." The "pernicious materialism" that had infected the German spirit had its roots in Marxism, and it could be dispelled only by restoring the rule of the marketplace. While many in the CDU in 1945, the year the party was founded, saw no alternative to massive nationalization of heavy industry and mining, Adenauer strongly opposed the managerial state as a threat to liberty and he kept postponing a party decision on the issue. By the 1950s in the changed political and economic climate of the Cold War, and the booming German economy, no one within his party was prepared to challenge Adenauer's orthodoxy.

From the day he alighted from the American jeep amidst the rubble of Cologne, the practiced political survivor was engaged in a two-front war, a battle with the Socialists for the allegiance of the German people and an equally portentous struggle with the conquerors over the identity of the new Germany. With great skill he parlayed his successes on one front into victories on the other. The British Military Government had banned Adenauer from taking part in any political activity when he was dismissed as Oberbürgermeister. But by the end of 1945 the ban was lifted and the wily septuagenarian became head of the new Christian Democratic party in the British Zone. In the summer of 1946 the official occupation publication *British Zone Review* was taking note. "By force of his quiet and dignified personality he has emerged as the outstanding figure of the CDU in the British Zone."

The Conservative wing led by Adenauer consists of business-men, industrialists and the farming community. The Left wing on the other hand is prepared to co-operate with the Social Democrats. The conservatives in the British Zone, however, are in the ascendant

and Adenauer's position is virtually unchallenged. His opponents accuse him of sepa-
ratism—and of opposing the reunification of Germany. He denies this, but adds that the
only future lies in the formation of a United States of Europe. His attitude to the
occupying powers is critical in some respects—but he enjoys his power and, for all his
apparent detachment, he is one of the astutest and most experienced politicians in
Europe.

Adenauer had outmaneuvered his potential rivals within the party, but the
British were to give him a great boost. Sir Brian Robertson, the military governor, in a move aimed at keeping the French from taking over the Ruhr,
proposed joining North Rhine and Westphalia into a single *Land* bigger than
Belgium. Schumacher, who had the sympathies of leading Labour government
officials at the time, opposed the plan, but Adenauer saw immediately that
giving a separate political identity to the industrial heartland would give him
and his party an extraordinary power base. He and Schumacher were flown to
Berlin on a Royal Air Force plane to talk about it. With his somber mien and
high starched collar, Adenauer was a formidable if not engaging figure. Whatever ideological sympathy the British Socialists may have had for Schumacher,
his abrasive personality helped to dispel. Adenauer always tried to paint the
SPD as "the military government party" or the "Royal British Social Democratic Party," suggesting that its members were discrediting themselves, by
becoming "lackeys of the kings of England." True, some in the Labour government saw the British occupation zone as a laboratory for Socialist ideas
that might then be adopted in Britain. Indeed, one reason the British authorities pressed so hard for *Mitbestimmung,* labor participation in industrial deci-
sion-making, was that they hoped to try something of the sort at home. But
while the Labour government expected to exert more influence if Germany
became a social democratic state and some saw the SPD as a "bulwark against
communism," from the British viewpoint Adenauer's vision of a decentralized
small Germany was infinitely preferable to Schumacher's nationalist vision of
a united Germany acting alone. Besides, General Robertson and his successor
as military governor, Sir Ivone Kirkpatrick, could not abide Schumacher personally, and Foreign Secretary Ernest Bevin had a distinctly "gloomy view"
of the SPD leader. Bevin thought Socialism was too good for Germans. According to his close associate, Kirkpatrick, he never forgave the German Socialists for having supported the Kaiser's war policies in 1914. "He felt
betrayed, and it made him more anti-German than anything else the Germans
did." Both Bevin and Kirkpatrick much preferred to deal with Adenauer.

In their political duels, both Adenauer and Schumacher tried to paint the
other as a jackal of the conqueror, but Adenauer, who in fact by 1947 had
attracted the favorable attention of influential Americans, including John Foster Dulles, the Republican party's leading foreign policy spokesman, and was
receiving direct support from Clay, used the tactic more successfully. Once
the Allies agreed to set up a separate German state, Adenauer's political fortunes rose dramatically. Had a united Germany embracing the Protestant traditional SPD strongholds of the East emerged in the late 1940s, it would have

almost certainly been Socialist. An aging conservative Catholic Rhinelander could have hoped for little more than a parliamentary platform from which to attack the evils of collectivism.

In September 1948, in the midst of the Berlin Blockade, Adenauer was elected chairman of the Parliamentary Council, the body charged by the occupying powers with drafting a constitution for a West German state. Overnight Adenauer became a national spokesman. As the first national election approached, he tried to outdo his opponent in dramatizing his independence from the occupiers. Speaking in Berne at a meeting of the Interparliamentary Union, he declared that only the Wehrmacht, not the German people, had unconditionally surrendered in 1945, and aroused a storm despite his insistence that he had been misquoted. Like Schumacher, he denounced the dismantling program in the British Zone as a scheme to eliminate competition. He cried *"Diktat"* when the Allies ceded a few yards of the Rhineland to Holland to rectify the border. In a clumsy attempt to ingratiate himself with the Berliners, with whom he never felt at home, he went to within a hundred yards of the Brandenburg Gate, where the Soviet sector of the city began, and declared that Germany's future lay in playing off the Western powers against the Russians. German cooperation would depend strictly on the attitudes of the West. As he spoke, a British or American airplane was landing every four minutes with food and supplies for the beleaguered Berliners.

Adenauer's most effective political stroke was to "destroy the halo," as he put it, Schumacher had acquired by appearing to force a crucial concession from the Allies in the drafting of the Basic Law. The socialists, Adenauer was informed, had been briefed in advance on the fallback position of the occupiers. Well aware that the Allies were under great pressure to have a West German state as the centerpiece in the grand design for Europe then taking shape, Schumacher could afford to be bold. But Adenauer succeeded in securing an official British admission that they had "intimated" to the SPD what sort of concessions they were prepared to accept, although General Robertson and his chief political advisers subsequently denied passing any information to the SPD. "We had to oppose the systematic attempts of the SPD to present history as though there had been only one patriotic party in Germany. . . ."

But the close election was probably won on economic issues. The inevitability of the class struggle, the dangers of clericalism, and the advantages of public ownership, the essence of SPD ideology in 1949, were no match for Adenauer's *Magenpolitik,* promises to fill the stomach once Erhard's bitter pills had done their job. Moreover, there was a growing perception of Adenauer as the American candidate and Schumacher as the British preference. As one German reader of the Paris edition of the *New York Herald Tribune* observed, "If a man has to have a master, it is better to have a rich one than a poor one."

Adenauer's campaign to restore German control of its own affairs now began in earnest. Politics, not economics, was his passion, and the task of transforming the Americans and British from conquerors into benefactors and

Allies now absorbed him. A few months after the Basic Law and the new Occupation Statute went into effect, the Allied military governors were replaced with civilian high commissioners. Sir Ivone Kirkpatrick, a professional diplomat and a Catholic, appreciated Adenauer's mordant style. Not a jolly man, Adenauer became deft at executing the gentlemanly jabs of boardroom wit. "He relished his brushes with the High Commission," Kirkpatrick recalls, "and he told me more than once that he had enjoyed our long and often dreary sessions over the Bonn treaties." Impassive for the most part but given to flashes of calculated anger—"that is what keeps me young," he told the British diplomat—he was "a redoubtable but charming adversary." Kirkpatrick's superiors in Whitehall, the Foreign Ministry, however, were hardly pleased with Adenauer's election eve remark that "it is no longer France which is the enemy, it is Britain which is the real enemy now." The French high commissioner, André François-Poncet, a small, pudgy but dapper man who had been French ambassador to Hitler from 1933 to the outbreak of the war and a senior official in Vichy, seemed to treat Adenauer with calculated rudeness for the sake of France, adding a touch of extra spite here and there for himself, but he reserved his fury for Schumacher, whom he publicly called a "Faustian Schizophrenic."

With John J. McCloy the battle of wits took on a different character. McCloy had risen from modest circumstances, and by the end of the war had become a senior figure of the American Establishment. Like Adenauer, he was the child of the lower middle class. His father, an auditor for an insurance company, died when the boy was six, and his mother, a nurse, struggled to put him through Amherst where he waited on tables. In various ways McCloy had become involved with Germany in public and private life. He made his reputation during the First World War as a lawyer investigating the mysterious explosions at the Black Tom oil refineries in New Jersey, supposedly the work of German saboteurs. As assistant secretary of war twenty-five years later, he had opposed the Morgenthau Plan for Germany. His wife was distantly related to Adenauer's second wife, although apparently neither knew of the connection when the high commissioner arrived to take up residence in Bad Godesberg. McCloy was strongly sympathetic to Adenauer's pleas to end the dismantling program which he considered contrary to U.S. interests.

By late 1949 even the anti-German British Foreign Minister Ernest Bevin was convinced that the exigencies of the Cold War required ending the schizophrenic policy of building up Germany and tearing her down at the same time. For three weeks the high commissioners bargained with the new chancellor in the Petersberg Hotel overlooking Bonn over an agreement to end the dismantling program, relax restrictions on German industry, permit the reestablishment of the shipbuilding industry, and authorize commercial and consular relations, all in return for two commitments Adenauer was most eager to make: Germany had to join the Council of Europe and certain other international bodies and, as Adenauer put it to the Bundestag, was required to maintain the demilitarization of Federal territory and to "endeavor to prevent the re-creation of armed forces of any kind."

Adenauer had excellent American contacts, principally well-connected Republicans who followed German policy closely and Reinhard Gehlen's intelligence organization which was already at work designing the new Bundeswehr, and he knew pretty much what the Allied terms were. As Charles Wighton, a British official in Germany at the time, puts it, Adenauer resorted to "inverse blackmail." He was a "weak chancellor" Adenauer told the high commissioners, who needed something easy to sell the Bundestag. In the CDU newspapers he launched a strident campaign demanding "precisely those Allied concessions which, he was tolerably certain from the hints of his American friends, were to be granted within the next few weeks." With the agreement in hand he announced with triumph that his persistence had netted "ninety percent of his demands." François-Poncet mused privately, "It is always a difficult business making gifts to the Germans, and a thankless task at that."

8

The chancellor understood that one commitment in the Petersberg Agreement —the pledge not to rearm—gave him enormous leverage over the Allies. High officials in the Pentagon were already of the view in 1949 that European defense required a major German contribution. Over the next five years he skillfully traded German soldiers, which after the outbreak of the Korean War were at a premium, for the restoration of sovereignty and the creation of a powerful new national identity for West Germany.

Adenauer had told his associates: "I think patience is the sharpest weapon of the defeated. I can wait." As he began the long campaign in late 1949 he discovered that the British were tapping his telephone and demanded an apology. (As late as 1962 he told the Bundestag that his phone was still being tapped but the British at once denied it.) He then went to Berlin and denounced the continuing interference of the Allies which, he said, "is extraordinarily great and not welcome to the Germans." About three weeks after Dean Acheson's visit in November 1949, in which the secretary hinted gently that a future defense contribution from Germany might be expected, the chancellor told the *Cleveland Plain Dealer* that there would be no "German mercenaries" serving in foreign armies, but he would consider recruiting German units for service in a European integrated army. The psychological moment for striking a bargain had arrived. Europe was in a "state of near-panic," as Sir Ivone Kirkpatrick described the mood in the aftermath of the Berlin Blockade and the Czech coup. (Indeed, one French minister was predicting that the Russians would be in Paris by the summer.) Thus, German troops—"bloodthirsty sheep," the chief of the British Imperial Staff had characterized them during the war— were now at a premium and could serve as impressive bargaining chips in the negotiations to decide Germany's future.

In the closing weeks of 1949 and on into the spring of 1950, the Bundeskanzler let slip one tantalizing remark after another. In his own mind the troop questions had been resolved. As he recalls in his memoirs, "Rearmament might be the way of gaining full sovereignty for the Federal Republic. This made it the essential question of our political future.'' An army was the key to equality with the victors and the glue with which to attach half of the old Reich to Western Europe, a unity more to be prized than *Wiedervereinigung* with the East, certainly one that came with a lesser price tag. Not the least important, German troops in place would ensure a permanent American force in Europe as protection against the Russians.

But there was considerable domestic opposition. Barely four years after the collapse, the widows, the legless veterans, the prospective conscripts, the Evangelical churches, who along with the SPD shared the fear that rearmament would doom reunification, and intellectuals with an eye for the catch-22 madness of the old *militarismus* and the skill to parody it unmercifully all together constituted a formidable antimilitary bloc.

By early 1950 the Americans knew what they wanted, a European army that included additional American divisions and a German contribution under the command of General Dwight D. Eisenhower. The British refused. Ernest Bevin was not yet ready to contemplate goose-stepping German troops. Adenauer tried a different tack in the spring of 1950. The East Germans had organized a Peoples Police, 48,000 strong with reconnaissance aircraft, and a formidable commander, the fabled "General Gomez" (Wilhelm Zaisser) of Spanish Civil War days. Why should not West Germany have an equivalent force? The response of the high commissioners was to authorize a 10,000-man increase in the existing small border patrol.

The Korean War accelerated everything. If Stalin could authorize Communist forces to cross a clear demarcation line in a divided nation of the East, why not in the West? Even though U.S. intelligence agencies quickly concluded there would be no attack from East Germany, from the moment Korean troops poured across the 38th parallel in the dawn of June 25, 1950, the mood shifted dramatically on the other side of the world. Adenauer ordered Hans Speidel, an ex-general who had been General Erwin Rommel's deputy in the Afrika Korps, to produce a memorandum on what it would take to provide security for the new German state. The answer, delivered in mid-August, was 15 German divisions, with a tactical air force and a small navy. Three days later Adenauer told the high commissioners he wanted a volunteer army of 150,000 men. By the end of August he was proposing a major German military contribution to a European Army in return for the restoration of sovereignty, an end to the occupation, and the establishment of normal diplomatic relations with the conquerors. Even to be discussing such matters as a future alliance on such an unequal footing was "grotesque." By October, the Pleven Plan was ready. A European Army would be created somewhat on the model of the Foreign Legion. Company-strength contingents of German troops would be scattered throughout a polyglot army, rubbing shoulders with French, Greeks, Americans, Turks, Belgians, or whatever nationalities could be induced to join.

The Pleven Plan which became the basis for the European Defense Community proposals, was an appealing political metaphor for leaders looking for German troops but who feared Germany. Yet it was a nightmare for the generals who would be asked to implement it. To make matters worse for the rearmers, there was now increasingly widespread pacifist and neutralist sentiment among the Germans. *"Ohne mich"* (the German rendering of the English malapropism, "include me out"), the slogan of the gathering movement, presaged in a way the anti-Vietnam War rhetoric of the 1960s. Moral passion against war, the effects of which were still around, was reinforced by the instinct for personal survival in a world gone mad. To prepare for another war while you were still cleaning up from the last one! One of Adenauer's ministers, Gustav Heinemann, who would later become president of the Federal Republic, suddenly resigned. God had twice dashed the weapons from the hands of the Germans, he said, and his people would do well to get the point. Heinemann immediately formed the All German People's Party dedicated to neutralism and continued German disarmament.

In the Bundeskanzler's negotiations with the Allies, none of this did any harm. In the next round with the Unholy Trinity, as the high commissioners on the Petersberg were known, Adenauer skillfully exploited the dangerous neutralist sentiment in the country to extract concession upon concession. His government had to be backed up. If a good German, like himself, could not deliver for his people, there were plenty of others waiting to take over. In reality, by the time the concessions were granted, the neutralist sentiment had crested. Schumacher himself now expressed readiness "to bear arms once again if, with us, the Western Allies take over the same risk and the same chance of warding off a Soviet attack, establishing themselves in the greatest possible strength on the Elbe."

Despite the technical problems, the Pentagon was convinced by the summer of 1951 that a European Army was the only context in which the French would accept German troops. McCloy sold the plan at the Pentagon and State Department and went back to Germany to see Adenauer. The chancellor, aware of how much Washington now wanted the troops, raised his price: Twelve divisions, a conscript army of 250,000 men; a coastal navy, a Luftwaffe of 2000 aircraft, and a revived German General Staff under a civilian minister —himself. The French, as was to be expected, were horrifed. Adenauer counted on American power and commitment to make his whole plan for German revival work. Earlier, he had given McCloy a memo and sent a copy to his friend Allen Dulles, in which he played on the Soviet threat and American fears of communism. Germany, unlike France or Italy, "is today still free from communist infection" and thus the most reliable long-term ally for the United States in Europe. McCloy played his cards. "No doubt we can defend Europe a little farther to the east with the Germans than we could without them." It was an accurate statement of how weak Adenauer's bargaining position was, but the chancellor persisted. He knew what his chief negotiating partner wanted.

The first six months of 1952 were undoubtedly the high point of Adenauer's long career. In negotiating the complex set of agreements to end the occupation, to put West Germany on an equal footing, and to rearm her, Adenauer was usually pushing against an open door. In just one of the agreements McCloy alone made 122 major concessions. The inevitable pun began to circulate: "Adenauer is the real McCloy."

No doubt McCloy's personal respect for Adenauer and even affection had grown—years later when he was President Kennedy's disarmament adviser, a word from "the chancellor" was enough to kill any new idea on arms control —but rearmament of Germany and her reintegration into Western Europe were now a cornerstone of U.S. global strategy, a grand design that squared neatly with ideas Adenauer had been carrying around in his head since the 1920s. McCloy himself had been deeply ambivalent about German rearmament not so long before. Writing his old boss Henry Stimson on June 28, 1950, three days after the Korean attack, he expressed nagging doubts whether German democracy was strong enough to contain a resurgent German military, particularly since there was much neutralist sentiment in the country and "an amoral business element that wished to trade with the Communist bloc." The same contradictory fears of a Germany at once too belligerent and too accommodating to the Russians would surface again and again in the next thirty years, along with its counterpart, a corresponding German view of an America that was provocative yet indecisive, belligerent yet unreliable.

On May 26, 1952, the Bonn Agreements were signed. The occupation would end when Germany joined the European Army. That would never happen. Why it did not happen and why it did not matter are part of another story, the making of America's Europe. By the spring of 1952 the momentum of German revival was unstoppable.

TWO

UNCERTAIN CONQUEST:

General MacArthur and the Remodeling of Japan

1

Better the patience of the East than the haste of the West, Douglas MacArthur had said as he waved off all suggestions from his staff that he summon Emperor Hirohito to his headquarters to demonstrate that the Supreme Commander Allied Powers was now the sovereign. "To do so would be to outrage the feelings of the Japanese people and make a martyr of the Emperor in their eyes. No, I shall wait and in time the Emperor will voluntarily come to see me." On September 20, 1945, barely three weeks after MacArthur had landed ostentatiously unarmed at Atsugi airport—"nothing will impress them like a show of absolute fearlessness," he had told his aides—the emperor asked to see the general.

The "emperor of heaven," dressed in a cutaway, top hat, and striped pants, arrived a few minutes later to be greeted on the threshold of the reception hall of the U.S. embassy by his conqueror wearing suntans open at the neck without decorations or insignia of rank. The lord privy seal, who had accompanied him from the palace and usually paraphrased his wishes for him —except from the throne the emperor never spoke for himself—was barred from the meeting. As the emperor, trembling, entered the hall, MacArthur gripped his hands, greeted him with a respectful "Your Majesty," and waved him to a chair. In thirty-eight minutes of stilted talk, each took the measure of the other. "I tried to make it as easy for him as I could," MacArthur recalls in his *Reminiscences,* "but I knew how deep and dreadful must be his agony of humiliation." MacArthur, who had been received by Hirohito's father at the close of the Russo-Japanese War, had already decided not to indict Hirohito for war crimes, but he expected the embarrassment of a personal plea for clemency. The emperor took quite a different tack: "I come to you, General MacArthur, to offer myself to the judgment of the powers you represent as the one to bear sole responsibility for every political and military decision made and action taken by my people in the conduct of war." MacArthur was "moved . . . to the very marrow of my bones." For the general, it was "painful to see a man once so high and mighty brought down so low," but "in that instant I knew I faced the First Gentleman of Japan in his own right."

In Germany all legitimate authority had dissolved as Hitler's bunker was captured and the arch Nazis scrambled for their suicide pills or surrendered to the conquering armies. But while Japan was in ruins—1,270,000 killed in action, 670,000 civilians dead from the bombings, 9 million homeless, a quarter of the national wealth destroyed—the imperial structure in whose name the war of aggression had been waged remained intact.

When the picture of the American general towering over the Son of Heaven was published in the newspapers a few days later, most Japanese could not believe it. The forty-four-year-old amateur marine biologist and poet with the receding chin and the straggly mustache was, so tradition had it, the 124th direct descendant of the emperor Jimmu Tenno; to look into his eyes for even an instant on his rare public appearances, so generations of children had been taught, would strike one blind. He liked bacon and eggs for breakfast instead of bean soup and fish, owned Western-tailored suits by the dozen (but, rumor had it, not one kimono), and insisted upon Occidental plumbing. Yet as MacArthur would tell his visitors, "The Emperor is to Japan what the Stars and Stripes are to the United States."

No emperor had actually ruled Japan for a thousand years. Indeed most of them since A.D. 823 were adolescents or babies. Twenty-six when he ascended the throne, Hirohito was the oldest mentally normal man since 1770 to sit atop the high, gold-brocaded dais in front of the six-paneled gilt screen. He had approved all the major decisions of the war, and he played a key role in ending it. He legitimated the first surrender of Japan to a foreign invader in its 2500-year experience in two sentences: "I cannot bear to see my innocent people suffer any longer. Ending the war is the only way to restore world peace and to relieve the nation from the terrible distress with which it is burdened."

What to do about the emperor had been a matter of considerable discussion during the war. A number of experts on the Orient, more familiar with China than Japan, such as John Carter Vincent of the State Department, Andrew Roth of Naval Intelligence, and Thomas A. Bisson of the Strategic Survey Board, thought that branding Hirohito a criminal would shock the Japanese out of superstition and bring them into the rational world of twentieth-century democracy. As the war ended, such views were widely circulated, particularly in the liberal press. A few years later with the onset of McCarthyism, the same views, since they happened to coincide with the Soviet position, would be taken as evidence of "crypto-Communism" and disloyalty.

The Japanese experts in the State Department, principally former Ambassador Joseph C. Grew, thought that Hirohito could be an effective tool of the occupation. There was a tradition in Japanese history of using the emperor as a harmless political symbol. When the shogun, Iyeyasu Tokugawa, ruled Japan at the beginning of the sixteenth century, he prohibited the emperor from interfering in matters of state, reduced his entourage, slashed his budget, and restricted him to ceremonial pursuits. The emperor's fate was still undecided when a few days after the capitulation Douglas MacArthur arrived in the capital to take up his duties as Supreme Commander for the Allied Powers (SCAP). He had made the trip to Tokyo, as William Manchester recounts it, in ''a fleet of decrepit, charcoal-burning sedans and trucks, led by a bright red fire engine'' on a road lined with thirty thousand Japanese infantrymen standing at parade rest with their backs turned, the traditional show of imperial respect. It seemed as though MacArthur were already the new emperor. George Atcheson, the acting political adviser in Japan, wrote President Truman that while it would be expedient to keep the emperor to sanction any new constitution the Americans would write, ''the Japanese people will never learn and follow the fundamental ways of democracy as long as the imperial institution exists.''

When Hirohito came to see MacArthur he was still considering abdication. After all, under the old regime, police officials who carelessly misdirected an imperial procession or school officials who stumbled over the words of an Imperial Rescript resigned in disgrace. Hirohito's cousin, Prime Minister Prince Haruhiko Higashikuma, had urged him to sign the surrender documents and then abdicate. Both ultranationalists bent on preserving ancient customs and the Soviets who thought the Communists might seize power in the chaotic aftermath were pressing for a quick end to Hirohito's reign. But Shigeru Yoshida and other conservative politicians familiar with the West advised strongly against it. It would confuse the occupation authorities and embolden the Communists.

Within days after his meeting with MacArthur, the emperor let it be known that he would not voluntarily leave his wood-and-paper palace surrounded by great gray stone walls and a lovely swan-filled moat. On New Year's Day, 1946, Hirohito issued an Imperial Rescript denying his divinity.

The ties between us and our people have always stood upon mutual trust and affection. They do not depend upon mere legends and myths. They are not predicated on the false conception that the Emperor is divine and that the Japanese people are superior to other races and fated to rule the world.

MacArthur, immediately announced that the emperor was under ''the irresistible influence of a sound idea. . . . democratization of his people.'' (Although the supreme commander had not been consulted in advance, a draft rescript denying imperial divinity prepared by General Ken Dyke, chief of the Civil Information and Education Section, had been given to the prime minister.) By the following March when the new constitution was promulgated in the emperor's name—there was more applause for Hirohito than for the constitution, critics noted—it was clear that *Showa* (''bright peace''), as he had named his reign, was far from over. Soon he was kissing babies, opening flower shows, and collecting lichens in public parks, behaving like a king of Norway, with an Oriental cast, a shade more democratic in bearing, perhaps, than an English prince.

To cut the emperor down to size, MacArthur dismissed 75 percent of the palace employees, but villages organized volunteer "sweeping parties" to look after the 1600 acres of palace grounds. The occupation authorities encouraged the emperor to travel around the country despite the annoyance of local officials who objected to the cost of receiving his ninety-man entourage and the anger of the Russians at what they took to be a "a capitalistic plot to fasten Emperor rule upon Japanese struggling to be democratic." General Courtney Whitney persuaded MacArthur that Hirohito was so unprepossessing—his tic, squeaky voice, and occasionally unbuttoned fly did little to evoke the samurai spirit—that the emperor himself was the best advertisement for democracy. But Hirohito's imperfections were not of overwhelming interest to the Japanese. He was, as were his predecessors, a symbol of the moral authority of the state and as such by 1948 he showed up in all the public opinion polls as the most popular man in Japan. When the palace was opened for New Year's Day in 1954, 380,000 people swarmed onto the grounds and 16 were trampled to death.

2

General Douglas MacArthur stepped easily into the old imperial role now abandoned after so many centuries by Japanese royalty. His "imperious aloofness and lordly graciousness," one Japanese historian observed, established the prestige of the occupation. Conscious of symbolism at every step, he located his headquarters in a six-story insurance building "across from the moat surrounding the emperor's palace," overlooking the Imperial Plaza where, according to Tokyo Rose's wartime broadcasts, he was to have been publicly hanged. He left all the ribbon cutting and elbow rubbing to others and was absent from Tokyo only twice in five years. But he was briefly visible to the Japanese four times every day, driving back and forth between the embassy and the headquarters in a 1941 Cadillac with five gleaming stars and fluttering flags on the fenders, traveling so slowly his aides worried for his safety.

Personal fearlessness, austere manners, and what biographer William Manchester calls "tinny" magniloquence were second nature to the sixty-five-year-old general. His rhetoric sounded like an Imperial Rescript: "Have our country's flag unfurled and in the Tokyo sun let it wave in its full glory, as a symbol of hope for the oppressed and as a harbinger of victory for the right." Combined with these qualities was a shrewd regard for the feelings of the conquered. His General Order No. One directed the Japanese commanders to disarm their own forces. The Japanese will provide our safety, he would say.

His statesmanlike speech at the surrender ceremonies aboard the *Missouri* impressed the spiritually devastated Japanese. Declaring that "we have had our last chance" to find peace through "the crucible of war," he called for "a spiritual recrudescence and improvement of human character that will synchronize with our almost matchless advances in science, art, literature and all material and cultural developments of the past two thousand years. It must be of the spirit if we are to save the flesh." Toshikazu Kase, the American-educated secretary to the Japanese foreign minister whose job it was to recount the surrender ceremony for the emperor, was "thrilled beyond words, spellbound, thunderstruck." Here was a victor over a "prostrate enemy" who could "impose a humiliating penalty . . . and yet he pleads for freedom, tolerance, and justice."

MacArthur was supreme commander in more than name. President Truman had appointed him without consulting any senior U.S. officials or any of the Allies. "You will exercise your authority as you deem proper to carry out your mission." The general took this broad mandate as a carte blanche. He was the only U.S. official abroad who could issue policy statements without first checking with the State Department. Ambassador William Sebald, political adviser during the occupation, in awe of "the wizardry of MacArthur," noted: "Never before in the history of the United States had such enormous and absolute power been placed in the hands of a single individual." The Soviet representative in Tokyo, Stalin complained to W. Averell Harriman, the U.S. ambassador in Moscow, in October 1945, was treated "like a piece of extra furniture." Perhaps the USSR should become "isolationist" and withdraw completely from what had so clearly become an American sphere. Harriman, eager not to set a precedent that would consign Eastern Europe irrevocably to Soviet domination, urged the creation of a control commission for Japan in which the Soviets would have a nominal role.

The Far Eastern Commission that was agreed upon two months later in Moscow included representatives of all the eleven nations that went to war with Japan, including the Soviet Union, but it functioned as a purely advisory group, along with an Allied Council made up of the United States, China, Britain, and the Soviet Union. Stalin had already agreed at Potsdam that an American commander would act as "the sole executive authority for the Allied Powers in Japan." When the Russians pressed for more authority, the general let it be known that if Truman backed down, he would "quit and go home." When the Allied Council met, the United States was often outvoted three to one by the Allies who wanted tougher policies for transforming the militarist institutions of Japan and for paying reparations. At the opening session MacArthur reminded the Allies that they had no authority whatever and gave orders to "talk the Council to death."

The general had dictatorial powers which, unlike Clay, he need not share with anyone. No businessman or newspaper correspondent could enter his domain without specific permission. (Offending reporters who left the country could be barred from returning.) The general set the rate by which army scrip was exchanged for yen. As in Germany, U.S. greenbacks were prohibited as legal tender. Foreign diplomats presented their credentials to the supreme commander. He never returned visits, not even Hirohito's call. He refused to brief ambassadors in Tokyo when the State Department requested him to do so. "And why, as a sovereign, should I? President Truman doesn't do so, nor does the King of England or any other head of state."

MacArthur's priorities for Japan were clearer and less contradictory than Clay's in Germany, for to a great extent they were his own. During the first week of the occupation he announced, "I am not concerned with how to keep Japan down but how to get her on her feet again." Anxious about maintaining order in the face of mass starvation, he cabled Washington for an emergency shipment of 3.5 million tons of food. "Give me bread or give me bullets." He saw no reason to forbid fraternization. Anyway, his father, who had been President William McKinley's general in charge of subjugating the Philippines, told him not to give orders he couldn't carry out. The population, eerily submissive, presented no danger. The people were "dazed, tottering, and numb with shock," the journalist John Gunther reported. "Not just the cities," the Harvard Japanese expert Edwin Reischauer wrote, "but the hearts of the people have been burned out." The struggle with the West had been painted as a spiritual contest, a test of will. More had been lost than lives and property.

MacArthur considered himself an expert on the "Asian mind" even though he once admitted that "even after fifty years living among these people I still do not understand them." Great battlefield generals of the past had failed as administrators—the duke of Wellington, Marshal Henri Pétain, and, especially, Napoleon, "The greatest soldier who ever lived . . . but in political affairs he listened to his advisers too much." He would not make that mistake. "Sometimes my whole staff was lined up against me. But I knew what I was doing. After all I had more experience than they. And most of the time I was right." His major advisers, he told a reporter, were George Washington and Abraham Lincoln.

His approach to the occupation was softer than Clay's in Germany. A generous peace, MacArthur calculated, would more quickly stabilize Japan and secure America's position in the Far East. There was a racist twist to his generosity as well. Japan could not be judged as harshly as Germany because the latter "were traitors to western culture." The Japanese atrocities, he told John Gunther, were in an old tradition going back to Genghis Khan.

For MacArthur, seated behind an immaculate desk in a small interior office of the Dai Ichi Building, the occupation was "the world's greatest laboratory for an experiment in the liberation of a people from totalitarian military rule and for the liberalization of government from within." He would use his dictatorial powers and the godlike awe in which he was held—"We look to MacArthur as the second Jesus Christ," one Japanese encountered by the writers Richard H. Rovere and Arthur M. Schlesinger, Jr., exclaimed—to make an artificial revolution in the name of "demokrashi."

MacArthur's broad objectives were not different from Clay's. Japan had to be disarmed, militarists and fanatics purged from its political life, its people reeducated for democracy—"myths" and "legends" were a special target—and the great industrial concentrations, the *zaibatsu,* that fed her warlike spirit, dismantled. But the pace and scope of the occupation were quite different. In Japan the U.S. authorities moved much faster to use local government to maintain order. The new Japanese constitution went into effect in 1946, three years before the Basic Law began to operate in Germany. The Japanese equivalent of "denazification" was a more streamlined process, with little emphasis on judicial hearings, findings of guilt, or punishment. In Japan 3.2 percent of the population were screened, as opposed to 21.7 percent in the U.S. Zone in Germany. There were 210,287 persons removed from office, whereas Clay had removed 418,307. The German elite that had staffed Hitler's war was not larger, possibly even smaller, than the Japanese equivalent. But in Japan the philosophy and style of the conqueror were different.

The Basic Law reconstituting part of Germany as the Federal Republic, although negotiated with the conquerors, was a German document, but the new Japanese constitution was a purely American product. The Potsdam Declaration had called for guaranteeing "civil liberties, respect for fundamental human rights and the removal of obstacles to the revival and strengthening of democratic tendencies." A little more than a month after the surrender ceremony MacArthur had decreed freedom of the press and women's suffrage. Giving more rights to women, the general believed, would strengthen the influence of the Japanese home and dampen the warlike spirit. It was theoretically possible, because of the elasticity of its language, to reinterpret the Meiji Constitution of 1889 so as to incorporate democratic ideas. However, the first inkling that the Americans would take a different course came in an Office of War Information overseas broadcast marking Bill of Rights Day in the United States to the effect that Japan ought to overhaul its basic law to incorporate fundamental freedoms. MacArthur began suggesting to the succession of prime ministers who briefly held the office in the first few weeks of the occupation that they draft such a law. The result submitted to the supreme commander in January 1946 was disappointing. It turned out to be, MacArthur recalls, "nothing more than a rewording of the old Meiji constitution. The power of the emperor was deleted not a whit. He simply became 'supreme and inviolable' rather than 'sacred and inviolable.' And instead of incorporating a bill of rights, the new constitution took away some of the few rights that already existed. . . . All that had to happen was for the old crowd of militarists or civil servants to get control of the Diet, and wipe out all the rights that were granted by the constitution."

The general wanted the issue settled before the next meeting of the Far Eastern Commission on which the Russians sat, since the Soviets were pressing to get rid of the emperor. MacArthur called in his longtime aide, Major General Courtney Whitney, now head of the Government Section in the occupation bureaucracy. "That committee is not catching its cue. They're not

moving. Step in and help them out." Thrilled at the prospect of turning the
Government Section into what he called a "constituent assembly," the bluff
Manila lawyer who worshiped MacArthur designated each officer "as a
Thomas Jefferson" and ordered the group to produce the constitution in three
weeks—in time, he hoped, to be announced on Washington's birthday. (The
drafts were to be ready by Lincoln's birthday.) The fiction was to be preserved
that it was a purely Japanese product, and when the news leaked some four
months later of how the document came to be written, Whitney launched an
investigation. But the emperor had gratefully sent each "Thomas Jefferson" a
commemorative medal and a special gift.

MacArthur gave no great guidance beyond four points he wrote on a
yellow pad. The emperor would stay. Feudalism would be abolished. Civil
rights would be assured. War would be forsworn and demilitarization would
become a permanent condition. MacArthur, a general in two world wars, believed that war was an obsolete institution. Despite his famous statement in
the Korean War that "there is no substitute for victory," he repeated some of
the pacifist ideas he had voiced on the deck of the *Missouri* to the end of his
life. The prime minister of the moment, Baron Kijūrō Shidehara, strongly
favored the antimilitarism clause, which became Article Nine of the new Constitution. Indeed, MacArthur later said that Shidehara had first suggested it.
The baron foresaw what a generation of Japanese politicians came to believe,
that Japan's security depended upon disarmament, not armaments. With the
empire gone and without significant resources in the home islands, the Asian
coprosperity sphere for which Prime Minister Hideki Tojo had fought was
more vital than ever. But it could be achieved only by peace, not war.

When the "constituent assembly" in the Dai Ichi Building had done its
work and MacArthur had approved it—"It is undoubtedly the most liberal
constitution in history. . . ."—Whitney took it to Foreign Minister Yoshida
and Dr. Joli Matsumoto, the archconservative who had drafted the document
MacArthur had found so unsatisfactory. When they seemed shocked by its
distinctly un-Japanese ideas—"essential equality" of the sexes, bureaucrats
as "public servants," collective bargaining guaranteed, parliamentary democracy, constitutional monarchy—Whitney threatened to go to the people over
the heads of the government. As they sat in Yoshida's garden, General Whitney recounts proudly, he suddenly decided "to employ one more psychological
shaft." Turning to Yoshida's aide, he remarked how much we "have been
enjoying your atomic sunshine." As if to punctuate his oafishness, "a big B-29
came roaring over us." "Your way is so American," the aide later wrote the
general, ". . . straight and direct."

There followed a few days of marathon negotiations over details, but the
emperor had insisted that the American draft be the basis for the new constitution. On March 5, 1946, MacArthur announced his "sense of deep satisfaction that I am able to announce a decision of the Emperor and the government
of Japan to submit to the Japanese people a new and enlightened constitution
which has my full approval."

3

MacArthur's reformers, far more than Clay's, were clear about their goals, but they were divided on how to achieve them. MacArthur's orders, like Clay's, ordered him not to "assume any responsibility for the economic rehabilitation or the strengthening of the Japanese economy," but he paid no attention. Governing was to be placed in the hands of the Japanese authorities to a degree unimaginable in Clay's headquarters. MacArthur's orders even required him to stand aside in the event of an internal revolution. Yet how could the mandate to bring democracy to the Japanese be carried out by the Japanese politicians who had fully supported Tojo in the war? Even the roots of democracy seemed to be missing. In the 1920s the electorate had amounted to less than 450,000 out of an adult population of over 30 million. Political parties had been dissolved in 1940.

"The only thing that will save your country is a sharp swing to the left," Major General Courtney Whitney was heard to lecture a Japanese politician. The alternative to a "revolution from above" appeared to be a revolution from below. "What we should fear most," Prince Fumimaro Konoye, the prime minister, had warned the emperor in February 1945, "is the possibility of a Communist revolution following defeat." When in October 1945 the Communist party was made legal for the first time since its founding in 1922, it could claim only six hundred members. But the Left was a serious force, MacArthur believed, since "many of the so-called liberal elements in Japan are Communistic." Scarcely a week after he had announced his directive ending curbs on civil liberties, the Japanese Left organized a hunger march in front of his headquarters calling for an end to hoarding. (As the government collapsed at the war's end politicians and industrialists had declared themselves dividends of billions of yen worth of food and raw materials.) By May Day there was a food rally in front of the imperial palace of more than 50,000, and some in the crowd tried to storm the gates. A second wave of demonstrations occurred throughout Japan a little over two weeks later. "Japan had been submerged under a sea of red flags," Shigeru Yoshida, the ex-diplomat who became prime minister through most of the occupation, recalls with the hyperbole he reserved for anything remotely red.

The Left, small as it was, could draw on the anger of a devastated people toward the military clique and the politicians and industrialists who had brought them to such disaster. With the end of the war, living conditions grew worse. The repatriation of Japan's armies and imperial establishments overseas swelled the population by six million. The disastrous postwar harvest was 60 percent of what had been produced while the fighting was on. Coal production was one-eighth of the prewar level. Eighty percent of the textile machinery had been uprooted from the factories and converted to war use; most of it was now rubble. The merchant fleet was gone. Two and a half million homes had been destroyed.

A purge of the old guard was a precondition for the "imposed democracy"

MacArthur wished to leave as his legacy to the nation he had subdued. How much of a purge was another question, one that deeply divided his staff. The Japanese conservatives, led by Yoshida, who had pressed for the surrender to avoid ruin and revolution, counted on Joseph Grew, the former U.S. ambassador in Tokyo and a personal friend, to set the postwar policy. But the "Japan Crowd" in the State Department faced a "China Crowd" led by Stanley Hornbeck, who favored a much tougher policy for Japan in order to provide breathing space for a strong China which could be the linchpin of American policy in the Far East. This split in Washington was mirrored in MacArthur's headquarters. His section included American professors, economists, and other specialists who quickly acquired a reputation for being left-wingers bent on bringing socialism to Japan. The curious label was pasted on the conservative general's domain as a consequence of bureaucratic infighting and skillful manipulation of the Communist issue by Japanese politicians.

The head of G-2 (Counter-Intelligence Section) was Major General Charles Willoughby, another longtime MacArthur aide, whose name originally was Von Tscheppe und Weidenbach. Indeed, so taken with right-wing militants was he that the supreme commander himself would refer to him as "my loveable fascist." Willoughby successfully protected some of Tojo's key officers. (In retirement he became an adviser to Franco.) Communicating in his native German with the Japanese generals who had been in the closest liaison with the Nazis, Willoughby even succeeded in putting some of them on the American payroll. For example, the former chief of military intelligence, Lieutenant General Seigo Arisne, was made a "historian" of Soviet troop deployments. (As early as September 22, 1945, the Soviet High Command communicated its alarm to the Soviet Far East commander in chief that MacArthur "repeats the same mistake that was committed in 1918 in relation to Germany.") Soviet concern about the American failure to conduct a wholesale purge of the Japanese military sprang from recent memories of more than 500 border clashes in Manchuria. In 1939 a Japanese offensive on the border was stopped by Soviet troops at an estimated cost of 25,000 Japanese lives and 9000 Soviet.

General Whitney, who wanted a much more thoroughgoing purge of the Japanese militarists, quickly found himself under attack as a cryptoleftist. As Harry Emerson Wildes, who worked for both Whitney and Willoughby recalls:

Certainly Whitney was no Communist, nor had he sympathy with Communist procedure; but the purge pattern that developed oddly paralleled the methods used in Iron Curtain countries, for one false step, one minor deviation, in the past cancelled out a lifetime of liberalism. The method opened the way to the worst excesses of backstabbing and delation, for an anonymous accusation of guilt, offered without proof, was sometimes accepted as sufficient evidence.

It did not help when Yoshio Shiga, a Communist editor who visited Whitney's offices regularly, declared publicly that "MacArthur's aides were Communists, and that the Occupation demanded support for Communist candidates.'' But then every splinter party trying to get organized was manipulating the Government Section. Racketeers raised campaign funds for a largely fictitious party on the strength of a careless endorsement of a GS officer. An archreactionary group invited Whitney's chief political adviser to a banquet and displayed photographs of the occasion to "prove" the real sentiments of the occupation.

By far the most skillful manipulator of the Americans was Yoshida. He would regularly warn MacArthur of the "Soviet menace" and "Red subversives." Did the general really wish to turn Japan Red? If not, he should watch the "New Dealers" and the "idealists" surrounding General Whitney and give more support to the "realists" like Willoughby. It was quite true that of all the political parties in Japan in 1946–47 the program of the Communist party most closely resembled occupation policies. "Loveable communism," as Communist party chief Sanzo Nosaka called his program, provided for "peaceful reformation through political action" and more thoroughgoing reform of militarist institutions and economic concentration than any other party. When SCAP began to dismantle the *zaibatsu,* limiting the profit of foreign traders, Colonel Robert R. McCormick, publisher of the *Chicago Tribune,* attacked MacArthur's "socialistic economic policies." Senator William F. Knowland, known in the 1950s as the senator from Formosa because of his close ties to the exiled regime of Chiang Kai-shek, demanded a congressional investigation. *Fortune* began attacking MacArthur's "Scapitalism."

Yoshida, aware of his allies in the United States, mounted a campaign for a counterpurge by exploiting the rivalry between the Whitney and Willoughby groups. He would go directly to MacArthur, dropping names of Japanese politicians of leftist tendencies who ought to be purged and relentlessly attacking the "New Dealers" within SCAP. He eliminated more than one politician by hinting that MacArthur was about to purge him. William Sebald, the State Department adviser, thought MacArthur underestimated the Communist danger in Japan and the supreme commander's reticence about making explicit public attacks on Japanese Communists in the early years of the occupation resulted in the growing charge that left-wingers were running his headquarters. Willoughby launched "searching personnel screenings" of the supposed left-wingers on the staff of the occupation, and many were sent home. In the mid-1950s some of them were called before the Senate Subcommittee on Internal Security. George Atcheson, John Stewart Service, and John K. Emmerson had to defend themselves a decade after their service in SCAP on charges of being Communists or associating with Communists. As in Germany, U.S. policy in Japan quickly became entangled in the ideology of the Cold War. Like Adenauer, Yoshida knew how to use the fever of anti-Communism to resist the revolution from above at the hands of American generals.

The Potsdam Declaration had called for the elimination "for all time" of Japan's war-making clique. The "Basic Initial Post-Surrender Directive" MacArthur brought with him when he arrived in Tokyo ordered him to arrest high military officers, "leaders of ultranationalist and militarist organizations" and to exclude "from public office and from any other position of public or substantial private responsibility" all active exponents of "militarism and militant nationalism." Many high-ranking officers were immediately arrested, but as one officer recalls, MacArthur "not only spared others who seemed to be of equal guilt but placed them on the Occupation payroll and gave them special privilege."

About one thousand Japanese, including Prime Ministers Hideki Tojo and Koji Hirota, were tried by an international war crimes tribunal. Seven men, including the former prime minister, were sentenced to death and secretly hanged with foreign diplomats looking on. (William Sebald left a dinner party to attend the execution.) MacArthur's principal adversaries on the battlefield, Generals Masaharu Homma and Tomoyuki Yamashita, were tried by court-martial on trumped-up evidence. "In the opinion of probably every correspondent covering the trial," *Newsweek* reported on the Yamashita trial, "the military commission came into the courtroom the first day with the decision already in its collective pocket." After Homma, the aging conqueror of Luzon had been brought before the firing squad, H. L. Mencken observed that MacArthur had killed "the man who beat him in a fair fight on Bataan." The evidence linking Homma to the atrocities of the Death March was shaky at best. The condemnation of Yamashita was, as two justices of the United States Supreme Court put it, simply a case of "legalized lynching." But a year after the war, the verdicts were upheld.

The purge of civilian leaders considered to be militarists but not war criminals was a responsibility of the Japanese; the Japanese government was expected to supply lists of potential "purgees." Tatsuo Iwabuchi, a purge administrator for the Japanese government, claimed that when a list of 3000 offenders was presented to Courtney Whitney, the general "complained that 300,000 Nazis had been purged under an identical program in Germany, and that Japan must match, if not exceed that total." In the zeal to amass a list of 210,000 "purgees," the ostensible purpose of the effort was forgotten. The new Japan would be "democratized" by police state methods. Men were convicted on the unsupported word of anonymous informers and were declared ineligible for public office if even distant relatives were tainted. The loose procedures offered considerable opportunity for Japanese looking to settle old scores or to get potential rivals for office out of the way.

When the purge was announced, about 100,000 politicians and bureaucrats throughout Japan quit their jobs. The Progressives, then the majority party, lost 247 of their 274 Diet members. The Liberals, also a conservative party, lost 20 out of 50 members, including the founder of the party, Ichirō Hatoyama, who was purged on the very day Premier Shidehara recommended him to MacArthur as his successor. The purge helped to reshuffle much of the older politicians and business leadership and thus propelled a new generation into key management positions. The forced modernization of government and business bureaucracy probably helped Japan to become more efficient and competitive. However, as John Montgomery, who wrote a detailed study of the occupation, *Forced to be Free,* concludes, "The purge as a political revolution failed to discredit the old Japanese elite or to enlist public support of the new leadership."

4

From the cubicles inside the Dai Ichi Building there blew a veritable hurricane of reform. Every phase of Japanese life was touched by the conqueror's directives. Only a relatively small proportion of the bureaucrats and reformers knew the Japanese language or history; what they lacked in knowledge they made up for in zeal. The results were predictably mixed. Contemporary observers attacked MacArthur from all sides. For *The New Republic* MacArthur seemed to be appeasing "the conservative social and economic elements in Japan which were behind this war." George Kennan, on the other hand, thought such SCAP policies as abolishing the central police seemed to have been devised "for the specific purpose of rendering Japanese society vulnerable to Communist political pressures and paving the way for a Communist takeover. . . ." The general ran a running battle with the press, but a succession of distinguished visitors—Philip Jessup, Henry Luce, Roger Baldwin, Philip La Follette, John Gunther—returned from encounters with MacArthur to sing his praises. *The New York Times* called MacArthur's administration "a model of government and a boon to peace in the Far East."

"The Japanese police problems," General Whitney recalls, "led to some of the longest discussions—not to say the most heated arguments—in SCAP offices during the entire occupation." Whitney's section favored not only the elimination of *Kempei Tai* ("secret police") and *Tokko* ("Thought Control Police") but the decentralization of all police. U.S. military intelligence opposed the idea for the same reason Kennan did. It would leave the country vulnerable to the Communists. Besides, decentralization went against the Japanese tradition. Since Pearl Harbor Day the police ranks had shrunk by about one-half. Ten thousand had been purged. However, high officials of the Thought Control Police resigned before the purge directives were issued and moved skillfully into other employment. Shigenori Hata, for example, who had run the Thought Control Division in the Tokyo Metropolitan Police Board during the war, was by 1946 a section chief in the Investigation Bureau of the Home Ministry. Other *Tokko* alumni were spread throughout the Education and Welfare ministries, and at least two served as prefectural governors. One was chief of the Labor Division—in a position to direct the growth of unions he was once charged with destroying—and another chief of the Wood and Charcoal Section in the Agriculture Ministry, a position of enormous power because charcoal was the critical household fuel. Hata told a reporter that he was not worried about being removed from his powerful position despite his past. "After all, my section has been set up at the request of your army."

Lewis J. Valentine, the former New York police commissioner, was called

in to work on a centralized police system. "These people drive you crazy," he
muttered as he set about modernizing the corps of bicycle-riding police who
carried swords and wore ill-fitting uniforms held together with safety pins. But
MacArthur favored Whitney's plan for an "autonomous" police force for
every city of five thousand people or more. That meant organizing 1605 separate police forces. Much of the financing was to come from the private subsidies of "crime prevention clubs," a traditional mechanism for bribery. The
plan was intended to encourage grass-roots democracy, but local communities
resisted the costs involved and the plan proved very unpopular. By 1950, with
the onset of the Korean War and the more militant tactics of the Japanese
Communist party, Yoshida succeeded in reversing the policy. In 1954 the
highly centralized police system under a national police chief was established
that has operated ever since. The re-creation of a national police agency provoked riots in the Diet itself and two hundred policemen were called into the
chamber to restore order.

Yoshida later blamed MacArthur's misguided police reforms for the Japanese government's failure in 1960 to control the hostile crowd that surrounded
and jostled the car President Eisenhower's press secretary, James Hagerty,
was riding in. Hagerty came as an advance man to arrange a visit for the
president, but the scary episode caused the presidential trip to be canceled.
Having been forced to "democratize" the force and "think twice before even
laying hands on a thief," Yoshida later snorted, "one could not expect it to
become suddenly efficient in protecting Mr. Hagerty. We had only the Occupation Forces to thank for that."

Other reforms lasted longer than the abortive effort at community control
of the police. Women were given economic and political rights, allowed to vote
and to hold property for the first time. Contract marriage, a form of legally
sanctioned matrimonial slavery, was abolished. Adultery was no longer a
crime. Previously it had been a crime only for women, a provision now inconsistent with the equal rights guarantees in the constitution. Whitney proudly
writes in his memoirs how wrong the advice proved to be of the Japan "experts" who said that women would never exercise their rights:

> The Japanese women were embracing their freedom in many ways. They sought
> and found jobs in almost every business and profession, even including the local police
> forces; there were nearly 2,000 women police by 1951. More than 1,500,000 women
> joined labor unions . . . Women also campaigned vigorously for equal *sake* and cigarette
> rations and an end to concubinage and family contract marriages; they bought their own
> property, took time out from their housework to read *Blondie,* learned to square-dance,
> and even listened to radio soap operas.

MacArthur's bid for lasting influence in Japan was to make what he called
"the greatest spiritual revolution the world had ever known." Not much of a
churchgoer himself, MacArthur was resolved to make the occupation "a practical demonstration of Christian ideals." When four Protestant leaders came to
see him in the fall of 1945, he told them, "Japan is a spiritual vacuum. If you
do not fill it with Christianity, it will be filled with Communism. Send me 1000

missionaries." Ten million Bibles were promptly imported. MacArthur told Billy Graham, who came to visit him, that the emperor had "declared his willingness to make Christianity the national religion of Japan," but the offer had been rejected because it was "wrong to impose any religion on a people."

But religion could be used as cultural propaganda for transforming "a race long stunted by ancient concepts of mythological teaching" and for creating a favorable climate for democracy. For democracy to take root secular education would also have to be reformed. Twenty-seven American educators were called in to give their advice on what the Japanese should learn. A Marine Corps officer, Donald Nugent, was put in charge of the program, and the supreme commander personally tried his hand at drafting the education bill. The overriding goal was to root out the educational influences of prewar Japan which had fostered militarism and ultranationalism, celebrated stratification, and created inequality. Before the war, school had been compulsory for only six years. The tracking system was exquisitely elitist. The top rung in the ladder was the University of Tokyo. With rare exceptions, the absence of a degree from that institution effectively barred the way to the upper reaches of the establishment.

MacArthur had barely settled in when he ordered suspension of all teaching of traditional Japanese values in what had been compulsory courses in ethics and morals. A diet of "civics" and "social studies" was substituted for Japanese history and geography. Compulsory education was greatly extended and universities were opened to the qualified. Textbooks would no longer be controlled by the Ministry of Education. Indeed the centralized hold of the ministry on the education system would be broken much in the manner of the police reform. And like the police reform, the imported system of elective local school boards was overturned soon after the occupation ended.

But the generals in the Dai Ichi Building took credit for having taught pacifism. General Whitney recounts a visit in 1953 from "Dr. Suess," the author of popular children's books, in which he asked Japanese schoolchildren about their career aspirations. Only one schoolboy in a fairly large sample aspired to a military career, and he wanted to be MacArthur! The supreme commander believed that he had wrought "a spiritual revolution . . . which almost overnight tore asunder a theory and practise of life built upon two thousand years of history and tradition and legend." Of course, that was pure legend itself. From the start Japanese politicians of the old school, especially Yoshida, conducted a rearguard action against the premises of the educational reform. They deeply resented the charge that their cultural tradition was un-democratic. The 1880 Imperial Rescript on Education was the embodiment of the "spirit of democracy," Education Minister Maeda Tamon insisted in October 1945, and he asked to have it read aloud in student assemblies to inculcate "spiritual composure." Yoshida believed that the country could not afford the elaborate system of near universal education SCAP was promoting and feared that the antimilitarist propaganda of the Americans was eroding "love of the country."

The traditionalists also worried about the excessive individualism that had been introduced by the occupation. In 1951 the education minister tried drafting a new code of ethics for the defeated nation, "a sort of moral minimum," Yoshida put it, that would reinforce the moral authority of the state. The conservatives who ran the government worried about the leftist bent of the teacher's union, and saw the classroom as a political arena in which a new generation could be subjected to subversive influence. Some of the fiercest political battles in postwar Japan swirled around education policy. Robert King Hall, who participated in the early reforms, noted thirty years later how ephemeral they were:

> The *Mombusho* [Ministry of Education] today has recovered all of its authority and again controls the standards of schools, the courses of study, the authorization of all textbooks used in elementary and secondary schools. . . . The intent of the Occupation policy was clearly not achieved."

The land reform abolished the institution of the absentee landlord and distributed land to two million small farmers. Five million acres changed hands. Almost 90 percent of the land now belonged to those who farmed it. In prewar Japan 70 percent of the peasants were tenants who were often forced to surrender the lion's share of their crop to the landlord. Now the law limited rents to cash payments which could not exceed one-quarter of the crop. The goal of SCAP's land reform was explicitly radical—"to break the economic bondage which has enslaved Japanese farmers through centuries of feudal oppression."

Carrying out a reform that would transform centuries of old habits and old relationships in a little over two years was a formidable task. The effort involved 36,000 bureaucrats, 115,000 poorly paid members of local land committees, and a quarter million volunteers. Within four years there accumulated 10 pieces of amending legislation, 31 ordinances, 51 ministerial regulations, and 120 ministry circulars all containing loopholes and exceptions for landlords adept at working the system. Because of land scarcity the peculiarities of Japanese farming created all sorts of hard cases. When the owner of an apple orchard, for example, had let another farmer cultivate a few square feet between the trees, as often happened, was that "owner" land or "tenant" land?

The essence of the reform was a government purchase program. The land was then resold in small plots to the tenants under thirty-year 3.2 percent mortgages. An acre cost about the price of a carton of black-market cigarettes. The favorite method of evasion for the landlord was to reclaim the land and become a working farmer himself. In just ten months there were 250,000 cases of landlords displacing their tenants so as to become beneficiaries of the reform.

Ending the extreme maldistribution of land that had characterized prewar Japan alleviated much of the desperate poverty of the countryside. Although the conquerors' plans were communicated to the Japanese in secret, everyone knew where the credit for what MacArthur called "possibly the most successful land reform in history" belonged. The supreme commander had burst a revolutionary bubble. "When I heard the news," Yamaguchi Tekehide, leader of a radical farmers union recalls, "I thought 'damn,' if they had not done that we should have had a revolutionary government in Tokyo in a couple of years." Certain effects of the reform were revolutionary in themselves. Although dependence of poor farmers on their relatively richer and more powerful neighbors for credit, firewood, or extra income was still considerable, tenant farmers were no longer "kept alive by the grace and favor" of their landlords. Peasant unions began to play an important role in transforming the myriad directives and hortatory lectures of Tokyo bureaucrats into what the British student of land reform R. P. Dore terms a change "which shook Japanese rural society by the ears." Yet the countryside remained overwhelmingly conservative, providing a reliable power base for the Liberal-Democrats, the conservative party that has, with one brief exception, ruled Japan since the war.

Unlike other reforms imposed by the Americans the effects of the land reform persisted. But the credit belongs less to the reformers from across the sea than to Japanese politicians and business leaders who understood that building a modern industrial society required the transformation of feudal structures. The old rural elites, hostile to the new industrial capitalists, had allied themselves with the military, hoping thereby to preserve their privileges by focusing the energies of the nation on foreign expansion. With the aid of the conqueror the great industrial families of Japan triumphed over the reactionary landed aristocracy.

5

In Germany there had been a political hiatus in the early years of the occupation; in Japan there was none. The rebuilding of the national political structures took years in Germany because for four years there was no national state. In Japan the cabinet and the bureaucracy continued to function even as the country was disarmed. Prewar parties and personalities reemerged, sometimes with new names and new reputations. The old Minseito and Seiyukai party machines turned themselves into the Progressive and Liberal parties. But their ranks were thinned in the purge, as were the Social Democrats, many of whose leaders also had given active support to the policy of conquest. Only the Communists had a consistent record of opposing prewar militarism and this, as in Europe, redounded to their credit in the immediate postwar period. Sanzo Nosaka, the Communist leader, had spent the war years leading a contingent of Japanese in China fighting side by side with Mao's armies. When MacArthur allowed him to return to Tokyo, he received an ovation from crowds in the street.

Despite freedom of the press guaranteed by the occupation authorities, a freedom used so vigorously to attack the conservative cabinet in power that SCAP imposed some restrictive "guidelines," the bases of power, neighborhood organizations, much of the labor movement, and the *zaibatsu* were in the hands of the conservatives. In the first postwar elections in April 1946, the old guard captured more than 300 of 466 seats. The Social Democrats managed to elect 92 members to the Diet and the Communists five.

Following Admiral Kantaro Suzuki, the prime minister at the moment of surrender, Prince Higashikuma headed the government for the first six weeks of the occupation. In the next seven years three former diplomats under the old regime held the office. One of them, Shigeru Yoshida, put his stamp on the era. Like Adenauer, he was near seventy when he became the towering national figure of the day. A proud man with a weakness for punning, famous for his imperious manners and imperial instincts, Yoshida was elected prime minister five times. Like Adenauer, he sensed the moment of national defeat as a personal opportunity.

He had a diplomatic career of middling success, having been consul in China and ambassador in London. Like John Foster Dulles, who would be his congenial negotiating partner for the treaty to end the occupation, Yoshida had been a minor functionary at the Versailles peace negotiations in 1919. Basically pro-Western, he had had a close personal relationship in the prewar years with the American ambassador Joseph Grew. Yoshida wrote the diplomat a touching letter and sent him food parcels after he was interned after Pearl Harbor. Throughout his career Yoshida was a patient imperial bureaucrat, fearful of the excesses of militarism and Communism alike, absolutely dedicated to preserving the old Japan by deft alliances with the most reliable centers of power in the world. He happened to believe, contrary to the prevailing orthodoxy, that these were Britain and America, not Nazi Germany. "I am not behind others in my admiration for Yoshida," Prince Konoye, the prewar prime minister in whose cabinet Yoshida served, remarked not long before he committed suicide to escape prosecution for war crimes, "but Yoshida's consciousness is the consciousness of the era of 'Imperial Japan,' and I wonder if that can go well in a defeated Japan."

Yoshida was born in 1878, two years after Adenauer, of a young samurai and a woman who was probably a geisha. On the day of his birth his father was in prison for plotting against the government, and at age nine days, the baby was adopted by Kenzo Yoshida, a close family friend. Because of his formidable manner Shigeru Yoshida was throughout his long career forever tagged with the nickname "Wan Man," a curious transliteration of the English "One Man." His abundant self-confidence, he wrote years later, was reinforced by his adopted mother, who would, he remembers, exclaim with delight: "This child is a proud child." Yoshida recalled with relish that he was always "egoistic and greatly troublesome. . . ."

His marriage into the family of a prominent diplomat gave his career a boost, and by 1928 he was a vice-foreign minister. He had favored all of Japan's earlier conquests, including the annexation of Korea in 1910 and the military intervention in Siberia in 1917, and he believed that Japan had rights in Manchuria and China, but he saw a great difference between Japan's Asiatic ambitions and warrior past and the new militarism of the 1930s. He had not hesitated to recommend military intimidation in support of Japanese objectives in China, but he made enemies among the ultranationalists by criticizing "crude army intrigues in China," and in opposing the ambitious plans of the navy at the time of the 1922 Naval Disarmament Conference. A deal could be struck with Great Britain and the United States, he told Yosuke Matsuoka the diplomat who would seal the Anti-Comintern Pact with Hitler, if only someone of stature would represent Japan in the League of Nations (meaning someone other than Matsuoka). When Matsuoka, a leading militarist, demurred, Yoshida offered typically forceful advice: "You should go to an insane asylum, douse your head in water, and then leave after you have cooled down a bit."

He strongly opposed the rapprochement with Hitler, and as ambassador to Great Britain worked hard at holding together Japan's fraying ties with the Anglo-Saxon world. As late as October 1941, after Japan had signed the Tripartite Pact with Hitler and Mussolini, Yoshida, now retired, visited Ambassador Grew three times and urged the United States to make a joint statement with Japan to keep hands off Indochina. But the plan to unleash an Asia-wide war had already been approved by the emperor on September 6. All during the war Yoshida conspired ineffectually with a circle of businessmen, peers, retired military, journalists, and diplomats who opposed the war to find a way to overthrow Tojo and make peace. By the end of 1944, with the defeat of Japanese forces in the Philippines and the final onslaught on the home islands imminent, Yoshida helped draft an appeal to the emperor to stop the war.

Recently, as the war enters a stage of crisis, voices calling for "one-hundred million fighting to the death" have gradually increased in strength. Those who make such pronouncements are the so-called right-wingers, but it is my estimation that the ones who are agitating them from behind are communist elements who ultimately are aiming at the goal of revolution by turning the country into chaos in this manner.

For his efforts Yoshida was arrested two months later by the military police and held in custody for forty days.

Shortly after the first U.S. units arrived in Japan, the former diplomat was summoned to Tokyo from his retirement villa at the seashore for what turned out to be an audience with the emperor at which he was made foreign minister. (He was unprepared for the meeting, and his borrowed, oversized shoes, he recalls, "emitted strange noises," in the imperial presence.) On the way to the encounter that would mark the beginning of his second career, he had met two American GIs whom he imagined to be "on some kind of marauding expedition," but they were merely hitchhikers and soon were pressing chocolates, chewing gum, and cigarettes on the future prime minister. He liked to tell the incident at SCAP, and General Whitney was convinced that the reason the occupation worked so smoothly is that the Japanese from the prime minister down had been overcome by the spiritual qualities nurtured in the American home.

Yoshida was prime minister for all but thirteen months of the occupation

years. An autocrat by disposition and ideology, he ruled the Liberal party with
an iron hand. "It is impertinent," he once said, "for party members to question what the party president does." Despite the efforts of the SCAP reformers
to transplant American parties in Japanese soil, Yoshida's characteristically
impatient remark reflected the political reality of Japan. Political parties dated
only from 1874, and they had always been much more vehicles for personal
rule of prominent personalities than machines for building a national consensus, as in the United States, or a political program, as in Europe.

Elevated to prominence by accident though he was—his forty days in jail
stood him in good stead as his rivals were purged—he savored his power. He
tripled the prime minister's staff, took up residence in a French Renaissance
mansion with expansive grounds, consorted with his neighbors, the Mitsuis
and Suimtomos, luxuriated in the imported whiskey, cigars, and the Rolls-
Royce to which his office entitled him, as he went about the country preaching
the virtues of thrift and hard work. His political genius was considerable, for,
quite literally, no one liked him. He betrayed his political mentor, by refusing
to give up his office as he had promised, once Hatoyama was "depurged."
Yoshida would crack an offending cameraman with his stick if the spirit moved
him, but he was such a stickler for etiquette that he fired a subordinate for
leaving a party before the Prime Minister. Although MacArthur came to respect Yoshida, the Prime Minister was no yes-man, and he carried on a continuing guerrilla warfare against what he considered the "leftists" in the Dai Ichi
Building.

Marvelously devious in navigating the minefields of Japanese politics,
Yoshida was steadfast in his goals. His principal objective was the preservation
of the "national polity" (*kokutai*), the historic legacy that made Japan unique.
That was why the retention of the emperor was so important. As the symbol
of the national destiny his continuation would mean that the "national polity"
had survived defeat. Yoshida was dedicated to preserving the old Japan, and
that required eliminating the threat of leftist revolution and restoring the traditional levers of power, the bureaucracy and the business establishment. The
"traditional diplomacy" from which the militarists of the 1930s had strayed
must be restored, and Japan should once again ally itself with the Anglo-Saxon
world. In eighty-six months in office Yoshida succeeded brilliantly in achieving
these objectives.

It was no small accomplishment, for Japan's conquerors landed with radically different notions of Japan's past and future. For Yoshida the war had
been a "historic stumble," a purely accidental consequence of conspiracy,
among militarists and Communists, and Japan's salvation was restoration, not
revolution. But the Americans called for radical changes. As Assistant Secretary of State Dean Acheson stated in September 1945, "The present economic
and social system in Japan which makes for a will to war will be changed so
that the will to war will not continue."

Yoshida took office under decidedly inauspicious circumstances.
"Hundreds of thousands of demonstrators denounced him in the streets.

Friends as well as foes urged him to withdraw, and both supporters and detractors scaled the walls around his residence to press their case upon him.'' Even some of the "Japan Crowd" in the State Department thought Yoshida was a "throwback." His first cabinet lasted a year. Most of it was spent in grudging implementation of MacArthur's revolutionary directives. The premier had not yet become expert in playing off the bureaucrats in the Dai Ichi against each other. As late as April 1948, MacArthur's private opinion of Yoshida was that he was "monumentally lazy and politically inept." Perhaps when Japan emerged from the occupation she could find something better than this "mediocre and uninspiring leader."

All through 1946 and the early months of 1947 the economic situation worsened. Inflation reduced the already precarious living standard. Unions grew in strength and militancy. The purge began to reach into the old guard, and four members of Yoshida's cabinet were forced to resign. When the Japanese went to the polls for the second time, despite an election law favoring the incumbents that was rammed through the Diet a few weeks before the election, the Socialists won a plurality of 143 seats. As Tetsu Katayama, the chairman of the SDP became premier, there was four days' supply of rice in government warehouses. Without any experience in government, unable to restrain the increasingly militant unions who were its chief source of support, the new cabinet lasted only ten months. When after seven months a hastily contrived coalition government collapsed because of graft and corruption on a heroic scale, Yoshida, now seventy, became premier again. Three months later he called an election and, despite his own continuing unpopularity within his party, led the Liberals to a smashing electoral victory.

In his first cabinet his strategy was already clear. He had observed that "history provides examples of winning by diplomacy after losing in war." One had to know how to be a good loser, Yoshida recalls his old schoolmaster, Admiral Suzuki, telling him:

> I thought this very true; but at the same time, I realized that it would not by any means be an easy task. I decided at any rate not to oppose everything that the Occupation said, nor to say yes to everything; since neither seemed to me in keeping with being a good loser. This meant that I was going to say all that I felt needed saying but that I would co-operate at the same time with the Occupation Forces to the best of my power. Whatever harm was done through the Occupation Forces not listening to what I had to say could be remedied after we had regained our independence.

For all his crusty conservatism he had bent considerably in the first cabinet. The man he appointed to run the land reform was an avowed Socialist. In the name of General MacArthur he had issued orders to strengthen the labor movement, cripple the bureaucracy, desanctify Japan's imperial past, and guarantee the personal freedom of the hated Communists. But in 1948 things would go better.

The Cold War was on and dramatic changes in occupation policy closely paralleled those that were taking place in Germany. In a speech to the Com-

monwealth Club in San Francisco, on January 6, 1948, Secretary of the Army
Kenneth C. Royall noted the "conflict between the original concept of broad
demilitarization and the new purpose of building a self-supporting nation."
The choice for the American taxpayer was to keep subsidizing Japan or to
remove the principal impediments to her own economic growth, the continued
exaction of reparations, and the efforts to break up and transform what
MacArthur had called the "private socialism" of the great family-held monopolies. The very same individuals who had posed these same choices in Germany, William H. Draper—Clay's adviser was now under secretary of the
army—and Joseph Dodge—the Detroit banker was now a special ambassador
in Japan—were instrumental in causing MacArthur to shift gears in Japan.

SCAP's initial policy toward labor was to encourage unions as an essential
institution for bringing democracy. Japan's few hundred Communist organizers had influence over the new labor movement far beyond their numbers.
Satomi Hakamada, head of the Communist party Labor Organization Committee, reportedly boasted that five comrades controlled 11,000 teamsters, 14
controlled 10,000 printers, and 110 Communist newspapermen dominated the
Newspaper Workers Union. Eager at first to stand aloof from internal political
squabbles, MacArthur avoided the Communist issue, referring to the union
radicals as "disorderly minorities." But Yoshida kept pressing for a tough,
explicit anti-Communist policy. The censors, he said, were too permissive.
Japanese moviemakers were allowed to release pictures like *Builders of Tomorrow,* a film celebrating a Communist union and predicting the coming of
the Soviets. The GI newspaper *Stars and Stripes* treated the Communist leaders with excessive respect. Many of these charges were echoed within SCAP
itself as growing splits developed between democratic reformers (either out of
New Deal consciousness or more leftist commitments), and the probusiness
military bureaucrats.

Mark Gayn's *Japan Diary* gives a picture of what was happening:

While the Labor Division was talking in pious phrases to Japanese union leaders, counterintelligence agents were breaking up labor demonstrations . . . Men big and small,
from sergeants in remote detachments to General Willoughby, have begun to remake
the U.S. labor policy for Japan. From time to time, the Labor Division tried to assert
its interest in the subject. It was quickly slapped on the wrist. Its chief, Cohen, a young
man with a pathological fear of being labelled Red (though Lord knows he is not), was
no match for his tough military opponents. At this point, not even Japanese labor pays
much attention to the Labor Division. It has learned at a bitter cost where the real
power lies in Headquarters.

All through 1946 the unions grew more militant and the Communists
gained ground in the labor movement despite some efforts at SCAP to stop
them. The high point of leftist militancy was the General Strike called for
February 1, 1947, that was to have involved four million workers. "I will not
permit the use of so deadly a social weapon in the present impoverished and
emaciated condition of Japan," General MacArthur announced a few hours

before the strike was to begin, ''and have accordingly directed them to desist from the furtherance of such action.'' Any confusion about the general's tolerance for mass action or Communist agitation as instruments of democracy disappeared. Yoshida was ordered, to his delight, to ban all strikes by public officials. The Communist party newspaper was censored. Literature from Communist countries was reduced to a trickle and Japanese contacts with what now was called the ''iron curtain'' were sharply restricted.

A ''reverse course'' now began in earnest. A new head of the Labor Division at SCAP, James Killen, a former official of the Pulp, Sulphite, and Paper Mill Workers, helped organize ''democratization leagues'' within Japanese unions to combat the influence of the Communists, and officials of the AFL helped organize *Sohyo,* the anti-Communist General Council of Japanese Trade Unions which affiliated with the anti-Communist international federation of unions then being organized in Europe by leaders of the U.S. labor movement and CIA officials.

By the end of 1950, 11,000 leftists had lost their jobs and a sizable number of suspected Communist sympathizers were soon fired from government employment. Three weeks before the outbreak of the Korean War in June 1950, twenty-four members of the Central Committee of the Communist party were purged from public life. More than 5500 Japanese unions disappeared, and membership declined by 880,000 in one year. After the Korean War broke out, the hunt for ''subversives'' in government and in the unions had a new legitimacy, one reason among many why Yoshida referred to the war as ''a gift of the gods.'' In all about 22,000 individuals were affected by the ''red purge.'' The ''depurge'' was now well under way; by the end of the occupation most of the 200,000 war accomplices were back in public life. In the elections of 1952, 139 ''depurgees'' were elected to the Diet, the nucleus of a coalition that, ironically, would ultimately put an end to Yoshida's long career.

In March 1950, a ''labor offensive'' of unions representing five million workers purged of ''irresponsible leadership,'' as the official euphemism put it, now posed an even greater threat than the Communist-led strike three years earlier. Over a quarter million coal miners had already struck for seventy-two hours when MacArthur stepped in again and ordered the unions to go to compulsory arbitration. SCAP would not permit strikes to last more than a few days. MacArthur's ban on strikes and the growing splits within the labor movement encouraged by SCAP crippled the radicals and did much to reinforce the conservative pro-business character of postwar Japan.

Yoshida watched with satisfaction as the Americans purged their own ''idealists'' and moved to a proper appreciation of the red menace in Japan. ''Loveable communism'' had given way to street violence, wildcat strikes, and a Stalinist vilification campaign which hit the Americans where they were weakest. The skillful propaganda campaign emphasized that Japan was becoming a colony under the heel of uncultured bullies who cared nothing for the glories of the Japanese past. American soldiers who were much in evidence made inviting targets for anger and ridicule; the few Soviet soldiers in Japan were mostly withdrawn to their quarters. The registered enrollment of the Japanese Communist party never reached 100,000, but in 1949 Communist candidates received 18 percent of the vote in Tokyo and 20 percent in Ōsaka. As MacArthur's policies became more overtly anti-Communist, the premier's world view and the general's began more and more to coincide.

Encouraged by SCAP, Yoshida passed a revision of the early occupation labor law that strengthened the hands of employers and tried vainly to get a law prohibiting general strikes. The premier's distaste for the Left extended beyond the Communists to the left-wing Socialists whom he likened to mermaids. "Their faces suggest that they are beautiful maidens, but their bodies are like fish. Yes, they smell of fish." By rendering the country vulnerable to leftist influences, Yoshida charged, the occupation had introduced a "thirty-eighth parallel" that had divided the population and had destroyed Japan's historic national unity. An "Un-Japanese Activities Committee," he thought, would be a good way to promote ideological conformity and preserve the national identity, but, like a number of antisubversive measures he proposed, the Diet voted it down.

6

"The tangled financial mess," as MacArthur called it, that faced the Americans in Japan posed the same sort of dilemmas Clay was confronting at the very same moment in Germany. The "Basic Initial Post-Surrender Directive" from Washington called upon MacArthur to demilitarize Japanese industry. An American oil tycoon, Edwin Pauley, arrived in Tokyo in December 1945 on a fact-finding mission for President Truman to facilitate the task. Like most such fact finders, he found what he was looking for. Japan did not need much of its industrial plant for a purely civilian economy. Factories could be removed to "neighboring Asiatic countries" to raise their standard of living. Eleven hundred plants were marked for dismantling. MacArthur objected. Whatever policies would be pursued in Japan, the American taxpayer would have to dig deep into his pocket to keep the population from starving. Crippling Japanese industry would make it worse. In the end, MacArthur and his successor at SCAP, General Matthew Ridgway, received about $2 billion from Washington, less than a half of what was spent on the much smaller population of the U.S. Zone in Germany.

Reluctant to engage in physical dismantling of Japanese industry, MacArthur was strongly committed to working a legal and social revolution to transform its structure. "It is the intention of the Supreme Commander," he declared on November 6, 1945, "to dissolve the private industrial, commercial, financial, and agricultural combines in Japan" so as to permit a "wider distribution of income and ownership" and to encourage "institutions of a type that will contribute to the growth of peaceful and democratic forces. . . ." Ridding Japan of the stranglehold of the *zaibatsu* was not economic interference but an essential measure of demilitarization, for the feudal industrial and banking combines, the conquerors believed, were sources of "militant nationalism and aggression." As the Edwards Report of 1946 put it:

. . . the low wages and concentrated profits which were produced by such a structure have been inconsistent with the development of a domestic market capable of keeping pace with the increased productivity of Japanese industry; and in consequence Japanese business felt the need to expand its exports. . . . This drive for exports and for imports of food and raw materials has been an outstanding motive of Japanese imperialism.

The *zaibatsu,* the report continued, "are to be regarded as among the groups principally responsible for the war and as a principal factor in Japanese war potential. The responsibility is primarily institutional rather than personal."

The *zaibatsu* were the family-dominated industrial and banking combines that played the key role in the modernization of Japan for over a hundred years. At the end of the war eleven feudal families controlled over 70 percent of Japan's industrial, financial, and commercial activity. Each combine was a family-run conglomerate of mammoth proportions. The Mitsui Trading Company, for example, the largest, was described by Eleanor Hadley, the antitrust expert who worked for SCAP, in these terms:

A comparable business organization in the United States might be achieved if, for example, U.S. Steel, General Motors, Standard Oil of New York, Alcoa, Douglas Aircraft, E. I. du Pont de Nemours, Sunship Building, Allis Chalmers, Westinghouse Electric, American Telephone and Telegraph, RCA, IBM, U.S. Rubber, Sea Island Sugar, Dole Pineapple, U.S. Lines, Grave Lines, National City Bank, Metropolitan Life, The Woolworth Stores, and the Statler hotels were to be combined into a single enterprise.

These peculiarly Japanese institutions go back to the Tokugawa era of the early seventeenth century when former samurai established the great business houses of Mitsubishi, Yasuda, and Okura. Takatoshi Mitsui, another feudal warrior who might have been expected to enter government service, chose instead to open a pawnshop and a sake and soy-sauce factory which the family built into a sprawling economic empire in a little over one hundred years. The Mitsui operation was run by a family council which had the last word on anything related to the affairs of their employees, personal as well as business. Marriages, divorces, investment rates, and profit distributions all fell equally within its jurisdiction. The Mitsui code promulgated in 1722 reads like a feudal version of a business school syllabus. "Managers are those persons whose essential role it is to guard the business of the house. They shall give appropriate advice if their masters' conduct is not good and correct blunders which might be made. Since people get slow and blunt in their old age, an age limit for members of the board of around fifty-five shall be considered proper."

In the nineteenth century the leading merchant houses assumed various government functions. The Mitsuis became tax collectors, exchange agents, and quartermasters for the army. Their relationship with government was so close that officials sold the entire output of the Miike coal mine, the richest in

Japan, to the Mitsuis at cost. As the pace of industrialization stepped up after
the First World War, the hold of the *zaibatsu* on the Japanese economy grew
ever tighter. While subordinates would not even eat at the same restaurants
patronized by employees of the other combines, so fierce was their loyalty to
their bosses, the top officials felt no such constraints. Further concentration of
power and influence was accomplished through the intermarriage of leading
figures in the Mitsui and Mitsubishi enterprises. Thus, for example, one such
Mitsui executive, Ikeda Seihin, married off his daughter to the son of the family
that controlled the Mitsubishis and then solidified the family's power by serving as minister of finance, governor of the Bank of Japan, and member of the
Privy Council. With steady government support, the Mitsuis achieved control
over a major chunk of the country's banking, trading, and mining. In 1940 the
Mitsui combine by itself accounted for 22 percent of Japan's exports and 10
percent of its total imports. In 1945 it employed 1.8 million employees inside
Japan alone. The other three major family holding companies held similarly
dominant positions in the Japanese economy. Profit rates were spectactular.
The Mitsui Life Insurance Company showed a profit of 862 percent for the
year 1939.

As in Germany there were divisions from the start within MacArthur's
headquarters about how fast and how far to go with decartelization. Japanese
resistance was much better organized than in Germany. By early November
the four top holding companies, Mitsui, Mitsubishi, Yasuda, and Sumimoto
had themselves proposed a "dissolution" plan which MacArthur promptly
accepted. The plan affected only the top levels of ownership and left most of
the complex structure untouched. Actually, the Mitsuis and Mitsubishis had
"almost perfect" control over subsidiaries in which they had as little as 7
percent of the stock because control was based not only on ownership but on
a culture of feudal loyalty. Each employee was required to swear an oath of
loyalty and secrecy much like a government employee. A subsidiary of Mitsubishi Mining, for example, required its employees to sign the following:

I shall never violate the orders of the president or the instructions of my senior
officers.

I shall sincerely and assiduously perform my duties, never bringing loss to the
company.

I shall never divulge to a third party any of the affairs of the company large or
small, trivial or important.

With respect to any business I transact I shall always follow the instructions of my
senior official, never undertaking any transactions on my own judgement.

Japanese politicians and industrial leaders fought a rearguard action all
during 1946 to forestall any radical moves against the *zaibatsu*. Shortly after
the surrender Yoshida told foreign correspondents, "It is a great mistake to
judge the *zaibatsu* as having only done bad things. It can be said that the
prosperity of the Japanese people has depended in great part upon the effort of
these *zaibatsu*. Thus, it is doubtful that the dissolution of these old *zaibatsu*

will really benefit the people." But MacArthur, who believed that free enterprise was the foundation of democracy, was persuaded that the great combines
had formed one of the three legs on which Japanese militarism had rested—
the others being the army and the bureaucracy—and was determined to extend
the purge into the economic arena. The Joint Chiefs of Staff had advised him
that anyone holding a high position in finance or industry after 1937 was pre-
sumptively an "exponent" of aggression. But actually the number of top businessmen who had worked openly with the Japanese militarists was rather
small, certainly less than in Germany. While some of the newer combines
seemed to benefit from military expansion more directly than the older established trading companies, the extraordinary profits of the entire highly concentrated industrial and banking sector depended in no small measure on
expansionism. As Ginjiro Fujihara, president of Oji Paper Company, wrote in
The Spirit of Japanese Industry:

> I am far from recommending the use of armed forces for economic expansion in an
> aggressive way, but I rely on the army and navy for the protection which our foreign
> trade needs. . . . We have a splendid opportunity to expand abroad; it is the manifest
> destiny of the Japanese nation. . . . The success of Great Britain in India, where the
> East India Company actively promoted her interests, was due to the combined efforts
> of the people and government for national expansion. . . . Nothing is more important
> than force in achieving this ambition. Diplomacy without force is of no value.

Cartelization and militarism were inextricably linked because concentration
had virtually destroyed small business and stunted the domestic market,
thereby creating enormous pressures for overseas expansion.

In January 1947, just as the political purge was about to be reversed, the
economic purge got under way. Key officers in 245 companies had to resign.
They were free to take subordinate positions, but Japanese tradition effectively
prohibited such a course. One does not serve under an equal. (In the civil
service it is even customary to resign rather than become a subordinate to a
classmate.) The economic purge lasted four years. By mid-1951 only those
convicted of war crimes were still ineligible for high corporate office. During
the four years in which the Zaibatsu Appointees Law was in effect, the Yoshida cabinet was inventive in devising delaying tactics to slow down its implementation. Yoshida passionately argued against the punitive premises of the
purge. "Just imagine you have been bitten by a mad dog," he consoled his
finance minister, Ishibanzi Tanzan, when he received word that he had been
purged. When the occupation ended in 1954, the Mitsuis, Mitsubishis, and
Sumimotos still dominated the coal, metals, engineering, shipbuilding, electronics, chemicals, fibers, glass, and warehousing industries. The level of economic concentration was about what it had been in 1937.

It was a defeat for MacArthur. He had considered it his mandate "to
reshape the Japanese life toward capitalist economy." If the "concentration of
economic power" were not "torn down and redistributed peacefully. . . .
there is not the slightest doubt its cleansing will eventually occur through a

blood bath and revolutionary violence." Like Clay, the supreme commander
believed that an engineered reform of the defeated enemy economy could head
off more radical solutions. But the Anti-Monopoly and Deconcentration Laws
promulgated by SCAP, bristling with fierce legal rhetoric though they were,
were no match for the skillful coalition that formed against them.

The reformers' theory was straight New Deal. Democracy is not safe,
Franklin Roosevelt had declared in 1938, "if the people tolerate the growth of
private power to a point where it becomes stronger than their democratic state
itself." Competition—between the public and the private sphere and within
the private sphere—was the precondition for democracy, so went the American creed, but Japanese tradition was totally different. The whole society
rested on hierarchy and subtle processes of consensus. Individualism of the
sort typified by American entrepreneurs was looked upon as antisocial. Thus
there was deep suspicion of what the Americans were trying to do. For Yoshida the attack on the *zaibatsu* was "the expression of a desire on the part
of the Allied Powers to retaliate on the leaders of the nation they had defeated. . . ." Japanese Marxists saw MacArthur's program as a campaign on
behalf of U.S. "monopoly capital" to replace the Mitsuis and Mitsubishis with
General Motors and U.S. Steel. The American trustbusters were viewed as
bent on "Morgenthauizing" Japan.

In September 1947, William H. Draper, now under secretary of the army,
made an inspection trip to Japan and immediately launched a devastating campaign against MacArthur's trustbusting policies. Japan would be a permanent
ward of the United States if the United States actually implemented FEC-230,
the deconcentration directive. James Kauffman, a lawyer who worked with
Overseas Consultants, Inc., an organization dedicated to opening up the Japanese market, attacked MacArthur's program for being "far to the left of anything tolerated in this country." How could Japan become "the workshop of
Asia," the lawyer wrote in *Newsweek,* if her industry were being atomized "as
effectively as the famous bomb destroyed Hiroshima?" Kauffman was convinced that Japan could be "a most attractive prospect for American industry
and a fertile field for American capital" if MacArthur would come to his
senses. Draper returned to Japan the following year with the head of the Chemical Bank and other top business figures from the United States and issued a
report calling for the drastic curtailment of the deconcentration program. Senator William Knowland, who shared the fear of many businessmen in the
United States that MacArthur's missionary zeal to reform the Japanese economy might find its way back to the United States, attacked the war hero on the
floor of the Senate for his "shocking economic policies . . . contrary to our
way of life." By mid-1948 the antitrust program was in reverse gear. Of the
325 firms selected for radical surgery, all but 19 escaped.

By 1953 the Anti-Monopoly Law had been radically revised in favor of big
business. The old *zaibatsu* gave way to new "enterprise groups" in which
banks played an ever more important role, but although family members themselves were no longer so prominent in high executive positions, the old family

"money cliques" continued to play a crucial part in the development of the new Japan. The new *zaibatsu* were looser, less feudal institutions than their ancestors. However, even as the occupation was ending, the Japanese government was actively promoting cartels. The Ministry of International Trade and Industry was "recommending" production curtailment in key industries and enforcing its views by controlling foreign currency and access to raw materials. The Bank of Japan also encouraged the practice of "collaborative production curtailment" by controlling credit. Despite the prevailing trustbusting ideology with which SCAP started, because of internal divisions within the headquarters and strong Japanese resistance, the American reformers were powerless to prevent the recartelization of Japan. The same sort of dual economy in which the government favored the giants at the expense of small, vulnerable subcontractors that had marked prewar Japan emerged again by the early 1950s. Bankrupt small businessmen began shooting themselves, but the Yoshida government refused to implement laws that supposedly kept the giants from squeezing the small firms. "It can't be helped," Ikeda Hayatom, Yoshida's economic czar, told the press, "if one or two businessmen commit suicide."

7

By 1952 the defeated enemies in Europe were on their way to becoming brothers-in-arms. Rearmament symbolized the radical shift that now tied the fortunes of the Germans and the Americans. American-Japanese relations took a similar course in the same period but with important differences. Pacifist sentiment in Japan was stronger; a visit to Hiroshima or Nagasaki or an encounter with a disfigured survivor in the throes of a slow and painful death or the collective memories of the fire storm that engulfed Tokyo all fed the strong popular revulsion from militarism in any form. In Germany the new military relationship was built on the physical defense of German territory by a large contingent of U.S. troops; in Japan the Americans would stay in bases throughout the island but the antiwar provision MacArthur had insisted on inserting into the new constitution was never in question, and neither the Japanese nor the Americans would maintain troops in sufficient numbers even to make a pretense of defending the islands against an all-out attack. But the third difference, of course, was that such an attack was less plausible than in Germany where Soviet armies camped just across the Elbe.

Nevertheless, the evolution of American policy followed the same general lines as in Germany, and Japanese politicians were as astute as their German counterparts in conceding real estate to the American military machine in exchange for the restoration of full control over the destiny of Japan. Americans underwent the same radical change of heart about Japanese rearmament as they were having in Germany. But again there were two important differences: much greater internal division inside the U.S. government between the

State Department and the military and much greater opposition from America's allies in the Pacific.

MacArthur himself was ambivalent and confusing when it came to Japan's future role in the Pacific. He seemed to have a much clearer conception of what he wanted to accomplish inside Japan than of the contribution the island power should make to American military strategy. As early as March 1947, he was telling reporters in Tokyo that Japan was ready for a peace treaty, that U.S. troops should not stay in Japan, and that the occupation should be quickly ended. (The State Department quickly repudiated such ideas. The occupation would in fact last five more years.) The general took pride in the antimilitary provisions of the MacArthur constitution and as late as 1949 continued to wax eloquent about the new "Switzerland of the East." On the other hand, less than a year after the war he termed the Pacific an "Anglo-Saxon lake" and explicitly included Japan in the nations' new expanded "defense" perimeter— the most important of "the chain of islands fringing the coast of Asia."

Back in Washington military planners were designing a new role for Japan which was acquiring great importance in the gathering bureaucratic storm inside the Pentagon. The proponents of a separate Air Force took the offensive at the end of the war, arguing that strategic bombing had defeated both Germany and Japan and that the future defense of the United States demanded a huge air force and a global chain of air bases surrounding the Eurasian landmass. On June 14, 1944, the Army Air Force staff officers circulated a long-range planning document for the postwar world based on the assumption that "peace prevails throughout the world," and that peace treaties with the enemies had been concluded. The Soviet Union was assumed to be not an enemy but a principal ally in keeping Germany disarmed, although, the writer warned, "our allies of today may be leagued against us tomorrow." A resurgent Japan was assumed to be the primary enemy. The United States alone would have the responsibility of keeping defeated Nippon under control, but bases in Alaska, the Philippines, Okinawa, and other Japanese-controlled islands of the Pacific would enable the Air Force to do the job. Curiously even the extravagant dreams of Air Force planners did not contemplate permanent bases in Japan itself. But by 1947 the Army, Navy, and Air Force, all skeptical of MacArthur's pacifist ideas, were circulating their "wish lists," for permanent bases in Japan.

The remilitarization of Japan proceeded in steps just as in Germany. In both cases the early moves were secret because they ran so counter to the popular mood in both countries. In November 1948, the National Security Council secretly approved a plan to rebuild Japanese paramilitary forces for internal security duty. But General MacArthur was unenthusiastic, and it was only after George Kennan had strongly urged the move after a visit to Tokyo that MacArthur took action in the immediate aftermath of the Korean invasion. In July 1950, he authorized the building of a 75,000-man National Police Reserve. As in Germany the remilitarization issue served a clear political purpose for a wily politician determined to preserve his country's national identity in the wake of a supreme disaster. It was a necessary component in the American decision to "reverse course." If the Americans were ever to abandon their efforts to control the culture and economy of Japan, the security issue would have to be settled. Yoshida was well aware that rising sentiment in the United States was calling for permanent bases in Okinawa and the Ryukyu Islands and for the conversion of Japan into a strong military ally. *Newsweek*'s foreign editor, Harry Kern, wrote in August 1947:

It might not be beyond the realm of possibility that the United States would then revive Japan not only as an industrial but as a military power as well. Many an American general in Japan talks of commanding a Japanese army equipped and staffed by Americans—a sort of wistful thinking right now. But the Japanese would probably welcome a chance to fight the Russians. . . . a Japanese army backed by the United States could probably take Russian Asia east of Lake Baykal.

Yoshida was aware that the internal disagreements within the U.S. government were prolonging the occupation. In 1947 the State Department had proposed a conference on a Japanese Peace Treaty, but the Soviets and the Nationalist Chinese were opposed. Within the U.S. government itself there were important disagreements. Secretary of Defense Forrestal, who thought MacArthur's economic purges and antitrust efforts were ruining a great industrial asset that could be used against the Soviet Union, wanted to keep as much sovereignty over Japan as long as possible. Hugh Borton, the official in charge of preparing peace treaty drafts, a historian of Japan with his eye on the past, strongly favored the demilitarization of Japan. But the State Department's Policy Planning Staff under George Kennan had its eye on the Soviet Union. Planning Japan's future would now be subordinated to the worldwide containment strategy then taking shape. That required at a minimum a Japan capable of protecting its own internal security. In Japan as in Germany, Kennan favored a military buildup as a "modest shield" behind which economic strength and public confidence could be restored.

In 1948 and 1949 the American emphasis shifted decisively from reform to recovery, and nothing was said or done about the peace treaty until Soviet Foreign Minister Andrei Vyshinsky suddenly demanded an early conference of the wartime Allies to arrange the end of the occupation. By this time the United States had evolved its global containment strategy and it was unthinkable that the Soviets would be invited to share in deciding the fate of strategic Japan. Containment, as some Americans defined it, was primarily a military notion, and Yoshida knew that some remilitarization of Japan was the price of the American alliance he believed to be the only alternative to American domination or a Communist revolution.

Yoshida, with his blunt manners, serpent's tongue, and bustling, unsteady gait, liked to play the crude and cranky septuagenarian. But he was a brilliant dissembler. Indeed he was so good that historians some thirty years later cannot be confident about what he actually believed. Most likely, he was, like MacArthur himself, confused in the early postwar years on the militarization question. He hated militarism but he worshiped power and believed that the national identity ultimately rested on military force. Britain, his favorite candidate for an alliance partner for fifty years, was now bankrupt, and so the protector had to be the Americans. In 1946 he took an extreme pacifist position. The new constitution, he argued, forbade even self-defense. Since "most modern wars have been waged in the name of the right of self-defense," he said on June 26, 1946, "to recognize a right of legitimate self-defense is, however unintentionally, to provide a rationale for provoking war." Even the Communists challenged him. But he stuck to his position. "Now that we have been beaten, and we haven't got a single soldier left on our hands, it is a fine opportunity for renouncing war for all time." When he finally left office in 1954, Japan had a small army, navy, and air force, about 180,000 strong, trained and equipped by the United States.

In later years Yoshida admitted that the extreme positions he took at the end of the war were dictated by political expediency. He deemed it necessary, as in Dower's paraphrase, "to erase the image of Japanese militarism in order to hasten Japan's return to the international community." Although he never expected Japan's disarmament to be "eternal," the famous Article Nine was an important tactical device to allay residual American fears of Japanese militarism. After all, MacArthur himself held the typical American view of the day, that "for centuries the Japanese people, unlike their neighbors in the Pacific basin—the Chinese, the Malayans, the Indians and the Whites—have been students and idolaters of the art of war and the warrior caste." But, as Yoshida put it in his memoirs, "the idea of rearmament has always seemed to be one verging on idiocy. . . . The necessary wealth is lacking, and even more than wealth, the necessary psychological background. . . . is just not there . . . the Japanese people . . . remember only too vividly what war is like and they want none of it again." Self-defense forces for use against domestic radicals he strongly desired, but military forces to engage a foreign foe he would accept only to the extent necessary to bind the new security relationship with the United States. His great fear was that a large Japanese force would be called upon for service in Korea. Thus while the Korean War made Japanese rearmament politically possible, it also made it politically dangerous. The bigger the army, the more intense the American pressure would be, he feared, to deploy it against the waves of Chinese that had descended upon Korea.

John Foster Dulles had been given the job of negotiating the Japanese Peace Treaty. That the Republican Wall Street lawyer had a job at all in the Truman administration was due to the intervention of Senator Arthur Vandenberg, the key Republican figure in forging the postwar bipartisan foreign policy consensus. Dulles, who had been Thomas E. Dewey's foreign policy adviser and had just been defeated by Herbert H. Lehman, a New Deal stalwart, in a particularly nasty campaign for a U.S. Senate seat, was hardly a favorite in the Truman White House. Secretary of State Acheson assigned him the responsibility for the Japanese treaty because with a high-sounding title and nothing to do, he might cause trouble. Besides, he had volunteered for a job no one else had seemed to be able to do in four years. "Why don't you give someone one year in which to get action, with the understanding that if he can't do it, he fails."

In approaching his task Dulles, the Presbyterian preacher's son, was driven by two ideas he happened to share with Yoshida. One was the implacable evil of Communism which served the two men equally well as a ready explanation for all varieties of the world's misery. The other was the need after a bitter war to make a generous peace. Both men had served as junior diplomats at Versailles and both came away convinced that the vindictive peace was responsible for Hitler and Tojo's war. But on another point there was a considerable gulf between the two. Dulles thought that the containment or, better, the "rollback" as he would later call it, of Communism could be effected by a worldwide military buildup. Like other Americans, he talked of the coming war with Russia and the risk of losing Japan in the encounter. A year and a half before the two men met for the first time, just three days before the Korean invasion, the secretary of the army, Kenneth Royall, had told journalists in Tokyo that Japan was indefensible and would be abandoned in the event of a conflict. Dulles argued that Japan needed at least 300,000 troops. Former high-ranking Japanese army officers of General Willoughby's entourage at SCAP proposed a twenty-division army. A Japanese admiral called for a three-flotilla navy and a big air force. Kimura Tokutaro, an extreme right-winger, who would later serve on the prime minister's advisory board on the "adaptation of democracy to actual conditions" and would become head of the National Safety Agency, proposed creating a secret private army of 200,000 vigilantes to be known as the "Patriotic Anti-Communist Drawn-Sword Militia."

Yoshida was determined, however, to go slowly in rearmament because he felt caught between two forces, each of which threatened the Japanese national identity. One was the internal communist threat—he always rated the possibility of external invasion low—and the other was a revived Japanese war machine. Ambassador John Allison, remembers telling the prime minister that "in the new Japan the military had none of the special powers they had in prewar Japan and that with civilian control the military could be the servant, not the master of Japan." But the old man, Allison recalled, "would look up at me with twinkling eyes and an impish grin and say, 'Yes, but they have guns, haven't they?' "

After one hundred thousand miles of negotiation Dulles' draft treaty was ready in the summer of 1951. Yoshida had by this time redefined his absolute position against self-defense, had authorized American bases in Okinawa and other former Japanese-controlled islands, begun the new Japanese armaments industry, and directed the recruitment of a small Japanese defense force. Frank Kowalski, the American colonel in charge of organizing and training what he called "a little American Army," who later became a U.S. congressman, was impressed by the "pure sophistry" of Yoshida's public stance. Like Adenauer's Germany, Yoshida's Japan was clearly rearming but pretending that it was not. Yoshida dragged his feet, however, in building up the force, afraid of public opinion and of the possibility of becoming involved in the Korean War. In the hysteria following the Chinese intervention into the Korean War, the practiced anti-Communist felt the need to cool public fears in order to resist American pressures for greater military involvement. "As far as Japanese skies are concerned," he wrote in *Foreign Affairs* in January 1951, "the Red star is receding." World War III was not imminent, he told the Diet. "We do not have the slightest expectation that the communist countries will invade Japan."

By the following April, MacArthur had been removed by Truman for insubordination. His failure on the battlefield—the war to destroy North Korea had been lost when waves of Chinese troops entered the fray in December 1950—and his willingness to lend public support to the rising chorus of Republicans out for blood—finally made the classic war hero a vulnerable target. "The son of a bitch isn't going to resign on me. I want him fired," Truman had exploded. The supreme commander was summarily dismissed with a curt cable from Washington. "Publicly humiliated," as he put it, "after fifty-two years in the Army." Yoshida, visibly shaken, told a nationwide radio audience that the general's accomplishments in Japan were "one of the marvels of history." MacArthur was the man "who has planted democracy in all segments of our society."

The Japanese Peace Treaty signed at a fifty-two-nation conference in San Francisco on September 8, 1951, was a triumph of American diplomacy. Not only did the U.S. position prevail over the vigorous opposition of the Soviet Union but also over deep misgivings of America's principal Allies in Asia—Nationalist China, Australia, the Philippines, and Britain. By signaling its intention to conclude a separate peace, the Truman administration forced the Russians to participate. By orchestrating the conference Dulles completely isolated the Soviets. (The vote for the treaty was 49-3.) The British, worried about future Japanese penetration of their traditional markets in South Asia, if the China market were closed to them, vigorously opposed the exclusion of the People's Republic of China from the negotiations, as indeed did a great number of conservative businessmen in Japan. But Britain was not in a strong position to resist American pressure in 1951. The wounded empire was facing its worst economic crisis since the war, and the hope for recovery lay with the Americans.

In 1951 America was obsessed with the Chinese revolution. The issue of the day in U.S. politics was "Who lost China?" The Chinese had humiliated the U.S. armed forces in Korea. The Republican party was dominated by a vocal "China Lobby" determined to isolate and to punish the ungrateful nation that had turned its back on generations of American missionaries and traders. Yoshida, for all his anti-Communism, saw China as a part of Japan's landscape, as essential to the islands' future as air or water. It was unthinkable that the Chinese market could be cut off forever. But on Dulles' insistence, he was forced to sign a letter to the Americans largely drafted by Dulles himself, promising not to "conclude a bilateral treaty with the Communist regime of China" and he also agreed to adhere to the strict embargo of China under the Battle Act of 1951. The letter was demanded because within four days of the signing of the treaty, Senator William Knowland had secured the support of fifty-six senators for the rejection of the treaty unless the Japanese made a clear statement about the People's Republic of China. Yoshida had been making contradictory statements in Tokyo, one day talking about establishing relations with Peking, the next day Taipei. Both Dulles and Yoshida believed that Communism was an "alien" and hence, a temporary phenomenon in China, but they differed on how to help the historic process along. Yoshida never believed that isolating China would restore capitalism. The better policy was to integrate her into a regional economy. But for almost twenty years Japan was forced under a secret 1952 agreement, known as "CHINCOM," to adhere to a stricter embargo on trade with China than was observed by the NATO Allies.

In Japan the United States faced the same inevitable limits on its power as in Germany. It could destroy and dismantle Japanese industry but not without doing permanent damage to the international capitalist economy, or it could make its watchwords "recovery," "reconstruction," and "stabilization" instead of the MacArthur slogans of "spiritual revolution," "democracy," and "reform," and thereby build up Japan into a formidable commercial rival. By 1949 the second course was in full swing. The need for radical change was clear. Despite an excellent harvest in 1946 the food crisis again became acute the following year since the rice had been diverted into the black market. Food prices jumped 300 percent in a year. SCAP's official ration was temporarily reduced to 997 calories a day. Rebuilding lagged. Wages were falling far behind rising prices. A quarter of the work force were employed by the government in the railroads, post office, salt and tobacco monopolies, and their conditions were miserable. Industrial production in 1947 was 45 percent of what it was in the early thirties and exports a bare 10 percent. Without a $300 million U.S. subsidy to meet the trade deficit, the economy would have ceased to function at all.

A parade of experts from the business world had examined the gasping Japanese economy throughout 1947. Most had been working in the German occupation. The heads of eleven industrial engineering firms and the former president of Republic Steel were appointed to an official commission to deal with the crisis. For a fee of $750,000 they issued a report calling for an end to the reparations program and the efforts at deconcentration and democratic reform. Paul Hoffman, the Studebaker president who was about to run the European Recovery Program, came to the same general conclusions. In December 1948, Joseph Dodge, a former car salesman who had worked his way up to the presidency of the Detroit Bank, became the czar of the Japanese economy. The "Dodge Line" was the Japanese version of the German austerity program. Its purposes were identical: cutting the inflation rate and imposing drastic limits on domestic consumption; building up an export industry; promoting productivity by eliminating small and medium enterprises that could not compete; keeping a lid on wages by repressing labor militancy. Unlike Germany, which had its own homegrown theory of the *Sozialemarkt Wirtschaft* and an effective economics minister, Japan had neither. The principal architect of the Japanese stabilization and recovery program was an American. The ideas were vintage McKinley. "There should be no fear of mass unemployment," Dodge scrawled on a note to himself as he wrestled with the inflation problem. "Get the country into hard condition for the struggle in the export market."

We are with you "from the bottom of our heart," Yoshida told Dodge, but privately, the conservative Japanese economic planners were in a state of panic. It seemed as though Dodge's patient would succumb from an overdose of strong medicine. Japanese economists compared the American banker to a juggler who promises to pull a rabbit out of a top hat big enough only to accommodate a rat. As in Germany the immediate results were disastrous. As the *Asahi Yearbook* for 1950 summarized the situation:

Under the drastic methods of the Dodge Line, the majority of enterprises, centering on the basic industries, were virtually strangled. Trade was the last resort, but foreign demand for commodities was also affected by the global recession, and thus bankruptcy occurred throughout middle and small enterprises as a result of rapid increases in inventories, accumulated goods, and unpaid accounts. Industry was being driven into an historic recession.

The Korean War rescued the situation. Japanese industry began turning out goods for the war effort. Dodge's earlier ideas of discouraging Japanese dependence on the dollar by restabilizing Japan's historic trading patterns, including even the China trade, were lost as the new global power alignments took shape. "Japan can be independent politically but dependent economically," Dodge told the Ministry of International Trade and Industry in November 1951. The Dodge Line was, as Finance Minister Ideda Hayoto told the Diet, "the first step to linking Japan to the international economy." Even before Korea, Dodge had seen Japan as a "springboard and source of supply for the extension of further aid to the Far Eastern areas." The workshop of Asia, as Acheson had called the defeated island empire, was now designated in the emerging American grand design as the "stabilizer" of Asia. Japanese economic policies had been tailored to meet U.S. security requirements. Nippon was once again encouraged to expand a "coprosperity sphere" in Southeast Asia and to tie its economy to the dollar. It would take almost a generation before the full effects of an American banker's cure for Japan would be felt in his own city of Detroit.

THREE

ATLANTIC CIVILIZATION AND ITS DISCONTENTS:

Mr. Acheson and M. Monnet Rebuild Europe

1

In 1947 two inveterate walkers and dreamers, both French, were obsessed with the same problem: how to create a new continent out of the ashes of the old. General Charles de Gaulle, restless and shorn of power, would pace the perimeter of his secluded garden at Colombey forty times a morning. Jean Monnet preferred to dress up in old ski pants and hike along the country lanes surrounding his elegant thatch-roofed cottage at Houjarray. Both men dreamed of a new Europe, but the dreams were as different as the dreamers.

As the leader of the Free French, De Gaulle had traveled to Moscow in December 1944 and informed Stalin that he wished to form "a European bloc, Moscow-Paris-London." The French-Russian alliance, he told the Soviet dictator, would be the essential link for keeping Germany in check. "At this time, there is nothing at issue between France and the Soviet Union. But we have always quarreled with Great Britain and will always continue to." De Gaulle never wavered in his demand that France be recognized as the leading European power in a new concert of nations that would stretch from the Atlantic to the Urals. Always thoroughly anti-Communist, in the midst of war the general saw Stalin as the key to the restoration of French power.

Yet it was Churchill who persuaded the Americans that France should have an occupation zone of her own in Germany. Both "Anglo-Saxon" leaders, as De Gaulle called Churchill and Roosevelt, distrusted the haughty general. "One thing I am sure," Churchill noted during the war, "that there is nothing that De Gaulle would like better than to have plenty T.A. ["tube alloy," the code name for the atomic bomb] to punish Britain and nothing he would like less than to arm Communist Russia with the secret." De Gaulle was incensed that Franklin Roosevelt had dared to invite him to a meeting in the French colonial city of Algiers—"How could I agree to be summoned to a point on the national territory by a foreign chief of state?"—and had excluded him from Yalta where, so legend had it, the superpowers had each helped themselves to half of Europe. A France true to her heroic past and her destiny of greatness could not flourish in the "Anglo-Saxon" half.

Jean Monnet was as loved and respected by the powerful and well-connected in New York, Washington, and London as De Gaulle was mistrusted and ridiculed. From the age of sixteen he traveled the world selling the family brandy, amassing a bigger vocabulary in English than in French, and impressing an array of political and economic leaders with his peculiar brilliance. At the age of twenty-eight he was France's representative on the inter-Allied purchasing commission that handled procurement in World War I, and after the war became deputy secretary general of the League of Nations. For the rest of his long public life he never held a top political office. Yet driven as he was by a single idea, he wielded enormous influence. That idea, which manifested itself in different forms throughout his career, was the obsolescence of national sovereignty. Europe exhausted itself every generation by pitting one indispensable part of itself against another. The choice, he believed, was a Europe united or a Europe forever at war.

Monnet was bold in thought and unencumbered by the orthodoxy of those who lionized him. He promoted national economic planning in France and voted Socialist, a capitalist modernizer who somehow managed to be a hero to conservatives like Winston Churchill, Konrad Adenauer, and John J. McCloy. In 1940 he had called for an Anglo-French union to fight the war, a "joint war cabinet" rather than De Gaulle's government-in-exile. For De Gaulle the idea was absurd. How, he asked, could you "integrate George VI and President Albert Lebrun, the *Garde Republicaine* and the Horse Guards?" France would be preserved by holding fast to the colonies. (Indeed De Gaulle's first brush with Roosevelt was over two tiny islands off the Canadian coast which De Gaulle claimed despite the fact that the United States had just agreed that the government of Marshal Henri Pétain in Vichy should retain them.) For De Gaulle the priority was to "save the honor of France"; for Monnet the only thing that mattered was to win the war by mobilizing the collective strength of the Allies. His principal task was to procure American planes by the thousands. In 1940 he visited Roosevelt at Hyde Park, and through his friendship with Harry Hopkins, Roosevelt's closest aide, he sold the president the idea of announcing in his 1941 State of the Union Message the seemingly absurd production goal of 50,000 planes a year. The slogan "America will be the great arsenal of democracy" originated with Monnet.

Using his superb contacts with the Americans to apply subtle pressures on both the American-backed General Henri Giraud and the man Roosevelt contemptuously spoke of as Joan of Arc, Monnet succeeded in 1943 in achieving the minimal cooperation necessary for military operations. (On the eve of the European campaign, rumors circulated that De Gaulle was preparing to shift the location of his French National Committee from London to Moscow.) In his memoirs Monnet considers his negotiations in Algiers one of his important accomplishments. In his, De Gaulle attacks "the inspirer with his panacea called fusion" for even "suggesting that the generals Giraud and De Gaulle be brought together in the same government." But De Gaulle agreed because he suspected what would happen, that he would outwit and finally eclipse the maladroit Giraud. However, he always believed that Monnet was working for his American friends, not for the soul of France.

With victory De Gaulle himself went into eclipse. The Resistance which he symbolized was dominated by forces far to the left of him. In the election of October 21, 1945, the Communists won 26.4 percent of the vote and the Socialists 23.8 percent. Communists now headed three critical economics ministries, and Maurice Thorez, the Communist boss, became minister of state. By January 1946, De Gaulle, exasperated by the leftward tilt of a paralyzed government not yet ready to submit to his direction, retired to his garden to organize a political movement and to await the call he knew someday would come. The immediate postwar years would bear the imprint of Monnet's dreams, not his.

Before resigning De Gaulle had appointed Monnet high commissioner to carry out a task Monnet had himself designed. "France must be modernized," he insisted, if the nation were ever to recover. But the only way to modernize was to develop a national economic plan. Monnet and his closest wartime associates moved into a modest house on the Rue de Martignac with a small budget—"No one must be jealous," Monnet warned—and began to draw up plans to transform France. They made an inventory of France's economic problems, a set of priorities for transforming the chaos into strength, and set production quotas. Horrified businessmen thought Monnet was introducing the Soviet Gosplan. "There were twenty of us working with Jean Monnet," recalls Bernard Clappier, later a high official of the Bank of France. "We took care of everything." In the cramped quarters Monnet and his fellow technocrats— bankers, engineers, and businessmen who had worked with him during the war years—tried to determine how best to use American loans to rebuild France. In planning domestic reconstruction Monnet became even more convinced that the recovery of each national state depended upon the economic integration of Europe. His dream was to build institutions, for "nothing is lasting without institutions." His success in creating and moving institutions was due not only to his special talent for hounding those he wished to persuade without giving offense, but to a shrewd cultivation of friends in high places, and a certain prescience in placing his own associates and disciples in strategic positions. Pierre Uri, one of his closest and most influential disciples, recalls: "Our greatest strength, when we had to launch the Coal and Steel Community, was that in all the key jobs we had men ready to back us up, men we had put there ourselves."

But it was Monnet's extraordinary friendships in the American Establishment that helped to define his reputation. The Catholic centrist governments that emerged in West Europe after the war regarded Monnet's connections as an asset because they made it easier to negotiate American loans. But for the Gaullists and the Left, both of whom feared American domination, Monnet was always under suspicion as Washington's man in Europe.

His "well-informed friends," as he called them, included the financier André Meyer, Felix Frankfurter, Robert Lovett, John J. McCloy, Dean Acheson, McGeorge Bundy, Walter Lippmann, James Reston, and Philip Graham of the *Washington Post*. On his regular visits to America he would make it a point to see as many as possible of these influential figures. He valued their judgment because they were practical men "who cannot afford to make mistakes." They in turn saw the little Frenchman with the gray mustache as a European untied to the past with whom a deal could be struck. Monnet had met John Foster Dulles at Versailles in 1919, and "since nothing important is done in the United States without lawyers," began consulting him in the 1920s on financial matters. The other lawyer who became a passionate devotee of Monnet was George Ball, whom the Frenchman originally met during the war in connection with Lend-Lease negotiations. In the late 1940s he became Monnet's legal adviser in the Planning Commission and in the 1950s the legal representative of the Coal and Steel Community in Washington. "I was one of Monnet's dialectical punching bags," Ball recalls. Working in his country house late into the night he would help refine Monnet's ideas. Years later when he was under secretary of state in the Kennedy and Johnson administrations, his enthusiasm for European integration was so great that he was once sharply reminded by a senator at a public hearing that he was no longer in the pay of Mr. Monnet.

Monnet did not, of course, invent the idea of European unity. For a flickering moment Charlemagne had achieved a unity of sorts. Indeed Monnet once toyed with the idea of re-creating Lotharingia, the kingdom of Charlemagne's son that embraced the ancestors of present-day Dutchmen and Belgians and the contemporary residents of the Rhineland, Saar, and Lorraine. They all shared the same mine basin. Why could they not again become a single state? Dante had dreamed of a United States of Europe. In the 1920s, French Foreign Minister Aristide Briand had preached European unity at the League of Nations. (The few American reporters who paid any attention to the speech thought it was a call for the troublemakers of Europe to "gang up" on the United States.) A United Europe was a favorite subject of Winston Churchill. In the 1920s he endorsed the tireless efforts of Richard Coudenhouve-Kalergi, a count of the old Holy Roman Empire, to promote a Pan-European political movement. The count had a knack for procuring enthusiastic endorsements from prominent persons who could think of no reason not to give him one, but he had no popular support. Churchill himself became the head of the United Europe movement of Britain, but his enthusiasm for cutting national sovereignty down to size on the Continent was noticeably absent when it came to the British Empire. "We are with Europe but not of it," he wrote in a 1930 article in *The Saturday Evening Post* endorsing European unity. "We are interested and associated but not absorbed."

In 1940 when the Nazi invasion had reduced France to a political corpse, Churchill had embraced Monnet's ideas for breathing life into her by proclaiming a Franco-British union, and three years later proposed a Council of Europe and even a European Army to keep the peace after Hitler's defeat. In September 1946, having been voted out of office, he went to Zurich and before an assemblage of heads of state sounded the call again: "We must build a kind of United States of Europe." It was the "sovereign remedy" that could make all Europe, "or the greater part of it"—he had already proclaimed the reality of a divided Europe in his "Iron Curtain" speech at Fulton, Missouri—"as free and happy as Switzerland is today. . . ." For the old Tory statesman European integration would achieve a historic goal of British diplomacy. It would offer the best chance of preventing any single continental power from dominating the rest. Indeed, it now appeared as if the historic Franco-German rivalry could not be ended without European integration. "Except within the framework and against the background of a United Europe, the problem of dismembered Germany," he said, "is incapable of solution. . . ." Having been the first Western statesman to warn of a Soviet threat to Europe, Churchill saw the unity of the West as an essential counterweight to Soviet power. But he never intended to sacrifice Britain's worldwide interests in the Commonwealth nor her "special relationship" with the United States to the effort. Ernest Bevin, foreign minister in the Labour government, a Yorkshire housemaid's son who never had a day of formal schooling after the age of eleven, was even more resistant to the idea of becoming a "European" than the famous descendant of the duke of Marlborough.

2

The United States emerged from the Second World War with the greatest accumulation of power in modern history, but its leaders had no clear ideas about how to use it. Wartime America was bombarded with inspirational slogans. In 1942, Wendell Willkie, the Wall Street lawyer who had run against Roosevelt two years earlier, took an airplane trip around the war-torn globe and returned to proclaim that the tortured planet was in reality "one world" and to sell one million copies of a book elaborating that thesis. *Time* publisher Henry Luce's contribution was "The American Century." Britain, France, and the continental empires were through, he wrote in 1941, and it was America's moment to "assume the leadership of the world." Vice President Henry Wallace had an equally grandiose but different vision. The national destiny was to use America's great economic power to feed the hungry masses of the planet and to usher in "the century of the common man."

Everyone had advice on how to run the postwar world. For Herbert Hoover, America should concentrate on becoming the sanctuary of the ideals of civilization; for Henry Luce, "the powerhouse from which the ideals spread throughout the world. . . ." In 1943 Walter Lippmann called for the United States to act as the guarantor of the "Atlantic Community" or face the prospect that Europe would fall under the pressure of an expanding Soviet Union and the "emerging peoples of Asia." Once having crushed the Axis, the secretary of the navy, Frank Knox, declared, the United States and Britain should "police the seven seas." His successor, James Forrestal, told the assembled bankers and financiers at the Bond Club of New York in 1943 that the "cornerstone in any plan which undertakes to rid us of the curse of war must be the armed might of the United States." In the hearings on Lend-Lease held that year, Republican congressmen Karl Mundt and Charles Eaton found themselves in agreement with old New Dealer Adolf A. Berle, Jr., that the United States must now seek world power "as a trustee for civilization."

In one way or another the postwar dreamers all sounded the note of "manifest destiny." Luce even used the term in "The American Century." But nowhere in evidence were tinkerers like Monnet. Franklin Roosevelt himself was a dilettante when it came to international institutions. He would throw out big ideas, illustrating them, as was his special gift, with homely metaphors. But details bored him. He thought the key to future peace was an international police force. He wrote Myron C. Taylor, his personal representative at the Vatican, that since disarmament might take "generations" to accomplish, the peace-loving nations "must be in a position to enforce non-aggression." He assured Stalin at Yalta in 1945 that American troops would leave Europe within two or three years of victory. At Tehran two years earlier where he had proposed that "four policemen"—Britain, Russia, China, and the United States —should enforce the future peace, he had told Stalin that the American contribution could be limited to air and naval units. Though the sea was his passion, FDR had become a convert to "victory through air power," and he envisaged that the real power of the international police force would be its air squadrons, located at semiautonomous bases throughout the world, which would deter or punish aggressors primarily through air raids on population centers. But the president was impatient with bureaucratic architecture. "Aren't you at least in favor of a world secretariat?" Cordell Hull, his secretary of state, asked him early in the war. With a laugh he replied, "I'll give you the Pentagon or the Empire State Building. You can put the world secretariat there." Roosevelt saw the postwar United States, much like the watchmaker God of the eighteenth-century rationalists, as the prime mover of a security system which would no longer require the day-to-day attention of the American government. Like a well-run town, this was to be a world where the policeman was always on call but not much in evidence.

Before the meeting at Tehran with Stalin, Churchill had vigorously argued for a separate regional organization for Europe, another for Asia, and a third for the Americas, in preference to a single universal organization like the League of Nations. Cordell Hull, who was suspicious of Churchill's influence on Roosevelt, was convinced that the Churchillian notion of "regional councils" was merely a scheme to preserve the British Empire and the system of imperial preferences which were the principal target of Hull's postwar planning. Deep within the bowels of the U.S. bureaucracy, papers on European unification were prepared, but the effort was abandoned when the Roosevelt administration became committed to a world organization based on cooperation with the Soviets. (It was clear even in 1943 that the Soviets would oppose any federalist notions for Europe because they would be incompatible with a Soviet sphere of influence in Eastern Europe.) In late 1944 the Council on Foreign Relations published a study, *Problems of a Regional Security Organization,* that reflected the consensus of the day. A European organization "presents many dangers and few advantages" the study concluded, largely because it would become a "military cover for Britain" and would be regarded as anti-Soviet.

If the American vision of postwar political institutions was somewhat murky, ideas about what the world economy should look like were considerably clearer. Yet it was the failure of the economic vision that led the architects of the postwar order to embrace the idea of an Atlantic Community.

Like Britain in the nineteenth century, the United States under Franklin Roosevelt had made free trade the national religion. "Free trade is itself a good, like virtue, holiness, and righteousness, to be loved, admired, honoured and steadfastly adopted, for its own sake," the British magazine *Economist* had intoned in 1843. But by the 1890s the world of free trade dominated by Britain was in shambles. Bismarck's Germany, Italy, and France had embraced protectionism and economic nationalism. It was all very well for Britain, with its manufacturing advantage, its huge navy and collection of colonies, to preach free trade, but free trade among grossly unequal partners, economists such as Georg Friedrich List began to argue, leads inevitably to the domination of the weak by the strong. Britain was attempting "to become to other nations what a vast city is to a country." In the nineteenth century the United States was the world's leading practitioner of protectionism, a policy designed to save the "infant industries" of the New World. By the end of the century, however, still surrounded by high tariff walls, the United States was calling for an "open-door policy" to guarantee free access to the markets of China and Latin America.

When Franklin Roosevelt moved into the White House and a tall, silver-haired former Tennessee congressman settled into the old State Department building across the street, the position of the United States in the world economy had radically changed, and so also its ideology. Indeed, as early as 1890 the United States had already become the world's largest economy. Protectionism had enabled American industry to challenge Britain in world markets. The breakdown of Pax Britannica in 1914 had led to trade wars, fierce economic rivalry, and ultimately to the bleeding of a generation in a war no one wanted. Cordell Hull sat in the cavernous office of the secretary of state for eleven tumultuous years of U.S. history, content to let others set U.S. foreign policy. But there was one thing—beyond being certain that the office itself was always heated to just under eighty degrees—that he cared about deeply. That was free trade. "When goods move, soldiers don't" was his creed. Roosevelt himself was not a true believer, but Hull single-mindedly labored to commit the United States to the principles of a liberal world economic order based on free trade and free movement of capital. The antagonist, as Hull saw it, was Britain, no longer the apostle of free trade but the architect of a pernicious system of "imperial preferences." The "sterling bloc," a closed system in which Britain traded with its colonies under advantageous terms denied to the rest of the world, would "induce economic conflicts with dangerous political repercussions."

The instrument for attacking the British imperial preference was Lend-Lease. In his memoirs Hull recounts proudly how Churchill, standing alone and desperate, had to sign the agreement that "promised the elimination of all forms of discriminatory treatment in international commerce" in order to get the planes and tanks he needed to keep Hitler at bay. Eleven other countries, including China and Russia, had to take the pledge too before they could get any help. It was American policy to regulate the flow of Lend-Lease in order to make sure that the British kept a dollar balance of no less than $600 million but no more than $1 billion. Churchill was furious. Three months before the landings at Normandy in March 1944, he dashed off a cable to Roosevelt:

> Will you allow me to say that the suggestion of reducing our dollar balances, which constitute our sole liquid reserve, to one billion dollars would really not be consistent either with equal treatment of Allies or with any conception of equal sacrifice or pooling of resources? We have not shirked our duty or indulged in any easy way of living. We have already spent practically all our convertible foreign investments in the struggle. We alone of the Allies will emerge from the war with great overseas war debts. I do not know what would happen if we were now asked to disperse our last liquid reserves required to meet pressing needs, or how I could put my case to Parliament without it affecting public sentiment in the most painful manner, and that at a time when British and American blood will be flowing in broad and equal streams and when the shortening of the war by even a month would far exceed the sums under consideration.

"You should make it clear," the prime minister instructed Anthony Eden, his foreign secretary later that year, "that we have no idea of three or four Great Powers ruling the world. . . . We should certainly not be prepared ourselves to submit to an economic, financial, and monetary system laid down by, say, Russia, or the United States with her fagot-vote China."

But submit they did. In June 1945, Lend-Lease was abruptly terminated in Europe. It was a "weapon of war" Harry Truman announced, and the war in Europe was over. Shortly after he succeeded Churchill, Prime Minister Clement Attlee told the House of Commons that the sudden cancellation had placed Britain "in a very serious financial position," and dispatched Lord Keynes to Washington to negotiate a loan. After months of tough negotiation Keynes succeeded in arranging a loan of $3,750,000,000.00. But the price was the abandonment or at least the crippling of the Keynesian vision for Britain. The heart of the Labour program was full employment, and while the Socialists were quite prepared, as Churchill was not, to say good-bye to India and to preside over the orderly liquidation of the colonial apparatus, they saw the imperial preference system, as the writers on political economy David Calleo and Benjamin Rowland put it, as the device to stabilize British exports and currency. "A modern form of mercantilism, by way of Keynesian economics, had come back into fashion." Keynes fought for an international monetary system that would make credit plentiful and relieve a country such as Britain of the necessity to solve its balance of payments problems by the traditional remedies, deflation and unemployment. The Americans saw the Keynesian proposal as a scheme to have the United States underwrite British Socialism, and that did not sell in Washington.

The price of the loan was a promise to make the pound fully convertible in dollars by 1947. In 1946 the British were doing quite well. Exports were running well ahead of their prewar level and imports had been successfully curtailed. But with convertibility there was a tremendous run on the pound, it being the only European currency that could be exchanged for dollars. Although they had used only a quarter of the loan before 1947, after convertibility the remainder was quickly exhausted. The pound was devalued and exchange controls were reimposed for another eleven years. "Whether or not the Americans intended to leave Britain impotent and bankrupt," George C. Herring concludes, "the effect was the same. The termination of Lend-Lease (in June, 1945) left the Labour government little choice but to accept American demands in return for a loan. Thus what Churchill called the 'most unsordid act' became indirectly the means by which Britain was reduced to dependence on her ally."

The hard bargaining over the new world economic order with John Maynard Keynes and the humiliating terms of what Americans considered a generous loan to the mother country left a permanent mark on the Anglo-American relationship. The events, remembered by very few Americans, became, like De Gaulle's exclusion from Yalta, a rankling symbol of inequality. But at the very height of its power the United States was unable to realize Hull's vision of a liberal world order. The nation was now roughly in the position Britain was in the mid-nineteenth century. "We need markets—big markets—around the world in which to buy and sell," declared William L. Clayton, a Texan who served as assistant secretary of state for economic matters. (As the owner of 40 percent of the world's largest cotton brokerage house, he could speak feelingly on the subject of exports.) "We ask no special privileges in any of these markets." But of course the privilege of world leadership is that one needs no special privilege. Exports and free access to vital resources—"Who knows how long we can go without importing oil?" Clayton asked in November 1946—were the indispensable preconditions of American prosperity. As the war ended most economists and politicians believed that the decade-long Depression that began in 1929 might well return once the stimulus of wartime spending was removed. The remedy was a massive export program. The target was set at $14 billion a year for the immediate postwar years—more than four times the 1939 level.

Yet by 1947 Britain, though teetering on the edge of bankruptcy and utterly dependent on the United States, stoutly refused to abandon imperial preferences. Hull and Morgenthau, the free-trade zealots, were gone. The Eightieth Congress, protectionist and isolationist to its core, did not share their vision. (Morgenthau, by the way, saw his plan to turn Germany into a pasture as a way to assure British prosperity for twenty years "because their principal competition for their coal and steel came from the Ruhr, and this ought to go a long way towards solving the economic future of England.") Most important, the Cold War presented a common interest that transcended the economic rivalries within the English-speaking world. High politics had relegated "the family quarrels over money" to the back burner. Who could be concerned about such mundane matters as exchange rates and tariffs when the very state of civilization itself was at issue?

3

In the autumn of 1945 John J. McCloy, winding up his duties as assistant secretary of war, made an inspection tour of U.S. military installations around the world and reported back to his colleagues on the War Council. "The world looks to the U.S. as the one stable country to insure the security of the world." The victorious Allies, as one European politician put it, were in reality a club of defeated nations. Only Britain and France refused to believe it.

President Truman, in announcing the development of the atomic bomb, declared that the United States would hold the ultimate weapon as a "trustee" for civilization. Franklin Roosevelt, who had once tried to name World War II "the war for civilization," believed that the successful alliance against the Axis powers had given humanity a last chance to defend civilization. For his successors it was self-evident that the United States was the only country with the strength and the energy to build that defense.

The new relationship between America and Europe that evolved in the postwar years grew out of a compromise between the liberal vision of a world economic order and what one senior U.S. military officer in 1945 called "the gospel of national security." The traditional isolationism and complacency of U.S. foreign policy had been stood on its head. In the past, as Walter Lippmann had put it, in the midst of the war, the "unearned security" that accrued from having two huge oceans between the New World and the quarreling nations of the Old had "diverted our attention from the idea of national security." But now no longer need foreign threats constitute a present danger in order to imperil American security; the ambitions, even the capabilities of unfriendly countries, were enough to demand a response. It could not be assumed, therefore, that the war against Hitler would be the last war any more than the Great War that preceded it had proved to be the war to end war. Another dictator could arise to challenge civilization, and now only the United States had the power to organize the response. If the United Nations (UN) did not work, James Forrestal warned in early 1946, "we face a world in which we must maintain such overwhelming military power as to make it abundantly clear that future aggressors will eventually suffer the ruinous fate of Germany.''

By the end of the war a new consensus on national security embraced a broad spectrum of American leadership. In January 1945, Senator Arthur Vandenberg, an archisolationist in prewar days, delivered a speech on the floor of the Senate calling for the end of isolationism. The speech had been drafted by James Reston and Walter Lippmann, who persuaded the senator that no one could look presidential in 1948—the "vain and pompous" senator, as Lippmann knew, was already feeling presidential in 1945—unless he embraced the new internationalism. Reston hailed the speech as "wise and statesman-like." Lippmann, not surprisingly, had good things to say about it too. The senator, suddenly a celebrity, looked "just like a pouter pigeon all blown up with delight at his new role in the world."

So by the end of the war one thing was clear. The United States would be involved in one sort of entangling alliance or another. For Lippmann logic demanded that it be an alliance of the victors, the United States, Britain, and Russia. "The failure to form an alliance of the victors will mean the formation of alliances between the vanquished and some of the victors," he wrote with considerable prescience in 1943. The story of the Cold War—another Lippmann phrase—is the tale of the substitution of one alliance for another. Wartime relations with the Soviet Union, even in the face of overriding common interest, were rocky at best. While Stalin could be charming, dealings with his terrorized underlings were frequently difficult. When a Soviet official complained during the war that the United States was "behind" in its Lend-Lease shipments and the American noted in rejoinder that the Soviets too were behind in fulfilling their commitments, the testy Russian reply became a Washington classic: "We are here to talk about my behind, not your behind."

Soviet officials were stubborn and boorish and backward, but only a few American officials believed that their ideology made them a menace, and some of the confirmed anti-Communists, like the career diplomat Loy Henderson, were deliberately kept away from U.S.–Soviet relations during the war. By the end of his life Roosevelt had had a sharp exchange with Stalin who had accused the United States of making a separate deal for the surrender of German troops in northern Italy. "Frankly, I cannot avoid a feeling of bitter resentment toward your informers, whoever they are, for such vile misrepresentations of my actions. . . ." But a few hours before he collapsed while sitting for a portrait in his cottage at Warm Springs, Georgia, FDR had cabled Churchill, "I would minimize the general Soviet problem." The friction with Stalin should be treated as a "minor incident." Churchill himself had left the Yalta Conference a few weeks earlier impressed, as he told his doctor, Lord Moran, by Stalin's humor, understanding, and moderation. "As long as Stalin lasted, Anglo-Russian friendship could be maintained," he told some cabinet colleagues on his return to London. "Poor Neville Chamberlain believed he could trust Hitler. He was wrong. But I don't think I'm wrong about Stalin."

Harry Truman had his first taste of high diplomacy at Potsdam, where outside the smoking ruins of Berlin he met with Stalin and Churchill. (In the midst of the conference Churchill was voted out of office and his place at the table was taken by Prime Minister Clement Attlee.) The wily Georgian in an immaculate white tunic with the resplendent regalia of a Soviet marshal agreed readily to enter the war against Japan on the date desired by the Americans. Even on the sticky reparations issue, Will Clayton, the U.S. negotiator, thought Stalin had been "pretty fair." Truman was elated on hearing of the successful test explosion of the atomic bomb in the New Mexico desert. "He was a changed man," Churchill noted of the session held just after he received the news. "He told the Russians just where they got on and off and generally bossed the whole meeting." Yet the new president liked the "old guy" as he would call the Soviet dictator in later years. "Stalin is as near like Tom Pendergast [the Kansas City boss who was Truman's political mentor] as any man I know. He is very fond of classical music." Stalin and Vyacheslav Molotov, the Soviet foreign minister, were "rough men" to be sure, but the new British foreign secretary, Ernest Bevin, the former head of the Transport and General Workers Union who had been battling Communists in the labor movement for forty years, was just a "boor."

Harry Truman was enthralled with history. Even in the Senate he would devour five or six books at a time, particularly biographies and chronicles of war. His was a storybook view of the past, as the historian of the Cold War Daniel Yergin calls it, that evinced a "rousing Fourth of July patriotism." Roosevelt, the country squire, talked Wilsonian idealism and practiced the horse trading of great-power diplomacy. But Truman, the Kansas City politician, found it difficult to see international politics in such pragmatic terms. He prided himself on an ability to make tough, quick decisions and to stand firm where it counted. His immediate coterie of advisers helped to stiffen his back. Admiral William Leahy, FDR's personal chief of staff, anti-Communist to the core, stressed Stalin's "insulting language" in his cables to Roosevelt; Truman reacted, Leahy was delighted to note, with "solid old-fashioned Americanism." Averell Harriman, the New Deal railroad heir who as Ambassador to Moscow saw Stalin more than any other American, was another strong influence. "How can a man with a hundred million dollars look so sad?" the Soviet diplomat Maxim Litvinov once asked. Back from Moscow, Harriman warned the new president that the United States faced a "barbarian invasion of Europe." Stalin's refusal to aid the Polish underground in its desperate uprising in August 1944 had convinced him that Stalin wanted to kill off the anti-Communist Poles in order to establish a subservient regime. The Kremlin was bloated with power Harriman had cabled from the embassy. Now at home he lost no opportunity to press his point. "Russian plans for establishing satellite states are a threat to the world and us. Our country," he told a sympathetic James Forrestal, "might well have to face an ideological crusade just as vigorous and dangerous as Fascism or Nazism." Harriman, Forrestal remembers, "said the greatest crime of Hitler was that his actions had resulted in opening the gates of eastern Europe to Asia. . . ." On his first day in the Oval Office,

Truman was given a memorandum from H. Freeman Matthews, director of the Office of European Affairs in the State Department that charged the Soviet government with having taken "a firm and uncompromising position on nearly every major question." Ten days later Truman had decided to have a show-down with the Russians. He wouldn't "baby" the Soviets anymore. Our agree-ments so far had been "a one-way street." If the Russians did not wish to join us, "they could go to hell." On April 23 in the late afternoon Molotov arrived at the Oval Office to be told in what Leahy described as "plain American language" that the Soviet Union had better follow the U.S. inter-pretation of the Yalta accords and permit the non-Communists to share power in Poland.

"What frightens me," Harriman had written in 1944, "is that when a country begins to extend its influence by strong arm methods beyond its bor-ders under the guise of security it is difficult to see how a line can be drawn." Stalin's intention to dominate Eastern Europe had been made rather clear, but how he intended to exert his influence in the region was less clear. In 1939 he had exchanged territorial shopping lists with Hitler, outlining Soviet interests in the region. Two years later, in the darkest hours of the war, he insisted on discussing minimum Russian territorial demands with Anthony Eden when the British foreign secretary visited him in Moscow.

In victory the United States adopted a much expanded, even a global definition of its security interests, but U.S. leaders were not prepared to accept the legitimacy of the regional security interests of the Soviet Union as the Soviet Union defined those interests. As the war in Europe was ending in early May 1945, Secretary of War Stimson and Assistant Secretary McCloy, who was in San Francisco, conversed by telephone about spheres of influence. Talking of Latin America, Stimson argued, "I think that it's not asking too much to have our little region over here which never has bothered anybody . . . [but] we don't go abroad unless there's a world war." The problem, as Stimson saw it, was to avoid being "immersed in what I used to call the local troubles of Europe." McCloy agreed. "Well you don't think that Russia is going to give up her right to act unilaterally in those nations around her which she thinks so darned—are useful, like Romania and Poland and the other things —you don't think she's going to give that up do you?" McCloy answered, "Uh, no, she will, no . . ." Experienced statesmen like Stimson who were not anti-Communist ideologues were prepared for a certain division of Europe— they knew that Stalin would never permit Eastern Europe to function once again as a *cordon sanitaire* to contain Soviet influence—but Truman's advisers were shocked by the way Soviet power was actually exercised in its sphere. "We must make the Russians understand," Kennan declared in 1946, "that they must confine their security demands to our concept of security demands." From the early months of the postwar era, American diplomats never suc-ceeded in persuading the Soviet leaders on that fundamental point.

With Hitler still a fresh memory it took only a short leap of imagination to conclude that if Stalin were playing by different rules from the West, then he too constituted a threat to civilization. In September 1945, Forrestal pronounced the Russians to be "essentially oriental in their thinking" and warned against trying to "buy their understanding and sympathy." That had been tried with Hitler. "There are no returns on appeasement." We were letting "the descendants of Genghis Khan . . . dictate to us when patently we could and should dictate to them. . . ." General George S. Patton wrote Stimson the same month.

In order to package the Russians as allies, it had been thought necessary to embrace the Soviet dictator as a morally acceptable leader. Stalin, who had sent millions of his own people to their death and had put the rest on a brutal forced march into the twentieth century, had been certified by a succession of wartime visitors from the West as a civilized, if inscrutable, statesman. Now the latent anti-Communism in the United States, fed by an outraged Catholic Church and millions of Americans of East European descent, burst the bonds of alliance before the fighting had stopped. "The objectionable feature of their foreign policy," John Foster Dulles wrote a pacifist clergyman about the Soviet leaders a year after the end of the war, "is that they are attempting in foreign affairs to do precisely what they had been doing at home for nearly 30 years."

The challenge was to build a bulwark for civilization. For the "trustee" of the post-Hitler world order the hard questions of the immediate postwar era concerned the strategy of containment. Could a Fortress America, armed with the bomb and a fierce determination to contain Communism, keep the peace? Or must a new grand alliance be built?

Even establishment easterners like Stimson worried about being drawn into the vortex of European quarrels. Twice in a lifetime tragic European errors had been redeemed with blood and treasure from the New World. Americans acknowledged the common heritage, but America's greatness was defined by the things that separated her from Europe: the opportunity, the mobility, the energy, the informality, the sense of possibility. The few Americans who felt at home in Europe because of strong commercial or family ties were not representative of a country that had been built by those fleeing the intolerance, conscription, and rigid bonds of class of the Old World. Yet influential dreamers of the past had planted the seeds from which the new relationship with Europe would grow. In 1893 Andrew Carnegie, applying the logic behind the great trusts, called for an Anglo-American merger. The influential geopolitical thinker, Admiral Alfred Mahan, also thought that the unity of the English-speaking races was essential in order to police the world sea-lanes. The supreme issue of the historical era was "whether the Eastern or Western civilization is to dominate throughout the earth and to control its future." When the United States entered World War I, Henry Adams, who, like Mahan, saw the unity of the English-speaking races as the bulwark against the barbarian East, welcomed the possibility of "building up . . . a great community of Atlantic powers. . . ." How strange it is, he thought, "that we should have done it by means of inducing those blockheads of Germans to kick us into it." Thirty years later one part of Adams' dream was a reality. The leadership of the English-speaking world had passed to the United States. Britain's imperial "responsibilities" were about to fall into American hands. This time the barbarians of the East themselves were the "blockheads" that made it all possible.

In the second winter after the Nazi collapse the war-ravaged nations of Europe were already struggling to rediscover themselves. The common bond for French, British, Dutch, and Italian politicians of the Center and moderate Left was the threat to civilization each perceived in Communism, the subversion of the old bourgeois order, now thoroughly shaken, by something alien and terrifying. Georges Bidault, the Gaullist who had worked with French Communists in the Resistance and had run the Foreign Ministry since the end of 1944, told the American ambassador shortly after the birth of the Fourth Republic in January 1947 that the goal of the Communists was "to eradicate Western civilization." Yet the fear of American domination was also great. "Our planet as it is today," General de Gaulle declared at the founding of his new political movement Rassemblement du Peuple Français the following April, "shows two huge masses both of which are intent on expansion but are driven by wholly different internal forces and also by different ideological currents . . . the preservation of our independence becomes the most burning and decisive issue." We are Occidentals, De Gaulle declared, "loyal supporters of a particular view of man, of life, of law and international relations." The man who three years earlier had proposed an alliance with Stalin now became increasingly anti-Communist. With Stalin's determination to build up East Germany, the natural alliance to keep Germany dismembered and weak had fallen apart. French obstruction of American plans for Germany began to disappear. For Georges Bidault, France's role as mediator between the Soviets and the Anglo-Saxons had come to an abrupt end when Stalin refused to support the French in their attempt to detach the industrial Saar from Germany and make it French. The "unconditional obedience to the orders of a foreign regime which is run by the leaders of a Slavic power," as De Gaulle put it, disqualified the Communists from running France. But the alternative to a Russian party had to be something other than an American party.

There were many in Europe who nourished the hope that the ancient civilizations of the Continent could liberate and modernize themselves by steering a course equally distant from the brutalities of Stalinism and the materialism of America. In Britain the left wing of the Labour party demanded that the Attlee government work for a "democratic and constructive alternative to an otherwise inevitable conflict between American capitalism and Soviet communism . . ." In Scandinavia, the Swedes, hoping to continue a policy of neutrality that had lasted 135 years, infuriated the American ambassador by equating "the two great power blocs" and seeking to build a defense alliance of the Nordic nations that would be independent of East and West. The Swedes should be told, the U.S. ambassador cabled from Stockholm, that the United States would not rescue them in the event of a Soviet attack unless they chose sides. "The issue in the world today," the secretary of state advised Truman to tell the Swedes, is "not a matter of choosing between two great power blocs . . . but is rather the question of the survival of nations which believe in freedom and democratic processes."

But the idea of Europe as a "Third Force" was very much alive in early 1947, embraced by many conservatives as well as leftists. (Indeed, as late as 1950 the great Scholastic philosopher Etienne Gilson wrote a series of passionate articles in *Le Monde* advocating neutralism. To underscore his point he resigned his chair at the College de France and left for Canada, determined, as he put it, not to face another war and another occupation.) Even many of those who believed that being a good European meant being tied to the United States preferred to tie the continental states to one another before forging transatlantic bonds. Weak nations by themselves were destined to be American satellites; only Europe could be a partner.

Yet it was extremely difficult for the European countries to follow such a strategy so dependent was each on the United States. The daily bread ration in France in 1947 was 200 grams per person, and the United States was the key to providing even that. The bread and dough ration for Italy was cut. The American ambassador in Rome was instructed to discuss with the prime minister ways to "minimize repercussions and avoid if possible furnishing issue of high propaganda and political value for extreme left . . ." On January 20, 1947, the Attlee government issued a startling White Paper on the state of Britain. The loan was running out. The economic situation was "extremely serious"; the coal shortage was "calamitous." Following the brutal blizzards of February, more than half of British industry came to a complete standstill. "The biggest crash since the fall of Constantinople—the collapse of the heart of the Empire—impends," *The New York Times* intoned. "It has projected before our imagination the picture of a world without Britain."

On February 21, 1947, the British first secretary called on the director of the U.S. State Department's Office of Near Eastern and African Affairs and the deputy director of European Affairs and handed these two senior Foreign Service officers a note. What the note said was that Britain could no longer maintain her forces in Greece or continue her economic support to that nation. What the note meant, as Joseph M. Jones, a career man in the State Department, comprehended it, was that "Great Britain had within the hour handed the job of world leadership, with all its burdens and all its glory to the United States."

A few weeks earlier the Eightieth Congress had taken its seats. The Republicans had won the Senate 51 to 45 and the House 245 to 118. In the autumn of 1946, Harry Truman's personal popularity had fallen to the unprecedented low level of 32 percent (it had been as high as 87 percent during the war). During the campaign the mere mention of the president's name had elicited boos, and after the election a senator of his own party, J. W. Fulbright, had publicly called for the president's resignation. There was a gathering mood in the country of frustration and resentment, fed by increasing impatience with lingering wartime controls, shortages, strikes, and racial disturbances. The Republicans, in control for the first time in eighteen years, were adamant for cutting $6 billion from Harry Truman's "astounding" $37.5 billion budget. They also demanded that tariff cutting under the Reciprocal Trade Agreements be halted and that the Export-Import Bank toughen its lending policies and restrict its loans to low-risk projects that "directly promoted American exports." At the same time, Republican leaders were charging the administration with being "soft on communism."

The immediate reaction of Secretary of State George Marshall to Britain's withdrawal from the eastern Mediterranean was annoyance that British "responsibilities" had been "dropped in America's lap." Most State Department planners, however, were "quite openly elated," one of them recalls, at the possibility of creating a "Greek-Turkey-Iran barrier" to keep the Soviet Union out of the Middle East. The plan to aid Greece and Turkey immediately raised fundamental questions of national purpose. Why should the United States, after spending so much money to fight the war, give more money to other countries? For the State Department professionals the answer was obvious. Britain's collapse meant a "power vacuum" in a strategic area of the world which the Soviet Union or some other adversary would exploit. Without an immediate infusion of aid, neither the Greek army fighting Communist guerrillas nor the Turkish army, which was being modernized in response to Stalin's suggestion that some disputed Turkish territory be ceded to the Soviet Union, could carry on.

But for the Republican congressional leaders balance-of-power diplomacy was not an obvious reason to spend money. When Secretary of State Marshall met with them, one asked, "Isn't this pulling British chestnuts out of the fire?" As Dean Acheson, then under secretary of state, recalls, Marshall, who usually radiated authority by speaking in a voice "low, staccato, and incisive," on this historic occasion "flubbed his opening statement." The general was too moderate in his appraisal of the danger and too humanitarian in his rhetoric for the crusty congressional potentates who came to the White House to hear him. "Is this a private fight or can anyone get into it?" Acheson asked his chief. Acheson then proceeded, as one witness describes it, to "pull out all the stops."

In the past eighteen months, I said, Soviet pressure on the Straits, on Iran, and on northern Greece had brought the Balkans to the point where a highly possible Soviet breakthrough might open three continents to Soviet penetration. Like apples in a barrel infected by one rotten one, the corruption of Greece would infect Iran and all to the east. It would also carry infection to Africa through Asia Minor and Egypt, and to Europe through Italy and France, already threatened by the strongest domestic Communist parties in Western Europe. The Soviet Union was playing one of the greatest gambles in history at minimal cost. It did not need to win all the possibilities. Even one or two offered immense gains. We and we alone were in a position to break up the play. These were the stakes that British withdrawal from the eastern Mediterranean offered to an eager and ruthless opponent.

Only two great powers remained in the world, he concluded. Not since Rome and Carthage had there been such polarization of power. The congressional leaders promised support if the president himself would sound the same note of alarm. "If FDR were alive," Acheson remarked, "he would make a statement of global policy but confine his request for money right now to Greece and Turkey."

Harry Truman followed Acheson's advice to the letter. His enunciation of the Truman Doctrine was immediately controversial. Some, like Henry Wallace, thought it too provocative to the Russians. Walter Lippmann thought that the hyperbolic rhetoric Acheson had used to sell the senators—the promise to aid "free peoples everywhere"—would come back to haunt the United States, as indeed it did. Lippmann and Acheson fought over it at a dinner party where Acheson, growing redder and ever more imperious as the evening wore on, accused the columnist of "sabotaging" his foreign policy. At issue was not the use of American military power but how global a commitment the United States was to undertake. (A year earlier, in fact, Lippmann had come up with the idea of sending the body of the Turkish ambassador who had died in Washington home on a battleship to impress the Russians.)

George Kennan, the chief of the Policy Planning Staff in the State Department, was concerned about the global reach and rhetorical flourish of the Truman Doctrine. It was becoming evident to a variety of government officials that a massive aid program would be necessary to stave off economic collapse in Europe and reverse the political trends on the Continent that had brought Communist ministers into the governments of France and Italy. The task was to use the aid program to help launch an alternative world security system now that FDR's "four policemen" vision was defunct, and to produce the sort of Europe the United States would like to see.

4

A little over a year after the bureaucratic whirlwind that culminated in the European Recovery Program, Charles P. Kindleberger, then chief of the Division of German and Austrian Economic Affairs, wrote a memorandum for the files which tried to trace its roots. His assistant in the Division of German and Austrian Economic Affairs, Walt Rostow, is given credit for having had a revelation a few months after the war "that the unity of Germany could not be achieved without the unity of Europe" and for the insight that unity could be best achieved "crabwise through technical cooperation in economic matters, rather than bluntly in diplomatic negotiation." (Both Kindleberger and Rostow later would become well-known economic historians, and Rostow would encounter prominence and controversy as Lyndon Johnson's chief adviser on the Vietnam War.) But, Kindleberger notes, Secretary of State James F. Byrnes was uninterested in Rostow's ideas despite a public prodding in the influential column of Joseph and Stewart Alsop.

In February 1947, Walter Lippmann wrote a series of articles on the British economic crisis, warning that a "forced and disorderly liquidation" of Britain's imperial responsibilities impended and that this threatened American interests. After talks with Acheson, Forrestal, and Will Clayton, Lippmann sounded the call in his column for a "large capital contribution" to European recovery, and the columnist was given credit for providing the inspiration for the Marshall Plan. But from his inside vantage point Kindleberger preferred to give the credit to James Reston. Reston's well-timed lunches with Acheson would invariably be followed by front-page stories in *The New York Times* about the "big planning going on in the State Department. This would give Mr. Kennan, who had just been appointed to the newly created planning staff in February, the jimjams. If there was public talk of all this planning in the department, and the planning staff had received so much publicity, maybe this was where the effort should be applied."

George Kennan, recently returned from a long tour of duty at the American embassy in Moscow, saw the European Recovery Program as the most effective strategy for implementing the policy of "containment" he had popularized within the government in a long telegram from Moscow on the nature of the Stalinist regime. Shoring up embattled democracies with economic and political support was congenial with his soon to be famous recommendation that "the containment of Russian expansive tendencies" . . . be carried out "by the adroit and vigilant application of counterforce at a series of constantly shifting geographical points." Those who promoted Kennan's ideas in government, like Forrestal, thought the logic of containment required a strong military response. Certainly the rhetoric suggested it. But Kennan's first memo as chief planner for the State Department written on May 23 made his position clearer. "The Policy Planning Staff does not see communist activities as the root of the difficulties of western Europe. It believes that the present crisis results in large part from the disruptive effect of the war on the economic, political, and social structure of Europe and from a profound exhaustion of physical plant and of spiritual vigor . . . American effort in aid to Europe should be directed not to the combatting of communism as such but to the restoration of the economic health and vigor of European society."

Four days later his views were considerably reinforced by Will Clayton, who had just returned from an inspection trip to the Continent. "It is now obvious that we grossly underestimated the destruction to the European economy by the war." The problem was not only the physical damage but the economic damage inflicted by the governments themselves—"nationalization of industries, drastic land reform, severance of long-standing commercial ties. . . ." The Marshall Plan from its inception was planned as an ideological weapon not only against Communists loyal to Moscow, but also against what Washington considered the doctrinaire notions of home-grown Socialists. Yet the thinking in the Truman administration was both more tentative and more subtle than many Europeans later believed. In July, after George Marshall had made the famous speech at Harvard that publicly launched the administration's effort, Kennan jotted these notes for the secretary:

1. Marshall "plan".
   We have no plan. Europeans must be made to take responsibility. We would consider
   European plan only if it were a good one and promised to do the whole job.
   Our main object: to render principal European countries able to exist without outside
   charity.
   Necessity of this:

   (a) So that they can buy from us;
   (b) So that they will have enough self-confidence to withstand outside pressures.

The essence of the idea was to direct large grants to the European countries as a substitute for loans. The purpose was to avoid the unending cycle of
the interwar period of floating new loans to repay old ones. In 1926 John Foster
Dulles, who was much involved with high finance in Europe, defended the
practice:

. . . our foreign loans primarily operate to provide payment in dollars here to our farmers and manufacturers for goods which they sell abroad and to pay debts previously
contracted for such purposes . . . Actually the dollar proceeds of foreign loans stay in
the United States. . . .

All during the interwar period the United States had used debt forgiveness and
private loans as the lubricant of the American export trade. The new element
in the Marshall Plan, beyond its magnitude, was that it was based primarily
on government grants and that the Europeans were now required to make internal changes in their economies to encourage the rebirth of a strong capitalist
order.
    By the time the Marshall Plan was announced, Communist ministers had
already been dismissed in France and had resigned in Belgium. The Soviets,
as had been generally predicted in Washington, had turned down the Marshall
Plan. The Communist parties of Europe, summoned to Poland by Stalin in late
September 1947, had been given a new tough line. When Jacques Duclos, the
leader of the French party spoke with obvious pride about the role his party
had played as "the party of order," he was savagely attacked by the Yugoslav
Milovan Djilas. The man who would later write *The New Class,* a devastatingly
influential critique of the Soviet system, was then more Stalinist than Stalin.
"The French delegates have turned into poor representatives of Soviet policy
before the entire French nation," he charged. A few days later the Cominform
was organized and with it the new Stalinist world view. The Marshall Plan
meant that the world was now divided into "two camps." Cooperation with
"the treasonable policies of right-wing socialists" must come to an end. France
had indeed become embarrassingly dependent on U.S. aid. The aid agreement
of January 2, 1948, furnished the country with 66 percent of the official bread
ration, 60 percent of the oil, and 20 percent of the country's coal requirements.
Communist parties must take the lead, Stalin's man Andrei Zhdanov now
demanded, in opposing "the global rule of American imperialism." In the
French Chamber of Deputies tempers flared. "There's the German pig,"
Jacques Duclos shouted as Premier Robert Schuman entered the chamber.

"Provocateur, you talk like Göring," Maurice Thorez, Duclos's successor as secretary-general, screamed at François Mitterrand, then a young minister.

The American-organized European Recovery Program meant the end of Europe as a neutralist "Third Force." It was precisely the American intention to force the European powers to choose sides and to arrest what Churchill had called the "slither to the left." But the Marshall Plan also meant that the West European nations whose recovery the United States had now deemed essential to its own national interest now had the power to frustrate America's traditional vision of a liberal economic order, for their very survival depended on the creation of a regional economic bloc. Neither free trade, abandonment of preferential trade with the colonies, nor freely convertible currencies were compatible with the new policy. The precious transfusion from America would not continue forever and it must not be wasted. Thus the Marshall Plan, contrary to all previous U.S. planning, became the catalyst for a movement toward West European unity.

In 1948, the year the European Recovery Program got under way, anti-American sentiment, the American ambassador to London reported, bordered on the "pathological." Britain's weakness and dependence were "a bitter pill for a country accustomed to full control of her national destiny." An irreverent ditty that made the rounds of London salons at the time touched on most of the irritants of the day:

> Our Uncle which art in America
> Sam be thy name,
> Thy navy come, thy will be done,
> In London as 'tis in Washington.
> Give us this day our Marshall aid,
> And forgive us our un-American activities,
> As we forgive your American activities against us;
> And lead us not into Socialism
> But deliver us from Communism,
> For thine is our Kingdom,
> The Atom power and the Tory,
> Forever and ever: G-men.

Churchill had pronounced Lend-Lease the most "unsordid act in history," but the gift had left Britain penniless and dependent, nonetheless. It was as naive to expect generosity as it was demeaning to accept it. Far better to stress the American self-interest behind every bag of wheat emblazoned with the seal of the United States and the picture of clasped hands across the sea. Immediately after Secretary of State Marshall proposed the European Recovery Program at the 1947 Harvard commencement, Ernest Bevin told the American chargé that the United States was really just following Britain's example. After all, the United States owned 50 percent of the world's wealth, while Britain held no more than about 30 percent at the end of the Napoleonic Wars. Yet, for eighteen years after Waterloo, Bevin told the American diplomat, Britain "practically gave away her exports," and this had resulted in "stability and a hundred years of peace."

In France the Left denounced the Marshall Plan, but an overwhelming majority of respondents in a public opinion poll in February 1948 expressed the view that the United States was the country that would help France most "to get back on its feet." In Germany, Schumacher denounced the aid plan, and in Italy, Pietro Nenni, leader of the Left Socialists, dismissed the European Recovery Program as an "economic tool of the Truman doctrine and Wall Street politics." (The American ambassador had been sufficiently alarmed the previous year about a Communist uprising in northern Italy that the Policy Planning Staff had prepared a contingency plan on protecting American interests in the event of a takeover.)

The taunt from European radicals that Americans were now forced to be generous in order to finance their exports of course had considerable truth to it. All the anti-American forces in Europe needed to corroborate the point was to follow the debates in the United States. The Council of Economic Advisers reported at the end of 1947 that without a significant new aid program, U.S. exports could be expected to decrease from $21 billion to $13 billion in one year. "It is idle," Secretary Marshall declared, "to think that a Europe left to its own efforts . . . would remain open to American business in the same way that we have known it in the past." The State Department planners understood that the greatest government aid program in history translated into enormous political power for the United States. The Marshall Plan agreements called for the recipients to set up "counterpart funds," 5 percent of which could be used by the United States, mostly to buy strategic materials, and 95 percent for domestic projects approved by the United States. It was a tool for influencing domestic priorities—enforcing sound economic practice, as the Americans saw it, tying our hands, as many Europeans saw it. The chief economic planner for the Marshall Plan was Richard Bissell, later the director of covert operations for the CIA. "One of Bissell's great contributions," a colleague later observed, "was the concept that the important thing is not the volume of our aid, but the effects in Europe and our influence in Europe upon national economic and financial policies." Never before, as the State Department publicly proclaimed at the signing of the aid agreements, had any nation agreed "to stabilize its currency, establish or maintain a valid rate of exchange, balance its governmental budget . . . create or maintain internal financial stability."

It was exhilarating for planners in Washington to believe that they were "present at the creation," as Acheson would later put it, of a new Atlantic Community, but the dreams had to be translated into policy country by country, and in the process fundamental differences among the members emerged. "We now have in our hands bargaining weapons we may never possess again," Clair Wilcox, the American trade negotiator, wrote Will Clayton in the summer of 1947. "What we must have is a front-page headline that says 'Empire Preference System Broken at Geneva.'" But Sir Stafford Cripps, the British negotiator, held fast. The United States could not afford to drive too hard a bargain, for Britain's collapse would imperil the whole postwar order.

5

The American planners working in secret had agreed, as Clayton put it, that American aid would be sent only if there was "a European plan which the principal European nations . . . should work out." There were at least three large ideas behind the Marshall Plan. The most immediate was relief. Without major stimulus the capitalist economies of Europe would continue to stagnate and the threat of Communist insurrection would grow. There was a remote possibility that such unrest might attract an army of "liberation." "The Russians need only a good pair of shoes to reach Brest," the American general Lyman Lemnitzer observed in the summer of 1947. The second concern was the "dollar gap." Even before the war had ended, economic planners in Washington had warned that postwar prosperity depended upon a huge increase in exports; massive sales of American goods abroad were believed to be the key to avoiding another bout of crippling unemployment. Europe was the obvious market, but it could not buy from the United States unless it could also make its own goods and sell them to Americans. In 1948 U.S. production was up 70 percent over 1929, but imports from a war-ravaged world were up only 5 percent. Massive grants would finance U.S. exports in the short run and over the long run would revive production in Europe. The third idea was as ideological as the others were practical. Money from America could be the instrument for producing European unity.

Why should Americans be interested in promoting the unity of Europe? For Charles Kindleberger, writing memos inside the State Department in 1947, the point was clear. "The symbols of nationalism in France and Italy and in Germany are essentially bankrupt and in danger of being captured by reactionary and neo-fascist political elements." A Europe united for recovery was a powerful idea to put up against Stalinist internationalism and pan-European Fascism. "There is a possibility of developing tremendous emotional drive in Western Europe behind the supranational idea of European unity." "In our propaganda and our diplomacy," he recommended, "it will be necessary to stress (even exaggerate) the immediate economic benefits which will flow from the joint making of national economic policies and decisions."

When the Foreign Assistance Act was signed on April 2, 1948, it reflected the curious mood of the moment, part missionary zeal for spreading the American success story to Europe, part atavistic fear that, unless reformed, the warring continent would once again disturb America's peace. Senator William Fulbright tried to add a specific provision in the act to the effect that "the policy of the people of the United States" was "to encourage the political unification of Europe." Federalism, the principle outlined in Madison's Federalist paper No. 10 that had turned a succession of migrations from the Old World into a strong community stretching across an entire continent, was the answer to the ancient nationalist rivalries of Europe. "We all know that the small compartments of Europe for hundreds of years have made difficulties that prevented humane understanding between people by which they could move forward," Senator H. Alexander Smith declared. "We have solved this particular problem in America by our economic unity and our political safeguards. Our experience may exert an ultimate influence on Europe. . . ."

The State Department traditionalists, George Kennan, Paul Nitze, and Livingston Merchant, were rather skeptical of putting much emphasis on regional cooperation; for them the building block of diplomacy remained the nation-state. Ever since the Peace of Westphalia in 1648, the stage for diplomacy was a world of borders. But the man Truman picked to run the Marshall Plan, Paul Hoffman, president of Studebaker Motor Company, had a different view. If mass production works in the auto industry, Hoffman reasoned, why shouldn't the principle of scale be extended to countries? Almost as soon as peace had come he had talked over the idea with Jean Monnet.

The Marshall Plan had a price which the Americans exacted slowly and in stages. The French eventually had to agree to the establishment of a new German state in the Western occupation zones, to give up the dream of controlling the Saar and the Rhineland, and to accept German rearmament. "France is the gainer in every way—economically, militarily, and in the furthering of European unity," Monnet rejoiced, as the French position on Germany softened. "We are merely being dragged along by the Americans," the new premier, Robert Schuman, sighed. "A distressing solution, but one we will have to accept," the president of France, Vincent Auriol, declared.

The second requirement was that the recipient nations must cooperate in distributing American largesse. The Organization for European Economic Cooperation (OEEC) was set up at the Château de la Muette in Paris under the directorship of a Monnet protégé, Robert Marjolin. With a Yale degree, an American wife, and an enthusiasm for Keynes, Marjolin was temperamentally suited to working with the Americans. Monnet's personal network helped to soften the assault on French sovereignty posed by the Marshall Plan agreements. He had known the United States representative David Bruce in the war—a "civilized man"—and he developed a close fatherly relationship with a twenty-eight-year-old economist from the Treasury Department, William Tomlinson, who became the key U.S. official for the Marshall Plan in Paris. Since Tomlinson "trusted me completely," Monnet managed in 1949 to secure 90 percent of the financing for his Modernization Fund from American counterpart funds. But the European organization of sixteen sovereign nations would not be enough, he wrote Georges Bidault. British objections had limited its authority. "I believe that only the establishment of a *federation* of the West, including Britain, will enable us to solve our problems quickly enough, and finally prevent war." On returning from Washington he wrote Robert Schuman of his impressions of America, hoping to allay the suspicion that hung over Europe concerning their new benefactor: "America is on the move but it is neither reactionary nor imperialist. It does not want war, but it will go to war if need be." He noted that "a great change occurred here recently: preparation to make war has given way to preparation to prevent it." The great need, he urged Schuman, was "a profound, real, immediate and drastic action that changes things and gives reality to hope in which people are now ceasing to believe.''

The $13 billion spent by the United States on Europe between 1948 and 1952 transformed the political economy of the Continent. True, it was less than half of what the European nations originally requested. But no one could guess at the time either the depth of the problem or the pace of recovery. ''The general opinion is that the gigantic task for the country's complete recuperation cannot conceivably be concluded until around 1975,'' journalist Janet Flanner had reported from Paris in *The New Yorker* in October 1945. At the time General de Gaulle was calling for ''a whole generation of furious work'' to repair the damage of war. But the pace of recovery was faster than anyone dared hope. By 1951 the ''dollar gap'' had been virtually closed. Exports from Europe to the United States were up sharply, and, contrary to the predictions of the Communists, imports from the United States were down. In four years, industrial production in France rose 32 percent, in Italy 54 percent, and in the Netherlands 56 percent.

Paul Hoffman, the administrator of the program, was intent on exporting ''skills as well as our dollars.'' He persuaded Sir Stafford Cripps, the ascetic barrister who had become chancellor of the exchequer, a man who for all his socialist convictions seemed more comfortable with an American businessman than with his hard-drinking colleagues from the unions, to set up an Anglo-American Council on Productivity. With the help of top officials from General Electric and the big U.S. unions, the British tried to figure out why productivity in the iron and steel industry was 50 to 90 percent higher in America. Under the technical assistance program, Turks would come to study road building, Norwegians to look at coal mines, and Dutch farmers to visit hybrid-corn experiments in Iowa. The long-term effects of this first conscious effort at technology transfer by the U.S. government would be felt over a generation.

Despite the end of the black market, a more stable currency, and the return of prewar amenities, life for French workers under the Marshall Plan worsened. They produced more with greater efficiency but their wages declined. ''The average Frenchman can now find in the shops nearly everything he wants except the means of paying for it,'' Janet Flanner reported. ''Parisians dine at home, on soup, and go to bed.'' Food consumption of urban workers was still 18 percent lower than before the war. The tax system took 70 percent of personal income, more iniquitous, *Le Monde* declared, ''than that which provoked the French Revolution.'' Unemployment doubled between 1948 and 1950. The Americans imposed a ceiling on the French budget and a ''commitment to cover all Treasury expenditures by non-inflationary revenues.'' Before the war, French industry had paid out 45 percent of its gross income for wages and pocketed 29 percent in profits. Under the new standard recovery policy pressed by the Americans and accepted by the centrist technocrats who had ridden the Marshall Plan to power, the workers' share fell to 34 percent and profits rose to 50 percent. As the European Recovery Program came to an end Averell Harriman confirmed the obvious before a

Senate committee—". . . certain classes of French society had improved their conditions more than the workmen did." In Italy the government pursued the deflationary programs with such zeal that Marshall Plan administrators called for special pump priming by the government. By early 1950 about 20 percent of Italian workers had no jobs. In Belgium unemployment, which had been about 2 percent in 1947, rose to 11 percent.

Within a year of the launching of the Marshall Plan, the United States faced a severe recession. In the first six months of 1949 profits fell nearly one-third, production dropped 15 percent, and unemployment shot up to nearly 7 percent, an unprecedented high for the yearly postwar period. An embargo was placed on agricultural imports. The Treasury pressed the British to de-value the pound, but the conservative Congress refused to lower U.S. tariffs. The effect was to make it much harder for the British to earn dollars; after devaluation they had to export 30 percent more goods to earn the same quantity of dollars as before, but the recession in the United States made it hard to sell their goods in the United States.

With all its problems and disappointments the Marshall Plan was pronounced a success. It was easy of course to puncture the myth of altruism. The tobacco lobby insisted that the U.S. taxpayer subsidize a shipment to Europe of 40,000 tons of tobacco although none was requested. A quarter of the wheat had to be shipped as flour, an expensive nod in the direction of the U.S. milling interests; 177 million pounds of unpalatable spaghetti were sent to Italy, a gratuitous assault on Italian stomachs that profited a few American companies. Congress insisted that 50 percent of the aid be shipped in American vessels and be insured by American companies. All such reports contributed to the popular belief that no real transfers had taken place, that the money had never really left America. Somehow it made everyone feel better to emphasize the self-serving aspects of the Marshall Plan. The conservative Congress and the restless American public were not in a giveaway mood. Europeans liked to minimize the debt. "A great lifting of the heart goes from us toward the generous American people and toward its leaders," so went the obligatory speech of the French minister of finance marking the first anniversary of the Marshall Plan. But the polemics of Pierre Emmanuel, writing in Paris's soberest daily, *Le Monde,* caught the anti-Americanism of the day:

For five years, American propaganda has been based only on fear [of Communism], a panic sign of impotence. Production-consumption is the diptych of American existence. America kills itself with work. It is a continent hostile to anyone who thinks. Publicity hammers the American brain just as propaganda does [in Russia]. Old countries like France, Italy, and England remind America of its inferiority complex.

The real significance of the Marshall Plan, which helped change the face of Europe, was not that the Americans were either altruistic or self-serving—they were both—but that the survival of the economic system in the richest nation on earth was perceived to require a systematic transfer of resources.

6

"We have no plan," Kennan had written in his notes to General Marshall. But the two French dreamers did. Monnet and De Gaulle had met on March 18, 1944, to discuss European unity in the postwar world. Monnet suggested that perhaps France, Holland, Belgium, and Luxembourg could get together. A four-power Europe? "It would be too small," the general replied. He spelled out his own "grand design" in a speech the following day in Algiers:

We believe that a Western association of sorts, organized by us, as broad as possible in membership and stressing economics, would be very advantageous. Such an association, extending to Africa and maintaining close relations with the East—especially the Arab states, which quite justifiably are seeking to pool their interests—and in which the Channel, the Rhine and the Mediterranean would serve as arteries, might constitute the major center of a global organization concerned with production, trade and security.

"But, of course," he told Monnet, "France must play the leading role."
In 1947 every politician in the western half of the Continent, except for a few diehard nationalists or Communists claimed to be a good European. The logic of integration was irresistible. But of what sort? And who was to be the organizing spirit? For De Gaulle the answer was obvious. France must be the "geographical and moral center" of an association of states, "each of which will preserve its body, soul, and image." And he, of course, as he told an American admiral a few days after the United States had joined the war, represented *"France eternelle,"* like Joan of Arc, Napoleon, and others who had risen from the French masses, propelled into leadership by the failure of others. He liked to confound Americans by emphasizing the mystical side of his politics. When Robert Murphy, Eisenhower's political adviser in Algiers, dared lecture him about what the French really think, on the basis of his three years' experience in France as consul, consul-general, and counselor of emassy, the general airily brought the conversation to an end. "What you say may be true, but I've been in France for a thousand years." Walter Lippmann, who "felt an admiration close to hero worship," found De Gaulle to be one of those rare leaders who actually incarnate their countries. "It's as if the country is inside them. . . ." It was precisely the impression the general wished to make.
The Marshall Plan years 1948–52 were a period of feverish diplomatic activity on the Continent—the Treaty of Dunkirk, a French-British alliance against Germany (1947), the Brussels Pact, an embryonic European defense organization headed by British Field Marshal Viscount Montgomery (1948), a European Payments Union, and the Council of Europe (1949), in which the driving force was Winston Churchill. De Gaulle attacked the council as a "caricature" of the integration process. Unification, he declared on November 14, 1949, must be gradual development. It should rest on an agreement "between the Germans and the Gauls without intermediaries"—meaning the "Anglo-Saxons"—and it should start with economic and political questions,

not defense. It was absurd, he snapped, to accept England, which had never been part of the Continent, as the driving force of a European movement. Yet so strong was the European idea four years after the war that he called for a "vast referendum" throughout Europe on the issue of continental unity.

For De Gaulle, Europe was an extension of France. There could be no unity unless France took the lead, and France would never do so unless she recovered a sense of "grandeur." For a thousand years, he told an American interviewer in his retirement years when he would refer to himself as the "sidetracked leader," France had been *the* world's leading nation and every Frenchman knew it. Once having been the star, he pointed out, Frenchmen were uninterested in playing a "walk-on" part. The problem was cynicism and despair, and the solution was to recover past glory.

General de Gaulle towered over those he would impress; Jean Monnet accomplished the same end by seeming to be in a state of perpetual bounce. No less driven, he would work a fourteen-hour day weeks on end, interrupting his endless cajoling, bargaining, prophesying, and planning only for one of his beloved walks. The press called him an economist and his enemies a technocrat, but he was neither. He was a businessman with a vision, "a happy combination of French logic and Anglo-Saxon practicality," as one of the many laudatory articles in *The New York Times* put it. As France began its slow recovery in 1949, having rejected "the decadence that threatened her," the chief planning officer reported to his government, it was clear that the nation could not achieve prosperity in a disorganized Europe. "The French could not become modern or great by themselves, alongside European neighbors and competitors who themselves would soon discover the limits of their home market and the cramping effect of national barriers. Tomorrow our steel production might be at the mercy of German coke deliveries; later, our agriculture might depend upon the whims of European importers." The obvious answer was to establish institutions to reflect the "community of interests between economies and peoples."

Monnet was an unapologetic Anglophile. From his earliest business experience selling brandy to the trappers in the Hudson Bay to his dramatic effort at French-British union in the darkest days of the war, he had always looked first to the English-speaking world. He had hoped that the OEEC and the Marshall Plan could be used to harmonize the national economic planning of France and Britain. "You won't reach agreement," he would say, "unless you make it your ultimate aim to merge the British and French economies." There were problems, to be sure. (French planning, Monnet notes in his memoirs, was a model of "Cartesian clarity" while the efforts of the British Socialists were rather sloppy.) Monnet's proposal to begin the French-British merger by trading British coal for French food was rejected out of hand by the British. "We'd won the war," Sir Edwin Plowden, the British negotiator later told Monnet, "and we weren't ready to form special links with the continent." At Strasbourg ambitious schemes for a federated Europe were presented. But Monnet paid little attention because he knew that the Council of Europe had no power. His consuming passion was "to invent new political methods and to hit on the right moment for changing the way people thought." The key to European integration, it turned out, was Germany, not England, and the right moment was a gift of Stalin.

In late 1949, Monnet feared that Germany was "about to become once again the most powerful nation on the continent." The Federal Republic had been proclaimed; Adenauer had been elected chancellor. The Americans, Dean Acheson, the U.S. secretary of state, told the French, were demanding "a German ally that is strong, highly industrialized, integrated into the Western system and ready to participate in the defense of the West. . . ." The Ruhr was once again under the control of the great coal and steel families, including Thyssen and Krupp. The French were still fighting a rearguard action to slow German revival and to prevent her rearmament.

"It would be such a good thing," Churchill had advised Georges Bidault, the French foreign minister two years earlier, "if you were to take the initiative in effecting a Franco-German reconciliation. For a former president of the National Council of the Resistance, everything is possible." Bidault established relations with Adenauer, but there was "something pathetic," Monnet recalls, about his growing isolation from the rest of Europe. His desperate efforts to overcome France's inherent weakness "gradually made him seem a man of the past."

Robert Schuman, Bidault's rival and successor in the French Mouvement Républicain Populaire (MRP), the Catholic centrist party, was born in Alsace-Lorraine when it was German, spoke French with a German accent, and had worn a Prussian uniform in his youth. He had been deputy mayor of the border city of Metz since 1918, had served briefly in the Vichy government, and had politely refused an offer of the Nazis to become gauleiter of Alsace-Lorraine. An introverted, deeply religious man with the face of a clown, exasperatingly slow of speech, and somewhat compulsive—he liked to collect bits of string— Schuman was dedicated to achieving "peaceful coexistence between two countries which have so often been at each other's throats." On January 15, 1950, he boarded a train for a pre-dawn meeting with Adenauer in the railroad station in Bonn. Five years after the war French-German tensions were still so great that the newly elected chancellor had had the station cleared and all the lights turned on for fear of an assassination attempt. "You want to annex the Saar," Adenauer greeted him with cold fury. "That would be another Alsace-Lorraine." Schuman tried to mollify him by speaking German, for which he was later much criticized at home, but Adenauer warned that amputating German territory would guarantee another revanchist movement in Germany. Schuman returned to Paris in despair.

A week later, Adenauer, sensing that he had gone too far, revived the idea he had first put forward in 1923 about merging French and German coal and steel production. France and Germany might eventually become one nation, he remarked to an American reporter on March 9, 1950, and have a single integrated parliament. Like the chorus of some Greek tragedy, as Monnet described it, General de Gaulle welcomed the proposal; its grandeur and vagueness guaranteed that it would never be realized.

If one were not constrained to look at matters cooly, one would be dazzled by the prospect of what could be achieved by a combination of German and French strength, the latter embracing also Africa. . . . Altogether, it would mean giving modern economic, social, strategic, and cultural shape to the work of the Emperor Charlemagne.

Jean Monnet paid no attention. Political unity could not be decreed, he told his associates. It had to be built. There could be no peace without German recovery, and no security for France with it, unless the old rivalries were transcended. The four powers were about to meet once again in London in May, 1950, to decide Germany's future. The tensions and political passions of the last war were still unresolved, but now added to these were the new dangers from the East

With less than a month to go before the meeting, Monnet began working at his Houjarray cottage with a few trusted associates, Paul Reuter, a law professor who consulted for the Quai d'Orsay, and Pierre Uri, and Etienne Hirsch, his two chief subordinates at the planning ministry. Reuter was the first to suggest a merger of coal mines and steel works on both sides of the Rhine. "Coal and steel," Monnet agreed, "were at once the key to economic power and the raw materials for forging weapons of war." There were 360 producers of coal, steel, and iron on both sides of the valley of the Rhine. If a High Authority could be set up to make the rules for the market, and enforce them, an iron and steel community based on free market principles could work. Although Monnet himself was not overly worried about centralized administration, the whole idea of bureaucratic planning was anathema to the German steel companies. The new German government was committed to the free market notions at the heart of Erhard's *Sozialemarkt wirtschaft*. The proposal had to blend the peculiarities of French and German economic practice. For Monnet, as he made clear in the final paragraph of his proposal, the objective of his complex scheme was political: "to make a breach in the ramparts of national sovereignty which will be narrow enough to secure consent, but deep enough to open the way towards the unity that is essential to peace."

Monnet sent off a copy of his memorandum to Bidault, the premier, but his aide delayed giving it to him. (In his memoirs Bidault says he did read Monnet's letter but did not respond. He was pushing another idea, an Atlantic High Council, a version of De Gaulle's notion of a "directorate" of the United States, France, and Britain to run the non-Communist world.) Hearing nothing from Bidault, Monnet then invited Schuman to lunch, presented him with the plan, and invited him to make it his own. "You would be believed. It would be regarded as an extraordinary proposal made by an honest man." Schuman was immediately enthusiastic, and arranged a secret meeting to try out the idea on the American secretary of state. Acheson was suspicious. "The arrangement could become a giant cartel controlling the basic necessities of an industrial society," was his first reaction. But Monnet worked on him, and secured the help of John McCloy in translating Monnet's "vagueness," as Acheson called it, into lawyerly prose.

In London, Acheson found Ernest Bevin in a "towering rage," visibly ill from the attacks of angina that would kill him within a year. He accused me, Acheson recalls, "of having conspired with Schuman to create a European combination against British trade with the continent." Conservatives welcomed the proposal and urged Britain to join the French and Germans, but the Labourites feared being overwhelmed by the combined power of French and German industry. They asked for a special relationship to the High Authority, even the chance to renegotiate the basic idea of the Coal and Steel Community, and were turned down. The National Executive Committee of the British Labour party issued a report attacking the notion of a "supra-national authority." For the Socialists of Britain, ideological fears reinforced nationalist sentiments. Britain's experiment with "cradle to grave security" must not be jeopardized by subjecting it to the whims of the coal barons of the Ruhr. The empire, though fading fast, still defined British identity. "In every respect except distance we in Britain are closer to our kinsmen in Australia and New Zealand on the far side of the world, then we are to Europe. We are closer in language and in origins, in social habits and institutions, in political outlook and in economic interest."

It took just over two years for Monnet's scheme to create a single free market for coal and steel for 160 million people in six countries to become a reality. On August 10, 1952, Monnet moved into a palace in Luxembourg, lately occupied by the local railroad administrators, as president of the High Authority of the Coal and Steel Community. For protocol purposes, the U.S. State Department decided, M. Monnet should be treated as a head of state outranking the foreign ministers of the six member countries. For three years he presided over marathon negotiations to standardize and lower tariffs, to give workers of the Six a common passport which would enable anyone to work anywhere in the Community, and to eliminate customs duties, quotas, currency controls, and double pricing. The supranational minigovernment he ran with its own Common Assembly, Court of Justice, and tax collectors fascinated American politicians who saw the federalist model as a flattering import from the New World. Monnet himself liked to stress his debt to America whenever he could. The "advantages of a huge unified market," he would tell reporters from the United States, came to him during the war when he was chairman of the Anglo-American Production Board and witnessed at firsthand the miracle of American plane production. "I swore to myself that, if I lived to see victory, I would employ my remaining years to create such a market in Europe." The Community was not a Third Force he insisted, but a way to build up a demoralized Europe fast. In 1913 Europe produced one-third of the world's industrial products, he told a *Newsweek* interviewer. "Now it produces only one sixth."

Coal and steel were only the beginning, he promised. The Common Market would next be extended to agriculture and to textiles. By 1960, his associate, Pierre Uri, predicted, Europe would have a common currency. Given a triumphant reception in America when he made a four-week visit in 1952 and admired by German industrialists and conservative politicians alike, Monnet was treated with suspicion by French industrialists who did not see how they could survive German revival without protectionism. The early years of the Coal and Steel Community coincided with a dramatic increase in production. The economic successes were impressive; political progress was much slower. In 1955 Jean Monnet decided to leave his palace in Luxembourg and to become once again a private prophet. "I knew my personal influence would not long survive my resignation from the High Authority," so he sought and found new authority in the Action Committee for the United States of Europe, a transnational lobby composed of influential politicians and businessmen. For the rest of his life he used his old boy network to push and prod the powerful to get on with the creation of a united Europe.

The moment seemed propitious. In France, Germany, Italy, and Belgium, politicians with a strong commitment to the idea of a united Europe were in charge. Schuman, Adenauer, Alcide De Gasperi, and Spaak shared a vision of Europe that was Catholic, conservative, and reformist. Old values could be preserved only by uniting against the barbarian East and by overcoming the decadence of the past. In their efforts to make Christian democracy a supranational ideology, the good Europeans had two powerful allies: the Vatican, which declared 1950 a Holy Year and stepped up its support for Christian Democrats everywhere, and the United States. By sheer coincidence the statesmen of Europe in 1950 shared a common religious world view, and each in his way was a political mongrel. Schuman was as German as he was French. Adenauer, always more at home in Alsace than in Prussia, also reflected the attitudes of a border politician. De Gasperi, who hailed from German-speaking Trent, spent his formative years in an Austrian political party and the war years as a librarian in the Vatican. Paul-Henri Spaak, the Belgian premier, already presided over a nation of two languages.

But the wave of euphoria passed. The European movement stalled. True, the Americans were now more enthusiastic than ever. John Foster Dulles, Monnet's old friend, was now secretary of state. Within days of Eisenhower's inauguration Dulles flew to Luxembourg to express his "inspiring faith" in Monnet's enterprise. "[A]bove all," Monnet wrote of the meeting, "he recognized in it the tradition which the Founding Fathers had enshrined in the U.S. Constitution, and which was so vividly alive in his heart." (At Dulles' funeral six years later, Monnet was the only foreigner to be a pallbearer.) But Winston Churchill, recently returned to power, showed no more enthusiasm than the Labourites for entering Monnet's Europe. "I love France and Belgium," he told his physician and confidant, Lord Moran, "but we must not let ourselves be pulled down to that level." The problem was the United States. "They have become so big and we are now so small. Poor England!" Moran remarked on the "sense of inequality" in the old man that "devours him like a cancer." It would only be aggravated by throwing in with the Six.

7

The North Atlantic Treaty Organization (NATO) was originally seen as a set of promises that an attack on one of the members would be considered an attack on all of them; in short, a guarantee pact, not a military organization in a permanent state of mobilization. But even this modestly conceived military alliance could not have been brought into being without a war scare. On February 19, 1948, Soviet Deputy Foreign Minister Valerian Zorin arrived in Prague. The Soviet Union was widely regarded as the liberator of the country. The Communist party was more popular in Czechoslovakia than anywhere else in East Europe and had won 37 percent of the vote in a free election in 1946. But the day after the Soviet diplomat arrived, twelve non-communist ministers suddenly resigned. Communist ministers were in charge of the police and they moved quickly to harass and intimidate political opponents. Panicked reports that divisions of the Red Army were about to roll into Prague circulated across the country. President Eduard Beneš, with all too recent memories of personal intimidation by Hitler and abandonment by the West, was too ill, tired, and demoralized to resist. On February 25 he authorized Klement Gottwald, Stalin's man in Prague, to oust the pro-Western members of the government. Within a month Jan Masaryk, the foreign minister, son of the nation's founding president, was dead. He had jumped—or, more likely, had been pushed—from a small bathroom window.

The consolidation of the Russian hold over Czechoslovakia hardly took the State Department by surprise. George Kennan immediately saw it as a defensive reaction to the political success scored by the Marshall Plan—Czechoslovakia had initially expressed interest in participating—and to the steps taken toward the creation of the Federal Republic. Laurence Steinhardt, the U.S. ambassador to Czechoslovakia, had predicted something of the sort. In December 1947 he told the National War College in Washington, D.C., that the "resentment that we are building up Germany too fast" would cause the non-Communists as well as the Communists to "feel they must look to the Russians for protection against Germany." There was another source of Russian political strength in Czechoslovakia which the Americans had miscalculated. The 1947 harvest had failed and the Czechs had asked Washington for 300,000 tons of wheat. But the United States, concerned that Czechoslovakia was already lining up with the Soviet Union in its foreign policy, refused to send a single ton of wheat without a commitment to back away from pro-Russian policies. The American refusal to give aid played into the hands of the Communists. "Those goddamn Americans . . . these idiots in Washington have driven us straight into the Stalinist camp . . ." Foreign Trade Minister Hubert Ripka fumed in Moscow as he accepted a well-publicized gift of 600,000 tons of Soviet wheat.

If some in the State Department had already written off Czechoslovakia, the Prague events were shocking enough to raise new fears. For the Americans and politicians of the center in Europe, the Czech coup raised the specter of

1848—a wave of insurrections across Europe. The Russian threat perceived in the West was not an invasion but the control by the Kremlin of local Communist parties, particularly in France and Italy, bent on subverting the political order. Headlines with the word Czechoslovakia touched raw nerves and guilty consciences. "We are faced with exactly the same situation with which Britain and France were faced in 1938–9 with Hitler," Harry Truman, vacationing in Key West, wrote to his daughter Margaret. "Things look black." General Lucius Clay added a little fuel to the gathering war scare by sending a cable to the director of Army Intelligence on March 5. There was a "subtle change" in Soviet attitudes and war could come with "dramatic suddenness." Clay admitted that he had no supporting data but "my feeling is real." (The editor of Clay's papers, Jean Edward Smith, says the primary purpose of the cable "was to assist the military chiefs in their congressional testimony; it was not in Clay's opinion, related to any change in Soviet strategy.") Nonetheless, the crisis atmosphere in Washington intensified. The chief of naval operations advised taking measures "to prepare the American people for war." Secretary Marshall, an aide scribbled a note, "is nervous—world keg of dynamite—HST shouldn't start it." The CIA advised the president that war was improbable in the next sixty days, but beyond that no one could say. The secretary of the army made inquiries of the Atomic Energy Commission on how long it would take to move atomic bombs to the Mediterranean. A few weeks later *Business Week* included a special section: "Economic Consequences of a Third World War."

On March 17, 1948, Truman gave a tough speech to a joint session of the Congress. "The tragic death of the Republic of Czechoslovakia has sent a shock wave through the civilized world." Marshall had wanted a "weak message" Charles Bohlen reported, "no 'ringing phrases'—nothing warlike or belligerent." But Clark Clifford, Truman's political adviser, believed that only a tough speech would ensure the passage of the Marshall Plan and the rearmament measures then being considered, especially the restoration of the draft.

A few hours before Truman spoke the Brussels Pact was signed. A full month before the Prague crisis Ernest Bevin had proposed such a "collective self-defense" alliance that included Britain, Canada, France, and the Benelux countries (Netherlands, Belgium, and Luxembourg). The pact was defensive in more than one sense. The political aggressor identified in its preamble was Germany. Of course the pact was also to be a show of strength to the Russians. But Bevin felt pressed to take action to preserve and expand the "special relationship" with the United States because the French had been making their own secret initiatives in Washington. Pierre Billotte, the youngest French general in World War II, De Gaulle's chief of staff, and the man who captured the infamous Von Chollitz—Hitler's general remembered for asking, "Is Paris burning"—had come up with an idea for a fifteen-nation Western alliance under a directorate of the United States, Britain, and France. It would be backed by the U.S. threat to use the atomic bomb in case Stalin moved against Europe. Based on ideas De Gaulle himself had developed in the war, Billotte's scheme was also influenced by his contact with General Marshall whom he had met in China when the American general was trying to mediate the Chinese civil war. Marshall had told him that if the Europeans could not pull themselves together, the United States "will be forced to abandon Europe."

On June 19, 1948, the Canadian prime minister, Louis Saint-Laurent, proposed a regional defense pact incorporating Canada, the United States, and Western Europe. Like many statesmen of the time, the Canadian leader was casting about for some alternative to the United Nations now stalled as an effective security arrangement because of the East-West split. A serious European initiative to protect itself was necessary to convince skeptical senators and congressmen that the Marshall Plan was more than a ceremonial transfusion to a dying victim. An American defense commitment would have no credibility unless the Europeans were willing to defend themselves, and such a defense commitment, State Department planners believed, was a necessary stimulus to economic and political recovery. From the U.S. standpoint, it was better for Britain to take the initiative than France; the more powerful France's role, the more difficult it would become to arrange German membership in the new alliance, an inevitable development in any effective security arrangement designed to contain the Soviet Union. The Brussels Pact creating the Western European Union, was, in Bevin's eyes, really little more than a carefully arranged trigger for an American commitment. Isolationism was still too strong for the United States to organize an alliance on the continent, but it could join one. On June 11, 1948, the Senate overwhelmingly passed the Vandenberg Resolution calling for the United States to associate with a regional "collective security arrangement" in Europe.

The proposed military buildup in Europe was designed to be a "modest shield," as Kennan put it, behind which recovery could take place. Its only military function, as Senator Vandenberg saw it, was to assure "adequate defense against internal subversion." "A general stiffening of morale in Free Europe is needed," the director of the Office of European Affairs advised Marshall on March 8, 1948, "and it can come only from action by this country." A revival of a military alliance just three years after the end of the last war would signal to the Russians that Europe had a will to live and that the United States was prepared to treat a threat to European security as a threat to its own.

Thus from the very first NATO was designed as a political response to a political threat. "Political and indeed spiritual forces must be mobilized in our defense," Orme Sargent, the permanent under secretary of the British Foreign Office, advised the prime minister. "I believe therefore we should seek to form backed by the Americas and the Dominions a Western democratic system. . . ."

No one—in authority—not the Joint Chiefs of Staff, not Secretary of Defense Forrestal, nor any other senior political or military official believed in 1948 and 1949 that the Soviet Union would invade Europe. All through 1946 the Soviet continued to tear up the railroad track across Poland. Feverish dismantling of this sort was quite consistent with Stalin's preoccupation of the moment—the rise of a revanchist Germany within a generation—but not with a secret plan to march west. With all the disclosures of Stalin's crimes by post-Stalinist politicians and Soviet defectors, it is noteworthy that not one bit of evidence has emerged indicating that Stalin planned a military attack on Western Europe in the late 1940s. At the hearings of the North Atlantic Treaty held in the spring of 1949, John Foster Dulles, then serving as senator from New York, summed up the prevailing view: "I do not know of any responsible high official, military or civilian . . . in this government or any other government who believes that the Soviet now plans conquest by open military aggression." The Soviets had demobilized in secret—from 11 million down to about 2.8 million men under arms. (The United States had 670,000 at the time.) The Pentagon assumed that the numbers were much larger; certainly the public was encouraged to believe in the existence of Stalin's 225 divisions ready and waiting to march to the English Channel. But given her 20 million dead, 70,000 villages destroyed, and the absence of usable railroad track across Poland, U.S. intelligence officials could be quite confident at NATO's birth that the invasion against which the alliance was ostensibly organized would not take place.

Unquestionably, American leaders had a cooler view of the military threat to Europe than was expressed in such public utterances as Winston Churchill's chilling assertion in 1950 that but for the atomic bomb the Russians would be at the English Channel. A CIA study of February 1950 questioned the assertion "[t]hat only the existence of the U.S. atomic bomb prevented the USSR from carrying out an intention to continue its military advances to the Atlantic . . . There is no reason to suppose . . . that the USSR had any such intention in 1945 or subsequently." The Air Force comment on the study considered this a "dangerous" way of looking at the situation, citing no evidence of an intention to invade other than Stalin's willingness to divide up Poland with Hitler. Many of Truman's advisers did not worry about an attack across the Elbe but about possible Soviet use of force on its periphery in some "year of maximum danger" when the Soviets had built up their atomic striking force to the point where it could neutralize America's "winning weapon." As early as the summer of 1946, Clark Clifford, who was special counsel to Truman, wrote a memo for the president summarizing the collective wisdom of the national security bureaucracy. The men in the Kremlin were "isolated, . . . largely ignorant of the outside world, . . . blinded by [an] adherence to Marxist dogma" and as a consequence the only language they understood was "the language of military power." Indeed, by the end of 1946, the Soviets had given up their demands on Turkey and Iran in response to explicit American pressure.

Ironically, some of the actions taken in 1946 and 1947 by the United States in that belief may well have enhanced the Soviet military threat to Europe. By 1948 two developments had taken place that must have alarmed Stalin considerably. One was the not-so-secret discussion within the U.S. government about deploying B-29 bombers, the carriers of the atomic bomb, to bases in

Europe within striking distance of the Soviet Union. The second was the Marshall Plan which Stalin read as a U.S. commitment to rebuild and eventually rearm Germany in order, as Dulles would later put it, to "roll back" Soviet control over Eastern Europe. Increasingly, military and economic moves by the West provoked by Stalin's hostility and designed to deter him reinforced Stalin's ideological and psychological predisposition to believe the worst about American intentions. Now he proceeded to take action in the name of "national security" which created a new military threat to Europe. In 1948, demobilization halted and military budgets rose.

Preparations for the war Stalin believed was coming demanded an offensive strategy. The war, if it happened, must be fought on the soil of Russia's enemies. Control of East Europe, even the rule of the Communist party in parts of the Soviet Union itself, were too fragile to withstand another invading army inside Russia two years after the most devastating war in history. The Berlin blockade accelerated plans to establish bomber bases in Britain from which the atomic bomb could be delivered to the Soviet Union; within days of the North Korean attack in June 1950, President Truman approved stockpiling of nonnuclear components for nuclear explosives at the British bases. If Britain and other parts of West Europe were now bases for atomic attack on the USSR, then in Stalin's eyes they were now legitimate Soviet targets. At a time when a U.S. secretary of the navy was openly advocating "preventive" nuclear war, Soviet military journals held out the prospect of a Soviet invasion of Europe as the principal deterrent of a U.S. nuclear attack on Russia.

The new secretary of state, Dean Acheson, with his imposing stature, his Groton speech, piercing eyes, beetle brows, fierce mustache, and impeccable Savile Row tailoring was a caricature of an anglophile. He looked, as more than one Midwest senator snorted, as if he had just emerged from a London club. Anthony Eden bestowed on the American secretary the ultimate accolade of a British gentleman: "I would not hesitate to go tiger-hunting with him." The Briticisms were no affection. His father had served in the Queen's Own Rifles before migrating to Canada and later settling in the United States where in time he became the Episcopal bishop of Connecticut. On the queen's birthday during that "radiant morn" Acheson calls his childhood, the Union Jack fluttered from the rectory flagpole as the bishop raised his glass at dinner to Her Majesty. Dean Acheson's anglophile prejudices were tempered by his awareness of Britain's sorry economic state. Despite his unusually close personal relationship with British Ambassador Oliver Franks, he was exceedingly skeptical that a government that made social welfare its priority could muster the strength to play the game of nations. Years after he left office, Acheson made a speech at Oxford lambasting the British for dissipating their power.

In 1949, Acheson saw NATO's armies as instruments for achieving a variety of specific political purposes. The principal objective was to help build a new Europe, not the "rickety fire-hazard of the past," as his successor John Foster Dulles called it, but a trading partner for America, strong and confident enough to contain the two potential outlaws—Germany and Russia. NATO's armies could, he believed, serve as glue to consolidate the power of a declining Britain and a recovering continent. Rearmament could provide what one 1950 memorandum in the German Affairs Office of the State Department called the "bold, hopeful acts" to overcome the "apathy . . . indecision and deep-running fears" that seemed so strong throughout Western Europe. Troops, tanks, and planes were tangible expressions of political commitment that could stir the public. In itself the modest buildup would not scare the Russians, but a transformed political climate might give them pause.

From the day the NATO treaty was signed, certain built-in contradictions haunted the architects. The most serious related to German rearmament. No European Army could be credible without a German contribution. Yet to admit Germany's crucial role would alarm the French who were not yet ready to accept it and would give enormous bargaining power to Adenauer in negotiating Germany's path to nationhood. Acheson had to walk a tightrope, and in his maneuvering he resorted to the time-honored tactic of the practiced diplomat, obfuscation. He made a complex reality perceived differently in every capital of the West "clearer than truth," to use his own words. If he did not deliberately conceal official intentions—from the French and from the U.S. Congress —he was a remarkably bad prophet. Henri Bonnet, the French ambassador, asked him on December 1, 1949, whether the rumors that the Pentagon favored German rearmament were true. "There is no intention," Acheson replied, "to seek German rearmament." Germany will remain demilitarized, the secretary told the House Committee on Foreign Affairs on June 5, 1950. Senator Bourke Hickenlooper, at the hearings on the North Atlantic Treaty, asked him: "Are we going to be expected to send substantial numbers of troops over there as a more or less permanent contribution?" The secretary replied, "The answer to that question, Senator, is a clear and absolute 'no.' "

For Acheson, the Korean invasion twenty days later, McGeorge Bundy writes, "was in part simply an opportunity to adopt openly a policy urgently recommended in private for some months previously." The possibility that a surprise attack in one part of the world might be repeated in another produced a moment of panic. Intelligence analysts quickly concluded that the attack across the 38th parallel was a "local affair," but the temptation to use the event to push European intregration to a new stage was irresistible. Acheson and the State Department planners regarded an American troop contribution to NATO as having a crucial political purpose in the United States. It would mark the end of isolationism and seal the victory of a Europe-oriented forward strategy for the United States over the dreams of a secure Fortress America then being proposed by Herbert Hoover, Senator Robert Taft, and Joseph P. Kennedy. "We have decided," as one State Department memorandum of November 1950 put it, "that the system of European defense can be made to work in a way that will best serve our interest. . . . the other alternative, namely the build-up of strength on the American continents, would have yielded a preponderance of potential to the Soviets which would present a less hopeful prospect than the forging of defenses in Europe. Moreover, the alternative would in itself have represented a 'retreat' . . ."

The culmination of the old prewar debate was at hand. Did the United States need Europe? Why did it matter who took over the Continent? Britain, to be sure, had built her empire on a balance of power notion, moving in quickly when any single European nation grew too powerful. But with two oceans protecting her and the atomic bomb still an American monopoly, why should America play that game? Worry about Iceland, not Berlin, the old isolationist Joseph P. Kennedy insisted. (In little over ten years his son as president of the United States would travel to the heart of that divided city and declaim, *"Ich bin ein Berliner."*) Like so many strategic discussions the so-called "Great Debate" about sending American troops to Europe that was resolved the following year had more to do with the battles of the past than of the future. The isolationists, committed to "Asia first"—the Pacific could be an American lake but Europe could never be anything but trouble—believed that America, armed with the bomb, could implement a global anti-Communist strategy far better by acting alone than by making dubious alliances with creeping Socialists looking for handouts. Acheson was the quintessential hard-liner as far as the Russians were concerned, but his name and imperious image became a political lightning rod attracting all sorts of skepticism about Europe now parading as anti-Communism. For the Democrats in 1951 it was crucial to win the Great Debate about troops for Europe to change the political climate not only in Europe but in the United States as well. Enthusiasm for NATO became the benchmark of American political orthodoxy because the alliance symbolized as nothing else did a permanent American commitment to exercise leadership over the industrial world.

The alliance was in "disarray" of one sort or another from the day the NATO treaty was signed because the partners always had different expectations and different visions of what they were doing. Confusion always centered on the NATO military forces. The stated function of the troops—to keep out Russian divisions which military analysts doubted were coming in any event—caused people to forget the real political purposes they were intended to serve. In 1950—after the Czech crisis had passed and before the Korean invasion—the idea behind rebuilding an Allied army on the continent was to breathe new life into the European integration movement which by that time showed signs of running out of steam. On March 7, 1950, Acheson and McCloy, having gathered in Washington for a policy review, were wondering how to regain the momentum. The European Payments Union was a fine thing, Acheson noted, but not the sort of thing to bring people out in torchlight parades. When McCloy suggested a set of articles of confederation for Europe, Acheson countered with the idea of setting up a secretariat for NATO with the full panoply of a healthy bureaucracy, castles, flags, green beige tables, parades, and, of course, platoons of generals and admirals to plan the war that no one quite believed in.

Monnet, too, saw that new forms of military cooperation were essential to save the European movement. Even before the attack in Korea he had concluded that functional integration—building political communities by emphasizing shared economic and social functions instead of geography, race, or language—would not get very far without dealing with the defense function as well. The test explosion by the Soviets of their first atomic bomb in August 1949 made the idea of extending American protection seem more urgent, but it also put the credibility of the American guarantees in question. The Korean attack ten months later gripped the non-Communist world in fear. When Douglas MacArthur's brilliant advance to the Yalu River on the Chinese border in late 1950 suddenly turned to humiliating retreat forced by waves of Chinese troops, the mood inside the U.S. government turned apocalyptical. One top-secret memorandum to the National Security Council by the chairman of the National Security Resources Board, Stuart Symington, argued the political necessity and moral justification for making an explicit threat to render the Soviet Union a radioactive ruin:

The United States and its allies of the free world are fighting a war for survival against the aggression of Soviet Russia.

The United States and it allies are losing the war, on both the political and military fronts . . .

The hour is late. The odds may be stacked against the free nations; but it is still possible to take the offensive in this fight for survival.

On the political front, the United States could make its greatest contribution to the defense of Western Europe and other areas of interest to the free nations by announcing, preferably through NATO, that any further Soviet aggression, in areas to be spelled out, would result in the atomic bombardment of Soviet Russia itself.

This action would accomplish the following:
  (a) Serve notice to the communist and the free world that the United States recognizes and assumes its role as leader in the fight against aggression.
  (b) Act as a deterrent to Soviet aggression.
  (c) Establish moral justification for use of United States' atom bombs in retaliation against Soviet aggression.
  (d) And thus afford the United States a measure of moral freedom it does not now have to use the atom bomb under circumstances other than retaliation out of what devastation might be left of this country after an initial Soviet atomic attack.

Even before the debacle at the Yalu, Monnet had recognized that Cold War tensions now made German rearmament inevitable and that this threatened all he had achieved with the Schuman Plan. The American goals seemed set. The United States would reinforce its divisions in Europe, Dean Acheson had told Schuman in New York on September 12, 1950, but only when the Europeans had raised sixty divisions. Of these, ten would have to be German. "There is no question of raising a *Wehrmacht*," the secretary assured the worried French foreign minister, "but simply of assigning these units to NATO under the unified command of an American general, probably Eisenhower." Schuman was appalled. The French position was extremely weak. Their own fighting forces were heavily engaged in Indochina, where in October they suffered their first major defeat, the fall of Caobang. The Schuman Plan was already beginning to unravel. American haste in calling for German rearmament and the implacable French resistance provided an opening to some of the powerful Ruhr industrialists to voice their opposition to the Coal and Steel Community.

The Monnet team went to work again. Convinced that France would be isolated and his dream of a united Europe wrecked unless France took the initiative, Monnet and his associates developed the idea of a European Army in a matter of days. Winston Churchill had raised the idea at the Council of Europe a few weeks earlier but, as he later told Anthony Nutting of the Foreign Office, "I meant it for them, not for us." According to Monnet, German troops would be "gradually integrated" into a European Army with a single high command—"not a coalition of the old type," he insisted, but "a complete merger of the human and material elements" necessary for an "Army of a United Europe." Once again "the inspirer" handed his idea over to a practicing politician to use as his own. On October 24, 1950, Premier René Pleven proposed a European Army under a European defense minister with a common European budget. The Americans, principally George Marshall, now secretary of defense, thought the European Defense Community was a French delaying tactic. Monnet worked on McCloy who in turn worked on Acheson to take the idea seriously. But Anthony Eden's judgment that Monnet's "hastily and ingeniously concocted" plan was something less than a masterpiece was fully shared by Acheson who saw the permanent prohibition of a German national army as a source of endless trouble. Meanwhile the wrangling over the European Defense Community was slowing down the transformation of NATO from a paper organization into an army. The administration pushed hard for Eisenhower's appointment as supreme commander and the authorization of four more American divisions. In the spring of 1951 just before the political storms erupted over the recall of General MacArthur from Japan, Congress gave the Truman administration essentially what it wanted.

When Dwight Eisenhower stopped by Acheson's office on January 4, 1951, for a briefing before taking up his duties in Europe, the secretary gave him a rundown of the enormous problems and contradictions that beset the fledgling alliance. Thirty years later it would all have a contemporary ring. First, there was the problem of defense costs. The U.S. Congress would not support a major effort in Europe if the Europeans did not pay their fair share. Yet heavy military expenditures would threaten European economic recovery, the very thing the army was supposed to make possible.

Realistic assessments of the military imbalance could only deflate and discourage. The Europeans did not believe that they could stop a Soviet attack with ground forces. The worse the conventional military balance looked, the more the American bomb looked like the critical factor in Europe's defense and more pointless seemed increased military spending by the Europeans themselves. Eisenhower believed that the Monnet myth could be a great energizer, a way out of what Monnet himself had called the "blind collapse" of conventional politics. In Rome a year later, after General Alfred Gruenther, Eisenhower's wartime chief of staff, had given what Acheson called a "hair-raising description of how devastating a Soviet attack on Western Europe would be," Ike sought to buck up the demoralized assemblage of politicians and generals with an inspirational speech on European unity.

But which Europe? Acheson made no effort to conceal his prejudices. The Nordic countries—Britain, Holland, Denmark, and Norway—were no doubt overly concerned with social welfare, but they were temperamentally stable. Compared to the moody southern countries like Italy, France, and Portugal, who did not know how to collect taxes or make themselves look like good credit risks, the northern tier was a good bet. Indeed the State Department in 1949 had been adamantly against inviting Italy to join NATO because then Greece and Turkey would ask to join too, and this would stretch the concept of "North Atlantic" to the breaking point. The idea that NATO was a band of blood brothers defending a common heritage and a common civilization was extremely important for securing congressional support. (Italy was admitted finally because France threatened to block Norway's admission unless the Latin component in the alliance was given its due.)

The separate concerns of the Benelux countries also served as a brake on European integration and a continuing problem for NATO. Having achieved considerable success in economic integration, they did not want to jeopardize it by being sucked into "the larger, more confused, and disparate economic affairs" of a larger Europe. In 1951 the ancient enemies, Greece and Turkey, were finally admitted over what Acheson dismissed as "the sulky resistance from our smaller associates." The two brothers-in-arms would once again go to war with one another over Cyprus a generation later, but it would not fundamentally disturb the strange alliance.

In his *tour d'horizon* for Eisenhower, Acheson omitted another huge set of problems that would plague the alliance in the years ahead. Major French military forces were already bogged down in Indochina. The Dutch were absorbed in preserving the last tatters of their once fabulous empire in the East Indies. The British were policing the remnants of theirs. The Portuguese were far more concerned to hold on to Mozambique, Angola, and Guinea-Bissau than to defend the Pyrenees, which they did not see as under imminent threat. Thus at the Lisbon Conference in February 1952 the French offered to raise their military expenditures to 12 percent of their gross national product, but they insisted upon cutting their troop commitment to Europe by two divisions because of the war in Indochina.

By the time of the Lisbon Conference a year and a half had passed since the United States had first called for the rearmament of Germany. Not one German soldier had yet been authorized. Both Britain and the United States had committed themselves to keeping forces in Europe even if the EDC never materialized. Acheson had approved a revised scheme for an integrated European army mostly to humor the French while plans for transforming NATO from a guarantee pact into a permanent military force continued. Predictably, negotiations among the Allies on the EDC concept stalled. "To sum it up," Eisenhower exclaimed after listening to Monnet, "what you're proposing is that the French and the Germans should wear the same uniform. That's more a human problem than a military one. . . . What Monnet's proposing is to organize relations between people, and I'm all for it." But the French government, still hoping for four-power talks with the Russians to settle the fate of Germany, dragged their feet, and the Germans refused to accept the built-in discrimination against them in the EDC. (The military discussions got off to a bad start when the German representative arrived at the Petersberg Hotel and was told he could not park his car in the convenient spot reserved for the occupying powers.)

In September 1951 Acheson told Schuman that American patience was coming to an end. No German army, no further American aid. Adenauer stepped up his pressure on Acheson. Were the Allies merely using the Germans "to back the Russians into a corner," threatening German rearmament in the hope of making a deal with the Russians that would preclude it? At Lisbon, Acheson achieved what he called a "grand slam." Aware that the steep increases in military spending would hurt the NATO partners severely because it would require cutting domestic programs on which each leader campaigned for office, Acheson relented. The United States would pick up more of the tab. The EDC treaty, its relationship to NATO, and the reduced financial commitments of the Europeans were agreed upon. "We seemed to have broken through a long series of obstacles and to be fairly started toward a more united Europe and an integrated Atlantic defense system." The very next day, however, Acheson stopped off in Paris for what he thought was merely a social call on Vincent Auriol, the president of France, only to be confronted by bitter denunciations of Germany. French indecision, Acheson lamented, was a threat to the very idea of a "strong Western European civilization," for the alliance could not work without a solid French-German relationship. Anthony Eden was right when he had exploded a few days earlier at a critical moment in the Lisbon negotiations. "In one telling sentence, he observed that no sooner did a crisis occur than some damned Frenchman went to bed."

8

In 1948 Harry Truman had peered over the rostrum at a Jackson Day dinner, the traditional Democratic party fundraising event, and told the skeptical party stalwarts that when the upcoming election was over there would be a Democrat in the White House and "you're lookin' at him." Four years later it was evident to Truman that his miracle victory in 1948 could not be repeated. After twenty years of Democratic rule it was, as the quadrennial Republican campaign slogan put it, time for a change.

When Dean Acheson saw "the boss" off at Washington's Union Station on the afternoon of January 20, 1953 to return home to Independence, Missouri, the former president was still smarting from the frosty ride he had just taken down Pennsylvania Avenue with the general to whom he had once offered his party's nomination. The Korean War, America's first defeat in living memory, the exchange of Democratic favors for mink coats and deep freezes, and the corroding fear of Communist enemies within had all contributed to the Democratic defeat and to the growing sense of unease in the country. But Truman and Acheson believed that the direction of U.S. foreign policy was set, perhaps for a generation. The heart of that policy was a commitment to the building of an Atlantic community, a metaphor for an American sphere of influence that stretched from Hiroshima to Hamburg. The irony that America's new security system rested on a triangle of power the two sides of which were the two nations lately pounded with American bombs escaped all but a few diehards, for the ideology of anti-Communism was sufficiently powerful to obscure it.

So crucial was the alliance in American thinking by 1952 that it had become an end in itself. The original purpose had been to build "situations of strength" as Acheson had called it, first to encourage the economic recovery of the West, and then to force the Russians to negotiate the reunification of a free, capitalist Germany. But in March 1952 Stalin offered a neutral, armed, and democratic Germany in which the government would be chosen by free elections. The East German regime was in such disarray that some members of the Politburo wanted to dismiss Walter Ulbricht, the intransigent party boss. Soviet leaders warned about the cost of maintaining a permanent unpopular regime in East Germany. Churchill thought the moment was right for a deal on reunification, but neither Adenauer nor the Americans would consider it.

Stalin's proposal to pull all foreign troops out of Germany was dismissed out of hand. "Here again," Acheson recalled, "was a spoiling operation intended to check and dissipate the momentum toward solutions in the West brought about by three years of colossal effort." No doubt Acheson had correctly assessed Stalin's motive. But years later many Germans, including Willy Brandt still believed that "a unique opportunity was lost here." Stalin's fear of a militarized West Germany bordered on the pathological. Perhaps the Soviet leader was sufficiently worried about the prospect of goose-stepping German divisions and the huge army that NATO was planning (but would never field) that he was ready for a deal that might have precluded forty years of military confrontations in the heart of Europe. But by the closing months of the Truman administration the Americans feared negotiation more than confrontation. An inconclusive negotiation with the Soviets would delay forward movement inside the alliance, but a successful negotiation leading to an East-West thaw could have more serious consequences. The danger Acheson saw was that a U.S.–Soviet deal would encourage neutralism, imperil the unity of the West, and dilute American influence in Europe. Twenty years later, in the era of détente, it all began to happen.

With the inauguration of Dwight D. Eisenhower, U.S. influence in Europe was at a high point. NATO had drawn up elaborate plans for a huge army, a vast "shield" to protect the West, but it was America's "sword," the atomic bomb, as everyone knew, that provided the real deterrent. Less clear was that which was to be deterred. The political influence of the Left in West Europe had declined sharply by 1953. Surely Stalin deserved most of the credit. Alternating between counseling excessive caution and demanding humiliating obeisance from his ideological cohorts in the West, the Soviet dictator now "spiritually drained, with all human attachments forgotten, stalked by fear," to use his daughters's words, succeeded in his paranoia in isolating and weakening the Communist movements of West Europe.

But the United States played far from a passive role in the process. The ideological tilt of West Europe was a far more serious matter for the United States than the mythical Soviet invasion, and at critical moments the Americans brought to bear the full panoply of their power to defeat the Left. That, of course, was one important purpose of the Marshall Plan. But other instruments of intervention, some blunt, some subtle, were used as well.

"It is the belief of the Italian intelligence services," American ambassador James Dunn cabled Washington on December 7, 1947, in a top secret message marked "urgent" that the Communists "are now preparing for action by force." The ambassador urged that covert military aid be immediately dispatched. The Vatican secretary of state, Giovanni Battista Cardinal Montini (later Pope Paul VI), warned the Americans that the Communists would make a major bid for power and that only a "strong stand" by the government could prevent Communist rebellion. The non-Communist majority in Italy, Domenico Cardinal Tardini assured the ambassador, "would welcome any necessary U.S. intervention in Italian internal affairs. . . ."

The moment for a major intervention came the following spring. The Communists were making "a major effort to take over the government," a report of the National Security Council concluded in February 1948, "either by winning the national elections now scheduled for April, by use of the general strike to create chaos, or by armed insurrection." The United States "should make full use of its political, economic, and, if necessary, military power" to prevent either eventuality. As the election approached, the embassy telegrams from Rome took on an ever more panicky tone. There was "large-scale hedging in the middle and upper classes"; well-to-do landowners and professional men were joining the Communist party. George Kennan proposed urging the Italian government to outlaw the Communist party and invite civil war "which would give us grounds for reoccupation [of] Foggia Fields or any other facilities we might wish." This would admittedly result in "much violence," Kennan noted, but "I think it might well be preferable to a bloodless election victory . . . which would give the Communists the entire peninsula at one coup. . . ."

A variety of lesser means was employed. The Truman administration orchestrated a huge letter-writing campaign among Italian-Americans, urging their relatives in the old country to do their duty at the polls. A special radio program by Hollywood stars was broadcast throughout Italy a few days before the election. It was "flattering," the embassy reported, that Bing Crosby, Walter Pidgeon, and Dinah Shore would take the time to learn a few lines of

Italian. Extra wheat was shipped to prevent any further cut in the bread ration. Official statements were communicated to the Italian public to the effect that a Communist victory would imperil the tourist trade and that Communists were ineligible for immigration to the United States. Prints of *Ninotchka,* Greta Garbo's 1939 movie satirizing life in the USSR, were rushed to Italy over the protest of the Soviet ambassador. The Special Procedures Group of the Office of Special Operations in the CIA spread money to various Italian centrist parties, a generosity that in time would be extended to politicians in Iran, Zaire, Chile, and many other places. James Jesus Angleton, who for years was head of counterintelligence for the CIA, got his postwar start in the Italian operation. His specialty was forged documents and letters purporting to have come from the Communist party that suggested that Italians would soon be suffering the fate of the Czechs and the Poles. The elaborate campaign produced results. When the Communists were decisively defeated at the polls, American propagandists and covert operatives quietly took the credits.

Clandestine activities were important elsewhere in the construction of the new Europe. In the years 1948–52 the new Central Intelligence Agency devoted much of its effort to paramilitary operations and preparations for even larger ones in Eastern Europe and the Soviet Union. General Lucian K. Truscott II, the first CIA station chief in Germany, had twelve hundred men under his command. Occupied Germany was a nest of spies, a command post for running operations to aid anti-Communist guerrillas in Albania and the Soviet Union, including regular overflights of Soviet territory. Told of the increasing futility of dropping agents by parachute into the Soviet Union—Kim Philby, the Soviet spy, knew about most of the operations in advance—Allen Dulles, then in charge of espionage operations for the agency, was philosophical. "At least we're getting the kind of experience we need for the next war." (At the war's end, Dulles, Richard Helms, who would one day succeed him as head of CIA, and Frank Wisner, head of covert operations for many years, all veterans of the Office of Strategic Services (OSS), the wartime spy agency, had shared a house in Wiesbaden.)

One part of the Central Intelligence Agency planned for war. Frank Lindsay, the Eastern Europe division chief was asked by the Air Force at the height of the Cold War to train and drop two thousand agents ready to sabotage Soviet airfields by "D-Day," which had been designated in planning documents as July 1, 1952. But the limits of U.S. power to wage secret war were becoming clearer, even to the gray spymasters themselves. Attention turned increasingly to what Ferdinand Eberstadt, a Wall Street lawyer called in by Forrestal at the end of the war to write what became the National Security Act of 1947, called "waging peace." In plain language this meant the use of secret operations to influence crucial segments of public opinion in Europe. In addition to working openly for the adoption of pro-American policies in Europe, the State Department provided cover for clandestine operations to influence public opinion; from its earliest months the CIA was preoccupied with the battle for Europe's soul.

The battle was fought on many fronts. Labor unions were crucial, for in every European country the labor movement formed the nucleus of a powerful political party. While World War II was still on, Sidney Hillman of the U.S. Congress of Industrial Organizations (CIO) had taken the lead to organize the World Federation of Trade Unions (WFTU) with participation by both Communists and non-Communist unions around the world, but Stalin's efforts to turn the organization into an instrument of Soviet policy and the American campaign to influence West European politics by supporting only non-Communist unions split the embryonic world labor movement. In France the Confederation Generale du Travail (CGT) was effectively under control of the Communist party. Strikes against deteriorating economic conditions grew in intensity in 1947–48, and the Communists, using their power in the labor movement, politicized them into protests against the Marshall Plan. Jay Lovestone, the former head of the American Communist party turned bitterly anti-Communist, and George Meany, president of the American Federation of Labor, organized a campaign to combat Communist influence in labor movements around the world, but the principal focus of their activities was Europe. As Meany put it in a 1964 speech to the Bond Club of New York, "[w]e played a major part in keeping the Communists from taking over [in France and Italy]. We financed a split in the Communist-controlled union in France." ("It is not a nice way of doing business," Irving Brown, the AFL chief operative in Europe had written an associate at the time, but the secret meddling in other countries' labor movements was "worth the fight for free trade unionism.") Thomas W. Braden, who ran the CIA's division of international organization activities in the early postwar years, provided the AFL with a "secret subsidy." Braden told an interviewer years later, "[i]t was my idea to give the $15,000 to Irving Brown. He needed it to pay off his strong-arm squads in Mediterranean ports so that American supplies could be unloaded against the opposition of Communist dockworkers."

In 1949 the AFL successfully organized the International Confederation of Free Trade Unions to do battle with the Communist-controlled WFTU. A number of the junior Marshall Plan officials were veterans of the radical politics of the 1930s, had worked with Lovestone in his earlier incarnation, and relished the opportunity to join the anti-Communist conspiracy. A system of labor attachés was organized to coordinate government and union activities in the labor war. But the effort did not always go smoothly. In Italy, Brown was hampered by an AFL regulation that forbade cooperation with church-controlled unions. In occupied Germany, Irving Brown fought with Clay who, an AFL report put it, "considered the unions as a sort of necessary evil." In the early postwar period Meany sent CARE packages to German union officials trying to subsist on 1100 calories a day, and pushed the German labor leaders to form one great federation. The "extensive educational activities" of American unions, the union leader David Dubinsky insisted in 1949, were responsible for keeping the Communists from controlling the German unions. When the threat of a Communist takeover quickly passed in Germany—unlike

France and Italy it was never very real—the German union officials began to resent the continued interference of the American unions.

The same sort of battle went on in the bizarre arena of student politics. Student movements were traditional instruments of Communist party agitation. Self-styled student leaders from Moscow, often perilously close to middle age, were accurately seen by the CIA as government officials. The American answer, which shocked the student generation of the 1960s when it was revealed in the midst of the Vietnam War, was to turn American students into agents too. The National Student Association was secretly funded for many years by foundations which were in fact CIA conduits. It regularly sent off American student leaders to the various youth festivals, congresses, and seminars to do battle with the Communist "youths" for the hearts and minds of young Europeans and later of student leaders in the Third World. For a few who were "witting," to use the CIA's term of art, it was flattering to be secretly enlisted into the national effort in the patriotic fight against Communism. But most who participated in the Manichaean "battle of ideas" orchestrated by two rival intelligence agencies did so without any inkling that they were being manipulated.

The "cultural cold war," to use social historian Christopher Lasch's term, had a wider dimension. In 1950 the Congress for Cultural Freedom was organized by Michael Josselson, an intelligence officer in the war, and Melvin Lasky, the editor of *Der Monat,* a German magazine launched by the American occupation authorities. (Similar magazines, *Encounter* in Britain and *Tempo Presente* in Italy, were organized by the congress. Irving Kristol and Stephen Spender edited *Encounter.*) The congress was launched in West Berlin with a series of speeches that sounded the American counterattack to the leftist and neutralist ideologies of Europe. "We are living in the last phase of an ebbing revolutionary epoch," Franz Borkenau, the former high official of Stalin's Comintern declared. (Many of the speakers had been members of Communist parties during the 1930s.) "No artist who has the right to bear that title can be neutral in the battles of our time," the film star Robert Montgomery warned the Europeans in the audience. For sixteen years the congress was funded by the CIA. Josselson, it later turned out, was still part of the American intelligence apparatus.

In 1951 Sidney Hook, James T. Farrell, James Burnham, and other former Communists formed the American Committee for Cultural Freedom to "counteract the influence of mendacious Communist propaganda." A seminar on "Anti-Americanism in Europe" was held. Major efforts were made to combat the two most successful Communist propaganda campaigns, one around the Rosenberg case, the other around the charge that the United States was resorting to the use of germ warfare in Korea. (When the Rosenbergs were executed in 1953, Jean-Paul Sartre, speaking for huge numbers of non-Communist intellectuals in France, called it "a legal lynching which stains an entire people with blood and once and for all uncovers in a flash the failure of the Atlantic Alliance. . . .") Thirty years later the guilt of the Rosenbergs is still a matter of controversy. But the germ warfare charge was "invented from A to Z," according to Pierre Daix, a journalist who participated in the campaign. When Matthew Ridgway, the former U.S. commander in Korea succeeded Eisenhower as NATO chief, the Communists staged a riot to greet the general they called *"La Peste."*

In 1977, *The New York Times* revealed how extensive CIA cultural penetration had been. For a generation U.S. and European journalists had been enlisted as spies and propagandists. More than a thousand books had been secretly subsidized, including a few scholarly works of interest to the agency from St. Anthony's College at Oxford. A network of newspapers, including Axel Springer's publishing empire in Germany, had been infiltrated by the CIA. Affectionately known inside the agency as "Wisner's Wurlitzer" in honor of the man who put it together, the "Propaganda Assets Inventory" was a vast communications network available for discreet use by the American authorities. No doubt the effort played a role in shifting European opinion away from neutralism and toward pro-American "moderation." But the United States paid a price. In the midst of the Vietnam War the professed American enthusiasm for pluralism and diversity had been shown to be shot through with fraud. In sedulously copying the unscrupulous methods of the Soviet secret police, the Americans succeeded not only in disillusioning young people at home, fueling the anti-Americanism of the Vietnam generation, but also in obscuring for a new generation of Europeans the moral distinction between the superpowers.

PART II

A TIME OF WRENCHING

FOUR

THE CAPTAINS AND THE KINGS DEPART:

Mr. Dulles Takes On World Responsibilities

1

The convivial general with the terrible temper seemed the perfect leader of the Western world. He had managed the biggest military enterprise in history and he had played bridge with the historic figures of his time. So bland did his political convictions appear to be and so amiable his manner that Republicans and Democrats alike had snatched at his coattails. He was, as Walter Lippmann wrote Lewis Douglas in 1948, "a kind of dream boy embodying all the unsatisfied wishes of all the people who are discontented with things as they are." Even Adlai Stevenson, the man who would run against him twice, believed in early 1952 that there was no one around who could beat Eisenhower, "and what's more, I don't see any good reason why anyone should want to."

Flattered, begged, and prodded by some of the richest and most powerful men in the country, Eisenhower had reluctantly agreed to reveal himself as a political partisan. "You don't suppose a man could ever be nominated by both parties, do you?" he once had asked. His views fitted the times. His instincts were conservative. "We think too much of luxuries," he declared in a 1949 speech while president of Columbia University on "the illusion of security." "We want to wear fine shirts, have caviar and champagne, when we should be eating hot dogs and beer. . . . I have seen many white crosses in many parts of the world, and the men under those crosses are there because they believed there was something more than merely assuring themselves they weren't going to be hungry at the age of 67." It was the sort of rhetoric to thrill his new coterie of friends and admirers, Philip Reed, chairman of General Electric, W. Alton Jones of Cities Service, and Robert Woodruff of Coca-Cola, who had

147

initiated the Kansas farm boy with the magnificent grin into the stag world of the corporate rich. And the general who after a long, humdrum military career had been catapulted by war into world stardom was equally impressed that America boasted men like Bob Woodruff, the Coca-Cola baron who kept seventy-five hunting dogs on his Georgia estate.

Yet he was no mossback. "How the hell is the American Medical Association going to stop socialized medicine?" he exploded in July 1954, if they opposed moderate bills on health insurance. He thought of himself as progressive and knew that the country had to change with the times in order to preserve the old values and keep the free enterprise system intact. But the changes looming in American society perplexed and pained him. Early in his administration, before the Supreme Court had handed down its 1954 decision on segregation, Chief Justice Earl Warren recalls Eisenhower taking him aside at dinner and asking for understanding of the segregationists: "These are not bad people. All they are concerned about is to see that their sweet little girls are not required to sit in school alongside big overgrown Negroes."

No prominent American had been more enthusiastic than Eisenhower for rearmament. He had chaired a Council on Foreign Relations study group in 1950 on the defense of Europe and had urged a major U.S. troop commitment for NATO. "Atlantic Union defense forces," he wrote his old schoolmate from Abilene (Kansas) High School, "Swede" Hazlett, were "the last remaining chance for the survival of Western civilization." At a moment when the Republican party was once again showing its isolationist leanings, Eisenhower sounded the one note that certified his acceptability to the East Coast bankers, lawyers, and industrialists who comprised the most powerful political force in the country. "Western Europe," he said in his first speech to the people of West Germany as NATO commander, "is the cradle of civilization as we know it."

His internationalism was unsentimental. To Edward Bermingham, a Dillon, Reed partner who frequently entertained the general at his Alabama plantation, he wrote in 1951: "I wish I could believe that we could . . . secure adequate supplies of manganese, uranium and a number of vital materials without the need for assisting in the defense of countries other than our own." Once in office he expressed his frustration to an old friend that people in the country were unable to "understand that our foreign expenditures are investments in America's future. No other nation is exhausting its irreplaceable resources so rapidly as is ours. Unless we are careful to build up and maintain a great group of international friends ready to trade with us, where do we hope to get all the materials that we will one day need as our rate of consumption continues and accelerates?"

Convinced that the United States was fated to wage a global ideological and psychological struggle against the Soviet Union, Eisenhower, like MacArthur, understood the absurdity of war, especially nuclear war. Human beings "ought to be intelligent enough to devise ways and means of avoiding suicide," he wrote to his friend Earl Schaefer, president of Boeing, not long after settling into the White House. He had spent his whole life "in the study of military strength as a deterrent to war," he wrote in another letter at the end of his first term. "[W]e are rapidly getting to the point that no war can be WON. War implies a contest; when you get to the point that contest is no longer involved and the outlook comes close to destruction of the enemy and suicide for ourselves . . . then arguments as to the exact amount of available strength as compared to somebody else's are no longer the vital issues." He had never been enthusiastic about nuclear weapons. Informed of the first successful test of the atomic bomb, he had told Stimson in July 1945 that he "hoped his country would not be the first to use this weapon." The explosions over Japan were "unnecessary," he had always believed, and they had made it more difficult to keep peace with Russia. "People are frightened and disturbed all over," he noted not long after Hiroshima. "Everyone feels insecure again." In his campaign Eisenhower promised a grand strategy, something more "positive" than containment, a projection of strength to be used with restraint aimed, as he repeated in his inaugural address, at the liberation "of all the world."

Standing just behind him with head bowed as Eisenhower took the oath of office was the figure who would symbolize the foreign policy of his administration. John Foster Dulles was a rumpled bear of a man with a drooping look, serious, suspicious, and self-righteous, the perfect foil for the popular general who hated war. The enormously successful Wall Street lawyer, now sixty-four, had been senior partner of Sullivan and Cromwell since he was thirty-eight. Through a long career of advising German bondholders, arranging corporate reorganizations, and orchestrating proxy fights, he made no secret of the fact that he would much prefer to be occupying the office once held by his maternal grandfather, John W. Foster, secretary of state in the cabinet of Benjamin Harrison, and by his uncle, Robert Lansing, who ran the State Department in Woodrow Wilson's time. Dulles was passionately committed to the ideas of Atlantic Community and European unity, but with the notable exception of his old friend Monnet and Konrad Adenauer, who found his hard-line views congenial and useful, most of the Europeans with whom he dealt took an immediate dislike to him. Richard Crossman, the Labour MP, met him in early 1952 and confided his reaction to his diary: " . . . an ecclesiastical type of man, with a lugubrious, pallid face, heavy black eyebrows and a twitch in his right eye behind his heavy glasses. Like Lord Halifax, he can lie as only a Christian can lie. But Halifax was really attractive and Dulles is not."

Eisenhower knew what he was getting. Dulles had laid out most of the ideas associated with his name before he took office, chiefly in a *Life* magazine article entitled "A Policy of Boldness." (In 1956 the secretary of state told his assistant that he had developed no new ideas in office.) The Truman containment policy was a "treadmill" that would eventually exhaust the country. It was not enough to develop retaliatory forces. (By 1952 the United States was committed to building the hydrogen bomb and would soon have one.) The United States must develop the "will" to use force in order to "retaliate instantly against open aggression by Red Armies, so that, if it occurred anywhere, we could and would strike back where it hurts, by means of our choosing." Communist "subversion" transgressed the "moral or natural law" by which God expects the world to run. "This law has been trampled by the Soviet rulers, and for that violation they can and should be made to pay." If the West were united and "firm," it would not have to fight on Soviet terms, and eventually the Russian hold on East Europe would weaken and "separation from Moscow" could be achieved without "bloody uprisings and reprisals."

Their style and temperament were different. The general, though moody and irascible at times, projected optimism and good humor, while the Calvinist clergyman's son always looked as if he were pondering the utter depravity of man. But the two thought remarkably alike. Both were determined to avoid war. Both believed politics was a moral struggle. "We sense with all our faculties that forces of good and evil are massed and armed and opposed as rarely before in history. . . . Freedom is pitted against slavery; lightness against the dark." These words of the thirty-fourth president spoken at his inaugural were pure Dulles—and pure Eisenhower. Both were convinced that in the nuclear age the packaging of military power was more important than hardware.

The legend quickly developed that Dulles was the Svengali of the Eisenhower White House. The benign general, critics believed, would never on his own talk about "going to the brink," or threatening "massive retaliation," or pressuring Allies with an "agonizing reappraisal." But, Eisenhower was essentially accurate when he insisted to a close friend that Dulles "never made a serious pronouncement, agreement or proposal without complete and exhaustive consultation with me in advance and, of course, my approval." Eisenhower was quite aware of the fact that "with strangers his personality may not always be winning," but there were advantages in conducting business according to the classic pattern. The more generous-spirited the client the tougher his lawyer needed to be. Eisenhower had not survived the minefields of army politics and arrived at the summit of power by fitting the contemptuous description of critics like the columnist Joseph Alsop—"just as provincial, just as well-intentioned as Neville Chamberlain. . . ." He was a practiced political dissembler, well aware that his extraordinary fame permitted him the appearance of transcending politics.

No sooner had Eisenhower taken the oath of office than the world seemed to spin faster. Within five weeks Stalin was dead. "Finally, cut off by his power, his glory, his semi-paralyzed consciousness, from life and people," his daughter Svetlana describes the terrible moment of liberation, "he sent them from his death bed what he could: a look full of terror and rage, and a threatening gesture of his hand." A little over three months later the first open revolt in the Soviet imperium had erupted; on June 17 riots broke out in the streets of East Berlin. The Dulles thesis that the successful stabilization of West Europe now challenged the stability of East Europe was confirmed. But the famous Eisenhower-Dulles strategy to "roll back" Soviet power was nowhere in evidence. Pictures of rioters burning Communist party banners along the Unter den Linden and pelting Soviet tanks with stones flashed across the world. When it was all over Dulles offered $15 million of free food which the Soviets, to the surprise of no one, rejected.

The Berlin incident was particularly frustrating for the new administration because it set such store by psychological warfare. Nine days before the inauguration, C. D. Jackson, the protégé of Henry Luce at Time, Inc. whom Eisenhower had appointed to head the Psychological Strategy Board, brimmed with enthusiasm about his job. The new president, Jackson assured a friend, was convinced that psychological warfare was "just about the only way to win World War III without having to fight it." Jackson's recommendation for an effective Cold War strategy—(1) "money, (2) no holds barred and (3) no questions asked"—was about to be implemented. The Eisenhower administration would put major emphasis on political warfare because, as Jackson put it, we now have "a Head of Government" who "appreciates that practically every other golf club in his bag is broken." There must be an American peace offensive to counter the Soviet peace offensive. But the problem was how to reach for the "hearts and minds" of the Europeans whose desperate yearning for peace Eisenhower understood without destroying the alliance on which the president so firmly believed all hopes for peace rested. The problem would recur again and again throughout the life of the alliance.

With Stalin's death, a CIA instant analysis concluded, the world had lost a ruthless, but cautious leader. "It would be unsafe to assume that the new Soviet regime will have Stalin's skill in avoiding war." But the new leaders made great efforts to appear conciliatory. By early June the Korean War was over. In July, Lavrenti Beria, the hated head of Stalin's secret police, had been shot. Georgii Malenkov, the new premier, declared that war was not inevitable, and the men who would succeed him, Nikolai Bulganin and Nikita Khrushchev, immediately hinted that they wished to visit in the West and to settle outstanding problems. Winston Churchill, now prime minister once more, called for a meeting "at the summit" to settle the affairs of the Continent. But for Dulles the new breezes blowing from Moscow meant, as he stated at a cabinet meeting, that "we ought to be doubling our bets, not reducing them—as all the Western parliaments want to do. This is the time to *crowd* the enemy —and maybe *finish* him, once and for all."

By the end of 1954 the Eisenhower bureaucracy had produced a top secret "Basic National Security Policy" reflecting the sober consensus of the national security professionals. "The stability of the USSR and its hold over the European satellites are unlikely to be seriously shaken." The various organizations for exploiting Soviet vulnerabilities, such as Radio Free Europe, Radio Liberation, and the Ukrainian émigré groups in Munich, should be supported. As early as 1954 CIA reports recommending efforts to exploit Sino-Soviet tensions circulated in the White House. The CIA drew up plans for an invasion of Albania with ships, planes, and thousands of troops. But the operation was scotched by Richard Bissell, the future architect of the Bay of Pigs disaster, who thought it was much too risky. After a number of abortive attempts to aid "dissident" groups such as a Baltic underground group known as WIN, the CIA began to realize that such "vulnerabilities" of the enemy were lures put out by the Soviet intelligence services to catch spies. Asked by Allen Dulles to develop a list of responses to a future crisis in the Soviet bloc, Bissell concluded after studying a long list of options that "very little could be done."

Indeed, the problem was Western vulnerability. Much had been done to stabilize Europe since the dark days of 1947–48, but the Basic National Security Policy document underscored the strains on the new alliance "resulting from growing fears of atomic war . . . differing attitudes on China, and greater receptivity by the allies to Soviet overtures." The world no longer faced a crisis that could electrify and unify the Allies but "a prolonged period of armed truce." The Allies, the paper warned, would be reluctant to take actions "which appear to them to involve appreciable risks of war. . . ." Eager to explore the "Soviet 'soft' line," the Allies "will probably wish . . . to go to further lengths than the U.S. will find prudent."

In developing a world strategy for projecting American power Eisenhower and Dulles faced serious dilemmas. The Russians had been "stopped" in Europe, if indeed they had ever been on the march beyond the territory occupied by the Red Army at the end of the war. Western Europe was recovering economically and settling politically. The contours of an Atlantic Community were taking shape. But the arms race with the Soviet Union was now inevitable. Eisenhower believed that the Soviet Union was "a backward civilization with a second-rate production plant." The United States was so far ahead in nuclear weapons that it "could reduce its atomic stockpile by two or three times the amount the Russians might contribute," the president noted, "and still improve our relative position." (For this reason his "atoms for peace" speech to the United Nations with its call to dismantle bombs, contribute fissionable materials to an international agency, and thus take the dangerous weapon "out of the hands of soldiers" made good propaganda with little risk, for the Russians could never accept the offer.

Clearly, the arms race would continue and with it the risk that the United States might spend itself into bankruptcy. Eisenhower believed in a balanced budget and adamantly resisted pressure from the Rockefeller wing of his party for massive increases in the defense budget, including a multibillion-dollar civil defense program. But the price of keeping military costs down, which Eisenhower did with remarkable success, was the "new look" in military doctrine. A terrible irony. The president who hated nuclear weapons and knew, as he told a gathering of Foreign Service officers in 1954, that "there is no longer any alternative to peace, if there is to be a happy and well world," ended by building bigger nuclear weapons than ever, equipping U.S. forces around the world with small, so-called "tactical" nuclear weapons, and relying on the threat to initiate nuclear war to keep the peace.

The Allies in Europe did not like the new emphasis on nuclear weapons.

At the Bermuda Conference in November 1953 Dulles told Eden that if the
Chinese broke the armistice in Korea the United States would have to attack
Chinese bases with its "most effective" weapons. The foreign minister was
horrified. Her Majesty's government would not support the use of atomic
weapons. The Cold War strategists at home didn't like the emphasis on "massive retaliation" either. Few moral scruples were expressed; that the national
interest demanded the annihilation of civilians was now widely accepted.
(Major General Emmett O'Donnell, Jr., commander of the Far Eastern Command, had told the Senate Armed Services Committee in 1951: "I would say
that the entire, almost the entire Korean peninsula is just a terrible mess.
Everything is destroyed. There is nothing standing worthy of the name." A
footnote to the political drama surrounding General MacArthur, his deadpan
report provoked no discernible public reaction.)

The new breed of psychological strategists now being spawned in think
tanks and universities were concerned rather that America would be the real
victim of the bomb—not that it would be dropped, but now that the Soviets
had exploded an atomic bomb of their own, it was undroppable. The battle-
ground with the Soviet Union was not Europe but the former European colonies of the Third World. The danger was "indirect aggression," a vague term
used to describe a variety of political developments from revolutionary nationalism to indigenous Communism. The Soviets would "nibble" America to
death by secretly subsidizing and arming revolutionary movements around the
world. Could you threaten to incinerate Moscow because the Egyptians had a
military coup or the Iranians nationalized their oil? Under the nuclear "umbrella" designed to deter that which was unlikely anyway—a big Soviet move
in Europe—a more aggressive strategy was developed for opposing political
and economic changes in the Third World deemed threatening to U.S. interests. All during his administration Eisenhower was subjected to considerable
pressure to build up conventional forces. A 1957 presidential panel on national
security known as the Gaither Report called for a massive increase in the
defense budget to fight limited wars, "especially in the Middle East and Asia."
John J. McCloy and Robert Lovett assured the president that he need not
worry about the fiscal effects. The arms buildup would have the "complete
backing" of business. But Eisenhower was not convinced. There had to be a
better way.

The answer was to invest in covert operations. The Eisenhower years
were dominated as much by Allen Dulles as by Foster. "A perfectly delightful
guy—so unlike his brother," a senior intelligence colleague described the
bluff, tweedy man Eisenhower had appointed to be director of the Central
Intelligence Agency. He had, as Thomas Powers describes it, "a deceptively
avuncular air, with his white brush mustache and his pipe and rimless specta-
cles and the bedroom slippers he wore to alleviate the suffering of gout." But
he was an experienced manipulator of spies, having been in the business off
and on since the First World War. Espionage was America's secret weapon
for keeping the world spinning properly. Purchasing friendly governments,

arranging coups, and fighting secret wars were effective and cheap ways to advance American interests. These the national security bureaucracy defined as keeping former colonial regions of the world free of anti-American nationalism or Marxist development, and open to American commerce. Behind the effort were two moral assumptions. Politics is a struggle of good and evil, and the United States by definition was the standard-bearer of virtue. Self-determination, the quintessential American slogan in an earlier day—the younger Dulles too had been at Versailles when Woodrow Wilson had passionately sounded the call for national independence—smacked of outmoded idealism in an era of Cold War. As Dulles himself put it:

. . . we cannot safely limit our response to the Communist strategy of take-over solely to those cases where we are invited in by a government still in power, or even to instances where a threatened country has first exhausted its own, possibly meager, resources in the "good fight" against Communism. We ourselves must determine when and how to act. . . .

2

In 1947 British officials had told the State Department that their grip on the Mediterranean was weakening. But by 1951 a series of shocking events dramatized the impending collapse of Great Britain's most successful imperial operations. In Iran, Dr. Mohammed Mossadegh, riding a gathering tide of anticolonial popular fury, was elected prime minister and promptly nationalized Iran's oil. Under the Anglo-Persian agreements signed in 1933—Anthony Eden, the under secretary at the Foreign Office had participated in the negotiations—British companies in 1950 earned 200 million pounds sterling; 50 million went to the British government in taxes, and the Iranians received 16 million pounds. Iranian oil was sold in Iran at a 500 percent markup. Iranian workers were barred from the Anglo-Iranian Company's hospitals, swimming pools, restaurants, and buses. Suddenly the tables were turned. What Eden in his memoirs describes as "a very valuable British asset" had become "stolen property."

Even more humiliating, all British employees had been expelled from the country in October 1951. "His Majesty's Government had moved land forces and a cruiser to the vicinity of Abadan, where the fate of the largest oil refinery in the world was at stake," Eden recalls. The temptation to intervene with force was strong, "but pressure from the United States was vigorous against any such action. The British staff was instructed to withdraw." The whole episode, the British Tory politician Harold Macmillan wrote in his diary at the time, seemed "calculated to destroy the last vestige of British prestige."

For Anthony Eden, who had specialized in Oriental languages at Oxford and read Persia's epic Book of Kings in the original, Britain's humiliation at the hands of " 'Old Mossy' with his pajamas and iron bedstead" was intolerable. "Alternatives" to this ridiculous figure, "the first bit of meat to come the way of the cartoonists since the war," had to be found. Eisenhower, on the other hand, while also contemptuous of Mossadegh's "tears and fainting fits and street mobs," saw him as someone to support because a continued impasse might drive him into the arms of the Soviet Union and end up delivering critical petroleum reserves of the West to the communists. He told Eden when the foreign minister came to see him in March 1953 that Mossadegh "was the only hope for the West in Iran," and that the Americans would try to placate him by sending his personal friend, Alton Jones of Cities Service, to "make the best arrangement he could to get the oil flowing again." Jones had already been to see Mossadegh the year before and had come close to making a deal. The strong American card was a reputation for anticolonialism. ("The free world knows the Iranians can manage their own oil industry," Jones had declared.) Dulles suggested sending in American technicians. Eden emphasized "in the strongest possible terms the deplorable effect on Anglo-American relations which the presence of Americans working in stolen British property would cause."

British and American intelligence agencies agreed that something drastic would have to be done, but the Americans preferred trying to manipulate Mossadegh rather than get rid of him. In the end the Iranian leader was deposed in the first of Allen Dulles' successful large-scale covert operations, at a cost of about $19 million. The CIA operative in charge, Kermit Roosevelt, grandson of President Theodore Roosevelt, rented a mob with a heavy representation of musclemen, gymnasts, and wrestlers recruited from Tehran's gyms and steam rooms. Major General George C. Stewart, director of the Office of Military Assistance, later testified that the U.S. military mission supplied the shah's supporters with "[t]he guns that they had in their hands, the trucks that they rode in, the armed cars that they drove through the streets, and the radio communications that permitted their control. . . ." (C. W. Woodhouse, the British intelligence officer in the Iranian coup, later described some of the problems of the alliance in conducting the secret war. The American candidate to replace Mossadegh, General Fazollah Zahedi, "had been regarded as a German agent. An operation to kidnap him and put him out of circulation" had been organized by British intelligence during the war.) But when the coup was all over, Mossadegh was in jail, Zahedi was installed as prime minister, and the shah was safely back on the Peacock Throne, "a new man," Roosevelt wrote his superiors in the CIA. "For the first time, he believes in himself because he believes that he is King of his people's choice and not by arbitrary decision of a foreign power." On hearing the news while cruising in the Greek islands, Eden "slept happily that night." Eisenhower was briefed by Roosevelt and found his report, as he noted in his diary, "more like a dime novel than an historical fact."

Now negotiations began in earnest. Eden insisted that the Anglo-Iranian Oil Company "should have by far the larger share of the consortium." The American companies would obviously have a large share not only because of the power of America but also because of the effective control over the world marketing and distribution that the U.S. oil majors had developed. The negotiations were conducted by Herbert Hoover, Jr., another president's son with ties to Iran. (As a geological engineer he had advised the Iranian government.) The American oil companies ended up with a share equaling that of Anglo-Iranian (40 percent). (The American majors under intense political pressure had to give 5 percent to eight smaller U.S. companies.) Royal Dutch, representing British and Dutch investment, was awarded a 14 percent interest, and the Compagnie Française des Pétroles took 6 percent. United States oil companies had now penetrated deeply into the Persian Gulf and Iran had acquired the expensive status of an American vital interest.

As the Eisenhower administration took office, tensions with France were also on the rise. France was expected to do her duty and approve the European Defense Community. After all, the idea had been French and the whole transatlantic relationship now depended on it. But the war in Indochina which would end by delivering a series of crippling blows to the alliance was already causing trouble. In October 1950, French President Vincent Auriol had noted the "violent anti-American mood" in no small measure caused by official American attitudes toward Indochina. "What they give us for Indochina while they say that we are defending this country against Communism is limited aid so that it doesn't look as if they were abandoning us." But their real policy, the president believed, was to promote an independent South Vietnam. "They give us money, and we pay for it with a piece of independence: that is infamous." To be sure, the NATO Council two years later passed a resolution expressing "its profound admiration for the courageous struggle being waged indefatigably by French forces and the armies of allied states against Communist aggression." But the French had been fighting the liberation movement in their colony for almost eight years. "[T]he defense of freedom in Indochina has practically cost us twice what we received" under the Marshall Plan and military aid, the French president had told a group of ambassadors a few weeks earlier. To Dulles, who had come to see him when he was still the Republican adviser in Acheson's State Department, Auriol offered a foretaste of the "domino theory" Eisenhower would adopt as his own. "We are the supporting pillar of the defense of the West in Southeast Asia; if this pillar crumbles, Singapore, Malaysia, and India will soon fall prey to Mao Tse-tung. You have understood that perfectly well and I thank you for it."

In the closing months of the Truman administration, Acheson had complained to Eden that the United States was now about to bear one-half of the cost of the French war effort in Indochina—it would soon rise to 80 percent—"yet to hear the French talk, one would think that his government were only supplying them with the odd revolver or two." The British ambassador reported that senior officers of the French general staff had already concluded that the war was lost. The goal was "respectable withdrawal" and American aid was crucial to that effort. Within four years, 1950 to May 1954, when the French lost the decisive battle at Dien Bien Phu, the United States supplied

$2.6 billion in aid. Much of it was in credits that could be used to keep France itself afloat as the Marshall Plan aid was coming to an end. The American financial help, Alfred Grosser concludes, constituted "a solid though unavowable reason for not ending the war in Indochina, even though it was not really supported by any part of the French public." So touchy were the French about American interference that a note from the State Department criticizing certain uses to which American aid in Indochina was being put was personally returned to the American ambassador by the prime minister in the presence of his senior cabinet advisers.

The French were aware that the United States now had no alternative but to help them. The National Security Council had concluded: "The loss of Indochina would be critical to the security of the U.S." These words had a special meaning for the Eisenhower administration. For Dulles, the fall of Indochina would signify a victory of Maoist China, now with Stalin gone the archsymbol of the evils of world Communism. Coming on top of the American failure to win in Korea, a Communist victory in Indochina would seriously erode American power in the Far East, which was something influential segments of the Republican party cared about above all else.

But there were two other objectives Dulles desperately wished to achieve in Indochina which had much more to do with Europe than with Asia. French colonialism must be brought to an end by something other than Communism. The stigma of colonialism played into Communist hands. It undercut the moral superiority of the West on which the whole Eisenhower Cold War strategy depended. "Our general tendency," Alexander Makinsky, the White Russian prince who lobbied European governments in behalf of Coca-Cola and patriotically shared his wisdom with the CIA, wrote at the end of 1954,

is to bet, throughout the world, on individuals and groups who are, rightly or wrongly, considered "reactionary," and whom we select or support simply because we feel at home with them: we find we and they speak the same language. . . . (I say this with regret, since I am probably myself a "reactionary"!) I do not think it is a secret to anybody today that Bao Dai [the French puppet emperor] has no following whatsoever in Indochina. . . . In the eyes of a great many people in Europe, we are identifying ourselves with "lost causes" whose only hope of survival lies in American support. Our association with those elements, however, brings grist to the Communist mill. . . ."

The stated purpose then from the first was to use American aid to loosen France's grip on Indochina. A second purpose was to purchase enthusiasm for the European Defense Community. "We have engaged to help . . . on a very major scale in Indochina," Eisenhower confided to his diary in October 1954, "in return for which France has irrevo[c]ably promised" to fulfill both American purposes. But the weak governments in Paris were unable to deliver, as it turned out, on either promise. Having fought for seven years the French army and the French people were exhausted, but the generals and imperial politicians could not afford to admit defeat. If Indochina could free itself, why not Tunisia, Morocco, and Algeria? By legal fiction these members of the French

Union were part of France itself. The dismemberment of France by freeing colonies held for more than a hundred years was scarcely a stirring war aim. If the freedom of the West required continued French resistance in Asia, then the Americans must give up their hypocritical moralizing.

For France in 1954 and 1955 her weakness was her only strength; French leverage on the United States consisted only in the power to surrender in Indochina. By the time the Allied foreign ministers met in Berlin in January 1954, it was evident that no French government could survive without negotiating a settlement. The question now was the use of American power to force an orderly substitution of a U.S. presence—guarantees, bases, dollars, but not ground forces—for the discredited and defeated French. In March, General Paul Ely, the French chief of staff, arrived in Washington. The garrison at Dien Bien Phu was under siege. The situation seemed hopeless without massive American intervention. France was now determined to settle.

Dulles was desperately eager to save the situation. At one point Admiral Arthur Radford, the chairman of the Joint Chiefs of Staff, wanted to try saving Dien Bien Phu with an air strike involving heavy bombers escorted by 150 fighters. Though pessimistic about saving the fortress, Radford was particularly eager to break through the "atomic threshold" so that nuclear arms could be a credible threat to use against China. The chiefs of staff disagreed, however, about the use of nuclear weapons, and Dulles thought that any military operation would be a "poor way for the U.S. to get involved" unless the French clearly renounced colonialism and the European Allies supported the effort.

The National Security Council Planning Board proposed lending one "new weapon" to the French to drop around the beleaguered fortress for its "psycho effect," but in the heated White House debates the State Department worried that use of nuclear weapons would alarm the Allies, causing "a great hue and cry throughout the parliaments of the free world. . . ." To the suggestion that the United States intervene alone if the Allies were too timid, Eisenhower angrily responded at a critical NSC meeting that this "would mean a general war with China and perhaps with the USSR" and that "[w]ithout allies and associates the leader is just an adventurer like Genghis Khan."

On April 4, Eisenhower sent a letter to Churchill proposing a coalition "to bring greater moral and material resources to the support of the "French efforts." A tentative date for a military operation—April 28—was set. If Indochina "passes into the hands of the Communists," the president warned, "the ultimate effect on our and your global strategic position with the consequent shift in the power ratios throughout Asia and the Pacific could be disastrous and, I know, unacceptable to you and me." The president attempted a Churchillian closing:

If I may refer again to history; we failed to halt Hirohito, Mussolini and Hitler by not acting in unity and in time. That marked the beginning of many years of stark tragedy and desperate peril. May it not be that our nations have learned something from that lesson. . . ?

Eden thought the United States plan made no sense. Even though a conference in Geneva had already been arranged to negotiate an end to the long Indochina war, Dulles continued to talk about "massive retaliation" with the scarcely veiled suggestion that if the Chinese entered the Indochina war in strength the United States would drop atomic bombs on China. Brandishing the bomb against China for unspecified future acts of aggression would not cause the Chinese to stop their present flow of military supplies to the Vietminh, and it might provoke a world war. A week later Dulles again urged Eden to support military intervention in Indochina and agreed to drop the ultimatum to China. Indochina was Manchuria and the Rhineland in one, and the place to stand. Still Eden resisted, arguing that British public opinion would not favor expanding a war a week before the opening of the conference that had been called to settle it. Dulles turned on the French. They had collapsed as a great power and thereby had left a "vacuum" which must be filled. Three days before the conference, Dulles made his final appeal for British support for an air strike at Dien Bien Phu. According to General Alfred Gruenther, it was needed to save the morale of the French garrison even if it did no more. Admiral Radford attempted to reassure the British about China. "[H]e had never thought that the Chinese would intervene in Indochina, nor had they the necessary resources available. If they attempted air action, we could eliminate this by bombing the Chinese airfields, which were very vulnerable." Dulles turned to French Foreign Minister Bidault, who was also present, and handed him a draft proposal which he had first shown briefly to the British. As Eden understood the proposal, the United States was prepared "to move armed forces into Indo-China and thus internationalize the struggle and protect Southeast Asia as a whole." Bidault hesitated for several minutes, then accepted the proposal. The French urged Eden to go along with Dulles' plans, but later in the evening they changed their mind. Bidault sent word to London that he was against American intervention. Churchill and Eden concluded that the Americans were asking them "to assist in misleading Congress into approving a military operation" that was both ineffective and provocative of a major war. Now Congress began to reflect increased nervousness about the still-rumored U.S. intervention. A rider was introduced in the House designed to limit the president's authority to send troops anywhere in the world.

As the Geneva Conference opened on April 26, the French had abandoned hope of military resistance and were looking for the least disastrous path of diplomatic extrication. "Bidault gives the impression of a man close to the breaking point," Dulles cabled the president from Geneva. In the midst of the conference the Laniel government, the fifteenth since the war, fell, and Pierre Mendès-France, in announcing the sixteenth, said that he would quit in thirty days if an honorable settlement had not yet been achieved. The new premier, a "brainy misfit," as Janet Flanner called him, had always been an outsider in French politics. A modernizer who made no secret of his rather Draconian ideas for making capitalism work in France, he was scarcely a passionate enthusiast for decolonialization. Unlike some of his advisers on the Left, repairing French relations in Indochina and North Africa was less a moral issue than a practical one that called for lawyerly arrangements rather than self-flagellation and hasty retreat. "France has been plunged into a deep sleep filled with nostalgic dreams and nightmares that have fed on the black future," he told the Chamber of Deputies. "We must wake her up."

At the Geneva conference, Vietnam was temporarily partitioned. The fate of the nation would be decided at free elections to be held in two years. While the United States refused to be officially associated with them, the Geneva Accords were seen by the signatories on both sides as a face-saving device under which the guerrilla army that had defeated a proud European imperial nation could take power with as little humiliation of the West as possible. Eisenhower wrote in his memoirs that Ho Chi Minh would get 80 percent of the vote in a free election throughout Vietnam. When the treaty he had fought so hard to prevent was signed, "Mr. Dulles thought it [non-Communist Vietnam] was not quite down the drain," Lieutenant General Andrew Goodpaster, an assistant to President Eisenhower, recalls. "Everyone else, I think, felt that it was. Even Dulles told General Lawton Collins, the army chief of staff, in November 1954, 'Frankly, Collins, I think our chances of saving the situation there are not more than 1 in 10.' "

In their very first effort to mount a concerted military operation, the Allies had failed at a crucial moment to carry it off because, for all their common interest in resisting national liberation movements and the expansion of Communist power, the distrust and disagreements among them were too profound. For Eden and Churchill, practiced diplomats that they were, John Foster Dulles' style—threats, calculated ambiguity, tactical feints—did nothing to inspire confidence. As far as Churchill was concerned, Dulles was "the only case of a bull I know who carries his china closet with him." The hero of the Battle of Britain had nothing against bluff as a political weapon, but bluffing with hydrogen bombs was amateurish. Neither the British nor the French shared Dulles' view of the People's Republic of China. At Geneva, Dulles refused to shake hands with Chou En-lai, recoiling as if from something contaminated. Unlike their American counterparts, British and French politicians believed the intelligence reports that established the independence of Ho Chi Minh from either Russia or China. The British suspected the truth—that Dulles wished to use the alliance as a cloak to legitimate a vast unilateral effort to establish an American security system in the Far East. (At one point in the crisis Eisenhower remarked that perhaps Britain was not "indispensable" to an Asian defense pact.) After the Geneva Accords had been signed, Dulles set about with lawyerly zeal to sign up the nations of Southeast Asia in a security organization (SEATO) which he envisaged as the Asian counterpart of NATO. Only one Southeast Asian nation, Thailand, joined, and when Walter Lippmann at a dinner party pointed out, "You've got mostly Europeans, plus Pakistan, which is nowhere near Southeast Asia," the secretary, never one to let geography interfere with high purpose, rose to the challenge. As Ronald Steel, Lippmann's biographer, recounts the incident:

"Look, Walter," Dulles said, blinking hard behind his thick glasses, "I've got to get some real fighting men into the south of Asia. The only Asians who can really fight are the Pakistanis. That's why we need them in the alliance. We could never get along without the Gurkas."

"But Foster," Lippmann reminded him, "the Gurkas aren't Pakistanis, they're Indians."

"Well," responded Dulles, unperturbed by such nit-picking and irritated at the Indians for refusing to join his alliance, "they may not be Pakistanis, but they're Moslems."

"No, I'm afraid they're not Moslems, either, they're Hindus."

"No matter," Dulles replied, and proceeded to lecture Lippmann for half an hour on how SEATO would plug the dike against communism in Asia.

On the cocktail party suggestion of Justice William O. Douglas, which was enthusiastically supported by the influential Senator Mike Mansfield, Dulles embraced Ngo Dinh Diem as the American candidate to run South Vietnam. Catholic and anti-Communist, Diem had a third virtue that endeared him to Dulles. He was passionately anti-French, exactly the sort of sympathetic nationalist with the legitimacy to preserve American interests in the area. Diem set about cutting away at French influence in Vietnam with increasing support from America. Dulles and Eisenhower now took steps to allocate U.S. aid directly, bypassing the French altogether. The National Security Council resolved to "work through the French only insofar as necessary," and the Joint Chiefs kept pressing for early withdrawal of French troops. Mendès, wishing to preserve some vestige of French influence in the former colony, vainly tried to resist Dulles' determined effort to convert South Vietnam into an exclusively American project. But he had no choice but to schedule the withdrawal of the French forces.

Dulles' anger at the French in the summer of 1954 bordered on fury. Just as the Geneva Conference was about to ratify the capitulation of Western interests in Asia, the French parliament delivered the crowning blow. On August 30 the National Assembly killed the European Defense Community on a procedural vote. French support for an idea devised by Frenchmen and initially scorned by the Americans had eroded as the reality of the scheme became clear in negotiation: The NATO commander, inevitably a U.S. general would have veto power over the deployment of French troops. A truly international army was acceptable in France as an inspiring myth but not as a reality.

Now Dulles made it clear that for the United States the goal of integration was paramount. European civilization, he said, could not survive "without a European Community in which will be combined, indissolubly, the interests and capabilities of two great nations at the heart of Europe, France and Germany. It would be difficult for me to exaggerate the anxiety with which our people await the consummation of this historic act." Playing to the growing ambivalence in Europe about taking the final steps to seal the East-West split, the Soviet Union in March 1954 had submitted a formal request to join NATO!

In any "defensive" alliance, the Kremlin asserted, the USSR should be welcome.

Dulles' threat of an "agonizing reappraisal" if the French turned their back on EDC—the word "agonizing" was a last minute flourish—had earned the scorn of diplomats and commentators but not many votes in the French parliament. "My own view," Walter Lippmann had written Dorothy Thompson a few months earlier, "is that Foster Dulles's real feeling about EDC is that of a man who has sat down on flypaper and can't think of what to do next." The issue, Raymond Aron, the influential French commentator observed, was more divisive than anything that had happened in France since the Dreyfus Case.

At stake in the parliamentary debate were a host of issues—whether France could compete economically if tied too closely to Germany, whether EDC would legitimize American hegemony over France, and whether the Germans should be forgiven for three wars.

Pro-EDC Frenchmen, *Le Monde* reported, felt closer to German supporters of the treaty than to their own countrymen who opposed it. The mystique of the European Defense Community was so strong that a Communist worker who opposed it, as all who followed the dictates of the party did, "felt closer to his boss or to an Army general, if his boss or the general was hostile to it, than to a fellow-workman who wanted E.D.C. ratified."

Mendès, on the other hand, was lukewarm about the treaty but wanted to have it passed to be rid of the issue. He tried to obtain agreement from the United States and Britain for sufficient modifications in EDC to give it a chance for passage, but Dulles and Adenauer, believing the political puffery of Monnet and his friends, were sure the votes were there for the treaty as it stood. When they were not, Dulles felt personally betrayed—by Mendès, not Monnet. The end unfolded in high drama. The honorary president of the Assembly, Édouard Herriot, eighty-two and crippled, in deference to his age and swollen limbs, was permitted to speak from his seat on the Radical Socialist bench instead of the podium. "On the threshold of death," he cried out, "let me tell you that EDC is the end of France . . . a step forward for Germany . . . a step back for France . . . *La C.E.D. est une aventure, ne la faites pas!*" When the vote was taken the triumphant Communists broke into the "Marseillaise," to which the defeated EDC proponents screamed, "Back to Moscow!"

The NATO military alliance was repaired with surprising ease, thanks in large measure to Anthony Eden's effective diplomacy at the London Conference called to pick up the pieces after the collapse of EDC, and to Adenauer's extraordinary gift for combining toughness and flexibility. Britain agreed to keep its Army of the Rhine and the Federal Republic accepted a permanent prohibition on producing nuclear weapons and was admitted to membership in NATO. Dulles agreed to renew America's pledge to defend Europe if Germany contributed twelve divisions to NATO. French resistance had dealt a harsh blow to European integration—there was, as would soon be evident, little that was supranational about the new army in the making—but the French had

Mr. Dulles Takes On World Responsibilities   163

succeeded in accomplishing what they feared most. A sovereign Germany would soon field the most powerful military force in West Europe.

3

As Eisenhower's first term was drawing to a close, it was evident that Dulles' foxy, pious ways, the recriminations over EDC, and the bitter aftertaste of the American-arranged withdrawal of French power from Vietnam and British power from the Persian Gulf had cast a pall over the alliance. In subtle ways the United States had used its anticolonial rhetoric and its minimal imperial record to its advantage. For the Eisenhower administration, the Middle East was the critical arena of political struggle, but there was no clear U.S. policy for the area except support for Israel, and many in the State Department bitterly opposed that. (Secretary of Defense Forrestal had warned at Israel's birth in 1948 that the price of support would be oil and that Americans would be forced to the ultimate humiliation, driving four-cylinder cars.)

The Americans, Her Majesty's ambassador reported from Cairo, seemed to think Egypt "was still a victim of British 'colonialism' " and wanted to make a deal at almost any cost. Generosity in giving up British assets seemed to come naturally to the Americans. "These considerations, combined with a horror of unpopularity and fear of losing their influence . . . and also an apparent disinclination by the United States Government to take second place even in an area where primary responsibility was not theirs, resulted in the Americans, at least locally, withholding the wholehearted support which their partner in N.A.T.O. had the right to expect. . . ." Dulles had set himself the task of extending a NATO-like alliance to the Middle East. It would involve simultaneously shoring up and replacing British power in the area. No policy could have been more successful in discouraging friends and winning enemies.

When Dulles set out for the Middle East on May 9, 1953, he was determined to show a greater evenhandedness in American policy toward the Arabs and Israel. It was a prerequisite for his grand design for the Middle East, a security pact for the area along the lines of NATO to keep the Russians out.

There was no sign of any Russians in the Middle East in 1953. But by the logic of the Cold War, they were coming. British and French power was collapsing. A week after the Iranians had thrown out the British technicians in 1951, the prime minister of Egypt had denounced the Anglo-Egyptian treaty of friendship, an alliance which still had five years to run. The next year the celebrated Shepheard's Hotel was set afire along with other British-owned buildings. In July 1952 King Farouk, the corpulent symbol of corrupt imperial rule, was overthrown, and Major General Muhammad Naguib, a British-trained soldier who had been wounded in the 1948 war against Israel, had become the head of state. But the power behind him was a group of colonels who were far more radical nationalists than he. Chief among them was Gamal Abdel Nasser, soon to succeed Naguib as president.

Dulles was dismayed by what he found in the Middle East. He had gotten off to a bad start by presenting a gold-plated Colt .38 revolver to Naguib, a bit of political symbolism which managed to insult the Egyptians, alarm the Israelis, and offend the British who worried that Dulles was sweeping into their domain with only minimal consultation. On his return to Washington he wrote an informal memo, "Conclusions on Trip," for the president.

British position rapidly deteriorating, probably to the point of non-repair . . . we find an intense distrust and dislike for the British . . . no respect for the French as a political force . . . United States position also not good . . . [This last was attributed to the American policy of friendly support for Israel, and to the tendency of the Arabs to associate the United States with British and French "colonial and imperialistic policies."]

. . . Also, almost entire area caught in fanatical revolutionary spirit that causes countries to magnify their pro[b]lems and depreciate soviet threat. . . .

. . . Efforts by the U.S., which by natural inclination and self interest finds itself somewhat in the middle between the British and Near Eastern positions, are increasingly resented by British. They interpret our policy as one which in fact hastens their loss of prestige in area. To some extent, regardless of efforts to the contrary on our part, this may be true. . . .

Anthony Eden had been dealing with the Americans on intimate terms since 1940, and believed in the "special relationship" with the United States. Whatever quarrels might arise within the English-speaking world, the bonds of culture, tradition, and common interest would withstand them. Surely, the Americans needed Britain, and without America, "we are alone," his mentor Winston Churchill never tired of repeating. When Eden finally succeeded Churchill as prime minister after serving in the old man's shadow for almost a generation, Eisenhower wrote, "I cannot tell you how delighted I am that my old friend Winston has been succeeded by an equally valued friend. . . ." But when he finally settled in at No. 10 Downing Street exactly fifteen years after his mentor, Winston Churchill, had told him in 1940 that "[t]he succession would be mine," Eden was a burnt-out comet. He had gone from political *wunderkind* to old man with nothing in between.

At age nineteen he had crawled through the mud at Ypres to rescue a wounded sergeant and emerged a war hero. A member of Parliament at twenty-six, by the time he was forty he had already resigned as foreign secretary to protest Neville Chamberlain's appeasement policies. The handsome figure with his elegant clothes and languid air still lived under the spell of empire, almost a caricature of the imperial aristocrat who still believed that Britain's choice was either to become another Netherlands, as one of Eden's Tory colleagues put it, or in Gladstone's words, "a great country, an Imperial country, a country where your sons, when they rise . . . command the respect of the world." How little had his long apprenticeship prepared him for what he faced. In 1955 wartime rationing in Britain had just ended. Taxes were discouragingly high and wages depressingly low. A strong face to the world was what it would take to "keep the lawns of England green for our grandchildren," Harold Macmillan, the chancellor of the exchequer, would tell him. But England had never seemed so small.

Eden was now fifty-six; Churchill still regarded him as a young man but not "a strong young man." He told Lord Moran a year before a succession of strokes finally compelled him to make way for Eden, "Anthony seems to me very tired. I detect strain in his telegrams. Sometimes he sends three thousand words in one day—and there is nothing in them." In truth, Eden was a sick man who suffered from a chronic infection in his bile duct in the wake of an incompetent gall-bladder operation.

Eden and Dulles had first met in 1942 over lunch at Eden's London flat. After listening to the American churchman, for it was in his capacity as chairman of the Federal Council of Churches' Commission on a Just and Durable Peace that Dulles had intruded on the foreign secretary's frantic wartime schedule, Eden worried in his diary that "it would be unfortunate for the future of the world if U.S. uninstructed views were to decide the future of the European continent." Alexander Cadogan of the Foreign Office, also at lunch, dismissed Dulles as "the wooliest type of useless pontificating American." Dulles and Eden met again at the United Nations and quarreled over the Japanese Peace Treaty in 1952. Before Eisenhower's election, Eden, presuming on their old association, confided his hope that he would not appoint Dulles as secretary of state "because he felt he would not work with him." Dulles reposed equal confidence in Eden. According to the two CIA officers assigned as Dulles' executive assistants, the secretary felt that the British were "clumsy and inept" in international matters and that the prime minister in particular "wasn't doing his homework." Eden's vanity and precious manners, Dulles believed, masked a bungler.

The old relationship between the nations had changed in ways the leaders themselves did not yet appreciate in part because of the atomic bomb. British scientists had played an important part in the joint research efforts that led to the explosion of the first bomb on July 16, 1945; indeed they had a head start on the Americans. At the Quebec Conference two years earlier Roosevelt had promised "full and effective collaboration" in nuclear matters, but when the bomb went off the United States passed the MacMahon Act which greatly restricted the sharing of atomic information. Prime Minister Attlee tried vainly to maintain the nuclear partnership but ended up in 1948 making a "real surrender," as members of his own party saw it, by acquiescing in the new state of affairs and accepting U.S. atomic bombs on British bases. In 1954 a controversy flared in Britain over the meaning of what had happened. Churchill, back in power, accused the Labourites in parliamentary debate of having sold out British interests. The Labour opposition, appalled at Dulles' hints to use atomic weapons and the horrifying reports filtering back from the Pacific atoll where America's first hydrogen bomb had been detonated—a Japanese fishing vessel eighty miles away had been deluged with radioactive ash—was internally split. Even the pacifist wing of the Labour Party shared the schizophrenia of the time about the American nuclear stockpiles—fearing equally that the bomb would be dropped in some American crusade and that it would not be brought to bear when Britain's survival was at stake.

Churchill, who had excluded American observers at the first British test conducted at Monte Bello Islands off Australia in October 1952, was determined to proceed unilaterally with a British superbomb since America might not be willing to risk using the weapon to protect anything but its own territory. Khrushchev was not the only world leader to appraise Dulles as a man who liked to talk about the brink of war but would never step over it. The hydrogen bomb, the retired chief of the air staff declared, was the key to Britain's remaining "a first-class power." Building the weapon was the only way to avoid becoming a "satellite," the archbishop of York agreed.

Dulles had come into office determined to repair relations with the Arab world and to avoid tilting too far toward Israel. This meant courting Gamal Abdel Nasser, the ardent young nationalist who in a letter written at age seventeen had cried out for a liberator "to rebuild the country so that the weak and humiliated Egyptian people can rise again and live as free and independent men." Eisenhower urged the British to evacuate their forces from Egypt and promised Nasser $27 million in military aid to encourage Egyptian concessions to make it happen. The American CIA agent in Egypt, Miles Copeland, and his superior, Kermit Roosevelt, were on a first-name basis with the Egyptian president, meeting him frequently in his private apartments. They advised him on how to deal with the American ambassador and even wrote paragraphs of speeches for him. In 1953 Roosevelt had delivered a $3 million bribe to the Egyptians to smooth the relationship. The British watched the wooing process with suspicion.

In 1955 while the Americans were trying to figure out what to do about Nasser, events moved fast. In February the Israelis, in apparent retaliation for an Egyptian raid against an Israeli outpost in which an Israeli soldier had been killed the month before, launched a bloody attack on an Egyptian army camp in the Gaza, killing twenty-two soldiers in a truck and another fifteen in the camp itself. Nasser became increasingly anti-Israel, increasingly suspicious of the United States, and increasingly bold in putting himself forward as a regional and even world figure. In April he attended the first Conference on Nonaligned Nations at Badung and had a long meeting with Chou En-lai, whom he asked to probe the willingness of the Russians to give him the arms the Americans had promised and never delivered. (In the end the Soviets would provide many times what Eisenhower termed the "peanuts" Nasser had requested from the United States.) As far as Dulles was concerned, Nasser had supped with the devil. In a phone conversation with Under Secretary Hoover, Dulles fumed, "We have a lot of cards to play with Nasser—although they are mostly negative. The waters of the Upper Nile: we can strangle him if we want to. . . . [We can] ruin the cotton market. We can switch this year's economic aid from Egypt to Iraq."

Nasser's nationalism now infuriated Dulles because it threatened his grand design for the Middle East, the Baghdad Pact, a Near Eastern NATO built around Turkey and Pakistan, with Iraq, then the most pro-Western Arab nation in the region, the centerpiece. Eisenhower was "delighted" when Iran joined, and he and Dulles strongly encouraged the British to press on. But the effort to organize the Middle East for an anti-Communist alliance provided fuel for Arab nationalism which Nasser was now seeking to personify. Nasser termed the pact "a new form of imperialism designed to imprison all the Arab people," pointing out to the numerous American envoys who came to see him that Israel, not the Soviet Union, was the nation against which the Arab states wished to form an alliance. He saw the alliance for what it was, an effort to prop up pro-Western Iraq as a counterweight to Arab nationalism. Eden charged ahead, seeking to enlist Jordan, despite a promise to Nasser that he would stop recruiting more Arab nations into the pact.

Eisenhower still hoped to come to terms with Nasser. He had sent Robert B. Anderson, a banker with a Texas drawl so thick the Egyptian could not understand a word he said, on a hopeless secret mission to Cairo. It soon became clear that the pact would never work. The British initiative had produced a series of reverses for the West. Radio Cairo regularly eviscerated King Hussein of Jordan for becoming a British-Zionist-Imperialist lackey, and in an effort to save his throne the king fired Sir John Glubb, the British commander of the Arab Legion for fifteen years, giving him exactly two hours to get out of the country. Egypt and Syria concluded a defense pact aimed at countering British-American influence. British prestige in the region had fallen to a new low. Dulles suddenly discovered all sorts of legal objections to the Americans joining the Baghdad Pact. "That terrible man," as Eden called Dulles, had, in Harold Macmillan's words, "used every possible pressure upon us to become full members," and then disappeared. It was an act of "vicarious brinksmanship," pushing others to the edge of the cliff while hanging back in safety.

The British blamed the Americans not only for reversing themselves on the Baghdad Pact but also for reneging on their promise to finance the High Dam at Aswān. Nasser's dream was a 15,000-acre irrigation project to make the desert bloom. If the United States were to foot the bill, Dulles made clear, Nasser would have to make political concessions, but the nationalist leader was suspicious even of standard bankers' conditions. The U.S. secretary of the treasury, George Humphrey, doubted that Nasser was a good financial risk. Senators from the cotton states were appalled that tax money was going to subsidize a producer that could be a potentially dangerous competitor in fifteen to eighteen years. The Israeli government and its supporters in the United States did not like the idea of strengthening the Egyptian economy. Dulles, feeling the pressure and increasingly angry that Nasser "was playing both sides," decided to cancel American participation in the project. Nasser's ambassador in Washington, Ahmed Hussein, a pro-American diplomat, begged Dulles not to withdraw the loan offer because, as he patted his breast pocket, "we have the Russian offer to finance the dam right here." "Well then," said Dulles, choosing to interpret the remark as a threat rather than the cry for help that it was, "as you already have the money, you have no need for our support.

The offer is withdrawn.'' Once again he had reversed course without telling the British.

On July 26, 1956, almost exactly one hundred years after Ferdinand de Lesseps had begun digging in the desert with Egyptian forced labor, Gamal Nasser retaliated against the United States and Britain by seizing the imperial jewel of the Middle East. Ever a master of symbols, Nasser used the name "De Lesseps" in his public speech announcing nationalization as the code word to signal the troops to sweep into the strategic points along the canal and occupy it. Although legal under international law, the seizure was an act to defy the established order of more than a century. A quarter of Britain's oil passed through the canal. In July 1956 Anthony Eden believed, wrongly as it turned out, that the nation had only six weeks' supply.

For Eden, Nasser had become the Moby Dick of Araby, the symbol if not the cause of all that was amiss in the Middle East. "But what's all this nonsense about isolating Nasser or 'neutralizing' him, as you call it?'' he screamed at his old friend at the Foreign Office, Anthony Nutting. "I want him destroyed, can't you understand?'' Though he could converse with Nasser in serviceable Arabic, the nationalist currents of the region meant nothing to Eden. Suez was the Rhineland. Nasser was Hitler. The sickness "which was eating away at his whole system" had turned the normally cool and subtle diplomat into an angry fanatic.

Between July and late October 1956, a few days before the U.S. presidential election, Britain, France, and Israel conspired to teach Nasser a lesson and to wrest back the canal. While the British and French engaged in inconclusive negotiations with the United States on the one hand and Nasser on the other, they secretly prepared an invasion of Egypt. Eden admitted to a friend that he was now "practically living on Benzedrine.''

On October 22, 1956, Foreign Secretary Selwyn Lloyd, David Ben-Gurion, Moshe Dayan, French Premier Guy Mollet, and his foreign minister, Antoine Pineau, arrived at a château in Sèvres amid elaborate secrecy to approve the final plans. For years afterward the participants would deny that the meeting had ever taken place. In the words of British Foreign Secretary Selwyn Lloyd, these plans called for Israel to launch "a real act of war" against Egypt, thereby providing a pretext for Britain and France to invade Egypt and reoccupy the canal. The French ambassador told Eisenhower after the Israeli attack had already started that he knew of no plan for France to join the conflict. "I will never again trust the word of a French ambassador," Dulles told him a few hours later after the true dimension of the conspiracy became clear.

Exactly a week after the meeting at Sèvres the Israelis mounted an invasion across the Sinai with 45,000 troops and rapidly approached the canal. As agreed, Britain and France issued an ultimatum for both the Israelis and Egyptians to withdraw thirty miles on each side from the canal. The Israelis agreed according to the plan to go no farther than they had originally intended, but Nasser knew what was afoot and refused to withdraw. Thereupon the British and French began bombing Egypt and landing paratroopers near the canal. On

November 5, Eden and Guy Mollet gave the go-ahead for an amphibious landing by 13,500 British troops and a French force of 8500. But within thirty-six hours, though the invaders were at one point six miles from Cairo, the United States had exerted enough pressure on Britain and France to force a cease fire.

"You will not get a dime from the United States government if I can stop it, until you have gotten out of Suez!" Secretary of the Treasury George Humphrey screamed at the British ambassador. "You are like burglars who have broken into somebody else's house. So get out! When you do, and not until then, you'll get help." Far from helping, the United States exerted intense pressure on the pound to make sure the British forces were promptly extricated from Egypt. The Federal Reserve sold off large blocks of sterling "far above what was necessary to protect the value of its own holdings," Foreign Secretary Harold Macmillan later observed.

I would not have been unduly concerned had we been able to obtain either the money to which we were entitled from the International Monetary Fund, or, better still, some aid by way of a temporary loan from the United States. The refusal of the second was understandable; the obstruction of the first is not so easy to forgive. We had a perfect right under the statutes to ask for the repayment of the British quota. . . . I telephoned urgently to New York; the matter was referred to Washington. . . . I received the reply that the American Government would not agree to the technical procedure until we had agreed to the cease-fire. I regarded this then, and still do, as a breach of the spirit, and even of the letter of the system under which the Fund is supposed to operate. It was a form of pressure which seemed altogether unworthy. It contrasted strangely with the weak attitude of the Americans toward Egyptian funds and "accounts" after the seizure of the Canal.

Eden and Harold Macmillan, the man who succeeded him as prime minister after the crisis was over, believed that Dulles had given them badly confused signals. The Americans were hardly in a position to be as high-minded as they suddenly appeared in November 1956. Had they not themselves used force to depose Mossadegh in 1953 and to overthrow the government of Guatemala the following year? Had not Dulles himself told Eden in August that "a way had to be found to make Nasser disgorge what he is attempting to swallow"? But it was all to be taken with a warehouse of salt, as the veteran diplomat Robert Murphy later explained. Dulles was doing anything to prolong the negotiations. He never considered using force but wanted the British to think that he had not ruled it out. Yet Eisenhower's own views were clear enough. In September he had written the prime minister, "I am afraid, Anthony, that from this point onward your views on this situation diverge. . . . I must tell you frankly that American public opinion flatly rejects the thought of using force. . . ."

But even when it was all over and the conspirators had bowed to the moral, political, and economic pressure of the United States—at one point the U.S. chief of naval operations had ordered the Sixth Fleet to be ready to "defeat them. The British, the French and the Egyptians and the Israelis, the

whole goddam works of them . . . ."—Dulles continued to send contradictory
signals. When Selwyn Lloyd came to visit him at Walter Reed Hospital where
he had just been operated on for cancer, Dulles asked with no trace of irony in
his voice, "Why did you stop?"

The Suez affair was a signal that the bonds of alliance on both sides of the
Elbe were loosening. In the more relaxed atmosphere following the Geneva
Conference where Eisenhower and Khrushchev met and pledged peace, the
British and French were ready to test the limits of the new alliance. And so
were the Hungarians. The event that kept the Western alliance from falling
apart altogether was the Soviet invasion of Hungary at the very moment the
British were pounding Egypt and a demand for a cease-fire had just been voted
in the United Nations. True, the British and French were furious that the
Americans treated them so much more severely than they treated the Russians;
they were forced to take humiliating action while the Soviets, merely condemned, consolidated their hold over Hungary. Students in Hamburg carried
signs reading: EDEN, MURDERER OF BUDAPEST, thus distilling in a slogan a
widespread view that the Anglo-French conspiracy had given the Soviets an
opportunity to crush the Hungarian resistance that they would not otherwise
have had.

But Hungary was a reminder of the limits of détente. When in the heat
of crisis the Kremlin had sent letters to London and Paris hinting that
rockets might fly, the security issue was dramatized anew. Although the threat
was not a major factor in the British and French decisions to withdraw, for
the CIA passed along the word that the Soviets lacked the means to carry
it out, the ominous rhetoric from Moscow suddenly made national survival
seem more important than lost imperial power. The United States had as
much interest in guaranteeing the one as in arranging the orderly takeover of
the other.

4

In September 1955 Konrad Adenauer set out for Moscow with a delegation
seventy strong, experts from the Foreign Ministry prepared to talk on anything. The chancellor of a West German state accorded its sovereignty by its
NATO Allies only four months before and still unrecognized by any of the
Communist countries was met at the airport by Prime Minister Bulganin, Foreign Minister Molotov, and an honor guard decked in blue and scarlet. In the
huge hotel room prepared for the chancellor, his hosts had thoughtfully placed
a grand piano.

More than two years had passed since Adenauer's triumphal tour of the
United States. He had found Dulles reassuring, a man of deep religious faith
and sturdy political convictions, hardly gullible about the Russians, not one to
entertain a deal with Moscow at Germany's expense. The two leaders shared

a common view of negotiation with the Communists, the less the better. Then why go to Moscow?

In part Adenauer's decision to sit down with men he considered to be brutal, atheistic, uncultured, and untrustworthy reflected his own new sense of confidence. Reelected with an absolute majority in September 1953, he was now the leading statesman of Europe. At least, *Time* magazine said so. His opposition at home had been smashed. Schumacher had died before the election, and the Socialists under his colorless successor were in disarray. He had dealt deftly with the "weight of the past." When General Otto Remer, the commander of Hitler's Wachregiment in Berlin, who had arrested the conspirators against Hitler in the July 20, 1944, plot against his life, formed the neo-Nazi *Socialistische Reichspartei* garnering a frightening 11 percent of the vote in Lower Saxony and Bremen, Adenauer had him indicted for slander and jailed. The chancellor was accused of being soft on former Nazis himself—his closest confidant, Dr. Hans Globke, had received a commendation under Hitler for drafting the Nuremberg "racial decrees" and writing a scholarly commentary thereon—but the chancellor was determined to root out any revival of Nazism as an organized political force. Both his own deeply held convictions and his moral credentials to be the restorer of Germany required it. He agreed to pay the Israeli government three billion marks to defray the costs of resettling refugees from Hitler in Israel, symbolic reparations for the Holocaust, about one half of what the Israelis had asked. (In the midst of the negotiations, according to Nahum Goldmann, the Israeli negotiator, a Jewish fanatic tried to kill Adenauer by handing two schoolboys on a streetcar a package with a bomb in it to mail to the chancellor, but they took it to the police instead, where it exploded and killed the demolition expert. Adenauer presented gold watches to the boys, and kept the identity of the would-be assassin a discreet secret.)

Erhard's miracle was working. The unemployment caused by his austerity policies dropped. The government financed the resettlement of several million refugees from the East and with an "equalization of burdens" tax, a 50 percent capital levy on all property surviving from the Nazi period, and loans of 50 billion marks. The German trade unions, haunted as all Germans were by the memories of the great inflation of the 1920s—a wheelbarrow of Reichsmarks for a loaf of bread—were remarkably accommodating in their wage demands. Adenauer himself participated in the drafting of the law on *Mitbestimmung,* worker codetermination, his answer to the socialization of heavy industry and one that the Social Democratic party came to accept. It was a time of hard work and social peace.

In foreign policy the great achievements were behind him. Germany, or at least the part that most mattered to Adenauer, was a sovereign nation again. The threat of a great East-West accord at the expense of an independent Germany was receding. Yet he was worried about allied diplomacy. Indeed his concern was the principal reason he was in Moscow. Two months before, Eisenhower, Eden, Edgar Faure, yet another French premier, and Bulganin had met at Geneva where Eisenhower had swapped war stories, with his old friend Marshal Georgi Zhukov. The Big Four had made speeches at one another and left after haggling over the communiqué on Germany, in a cloud of official good feeling with nothing resolved. Adenauer shared Dulles' concern that the "spirit of Geneva has certainly created problems for the free nations." As Nelson Rockefeller, then serving as Eisenhower's adviser on Cold War strategy, put it, NATO could not remain "the core of U.S. European policy" if the sense of common danger passed.

Adenauer was particularly unhappy with the plan Eden had put forward at the Geneva Conference for a mutual withdrawal of NATO and Warsaw Pact forces from the center of Germany. Although he had talked with Harold Macmillan a month before about demilitarized zones in Germany if the Russians should ever decide to abandon East Germany and agree to reunification on Western terms, Adenauer was always against purely military arrangements that were limited to Germany alone. Any agreement would have the unfortunate effect of according to the Soviets the "moral and social equality" they had demanded at Geneva, thus abandoning the posture of moral superiority on which he and Dulles banked so heavily. More important, all such agreements would place the Western imprimatur on the status quo. Even if Adenauer, as his political opponents charged, was more interested in integrating the *Länder* of the West into an Atlantic Community than in re-creating Bismarck's Prussian Reich, he could scarcely afford to say so. The German electorate was now filled with enough Germans from the east to force any German politician to make reunification the sacred national goal.

A year before his trip to Moscow, Adenauer had hinted that the time for a German-Soviet rapprochement might well be at hand. In London, Washington, and Paris, the allergic reaction was so pronounced that the chancellor insisted, as he often did when his trial balloons were punctured, that the press had taken liberties with his words. But Adenauer knew that the specter of Rapallo—the 1922 treaty under which the European pariahs, defeated Germany and the Bolshevik state, briefly arranged to recognize one another and to enter into a secret military collaboration—was an effective political weapon to use against his new allies. The Americans, particularly, must have confidence in the loyalty of the new German state, but not too much. Indeed, one of the strong arguments in Washington for making the Federal Republic the linchpin of the Western alliance was the threat that Germany would otherwise make a deal with Moscow. Acheson argued that American troops in Germany were as much a guarantee of German good behavior as of Soviet prudence. Without the presence of American troops in Germany to monitor the continued integration of Germany into the West, the architect of the alliance wrote in *Foreign Affairs,* we should continually be haunted by the spectre of "a sort of new Ribbentrop-Molotov Agreement." Testifying shortly before his death, Dulles urged ever closer ties with Germany; otherwise the Germans "would be under an almost irresistible temptation to play one side or the other." For Adenauer the Allies seemed to be wavering; the Russian smiles and their concessions that had produced the Austrian State Treaty and the withdrawal of the Red Army seemed to portend a new stage in the Cold War. It was time for an independent initiative. At the very least, he could prove to Dulles that any optimism about the Soviet leaders was unfounded.

The negotiations at the Spiridonovka Palace between the Kremlin high command and the first anti-Communist German official to arrive in Moscow since the war got off to a frosty start. When Adenauer mentioned reunification, Khrushchev shook a fist at him. But Adenauer tried to be pleasant. When he made a point of telling his hosts that Molotov had surprised him by appearing so intelligent, Khrushchev and Bulganin broke into smiles. "You're certainly the first person ever to say that," Bulganin exclaimed. Refusing to be intimidated by denunciations of the "revanchist" Federal Republic, Adenauer acidly noted that it was the Soviet government, not he, that had signed a pact with Hitler. Adenauer's real purpose in making the trip was to obtain the release of about 10,000 prisoners of war still incarcerated in Russia ten years after the collapse of Hitler. Bulganin and Khrushchev kept insisting that these were war criminals who would never be released until they had served their sentences, but over vodka one night Bulganin told Adenauer he could have the prisoners in return for establishing normal diplomatic relations. The chancellor, who had sworn before going to Moscow that he would never make such a deal because it would undercut the possibilities of reunification, accepted.

Adenauer's visit to Moscow was one straw in the wind, signaling the start of a slow process of political settlement in Europe that would take a generation and more. Another was a memorandum George Kennan wrote in May 1956. The architect of "containment," who had been expelled from Moscow as the U.S. ambassador at the end of the Stalin era, now pointed out that Soviet control over Eastern Europe was a reality which the West must now accept, peaceful coexistence was a necessity, and German rearmament probably a mistake. Kennan's views made Adenauer extremely nervous. The nervousness grew as Kennan developed his views the following year into an eloquent plea for "disengagement" in Europe. The Soviets endorsed the "Rapacki Plan" in October 1957, a scheme for a nuclear-free zone in Central Europe, including the two Germanys, Poland, and Czechoslovakia. Adenauer worried that such plans—Hugh Gaitskell, the leader of the Labour opposition in Britain, Eden, Macmillan, and many others put forward their own versions all during the late 1950s—would feed neutralism in Germany and create a dangerous "power vacuum" into which Communism, like poisonous gas, would flow.

Nikolai Bulganin, the Soviet premier, with his trim beard, looked like a kindly, old-fashioned Russian uncle except for his steely blue eyes. He was no match for Nikita Khrushchev, his rotund, impetuous, and wily partner in power. By 1956 Khrushchev had used his office as secretary general of the Soviet Communist party to eclipse Bulganin and to emerge as the preeminent figure in the Kremlin. In February 1956 he gave a secret speech at the Twentieth Party Congress denouncing the "crimes" of Stalin. So perfect a confirmation of his own world view was this confession that Dulles signed a priority cable to every embassy demanding that a copy of the text be procured. Mossad, the Israeli intelligence agency, produced a copy of the speech for the CIA in return for a cash payment and an agreement to swap information. Khrushchev's recitation of Stalin's barbarism had an electrifying effect on Communist parties around the world, produced numerous defections, and raised fundamental questions about the legitimacy of Moscow's leadership of the Socialist camp, all of which fed the confidence of the West but complicated the task of building the alliance.

With a Soviet invasion even less plausible in the mid-1950s than it had been six years earlier, the military arrangements in NATO for doing battle with the Russian hordes were really a metaphor for the political struggles taking place within the alliance itself. Adenauer had used the promise of 500,000 troops to whet American appetites for a rearmed, sovereign West German state. Franz Josef Strauss, the pudgy, energetic Bavarian who had not so long before been an advocate of German demilitarization and neutrality, took over the Defense Ministry and concluded that 172,000 was a more "realistic" target. No other country had met the ambitious goals for its contribution to the seventy-division army that had been planned at the 1952 Lisbon Conference. The United States was hardly now in a position to object, since the Eisenhower economy drive contemplated cutting American forces too.

In July 1956 the testimony of Admiral Arthur Radford, the chairman of the Joint Chiefs of Staff, before a secret session of a Senate subcommittee was leaked to *The New York Times*. The Pentagon had prepared a memorandum to the effect that the United States could cut 800,000 men from its forces, increase its reliance on nuclear weapons (which, as far as Radford was concerned, were now "conventional"), and save money without endangering security. Tactical nuclear weapons, designated in the press as "small," though most were at least the size of the bomb that obliterated Hiroshima, would now play a greater role in NATO defense. Dulles then spoke privately with reporters and suggested that he approved the idea of "reforming . . . the defense pattern of NATO."

Adenauer reacted strongly. He was worried that the Republicans in the American Congress who had opposed the permanent stationing of American forces in Germany in the first place would now eagerly embrace the "new look" in military doctrine and call for the withdrawal of half the American forces from Germany. When Allen Dulles visited the chancellor in Bonn, Adenauer warned him that NATO was threatened with "senility" and would end up being "just an officers' club." Only now had he just succeeded in overcoming the antimilitarist sentiment in Germany and in paving the way for the twelve divisions he had promised. An American withdrawal would jeopardize everything.

For Adenauer the level of U.S. troop commitment symbolized the seriousness of the American commitment to defend Europe, and without that commitment the incorporation of the western half of Germany into an Atlantic Community could never be secure. He began a campaign to make sure that the

"Radford Plan" never became official policy. Felix von Eckhardt, his press spokesman, was dispatched to enlist the support of prominent Democrats, including Harriman, Stevenson, and Lyndon B. Johnson, in fighting the Radford Plan. Dulles was impressed. Indeed, he came to the conclusion, as Eckhardt later recalled, that "if the Federal Government rejects such a military development as strongly as this, it really cannot be carried out. . . ."

Now that John Foster Dulles, enfeebled by recurrent cancer, no longer exercised the influence on Eisenhower he did during the first term, Adenauer emerged as the arch cold warrior of the West. His goal was ambitious, nothing less than to exercise a veto on American policy in Europe. In this he was remarkably successful. Professing to believe in disarmament in principle, he vigorously opposed any sort of scheme for arms limitation or control in Europe. Harold Stassen, Eisenhower's disarmament negotiator, bothered him greatly because unlike most diplomats who attended disarmament conferences the former Minnesota governor passionately wanted to achieve an agreement. The chancellor complained about Stassen to anyone he could find, including the columnist James Reston; and Dulles at a critical moment in the negotiations swooped down on Stassen and ended his peacemaking activities. Dulles had his own reasons for getting rid of Stassen, but Adenauer's opposition was an important consideration. Adenauer hired a public relations firm to influence U.S. opinion and did not hesitate to let powerful private citizens like John J. McCloy and Dean Acheson know when he was displeased at what the American government was thinking of doing. Foreign Minister Heinrich von Brentano could scarcely conceal his euphoria at the influence the German government seemed able to exercise in Washington. Stopping off to visit the Grand Canyon in 1957, he wrote the chancellor: "I believe that it is . . . largely within our power to determine the policy of the United States during the next few years. The growing strength of Europe ties the Americans closer to us."

But the military issues that threatened to divide the alliance were inherently insoluble. There has always been a stubborn contradiction in the Western alliance: Military ties are the *raison d'être* of the North Atlantic Treaty Organization, but no military strategy has ever existed to inspire the confidence of the members. The earliest military plans drawn up by NATO before the Korean War amounted to little more than an evacuation plan. It contemplated a series of rescue operations, much like the British had carried out at Dunkirk during World War II, and perhaps a stand at the Pyrenees. When Eisenhower arrived as supreme commander, the planning had become more ambitious. With a hundred divisions, the NATO forces might hope to fight off an attacker for some time, since the aggressor needs a three-to-one superiority over a well-entrenched defender. The theory at the Lisbon Conference in 1952 was that a large enough conventional force could be raised to prevent the Soviets from racing to the Channel. The prospect would deter them. Being deterred would make them less ominous neighbors.

The planners envisaged World War III as a more mechanized version of World War II. Although the military experts thought it made sense to locate the defense. line at the Rhine River, a natural barrier, the politicians pointed out that the defense of France was scarcely a goal for which a German chancellor could stir his countrymen to rearm. There had to be a "forward strategy," a commitment to defend German territory at the Elbe, the new East-West frontier, not the Rhine.

By the end of 1953 progress had been made. NATO had fifteen divisions in the field, enough to force the Soviets to reinforce their twenty-two division forward army in East Germany in the event they ever wished to attack the West, thus giving a sufficient warning for the United States to launch the bombers of the Strategic Air Command on their mission of annihilation. In December 1954 the NATO planners were authorized to base their war plans on the use of atomic weapons. Reliance on nuclear weapons for the defense of Europe was politically compelling, for the cost was prohibitive of maintaining conventional forces big enough to be a credible deterrent to the Soviet attack no one quite believed was coming. In 1951, when Britain, still struggling to recover from the war, was spending 14 percent of the national income on the military, Aneurin Bevan, the leader of the left wing of the Labour party, resigned from the government in protest, and the party lost the election, a lesson that all European politicians noted.

Rearmament in France contributed to the economic crisis. Inflation, increased speculation against the franc, and a precipitous drop in monetary reserves followed. To be a good ally of the United States and contribute to the common war effort required the French to adopt other policies which Washington opposed. Efforts at trade liberalization were abandoned and import quotas introduced. For Britain the damage caused by the Korean War rearmament was longer lasting. While British factories turned out arms, the new West German plants produced high-quality machinery, refrigerators, and optical equipment for export and built its new prosperity to no small extent by capturing British markets of the past. The Netherlands foreign minister, though a NATO enthusiast, worried about the political and economic effects of rearmament. He warned that "any further lowering of the present standard of living in Europe . . . would endanger the social peace on the home front. . . ." Nuclear weapons had made annihilation a bargain. If the function of the military was deterrence, a single weapon that killed more people than a combat division ever could was "cost-effective."

Of course by the mid-1950s, when NATO developed its nuclear strategy, the Soviets had nuclear weapons too. At the very moment when economics was forcing the alliance to think in nuclear terms, the strategic reality had already rendered a nuclear strategy hopeless. In June 1955 the NATO exercise "Carte Blanche" was held in West Germany. The players were asked to assume that in West Germany, the Lowlands, and northeastern France, 335 nuclear bombs had been dropped and then to calculate the consequences. The umpires reported that within 48 hours over 1.5 million Germans would have been killed in any such attack and 3.5 million wounded. These impressive results were published. A new era of warfare had indeed arrived. Every European statesman was shocked. German politicians immediately questioned the need for recruiting German troops since NATO was planning to use atomic weapons immediately in a war and these would destroy Germany, troops, civilians, and all. In public opinion polls the German public overwhelmingly rejected the idea of being "defended" with catastrophic weapons.

The decision to store nuclear weapons in Europe had torn at the alliance from the very first moment in 1952 when Pentagon planners had publicly envisaged the idea of unleashing mushroom clouds, radioactive fallout, and small-scale fireballs over what they called the "battlefield," and Germans called Mainz, Hannover, and München. Not only were nuclear weapons hopelessly destructive for their intended purposes, but they were shrouded in a secrecy that served to underscore the point that one ally was more equal than all the others. Under U.S. law, Marshall Juin, the French general in charge of NATO's ground troops, was prohibited from knowing the number and character of atomic arms with which his troops might be equipped. (Only when the stream of nuclear weapons to Europe threatened to assume flood proportions did Congress change the law in 1954 to provide minimal information to the Allies. But legal control and the decision to use such weapons has remained with the United States to this day.)

The nuclear weapons issue shook the alliance in the 1950s just as it would thirty years later because of two huge gaps in perspective, one between the Americans and the Europeans, the other between the military and the politicians. Profound differences existed on the two sides of the Atlantic on the very purpose of NATO. For the Europeans, NATO was essentially an insurance policy, a way of committing the United States in advance to their defense, so that the terrible uncertainty of the two world wars when America hung back while Europe bled would never be repeated. It was the certainty of the American response that provided the deterrent against any possible Soviet aggression. But for the Americans, NATO was a geopolitical instrument for restoring a power balance on the European Continent to contain the forces of the East. For this reason the Americans could not afford to use military power merely to make a symbolic point, which at heart was all the Europeans were interested in, but had to treat the security problem in Europe as a real military task, for which solutions must be found. But in the classic military sense there never were any such solutions.

The gulf between the military planners, on the one hand, and the politicians was just as wide. By the mid-1950s NATO had become an impressive bureaucratic institution. Its sixty-acre headquarters at Rocquencourt, near Paris, was resplendent with the flags and insignia of fifteen countries. But in reality it was an American headquarters. Almost half the officers were American. Critical documents were stamped AEO—"American Eyes Only," or NOFORN. There was a secretariat organized by Sir Hastings Ismay, one of Churchill's former military staff officers in World War II, who became the first NATO secretary-general. Under his successor, Paul-Henri Spaak, the NATO bureaucracy mushroomed. In his youth the former Belgian prime minister had been the editor of a Marxist journal, but he was now one of the leading "good Europeans" who tried vainly to turn NATO into what it could never be: an instrument for integrating Europe into an Atlantic Community. There was a military committee made up of the chiefs of staff of all the NATO countries, but it rarely met. A "Standing Committee" of military ambassadors from the fifteen NATO countries was established in what one French member called a "gilded cage at the Pentagon." But the planning exercises, though time consuming, were largely futile, since the "national guidance" the members received from Paris, London, and, most important, from the inner recesses of the Pentagon itself determined the policy. While duty at NATO provided respectability for German officers and helped to overcome the resistance among the European military to the birth of another German army in the making, for most non-Americans assignment to NATO remained what Eisenhower once called it, a thorn, not a plum. Nevertheless, the impressive quantity of military busywork created the impression that a real defense was in the making.

All this was taking place at a moment when the most perceptive statesmen were beginning to realize that the atomic bomb had rendered the classic military concept of defense an anachronism. In 1953 the Soviet Union exploded a hydrogen bomb. Winston Churchill immediately declared that "the entire foundation of human affairs was revolutionized" and the problem of defense "fundamentally altered." He was astonished, he told the House of Commons, how little reaction there was to the disclosure that the hydrogen bomb created an area of destruction six miles in diameter! The Soviet capacity to annihilate American cities was now just a matter of time. The American threat to initiate the use of nuclear weapons in the defense of Europe had become a threat to commit suicide. Yet so out of phase was the military planning and the political reality that NATO military planners talked as if nothing had changed. "I want to make it absolutely clear," Marshal Montgomery, the deputy supreme commander of NATO, declared at the Royal United Service Institute in 1954, "that we at SHAPE [Supreme Headquarters Allied Powers Europe] are basing all our operational planning on using atomic and thermonuclear weapons in our own defense." General Alfred Gruenther's "cosmic top secret" study was leaked to the press: according to the supreme allied commander, any future war in Europe would "inevitably be atomic."

Khrushchev announced in 1956 that the Soviet armed forces had been reduced by more than 1.8 million troops. But the Soviet Union now had nuclear-tipped intermediate-range rockets aimed at West Europe. Britain was finding the military burden so severe that in 1957 the government instituted a program to cut the armed forces almost in half and to reduce substantially the British army of the Rhine. Since 1954 the French had pulled out most of its NATO troops from Europe and sent them to fight in Algeria, where, a succession of French statesmen insisted, the battle to defend Western civilization was now joined. The more NATO searched for a credible military strategy, the greater the friction within the alliance.

In 1957 a thirty-four-year-old German refugee, who had recently been denied a tenured teaching post at Harvard, landed a position as secretary to a prestigious study group at the Council on Foreign Relations. Henry Kissinger turned his report of the discussions at the Council into a best-seller. *Nuclear Weapons and Foreign Policy* was an attack on "massive retaliation" and offered the solution that Americans had been looking for. There could, he assured his readers, be such a thing as a "limited nuclear war." If the United States were prepared to fight one, the Russians would be deterred. Two years later he changed his mind. Dulles, too, had briefly subscribed to the idea of limited nuclear war. Yet the limitations of fighting a nuclear war of any kind were becoming more apparent. At his confirmation hearings, Christian A. Herter, after being appointed to succeed Dulles as secretary of state, caused alarm in Europe when he remarked on April 21, 1959, as if restating the obvious, that he could not "conceive of any president engaging in all-out nuclear war unless we were in danger of all-out devastation ourselves." In a sentence the new secretary had blown away the solemn assurances of a decade. Adding to the confusion was the statement of the American commander of the Sixth Fleet a few months earlier: "I would not recommend the use of any atomic weapon, no matter how small," Vice Admiral Charles R. Brown declared, "when both sides have the power to destroy the world." General Maxwell Taylor, wishing to point out an equally obvious aspect of the new reality, that the presence of 250,000 U.S. soldiers and thousands of dependents precluded the use of tactical nuclear weapons in the front lines, encountered the blue pencil of the Pentagon censor. The illusions of nuclear defense must not be disturbed.

A common defense against a common enemy is the traditional unifier of nations, but by the end of the Eisenhower years, Adenauer, who had seen German soldiers as the currency with which to buy back German sovereignty and equality, realized that the military arrangements in NATO symbolized the inherent inequality of the partners. Germany was forever barred from producing nuclear weapons by the terms of the treaties that created the Federal Republic. Britain was now about to have the bomb, and since the mid-1950s the French government had been working to the same end. One of Monnet's associates, Felix Gaillard, who had been in charge of atomic matters in the early 1950s, gave the final go-ahead to produce a French nuclear weapon on April 11, 1958, during his brief service as prime minister. (Operation "Gerboise Bleue" produced an explosion in the Sahara in early 1960.) Adenauer publicly demanded that Germany be given a share in control over the tactical nuclear weapons in Europe. They were, after all, he argued, nothing more than an advanced form of artillery. Franz Josef Strauss insisted that Germany deserved equal access to the weapons; anything less amounted to intolerable discrimination. Adenauer began talking to the French government about possible collaboration in atomic matters. Why, indeed, could not Germany produce rockets and France the nuclear warheads? On March 31, 1958, the defense ministers of France and Germany signed an agreement to conduct joint nuclear research at an institute at Saint-Louis in Alsace. Strauss took a mysterious trip

to the Sahara, the site of the French testing ground. It was American unreliability, Adenauer told his associates, that made such a Franco-German initiative
desirable. But the French-German project did not get off the ground. De Gaulle
returned to power in June and made it clear from the outset that the French
would cooperate with no one in developing nuclear weapons. The French
bomb would be the symbol not of continental cooperation but of French *grandeur*.

Once again the Soviets would put the alliance to the test. By November
1958 Nikita Khrushchev had humiliated and scattered his Kremlin rivals—
Bulganin, Molotov, Kaganovich, Shepilov, now known in official lingo as the
Anti-Party Group. Advances in Soviet rocketry had given the USSR the distinction of putting the first satellite into orbit. On November 3, 1957, a Soviet
Eskimo dog named Laika had the honor of being the first living thing to orbit
the earth in space. In the West, the friendly-faced husky had an ominous look,
for if Soviet science had reached such a point it meant that intercontinental
missiles capable of landing on New York or Washington would soon be ready.
The post-Stalin liberalization was in full swing. In the Third World the influence of the Soviet Union had never been greater. Soviet technicians and military advisers in Egypt were establishing a strategic foothold in the Middle East.
In Indonesia the Communist party had acquired a key role in President
Achmed Sukarno's "guided democracy." Relations with China had cooled
almost to the point of open enmity; yet Mao seemed to be speaking for the
whole anticapitalist world when he declared in the Kremlin in 1957 that "the
East Wind prevails over the West Wind." In Britain, Richard Crossman worried that the American panic over Soviet successes in rocketry would mean
"increasing polarization, another period of cold war and gigantic arms expenditure, and Western Europe tighter than ever in the Atlantic system." Three
days after the Soviets had sent Laika on her well-publicized travels in space,
Crossman recalled his meeting with Khrushchev and feared that he would
exploit "this fantastic new dominance they have acquired for aggression and
expansion."

. . . He seems to be a boss and a bully, who doesn't believe in world expansion with his
brain but will practise it in a quite sincere effort to make Russia safe. I will never forget
his contemptuous attitude to us, his couldn't-care-less suggestion that we should join
the Russians because, if not, they would swat us off the face of the earth like a dirty old
black beetle.

. . . So back we come to the idea that it might be better to opt out of that race, reckoning
that the Russians have nothing much to gain by mopping us up and could well be induced
to leave us alone. Of course, that's the sort of thing one can write in one's diary, but it
isn't the sort of thing which one can publish. . . .

On November 10, 1958, Khrushchev announced that the time had come to
end the "abnormal" state of affairs in Berlin. The occupation should be terminated. West Berlin should become a "free city" and all formalities concerning access to this enclave of capitalism deep inside the German Democratic

Republic (GDR) should be handled by the East German government. If no
agreement were reached in six months, Khrushchev explained, the Soviet
government would make its own treaty with East Germany, and the Western
Allies, whose right of access to Berlin rested on nothing more secure than
verbal wartime agreement, would have to make their own deal with the East
Germans. Khrushchev's goal was an East-West summit to retard the frightening prospect of the new German army which was now being equipped with
missiles capable of carrying nuclear warheads. (Soviet intelligence undoubtedly reported that World War II veterans recruited for the new, democratic
German army avoided wearing campaign ribbons earned on the Western front
out of deference to their new allies, but medals earned in the Soviet Union
were displayed with pride.)

The U.S. Joint Chiefs of Staff recommended that on the very day the East
Germans should stop a truck convoy, the United States must dispatch a division to shoot its way into Berlin if necessary, and to reinforce the 13,000-man
American garrison in West Berlin. Neither the French nor the British liked the
idea of negotiating with the Russians under threat, but the idea of starting
World War III over whether a passport would be stamped by a Russian soldier
or an East German bureaucrat seemed absurd. Willy Brandt, the mayor of
West Berlin, did not reject the "free city" idea out of hand. Even Dulles, who
told the Joint Chiefs that world opinion would never support the Americans
fighting a war over Berlin because of a stamp in a passport, appeared to be
willing to accept the idea of East Germans acting as "agents" for the Russians.

When Adenauer heard Dulles' surprisingly conciliatory response to
Khrushchev's ultimatum, he was meeting with General Charles de Gaulle,
now once more in power. (The Kurhaus in Bad Kreuznach, once used as
Kaiser Wilhelm's wartime headquarters, had been selected for the encounter
because it was almost exactly equidistant between De Gaulle's home at Colombey and Adenauer's residence on the Rhine.) The chancellor was shocked
that Dulles had not consulted him. To recognize East German bureaucrats for
any purpose would lead inevitably to the recognition of East Germany. So
strongly had he always felt that nothing must be done to legitimate the East
German state that he cut off relations with any government that dared to
recognize the German Democratic Republic! The Americans, Adenauer was
convinced, intimidated by Khrushchev's bluster, were weakening. In the
congressional elections of 1958 a number of liberal Democrats had won. The
solid anti-Communist consensus was crumbling.

Adenauer and De Gaulle immediately perceived their common interests.
"England is like a rich man who has lost all his property but does not realize
it," Adenauer told De Gaulle with obvious pleasure. Changes were taking
place in America, Adenauer warned. "We cannot count on the help of the
United States forever." The two men sought to flatter each other by taking the
trouble to speak a few words of the other's language, though Adenauer's
French was so execrable that the general could scarcely feign comprehension.
Adenauer had been suspicious of this "second Joan of Arc," too military and

mystical for his taste, but he found him, according to Adenauer's daughter who accompanied him, "a pleasant surprise." The general was, to be sure, a bit dramatic for Adenauer, but he was of a moral, upright character, and shrewd enough to flatter the sensitive octogenarian about his "youthful spirit." Power, Adenauer assured De Gaulle, would keep him young too.

5

Having personally negotiated the Japanese Peace Treaty, John Foster Dulles knew what he wanted from Japan. It should "stand on its own feet" economically, provide "a safe base for American military activity," as the American ambassador John Allison put it, and function as the Asian bastion of the Free World. In the early Dulles years U.S. and Japanese diplomats acted literally as ships passing in the night. Arriving in Washington with requests for substantial economic concessions, the visiting Japanese would be politely informed that if money was the problem, the Japanese should open their economy to U.S. private investors, who, incidentally, would be greatly reassured if Japan were to field a serious army. Descending on Tokyo with elaborate plans for rearmament, the Americans would be told that Japanese opinion would not support it. Indeed, the substantial Socialist minority and the left-wing students were already picturing the ally across the Pacific as "war-loving America." As U.S.–China tensions rose, more and more Japanese worried about being drawn into America's battles. Dulles' recommendation that American security could be served by letting "Asians fight Asians" was known in Japan, and thus his taunt in Tokyo that the Koreans had a bigger army than the newly established Japanese Self-Defense Force had actually the opposite of the effect intended.

With the end of the occupation and the ebbing of the Korean War boom, Japan in the mid-1950s was trying to define its security policy. The conservative majority in the Diet opposed neutralism. With the huge Soviet Union and the People's Republic of China as neighbors, conventional prudence dictated that Japan huddle under America's "nuclear umbrella," despite the widespread revulsion against the atomic bomb. But from the first the Pacific alliance was beset by contradictions more serious than its Atlantic counterpart. The most vulnerable of the great industrial countries, dependent upon massive imports of fuel, food, and industrial raw materials, Japan had no choice but to revive its prewar policy: Japan could be secure only within some sort of Asian "coprosperity sphere." The means for creating such a community would be peaceful, but Japan's long-term interests required her to act independent of her protector and sometimes even in subtle opposition. As the shock of defeat was wearing off, the presence of large numbers of American troops on the home islands was becoming an increasingly distasteful reminder that Japan's fate was not yet completely in her own hands. The rapes, homicides, and traffic accidents that are the inevitable by-product of even well-behaved armies—and the U.S. garrison in Japan during the Korean War was not especially well-behaved—now began to fan old feelings of nationalism and hurt pride. When the Americans decided to expand the air base at Sunagawa, Japanese farmers in the area formed a human chain to prevent the Japanese government from even surveying the areas. Residents near Mount Fuji protested the incessant artillery practice under the shadow of the mountain. "You Americans forced us to disarm not only physically and legally but spiritually. Then Dulles reviled us for not rearming faster!" a cabinet vice-minister complained to a visiting professor in 1953. "The occupation wanted to destroy Japanese militarism, but went so far as to undermine the patriotism on which any nation's self-defense must be built. Can you blame us for being confused and a bit angry when America has pushed us in such opposite directions over the past few years?"

On March 1, 1954, the tuna boat *Lucky Dragon,* well outside the designated fallout zone announced by the United States in advance of the first hydrogen bomb test at Bikini atoll, received a heavy dose of radioactive volcanic ash. The radio operator died of radiation effects and several others were seriously injured. The Japanese government protested, but infuriated many Japanese by publicly endorsing further tests "in order to protect the security of the free nations." The incident gave a focus to the still deep antinuclear anxieties and fanned the growing anti-American sentiments. With the end of the Korean War and the death of Stalin, skepticism about the American protector, as measured in public opinion polls conducted by the huge national daily, *Asahi,* was rising steeply.

Eager to restore the huge China market as a major outlet for its exports, Japanese politicians resisted the trade embargo which the United States had urged on all its Allies. Dulles argued strenuously for opening up the U.S. market to Japan to deflect her interest from China, but Eisenhower, worried about Japanese goods flooding the country, had different ideas. At a cabinet meeting on August 6, 1954, Ike expressed the view that Japan should be encouraged to trade "with the neighboring Red areas in Asia. . . . If China, for example, finds that it can buy cheap straw hats, cheap cotton shirts, sneakers, bicycles, and all the rest of that sort of stuff from Japan, it would seem to me that that would set up the need within China for dependence upon Japan. . . . [A]nyone who says that to trade with a Red country is in effect advocating a traitorous act just doesn't know what he is talking about."

In the Dulles State Department, however, the influence of the "China Lobby" was strong; there was considerable pressure to look at Asian problems through the eyes of Chiang Kai-shek, the deposed leader of the Nationalist regime. The worry was the Communist enemy on the mainland, not Japan, which was viewed primarily as a piece of strategic territory that could be critical in a future war. Your country is Russia's "most desired prize," an assistant secretary of defense told Japanese cabinet officials in 1953. Unless the defeated nation speedily rearmed, Soviet and Chinese forces 500,000 strong would probably "come into Japan with lightning attack." Japan being a staging area for the Korean War had left the economy with islands of prosperity. Between 1951 and 1953 Japan received an infusion of $2.2 billion for machinery, metals, chemicals, lumber, and textiles needed for the war effort. Arsenals, weapons research laboratories, and factories for producing tanks, aircraft, machine guns, ammunition, and sophisticated military communications equipment confiscated during the occupation, were returned to their owners and began producing for the Americans. Soon 72 percent of the productive facilities of the nation were devoted to the manufacture of weapons.

But the Japanese had not yet attained prewar living standards. Japanese politicians understood that maintaining large-scale military forces would ruin the chance to turn the still shaky economy into something solid and would alienate most of the population in the process. Most Japanese were strongly anti-Soviet, for the USSR had refused to give back the southern half of Sakhalin Island and the Kuriles, whose territorial waters had been the source of half the prewar Japanese salmon catch. But they did not believe that the Russians were coming to Japan.

Having cabled ahead to Tokyo to make sure that there were throngs of Japanese schoolchildren waving Japanese and American flags along the fifteen-mile route from the airport, Richard Nixon arrived in late 1953. In a speech at a Tokyo luncheon, the vice president declared flatly that General MacArthur's contribution to the Japanese constitution, the antiwar provision, was a mistake. Nixon's public intervention into an internal Japanese controversy showed that, psychologically speaking, the occupation had not ended. In the words of the U.S. ambassador at the time, John Allison, Washington officials looked upon Japan as "a forward bastion of American strategic strength with the Americans calling the tune and the Japanese meekly accepting their secondary role."

In 1954 the pro-American Prime Minister Shigeru Yoshida finally retired. The man who helped ease him out of office became the dominant political figure of the late 1950s. Nobusuke Kishi was a cold, intense figure with outsized ears and a crumpled chin whose toothy look soon became a cartoonist's cliché. As conservative and anti-Communist as Yoshida, his prewar experience left him with a quite different view of the world. As Yoshida had bravely opposed the war, Kishi had been instrumental in planning it. A protégé of the wartime prime minister Hideki Tojo, for whom he had worked in developing Japanese industry in occupied Manchuria, Kishi was minister of industry and commerce. He believed that Southeast Asia with its material resources, especially oil, had to be gathered into Japan's rapidly expanding "coprosperity sphere" by force of arms and that if the United States tried to obstruct this security strategy, war was unavoidable. Descended from a family of warriors, Kishi was well-connected. His uncle, Yosuke Matsuoka, who had run the Manchurian railway, became Tojo's foreign minister and concluded the Axis agreement with Hitler. Kishi strongly supported the decision to attack Pearl Harbor and then threw himself wholeheartedly into running the Japanese war industry. But by the time the Americans had captured Saipan in April 1944 he knew the strategy had failed. He went to Tojo and told him to his face that surrender was unavoidable. But when the enraged warrior politician refused even to consider such a course, Kishi helped engineer his old mentor's removal. For Japanese diehards Kishi was a defeatist, but as far as the occupation authorities were concerned, he was a Class A war criminal. For three years he sat cross-legged in a prison cell awaiting trial, writing wistful poems, and devouring disturbing reports of MacArthur's revolution. Then suddenly he was a free man. On December 24, 1948, Kishi walked out of Sugamo prison, the beneficiary of a sudden shift in U.S. policy. With China revealed as a hopelessly corrupt and ineffectual ally and about to fall to the Communists, the Americans were no longer interested in punishing or reforming Japan but in "cranking up" Japan as the principal Asian ally in the Cold War. Kishi was taken from the prison in an army jeep to the prime minister's residence, where his brother, Eisaku Sato, served as Yoshida's chief secretary. His business friends immediately offered him directorships in several companies, and for several years he repaired his fortune while waiting to be "depurged."

As the occupation ended, he officially reentered politics. "I have buried my past," he announced. Determined to get rid of the MacArthur constitution, Kishi was committed to restoring Japan's national pride. The "coprosperity sphere" was still essential, but it could not be achieved with arms. The key to prosperity in Asia, he once said, was "American capital, Japanese technology and local resources." In his campaign to make himself a key political figure once more, he set off in February 1953 on a fact-finding visit to Germany. Impressed that Germany still had national pride and faith in the future, he told a radio audience on his return:

The Germans say they have little respect for American culture and do not like many of the Americans, but that they do not show their anti-Americanism because they need America's aid to reconstruct the country. The Germans have mature minds. They are adults. . . . Of course, as Germany has been defeated many times in the past and after each defeat has reconstructed itself, the people don't feel so deeply about being beaten. On the other hand, Japan was defeated in the last war for the first time in its three-thousand-year history, so it is natural that we should be more dejected and timid. Moreover, General MacArthur's policies helped to foster an inferior feeling. But now that foreign countries are beginning to accept us as equals, this feeling should be eliminated. . . .

Kishi refused a portfolio in the cabinet of Prime Minister Ichirō Hatoyama, the man who succeeded Yoshida, but behind the scenes he pressed his policy: independence but with a pro-American tilt. To dramatize the independence he supported the government's decision to reestablish relations with the Soviet Union. In 1955 he went on an official mission to Washington to reassure Dulles about what the Japanese meant by "independence" and to press for a revision of the security treaty with the United States, then barely four years old. The State Department was concerned that Japan might increasingly tie its economy to the China trade, particularly since the end of the Korean War had brought a potentially serious recession. To strengthen Japanese ties with the West, the Eisenhower administration offered aid in financing the buildup of

Japanese security forces and promised to keep military procurement dollars flowing to Japan. But on the symbolic issues about which Kishi cared most deeply—the American military presence in Japan, the Bonin and Ryukyu islands, especially Okinawa—the Americans refused to budge. Indeed, the prospect of an undefeated army in North Korea, the shock of the recent French debacle in Indochina at the hands of the Vietminh, and the memories of the waves of Chinese troops pouring across the Yalu River, reinforced the determination of U.S. military planners to keep the bases in Japan and in Okinawa as long as a "Communist threat" existed. Dulles had been prevailed upon not to push so hard for rearmament by wiser State Department hands, who knew that promilitary Japanese politicians were not necessarily pro-American, and by Japan's nervous Asian neighbors, but this shift in emphasis made it seem all the more necessary to retain a large U.S. military presence. Kishi returned to Tokyo with his flattering clippings from *Newsweek*—"unlike most Japanese [he] moves swiftly and boldly"—and a new argument for unifying the conservatives of Japan: the United States would not listen to Japanese politicians unless they spoke from a position of domestic strength.

Two years later the former war planner was prime minister. Yoshida had seen the American alliance as the key to Japan's strategy of recovery; Kishi saw the elimination of the last vestiges of the occupation as the mark of Japan's complete rehabilitation. During a visit with Eisenhower in 1957 that included a round of golf with the president, Kishi repeated the demands he had politely put forward two years earlier: U.S. ground troops should leave Japan. Okinawa should be returned to Japan. United States bases in Japan could be kept, but the Japanese government would have to be consulted before they were used for war purposes. He desperately wanted a new security treaty embodying these provisions that would crown his career.

Fortunately the Americans were now ready to make all the major concessions asked of them except for Okinawa. The Japanese would be accorded "residual" sovereignty, but the island would remain in the hands of the U.S. military for the indefinite future. In January 1960 Kishi flew again to Washington to sign the new treaty, now happily free of the condescending language Dulles had insisted upon nine years earlier. To dramatize the new stage in U.S.–Japanese relations, Crown Prince Akihito and President Eisenhower agreed to exchange state visits.

When the original security treaty was signed in 1951, there had been little opposition. The text was kept secret until the signing, and its demeaning provisions had little impact because public attention was focused on the good news that the occupation was at last over. But in 1960 the situation was different. While most business leaders strongly supported the treaty on the ground that the American alliance was essential to prosperity, a growing number of intellectuals, religious organizations, labor unions, and, especially, the Socialist party of Japan disapproved the treaty largely on the ground that it might well drag Japan into war. The United States and China were engaged at the time in a war of words over Quemoy and Ma-tsu, tiny islands off the coast of

China still occupied by the Nationalists. The Soviets had just shot down an American spy plane over the Soviet Union, and the Paris Summit meeting in the spring of 1960 between Eisenhower, Macmillan, De Gaulle and Khrushchev had ended in angry words. All this heightened the fear of war in Japan. To tie up so closely with "war-loving" America when China was the closest neighbor involved great risk that Japan could become the Quemoy and Ma-tsu of the 1960s. The press began to attack the treaty. A group of presidents of corporations in the textile and machinery field eager to do business with China joined the opposition. As the day for the ratification vote in the Diet approached, thousands of petitions with almost two million signatures denouncing the treaty arrived at the parliament.

Kishi, who had already scheduled the triumphal visit of the American president, grew desperate. On May 19 the treaty was hurriedly approved in committee with only members of Kishi's party present, and when it was brought to a vote on the floor the Socialists staged a sit-in. Five hundred policemen removed the Socialists from the chamber, whereupon the treaty was unanimously approved by the remaining Liberal-Democrats. Most of the business establishment publicly supported Kishi in this naked bid to establish one-party rule, but privately many feared that his high-handed methods jeopardized conservative control of Japan. The national dailies began withering attacks on Kishi, demanding his resignation. On June 4 all mines and transportation services across the country were shut down for two hours. The Socialists continued to boycott the Diet. Hundreds of the leading professors in the country called for the prime minister's resignation, and three former prime ministers called for the postponement of Eisenhower's visit. In the United States, Senator Warren Magnuson reported that he had received word from Japanese business leaders urging the president not to come.

However, Secretary of State Herter told the Senate Foreign Relations Committee in closed session that Kishi's survival depended upon the president's visit and warned that "if a government friendly to the United States were to fall because of pressures brought to bear by International Communism, it would have a serious effect on America's prestige and the defense of Asia." James Hagerty, the president's press secretary, arrived in Tokyo on June 10 to make final preparations. As his limousine reached the main gate of the airport, a mob of 10,000, mostly left-wing students carrying sticks, chanting the "Internationale," and screaming curses at Eisenhower, descended upon the car, beating at the windows, clambering onto the roof, tearing at the antennae, and rocking it from side to side. It took almost a half hour for a helicopter to whisk Hagerty and the American ambassador away from the howling crowd.

Kishi promised to clear the entire city, stop all traffic, and have 27,000 policemen patrol the streets if the president would still be willing to come. But the crisis grew. Five days later a crowd of 7000 organized by the left-wing student group Zengakuren forced their way into the Diet, despite the presence of some 19,000 policemen in the area, and a young woman was trampled to death in the rush. Advisers to the emperor's household began worrying about

Hirohito's safety, for he was scheduled to ride with Eisenhower. More than 5 million workers went out on strike. Kishi now had no alternative but to cancel the invitation. As 22,000 students surrounded his residence threatening to storm their way inside at the stroke of midnight when the treaty was to go into effect, Kishi made his decision to resign. But the crowd dispersed, and the prime minister spent the next four days in office rounding up his ministers at teahouses to get the necessary signatures on the instruments of ratification before announcing his resignation. As he was about to hand over his office to his successor, Kishi was stabbed five times in the thigh by a right-wing nationalist.

6

A year had passed since the debacle at Suez. Harold Macmillan, the new prime minister, had managed to establish a much improved working relationship with Eisenhower and Dulles. "Foster Dulles . . . realizes that America cannot stand alone, still less 'go it alone'," Macmillan noted in his diary on October 23, 1957. "I responded with quite a romantic picture of what U.S. and U.K. could do together. . . . not to rule but to serve the world." The Republican administration was under increasingly severe attack, the prime minister noted with some satisfaction, and now "realises that their attitude over the Canal issue was fatal and led necessarily to the Suez situation." Eisenhower and Dulles realized no such thing, but they were indeed interested in repairing relations with Britain. Macmillan's sensitivity to the "ominous note of confidence and truculence" in Khrushchev's diplomatic pronouncements was shared in Washington. Eisenhower stunned the prime minister by his new willingness to share certain atomic secrets with Britain, a recognition to be given no other country. For *The Times* (London) the sudden burst of sunshine in Anglo-American relations evoked memories of the great wartime conferences of Cairo and Casablanca. The queen had visited the United States, too, and left in triumph. "She has buried George III for good and all," the British ambassador reported to London.

With France, however, the situation was different. In the midst of World War II the United States had staked out certain interests in North Africa, and these increasingly began to clash with French interests. The bases which the United States established in Morocco during the war were expanded in the 1950s at a cost of about $500 million, despite continuing French efforts to limit the number of U.S. military personnel in their protectorate. A surprising number of Americans who had been stationed in Morocco decided to stay and go into some sort of export-import business. Under an 1836 treaty, American traders in Morocco were exempt from local law, and every American administration until Moroccan independence was granted insisted on retaining the rights of extraterritoriality. So suspicious of American designs were the French that they refused all U.S. technical assistance for North Africa under the Marshall Plan.

Meanwhile, a national independence movement grew. Enough well-placed bombs exploded in the cities to convince the French that a full-scale guerrilla war was in the offing, and they decided to pull out of Morocco. Independence was granted on March 2, 1956. In Paris the satisfaction of the United States was apparent—and irritating.

The United States had no military bases in Tunisia, and the State Department loyally supported the French in the United Nations in the early 1950s whenever the issue of Tunisian independence was raised. But the French, having decided that the real stand on behalf of French influence in North Africa must be made in Algeria, also gave Tunisia its independence in 1956. Habib Bourguiba, the fiery nationalist leader who became president, was openly and enthusiastically pro-American. Vice-President Nixon visited Tunis and offered a few small arms, a slap in the face to the French, who had refused to provide any because the Tunisians were supporting Algerian independence. When the arms shipment to Bourguiba of 500 M-1 rifles and 50,000 rounds of ammunition and a few British machine guns was announced, anti-American feeling in Paris ran so high that 500 steel-helmeted police from the riot squad were ordered to form a phalanx in front of the American embassy. "We cannot be the ally in Europe and the scapegoat in Africa," the acid comment of the ex-premier Georges Bidault summed up the popular feeling.

By 1957 the war in Algeria had imperiled French society much in the way that the Vietnam War would shake American society. Ten years later French observers would cheerfully point out the similarities. Across the political spectrum it was widely believed that keeping Algeria French was a strategic necessity. The Allies "have not understood it with sufficient clarity . . . that meanwhile the Mediterranean has become the axis of our security," François Mitterrand declared in the Assembly on September 30, 1957. "It is no longer the Rhine." The Americans were, of course, quite aware that the French had an army in Algeria close to 500,000 men and that only a handful of French troops remained to man the NATO ramparts in Europe. Just as the French would dismiss Lyndon Johnson's rhetoric a decade later that in Vietnam he was defending San Francisco, so in 1957 the idea, as an article in Le Figaro put it, that "by taking sides against us in Algeria, you abandon North Africa to the Russians" was greeted with skepticism in Washington. The private American analysis was exactly the opposite. Supporting Algerian national independence was the best way to keep the Russians out.

According to French law, Algeria was part of France. Hundreds of thousands of Frenchmen had lived there for a century. Even the French Communist party, until finally ordered by Moscow to do so, could not bring itself to support the dismemberment of France. Yet even before the Second World War had ended, the military had left such bloody traces in Algeria that many Frenchmen could not reconcile empire and conscience. While the victory celebrations were under way in Paris during the first week of May 1945, French artillery and aircraft were turned on Muslim crowds in Algiers demonstrating for the release of a nationalist leader from prison. When calm was restored, 1500 lay dead, according to official estimates; the nationalists themselves claimed that 45,000 had been killed. As the Algerian uprising spread after 1954, French repression grew. Robert Lacoste, the minister for Algeria, always claiming that the war is "in its last quarter of an hour," increasingly encouraged the use of torture to break the revolution. "French policemen can recall by their behavior the methods of the Gestapo," the director of the Sûreté Nationale in Algiers wrote his superior in Paris.

French authorities believed that the alliance obligated the United States to support their effort to put down insurrection in the "French departments of North Africa," as the NATO treaty itself had described Algeria, Morocco, and Tunisia. Indeed, one of the most important original contingencies for which NATO military forces were established was the suppression of domestic rebellion. But the world did not consider what was happening in Algiers to be a domestic fight. Thus while the United States publicly supported France and dutifully abstained from votes in the UN to condemn French "genocide," CIA operatives were making contact with the leaders of the National Liberation Front (FLN) the Algerian revolutionary movement. Aware that the nationalist movement in Algeria was more proletarian and more radical than its counterparts in Morocco or Tunisia, the CIA operatives were convinced that, despite FLN leader Ahmed Ben Bella's visit to Khrushchev, the Russians had little influence and that revolutionary Algeria need not be anti-American. So solicitous of the FLN was the Central Intelligence Agency that in 1961, at a critical stage of the final negotiations with De Gaulle for ending the war, the agency flew Frantz Fanon, the brilliant theoretician of the movement who was dying of cancer, to the National Institutes of Health near Washington for a final heroic effort to save his life. When he died, a CIA officer flew from Europe to attend the funeral. The modest clandestine efforts in behalf of the Algerians infuriated De Gaulle.

In July 1957 Senator John F. Kennedy made a speech in the Senate in which he declared that Algeria was no longer a French problem alone and that if the West was to have "a continuing influence in North Africa . . . the essential first step is the independence of Algeria." Dean Acheson attacked him for imperiling the unity of NATO; De Gaulle took note of this impetuous young man so ready to be a crusader in other countries' wars.

On May 13, 1958, a coup took place in Algiers, "the most peculiar colonial rebellion of modern times," Janet Flanner called it, because it was a rightist movement in behalf of a million French *colons,* not for independence, but to prevent it. Unlike the usual riot in Algiers when Frenchmen would set the torch to the Moslem quarters, this time the target was the French government building. General Raoul Salan, the commander in Algeria, established a Committee for Public Safety and called for General de Gaulle to assume power. The French president, René Coty, urged the country to accept the general as the only salvation for France. Communist demonstrations against him were swiftly organized. "Put the giraffe in a zoo!" "Down with De Gaulle!" From Colombey the general wrote that he would take power only under a new constitution. Warning of civil war and anarchy, he declared that those who would "prevent me once more from saving the Republic will bear a heavy responsibility." Narrowly invested with the power he demanded, De Gaulle went to Algiers, and from the balcony of the Forum delivered the Delphic phrase that would drive some of the same cheering *colons* assembled below to attempt his assassination. "I have understood you." He thereupon proceeded to initiate the process of Algerian independence which culminated in the Evian agreements of 1962 and the mass exodus of the *colons* from Algeria. An issue that threatened to split the North Atlantic partnership was thereby removed. But the general had his own ideas in mind for the alliance.

7

With the EDC in ruins, the indefatigable Jean Monnet had taken up the fight for European unity in a new guise. Meeting in Messina in June 1955, the foreign ministers of the Coal and Steel Community nations at his prodding laid the basis for an ambitious Common Market, which two years later came into being with the signing of the Treaty of Rome. The elaborate structure for encouraging the free market of goods, capital, and workers within the European Economic Community (EEC) was intended by Monnet as a critical step toward political union. Dulles had given strong support to the Common Market largely for political reasons. A Common Market within the "Atlantic Community" was an alternative political vision to a reunified Germany, now increasingly seen in Washington as both unattainable and undesirable. Speaking to an American television audience but directing his veiled threat to Europe, Dulles, in his first statement as secretary of state, noted that the United States "has made a big investment in Western Europe on the theory that there could be unity there" and promised to do "a little rethinking" if unity were not possible.

The conventional wisdom in United States government circles was that the EEC was a wholly positive development. It provided an economic straitjacket for Germany which the Germans themselves would welcome. It would legitimate and encourage the development of liberal capitalism in Europe. Expanded trade would lead to greater efficiency and productivity and so build broad public support for the free enterprise system. Neither advantage could be stated too crudely. The United States was still officially committed to the reunification of Germany. And American diplomats were well aware that Socialist opposition in France had killed the EDC. Therefore, as Lawrence B. Krause of the Brookings Institution notes in his study *European Economic Integration and the United States,* "the promoters of the EEC went out of their way to play down the free enterprise characteristics of the treaty and emphasized that the Community would be perfectly compatible with national planning of the French type. . . ." (After all, Jean Monnet was the architect of both.) The Pentagon was all for the EEC because it would stabilize European recovery and because a prosperous Europe would be willing to pay more for defense. The Common Market also reinforced the ideological commitments of the NATO members. Since the stated purpose of the alliance was to defend a somewhat ineffable "Western civilization," the more concretely the liberal values of "the West" could be embodied in institutions that kept men free while they made them rich, the better it would all be for the global balance of power.

The problems which the American planners had foreseen were almost entirely political. The European Economic Community might come to see itself as a Third Force: for this reason virtually every American endorsement was premised on the revitalization of the "Atlantic Community" or development of "Atlantic Partnership." The attraction of East-West trade, it was feared, might also weaken anti-Communist zeal. But the economic implications for the United States were, as Krause concludes, "given very little weight." Indeed Christian A. Herter, writing in 1963, concluded that "little attention had been given in this country to the European Common Market and to its far-reaching implications."

Ironically, the Common Market for which the United States had so vigorously pushed—American ambassadors in key European capitals quietly lent their services to Jean Monnet by pressing recalcitrant businessmen and politicians to support the new Europe—actually helped to split Europe. Britain, for essentially the same reasons that she had refused to join the Coal and Steel Community, remained aloof, and by the time she sought to enter, De Gaulle barred the way. Because Britain was not a member, her traditional trading partners such as Portugal and the Scandinavian countries also stayed outside. Since Monnet always trumpeted the EEC as more a political than an economic union, traditional neutrals such as Sweden and Switzerland and the recently neutralized Austria felt that they could not join.

The Swedes took the initiative in the late Eisenhower years to create a European Free Trade Association embracing Britain, Portugal, and her Scandinavian neighbors. "We must not be bullied by the activities of the Six," Prime Minister Harold Macmillan wrote the chancellor of the exchequer as he launched his own diplomatic offensive for "Plan G," an effort to link the Six with the rest of Europe in a wider free-trade area. But the British, it soon developed, were being squeezed by an unlikely coalition of "good Europeans," who refused to extend the economic privileges of the Common Market to any nations unwilling to assume its political obligations and ideology, and of Gaullists who saw Britain as an American Trojan horse that would undercut the very political and economic independence which for them justified the EEC's existence. Three months before De Gaulle assumed power, Reginald Maudling, the British negotiator, had concluded that the French were "determined to wreck" the negotiations "partly out of weakness, but mostly out of jealousy and spite." The French, Macmillan was convinced, "have been pouring . . . poison" into Adenauer's ears. De Gaulle, "grown rather fat, calm, affable, and rather paternal,'' as the prime minister found him soon after his accession to power, was "neither interested nor impressed" with the British arguments. That was to be expected, perhaps, but the Americans seemed more interested in negotiating tariff agreements for themselves and pressing for political federation with the Common Market countries than in healing the split in Europe and heading off what Macmillan believed to be the devastating trade war in the offing. "I am an expansionist," he wrote Eisenhower's secretary of treasury George Humphrey in November 1958. "I do not believe the Free world will ultimately stand up against Communism unless the overall level of our trade keeps going up. Nor shall we attract the underdeveloped countries if we pay them wretched prices for their raw materials, and occasionally give them loans."

In a memo to the foreign secretary, the prime minister noted, "The Germans and French have made an unholy alliance against the British" and the United States "seem uninterested. . . . In April we are to celebrate a jubilee of NATO [the tenth anniversary]. It will be a rather hollow ceremony as far as we are concerned." In March 1960, two months before a summit conference with the Soviets was scheduled to begin in Paris, Macmillan flew to Washington to plead with Eisenhower to come to Britain's aid and to head off the forces on the Continent that were once again, as in the days of Napoleon and Hitler, ganging up on the island power. But Eisenhower was far more interested in the approaching meeting with Khrushchev and the resolution of the Berlin crisis than in the complexities of tariffs and trade, and he turned a deaf ear. By the time his young successor had had his rocking chair moved into the Oval Office, it was clear beyond doubt that the United States lacked a practical view of the new Europe and how the world's most powerful nation-state should relate to it. The thirteen-year enthusiasm for European integration had produced neither a united Europe nor, as it would soon become clear, one easily subjected to American power.

FIVE

YOUNG MEN'S DREAMS AND OLD MEN'S VISIONS:

Mr. Kennedy and General de Gaulle

1

"He is quick, well-informed, subtle . . . proceeds more by asking questions than by answering them," Harold Macmillan noted in his diary after a dinner at Buckingham Palace with President Kennedy in June 1961. The prime minister, battling gout and feeling his age, had expected that he "should inevitably appear a 'stuff-shirt' or a 'square' " to the young American leader, and he was grateful for Kennedy's unfailing courtesy. When the election results had arrived in London seven months earlier, Macmillan had dashed off a note to the foreign secretary on how to handle Kennedy. With Eisenhower, whom he had known for twenty years, one could "appeal to memories." With this new president we must "make our contacts in the realm of ideas."

But though he was at home with ideas, John F. Kennedy did not come to the White House burdened with many. Unlike Eisenhower, who brought with him a curious mixture of conventional prejudice and astute insight gathered in a long career, John Kennedy came with little of either. He was clear about what he admired. Physical and moral courage. He had won a medal demonstrating the first when his PT boat had been cut in two by a Japanese destroyer during the war and a Pulitzer Prize writing *Profiles in Courage* about the second. A certain high-powered intellectual style. He was attracted to fast talkers; the Kennedy aides, Bundy, Rostow, Sorensen, perfected a machine-gun patter for delivering their advice. He himself could read 1200 words a minute and was impatient with those who spoke too slowly or too much. A Whiggish detachment. He was charmed by the cool wit and offhand elegance he had found as a young man in the country homes of prewar England. Fiercely competitive, he had a tragic sense of how little could be done. His jottings in his reporter's notebook at the San Francisco conference to establish the United Nations reveal a cool pessimism at odds with the euphoria of the day. "Danger of too great a buildup. Mustn't expect too much. . . . There is no cure all." In the presidency, Kennedy was determined to project an image of vigor, dynamism, and health, though he was often perplexed and almost always in pain. So little had he developed his own world view, indeed so resistant was he to thinking in ideological terms at all, that by the time he ascended to power he found himself embracing the Cold War wisdom of the elder statesmen of the Democratic party, leavened by the tactical advice of the young professors from Harvard and the Massachusetts Institute of Technology (MIT), who spoke of themselves without irony as practitioners of excellence.

The world view of Kennedy's New Frontier rested on a few fundamentals. The country must "get moving again." This required expansionary economic policies at home and these in turn required a new and more solid politico-economic relationship with Europe. For George Ball, Monnet's old friend and lawyer, this was the historic moment to rebuild the Atlantic Community. De Gaulle was the spoiler who must be artfully exposed. For Dean Acheson, it was a time for the new president to correct the impression of weakness that Eisenhower had given. Dulles' ineffectual bluster had emboldened Khrushchev to threaten Berlin. Since the 1960 campaign had been fought in part on the existence of a dangerous "missile gap," all advisers agreed that there must be a big new push in defense spending. It soon developed that there was no missile gap, but by that time a new rationale for a major defense buildup had been accepted by the administration.

The Kennedy strategists were shocked at the Eisenhower "wargasm" strategy. The supersecret SIOP (Single Integrated Operational Plan), the targeting plan for nuclear weapons, dictated that in the event of war they would all be fired. Indeed there were technical difficulties in doing anything else. Franz Josef Strauss, the German defense minister, reminded the Kennedy officials that Admiral Radford, the chairman of the Joint Chiefs of Staff, had personally assured him that "if a single communist soldier stepped over the frontier into the west, the United States would respond immediately with all-out nuclear war against the communist bloc." That was the strategic absurdity that had caused Maxwell Taylor to resign as chief of staff of the army. Now he was back as Kennedy's personal general committed to the idea of limited war as the answer to Khruschchev's strategy.

The Soviets, as Kennedy himself had noted in the Senate two years before his election, were not going to start a nuclear war but would resort to "Sputnik diplomacy, limited brushfire wars, indirect non-overt aggression, intimidation and subversion, internal revolution." Taylor's recommendation that "we must have the means to deter or to win small wars" meant that the new administration would build up conventional forces in Europe, antiguerrilla forces for the struggle in Asia and Africa, and a new generation of nuclear weapons that could be sufficiently controlled for a "flexible response." "The greater our variety of weapons," the president said, "the more political choices we can

make in any given situation." Eisenhower had worried that the Soviet goal
was a "bankrupt America," but the neo-Keynesians thought that the balanced
budget was a Republican superstition and that vast public spending programs
emanating from the Pentagon could be a tonic for the sluggish economy which
Eisenhower had left them.

Elected by a paper-thin margin, Kennedy knew that there was no consensus on domestic policy. So pervasive was the sense of drift proclaimed in the
Eisenhower years by columnists and social critics that Ike had directed a
Commission on National Goals to articulate a national purpose that might
galvanize the country. But its windy reports, though heavily publicized, electrified no one; intellectuals and commentators greeted them with derision. Now
the torch had passed, as Kennedy had put it in his inaugural address, to a new
generation, tempered by a disillusioning war and a "hard and bitter peace."
The men of the New Frontier knew what the national purpose was: to continue
the fight for civilization against Communism just as in Dulles' time. But while
the old moralist saw Moscow as a unique evil, the Kennedy pragmatists, as
they liked to call themselves, saw the Soviet Union as an inevitable historic
adversary, neither a soul to be converted nor a disease to be eradicated, but a
formidable competitor to test the cunning and nerve of America's new leaders.
The most crucial arena of conflict, Kennedy believed, would be the fight for
the soul of the developing nations of Asia and Africa and Latin America. How
they organized themselves—whether they would be open to U.S. ideas and
U.S. capital—would decide the global balance of power, perhaps for the rest
of the century. Khrushchev's boasts about "overtaking" the United States,
the Soviet space exploits, and his exuberant declaration two weeks before
Kennedy took office that "there is no longer any force in the world capable of
barring the road to Socialism" seemed to pose a historic challenge and to
provide a made-to-order national goal.

An admirer of style, Kennedy loved listening to his wife read aloud from
De Gaulle's memoirs. He even tried incorporating into his own speeches some
of the grandiloquence of the general, a figure to emulate but impossible to deal
with. What do you do with a man who kept saying that he was France? (If I
were not, De Gaulle had snapped at Churchill during the war, why would you
be talking to me?) Tall, grave, and unbending, so perfectly did De Gaulle
master the powerful passions within him that he rarely displayed emotion
except for effect. "The man of action," the young tank officer had written in
1932, "is inconceivable without a strong dose of egoism, pride, hard-hearted-
ness and guile." He had shown exemplary heroism in the First World War and
extraordinary prescience in the second. The Maginot Line, the chain of fixed
fortifications that was the pride of the French army, struck him as a strategic
delusion, and he had predicted exactly where the Nazis' tank battalions would
strike. His political career that began when he was forty-nine was built on risk
and rebellion. After the fall of France he broke ranks and escaped to London,
and from a BBC studio proclaimed that France had merely lost a battle but
would win the war. During the battle for Europe he continually jousted with

Churchill, Stalin, Eisenhower, and Roosevelt over the future of France, always reaching for that special "something," which he had written long before, "others cannot altogether fathom, which puzzles them, stirs them, and rivets their attention." Great leaders like Caesar and Napoleon "have always stage-managed their effects."

The cultivation of mystery came easily to him. France was "like the princess in the fairy stories [or] the Madonna in the frescoes." No large-scale human endeavor could be anything but "arbitrary and ephemeral" without the seal of France. But, as the writer François Mauriac noted, De Gaulle had an eccentric view of the nation; he never confused France with the French. Indeed, for De Gaulle, great nations like China, Russia, and Germany were immutable; they put on ideologies like clothes and sooner or later they would take them off. While the French people were trapped in the mediocrity of the Fourth Republic, he alone was the incarnation of France. On January 29, 1960, at the moment of the uprising of the *colons* in Algiers, he appealed for support in the name of "the national legitimacy that I have embodied for twenty years," a legitimacy that resided not in the office he had held but in his person. He refused a medal at the end of the war on the ground that the state cannot decorate itself. "As you know," he told a visiting delegation from the Académie française that had come to offer his election to that august body, "De Gaulle cannot belong to any category, nor receive any distinction."

Unlike Kennedy, for whom the presidency was a high-pressure schoolroom that offered his first serious experience in world affairs, De Gaulle had spent a lifetime thinking about the future of Europe, and much of the previous twenty years plotting strategies for assuring France's greatness by challenging the Great Powers, particularly the Americans. Though he had boundless confidence in her possibilities, he had a realistic assessment of France's present limitations. It is not, he would say, the France of Louis XIV or Napoleon. But, like Victor Hugo, he believed that one day Paris would be the spiritual capital of a Europe forged neither by marching armies nor by the supranational schemes of ambitious technocrats, but by the historic pull of a common civilization. This Europe would be the natural extension of France and would take its place as the world's third superpower.

This was what we were aiming for in the vast arena of Europe. . . . Being all of the same white race, with the same Christian origins and the same way of life, linked to one another since time immemorial by countless ties of thought, art, science, politics and trade, it was natural that they should come to form a whole, with its own character and organization in relation to the rest of the world. . . . It was my belief that a united Europe could not today, any more than in previous times, be a fusion of its peoples, but that it could and should result from a systematic *rapprochement*. Everything prompted them towards this in an age of proliferating trade, international enterprises, science and technology which know no frontiers, rapid communications and widespread travel. My policy therefore aimed at the setting up of a concert of European States which in developing all sorts of ties between them would increase their interdependence and solidarity. From this starting-point, there was every reason to believe that the process of evolution might lead to their confederation, especially if they were one day to be threatened from the same source.

De Gaulle, as he explained in his memoirs, saw NATO as the price the Americans had exacted for the Marshall Plan. The U.S. guarantee to defend Europe, vague and ultimately unreliable as it was after the Soviets acquired their own nuclear weapons, was nonetheless an insurance policy. It would be imprudent to reject it out of hand. Thus De Gaulle never wavered in his commitment to the idea of a Western alliance. But NATO as an organization was too costly a premium because the so-called integrated command was completely subject to the direction of the Americans and membership greatly circumscribed the freedom of the members to pursue their own policies. Europe united around supranational institutions would inevitably be "a stateless system, incapable by its very nature of having its own defense or foreign policy" and hence "would inevitably be obliged to follow the dictates of America."

My aim, then, was to disengage France, not from the Atlantic alliance, which I intended to maintain by way of ultimate precaution, but from the integration realized by NATO under American command; to establish relations with each of the States of the Eastern bloc, first and foremost Russia, with the object of bringing about a *detente* followed by understanding and co-operation; to do likewise, when the time was ripe, with China; and finally, to provide France with a nuclear capability such that no one could attack us without running the risk of frightful injury. But I was anxious to proceed gradually, linking each stage with overall developments and continuing to cultivate France's traditional friendships.

In September 1958 he had begun his campaign to break the American hold on Europe. He sent off a memorandum to Eisenhower and Macmillan proposing a triple-headed directorate for the alliance to replace the "special relationship" of Anglo-Saxons that now set the global strategy for the West. If his proposal were not accepted, De Gaulle made it clear that he would reserve the right to renegotiate the alliance or leave it. "As I expected, the two recipients of my memorandum replied evasively. So there was nothing to prevent us from taking action." Step by step he disengaged. In March 1959 he withdrew the French Mediterranean fleet from the NATO command. He put a ban on American atomic weapons in France while he stepped up efforts to produce his own. The troops returning from North Africa did not rejoin their NATO divisions. De Gaulle kept reiterating the point that the defense of France must be in French hands, as he told the students at the Military Academy on November 3, 1959. "In everything that constitutes a nation, and principally in what constitutes ours, nothing is more important than defense."

When Macmillan visited De Gaulle just before the ill-fated Paris summit in early 1960, he had asked the general why he "continually harped on the theme of the 'Anglo-Saxons.'" De Gaulle's "retentive mind" immediately dredged up grievances going back to Roosevelt's snubs, Churchill's taunt, "Whenever I have to choose between you and Roosevelt, I shall always choose Roosevelt," and a long list of personal affronts of which the "betrayal" of France at Yalta was only the culmination. In the volume of his memoirs published in the year of his death, he reached back to November 1918 to blame "the 'Anglo-Saxons' cry of 'Halt' " for preventing the French from plucking "the fruits of victory" in the Great War. Yet he respected Eisenhower and his private hope was that Richard Nixon would succeed him. Just as the Summit Conference of May 1960 was collapsing amid Khrushchev's fiery denunciation of the Americans for sending a U-2 spy plane over the Soviet Union, De Gaulle had touched the American president on the elbow and murmured, "Whatever happens, we are with you." But now John Kennedy was in the White House intent on developing some plans that were distinctly at odds with the Gaullist vision. The new American president struck the general as "somewhat fumbling and over-eager."

2

There are two things that scare me most, John F. Kennedy would tell his advisers as he settled into the White House, nuclear war and the payments deficit. What to do about the dollar had become as troublesome as what to do about the bomb. Each a supreme symbol of power, each became the center of controversy. "What really matters," Kennedy once put it, "is the strength of the currency. . . . Britain has nuclear weapons, but the pound is weak, so everyone pushes it around. Why are people so nice to Spain today? Not because Spain has nuclear weapons but because of all those lovely gold reserves." By the time Kennedy arrived in the White House the United States was losing gold at the rate of more than $1 billion a year. The continental economies had recovered and all major European currencies were fully convertible into dollars. Thus the principal postwar American goals had been achieved. But success had brought with it adverse consequences for the United States. European factories were booming, and Common Market tariffs discriminating against American goods were in force throughout much of the Continent. That had been foreseen. What had not been foreseen was how much it would really matter.

The changing balance of economic power posed a challenge to American leadership. Under Dwight D. Eisenhower the United States had extended its influence in strategic areas of the world by quietly promoting its detachment from the British and French empires. American global hegemony, if not accomplished in quite the same fit of absentmindedness in which Britain supposedly acquired its empire, flowed naturally from the peculiar conditions of the planet following the most destructive war in history. With all the Cold War talk of the Red menace flowing into the "power vacuums" left in the wake of the global struggle, the United States was the real beneficiary of the collapse of the old empires. But John F. Kennedy was the first American president who had to design policies for an America on the decline. Despite the expansionist rhetoric of the New Frontier, the historic moment called for a politics of adjustment to a changing world order no longer quite so subject to the dictates of what the young president's more extravagant successor liked to call the Number One Nation.

The United States emerged from World War II with about 59 percent of the world's gold, much of it refugee riches from Europe. Because virtually all other currencies were nonconvertible, purchases of U.S. goods could be made only with dollar credits or gold. As a consequence, by 1949 United States gold stocks stood at 72 percent of the world's total. There is one obvious difference between dollars and gold. As De Gaulle put it, gold has no nationality. Serendipity, luck, and hard work determine the physical availability of gold, and these are no respecters of boundaries. Dollars, on the other hand, though they travel far and wide, are creations of the U.S. Treasury. In the 1950s, far more than today, the president of the United States was the most powerful man on earth, not only because he had his finger on the nuclear button but because he also exercised a certain influence over the printing press at the Mint.

By 1958 the Europeans had more dollars than they knew what to do with. The European nations had been given billions of dollars through the Marshall Plan and military aid, attracted billions more by creating a favorable investment climate for American firms, and earned still more by producing goods that competed on the world market. The liquidity problem that had so worried the postwar planners in Washington had disappeared. There was now a "dollar glut" which became a problem for the United States as soon as the European banks decided to cash in their dollar reserves for gold. Between 1949 and 1959 the United States sold $5.7 billion worth of gold to foreign countries and increased world reserves through its balance-of-payments deficits at the rate of $600 million a year. If the Europeans cashed in even more of their dollars, as they had a legal right to, there would be a "run on the bank." Gold was pegged by agreement at $35 an ounce, and the United States did not have in the great vaults at Fort Knox enough of it to pay all the outstanding dollar obligations.

It was largely because of the gold hemorrhage that Kennedy had appointed Douglas Dillon of Dillon, Read to be his secretary of the treasury. An "affable easy-goer," as Senator Albert Gore of Tennessee, who coveted the appointment himself, conceded, rich enough to own Château Haut-Brion, perhaps the greatest vineyard in France, the Republican investment banker was committed to the Kennedy goal of getting the economy "moving," and his style and the ring of his name were soothing to nervous bankers. Strongly pushed by Philip Graham, the publisher of the *Washington Post,* Dillon promised the president's brother Robert, who wondered about having a Republican banker in perhaps the most sensitive position in the administration, that "if he felt he had to resign, he would of course go quietly." Though several leading monetary experts now questioned whether the dollar could continue as the world currency, Dillon insisted, "The United States should continue as banker for the world."

As under secretary of state in the Eisenhower administration he had gone to Europe with the secretary of the treasury to ask the help of European bankers in alleviating America's balance-of-payments crisis. *Fortune* magazine had then noted, "When a banker is forced to advertise the fact that he is in a bad way, he does not inspire confidence in the people who have money on deposit." Confidence was precisely what John F. Kennedy worried most about. His father, having what Arthur Schlesinger, Jr., calls "the orthodox business reverence for the Eleusinian mysteries of the international monetary system," urged him to do nothing to upset Wall Street or the gold would drain away. The president announced, "The United States must in the decades ahead, much more than in any time in the past, take its balance of payments into account when formulating its economic policies and conducting its economic affairs." That was precisely what the European central bankers wanted to hear. But the practitioners of neo-Keynesian "new economics" who preached expansionary economic policies at home balked. James Tobin of the Council of Economic Advisers, noting that the central bankers on the Continent "by occasional withdrawals of gold and constant complaints . . . have brought tremendous pressure for 'discipline' upon the United States," concluded that international financial policy was "too important to leave to financiers." The historic function of gold in international trade has been to force nations to live within their means.

Human beings have accepted gold as money for about four thousand years. Since national currencies need to be backed by gold—until 1968 every dollar was backed by 25 cents worth of the precious metal—shipping gold bars abroad to settle debts meant that the national money supply would contract, interest rates would rise, domestic investment would slow down, and incomes would fall. In short, the discipline of gold would force domestic austerity policies upon countries unlucky enough to have a payments deficit. This is precisely what happened to England when sterling was the key currency in the world. The British supported the value of the pound by adopting drastic deflationary policies that brought with them unemployment and business decline. The United States, however, saw no need to curtail domestic spending as long as foreign banks could be induced to accept dollars rather than gold. "Of the $8.5 billion increase in world reserves in the years 1949–1959," Robert Solomon, formerly of the Federal Reserve Board, notes in his history of the postwar monetary order, "the United States provided $7 billion through the increase in its liabilities to foreign monetary authorities."

While the balance-of-payments crisis ebbed and flowed in the early 1960s, the Europeans had little choice but to finance expansionary fiscal and monetary policies in the United States by accepting what amounted to American IOUs. To do otherwise would threaten the dollar in which much of their own wealth resided. Moreover, there was no other reserve currency that would gain wide political acceptance. Most important, as long as the nations of West Europe and Japan believed that their physical survival was dependent upon the United States nuclear "guarantee," they were not able to deal with the United States as a conventional commercial partner.

The arcane and immensely technical discussion of gold that kept lights burning late in the Treasury masked quite simple issues of power. The gold traffic mirrored some new facts of economic life. Between 1952 and 1960 industrial production in Europe increased by more than 60 percent. In Japan the rise was even more staggering—144 percent between 1952 and 1959. Because of lower wages, productivity (output per worker hour) was increasing at a substantially higher rate in Europe than in America all during the 1950s—an increase of 6 percent a year in Germany and almost 4 percent in France, compared with 2.4 percent in the United States. All this meant that the European plants were now in a position to compete with goods produced in the United States. The U.S. share of world production began to drop precipitously and the U.S. trade balance was affected adversely. Despite the high U.S. tariffs, European goods were streaming into the American market. The dream of an "outward-looking" European Community with low tariffs had not materialized. The Europeans saw no reason to lower the tariff barriers to accommodate a United States that in critical commodities was still highly protectionist. Behind the gold crisis was a basic issue: How much would the United States modify its quest for domestic economic growth in order to play by the rules of international finance? Or, to take up the other side of the same question, how much more bargaining power to enforce the rules on the United States did the suddenly prosperous Europeans now have?

While the invasion of Europe by U.S.-based corporations in the late 1950s and early 1960s was facilitated by the Marshall Plan, the vast outpouring of private investment was stimulated as much by the limitations of the American aid program as by its successes. By 1952 it had become politically impossible to sell the U.S. Congress on handouts for Europe in the billions of dollars even if U.S. companies were obvious beneficiaries. United States exports were dropping precipitously. Unemployment hovered around 7 percent. As the Truman administration was coming to an end, isolationist and protectionist feelings were once again running high. The United States had insisted that Marshall Plan recipients should not be eligible for International Monetary Fund (IMF) loans while they were receiving grants.

Whence would the investment capital for Europe come? NATO rearmament was seen as one way to save stagnating industries such as machine tools and airframe companies. (A presidential commission concluded that the "impact of United States rearmament will be to enlarge greatly the available markets for European exports and the ability to earn dollars.") But European integration and U.S. private investment were now the key to U.S. economic strategy. With a big market on the U.S. scale available to them, the Europeans could expand their trade with one another and earn dollars to buy American goods, all of which would lubricate the export trade on which U.S. prosperity would increasingly depend. Now that the U.S. domestic market was becoming saturated, American firms could expand their horizons by participating directly in the booming European economy.

The twin policies of the 1950s—rearmament and European integration—depended on each other. As the U.S. economy became more dependent on commercial relations with Europe and more vulnerable to economic retaliation from the Continent, the more the United States pressed the security issue. The troops in Europe were themselves responsible for a significant part of the balance-of-payments problem. But their presence symbolized the political dependence of Europe. In the economic realm the recovered Continent was acquiring interests that diverged from those of the United States and, also, options to close itself off from the United States—to become, in the bureaucratic jargon of the day, "inward-looking." But the security tie based on a shared perception of common dangers made it seem safe for the United States to encourage what it had always feared—a European trading bloc.

The transformation in the landscape of international capitalism was remarkably swift. As late as 1956 the holdings of European companies in the United States actually exceeded the investment of U.S. companies in Europe. But between 1950 and 1969 the book value of U.S. foreign direct investments in Europe rose from $1.7 billion to $21.5 billion. By 1964 U.S. companies owned more than 6 percent of all the industrial development in the countries of West Europe that belonged to the Common Market. More than 10 percent of new capital invested each year in the national economies of the Benelux countries came from American companies. By the mid-1960s, according to a study of the German Automobile Association, 25 percent of the production of autos in the Common Market countries was controlled by U.S. firms. A fourth of the French chemical industry sales for 1963 were attributable to foreign companies, mostly American. A 1968 study of the Atlantic Institute estimated that two-thirds of U.S. investment in Europe was held by twenty companies; indeed, Ford, GM, and Exxon (then called Standard Oil of New Jersey) owned 40 percent of all the direct U.S. investment in France, West Germany, and Britain. Because European central banks and private investors saw no alternatives but to pile up and relend their surplus dollars, American corporations could use the huge balances in Europe, the so-called "Eurodollars," to buy up French, British, German, and Italian companies. The process began in the late Eisenhower years and accelerated greatly during Kennedy's thousand days in office. This American Challenge, as Jean-Jacques Servan-Schreiber called it in his best-selling book of 1967, was nothing less than a bid to take over the industrial plant of Europe. That which the Nazis had tried to take, the Americans were busily proceeding to buy.

The onslaught of the U.S. multinationals in the early 1960s was actively encouraged and to a degree underwritten by the U.S. government. "Faced with a deteriorating balance-of-payments situation," the Princeton political scientist Robert Gilpin has noted, "the United States government began to regard the multinational corporations and their growing overseas earnings as the means to finance America's hegemonic world position." Immediately after the war American companies had been wary of making heavy investments in Europe. The inflation and monetary instability that characterized Britain, France, and Italy made investment unattractive, since the inflation-ridden economies resorted to exchange controls which interfered with the repatriation of profits. But the U.S. government had agreed to subsidize private risk-taking.

If corporations would invest in Europe the U.S. Treasury would not only insure them against the risk that local governments would seize their factories or impound their profits but would also provide major tax incentives. Perhaps most important, official American support for the Common Market helped bring into being a huge continental market that rivaled the American market itself. To produce behind the tariff walls in Europe was so obviously preferable to paying formidable duties for the privilege of exporting from America that Monnet's dream led inexorably to the transplantation of America's largest companies.

3

In 1949 the National Assembly of France passed a law empowering the minister of health to regulate all drinks that contained "vegetable matter." The target was Coca-Cola, which had been drunk in France since 1919 but which had become, thanks to an efficient alliance of Communist party propagandists and local winegrowers the symbol of "Coca-Colonialism." The peculiarly American product originally marketed in the South as a temperance drink despite being laced with cocaine had become a political litmus test. "As American as Independence Day," proclaimed an early postwar ad. At the first international conference of Coke bottlers held in Atlanta in 1948 signs festooned the meeting room: "When we think of Nazis, we think of the Swastika, when we think of the Japs we think of the Rising Sun (that set) and when we think of Communists, we think of the Iron Curtain, BUT when THEY think of democracy, they think of Coca-Cola." Communists in Belgium charged that Coke drinking produced Fascism, and in Austria in addition to the usual charge of addiction—"Ten bottles will make the user a helpless slave of Coca-Cola for life," one Viennese newspaper declared—the local functionaries spread the story that the neighborhood bottling plant was actually making atomic bombs.

James A. Farley, the brilliant political entrepreneur who could, so legend had it, recall instantly the first name of anyone he had ever met, had managed two electoral victories for Franklin D. Roosevelt. But in 1940 he broke with FDR and transferred his loyalty and skills to Coca-Cola, for which he was determined to mount an equally hard-driving campaign. His staunch anti-Communism, his status as a prominent Catholic layman, and a lifetime dedicated to the collection of important people, made him a formidable figure. The former chairman of the Democratic party and four other Coca-Cola executives met with the pope, and the Communists twitted the faithful that a conspiracy was being hatched to substitute Coke for sacramental wine. Farley's direct intervention with the American ambassador in Paris and the French ambassador in Washington, backed by threats by U.S. congressmen of boycotts of French perfume, turned back the anti-Coke campaign in France. The discriminatory legislation failed to pass the upper house.

In the United States the company victory was viewed as an ideological triumph. "You can't spread the doctrines of Marx among people who drink Coca-Cola," one columnist exulted with only a touch of irony, "it's just that simple." Coca-Cola had been bottling its product in England since 1900 and its Frankfurt plant had sold millions of cases on the occasion of the 1936 Olympics despite the frowns of Nazi health authorities. But with the ideological battles of the late 1940s behind him, Jim Farley's Cola-Cola Export Company went into high gear. Bottling plants appeared all over Europe. By the late 1950s Pepsi-Cola, the archcompetitor, had joined the invasion, and in the 1960s, having made alliances with famous European bottlers such as Schweppes, Heineken, and Perrier, the company slogan "Have a Pepsi Day" now appeared in virtually every European language. The smaller but more agressive company had acquired the services of its own well-connected politician, former Vice President Richard M. Nixon.

Coke was a unique symbol of American cultural penetration of Europe, and for that reason produced the early postwar storms. But the president of Coca-Cola was right when he described his worldwide operation as more "multilocal" than multinational. It was an alliance of local bottlers, dealers, and entrepreneurs orchestrated in Atlanta. The Coke and Pepsi signs may have altered the landscape and ancient drinking habits, but the massive investment in American-controlled factories to produce computers, autos, and electrical goods on the continent that began in the late 1950s transformed the European economies.

The early postwar investors from America were the giants who had been in Europe for years. American bankers and industrialists had been interested in Europe for a long time. Indeed, in response to J. P. Morgan's purchase of a sizable share of the Leyland shipping group, books with titles like *The American Invaders* and *The Americanization of the World* were being published in London as early as 1902. In 1929 GM purchased Opel at an absurdly low price, so eager were local investors in that inflation-ravaged country for solid American stock certificates. Thomas J. Watson, the country peddler who turned his wizardry in selling cash registers into the world's most successful high-technology corporation, had established International Business Machines (IBM) on the Continent in the 1920s. In 1937 IBM had a thriving punch card and typewriter business in Europe, and Watson was president of the International Chamber of Commerce in which capacity he received the Order of Merit of the German Eagle with Star from Adolf Hitler. (On the eve of Hitler's invasion of Poland he sent it back, registered mail.) Watson acquired for IBM not only a historic building on Place Vendôme in Paris but the services of the enterprising Baron Christian de Waldner who, having married into the Michelin tire family, used his connections and energies so tirelessly in behalf of the company that he was known everywhere as Mr. IBM of France.

The baron organized a thriving office-machine and punch-card business in the French empire—Madagascar, Indochina, and North Africa—and in just ten years built up IBM France from a skeleton operation of 410 employees to which it had been reduced by World War II to one with more than 2000 employees. By 1960 French-produced IBM equipment was being sold in sixty-four countries. When the computer age arrived, IBM sold more computers in France than the leading French manufacturer, Machines Bull, sold in all the world. Eventually, despite De Gaulle's efforts to save the pride of French technology, IBM garnered 80 percent of the European computer market in the 1960s and put Machines Bull out of the running, forcing it to sell out to another American giant, General Electric. The humiliation for De Gaulle was particularly sharp because at the moment of collapse the French company was selling a more advanced computer than IBM and achieving a phenomenal growth in sales, but it lacked the capital to compete with IBM. Its annual sales combined with those of Olivetti, Telefunken, and a large British computer company, ICT, did not equal the cash flow of IBM.

By and large only the largest U.S. companies such as IBM had the risk capital, the self-confidence, and the managerial know-how to operate in a strange and prickly environment. Smaller firms were not in a position to take advantage of the great economies of scale offered by the newly created market that stretched from the Pyrenees to the Elbe. But not every major U.S. company that ventured abroad succeeded. Betty Crocker cake mix, for example, launched a big campaign in Britain—"Betty Crocker is here"—but no one seemed to care. Yet while European firms were strapped for cash, the big American firms—with the help of government subsidies and tax write-offs— were able to generate huge cash flows with which to acquire both companies and markets in Europe. In key sectors they knew how to advertise and market better than the European firms, were more efficient, and more profitable. A group of French industrialists calculated in 1965, for example, that General Foods could destroy the French bonbon business anytime it wished by selling its sweets at a 10 percent discount or by plowing 10 percent of its sales into a massive advertising campaign. Company profits might fall 6 percent, they informed a round table sponsored by the minister of industry, but in three years the French firms would be out of business. "In fact," they concluded, "it is the very existence—or independence—of a large part of French industry that may one day become the critical question."

If there was one U.S. company that had been a handmaiden of government throughout its life, it was International Telephone and Telegraph (ITT). Founded in August 1933 by Sosthenes Behn, a colonel in the U.S. Signal Corps in the First World War, the small telephone company with the global name soon developed into a major international enterprise by following its own foreign policy. "International trade and good will should not be stifled and throttled by a bugaboo of national defense," Behn testified before a congressional committee a few years before purchasing 28 percent of Focke-Wulf, a company that made bombers for the Luftwaffe. Although ITT's German connections were a matter of recurring concern for the U.S. government all during the War, ITT actually received $5 million from the U.S. government in 1967 for damage to its Focke-Wulf plants in Nazi Germany inflicted by American bombers! The company's international contacts were of such use to U.S. intelligence that, according to one history of the company, Allen Dulles "helped to arrange ITT's return to Europe via the American Army. . . ."

By 1963, however, ITT President Harold Geneen was circulating a private memo to the board of directors on what was happening in Europe and how little further help the U.S. government was likely to be. "[T]he tides of U.S. prestige are admittedly running lower than ever before throughout Europe in particular." The Christian Democrats in Italy were "committed to a semi-Leftist approach." France and England were becoming nationalistic and anti-American. The Common Market communications ministers were threatening to get together and to introduce underhanded practices like competitive bidding. ITT should concentrate, Geneen told the board, on acquiring solid American properties that could not be nationalized.

By the mid-1960s, the complaints of politicians, writers, and businessmen about the American "takeover" had become a roar. As one British industrialist complained, "Between your products, your techniques, and your movies, we risk becoming just another bunch of bloody Yanks." In Germany the mass magazine *Der Stern,* noting that 90 percent of the office equipment and computer business, 65 percent of the razor blades, and 40 percent of the auto industry were dominated by American multinational giants, charged that not even in the age of imperialism "did a colonial power derive such wealth from a single colony as the American companies are drawing in profits from their operations in West Germany." The American corporate mammoths—GM being larger than the seventeen largest German companies put together and exceeding the gross national product of the Netherlands—would destroy European competition. Gaston Deferre, a Socialist candidate for the French presidency, wrote in *Foreign Affairs* at the height of the De Gaulle era that economic invasion by the United States was a greater danger to France than Soviet expansionism.

The "Americanization" of Europe seemed overwhelming, and the consequences humiliating. "There, Mr. President, is our enemy," Pierre Dreyfus, head of the Renault company said to General de Gaulle as they stood together before the General Motors exhibit at the Salon de l'Automobile. De Gaulle replied that he had been saying the same thing for twenty years. American commercial culture and American economic power coming together, so some critics contended, threatened to snuff out a thousand years of European culture. France's *mission civilisatrice* was her *raison d'être,* but the missionaries on the move now were the chewing-gum salesmen—1.6 billion packs sold in France in 1966—and the fast-food hustlers. In 1948 there were two "drugstores," as the French call them, in all of France; in 1966, 9957 self-service eateries. The flight attendants on Air France mimicked the inflection of the American airline patter. Aunt Jemima Pancake Mix, Minute Rice, Gillette blades, Camay soap, and Helena Rubinstein lipsticks soon became indispensable amenities for "upwardly mobile" families—U.S. academic jargon was also a major import—available in old-fashioned shops and the new American-style supermarkets that were springing up from Amsterdam to Milan. France, Italy, and Germany had their own news magazines each patterned after *Time*. *Hörzu*, the German version of *TV Guide*, hired a *Saturday Evening Post* illustrator to reproduce the blend of nostalgia and modernity that had made the defunct magazine so popular in prewar America. Discount stores, trading stamps, and the mail-order business altered the commercial landscape of Europe. The automobile produced even more of a transformation. By the mid-1960s five million new ones a year were clogging the narrow streets of Europe's ancient cities, and growth in the countryside was even faster. The English are now polishing cars instead of tending gardens, one American observer reported in 1964.

There was indeed scarcely any aspect of daily life in Europe that did not bear some American stamp: instant coffee, TV jingles, blue jeans, Elvis Presley records, deodorants, and dark leather jackets right out of *West Side Story*. There was an advertising explosion. In 1962, $16 was spent by advertisers for each person in Germany, much less than the $65 per person then being spent in the United States, but investment in commercial enchantment rose each year at a rate of about 10 percent. For French intellectuals the most grating import was *franglais* ("*Je passe le weekend avec la girlfriend*"). Artists in Paris railed at the influence of New York's Museum of Modern Art; control of the traffic in creativity had passed to the Rockefeller brothers. Playwrights and filmmakers looked to Broadway and Hollywood with contempt and envy.

But while nationalist feelings ran high, too many local entrepreneurs and capitalists shared in the American boom in Europe to make economic nationalism a serious political option. As the invasion began, European governments welcomed the capital, technology, and managerial know-how that flowed into the Continent from America. In the 1950s American companies were ready to invest in new growth industries in France while conservative French investors preferred the safety of a solid portfolio. Local communities in the provinces could attract American companies and provide jobs for depressed regions. Thus while the French government complained about the multinationals, the Gaullist Prime Minister Chaban-Delmas, who doubled as mayor of Bordeaux, welcomed the Ford Motor Company's decision to build a plant in his city.

4

"We, my dear Crossman, are Greeks in this American empire. You will find the Americans much as the Greeks found the Romans—great big, vulgar, bustling people, more vigorous than we are and also more idle, with more unspoiled virtues but also more corrupt." The scene was wartime Algiers. Harold Macmillan, erstwhile publisher, Conservative member of Parliament, and now Churchill's top agent in North Africa, was lecturing the young director of psychological warfare. In his critical months in Algiers, Macmillan had impressed Eisenhower and tangled artfully with De Gaulle. The memories of these associations would become important almost twenty years later during the seven years Macmillan served as prime minister. The donnish politician who devoured Trollope novels did not, except for his looks that suggested a slightly puzzled lion, fit the mold of a Conservative leader. Indeed, in his youth he had been a staunch admirer of Keynes and an enthusiast of national planning. Toryism, as he understood it, was "a form of paternal socialism." As his political associate "Rab" Butler put it, Macmillan had "the strong determination to help the underdog and the social habit to associate happily with the overdog." He had the Edwardian air of a man at home with foxhounds, who could settle comfortably into an overstuffed chair of a London club. Yet he was not always what he seemed, for he was an excellent actor.

As prime minister his attentions were focused on the problems of being Greek in a Roman century. Chastened by the Suez debacle, he saw as his task the careful detachment of imperial possessions and responsibilities that could no longer be retained. A less embattled Britain, he hoped, could play a larger role on the world stage, and by virtue of its "special relationship" with the United States even act as a linchpin in forging new relations between the superpowers and Europe. But that would require Britain to throw a thousand-year tradition to the wind and end its isolation from the Continent. No more could Britain be merely "with" Europe, but she must be "of" it.

"People often don't realize that the Victorian age was only an interruption in British history," he told an interviewer in 1961. "The hundred years of British domination which ended in 1914 was a very rare thing in history. . . . They talk a lot about the glories of the old Elizabethan Age, but they forget that that was a time when Britain was politically very insecure, between much greater empires. We only kept the country going then by taking tremendous risks and adventures. It's more like that today—it's exciting living on the edge of bankruptcy." Macmillan's task as he saw it was to cut Britain's enormous defense commitments without giving up the pretensions of power. He would use his conservative bearing and political agility to disguise the continuing historic retreat from Suez. Britain's defense establishment, the largest in Europe, helped explain its extremely poor rates of growth all through the 1950s (2.6 percent a year compared with 7.6 percent for West Germany, 5.9 percent for Italy, or 5.1 percent for Switzerland).

The British hydrogen bomb was first exploded at Christmas Island in May 1958, only a few months after Suez. Randolph Churchill taunted the American Chamber of Commerce in London: "Britain can knock down twelve cities in the region of Stalingrad and Moscow from bases in Britain and another dozen in the Crimea from bases in Cyprus. We are a great power once again." But Britain's independent deterrent required a great deal of American help. The missile age had arrived and Britain had no missiles that could deliver the city-smashing bomb. At Camp David, the presidential retreat in the Maryland hills, Eisenhower had promised to provide Britain with the Skybolt missile which could be fired from Royal Air Force bombers. Although the Polaris submarine, a far more efficient and less vulnerable missile platform, would soon be ready, that would have required the Royal Navy to put its reduced budget into submarines instead of aircraft carriers, a prospect that did not sit well, since the primary function of Her Majesty's fleet was to show the flag at the edges of the fading empire and the whole point of nuclear submarines is not to show the flag at all. Thus in return for opening the naval base at Holy Loch in Scotland to U.S. submarines bristling with nuclear warheads, thereby, as Macmillan knew, courting local anxieties about being blown up, Britain would get the Skybolt. The whole theory of British defense now depended critically upon this weapon.

Robert McNamara, Kennedy's secretary of defense, was bent on using his considerable reputation for efficient management—he had been briefly president of the Ford Motor Company—to gain control of the ungainly Pentagon. His instrument was something called "cost-effectiveness" analysis and to this awesome accountant's tool the Skybolt fell victim. It would cost too much and it might well not work. When the British minister of aviation, Julian Amery, came to lunch at the White House in January 1962, Kennedy expressed his doubts about the weapon. Amery's response was that it had to work since it was the basis of Britain's nuclear defense. McNamara recommended cancellation of the project, seeing it as a purely technical weapons decision. But the British saw Skybolt as the symbolic linchpin on which the two poles of their national security policy rested: the "special relationship" with the United States and their own independent nuclear deterrent.

Within the Kennedy administration highly placed officials were skeptical of both. The enthusiasts of European integration, notably George Ball, were impatient with making too much of the "special relationship" because it was an obstacle to Britain's joining Europe as a member of the Common Market. McNamara, struggling to develop the doctrine and hardware to improve "command and control" over nuclear forces, publicly attacked "relatively weak national nuclear forces with enemy cities as their targets" as a threat to peace. As far as he was concerned, the "interdependence" of U.S. and European security interests required a "unified" NATO command all of which was easily decipherable code for keeping an American finger on all nuclear weapons of the alliance. Nuclear proliferation "with all its attendant dangers" had become a major American preoccupation.

Despite the succession of hints from Washington, the British did not react until McNamara arrived in London to see the minister of defense, Peter Thorneycroft, who lashed out at the American secretary. The meeting, the British official recalls

was the first time I realized . . . that he was going to cancel Skybolt and wasn't going to offer anything in return. So I then said to him that this cancellation—as I had warned him—went deeper than defense policy, and went to the very root of any possibility of the British trusting America in defense dealings again; because you do not twice ever commit your whole strategy to a country in weapons and then have the carpet taken from under you. . . .

At a meeting in Nassau in December 1962, Macmillan and Kennedy met once more. The conference had been called for other purposes, but the Skybolt affair preempted all else. On the plane to Nassau, Kennedy, clad in pajamas, worked out with the British ambassador, David Ormsby-Gore, an old friend from his days in England, a new agreement to save Skybolt. "I trust David as I would my own Cabinet," Kennedy once remarked. But Macmillan's new view, unknown to his ambassador, was that the Skybolt was now a "compromised lady" in view of the disparaging public statements about it made by Kennedy and McNamara, and he rejected Kennedy's proposal as soon as the plane landed in the Bahamas. The London *Sunday Times* correspondent attending the conference noted a "resentment and suspicion of American intentions such as I have never experienced in all the Anglo-American conferences I have covered over the past twenty years." Macmillan told the president that Britain would stay a nuclear power and if the price was a decisive split with the United States and the cultivation of anti-Americanism at home, so be it.

The Americans had underestimated the importance of the nuclear issue in British politics. In a speech at West Point just before the Nassau meetings, Dean Acheson, who had spent years fending off charges that he was soft on Britain, taunted the Tory government: "Great Britain has lost an empire and has not yet found a role." (Macmillan wrote off notes to a group of fuming British leaders that in underestimating the island power Acheson had fallen into the error of Napoleon, Kaiser Wilhelm, and Hitler.) The decision to proceed with an independent nuclear deterrent had been preceded by a wrenching debate. On both moral and practical grounds opposition to the British bomb had been formidable. (Indeed, it never disappeared and surfaced again with great force in the 1980s.) By the late 1950s the Campaign for Nuclear Disarmament was organizing mass marches to demand unilateral British nuclear disarmament. Even in the military establishment there were many who thought it made no sense for Britain to put limited resources into missiles and H-bombs. As if to confirm their view, the government, after spending £60 million on developing its own Blue Streak missile, abandoned the project as impractical. In his memoirs Macmillan throws up his hands at the "technicalities and uncertainties" of sophisticated weapons for which politicians have no experience on which to make judgments. But the abandonment of the British missile for the "independent" deterrent revealed the limits of independence, and now if the Americans refused to help, the embarrassment of the government would be complete. Thorneycroft was convinced that the Americans "wanted to get us out of the deterrent if they could, and this was one way of doing it."

The Kennedy advisers understood little of this. Secretary of State Dean Rusk proposed renaming the infelicitous-sounding Hound Dog missile "Skybolt II" and giving it to the British, prompting a comment from McNamara that the secretary of state would have done very well in the automobile business. Indeed so unprepared was the whole administration for the misunderstandings flowing from what the Americans considered a "back-burner" technical issue, and the British saw as a political watershed that the president asked Richard Neustadt, a Harvard political science professor, to do a study of the incident. "He should have warned me of the dangers," Kennedy later complained about Macmillan. The denouement to the Skybolt fiasco was to give the British five Polaris submarines under NATO command with a provision that the British could use them independently in a purely British emergency. It was a face-saving solution for Macmillan, whom Kennedy liked personally and worked to accommodate. But the solution helped to shatter John Kennedy's "Grand Design" for Europe before it ever took shape. Even as the president's plane was winging toward Nassau, William R. Tyler, the assistant secretary of state for European Affairs, wrote a handwritten note predicting "that any agreement to replace Skybolt with Polaris would be used by De Gaulle as a pretext for vetoing Britain's EEC application."

According to Theodore Sorensen, Kennedy's closest adviser, the president tended to look upon the Western alliance "in somewhat the same light as he looked upon the Congress—as a necessary but not always welcome partner, whose cooperation he could not always obtain, whose opinions he could not always accept and with whom an uneasy relationship seemed inevitable." The State Department NATO enthusiasts irritated Kennedy on occasion because they "had led us to think of every problem of foreign policy in terms of the Western Alliance when it was no longer as central to all our problems as it once had been . . ."

Since the New Deal, each Democratic administration had searched for a slogan that would capture the essence of its policy. The "Grand Design" was the contribution of a worshipful columnist, Joseph Kraft, who wrote a small puff piece on Kennedy's first year under that title. He accurately recorded Kennedy's hopes. North America and Europe would, in Arthur Schlesinger's words, be "happily joined by policies and institutions in common pursuit of economic expansion and military defense." Kennedy saw a recovered Europe as a crucial partner for much expanded trade. He believed that European unity improved that prospect. He favored British membership in the Common Market for the same reasons that De Gaulle would prevent it: because of the "special relationship." Britain's membership would serve as a restraint that would keep the European Community from veering off in an anti-American direction. Translated into De Gaulle's French, Britain would act as America's Trojan horse. According to Schlesinger,

He simply felt that Europe would work toward unity in its own way. As for the character of this unity, he did not think nationalism altogether a bad thing. He knew that the United States would not lightly renounce its own sovereignty; this made him a bit skeptical of rigid supranatural institutions in Europe. Though he had the greatest affection and respect for Jean Monnet, he was not tied to Monnet's formulas—or to those of anyone else. His support of the trade expansion bill did not commit him to the theology of partnership any more than his support of the unified deterrent committed him to the theology of interdependence.

While there were some in and around the Kennedy White House who spoke with evangelistic fervor about the new "partnership" for an ever greater Atlantic Community without which the United States might have to "resign from history," Kennedy himself, though he resorted to such public rhetoric himself at times, was rather cool and open about these matters. In contrast to the older generation like Dean Acheson, who spoke with reverence of NATO as the embodiment of profound spiritual ties, Kennedy was skeptical. He would quote Napoleon, who attributed his triumphs to the successful battles he fought with his allies. In moments of exasperation over the Berlin crisis, Sorensen recalls, he would refer to Churchill's dictum that "the history of any alliance is the history of mutual recrimination."

In reality, by the 1960s the Americans had little opportunity to impose a Grand Design on Europe even if they had had one. When John Kennedy came to office, the statesmen of Europe had been busy for over two years with an assortment of plans for rearranging the face of the now recovered Continent. In West Germany, Konrad Adenauer was searching for a political role commensurate with his country's new economic power. Now rearmed, Germany was still a nuclear pariah forbidden by treaty to produce or to control the superweapons. The symbolism of "nuclear-sharing" appealed to him. The suggestion that Germany might acquire some rights over nuclear weapons scared the Soviets and could be a bargaining chip or a deterrent in dealing with Khrushchev. Even a symbolic sharing of control over nuclear weapons which the Americans had begun to talk about at the end of the Eisenhower administration offered prestige and would signify the end of Germany's period of penance.

De Gaulle's proposal for a "directorate" of NATO in the form of an Anglo-Saxon–French partnership did not of course sit well in Bonn. Germany, the French president had told the Americans, "was not yet a major Western power" and therefore Adenauer was not entitled to a finger on the button. By proposing a global role for himself which would leave the rest of the Continent in a permanently inferior status, De Gaulle undercut his own claim to be speaking for Europe. The French president considered Adenauer's enthusiasm for political integration to be naive. Transnational economic ties, even dependencies, could grow even as political nationalism grew stronger. Europe could not be created by bureaucratic tinkerers, certainly not by the new breed of American-trained political scientists who wrote rhapsodically of the revolution in human affairs to be staged by commissions, authorities, and parliaments, but only by a historic process of organic evolution. Alfred Grosser summed up their differences: as Adenauer saw it, De Gaulle wanted a Europe with a loud voice but no body, whereas De Gaulle thought Adenauer was so attached to the body that he would sell Europe's soul to the Americans.

Still and all, despite De Gaulle's show of independence—at a press conference on March 25, 1959, he expressed the view that a reunified Germany would have to recognize the Oder–Neisse Line and reconcile itself to the permanent loss of the eastern territories of the old Reich to the Poles and the Russians—the two leaders cooperated closely in trying to define the new Europe. The key issue that brought them together was the British connection.

Adenauer shared De Gaulle's classic continental view of perfidious Albion. British policy toward the Continent had been "one long fiddle," a record of exploitation of "us poor dumb Continentals." He thought Harold Macmillan's growing interest in nuclear disarmament and his proposals for "thinning out" troops in Europe were designed to win votes at home and demonstrated Britain's unreliability as a partner. Harold Macmillan had his first extended talk with Adenauer in June 1954. The chancellor delivered "a long and fascinating discourse, covering not merely the immediate problems but the whole history of the German peoples from Roman times until the present." Regrettably, Macmillan added, during the next nine years, "I was destined to listen to it on every occasion when we met."

By the time he first met Kennedy, Harold Macmillan had decided that Britain should enter the Common Market. It was an extraordinary about-face. When the Common Market was first established and Britain invited to join, Macmillan rose in Parliament to voice the conventional reaction: "Our people are not going to hand to any supranational authority the right to close down our pits or steel works. We will allow no supranational authority to put large masses of our people out of work. . . ." The Labourites were even more strongly against it. In the glow of the Marshall Plan, Averell Harriman over lunch prodded Sir Stafford Cripps, foreign minister in the Attlee government, about going "into Europe," only to be told that England relished getting into bed with France about as much as the United States would favor a marriage with Brazil. But Macmillan's close associates, Edward Heath and Lord Home, both of whom would succeed him as prime minister, were now all for it. More importantly, the Federation of British Industries was demanding Britain's entry into the EEC in the hope that access to a larger market would reverse the depressing performance of British business. Kennedy too was eager for Britain to join the Six to stabilize the Continent in the face of the unsettling figure now running France. De Gaulle, the president suggested, could be handled with a variety of symbolic gestures. He thought that Macmillan's suggestion that the United States help De Gaulle get a nuclear force and then persuade him to put it into an American-controlled "trusteeship" might work. Perhaps the British might be allowed under U.S. law to pass American nuclear secrets on to the French. He spoke about all these things, Macmillan noted, "in a rather detached way. Perhaps because it is his character to be ready to listen to anything."

For almost four years Macmillan worked tirelessly to arrange Britain's entry into Europe. It was his initiative that gave credibility to Kennedy's articulation of an American vision. On July 4, 1962, in Independence Hall in Philadelphia, the president delivered a ringing "Declaration of Interdependence." The speech was designed to muster support for his trade bill, which was to be the centerpiece of the "Grand Design." The Trade Expansion Act, passed the following month, gave the president sweeping authority to create what amounted to a free trade area embracing the United States and the Common Market. In his speech Kennedy promised that the United States would "discuss with a United Europe the ways and means of forming a concrete Atlantic partnership, a mutually beneficial partnership between the new union now emerging in Europe and the old American Union founded here 173 years ago." Five days later Macmillan sent his enthusiastic congratulations but warned the president that the "Europeans are in a rather touchy mood."

The Kennedy speech was an exercise in the eloquence of ambiguity. There was no common agreement on what a "United Europe" was, much less an "Atlantic partnership." De Gaulle's vision of a United Europe, a Europe of States, had been put forward as the Fouchet Plan at the Brussels negotiations of the EEC. Belgium and the Netherlands, fearing De Gaulle's ambitions, pressed hard for a United Europe based on two ideas that were totally unacceptable to the general: British membership and a highly integrated supranational directorate. Paul-Henri Spaak, writing in a French periodical, attacked De Gaulle's idea that an integrated Europe could or should become "a third world power." The general, in turn, scoffed at the idea of a supranational Europe. It would require a federator, "but the federator would not be European." The Fouchet Plan was rejected, and General de Gaulle resolved to take drastic action to keep Europe free of American "hegemony."

Harold Macmillan faced formidable obstacles in reversing what the Labour leader Hugh Gaitskell called a thousand years of history. While the multinationals and civil servants were all for the Common Market, the right-wing Tories and the left-wing Labourites had formed a coalition against it. In calling for a British application to join the Common Market, Macmillan had deliberately masked his historic decision by making it sound as boring as possible. Kennedy, on the other hand, who wished to keep the basic relationships of the West intact while appearing to make great changes, was given to flights of rhetoric.

In November 1961, shortly after applying to join the Common Market, the prime minister entertained the French president at his country house in Sussex. Although the attempted coup by the disgruntled generals in Algeria had failed the previous April, De Gaulle, still fearing assassination, arrived with quantities of blood plasma, much to the consternation of the Macmillan cook who resisted having it put in the family refrigerator. Macmillan found him charming, mellow, and remote, a man who "hears nothing and listens to nothing." In his diary the prime minister vented his frustration:

> The tragedy of it all is that we agree with de Gaulle on almost everything. We like the political Europe (*union des patries* or *union d'etats*) that de Gaulle likes. We are anti-federalists; so is he. We are pragmatists in our economic planning; so is he. . . . We agree; but his pride, his inherited hatred of England (since Joan of Arc), his bitter memories of the last war; above all, his intense 'vanity' for France—she must dominate —make him half welcome, half repel us, with a strange 'love-hate' complex. Sometimes, when I am with him, I feel I have overcome it. But he goes back to his distrust and dislike, like a dog to his vomit.

Adenauer had promised Macmillan to plead Britain's case with De Gaulle, but, partly to ingratiate himself with the general, partly out of the animus he bore his longtime antagonists, he managed to say exactly the right words to reinforce De Gaulle's prejudices. His ambassador in Washington, the chancellor told the French president in Paris in July 1962, had reported a bit of gossip to the effect that Macmillan had proposed an economic union with the United States and had been turned down by Kennedy. The conversation never took place, but the story provided further corroboration of De Gaulle's Trojan horse theory. Adenauer then switched his tack and suggested that Britain's real motive in joining was to split Franco-German unity.

In so complex a negotiation with seemingly insuperable problems, especially the challenge of developing a common agricultural policy for a group of nations each of which protected its own farmers in a different way, it was easy for De Gaulle and Adenauer to come up with endless reasons for rejecting the British application. But at the heart of their common decision were quite different assessments of the consequences. De Gaulle believed that with Britain out of Europe, American influence could be resisted and France could play its own "hegemonic" role in Europe. (He called it *grandeur*.) Adenauer believed that a reduced role for Britain would reinforce West Germany's position as America's leading ally. The real "special relationship" was between Washington and Bonn. On January 14, 1963, in the midst of the many-sided negotiations, De Gaulle called a press conference and in categorical terms announced his veto of Britain's entry into the Common Market. Though not entirely unexpected, the desired histrionic effect was achieved. Washington was stunned and confused. Macmillan was crushed. For a moment France had become the deciding voice in the affairs of the West.

5

The mushroom cloud that rose over Hiroshima fundamentally changed not only the nature of weaponry but its function. Arms have always been used as symbols of strength, but throughout history the calculus of power was usually made in the actual heat of battle. Now political leaders recognized that the battle had to be avoided. Despite occasional rhetorical statements to the contrary by enthusiastic generals and lugubrious scenarios prepared by defense intellectuals, as they called themselves, depicting the rewarding life to be lived in the "post-attack environment," political leaders took as their operating premise the conviction that a nuclear war would have no winners and that, in Khrushchev's words, the survivors would envy the dead. On January 23, 1956, President Eisenhower had noted in his diary the conclusions of a briefing given him that day by an Air Force general: "It was calculated that something on the order of 65% of the population would require some kind of medical care and in most instances no opportunity whatever to get it." Despite America's nuclear superiority at the time, Eisenhower believed that the United States would suffer a "total economic collapse."

As nuclear weapons became less usable in a military sense they acquired ever more political importance. No longer was the test of power the capacity to incinerate millions. Destructive power had developed to a point that dwarfed the lethal efforts of two world wars. In strictly military terms the atomic bomb had become a depreciated currency since it could not be used without suicidal consequences. Many nations could now acquire these weapons, and no nation was powerful enough to defend its own territory in the classic sense. Thus while nuclear weapons were steadily integrated into military forces, they were regarded more and more by politicians as metaphors. What a nation did with nuclear weapons or what it said about them signified how prepared it was psychologically to face nuclear war. The high rollers in the game would be the winners—at least until the war.

In the late 1950s there was a flurry of interest in the subject of controlling nuclear weapons. Harold Macmillan, though he put considerable effort into promoting disarmament negotiations, believed that any country aspiring to the status of a front-rank power must control its own nuclear weapons. Precisely because Britain had lost the empire she must acquire the bomb. De Gaulle and Adenauer, each concerned with establishing the sovereignty of his nation, saw nuclear weapons as political statements. For the Gaullists, as Michel Debré, De Gaulle's first premier, wrote, the American reluctance to share nuclear technology proved that the United States did not "wish France to remain an African or Saharan power . . . [nor] recover her political independence."

Actually the U.S. military had been wrestling with the issue of nuclear sharing for a long time. In 1940, when British nuclear scientists were considerably ahead of the Americans, the question of merging the two programs arose, but the British rejected the idea because they lacked confidence in American security procedures. Just after the war Lauris Norstad, a colonel in the Pentagon at the time, proposed a throughgoing nuclear collaboration with Britain, but Klaus Fuchs, the Soviet spy, had just been caught in England, and it was now Washington's turn to reject the British on security grounds. In the early days of the nuclear era, the U.S. Congress, believing that the U.S. monopoly could continue indefinitely if only the "secret" were not compromised, erected elaborate legal obstacles to passing nuclear information on to any other nation. Since the British had started ahead of the Americans and had cooperated to an important degree in the Manhattan Project, U.S. reticence about nuclear sharing was a sore point.

De Gaulle intended his Washington-London-Paris directorate to mean that France would have a veto on the use of nuclear weapons anywhere. The general had told Dulles that unless France felt herself to be a world power, "she would degenerate internally." Dulles and Eisenhower had tried to head off the rising pressures in Britain and France for independent nuclear forces with a variety of cosmetic arrangements. They offered NATO members "access" to nuclear weapons stored on the Continent under a "double veto" arrangement. The Europeans would control the missiles and the United States would control the warheads. The Pentagon was pushing the idea of transplanting the already obsolete Thor and Jupiter missiles to the Continent under the control of the "host countries." Since 1953 the United States had been unsuccessfully seeking permission to store its nuclear warheads in France, and the IRBM (for Intermediate Range Ballistic Missile) program, as it was called, would allow that to happen. The Soviets now had a variety of intermediate range nuclear rockets of their own aimed at Western Europe. That was a strong selling point for the program in the United States, but an equally strong one was the balance-of-payments problem. Far better to export old missiles than gold! The European military, however, looked with skepticism on what was certain to be the last generation of liquid-fuel missiles. (Unlike the later generation of solid-fuel missiles, these involved a lengthy, easily detectable, firing procedure which could alert the enemy and possibly cause him to strike first.) Since sea-based missiles were much less vulnerable, the premier of the Fourth Republic, Félix Gaillard, asked instead to buy the guidance system for the Polaris missile, but he was promptly turned down by Eisenhower.

The Kennedy advisers were deeply split on what to do about weapons sharing. General Lauris Norstad, now the NATO supreme commander, wanted NATO to become the fourth nuclear power with a nuclear arsenal completely independent of American control. The idea found few supporters in Washington, and he resigned. A number of Kennedy advisers at the Pentagon favored a big military sales program for France. If the French bought quantities of nonnuclear weapons technology, it would cement relations with De Gaulle and help with the U.S. balance-of-payments problem. But the minister of defense arrived from Paris with a shopping list of samples and parts of the most advanced American equipment, much of it of obvious application to the *force de frappe* and a token budget of $50 million. The political generals in Washington like Maxwell Taylor and James Gavin, wanted the United States to be more forthcoming in aiding De Gaulle's program, but they failed to realize how little the general would be deterred from his vision of an independent Europe by minor changes in the symbolism of nuclear weapons. At a press conference in November 1959, he had laid out the logic of his position. Neither American charm nor cosmetic arrangements would change his mind:

Who can say that if in the future, the political background having changed completely—this is something that has already happened on earth—the two powers having the nuclear monopoly will not agree to divide the world? Who can say that if the occasion arises the two, while each deciding not to launch its missiles at the main enemy so that it should itself be spared, will not crush the others? It is possible to imagine that on some awful day Western Europe should be wiped out from Moscow and Central Europe from Washington. And who can even say that the two rivals, after I know not what political and social upheaval, will not unite?

The NATO traditionalists in the State Department were against making concessions on nuclear weapons to France which could not lawfully be made to Germany, for the principal justification for the alliance was the political webbing within which it enmeshed the labile Germans.

The NATO enthusiasts had an ally in Robert McNamara, whose genuine horror at the spread of nuclear weapons expressed itself in ways calculated to offend virtually everyone. The hard-driving secretary of defense, a complex man with a complicated view of the world he habitually simplified with a succession of *idées fixes,* flew to Athens in May 1962 and put forward "with equal vigour and clumsiness," to use Macmillan's words, "a powerful condemnation of all national nuclear forces, except, of course, those of the United States." McNamara was determined to build up conventional forces in Europe to avoid the necessity of early resort to nuclear weapons in a conflict. Since the Europeans now knew how utterly destructive a nuclear war on the Continent would be, the new strategy should please them, he reasoned. But of course, it didn't. As a military strategy for fighting a war, the McNamara proposals, which required the French, Germans, British, and the others to devote more of the fruits of their new prosperity to defense (and, incidentally help the U.S. balance of payments by buying large quantities of American conventional weapons), made sense in Washington. But from the European perspective, they communicated the wrong signals. Raising the "nuclear threshold," as the strategic jargon called it, was a way of saying that the United States was not quite so ready to protect Europe by threatening Russia with nuclear war. It was also saying that just at the moment when the nations of Europe were within reach of acquiring their own nuclear weapons, these symbols of power were not as important as in the past. In his diary Macmillan explodes. The Americans were stepping into the diplomatic nettle of Europe without knowing what they were doing:

McNamara's foolish speech about nuclear arms has enraged the French and put us in a difficulty. . . . I shall have a chance to tell Rusk on Sunday what terrible damage the Americans are doing in every field in Europe. In NATO, all the allies are angry with the American proposal that we should buy rockets to the tune of umpteen million dollars, the warheads to be under American control. This is not a European rocket. It's a racket of the American industry. So far as the Common Market is concerned, the Americans are (with the best intentions) doing our cause great harm. The more they tell the Germans, French, etc., that they (U.S.A.) want Britain to be in, the more they incline these countries to keep us out. Finally, at a time when the dollar is weak and may, in due course, drag down the pound and bring all Western Capitalism into confusion, they go round the European capitals explaining their weakness and asking for help. So gold price (and gold shares) go up. It's rather sad, because the Americans (who are naive and inexperienced) are up against centuries of diplomatic skill and finesse.

The *deus ex machina* that could hold back the disturbing political tides of Europe and restore the alliance to "health," some of the NATO enthusiasts in the Kennedy State Department believed, was the Multilateral Force (MLF). The idea had been first proposed at the end of the Eisenhower administration for a small flotilla armed with the same missile that the United States had on its submarines but manned by a polyglot crew of Germans, British, Belgians, Greeks, and Turks. Kennedy himself was somewhat skeptical, and the Joint Chiefs of Staff thought it was a nightmare on technical grounds. But the European integrationists liked it for the same reason that they had favored the European Defense Community ten years earlier. A military relationship could be used as political glue. The macabre surface vessels, with their lethal cargoes, their crews chattering away in languages incomprehensible to one another, and the ships' stores stocked with everything from stout to ouzo, made perfect targets for bureaucratic sniping. Yet such was the fervor of their proponents, indefatigable bureaucrats like Henry Owen and Robert Schaetzel, who believed that integrating a boat was a step in the direction of integrating a continent, that with the prodigious efforts of weighty men like George Ball and Jean Monnet the MLF moved inexorably like an armored personnel carrier down the corridors of power.

The MLF was to be NATO's answer to De Gaulle. It would symbolize the fact that there were now many fingers lurking near the button if not actually on it, for the United States retained effective control over the decision to go to nuclear war. But as a further enticement to the Europeans not to develop further their own national deterrents, McGeorge Bundy gave a speech in Copenhagen in September 1962 to the effect that eventually the Europeans could have their own MLF without American participation provided it was "integrated" with the U.S. defense effort. The United States never intended to give up the veto, and the scheme was, as Kennedy himself considered it, "something of a fake."

He was dubious about repairing relations with Europe with a device like the MLF. "The whole debate about an atomic force in Europe," the president told Paul-Henri Spaak seven months before his assassination, "is really useless, because Berlin is secure, and Europe as a whole is well protected. What really matters at this point is the rest of the world." The architectural pretensions of the Atlanticists, with their elaborate efforts to evoke a picture of the intercontinental relationship with such metaphors as dumbbells and pillars, irritated him. The president genuinely admired De Gaulle as a great figure, and he came to regard the view of some State Department officers that the general was just "a bastard who is out to get us" as ignorant. He had gotten on well with the general on his stopover in Paris when he had been in office less than six months. His entourage, especially his wife, had impressed De Gaulle with their familiarity with French civilization. (Jacqueline Kennedy had carried on a spirited discussion at dinner in her excellent French on the Duc d'Angoulême and the later Bourbons, showing, as De Gaulle told the president, that she knew more about French history than most Frenchwomen.) As he walked with André Malraux to the ballet inside the Louis XV theater, Kennedy himself had scored points by admiring a statue which the brilliant writer, now De Gaulle's minister of culture, considered the only genuine work of art in the place.

At their first meeting, De Gaulle reconsidered his first impressions of the new president. They agreed on almost nothing. The general quizzed Kennedy on exactly what the nuclear strategy would be in the event of war. "[I]n answer to the specific questions I put to him, he was unable to tell me at what point and against what targets, far or near, strategic or tactical, inside or outside

Russia itself the missiles would in fact be launched.'' The general snorted that he was not surprised, since "General Norstad, the Allied Commander in Chief . . . has never been able to enlighten me on these points, which are vital to my country.'' It was evident, De Gaulle wrote later, that Kennedy had set his heart on "the maintenance of his country's dominant situation in the defense of the West.'' Revising his earlier skepticism about the young American leader, De Gaulle pronounced him to be a man who "seemed to me to be on the point of taking off into the heights, like some great bird that beats its wings as it approaches the mountain tops.''

After De Gaulle's dramatic attack on the Atlantic vision, Kennedy had wanted to avoid the appearance of panic. When De Gaulle and Adenauer signed a treaty of cooperation a week after De Gaulle had announced his veto, Kennedy was philosophical. Was not the whole object of U.S. policy "to tie Germany more firmly into the structure of Western Europe. Now de Gaulle is doing that in his own way.'' He looked forward to the meeting he was scheduled to have with the general early in 1964. "I think that we will be able to get something done together.''

While U.S.–French relations grew colder, the MLF enthusiasts launched a major campaign to sell their new military arrangements to the Europeans. One of the big selling points of the MLF in Washington was that it would satiate the German appetite for nuclear weapons. But the Germans, as Henry Kissinger, the Harvard professor who was serving as a consultant to the president, reported, showed "no signs of any domestic pressure . . . for a national nuclear-weapons program.'' Indeed, public opinion in Germany had been overwhelmingly against furnishing tactical weapons to the Bundeswehr when the Eisenhower administration had proposed it in 1957. (The fiction was that legal and physical control over the actual use of the warheads would remain with the Americans, but the missiles would be distributed throughout the German army.) Public opinion in the Federal Republic was overwhelmingly against putting nuclear missiles in Germany. According to one poll in March 1958, only 13 percent of the country were for it. The SPD had carried on its *Kampf dem Atomtod* in 1957–58, playing on the same genuine revulsion against nuclear weapons that would surface again in Germany in the 1980s.

But Franz Josef Strauss, Adenauer's minister of defense, did push hard for "small" nuclear weapons for battlefield use by the Bundeswehr and for intermediate-range missiles on German soil. Moreover, he resisted strongly the Kennedy rhetoric of "raising the nuclear threshold" for it suggested a pusillanimous attitude toward using nuclear weapons in Europe. Unless the alliance kept insisting how ready it was to use nuclear weapons immediately in a crisis, he believed, the Soviets would nibble away at Germany. Since actual warfare was unlikely, a tough nuclear stance symbolized the will to prevail over the Soviets in the endless war of nerves. "I can guarantee that there will be no German nuclear weapons for three, four, or even five years,'' Strauss told Richard Crossman, the Labour party politician in 1958. "But after that, if other nations—particularly the French—make their own H-bomb, Germany may well be sucked in too.'' After all, Dulles had told him when Germany had renounced nuclear weapons in 1954 that the venerable escape hatch from disagreeable treaties perfected by international lawyers under which agreements cease to bind when conditions change—the so-called *clausula rebus sic stantibus*—could be taken advantage of if the other European powers went nuclear.

The transatlantic dialogue on when to use nuclear weapons was bloodcurdling, certainly to anyone who knew what a nuclear weapon really was, but under the guise of strategic analysis, real issues of power were being argued out. Strauss tried and failed to get what amounted to a "special relationship" with the United States on nuclear weapons, the recognition of a sort of special obligation of the United States to use them when Germany wanted them used. At the same time he and Adenauer stoutly resisted any "discrimination" against West Germany with respect to nuclear weapons. All ideas for a nuclear-free zone in Central Europe were anathema because they symbolized that in the atomic age the Federal Republic was less than a nation.

The highly theoretical and symbolic dialogue about nuclear weapons provided endless employment for the NATO establishment that had grown up in every member nation. Politicians, defense experts, generals, and commentators shuttled from conference to conference and wrote learned articles for one another. But they either skirted or refused to consider the implications of certain stubborn facts. The war against which the strategies were being devised was not a credible threat. Nor were the strategies to meet the threat any more credible. Europe could not be saved by a nuclear war and hence all proclamations of a readiness to start one on the plains of Germany dramatized the weakness of the West. The ability to replay World War I, a prolonged defense with conventional weapons, if indeed the Soviets ever considered marching across the Elbe, would have been the best deterrent, but neither the economic resources nor the spirit were available for a long war of attrition.

6

In the midst of the theological debate a real crisis arose to test theories and nerves. Nikita Khrushchev had promised Eisenhower and Dulles that he would bring up the matter of Berlin again, and on this he was as good as his word. On February 17, 1961, barely three weeks after Kennedy took office, the Soviet leader dispatched an *aide-memoire* to Bonn warning that "all the time limits have expired for understanding the need to . . . solve the problem of the occupation status of West Berlin, making it a free city." The Soviet strategy was becoming clearer. The vulnerable western half of Berlin would be the lever to pry the agreement of the Allies to the status quo in Europe. Access to West Berlin would be at the sufferance of the East German state; the world would be compelled to recognize the eastern half of Berlin as its capital. A new status for Berlin was urgent before "Hitler's generals with their twelve NATO divisions" got their hands on nuclear weapons, Khrushchev told Walter Lippmann when the columnist and his wife visited his villa at Sochi for a monumental buffet lunch worthy of a medieval czar. Khrushchev's fears were not entirely groundless. In 1960 members of the Joint Congressional Committee on Atomic Energy on a European inspection tour were incensed to discover U.S. fighter aircraft "loaded with nuclear bombs sitting on the edge of runways with German pilots inside the cockpits and starter plugs inserted." The only indication of American control "was an American officer somewhere in the vicinity with a revolver." Given the skill of Soviet intelligence it is virtually certain that Khrushchev was aware that de facto control of nuclear weapons had already begun to pass to the Germans. It is unlikely that he was any more pleased about it than the American congressmen.

Kennedy came to the White House expecting "a test of nerve and will" over Berlin. Exactly because it was the weak spot in the West, it was the symbol of American power. To give up Western rights in Berlin would signal the world that the shift in the world balance of power Khrushchev boasted of had indeed occurred. For an administration that embraced the "domino theory" with greater fervor than its predecessor, Berlin was the quintessential domino.

Konrad Adenauer was at least as apprehensive as De Gaulle about Kennedy's accession to the presidency. The new American leader appeared to him to be "a cross between a junior naval person and a Roman Catholic boy-scout," a man, as the chancellor insisted to De Gaulle, with a weakness for surrounding himself with prima donnas. During the campaign a three-page secret memorandum prepared for Franz Josef Strauss by the Defense Ministry warning that Kennedy spelled trouble for the Federal Republic had been leaked to the *Baltimore Sun*. Within hours of the new president's election, Adenauer announced that he would meet him in February. Politely told by the White House that he must wait his turn, the visit was deferred to April. "The real trouble is that he is too old and I am too young for us to understand each other," Kennedy mused after their first meeting. "I sense I'm talking not only to a different generation, . . . but to a different era, a different world." Perhaps the chancellor was, as Kennedy once exclaimed, "a greater man than De Gaulle" because he had principles that transcended "the aggrandizement of his nation." But it was a chore to deal with him, for he was given to long rambling lectures and seemed in constant need, as Sorensen put it, of "repetitious reassurances of our love and honor." But Adenauer considered Kennedy "intelligent and far-sighted," he wrote Foreign Minister Von Brentano, and he thought Wilhelm Grewe, his ambassador in Washington, was overly critical of Kennedy and should be transferred. So did Kennedy, and he was.

Kennedy was fascinated by Adenauer's political longevity and quickly calculated that if he were still in office at the chancellor's age he could preside over the dawn of the twenty-first century. But by the time they met Adenauer had lost his old verve along with much of his reputation. The latter he had damaged rather badly two years earlier by suddenly deciding to run for the presidency of the Federal Republic and then almost as suddenly deciding not to run. At first he thought that he could convert the ceremonial office by the sheer force of his personality into a presidency of Gaullist proportions. Some politicians who wished to ease his passing from the center of power encouraged him in this illusion. But the thought of being succeeded as chancellor by Ludwig Erhard was more than the old man could stomach, and he used Dulles' death as a pretext for changing his mind. He was now, he said, more than ever indispensable to the West.

The storm of criticism aroused by his behavior helped to undermine Adenauer's political position. His political power rested in no small measure on the myth of immortality. The Federal Republic was largely his creation; the man and the new state had endured together for so many years. But now, it seemed, the Adenauer era would soon be coming to an end. Ironically, the success of his policies had clouded his political future. By 1958, according to public opinion polls, 74 percent of the West German population appeared resigned to living in a divided Germany for the indefinite future. So successful had Erhard's economic policies proved to be that in 1959 the Social Democrats finally turned their back on Schumacher. In their party program adopted at Bad Godesberg, they jettisoned such classic Socialist planks as state planning and nationalization of heavy industry and dropped their long opposition to NATO and rearmament. In 1960 Willy Brandt, the dynamic, popular mayor of West Berlin, became the party leader. As Adenauer prepared for the election of September 1961, he faced an opposition that could now appeal to his supporters with policies not so different from his own but with a vigorous leader little more than half his age. Adenauer's new political vulnerability would influence his behavior in the coming crisis over Berlin.

In April, Kennedy asked Dean Acheson to prepare a paper on how to handle Khrushchev on Berlin. The former secretary argued vigorously that the Soviets were using Berlin as a pretext for testing the West. There was only one issue for Acheson: how best to demonstrate the will of America's new leadership. He recommended sending a division down the *Autobahn* if lesser military measures failed of his purpose. Khrushchev was not sufficiently afraid of nuclear war. A major U.S. buildup of both conventional and nuclear forces might encourage him to be more cautious in challenging the United States, but, of course, "there was also a substantial possibility that nuclear war might result." When Lord Home, the British foreign secretary, suggested that the legal position of the West based on the right of conquest was wearing a little thin, Acheson retorted that "perhaps it was western power that was wearing thin." It was not a legal issue. "Many Americans are in the grip of the illusion inherent in the American Bar Association slogan 'World peace through world law,' " he wrote the president. "No one else is; and we really do not believe it either."

John Kennedy met Nikita Khrushchev in the music room of the American embassy in Vienna on a gray, rainy Saturday morning in June 1961. He had with him an enormous briefing book which should have prepared him for what he was to encounter. Ambassador Llewellyn Thompson's dispatches from

At Yalta, Joseph Stalin, Franklin Roosevelt, and Winston Churchill made the decisions that led to the division of Europe, the end of the Grand Alliance, and the birth of a new alliance. UPI

"We come as conquerors," declared General of the Army Dwight D. Eisenhower. But the Americans found themselves compelled by economics and Cold War politics to put reconstruction ahead of punishment.   UPI

The "Big Four" (left to right): Ernest Bevin (U.K.), General George Marshall (U.S.), Vyacheslav Molotov (USSR), and Georges Bidault (France). Each of the "Big Four" had different plans for defeated Germany.   UPI

Japan lost more than lives and property in the war. The devastation of Hiroshima and elsewhere produced a spiritual crisis which Supreme Commander General of the Army Douglas MacArthur saw as an opportunity to remake the nation. His plan for remodeling Japan began by remaking the image of Emperor Hirohito.   UPI, UPI

Dean Acheson (right), secretary of state in the Truman Administration, was a principal architect of the Western Alliance. He is shown here with Shigeru Yoshida (left), the Japanese Prime Minister who contained the MacArthur revolution in Japan and set the stage for his nation's extraordinary recovery.   UPI

Konrad Adenauer (right), the first chancellor of the Federal Republic of Germany, shown here with his friend John Foster Dulles, was the principal architect of his nation's rehabilitation and recovery. UPI

Although John J. McCloy (left), the U.S. High Commissioner, and his predecessor Lucius Clay (right) had dictatorial powers over occupied Germany, Adenauer exercised extraordinary influence over U.S. foreign policy. McCloy and Clay are shown here with Theodor Heuss, president of the West German Republic. UPI

The Berlin Blockade helped to create a new nation in West Germany. U.S. planes flew in 13,000 tons of food in a day, and overnight the conquerors became saviors. UPI

The $13 billion spent by the United States on Europe between 1948 and 1952—a shipment of dry eggs is shown here—transformed the political economy of the Continent. UPI

Jean Monnet, the driving force on the Continent for a United Europe. UPI

The most popular postwar U.S. president and his controversial secretary of state, John Foster Dulles, solidified the NATO alliance even as they challenged the new Allies in Iran, Indo-China, and Egypt. UPI

Eden (right) wrote to Eisenhower not to appoint as secretary of state the man his foreign office colleague called the "wooliest type of useless pontificating American." Dulles thought that Eden's vanity and precious manners masked a bungler. UPI

French troops shown here at Suez helped precipitate the most acrimonious crisis in the history of the alliance. "You are like burglars. ...So get out!" the U.S. secretary of the treasury screamed at the British ambassador. UPI

President John F. Kennedy admired General Charles de Gaulle even though the French president frustrated the American "grand design" for Europe. UPI

U.S. tanks at "Checkpoint Charlie" move into position to confront Soviet tanks during the August 1961 Berlin crisis. UPI

John F. Kennedy riding with West Berlin Mayor Willy Brandt in 1962. UPI

The erection of the Berlin Wall in 1961 dramatized the division of Germany, Soviet political vulnerability in Eastern Europe, and the failure of Adenauer's tough policy to achieve reunification. For Willy Brandt, shown here with Kennedy, the logic of what became *Ostpolitik* was now apparent. UPI

The permanent stationing of 300,000 troops and 200,000 dependents symbolized U.S. commitment to the defense of Europe, but their presence strained U.S.–German relations. Large-scale maneuvers like the one shown here brought a taste of war to the German countryside. UPI

Though the NATO alliance was an international organization and the members conferred regularly at meetings such as the Paris summit conference shown here, the Americans controlled the key decisions, a fact of life that caused increasing concern in Europe. UPI

American-Japanese relations infrequently commanded presidential attention in the Eisenhower, Kennedy, and Johnson years. The dramatic circumstances that forced the cancellation of Eisenhower's visit to Japan were an exception. Here the president meets in Washington with Prime Minister Kishi. UPI

Vice-President Lyndon B. Johnson enter-
tains Konrad Adenauer at the LBJ Ranch
in April 1961.   UPI

The "living room war" in Vietnam divided the alliance and the United States
itself.   UPI

President Lyndon B. Johnson,
shown here with Secretary of Defense Robert McNamara in late
1966, tried unsuccessfully to enlist
the support of the NATO Allies and
Japan for the American military operation in Vietnam. How to react to
the first televised war caused deep
divisions in Europe and Japan.
UPI

In 1968, demonstrations by students erupted in New York, Paris, Tokyo, and, as shown here, in Bonn, West Germany. UPI

Richard Nixon and Henry Kissinger plan for a "Generation of Peace" and worry that the new German chancellor, Willy Brandt (shown below, at left, with Helmut Schmidt), is moving too fast toward *Ostpolitik*. UPI

Secretary of the Treasury John Connally closes the "gold window" and imposes a surcharge on America's allies. "We have a problem and we're sharing it with the world—just like we shared our prosperity. That's what friends are for." UPI

Richard Nixon unfolds his "secret plan" for extrication from Vietnam. UPI

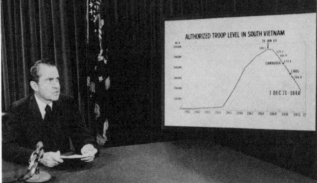

But opposition to the war grows, further straining the alliance. WAR RESISTERS LEAGUE

As Nixon and Brezhnev toast détente in the Kremlin, the Allies worry about a super-power deal even as they welcome the thaw in the Cold War. UPI

Prime Minister Edward Heath with President Nixon, now mortally wounded by the Watergate cover-up scandal as the ill-fated "Year of Europe" comes to an end. UPI

Prime Minister Sato of Japan visits Nixon after the shock of the sudden opening of doors to Communist China. UPI

Americans discover the energy crisis, but the Allies, much harder hit, complain about America's cheap gas, wasteful habits, and growing oil imports from the embattled Middle East. UPI

Portugal's briefly festive revolution caused panic in the White House because of the prominence of Portugal's militant Communist party. UPI

The new U.S. president, Gerald Ford, shown at right with the new French president, Giscard d'Estaing, suggested that Portugal be expelled from NATO. UPI

The fraying of NATO at the edges continued as two Allies, Greece and Turkey, went to war with each other over Cyprus. Archbishop Makarios, a central figure in the conflict, is shown here with Under Secretary of State George Ball, one of the senior figures of the national security establishment periodically dispatched to deal with "the Castro of the Mediterranean." WIDE WORLD

The Shah of Iran, shown here as President Jimmy Carter received a whiff of tear gas used to control angry demonstrators, was a pillar of U.S. foreign policy in the Middle East. His fall in 1979 was a severe upset to American strategy.   UPI

The taking of hostages at the U.S. Embassy in Tehran caused further strains in the Alliance.   UPI

The Soviet invasion of Afghanistan in December 1979 dealt a death blow to the tottering U.S.–Soviet détente and exposed profound differences among the Allies about how to treat Soviet Russia.   UPI

National Security Adviser Zbigniew Brzezinski looks through the sight of a Chinese-style AK-47 machine gun near the border of Afghanistan.   UPI

Slow economic growth and periodic recessions heightened trade rivalries among the Allies. Japanese cars, shown here waiting for shipment to the U.S., captured 20 percent of the American automobile market, exacerbating the severe unemployment in the industry. UPI

The Carter Administration was dedicated to closer cooperation with the other industrial nations but did not succeed. The Trilateral Commission, here being addressed by David Rockefeller (right), was a source of ideas and bureaucrats in the Carter presidency and a favorite target as a "conspiracy." UPI

The call for the coordinated management of the increasingly interdependent market economies of North America, Europe, and Japan was regularly sounded when the leaders of the Alliance met, but competitive nationalism was on the rise everywhere. Shown here at the Guadeloupe conference in January 1979 are (from left) West German Chancellor Helmut Schmidt, British Prime Minister James Callaghan, U.S. President Jimmy Carter, and their host, French President Giscard d'Estaing. UPI

Ronald Reagan came to the White House determined to restore American prestige and power. He is shown here with Queen Elizabeth II of Great Britain, with François Mitterrand, the first Socialist President of France (right), and with Prime Minister Zenko Suzuki of Japan (below).
UPI

The call for major increases in military spending and the sharp deterioration in U.S.–Soviet relations sparked a strong public reaction in the U.S. The peace demonstration in Central Park in June 1982 was an echo of massive demonstrations in Europe such as the one shown (right) in Frankfurt.   WAR RESISTERS LEAGUE, UPI

The imposition of martial law in Poland in response to the Solidarity movement led by Lech Walesa (shown above) elicited sharply different reactions among the Allies.
UPI

Moscow predicted that the Soviet leader would take a tough tack on Berlin. The Soviet leader had seemed determined to demonstrate that the Soviet Union was now in its most dynamic stage of its history, ready to "overtake" capitalist achievements in the economic arena and to lend its support to revolutionary struggles around the world. Kennedy's rhetorical stance, with his emphasis on getting the country "moving," was to show an American determination to retake the initiative. "I go as the leader of the greatest revolutionary country on earth," he told a Boston audience a few days before his departure.

It was a mark of his personal flair and the yearning of so many to believe in the debonair young leader that Kennedy arrived in Vienna with his prestige largely intact. Barely six weeks earlier he had fallen into a disaster by authorizing a hopeless invasion of Cuba which failed spectacularly. Acheson was in Europe at the time of the Bay of Pigs fiasco sounding out the Allies on whether they would cooperate on his ideas for a tough stance on Berlin. "The European view," he reported to Kennedy on his return, "was that they were watching a gifted young amateur practice with a boomerang, when they saw to their horror that he had knocked himself out." Kennedy, Acheson recalls, "didn't like this at all." In his performance in Vienna, he knew, he would be playing for other audiences besides Khrushchev. Like Truman in Korea and Eisenhower over Suez, he had given the Allies reason to doubt the steadiness and nerve of the American leadership. He must now recoup.

Kennedy's first impression of the Soviet leader was a man who for all his heavy jokes was full of "internal rage." "Ah, a capitalist, not an incendiary," Khrushchev smiled at dinner as Kennedy assured him that the match he had flung behind his chair after lighting up a cigar was not meant to set the chairman on fire. The president complimented Khrushchev on the Lenin Peace Prize medals dangling from his lapel. "I hope you keep them," he laughed wryly. But when the subject of Berlin came up, all banter ceased. Khrushchev restated his position. The situation in Berlin was "abnormal." Eisenhower had even admitted that. The German militarists were gaining ground. The peace treaty "normalizing" relations between the occupying powers and East Germany must be signed by the end of the year. If U.S. troops were to stay in Berlin, it would have to be at the sufferance of the German Democratic Republic. "If that is true," the president retorted, "it will be a cold winter." Any attempt to block the Western access routes to Berlin would mean war.

Khrushchev left the meeting with the impression that Kennedy was too "reasonable" to start a war over Berlin. Kennedy left Vienna believing that he was being challenged around the world by the Russians and that the supreme test of whether the United States would fight for a "vital interest" was Berlin. The "prospects for nuclear war were now very real," the president told newsmen. He so "overmanaged" the news, as his confidant Theodore Sorensen later wrote, in an effort to combat the euphoria that had followed previous summits and to create the mood for the big military buildup that he was convinced was necessary, that rumors flew in every major capital describing the president as having been thrown into a panic by the dumpy, excitable Khrushchev.

Back in Washington, Kennedy gave three speeches that sounded an increasingly strident note of crisis. The conference had been a "somber" experience. The nation would now be tested. Berlin was not "indefensible" if free men were determined to defend it. The few American troops there were "hostages," Kennedy said at a press conference to underscore America's determination to risk nuclear war for its rights in Berlin. Khrushchev gave a speech on June 15 reiterating that the United States had just six months to come to a new agreement. On the same day Walter Ulbricht, the leader of the East German state, speculated that the Tempelhof Airport in West Berlin just might have to "close itself down" unless East Germany were recognized. ". . .air safety service must now be agreed upon within the representatives of the state exercising air sovereignty."

The war of nerves was on. The issue that divided Kennedy's advisers was how to fight it. The president had gone to Vienna in part to see whether he could avoid a miscalculation over Berlin and defuse the issue while the United States carried out a major military buildup across the board. With the crisis starting to boil, his fervent wish was to find a diplomatic solution. But diplomacy would fail, he was repeatedly told, if he appeared too eager to avoid war. United States vital interests worth risking nuclear war must be kept to the absolute minimum and must be precisely communicated. Thus from the start the issues were the presence of U.S. troops in Berlin, access for the American garrison, and the security and political freedom of West Berlin. The United States was committed to the defense of the status quo, yet the rights of the Four Powers in East Berlin were scarcely mentioned. Acheson and other hardliners argued that diplomacy would only dilute the message that must now be sent "loud and clear": the United States was prepared to take greater risks than the Soviet Union over the fate of Berlin.

The president authorized a "two-track" strategy, but the magnitude of the military buildup overwhelmed the hesitant peace efforts. On July 25, 1961, Kennedy called for increasing the draft, calling up reserves, and substantially increasing the defense budget and the size of all three military services. In addition, having been barely talked out of sending a personal letter to every American home advising the immediate construction of a backyard fallout shelter, he called for a major civil defense program. At a National Security Council meeting Lyndon Johnson and Dean Rusk urged the president to declare a national emergency, but Kennedy refused to take such a drastic step. Yet he was determined to show resolve. "That son of a bitch won't pay any attention to words," Kennedy exploded. "He has to see you move." In Washington anxious bureaucrats began stocking their cellars with toilet paper and peanut butter. By late summer macabre discussions of likely fallout patterns in the metropolitan Washington area were familiar features of dinner parties in Georgetown and Cleveland Park.

All through July and early August the Pentagon was plunged into feverish

preparations for what Paul Nitze, assistant secretary of defense, later described to a German audience as "a really serious non-nuclear probe in the air
corridors or along the autobahn in the event of Soviet actions against Western
interests in Berlin." Nitze made a point of inviting Soviet Ambassador Mikhail
Menshikov to lunch at the Metropolitan Club to tell him how much of the
USSR would be devastated by the multi-megaton attacks called for in U.S.
war plans.

For McNamara, Berlin was the place to test the new "flexible response"
doctrine he was trying to have adopted as the new NATO strategy. Only after
the Soviets had repulsed a "probe" by ground forces down the autobahn would
nuclear weapons be introduced. This strategy would provide a "pause" in the
rush of events to permit everyone to come to his senses before all-out war
occurred. Endless discussions of the theory and practice of "escalation" went
on in pastel, windowless offices throughout the city. The problem was perceived as the education of Khrushchev, and the means ranged from harassing
the solitary eighteen-year-old Soviet soldier guarding a Soviet monument in
the British sector of the city to dropping the bomb.

Ostensibly the contingency planning effort involved all the NATO countries, but in reality the strategy was strictly a U.S. creation. Kennedy admitted
as much when he referred in his speech of July 25 to the "decisions" taken by
the administration. The Allies had been consulted but the strategy bore an
American stamp. Not only was there no consensus on what to do, but the
American military strategy alarmed all the Allies. The British wanted the immediate use of tactical nuclear weapons; they opposed the idea of a long
"ladder of escalation." Khrushchev should get the point right away. At the
same time Macmillan was insistent that serious negotiations begin promptly.
At the NATO Foreign Ministers Conference the previous May, German Foreign Minister Von Brentano declared that the West should "not hesitate to use
atomic weapons" over Berlin. The idea of doing anything else, Franz Josef
Strauss added, would give him "holy terrors." De Gaulle had told Eisenhower
and Macmillan two years earlier, "[y]ou do not wish to die for Berlin, but you
may be sure that the Russians do not wish to either." Worried that a soft
position on Berlin might eventually drive the Federal Republic into an accommodation with the East and change the balance of power of Europe, the general
pressed Kennedy to take a tough position. "[W]hen Khrushchev summons you
to change the status of Berlin, in other words to hand the city over to him,
stand fast! That is the most useful service you can render to the whole world,
Russia included." He had given his own icy warning to Khrushchev whom he
had invited to Paris in 1959: "The three Western powers will never allow their
troops to be insulted. If it leads to war, it will be entirely your fault."

John J. McCloy, now serving as a special adviser to Kennedy on disarmament, was visiting Khrushchev at Sochi when the Soviet leader received
word of Kennedy's tough speech on Berlin. Khrushchev's voice quivering with
emotion, he told the American, whom he had just lent a pair of his own oversized bathing trunks, that Kennedy was threatening war and that if war came

"he would be the last president." The Soviet Union, he wanted Kennedy to know, had developed a hundred-megaton bomb. On August 7, Khrushchev went on television and gave an excited speech about the danger of war. He too was calling up the reserves. Now the mood in Washington was shifting. Acheson's influence was waning. The president's principal advisers wanted an early meeting with the Russians at the foreign minister level to begin negotiations.

On August 6, the day after the foreign ministers of the United States, Britain, France, and West Germany met in Paris to discuss negotiations with Khrushchev, 2305 persons arrived in West Berlin from East Germany. It was the biggest daily influx of refugees ever. In 1960, 152,000 East Germans had escaped via Berlin, almost half of them under the age of twenty-five. Many of the refugees were skilled workers or technicians. Given the accelerating rate of exodus, the German Democratic Republic was now threatened with the loss of more than a half million people a year. As the war clouds gathered, more and more were "voting with their feet" as the Western propaganda broadcasts phrased it. The propaganda victory for the West was putting enormous strain on the Federal Republic. For Khrushchev and Ulbricht the flood of refugees was more than embarrassing. It threatened the very stability of the East German regime.

The NATO foreign ministers departed from Paris without any agreed upon position. De Gaulle refused all negotiation and, as the September elections approached, Adenauer appeared to be against negotiating with the Russians, against risking war, and, as Sorensen put it, against "seemingly everything else." The crisis was building. Khrushchev, who had dressed himself in his wartime lieutenant-general's uniform to make an earlier speech on Berlin, now warned that if war came, the Acropolis would be "in the line of fire" and the culture and art of Italy would be destroyed. "Come to your senses, gentlemen," he cried.

On August 13, shortly after midnight, columns of Soviet tanks, East German police cars, and trucks with special platoons of factory workers carrying machine guns broke the silence of the night. Tanks and armored cars took up positions by the Brandenburg Gate. Under floodlights, barbed-wire fencing was unrolled and installed at Potsdamer Platz. At every crossover point to West Berlin, soldiers stood guard with automatic weapons as workers dug deep ditches. The Western military traffic between the cities was undisturbed, but no German could henceforth enter or leave the eastern half of the city without "special permission." In the first forty-eight hours after the skeleton of what would soon become The Wall was already in place, about ninety Berliners escaped under a hail of gunfire by swimming the canals and the river. Erwin Shabe, a twelve-year-old schoolboy who lived in Eiskeller, a minuscule West Berlin enclave inside the Soviet Zone, was told by the East German authorities that he could not get to his school in West Berlin. Unlike most of the other Berliners who lived in one part of the city and worked in the other, Erwin Shabe because of a geographical quirk had become a symbol of Allied rights in Berlin. A British Army armored vehicle was assigned to follow his bicycle on the daily three-mile ride to the schoolhouse.

Konrad Adenauer was informed of what was happening in Berlin at 7:00 A.M. and he went to Mass. Urged by the visiting U.S. Senator Thomas Dodd to fly to Berlin with him at once, he shook his head. All day he remained in seclusion, emerging only to make a television speech urging calm. Willy Brandt, notified aboard the Munich–Kiel express, immediately made arrangements to fly to Berlin. He fired off a letter to Kennedy demanding a strong U.S. response and in an obvious campaign ploy made it public, much to the annoyance of the president. Kennedy was aboard his cabin cruiser *Marlin* off Cape Cod for a midday cruise when he received word by radio to return to shore for an urgent message. He quickly concluded that the crisis did not require his immediate return to Washington. Indeed, neither the British prime minister, the foreign secretary, nor the French premier, Michel Debré, permitted the events in Berlin to interrupt their weekend.

The president had understood that East Berlin was a "vital interest" for the Russians and that any move limited to East Berlin would not be an issue on which "I can get the alliance to move." Yet he worried that the sealing of East Berlin might be only the first step in a larger Soviet plan. Shortly after his arrival back in Washington, at a hurried meeting of top advisers in his bedroom in the White House, Kennedy, still in pajamas, quickly concluded that providing a psychological lift for Berlin was the only response to be made and he ordered 1500 additional U.S. troops for the American garrison. When informed of Kennedy's decision by Allen Dulles, Dwight Eisenhower thought Khrushchev "would merely chuckle." The chances of a "nuclear exchange," Schlesinger recalls Kennedy saying, were now one out of five. By the time Adenauer made his first appearance in Berlin on August 22, Vice President Lyndon Johnson had come and gone. Greeted by hecklers, "You have come too late, Herr Bundeskanzler," the cry was taken up by writers and politicians across Germany. The divided city that symbolized the Cold War now dramatized Adenauer's failure. As the cinder blocks replaced the barbed wire and the ugly watchtowers went up over Potsdamer Platz, the wrenching of Germany seemed complete and permanent.

At one point East German police trained water hoses on American soldiers who reached for their grenades. On another occasion, the East Germans attempted to rush an American civilian car "exercising rights" in East Berlin. The Americans feared that the authorities were trying to cause an accident that would serve as a pretext for controlling the traffic. Lucius Clay, the hero of the 1948 airlift, now once again in Berlin as Kennedy's special representative, sent a car with an armed escort for a tour of East Berlin on two successive days. But ten minutes after the vehicle left East Berlin, Soviet tanks moved up to block the Friedrichstrasse checkpoint. Amid the growing alarm of the British and French, Kennedy called off the probes by armed vehicles. General Clay then moved ten U.S. tanks up to the border, and the Soviets responded with ten of their own, then twenty. Again Clay matched them. As the U.S. and Soviet tank drivers stared curiously at each other across the barbed wire munching sandwiches, Kennedy called Clay, "Tell me, are you nervous?" "If anybody's nervous, Mr. President," he replied, barely disguising his contempt for the dovish diplomats in the State Department he was convinced were sabotaging his efforts, "it will probably be people in Washington." Kennedy assured the general that he wasn't nervous. But alarming headlines appeared around the world about the impending tank duel in Berlin. For Brandt the appearance of Soviet tanks within two hundred yards of American occupied territory undercut the official Soviet position for it "confirmed that they still had the 'last word' in the Eastern Sector."

The Kennedy administration operated on the premise that they could do nothing to reverse the Soviet *fait accompli*. (Brandt, who blamed the "Protecting Powers" for their slow reaction, had no military strategy for tearing down The Wall.) In Washington the emphasis was on limiting the damage by shoring up the morale of West Berliners. Edward R. Murrow, the famous war correspondent now head of U.S. propaganda activities, had by chance been in Berlin on the night the barbed wire went up, and he returned to Washington with renewed determination to send in cultural reinforcements—the Santa Fe Symphony, Igor Stravinsky, even Harry Truman. "Why not in this summer of our discontent and as marvelous pre-negotiation propaganda," one of the professorial strategists in the White House basement mused in a memo, could we not have "an inspired widely publicized big circulation magazine (Time-Life-Sat. Eve Post) do the story of Ulbricht—murderer, betrayer of his country, hated by his people, completely unprincipled political eel. . . ."

The president's brother, the attorney general, also thought that the times called for manipulating opinion. On August 17 Robert Kennedy sent a memo to the president urging "greater steps to stimulate activity among students, university professors, labor leaders and businessmen" in the propaganda war with the Russians. "Allen Dulles says that he has spent ten years forming groups that can perform these kinds of functions," but to Robert Kennedy they sounded "more like paper organizations than anything else." Lyndon Johnson's visit to Berlin had been a propaganda success even though the vice president had not endeared himself to his hosts. Johnson had heard that the Staatliche Porzellanwerke in Berlin made famous blue dishes and he wanted some. When told by Brandt that it was Sunday and the factory was closed, Johnson exploded. "Well goddammit. You're the mayor, aren't you? It shouldn't be too difficult for you to make arrangements so I can get to see that porcelain. I've crossed an entire ocean to come here. . . ." The hapless manager was dragged from his bed by protocol officers and the vice president ordered a couple of sets of dishes. Watching Johnson glory in the crowds that came to hear him, kissing babies and patting dogs, Egon Bahr, Brandt's confidant, decided that Lyndon Johnson was already running for president of the United States.

Like the Berlin Airlift thirteen years earlier, The Wall was a historic turning point—for individuals and nations. Lucius Clay, who kept pressing for a tough response, was continually frustrated by what he considered a weak reaction of the West and resigned in disgust. Adenauer, panicked that the crisis had given new visibility and stature to his opponent, Willy Brandt, dropped his statesman's mantle and made certain that every German knew that Willy

Brandt "alias Frahm" had been born a bastard. In the election the CDU received 700,000 fewer votes than in the previous election and lost its absolute majority in the Bundestag. Though reelected for the fourth time as chancellor, Adenauer was shaken and damaged. The remainder of his time in office would be largely spent in discussing how he would leave it. For Willy Brandt the incident dramatized the limits of Western power and commitment to Berlin. In December 1961, hinting at the direction of his future career, he declared that the great task of German foreign policy was to enter "a new relationship with the Great Power in the East."

The building of The Wall solved Khrushchev's most pressing problems and thus, also, Kennedy's. Once the Ulbricht regime was less vulnerable, Khrushchev's interest in fanning the crisis waned. Acheson's notion that Khrushchev's motives were primarily to test Kennedy rather than to stabilize his domain in East Europe had proved wrong. Within two months Khrushchev had withdrawn his deadline, ostensibly because "the western powers were showing some understanding of the situation, and were inclined to seek a solution. . . ." When the crisis had subsided the United States adopted NSAM 109, a contingency plan for protecting the access to Berlin with nuclear weapons once nonnuclear measures failed. The top secret paper signed by the president stated:

If, despite Allied use of substantial non-nuclear forces, the Soviets continue to encroach upon our vital interests, *then* the Allies should use nuclear weapons, starting with one of the following courses of action but continuing through C below if necessary:
A. Selective nuclear attacks for the primary purpose of demonstrating the will to use nuclear weapons.
B. Limited tactical employment of nuclear weapons to achieve in addition significant tactical advantage such as preservation of the integrity of Allied forces committed, or to extend pressure toward the objective.
C. General Nuclear War.

The Berlin Crisis did not finally recede, however, until it was overtaken by an even more formidable crisis which Khrushchev precipitated by placing nuclear rockets in Cuba. Until that crisis Khrushchev maintained pressure on Berlin. On one occasion a special U.S. plane carrying Lucius Clay and Willy Brandt was buzzed in the Berlin air corridor. Troop concentrations in East Germany so alarmed the mayor that he drove home one afternoon to have a "serious chat with my fourteen year old son Peter." He should be prepared to become "the man of the family," for it was possible "that his father would be away for some time." The Berlin public knew nothing of Brandt's concern.

The Cuban Missile Crisis of October 1962 transformed the Western alliance. What had been implicit suddenly became frighteningly explicit. The American president had calculated the odds as "somewhere between one out of three and even" that if he were to order an attack on the Russian missiles in Cuba there would be a nuclear war. But as each day passed he moved closer to that decision. As his brother Robert later put it, "[W]e had to be aware that we were deciding, the President was deciding, for the U.S., the Soviet Union, Turkey, NATO and really for all mankind. . . ." The confrontation ended in what seemed a smashing victory for the United States. Khrushchev, who had most likely placed the missiles in Cuba as a prelude to a global negotiation to establish the "equality" of the USSR as a nuclear superpower and to force acceptance of the status quo in Europe, backed down. Despite Kennedy's efforts to help him save face, the Soviet leader was humiliated and his power broken.

The Allies applauded the outcome, admired Kennedy's nerve and coolness under fire. He had thrown off the image of the wavering leader that he had earned at the time of the Bay of Pigs affair. But, as Dean Acheson made clear in the early hours of that fateful week when he flew to Europe with secret photos of the Soviet missile sites to brief De Gaulle and other leaders of the alliance, the Allies were being "informed," not consulted. Scanning the photos taken from 65,000 feet with a soldier's fascination, De Gaulle told Acheson, "If there is a war, I will be with you. But there will be no war." Macmillan pledged public support but was deeply troubled by the mounting confrontation. The *Economist* warned against "forcing a showdown" and a number of prominent intellectuals, including A. J. Ayer, A. J. P. Taylor, and Richard Titmuss, called for British neutrality in the crisis. Kennedy and Macmillan had several long telephone conversations in which the president kept asking the prime minister what he would do. In his memoirs Macmillan offers the conversations which he quotes at length as evidence of the persistence of the "special relationship." In fact, Kennedy was using the older man as a sounding board. When it was over, Macmillan remarked that Kennedy had earned his place in history.

But the "eyeball to eyeball" confrontation, to use Dean Rusk's celebrated phrase, had unanticipated and unintended consequences. While the victory over Khrushchev helped the Democrats the following month in the congressional elections, it also helped to destroy the Kennedy Grand Design. Within two months General de Gaulle vetoed Britain's entry into the Common Market and proceeded to turn Germany into a junior partner in his campaign to resist American influence over the Continent. Now that Kennedy had stood firm against the Russians, it was safe to explore détente. As much as he cheered Kennedy on, the general found it quite intolerable that the security of France should depend upon American nerves. The missile crisis gave a push to the Soviet rearmament program. Khrushchev's effort to substitute bluster and drama for a massive expenditure on the military had failed and his successors resolved to challenge American nuclear "superiority." But the victory of the West in October 1962 provided De Gaulle with a powerful argument for building up France's own nuclear force and for disengaging from an alliance he could not shape.

The Cuban missile crisis was crucial to the Kennedy legend. He had gambled for the highest stakes and won, or so it seemed. Somehow there attached to his person the relief, even the gratitude of the world. The legend grew with his final European tour a few months before his death. Within sight of the Wall Kennedy cried, "*Ich bin ein Berliner*," and the crowd went mad. He said later that if he had told them to "[M]arch to the wall—tear it down," they would have done so. Kennedy noted this with those mixed feelings of exhilaration and anxiety that irrational crowds always evoked in him. He was a man who could "project a vision of the future without moving an inch away from the reality of our time," the influential commentator Countess Marion Dönhoff wrote in *Die Zeit*. "In the summer of 1963," Arthur Schlesinger, Jr., later wrote, "John F. Kennedy could have carried every country in Europe."

SIX

THE TEST OF VIETNAM:

Mr. Johnson Looks for Friends

1

Within seventy-two hours of the death of John F. Kennedy eight chiefs of state, eleven heads of government, ten monarchs and princes, thirty-four foreign ministers, and other dignitaries from seventy nations gathered in Washington to do honor to the fallen president and to take the measure of his successor. So spectacular a funeral had not been seen since the rites for Edward VII in London a little over fifty years before. But how the look of power had changed. On the eve of the First World War companies of royal cousins from the continental monarchies—a splash of kings, dukes, earls, counts, and generals with plumed hats—had paraded in full pomp before a breathless crowd. But now Washington was the center of the world. Despite the sprinkling of royal regalia, the congregation of mourners from around the globe did not match the pageantry of the dying Edwardian age, yet the crowding of the world's political leaders into one reception room was an awesome event.

Official funerals offer irresistible moments for discreet diplomacy. Lyndon B. Johnson welcomed his talk with Charles de Gaulle, pleased that the imperious figure, now a bit stooped, had made the gesture to come to Washington. "I think he likes me. I'm going to try to work with him—not force something down his throat. . . . I've told everyone who has anything to do with it: stop telling Europeans that they have to do this or that—or else." But the new president got off to a bad start by telling reporters that De Gaulle had agreed to return to Washington the following year, only to be corrected publicly by the French ambassador a few days later: Johnson was now the junior leader of the alliance; he would be received in Paris should he care to come. As he circulated among the guests in the banquet hall of the State Department after the funeral, supplied with three-by-five cards on the most

234

important of them, an anxious Dean Rusk at his elbow, Lyndon Johnson revealed nothing of himself. Even in private conversations with the leaders of Britain, Japan, Germany, and the Soviet Union he remained largely unfathomable.

He served as president for almost six years, but the real Lyndon Johnson was as elusive on the day he left office as on the day he took the oath. One thing was sure. He was not what he wished to appear. Behind the public man, whose oily phrases and embarrassing pieties soon earned him the name of "Ole' Cornpone" in Georgetown and London salons, was a maddeningly complex personality. No president in recent memory was so tirelessly devoted to personal enrichment nor so impulsively generous. None was so full of sentimental concern and none found it easier to lie. He craved love and adulation more than most leaders, but he abused the subordinates on whom he most depended. "Mr. President, you don't pay these men enough to talk to them that way," Dean Acheson, having just been needled himself, once reminded the president at a meeting of high-level advisers. Johnson projected fierceness and determination but he was plagued by self-doubt—especially about the war that would consume his presidency—and in the end he was afraid. Despite the image-building paraphernalia of the White House, people around the world sensed this even if they did not know it. By the time he was forced out of office, Lyndon Johnson had become the lightning rod for anti-Americanism around the world. As Kennedy had come to symbolize the hope of America, LBJ came to stand for the hypocrisy, self-deception, and murderous rage of imperial America.

Lyndon Johnson was a student of power, indeed a power addict. "The President comes into a room slowly and warily," Michael Davie of the London *Observer* reported in 1966, "as if he means to smell out the allegiance of everyone in it. There is a faint air of a barroom strategist." Seeking power had consumed his life. Painful childhood memories—at times the only food in the house was what neighbors brought—propelled him all the way to great riches and high office. He would use the power to help the powerless. From his early days as a teacher of poor Mexicans, he cared about the poor. Cynics would say that most of the concern about poverty was personal; by the time he reached the White House he had amassed more than $14 million, some of it by questionable practices. Even in the highest office, according to his biographer Robert Caro, "Johnson personally directed his business affairs, down to the most minute details, not infrequently working on those affairs, according to some of his attorneys, for several hours a day." But what the press called his "populism" was as genuine as his greed. His dream to create an America in which every cottage would have "a picture on the wall and a rug on the floor" was a heartfelt power fantasy that sounded like political hokum. "I realized that if only I could take the new step and become dictator of the whole world," Johnson confided to his biographer Doris Kearns in retirement, "then I could really make things happen. Every hungry person would be fed, every ignorant child educated, every jobless man employed. And then I knew I could accomplish my greatest wish, the wish for eternal peace."

All that the world intelligence agencies knew of Lyndon Johnson were colorful snippets: this huge, gangling figure of coarse manners and domineering ways played the part of an innocent abroad. As vice president he had let loose with a yahoo scream in the Taj Mahal to test the echo. While still vice president-elect he had abruptly left a hastily assembled dinner in his honor at the home of the foreign secretary attended by the British power elite for a highly publicized visit to a London nightclub. He haggled shamelessly with a local artist over the purchase price of paintings in a Copenhagen hotel room, ordered CIA agents to assist him in his ceaseless search for bargains, and sent a navy plane on a round trip from Hong Kong to Taipei to pick up his favorite Scotch. His imperious ways abroad contrasted sharply with his uncharacteristically self-effacing manner at home. For more than three years he was rarely heard in Washington speaking above a throaty whisper. "Every time I came into John Kennedy's presence," he told Doris Kearns years later, "I felt like a goddam raven hovering over his shoulder. Away from the Oval Office, it was even worse. The Vice-Presidency is filled with trips around the world, chauffeurs, men saluting, people clapping, chairmanships of councils, but in the end, it is nothing. I detested every minute of it."

Like the rest of his generation his world view was formed by the crusade against Hitler. "If you let a bully come into your front yard one day," he would say over and over, "the next day he'll be up on your porch and the day after that he'll rape your wife in your own bed." The United States had to show strength to avoid looking "fat and fifty, like the country-club set." Johnson shared none of the Eastern ideology of Atlanticism. Foreigners were just "not like folks you were reared with." But he was strongly behind NATO for the same reasons the State Department had been for it in 1949. Only he expressed it differently: If the Germans were not restrained by the alliance and given their due within it, they would "break out again like Kaiser Bill and get us into World War III. . . ."

Johnson had not been above using anti-Communism to attack political foes in the McCarthy era, and he shared the conventional skepticism of the Soviet Union. But he was passionately committed to search for peace, for not only was he frightened by the prospect of war, but he was certain that his dream of extending the New Deal—ending poverty, integrating the blacks, making government humane—required the relaxation of tensions. Within three weeks of taking office he went before the United Nations with a plea "to see the Cold War end once and for all." He worked hard to expand the post–missile crisis détente. Kennedy had given a considerable lift to détente with a speech at American University five months before the assassination, in which for the first time in almost twenty years a U.S. president talked sympathetically about the Russians and how they saw the world. The Partial Test Ban agreement had then been signed. Now Johnson was determined to press on with arms control negotiations and the private correspondence Kennedy had been conducting with Khrushchev. He kept the Kennedy aides, Bundy, McNamara, Sorensen, at their desks, and stressed "continuity."

Lyndon Johnson had been an important power broker in the Congress since 1937 when he landed a seat on the Naval Affairs Committee. In his years as Majority Leader of the Senate during the Eisenhower presidency, he was a master horsetrader, equally expert at subtle intimidation, flattery, outright threats, and the arts of compromise. Foreign leaders. he believed, were susceptible to the same treatment as American politicians. The traditions were different, but the global political elite constituted a club like the Senate, not even as big. His instinct for political self-preservation, not geopolitics, had prompted him to play the decisive role in keeping Eisenhower out of a military intervention in Indochina in 1954. Foreign policy issues were something political enemies could use to stir up the country and destroy even a great leader's chance to remake the society. The American people, he told Doris Kearns, were "not only peaceful but apathetic," concerned mostly with their own affairs, but the deep hunger for security, if played upon, could provoke "a mass stampede, a violent overreaction to fear, and explosion of panic." Explaining his persistence in the Vietnam War long after the disastrous consequences had become apparent, Johnson would plead that his own identity and the national destiny were equally at stake. In his dreams he saw thousands of people rushing toward him, crying, "Coward! Traitor! Weakling," and he was "as sure as any man could be that once we showed how weak we were, Moscow and Peking would move in a flash to exploit our weakness."

When Lyndon Johnson talked about power in private, everyone understood him. "What does he need?" "What does he want?" he would say of a foreign leader on the eve of his visit. If he could get into a room with a man, judge his strengths and weaknesses, he could come out with agreement, even with Khrushchev. But when he enunciated high principles in public, particularly as the Vietnam War boiled up, his credibility collapsed.

The Johnson legend was an instant creation of the press. "[P]urely and aggressively American . . . infinitely more alien and complex than was President Kennedy," a British observer reported. Here was a peculiar American superman, a Paul Bunyan with a foul mouth. Given to making public utterances in whiny, sanctimonious cadences, his private speech was peppered with sexual metaphors and scatological allusions as to impress a drill sergeant.

He was known for the restless energy that kept him at work most of the night, but what was not known were the self-doubt and inner conflicts that kept him from sleeping. Years later he recalled his feelings in his first weeks in office. "I was still illegitimate, a naked man with no presidential covering, a pretender to the throne, an illegal usurper." He feared, resented, and admired the Kennedy advisers on foreign policy, but he felt he needed them all, especially McNamara. His classmates had described the young Johnson in his college yearbook as "a master of the gentle art of spoofing the general public." But as he strained to be believed, angry crowds around the world refused to listen.

2

As Johnson took office the relationship with Europe was no longer the obsession of the foreign policy establishment as it was in the Marshall Plan days or even in the Eisenhower years. By 1964 the disintegration of the prewar European empires which had absorbed so much of Dulles' attention was about over. Except for some residual colonies and bases east of Suez, Gibraltar, and a few other vestiges of her imperial past, the "little England" long sought by British anti-imperialists was now a reality. France talked increasingly of grandeur but kept shedding territory. John F. Kennedy had proclaimed that the arena of the Cold War was no longer Europe but the new nations of Asia and Africa and the "neglected" neighbors of Latin America. With the collapse of the Khrushchev challenges over Berlin and Cuba a de facto détente had arrived. Johnson and Erhard repeated the ritualistic commitment to reunification, but by this time almost no one on either side of the Elbe believed in the possibility of a reunited Germany, and fewer and fewer seemed to care. Twenty years after the cataclysm the Continent was settling. Neither war nor diplomatic breakthrough nor radical political changes in either half appeared likely.

Preoccupied as he was in the early months with making Kennedy's stalled domestic program his own monument, Johnson was, nevertheless, faced with the need to come up with a new strategy for dealing with the Allies, particularly since he hoped soon to approach the Russians for an arms limitation agreement. "Disarray," the inevitable word used by journalists and scholars to describe the state of the alliance, was now equally applicable to West Europe as a whole. The European economy was at its most dynamic stage, but all political movement was stalled. De Gaulle, despite the Johnson efforts to defuse U.S.–French tensions, was energetically pursuing what the State Department Atlanticists considered a huge wrecking operation. Acheson's advice that it was impossible "to persuade, bribe, or coerce" the general was no doubt sound. "The power of the United States to shape the inevitable for General De Gaulle is immense," the senior statesman assured the president. But it was not clear how. De Gaulle was seeking to lure the Germans to his side, at the very least creating an explosive division inside Germany between the pro-American faction led by Erhard, and the "Gaullists," led by former chancellor Adenauer who retained his post as party leader and seemed eager to do what he could to make Erhard regret the succession as much as he. In Britain the Tories had been rocked by the Profumo Affair. The secretary of war, John Profumo, had been indiscreet enough to share a mistress with the Soviet naval attaché and to lie about it to the House of Commons. Macmillan, in bad health, stepped down soon thereafter, musing, as he put it in his memoirs, about how respectable and disreputable people "now seemed to be all mixed up together." In October 1964 Labour narrowly won the election and Harold Wilson became prime minister. Politically divided, the pound once again imperiled, England even more than Germany now seemed incapable of mustering the power to oppose De Gaulle. Meanwhile the general was playing his role as the leader of independent Europe with ever more feeling, for he knew as the State Department ideologues did not, that for all his fustian style he spoke for many in Europe who believed that the Continent must find its own voice.

At the Kennedy funeral Ludwig Erhard, who had become Bundeskanzler barely a month before, had eagerly accepted an invitation to visit the LBJ Ranch in Texas right after Christmas. Amidst rides at breakneck speed in presidential limousines through the hills of central Texas, darting visits to German-American communities nestled in the countryside surrounding the ranch, and a little deer hunting, Johnson began to experiment with diplomacy. (He also took time out from the visit to sit behind closed doors "browbeating a group of businessmen in connection with a television option agreement . . . he had won through his behind-the-scenes influence over the Austin City Council. . . .")

The United States, Johnson told Erhard, was "going down the road to peace" toward détente with Russia "with or without others." The chancellor would have to be more flexible than Adenauer about Eastern Europe. No one was more committed to Berlin than he. After all, he had gone there to represent the American commitment within days of the erection of The Wall. In fact Johnson had been reluctant to go, fearing that the trip would be personally damaging to him, and he had had to be ordered by Kennedy to undertake the mission. Erhard warmed to the new president and seemed much more forthcoming than Adenauer. (The old man had been a guest at the ranch, too, in 1961 during Johnson's vice presidential days, a "nice and peaceful" occasion, the chancellor later termed it, complete with a barbecue and the inevitable gift of a ten-gallon hat.) But Erhard, who had clashed with *Der Alte* inside the cabinet over Adenauer's Gaullist leanings, was acutely aware that German policy would have to change. The Social Democratic opposition was growing and with it popular sentiment for a new Eastern policy. Johnson and Erhard felt a certain common bond. Each was a stand-in for a famous figure, suddenly elevated to highest office, each waiting for an election that would legitimate his power. Erhard promised that he would buy larger amounts of military equipment from the United States as a discreet way of helping the U.S. balance-of-payments problems arising from the maintenance of six American divisions on German soil. But the president must promise not to make the agreement public because any suggestion that the Germans were "paying" for their protection would not sit well at home. Johnson agreed, and Erhard promised to raise the West German defense budget as well. He also agreed to stop shipping goods to Castro even though all the NATO partners regularly violated the embargo on Cuba which the United States pressed upon them.

Johnson was elated. He had threatened Erhard with congressional retaliation if Germany did not stop the "chicken war"—high tariffs and dubious health restrictions aimed at American poultry. J. William Fulbright, the chairman of the Senate Foreign Relations Committee, he reminded the chancellor, might be a scholarly enthusiast of European integration, but he was first and foremost a senator from Arkansas, one of the leading poultry-producing states. The German took it all so well that to the end of his term Johnson would refer to Erhard as his favorite foreign leader. "I love President Johnson, and he loves me," the chancellor exulted to a German reporter as he left the ranch.

The State Department answer to the new currents in Europe remained the Multilateral Force. Kennedy had turned increasingly skeptical shortly before his death, but the enthusiasts saw Johnson's accession as a chance to revive the scheme. Johnson was much concerned that Germany would acquire the atomic bomb. If the Germans did not have some way out of their "second-class citizenship" with regard to nuclear weapons they would get their own. If he were running things in Germany, that's what he would do. In April at a review of the idea at the White House at which the enthusiasts were present and skeptics like Bundy and McNamara were out of town, Johnson seemed to support it, and in a speech to newspaper editors later that month he declared, "We support the establishment of a multilateral nuclear force composed of those nations which wish to participate." On Erhard's second visit in June the communiqué expressed the hope that the MLF agreement would be ready by the end of the year. Meanwhile the U.S.S. *Claude V. Ricketts,* a vessel with a mixed crew from eight nations, was sailing the Mediterranean to prove that it could all be done.

By the end of the year, however, the MLF was dead. Despite the quasi-religious zeal with which the proponents presented the notion—to their growing number of antagonists they were known as "theologians"—the symbolism of multinational nuclear missile platforms roaming the high seas bothered conservatives and liberals in Congress. The former were against any nuclear sharing; "slippery-slope" arguments came easily to them. Liberals feared any move that put Germans and nuclear weapons together, for surely it would make it harder to come to arms agreements with the Soviets. Domestic political changes in Germany and Britain strengthened the opposition. Adenauer had proposed to Kennedy that they sign a provisional agreement on his European trip in June 1963. The chancellor did not like the idea that the control over the MLF had to be by unanimous agreement, not because he feared a U.S. veto so much as that of one of the European countries, but he suggested that this thorny issue could be decided later. Under increasing pressure from Adenauer and Franz Josef Strauss, Erhard wrote Johnson in October proposing that their two countries not wait for the British but sign a bilateral German-American agreement. The German ambassador made it clear that the issue should be settled well before the next parliamentary elections scheduled for a year hence. Surprised by a reporter's question, Erhard, before Johnson had replied to the letter, revealed the idea without apparently meaning to at a press conference in Berlin. That was enough to kill the German initiative and to reinforce the growing suspicion in Lyndon Johnson's mind that the MLF scheme spelled trouble.

In Britain nuclear-sharing had become an increasingly divisive issue. Before the October elections no action could be taken, and after the elections,

Harold Wilson, the second leader of a Labour government in British history, came to power on a platform that opposed it. The MLF enthusiasts argued that while Wilson's party was officially against the idea as too full of pro-German and anti-Russian symbolism for their leftist constituency, as a practical matter the polyglot fleet offered a convenient dumping ground for Britain's independent deterrent which the Labourites, on paper at least, were committed to dismantling.

Harold Wilson's visit to Washington a few weeks after Johnson's electoral triumph in November 1964, and his narrow victory a few days earlier, provided the occasion to resolve the issue. Reaching major decisions is a problem for any alliance of democracies; it is difficult to get the attention of all the relevant leaders at the same time. Political cycles vary from country to country. Someone is always about to face an election or has lost one. Weak governments, as in Italy, are reluctant to commit themselves, and when they do, they are soon gone. Harold Wilson was fully conscious of his political frailties as he sat down with Lyndon Johnson who was at the peak of his popularity.

Wilson was a creature of accident as much as Johnson. Each had arrived at the highest office by the sudden death of an established leader. In Wilson's case the prime ministership would not have been his except for the unexpected demise of the long time Labour leader Hugh Gaitskell and the well-publicized incompetence of Harold Macmillan's successor. During his short stay at No. 10 Downing Street, Alec Douglas-Home, a hereditary earl who relished grouse hunting more than politics, always seemed, according to his colleague "Rab" Butler, to be escaping in the midst of a crisis to arrange flowers. He was no match for Wilson, the shrewdest television campaigner in Britain who knew how to make Socialism sound reassuringly dull to swing voters. As it was, the plump, gray-haired, cold-eyed, rather prudish man who was now prime minister had the narrowest support in Parliament of any British leader in more than a century. He had gone from a lower-middle-class Yorkshire childhood to a flashy career as an Oxford don. Three prominent members of the Kennedy administration had been his students before the war. "Though enormously intelligent," Richard Crossman, another former don and a close political ally, wrote in his diary in early 1963, "he is certainly not an intellectual. He is a supremely professional politician—in this he resembles Kennedy. But he is also an agile manoeuvrer and something of the demagogue, and therefore a wonderful listener who can pick the brains of skillful people. . . ." Like Kennedy, Wilson used his sponge of a mind to dazzle; he had an uncanny ability to bring forth the exact date of a speech or a meeting, thus giving the disquieting impression to political foes that he knew much more about critical events than he did.

When the two politicians met at the White House, Wilson recalls, Johnson evinced "a professional's interest in the political problems of his guest." Johnson knew what "our smallest-ever parliamentary majority" meant. He, too, had worked with an unreliable majority in the Senate and knew what could be done through sheer determination. Wilson was aware that the president had recently told a British editor that he would never trust a British prime minister again "because they use their visits to Washington for electioneering." (The last British leader, Alec Douglas-Home, had created the impression on returning home that he had banged the table and lectured the president on the right of the British to sell Castro buses if they wanted to, when in fact he had barely mentioned the matter at all.) Wilson was determined to present himself as a dependable but resourceful ally.

The new government offered to play a "special role" in Africa "through our close relations with Commonwealth countries." Wilson recalls that Johnson was pleased since the Americans "had little leverage there, and at the same time had to face considerable domestic pressures on African problems." But when the president gently raised the question of "token" cooperation with him in the rapidly escalating war in Vietnam, "I made it clear that we would not enter into any such commitments." The prime minister did, however, offer "the use of our jungle training team in Malaya and also our teams for anti-subversive activities." The Americans, Wilson explained to his colleagues in the cabinet, did not care so much about having British soldiers for their war, but wanted the British flag. No pistol had been put to his head, but the Americans hoped that Britain would continue to take on a "world-wide role." As Defense Minister Denis Healey, who had accompanied Wilson to Washington, explained it, the Americans wanted Britain to keep a "foothold in Hong Kong, Malaya, the Persian Gulf to enable us to do things for the alliance which they can't do. They think our forces are much more useful to the alliance outside Europe than in Germany." McNamara had put forward these ideas on a long plane ride to Strategic Air Command headquarters, and since they suggested that British imperial swagger still had a role in Pax Americana, indeed a more important one than that served by the enormously expensive British army of the Rhine, the American notions were doubly welcome.

The critical issue to be decided at the Washington meetings was the fate of the MLF. George Ball and Richard Neustadt had visited Wilson in November to warn him that he was "on a collision course" with the president if he rejected the basic idea of a surface fleet. McGeorge Bundy reminded Johnson that he had all the cards. Wilson's position was weak. However, a "fallback" position was prepared in case Wilson should prove adamant: The MLF should be allowed to die "in such a way that responsibility for its demise accrued to the European allies rather than to the United States."

The prime minister began the discussion by insisting that the Russians really did believe that MLF meant having a German finger on the nuclear trigger because Bonn would now be in a position to push Washington toward war. (Gromyko once demonstrated his concern when Wilson was in Moscow by pressing the finger of one hand with a finger of the other.) Many in Britain, on the other hand, were concerned, Wilson told the president, "that the world might one day be plunged into nuclear war by a unilateral decision in the White House." New forms of consultation on nuclear matters were necessary to deal with the twin fears that haunted the Continent—that the U.S. president would involve Europe in a needless nuclear war or else would in a crisis in which Europe's fate hung in the balance appear to shrink from using the ultimate weapon.

The dilemma of which Wilson spoke was insoluble and remains so, but he purported to deal with it in a proposal he submitted to the president for an Atlantic Nuclear Force made up of already existing bombers and submarines instead of a new surface fleet. Under his proposal the Europeans and the Americans could in effect veto each other. The German role would be reduced. But the major advantages from the British standpoint were political. The Atlantic Force would include British bombers and Polaris submarines. The financial contribution demanded for the proposed new surface vessels could be saved and the political risks in stopping the British Polaris program could be averted. (Two submarine keels had already been laid at great expense.) If the Americans were really so worried about the Germans being the nuclear step-children of the alliance, the British had suggested in advance of the White House meeting, why not have Germans participate in the Minuteman crews in Colorado and the Dakotas? It was a nice debating point to needle the Americans for whom the idea was about as acceptable as having bobbies and *carabinieri* guard the White House.

By the time he met Wilson, Johnson had become convinced that an MLF treaty would never pass the Senate. Worried that the Kennedy advisers were leading him into a political trap, he rejected the argument that he was already committed to the MLF and that his own prestige as well as the national honor were at stake. The anti-MLF faction in the government closed in for the kill. The day before the talks were to begin, a cable from the American embassy in Bonn arrived with the startling information that the German defense minister, Kai-Uwe von Hassel, presumed to be a staunch supporter, now wished to delay the project because of De Gaulle's increasingly vocal opposition. Johnson made his final decision while Wilson was left waiting in the cabinet room. All deadlines were off. The United States would support no arrangement that did not have the support of Britain and Germany and would seek to avoid further confrontation with France. He would listen sympathetically to Wilson's ideas but would remain noncommittal.

The prime minister was elated. In his memoirs he crows a bit about the encounter. The "authoritative" London *Sunday Times* reported that he had given all the advisers present "something of an inferiority complex by his command of the substance discussed" and the cartoonist of the *Christian Science Monitor* had shown him as the submarine skipper who had torpedoed the MLF. In reality Johnson's political instincts rather than Wilson's brilliance were responsible for the decision. The United States was beginning a process of disengagement; under the exigencies of a Pacific war the Eurocentered alliance policies of a generation were giving way to a new geopolitical structure in which intra-European problems would no longer be the major preoccupation of American diplomacy. But the nuclear-sharing issue dragged on. A year later Ludwig Erhard returned to press it again. But by 1966 the Germans seemed too divided over the question of their national role to be worrisome, and Lyndon Johnson was already engulfed by the war in Vietnam.

3

Ludwig Erhard called himself an "American invention." He had worked with the Americans since the earliest days of the occupation, and he could not conceive how Germany's interests could be served other than by accepting the role of an American "protectorate," as De Gaulle called it. The only road to independence was to build up his country's phenomenal economic strength. He had no taste for the diplomatic style his predecessor had used so successfully to exert extraordinary influence over the United States. Indeed he had little taste for politics at all. It was only after fourteen years in the Bundestag and the cabinet that he applied for membership in the CDU. An obese, mildmannered, and patient man, with the enduring aroma of the fifteen huge cigars he smoked each day, Erhard brought to the chancellor's office a style so different from Adenauer's authoritarian ways that he quickly earned the not altogether complimentary nickname of *Gummilöwe* ("Rubber Lion"). When Lyndon Johnson asked for public expression of support on Vietnam and increased aid for South Vietnam, the chancellor, despite rising opposition within the cabinet, unhesitatingly gave it.

He had never shared Adenauer's enthusiasm for supranational institutions in Europe. Since Germany exported more of its production to the non-EEC countries of Europe than to the six members, Erhard had opposed a high tariff aimed at nonmembers. He understood that French industrialists who stood to benefit from a protected market limited to the six member nations did not have the same interests as German industrialists. He was also against the efforts of the French to promote a common agricultural policy which would open the German market to heavily subsidized French food products. These practical problems meant much less to Adenauer than the challenge of effecting a historic reconciliation, and so the Bundeskanzler frequently lined up with De Gaulle against his own economics minister. As chancellor, Erhard's preoccupation was the same as it was during his long years at the Economics Ministry: to build up industrial power and to resist fanatically anything that could lead to another catastrophic inflation.

By the mid-1960s the familiar postwar order was changing. Indeed, it had changed during Adenauer's last years in office, but the old man was not ready to accept it. The Franco-German Treaty, which the last surviving "good European" saw as the enduring monument of his career, had alarmed the British and the Americans in 1963 when it was announced because it seemed to be the backdrop for De Gaulle's renewed attack on the Anglo-Saxons. The Adenauer-De Gaulle relationship produced much symbolism: The general's arrival in Bonn with a huge entourage—the emperor's review of the Eastern provinces, some Germans called it—a High Mass attended by the two leaders in Rheims

Cathedral, and a Franco-German youth project which arranged three million exchange visits in ten years. But De Gaulle, who had seen the treaty as a way to exert influence over Germany without having to deal with *Der Alte*'s forty-year dream of a Franco-German union, soon lost interest when the Bundestag insisted upon attaching a preamble reaffirming the American connection. "Treaties are like maidens and roses," he is supposed to have said, "they each have their day."

The French president, having wooed Adenauer with promises of support for Bonn's Eastern policy, had taken the toughest rhetorical stance of any of the Allies in the 1961 Berlin crisis. But three years later he was making ostentatious gestures to Moscow. With calculated effusiveness he noted the twentieth anniversary of the Franco-Soviet alliance pact he had signed during World War II, and extended seven-year credits to the Soviets in a trade agreement. In 1966 he went on a state visit to Moscow to discuss his vision of a new Europe "from the Atlantic to the Urals." What Alfred Grosser calls the "gentlemen's agreement" between Adenauer and De Gaulle—an exchange of French support of Germany's tough line on Russia in return for discreet German backing of France's anti-Atlanticist policy—had been quietly forgotten on both sides.

American policy toward Germany had begun to change too. The strange power that Adenauer had exerted on the Republican administration had weakened in Kennedy's time, in no small part because Adenauer was viewed by the New Frontier as an Eisenhower holdover. But more than a clash of personality and style was involved; the sources of Adenauer's power had eroded. Once the German army was a reality, the promise to produce one was no longer much of an asset. More important, the Americans now had new reasons to push détente with the Soviet Union. Kennedy saw it as the only real alternative to future confrontations. He believed that the human race could not survive many more incidents like the thirteen-day Missile Crisis. By the time Johnson had decided to escalate the Vietnam War, there was a more immediate and compelling reason for not provoking the Russians. The last thing Johnson wanted was to alarm the Soviets by taking a hard-line position on Germany at a time when he was bombing a Soviet ally in Asia. By the end of 1966 there were 267,000 American troops in Vietnam.

Under Johnson, even more strongly than under Kennedy, U.S. policy moved toward acceptance of the status quo in Europe. In the final months of the Kennedy administration, ideas had percolated in the White House for encouraging more contact between the two Germanys, and Egon Bahr, the future architect of Willy Brandt's *Ostpolitik,* put together in July 1963 a "change through contact" *(Wandel durch Annäherung)* program for the SPD "based on a point-by-point examination of the Kennedy administration's ideas on East-West relations." On October 7, 1966, Lyndon Johnson gave a speech on "peaceful engagement" with Eastern Europe written by Zbigniew Brzezinski, a young Columbia professor. "We must improve the East-West environment in order to achieve the unification of Germany in the context of a larger, peaceful and prosperous Europe.'' Change in Eastern Europe would come more easily and more quickly by a process of gradual contacts than by confrontation. Indeed, the blocs now showed signs of cracking. Rumania appeared to be becoming Russia's France, cloaking the most Stalinist domestic policy in Eastern Europe with an amazing tilt toward the West in foreign policy, including open support for Israel. "Put yourself in the place of the Russians,'' Lyndon Johnson observed to the Munich weekly *Quick*. "Try to understand their feelings. They are worried about the Germans and that is understandable.''

But equally understandable were German worries about their ally in Washington. For years Adenauer had played on German fears of a "deal'' between Washington and Moscow which the leaders in the two capitals were emotionally incapable of making. But now the prospect of such an entente was more real. The United States, having buried the MLF, was promoting the nuclear nonproliferation treaty as its major objective in nuclear diplomacy. The treaty consisted of a pledge by the nuclear powers not to assist nations without the bomb to acquire such weapons, together with a self-denying ordinance which all nations, great and small, would be pressed to sign. Since it was clear from the outset that neither France nor China would sign it, the major effect of the treaty was to dramatize the overriding common interest of the nuclear giants in preserving their unique status as potential destroyers of the world. But for the Federal Republic to sign the nonproliferation treaty meant giving up a number of diplomatic options, including the use of the threat to acquire nuclear weapons as a bargaining chip with the Soviets. Shortly before his death, Adenauer called the treaty a "Morgenthau Plan squared.'' For Franz Josef Strauss it was a "Versailles of cosmic proportions.''

In the waning months of Adenauer's chancellorship, Willy Brandt's party emerged as the staunchest NATO supporter, for the SPD was worried that the old man was throwing over the crucial relationship with America for the dubious protection of De Gaulle. Erhard, concerned that the United States was rethinking its policy in the light of Adenauer's flirtation with the French, opted for an unashamedly pro-American stance. Johnson's war in Vietnam, his dispatch of marines to the Dominican Republic in April 1965, and his demand for more economic help from the Germans for the common defense were all warmly supported by Erhard, but the chancellor's public embrace of an increasingly controversial American president hastened his political disappearance.

Erhard sought to accommodate both the Americans and rising sentiment within Germany by modifying Adenauer's rigid Eastern policy. Gerhard Schröder, who had been one of Hitler's Storm Troopers in 1933, was now the foreign minister. Calling for an "opening to the East,'' he established trade missions in Budapest, Sofia, Warsaw, and Bucharest. "There is a growing understanding of the German problem,'' he reported. But toward East Germany there was little change. Indeed, when Khrushchev's son-in-law Alexei Adzhubei returned to Moscow from a visit to Bonn "extolling the wisdom of

Rapallo,'' GDR officials feared that Khrushchev might be selling them out, and Politburo members Mikhail Suslov and Leonid Brezhnev issued veiled warnings. After Khrushchev's fall from power soon thereafter, trade between the Germanys increased markedly, but political relations remained as frozen as ever.

Despite his continued personal popularity as the father of the "miracle," Erhard seemed stalled on all fronts. His concessions to Johnson had produced virtually nothing in return. As the U.S. balance-of-payments position worsened, American officials kept pressing the Germans to buy more U.S. military equipment to offset the costs of the American troops in Germany. Erhard had promised to purchase almost a billion and a half dollars worth in two years. But although U.S. officials insisted—the assistant secretary who handled these matters was soon known in Bonn as "Basil Zaharoff Bundy," after the famous munitions king of an earlier era—the Germans balked at fulfilling their commitment. When McNamara pressed on them new helicopters and long-distance troop transports for which they had no obvious uses, German officials were undiplomatic enough to point out that fifty-six crashes of Starfighter jets had occurred within a little over a year. Discussions became more acrimonious. McNamara threatened to pull troops out of Germany if the Germans didn't buy enough weapons, and in April 1966, 15,000 U.S. soldiers were actually withdrawn.

Germany had secured nothing in the way of even symbolic control over nuclear weapons. (Indeed, the Americans were showing increasing concern about de facto control—the access of German personnel to nuclear weapons stocks in Germany—and were determined to improve security procedures.) The MLF and Wilson's Atlantic Nuclear Force were both dead. But despite these disappointments, McNamara and German Defense Minister Kai-Uwe von Hassel had a good working relationship. The Federal Republic was invited to sit as a member of a Nuclear Planning Group to discuss nuclear strategy, and the Erhard government was less apprehensive than Adenauer had been about McNamara's ideas for "raising the nuclear threshold," that is, building up conventional forces so as to avoid the use of nuclear weapons.

However, Erhard's poor showing in Washington cost him political support at home. Franz Josef Strauss, who had been forced to resign from Adenauer's cabinet over the *Spiegel* affair, was seeking to make a comeback as a "Gaullist." (In 1962 the defense minister had publicly condoned a Nazi-like mass arrest of the editors of the most consistent and telling critical voice in the country against his policies.) The Americans, Strauss now thundered, were giving the Germans nothing and were about to make deals with the Russians at German expense. The German "Gaullists," though sharing the general's skepticism about the United States, did not like his growing cordiality to the Soviet Union. While Strauss was attacking from the right, Erhard's coalition partners, the Free Democrats (FDP), which had always put greater stress than Adenauer on reunification and closer relations with the East, was pressing the chancellor to move faster in his small steps toward a new *Ostpolitik*. To make matters worse the neo-Nazi National Democratic Party was making worrisome gains in local and regional elections in 1965 and 1966. Adenauer warned of "diplomatic encirclement." De Gaulle, it seemed, shared the views of François Mauriac: "I love Germany so. Every day I thank God that there are two of them."

The sense of drift in Germany worried the State Department. Rumors floated that Strauss and the "Gaullists" might form a "grand coalition" with the SPD. For the first time since the "miracle," the German economy was in trouble. Growth slowed. Unemployment threatened. The president of the Bundesbank, Karl Blessing, warned of "imported inflation." Germany's large trade surplus meant that "sound marks" were being exchanged for "consumptive" francs. This involuntary financing of "De Gaulle's expensive dream to become the world's fourth atomic mushroom," the German banker warned, was heating up the German economy.

By 1966 De Gaulle was ready to announce the decision that he had already telegraphed in so many ways. France would desert the formal alliance structure. All foreign troops should leave France forthwith. "When a man asks you to leave his house," Johnson told McNamara, "you don't argue; you get your hat and go." NATO headquarters was moved from Paris to Brussels. De Gaulle negotiated a bilateral agreement with the Germans to keep his troops in the Federal Republic. Meanwhile the balance-of-payments crisis for the United States and Britain was worsening, and the Senate Majority Leader Mike Mansfield began proposing that the United States bring home "substantial" numbers of troops from Europe. In Britain members of the Wilson cabinet were demanding that the Army of the Rhine be withdrawn unless the Germans were prepared to pay more to keep them. De Gaulle "began whispering on the diplomatic cocktail circuit," Lyndon Johnson recalls, "you see, you can't really depend on the Americans for your security."

Once again a president turned to John J. McCloy. He was to negotiate an arrangement between Germany and the NATO partners to stop the unraveling of the alliance. Since the Americans were financing the Vietnam War and the good life at home with inflation, they failed to appreciate how vivid the memories remained in Germany of the horrors of depreciated currency. Nor were the Americans shy about exacting heavy dues for the alliance. In 1964 U.S. pressure forced the cancellation of a large sale of German steel pipe to the Soviet Union and two years later the Erhard government was compelled to cancel a $150 million steel plant to be built in China after influential U.S. senators expressed their displeasure. When Erhard arrived in Washington for the last time, the atmosphere was a good deal more strained than on his first visit. The chancellor was informed that to help American balance-of-payments problems he would have to carry out his agreement to buy weapons. Johnson's offer to Erhard for a "hot line" telephone linking their two desks was not enough to lift the chancellor's spirits. He returned to Bonn with the sad news that another billion dollars or more would have to be added to the budget to pay off the Americans. The FDP cabinet members resigned, and within a month Erhard was gone.

4

Lyndon Johnson was becoming much too preoccupied with Vietnam to prepare the "inevitable" for General de Gaulle, as Dean Acheson had advised. Indeed, the shoe seemed to be on the other foot. From the flurry of activity of the French president in the mid-1960s emerged a global policy that was inexplicable except as a giant game plan to contain American power. In January 1964 relations were reestablished with America's archenemy, China. Then followed visits to South America, where the president encouraged the people to remember that they were more Latin than American and to Canada where he ended a rousing speech in Montreal with the meddlesome cry, "Long Live Free Quebec!" (He had previously dismissed Canada as an "appendage" of the United States.) French attacks on American foreign policy were stepped up as the marines arrived in Santo Domingo and the Americans dropped ever-increasing quantities of bombs on Vietnam. "[N]ever before have the misunderstandings between France and the U.S. been as profound," the French ambassador, Hervé Alphand, had scrawled in his notebook even before Kennedy's death. But by the end of Johnson's term, "eternal France" had established cordial relations with "eternal Russia," De Gaulle had blamed the United States for the Arab-Israeli War—"One conflict always produces the next"—had turned against Israel, and presented himself to the world as the advocate of Third World independence against American imperialism.

All this high drama infuriated officials in Washington, as it was intended to do. But the damage was slight compared to the French president's gold offensive. Here was the American weak point and De Gaulle's chance to go beyond words. An ambitious aide in the Ministry of Finance had come up with a quote from Cosmas, an early Alexandrian writer: "The true sign of the power of the Romans, was that their money was accepted everywhere in the civilized world." The Americans would remain the Romans of the mid-twentieth century as long as the dollar was accepted everywhere. But with the huge Vietnam War deficits, U.S. currency was vulnerable. In Washington the Johnson administration tried emergency measures to shore up the dollar. Foreign tourists were wooed with special fares and discounts and U.S. tourists were limited in what they could buy abroad duty-free. A Buy American Act was passed, and government bureaucracies were required to purchase at home unless the items were considerably cheaper abroad, which did nothing to help the mounting inflation. The European boom was attracting the investment dollars of U.S. citizens and adding to the balance-of-payments deficit. So an Interest Equalization Tax was passed which was designed to make the rates of return on foreign securities equal to that of U.S. securities in the hope that the investment funds would stay in the country. But it was relatively easy to get around the Interest Equalization Tax; indeed the tax actually encouraged the buildup of the huge Eurodollar funds abroad. The most severe and effective measure was the program of mandatory controls on foreign investment. (A voluntary

program tried earlier had proved ineffective.) United States direct investment
on the European continent was prohibited. American banks were ordered to
reduce their loans abroad. Protests from the business community were "immediate, violent, and prolonged," and the unhappiness at having to restrict
investment in Europe in the midst of a boom had a good deal to do with the
rising sentiment on Wall Street against the Vietnam War that was causing the
crisis.

De Gaulle began cashing in dollars for gold. Indeed he refused to follow
the conventional practice; instead of permitting trucks to bring the gold ingots
from Fort Knox to the subterranean vault of the Federal Reserve Bank in New
York where the holdings of the Western nations were usually held, the French
government dispatched special Air France planes to pick up the gold and take
it to Paris.

In 1965 the French government converted $300 million of its dollar hold-
ings into gold and increased its monthly purchase of gold from the United
States. Influenced by Jacques Rueff, one of the few economists elected an
"immortal" of the Académie Française, De Gaulle suddenly called for a return
to the gold standard of the 1920s.

Truly it is hard to imagine that it could be any standard other than gold, yes gold,
whose nature does not alter, which may be formed equally well into ingots, bars, or
coins, which has no nationality, and which has, eternally and universally, been regarded
as the unalterable currency par excellence.

A return to the gold standard, according to Rueff, would make possible a
devaluation of the dollar. The precious metal could be pegged at, say $70 an
ounce instead of $35 so that the limited world gold reserves would be sufficient
for expanding world commerce. But if the dollar were no longer the world
reserve currency, then the unique privilege of the United States to finance its
domestic prosperity by printing greenbacks would be ended. The Europeans
would no longer have to pay for America's wars nor permit U.S. corporations
to use the huge dollar balances in Europe to gobble up French, German, and
Italian firms. Inflation would be controlled, for gold, limited in quantity, would
limit the money supply. In Rueff's words, gold "is a forceful but unobtrusive
master, who governs unseen and yet is never disobeyed . . . an absolute but
enlightened monarch. . . ." Here was an economic *Weltanschauung* made for
the general. Valéry Giscard d'Estaing, who had become De Gaulle's minister
of finance at age thirty-six, was not a true believer—he wanted to reform the
international monetary system but with something more than the "discipline
of gold"—and he was replaced.

In 1965 and 1966 Lyndon Johnson poured hundreds of thousands of troops
into Vietnam and produced a war boom. Manufacturing facilities in the United
States were running at 91 percent of capacity, and by the first half of 1966
wholesale prices jumped 3.4 percent. To a generation accustomed to "double-
digit" inflation the figure may not be impressive. But the extraordinary prosperity of the first postwar generation had been built on an inflation-free

economy. The president was told by his Council of Economic Advisers to raise taxes fast. But Johnson, fearing that a war tax would trigger a referendum on the increasingly unpopular military operation in Southeast Asia, held off. It was, as his budget director, Kermit Gordon, later put it, the worst economic blunder since the end of World War II. The tax increase was not enacted until June 1968, by which time the huge military expenditures abroad, the enormous borrowings in Europe by U.S. multinational banks, and the huge increase in imported goods eagerly purchased by Americans with their inflated dollars had all contributed to a balance-of-payments crisis and a gold rush. The monetary system was coming apart, and investors were scrambling to protect themselves against the galloping inflation from America of which De Gaulle warned. A wave of speculation swept over Europe. By November 1967 the Gold Pool, the consortium of allies formed to intervene in the gold market to keep the price from rising too far above the pegged price of $35 an ounce, had to sell $800 million in just one month. United States Air Force planes were used to rush the gold to London. On a single day, March 14, 1968, $400 million worth of gold was sold before nightfall. American officials kept insisting that the price of gold would remain immutably at $35 an ounce, but speculators did not believe it.

The world monetary crisis was a reflection of shifts of power. By 1967 the pound was under severe attack because Britain's status as a former empire and once great industrial nation was becoming clear. The closing of the Suez Canal had been expensive. The vestigial military commitments east of Suez were extremely costly and the Labour government moved to get rid of them. Britain had grown to world power by integrating a middle-sized island into a world imperial system, but once the imperial system ceased to exist the island found itself with problems. The island economy grew faster in the early 1960s and gains in productivity were greater than in the first five decades of the century. But the gains were minuscule compared with the rapid growth of the other industrial countries. During the 1960s, for example, Italy showed a rate of growth per capita that was almost twice Britain's. The British share of world manufacturing fell sharply. (By 1975 it was little more than half what it had been in 1960.)

The pound was still used as a reserve currency in the so-called sterling bloc—the Commonwealth countries which continued to be tied into the British world economic system. Before the war, sterling had been a world reserve currency and the memories of the collapse of the pound at the end of World War II did nothing to encourage countries in the troubled sixties to keep their balances in sterling. Because of chronic foreign exchange problems, successive governments kept borrowing heavily from the International Monetary Fund, where Britain retained a privileged place, and from the central banks of Europe. Beginning in 1965 De Gaulle began attacking the pound by withholding the short-term credits traditionally used to stabilize British currency. Central banks are supposed to act reasonably independently of their respective governments, and the action of the French bankers in putting Gaullist diplomacy ahead of the needs of the international banking fraternity was unsettling. By 1967 the assault on the pound intensified. De Gaulle had made it clear that the pound could not continue to be a reserve currency if Britain were finally to be admitted to the Common Market. Michel Debré, the finance minister, embarked on a campaign to make Paris the financial center of Europe instead of London. The foreign minister, Couve de Murville, began hinting that Britain should devalue, and *Le Monde* featured Britain's economic plight on the front pages.

According to the traditional rules of diplomatic decorum, it was a distinctly unfriendly act for one sovereign nation to tell another, especially in public, that its currency wasn't worth what it was set at. To harass a country to change its currency was a little like telling it to change the flag or move the capital. Whenever keepers of the exchequer are bombarded with suggestions to devalue, there is an implicit accusation that they have frittered away the nation's wealth. But worse for the British than unsolicited French advice was public speculation by high French officials that the troubles at the Treasury would inevitably cause the devaluation to occur. Traditionally, British newspapers avoided even discussing such matters. Everyone was expected to conform to the classic ritual which demanded that an impending devaluation be denied right up to the very moment of its announcement. To do otherwise would invite a run on the pound. But now the French served notice that they were playing by different rules.

A week after the Six Day War in the Middle East, Harold Wilson visited De Gaulle at Louis XIV's magnificent palace, le Petit Trianon, which the general had just had renovated at considerable expense. A month earlier De Gaulle had once again vetoed Britain's membership in the EEC, this time striking a tone more of sadness than anger. If only Britain could undergo the "historic transformation" that would make it possible to join Europe! The June war in the Middle East had left the general singularly depressed, "None of us—not Britain, not France, not America, not Russia," Wilson recalls his despair, "was holding the reins any longer, nor likely to do so. No one could say how long this would last, still less how it would end. Nobody was in control of the situation."

At seventy-six, De Gaulle's confidence seemed to have deserted him. It was somewhat pointless to talk of Europe ten years hence, he told Wilson, since he would not be there, and when he was gone the prospects for his country were *"les delices de l'anarchie."* The French always responded to a period of strong rule by "a relapse into anarchy." Now that the United States was perpetrating "the greatest absurdity of the twentieth century in Vietnam . . . ," he said, "he thought we might well be involved in a world war by September." Wilson argued for closer Franco-British cooperation in technology and nuclear matters, for the alternative was an ever stronger U.S.-German alliance. Yes, De Gaulle agreed. *"Les Allemands seront toujours les Allemands."* He listened as the British prime minister conjured up a picture of a post-Gaullist Europe with an ascendant Germany dominating a weak and divided France by virtue of its ties with Washington. Surely this was an argument for greater British involvement on the Continent, for the island had always thrown its weight behind the weaker European power. But Wilson's appeal to the general's sense of history was of no avail. As much as he dreamed and talked of France *eternelle,* the general now seemed more impressed with the transient nature of French power: Could there be a glorious France without De Gaulle? Whatever might happen in the post-Gaullist *"anarchie,"* the reality now was that Europe was being sucked into an "Atlantic" orbit and that Britain, for all Wilson's appealing talk, was powerless to oppose it.

By November 1967 the British finally felt compelled to devalue the pound. When Sir Patrick Dean, the British ambassador, informed Johnson of the decision, the president likened the not unexpected news to "hearing that an old friend who has been ill has to undergo a serious operation." More than fraternal concern was involved. As Fred L. Block puts it in his study of *The Origins of International Economic Disorder,* "the pound served as both a lightning rod for speculative pressure and a bulwark in defense of the dollar."

As long as the pound was relatively weak, speculative pressure was likely to concentrate on the pound, since a devaluation of the pound with its potential for speculative profits was much more likely than a devaluation of the dollar. But, at the same time, it was recognized that once the pound was devalued the speculative assault would then turn against the dollar with greater intensity. Hence, the defense of the pound at its existing rate was a central part of U.S. international monetary policy between 1964 and 1967.

De Gaulle chose this moment of vulnerability to deliver another blow. Two days after the devaluation was announced, the general made public a decision he had privately communicated to the Americans several months earlier. He would no longer participate in the Gold Pool; he was, in effect, announcing his intention to force the United States to raise the official price.

The response from Washington was to secure the pledge of the Allies to maintain the price and to end the free market in gold. As Johnson explains it,

We agreed to continue to sell gold at $35 an ounce to other central banks, but henceforth neither we nor they would buy gold in the free market. Gold for industrial or technical purposes, or for speculation, would have to be bought in a separate commodity market. This plan was called the "two-tier system." The experts were confident that once official sales were separated from the private gold market, the price of gold in the latter would drop.

A new international currency issued by the International Monetary Fund, called Special Drawing Rights would now be used to expand monetary reserves. The wind had been taken out of the gold speculators' sails. A momentary calm prevailed in the international monetary order. The United States even began to show a balance-of-payments surplus.

5

In 1967 Jean-Jacques Servan-Schreiber, the editor of the Paris weekly *L'Express,* alarmed and entertained huge audiences on both sides of the Atlantic with his prophecies: Europe was being "colonized" by the Americans; Frenchmen, Germans, Danes, and Dutch were all in danger of becoming "sub-Americans." The IBM laboratory in Nice, he argued, was the real center of the American occupation, not the NATO headquarters that De Gaulle had expelled. "French money . . . French brains; on French ground they're thinking up new things and every time they come up with something it goes via Telex to New York where the decisions are made. That's the new colonialism." Harold Wilson joined the argument. The takeover of Europe by American corporations meant that the British would soon be reduced to acting as the "woodcutters and water carriers of industrial society." At a moment when Lyndon Johnson was being burned in effigy in antiwar demonstrations throughout Europe, the "American Challenge" thesis found a ready audience.

Yet behind Servan-Schreiber's warning against "American industrial imperialism" was adulation, not hostility. The book was profoundly pro-American which is why so many Americans bought it. The reason why U.S. corporations were taking over the world was simply, as the French editor told a Dutch TV audience in March 1968, that they "put their money and their brains to better use than we do. . . ." The Americans understood the secrets of industrial civilization and knew how to manage. Unless the Europeans learned them too, they would be out of the running. America would rob Europe of its dreams; ten-year-olds would be doomed forever to watch American astronauts on TV conquering new worlds they would never see except through American eyes; how "crippling" it was that little boys in France knew that they were fated to be "second-class citizens of the world."

The first French astronauts blasted off with their Soviet partners in 1982. Servan-Schreiber's prophecy about the American takeover was equally prescient. Indeed, by the late 1970s the fashionable topic in the business press was the "non-American challenge." The spectacular performance of the Japanese, German, and other European corporations under the worsening conditions of the 1970s had produced a profusion of articles and books on the "secrets" of Japanese management. Foreign firms of all sorts seemed to be outcompeting the Americans. Indeed a "decline" of American power had occurred instead of the vaunted takeover. Was it true, as many in the business world suspected, that with the loss of American prestige and power in Southeast Asia, American multinationals had been nosed out, principally by the huge industrial combines of the defeated enemy nations of the Second World War?

As the issues of political sovereignty and common defense dominated the alliance in the first fifteen years of its life, so the management of economic rivalry within the non-Communist world became the key controversy of the 1970s. In the decade during which "détente" became official (1969–79), the question of economic power increasingly defined the relationship between the United States and its Allies. A new world economy was taking shape in which the role of the United States was different from what it had been in the earlier period, and multinational corporations, whatever flag they might be flying, were becoming increasingly independent actors.

It is worth taking a deeper look at what was actually happening in the previous decade—the years of the "American Challenge." American investment indeed poured into Europe. In the six years between 1958 and 1964 the U.S. share of industrial investment in the Common Market countries rose from 4.5 percent to 6.3 percent. Writing in 1968, Hoyt Gimlin noted in his study, "American Investments in European Industry," that American-affiliated companies control "three-fourths of the European computer market, produce one-half of France's telecommunications equipment, own one-third of Germany's oil refining capacity, and employ 6% of Britain's work force turning out 10 percent of that country's goods." More than 400 U.S. companies had invested over $3 billion in Germany by the end of the 1960s and controlled 40 percent of the automobile industry, 33 percent of chemicals, and 20 percent of the tire industry.

Contemporary explanations for this phenomenon ranged from Servan-Schreiber's thesis that the Americans were smarter than Europeans to De Gaulle's charge that the U.S. Treasury, by flooding Europe with the inflated dollars, was in effect giving subsidies to its nationals to buy up European industry. With so much American money available, a company like General Electric could afford to buy a losing venture like Machines Bull just to put a local competitor out of business. Still others emphasized the "brain drain." The United States "is stripping other countries of their technologists," charged the head of Manchester's Institute of Science and Technology. About 13,000 technical and professional workers a year migrated from Europe to the United States. The original research for the swing-wing plane, the hovercraft, and most of the basic inventions for office copying machines had been done in Europe, but nevertheless, U.S. companies dominated the office equipment and aerospace industries. Some European intellectuals were convinced that cultural traditions would keep Europe forever out of the running in the contest for riches. Families were too tight, ancient hierarchies too immovable, to meet the demands of the new industrial society. Georges Suffert wrote in *L'Express* that in France "making money is almost as dishonorable as going bankrupt."

Yet the genteel abhorrence of making money was brilliantly overcome. Clearly, it was never a German disability. The West Germans increased their share of world trade between 1950 and 1966 from 7.3 percent to 19.7 percent, while the U.S. share fell from 27.3 percent to 19.5 percent in the same period. American firms were indeed buying up European industry, but European firms were by and large growing faster and European investment in the United States was proceeding more rapidly than U.S. investment in Europe. Indeed, as Stephen Hymer and Robert Rowthorn showed in their study of the five hundred largest industrial organizations across the planet, the American Challenge the-

sis was based partly on myopia: The U.S.-based firms were indeed increasing
their share of the European market, but the European firms with the lion's
share were deriving even greater advantage from the rapid growth of those
economies, and together with the Japanese were taking an ever increasing
share of the world market.

There are 156 multinationals (MNCs) that dominate the 13 major industrial
sectors of the world economy, such as petroleum, metals, autos, and so forth.
In 1959 111 of them had their headquarters in the United States. By 1976 only
68 of the largest and most powerful multinational firms were flying the American flag. The number of European and Japanese firms ranking among the top
12 companies in each sector equaled or exceeded the number of American
companies. By the mid-1970s it was becoming clear that European and Japanese firms were outcompeting U.S. corporations not only in older industries
such as steel and shipbuilding but in the product on which one American job
out of every six depended: the automobile.

The American Challenge was not invented, but it was misperceived.
Americans started the period of postwar industrial competition with Europe
and Japan with some important advantages inherited from the Second World
War. One 1968 report estimated that government research subsidies in the
United States were three times what the European governments were
spending. But the development funds were heavily concentrated in certain
industries. The aerospace industry lived off its military contracts. (The first-
generation jet aircraft, the Boeing 707, was a KC-135 military tanker that
carried people instead of fuel.) The computer and telecommunications industries were also heavily subsidized by the Pentagon. But older industries, such
as steel, shoes, or automobiles, were in fact subsidized more heavily in Europe
and Japan. The Allied air forces had accomplished a stunning modernization
program for the former Axis powers. No government or firm would have voluntarily razed the production facilities of whole industries, but the effect was
to give a unique advantage to the defeated nations. German and Japanese steel
companies started off the postwar competition with the obsolete turn-of-the-
century forges of Youngstown, Gary, and Pittsburgh, from which most of the
world's steel came, by developing new production processes with more efficient technology. Just as the United States firms innovated at the frontier of
technology, notably computers, where huge amounts of capital had to be assembled, the Europeans and Japanese concentrated on making old products in
new ways. The German shipping industry had been completely destroyed. In
1945 the largest German vessel afloat was a 1500-ton coastal steamer. Forbidden by the Allies to have a merchant marine of its own, the German government decided early on to promote shipping as an export product. Huge
amounts of capital were raised; all funds invested in the shipbuilding industry
were free of tax. By 1953 the Hamburg shipyards were turning out enormous
tankers for Aristotle Onassis, the Greek shipping magnate. By the end of the
decade Germany was the number two shipbuilder in the world—just behind
Japan.

German industrialists understood how to use American capital and technology. The key figure in the steel industry, Hans Gunther Sohl, who had run the raw materials division of Krupp before the war and became an important aide to Albert Speer for war production, was appointed by the Allied Powers to be trustee of the August Thyssen steel complex which had been scheduled for dismantling. Not only did he persuade the occupation authorities to halt the dismantling, but he convinced the Americans to put millions of dollars of Marshall Plan funds into the most modern steel plant in Europe. Working with Robert Pferdmenges, a Cologne banker who was one of Adenauer's closest friends, he secured a variety of loans, including a $10 million credit from the U.S. Export-Import Bank, to purchase equipment and expertise from Armco and U.S. Steel. When Sohl went on to become president of the Federation of German Industries in 1973, his old firm had become the third largest steel company in the world, and one of the most profitable. Anyone who can't give the stockholders 14 percent return and salt away another 14 percent profit, he liked to say, shouldn't be in the steel business.

The process of product development itself offered certain advantages to the Europeans and Japanese in competing with U.S.–based firms in consumer goods. By the end of the war American firms had already invested millions in the development of television. (RCA placed its first ad for TV sets in September 1929, predicting their imminent availability.) When the TV era arrived in the late 1940s, U.S. firms spent millions more exploring the market and how to cultivate it. Latecomers could benefit from the expenditures already made by the industry pioneers. Considerable technology was licensed by U.S. firms to Japanese and German companies in the 1950s. For the Americans it was an obvious way to squeeze extra return from capital already invested. But it changed the nature of competition in a number of industries, electronics in particular, and gave a boost to the non-American challengers. The significance of the licensing agreements should not be exaggerated, however. Much of the technology of consumer goods was available to anyone. The pioneers had to start from scratch in the laboratory; the latecomers could duplicate much of that effort simply by buying a television set. If U.S. firms were coming to the Common Market countries to take advantage of societies which in the late 1950s and early 1960s had lower wage rates and higher productivity gains, why could not local firms imitate their efforts but derive added advantages from the favored relationship they enjoyed with their own government?

The key to understanding the nature of economic competition within the Western alliance is the relationship of the modern industrial state to the multinational corporation. Within what is loosely called the free-market or capitalist system that relationship differs greatly. The variety of capitalist experience helps to explain why the American takeover did not occur.

Germany had its industrial revolution after Britain, and it never accepted the ideology of the "invisible hand." As Andrew Shonfield put it in his survey *Modern Capitalism,* the Germans favored organized commercial combat rather than the "blind hand-to-hand encounter" of small businessmen struggling with one another in the marketplace. Under Hitler, German industry was organized like an army. National industrial associations that began in imperial Germany were renamed *Reichsgruppen,* and they managed the industrial effort as the agent of the state. Because of the Hitler experience, German politicians and industrialists were especially allergic to the idea of centralized direction of the economy or even the suggestion of national economic planning; yet under the banner of Erhard's strong free-market rhetoric, the old national industrial federations were retained and given special "consultative" status in the Bonn constitution.

Despite the Allied decartelization program, economic concentration remained. The hundred largest firms in 1960 produced 40 percent of all the goods and services, employed one out of every three industrial workers, and were responsible for 50 percent of Germany's mushrooming export trade. The *Verbände* (federations) provided a forum for collective business decisions affecting an entire industry that has no counterpart in the United States. The close relationship between large industry and large banks offered a means for assembling capital quickly. Thus while the industrial corporations by themselves could not match the capital available to their American counterparts, their special relationship with large banks made them formidable competitors.

Lucius Clay had arrived in Germany in 1945 convinced that the dissolution of the Big Three, Deutschebank, Dresdner, and Commerz, was "essential," but within ten years of being broken up into smaller banks, the Big Three were back in business. Since in the early postwar years foreign capital, except for Marshall Plan money, was unavailable, the banks played a key role in the reconstruction of Germany. Under German law and practice the banks had a virtual monopoly of the money market. They could assemble huge amounts of capital quickly and they were risk takers. They financed the resettlement of companies such as the Carl Zeiss Optical Works when the famous Jena plant was taken over by the Russians. The Americans evacuated a hundred or so technicians and executives to the West, and the Deutschebank financed a new plant for them without collateral of any sort.

In 1962 when it was evident that the steel industry required another round of major investment, there was an industry-wide surplus which discouraged the needed capital infusion. However, with the help of the big banks—Deutschebank had one of its directors or senior executives on the board of virtually every important steel company—an agreement for rationalizing the industry and dividing up functions among the firms was reached. Shonfield describes how it worked:

... [T]wo of the largest steel companies, Thyssen and Mannesmann, were dissuaded from going ahead with separate and expensive hot strip mills for the production of wide steel sheets. Instead, it was agreed that one of them, Thyssen, would set up a single large plant with an annual capacity of nearly 1-¾ million tons, and be given an eight-year contract for "hire-rolling" by the other. Under the contract, Mannesmann supplies its own steel slabs to be rolled by Thyssen and to be returned to it in the required form, paying merely for the use of the capacity "hired" from Thyssen. Mannesmann for its part committed itself not to put up a plant of its own. Finally, in order to make the Thyssen operation larger and more economic, a third company was brought in, Hütten-werke Oberhausen AG. (HOAG), to share in the long-term contract for hire-rolling.

Without the industry-wide agreement the German steel industry could not have so successfully beaten out the American steel giants in the world market.

The strategic position of the German banks has given them a degree of control over the economy unknown in the United States. In 1960 banks con-trolled 70 percent of the total value of about three-quarters of all publicly traded companies. The Big Three banks voted 70 percent of all shareholders' proxies. As strategists of German industry the Big Three played a key planning role. Siemens, for example, the biggest employer in German industry, engaged in systematic five-year planning in collaboration with the Deutschebank. Kre-ditanstalt, a public bank effectively controlled by private bankers—Herman Abs, the leading figure in postwar German banking, had a continuing role either as director or supervisor—placed strategic investments which the commercial banks did not wish to undertake.

The use of public investment funds was but one example of the active intervention of the new German state in the economy. Even as Adenauer denounced planning, his ministers were practicing it. The so-called free market boom in Germany rested on the heaviest tax burden of any advanced Western country: in 1961, 35 percent of the nation's output was taken in taxes. The taxes to support the greatly expanded social security system Germany adopted in the late 1950s by themselves equaled 10 percent of the gross national prod-uct, a burden comparable to that of the military budget on the U.S. economy at the height of the Cold War. The high taxes made selective tax relief a particularly potent weapon. In the early 1950s special tax benefits went to favored industries: iron, steel, shipbuilding, housing, and so forth. But the benefits were substantially removed by the end of the decade. The high taxes kept consumption down, an important factor in producing a rate of savings four times that of the United States.

German industries entered the era of multinational competition in a partic-ularly strong position, not only because of the shrewd interplay of public and private investment decisions, but also because of a tacit social contract in which German labor made major concessions. In the late 1950s the number of days lost from strikes in Germany was less than an eighth of the number lost in Britain where the work force and population are roughly the same. Unem-ployment in the early 1960s was less than 1 percent. The unions put great stress on *Mitbestimmung;* union officials who were put on the boards of, say, a large steel company might be furnished a Mercedes or a Christmas bonus many times what they once earned as workers. The militant stance of the labor movement had been broken by Hitler, and the postwar union officials were open to ideas which the radical founders of the German labor movement would have dismissed as "class collaboration." Thus when signs of unemployment appeared in 1966, the leaders of the Deutscher Gewerkschaftsbund, the um-

brella labor organization, embraced the notions of Karl Schiller, the right-wing
Socialist who had become economics minister. *Konzertierte Aktion,* a process
of ongoing negotiation between labor and capital to set wages and prices,
continued into the seventies. The bargain as Heinz-Oscar Vetter, the head of
the German labor organization, explained it in the recession of 1975 is to hold
down wage demands "to give industry a chance to make the investments that
will create new jobs." The head of the Federation of Employers commended
the unions for "showing a great deal of responsibility." Workers themselves,
for whom the tax burden was especially heavy, complained that the sacrifice
for prosperity had fallen too heavily on them. But West Germany's competitive
edge in the world export trade during the 1960s and 1970s rested in no small
measure on labor's acquiescence.

There was another important factor in derailing the American Challenge.
Every European government encouraged mergers and cooperative arrangements for its domestic firms in order that they might acquire the power to
defend the home markets and challenge the Americans elsewhere in the world.
German industrial life was already organized for cooperation through the industry associations and the close relationships with the big banks. In England,
Wilson established an Industrial Reorganization Corporation to make "effective use . . . of our resources and skill, management, and capital." In 1967 and
1968 5000 British companies were merged, 10 of them into the automotive
giant, British Leyland Motor Corporation. In France, another highly centralized economy which was growing at the rate of 8 percent a year during the
1950s, the Gaullist bureaucrats arranged 2200 corporate marriages in the year
1968 alone.

The vigor of the French industrial economy took Americans by surprise.
Before De Gaulle, the country had a reputation for being backward and hopelessly entangled in political turmoil. Yet even in 1929 France was producing
more cars than any other European country and about as much steel as Britain.
The state had been deeply involved in heavy industry—energy and chemicals,
especially—since the First World War. After the Second World War, Jean
Monnet's planning operation evolved into what Shonfield calls "a conspiracy
in the public interest."

. . . It was a very elitist conspiracy, involving a fairly small number of people. One of
the senior officials of the Commissariat du Plan once described the actual process of
planning during the 1950s as "a rather clandestine affair." It relied essentially on the
close contacts established between a number of like-minded men in the civil service and
in big business. Organized labour, small business, and, most of the time, the ministers
of the government of the day were largely passed by.

The planners endeavored to rationalize French industry by merging or
killing off smaller firms deemed to be inefficient. *"Un vrai holocauste,"* an
official of the Commissariat du Plan exclaimed with evident satisfaction. The
postwar planning mechanism gave the French government a new weapon in its
campaign to promote the export capabilities of its major industries. But the

biggest firms could easily raise capital privately and were immune to government blandishments such as assistance in arranging loans. Indeed, in the 1960s even the nationalized enterprise Renault refused to cut back its investment in automobiles when the planners sought to persuade them to do so. De Gaulle invested heavily in certain projects that promised more *grandeur* than profit. *Le Plan Calcul,* a government-inspired merger of computer and office equipment companies to do battle with IBM, never succeeded in even blunting the most dynamic thrust of the American invasion. Four years after De Gaulle's death Compagnie Internationale pour l'Information was sold to Honeywell. The supersonic passenger plane, the Concorde, represented a higher state of technology than the Americans had developed, or, as it turned out, would develop. But not until the 1970s did the European airframe industry develop the transnational base of support to challenge the Americans in an industry with huge capital requirements.

Japan handled the American challenge by repelling the attempted American corporate invasion before it even secured a foothold. Starting with the Truman administration, U.S. officials kept urging the Japanese to open up their economy to U.S. investment. But from the mid-1950s on, when Japan began to experience the fastest growth rate in the industrial world, the interest of U.S. companies grew more intense. The Americans had been understanding about Japanese protectionist instincts in the early postwar days when the economy was in shambles, but now as a prosperous member of the Free World, Japan was expected to adopt the liberal ideology of free trade and free movement of capital. Indeed, Japanese resistance to the U.S. multinationals was all the more infuriating since the United States had sponsored its former enemy in becoming a member of such international organizations as the International Monetary Fund which were premised on the liberal vision of a world without investment barriers.

Nonetheless, the Japanese held firm in keeping the American companies out. Between 1950 and 1966 Japanese corporations entered into over four thousand licensing agreements with U.S. companies, but happy as they were to purchase technology, they were reluctant to turn over any portion of the economy to foreign firms. United States multinationals could buy into Japanese firms, but they could not acquire a controlling interest. In 1967, bowing to growing pressure, the Japanese made a liberalizing gesture in their investment policy by allowing 100 percent foreign ownership in a few sectors where Japanese strength in the home market was unassailable, such as beer, motorcycles, and shipbuilding. A year later there were about thirty such companies. Except for IBM, which was virtually the only foreign manufacturer with a healthy share of the domestic market—about 40 percent in 1967—and for the foreign oil companies who controlled 70 percent of the Japanese market, Japanese restrictions became, if anything, even tighter.

To the superficial observer, Japan began to take on an American look. The same fast foods, movies, and dress styles that were transforming Boston, Berlin, and Paris were giving Tokyo a new look in the 1960s. Some American businessmen were flattered and others were alarmed that the Japanese seemed to be copying American management and marketing techniques in the race to catch up with the industrial giants. But the explosive growth of the Japanese economy rested on a strikingly different model of industrial development from that of the American colossus. To be sure, there were the same rags-to-riches stories. A young mechanic named Soichiro Honda decided in 1948 to build a cheap motorcycle and in ten years he was the world's leading manufacturer before he turned his hand to automobiles. In 1958 Masaru Ibuka started a company with $500 and seven workers which he called Sony. His rival for the electronics market, Konosuke Matsushita, was a former bicycle repairer who had developed an electric machinery business before the war. In the darkest days of defeat, he reasoned that the Japanese would one day reach for the easier life that consumer gadgets could bring. Starting with an electric rice saucepan, he revolutionized the Japanese household with everything from re-frigerators to massage machines and built his firm into the fourth largest in the country.

But the Japanese industrial buildup scarcely depended upon these individual success stories so reminiscent of American frontier capitalism. On the day after the surrender ceremony on the *Missouri,* the leaders of the largest corporations and banks met to work out a strategy for maintaining tight control of the economy in the face of MacArthur's certain attempt to break up the *zaibatsu.* The old family-controlled cliques were shaken up, but they soon re-emerged in new form. Centralized family control was largely over, but new enterprises formed around the old *zaibatsu* using the old names. By the end of the 1960s there were forty-six Mitsubishi companies, including the world's largest shipping company and largest-selling brewery. Describing the phenomenon for an American audience, *Asahi* correspondents compared the $10 billion a year enterprise to a company made up of Sears, Monsanto, General Electric, National City Bank, and a dozen other Fortune 500 companies, run by a collective of their respective presidents who set policy at weekly meetings.

Held together by interlocking directorates and common financing, the postwar *zaibatsu* were not monopolies because they competed with one another for shares of the same markets, but the competition was mysteriously guided by a government completely sympathetic to big business. Thus the economy that emerged after the occupation was concentrated and orchestrated from the top as in the prewar days. By 1959, six conglomerate groups, each built around powerful banks and transnational conglomerates (Sogo Shosha), dominated Japanese business. While the great families had lost much of their power, it had been taken by *zaikai,* a postwar term for the "business community," meaning the leaders of the largest corporations and banks. *Zaikai* had controlling influence over the Liberal-Democratic party and held an effective veto power over the appointment of the prime minister. Hayato Ikeda, a former tax bureaucrat who reached that office with the help of business leaders grateful for his forgiving nature when it came to collecting inheritance taxes, once said that the government was the captain but *zaikai* was the compass.

The highly organized Japanese industry quite consciously diverged from the American model in one crucial area. Between 1954 and 1963, the years when Japan's postwar industrial base was organized, U.S. industry was devoting about 18 percent of the gross national product to plant modernization and production growth, but year after year the percentage in Japan was almost double. Individual frugality was even more impressive. In 1961 when Americans were saving about 7 percent of their income, the Japanese had a savings rate of more than 22 percent. While U.S. and European steelmakers derided this "kamikaze" rate of investment, the Japanese persisted. We have a bicycle economy, Japanese businessmen would say. If we slow down, we will topple. To finance the expansion the great firms piled up huge debts; 70 to 80 percent of company financing was in the form of debt rather than equity, roughly the reverse of the situation in the United States. Between 1950 and 1966 there was less than $300 million in foreign capital coming into Japan. (In the same years U.S. investment in Britain alone was $1.8 billion.)

Thus instead of the Americanization of world business a historic division of labor was taking place. The process was misunderstood in the United States as well as in Europe because the multinational corporation itself was wrongly seen as a kind of commercial foreign legion serving the home economy. In a National War College study, for example, the U.S. multinationals were likened to a "growing arsenal . . . working for us around the clock" representing "a tremendous lever" for promoting "our values and life styles." But while the companies argued in Washington how much their foreign operations served the national interest, their representatives abroad minimized their American ties. The Dow Chemical Company, the president of its European subsidiary declared in 1967, is "a global company whose headquarters happen to be in Midland, Michigan." To be sure, at a time when antiwar demonstrators were burning American flags, companies had good public relations reasons not to fly one. But the Dow Chemical Company executive was fundamentally correct.

General Motors, IBM, and other multinational giants were hardly extensions of the American government. Their expanding influence did not mean increased influence in the world for the United States. Indeed, the opposite could be more plausibly argued, for the foreign operations of U.S. multinationals disrupted their country of origin even as they enriched it. During the years of spectacular growth of the multinationals—1957–70—the explosion in the U.S. gross national product was due to a very great extent to foreign acquisitions and domestic mergers. The firms prospered, but the long-term health of the U.S. economy was imperiled because investment in productive facilities within the United States lagged. The ability of multinational corporations and banks to borrow abroad in the uncontrolled Eurodollar market undercut traditional Keynesian remedies. Controlling interest rates and raising or lowering taxes no longer produced the desired response from business because, increasingly, corporations were able to evade the regulations of any single government, including that of the home country. Even stimulating investment in production did not produce more American jobs because the companies preferred to employ cheaper labor abroad. The fiscal crisis and the employment crisis of the 1980s had their roots in the twin strategies which the largest and most powerful units in the American economy pursued twenty years earlier: globalization and merger. As European and Japanese multinationals moved more of their own production overseas and engaged in currency speculation that frustrated the policies of central banks, the realization grew that the multinational corporation was not necessarily an instrument of national power.

It was hardly surprising that the historic transformation of the world economy that began ten years after the Second World War should have been seen as an *American* Challenge, for the new, immensely powerful international culture began in America. But the spread of fast foods and supermarkets transformed the landscape of Europe and Japan only a few years after the new corporate culture had changed the face of the United States. By the end of the 1960s new products, slogans, and business techniques introduced into the United States were showing up within months in Paris, Frankfurt, and Tokyo. Unlike the colonial era, when venerable British and French traditions, habits, language, and culture were imposed on Africans and Asians, and local elites aped British civil servants and French intellectuals, the new mass-consumption culture was more of a global phenomenon than a transfer of values from one national culture to another. To be sure, the new universal language of advertising was heavily influenced by American values—the celebration of youth, speed, mobility, and individualism—but these were neither identified nor promoted as such.

Intellectuals, businessmen, and politicians all across the political spectrum worried about the power of the multinational corporation. They were right to worry, for the power was disruptive of the local culture in a thousand ways. But the power was not national and the challenge transcended America.

6

As 1967 wore on, Europeans, no less than Americans, sat riveted before their television sets watching the "living-room war." To see helicopters spraying death and children turned into human torches day after day made this distant American operation seem everyone's war. For French doctors, German professors, Italian businessmen, Dutch workers, and Danish farmers, the sight of tall, well-built GIs laying waste to whole villages and herding tiny, dark, and frightened Asians into refugee compounds demonstrated that the Americans were not only brutal but incompetent, for the resistance kept growing bigger, not smaller. Europe was less united on its economic and political future than at any moment since the immediate postwar days, but fully 80 percent of the West European public, American officials admitted to *The Wall Street Journal* in May 1967, "is against what the U.S. is doing in Vietnam." The typical European, a survey by the paper's correspondents concluded, "simply wants the U.S. to quit fighting and clear out."

Once Lyndon Johnson had decided that the United States could not afford to lose in Vietnam, he had pressed America's allies to support the war effort. He needed their seal of approval to overcome the growing sense of moral isolation; if the world's democracies would rally to the cause, the bombing, village burning, and search-and-destroy missions could not be said to offend the decent opinion of mankind. As a politician comfortable with the Atlanticist leanings of his inherited advisers, he feared the isolationist reaction from an American public shocked at discovering that America's friends were abusing the nation for its sacrifices in Southeast Asia. If the Europeans would not help America in her hour of need, why should Americans continue to defend Europe? European support was critical not only for keeping support for the war at home but also for holding NATO together.

It was expected that France would attack Johnson's policy in Vietnam. Speaking to 100,000 cheering Cambodians in the National Stadium at Phnom Penh in September 1966, De Gaulle proclaimed that there was "no chance that the peoples of Asia will submit to the law of foreigners from across the shores of the Pacific, whatever their intentions and however powerful their arms." But Britain's "special relationship" and her dependence on American efforts to shore up the pound should surely count for something. "If you want to help us some in Vietnam," Johnson had growled at Wilson over the transatlantic telephone when the prime minister had offered to fly to Washington with advice in February 1965, "send us some men and send us some folks to deal with these guerillas and announce to the press that you are going to help us." In Italy the Christian Democrats had ruled for almost a generation as the acknowledged "American" party, a collection of accomplished, if corruptible, politicians who could always count on being well received in Washington. Surely the American aid and the support one American administration after another had given the rotating band of loyalists in Rome would be reciprocated. In parliament Premier Aldo Moro expressed "understanding" for the U.S. position in Vietnam but the foreign minister, Amintore Fanfani, annoyed Johnson by encouraging the mayor of Florence in his efforts to mediate the war. There were plenty of intermediaries. Johnson wanted commitment. In Germany, Erhard was prepared at increasing political risk to make statements of support but not to send a single soldier. By 1966 Johnson's appeals for an Allied "presence" in Vietnam had produced twenty-three professors from Germany, two Dutch surgical teams, and eleven British police instructors, *U.S. News & World Report* noted indignantly.

Johnson had not failed in his efforts for lack of trying. But as the war escalated and popular opposition grew, the Americans gave up the effort to enlist enthusiasm in Europe for the Asian war and concentrated instead on damage limitation. It was crucial to Johnson's political plans to keep European grumbling private. In June 1966, having decided to bomb Hanoi and Haiphong, he dispatched a colonel to see Prime Minister Wilson, hoping, as Wilson puts it, "that I could still be persuaded, at any rate to mute my criticism, if not to support the policy." The emissary "produced map after map, with the target areas marked: the calculation of his macabre computer, with the grisly details of the material fed into it, of the likely civilian death toll. There was a x percent possibility of twelve deaths and a y percent probability that two would die." The colonel seemed rather humane, Wilson thought, and the prime minister was hardly equipped to challenge the Pentagon computer, but he "dissociated" the British government from the escalation. Yet the mild criticism did not satisfy the growing opposition within the Labour party or among the public. By the end of the year, Wilson recalls wearily, yelling mobs of demonstrators "became a familiar routine." Demonstrators beat the hood of the prime minister's car with clubs, broke the radio antennae, threw eggs, and manhandled Mrs. Wilson. The cabinet split. To his colleagues who urged him to drop Johnson fast, George Brown, the foreign secretary, retorted, "The communists do not ask me to cut myself off from the Americans: the Russians ask me to keep in contact with the United States and keep our association. It's only nice chaps like you who want us to dissociate." Richard Crossman exploded in his diary: "I never imagined that he would talk quite such tripe as that." Wilson, ineffectually trying to play a mediator's role, was showing strain. "I don't like the fact," Crossman noted, "but he now sits at the Cabinet table sipping whiskey instead of water."

In April 1966 the right-wing anti-Communist publisher Axel Springer published an editorial in *Bild Zeitung:* "We should tell Washington quite clearly that the Germans don't want to go to Vietnam." The country should "stand aside from this 'dirty war.' Very far aside." You have destroyed the "last bit of confidence in our nation by its ally," Fritz Erler, the deputy SPD leader, accused the publisher, and he and Willy Brandt flew to Washington to express the private support of German Social Democrats for America's crusade. Obedience, a well-known German professor reminded his countrymen, is the price of American protection.

But as the war grew bloodier and seemingly more hopeless, opposition spread in Germany as elsewhere on the Continent. By 1968, 66,000 American troops had been withdrawn from Europe, many of them redeployed to units in Kansas and Idaho, scheduled for airlifting to the European theater in time of crisis. But for many, the double-barreled example of American unilateralism —prosecuting an exclusively American war in Asia while removing troops from Europe—seemed to prove De Gaulle's point: The alliance was a one-way street. In Vietnam the Americans were doing what the French had tried. Even their military strategy and political game plan were similar. NATO had resisted the French in their efforts, not aided her. If the alliance was a collection of sovereign equals, why should the Americans expect different treatment? But the Federal Republic, unlike most of the rest of the European Allies, kept conscription. While the public debate about America gathered force, official relations actually improved.

After Erhard fell in late 1966, a Grand Coalition of the two major rival parties, CDU and SPD, took office with Kurt Kiesinger, a silver-haired former Nazi with elegant manners, as chancellor, and Willy Brandt as foreign minister. The new government took a far more flexible stance toward Washington. Lyndon Johnson's initiatives affecting Europe—removing U.S. troops, raising the "nuclear threshold," inviting Premier Aleksei Kosygin to Glassboro, New Jersey, for talks that would open up a détente even in the midst of America's war on Russia's Asian ally, and laying plans for an antiballistic missile that theoretically could leave the superpowers unscathed in a nuclear war—all would have touched raw nerves in Adenauer's time. But in July 1967, Senator Mike Mansfield had forty-nine votes for his resolution to pull most of America's troops out of Europe. Senator Stuart Symington, an important Democrat on the Armed Services Committee, called for reducing the American forces to 50,000, in effect as punishment for the failure of the Europeans to live up to their end of the collective defense bargain. After all, even General Eisenhower had written in a popular magazine that one or two U.S. divisions in Europe were enough to deter the Russians. The new German government, primarily concerned with cutting domestic spending and reversing the recession that had baffled Erhard, approached Washington gingerly.

The cabinet was distinctly less "Atlanticist" than in Erhard's time. It even had a former Communist, Herbert Wehner, in the sensitive position of minister of all-German affairs. But while Kiesinger talked of setting a more independent course and grumbled about the "atomic confederacy" between the United States and the Soviet Union that was being put together behind the backs of the NATO Allies, he was forthcoming in the negotiations with the Americans over balance-of-payments problems. Relieved to have McCloy, known for his pro-German sympathies, to deal with rather than the hard-driving McNamara, the new German government agreed to buy $500 million worth of U.S. securities to cover the support costs in Europe, provided the Americans would stop trying to unload huge quantities of military hardware. The head of the Deutsche Bundesbank pledged publicly not to convert its dollar holdings into gold. Visiting Johnson in August 1967, Kiesinger pronounced himself "very satisfied" with his relations with Washington.

The hateful war continued to be an irritant in U.S. relations with its European neighbors but with Japan it produced more serious strains. The newly prosperous nation was benefiting greatly from the billions that the United States was spending in the Far East. But the Japanese public, worried about being drawn into a wider Asian conflict, strongly opposed what the Americans were doing. As early as 1965, according to a poll conducted by the huge daily *Nainichi,* 40 percent of the population wanted an immediate American withdrawal from Vietnam. Only 4 percent approved the bombing of Vietnam. The war was too close for comfort, particularly since B-52 bombers took off to bomb Vietnam from what Japanese considered their own territory, the island of Okinawa.

Captured in a bitter World War II battle in which 12,000 Americans died, Okinawa was in the eyes of the Pentagon a great strategic prize bought and paid for with American blood. Even before the war ended, military planners were building their Asian defense strategy on the assumption that the Ryukyu

Islands chain of which Okinawa was the jewel would become permanent bases. In the euphemistic language of the UN Charter the United States agreed to act indefinitely as "trustee" of this valuable real estate. But the people of Okinawa considered themselves Japanese. The United States had promised in the security treaty to recognize the "residual" sovereignty of Japan over the island, but as protests grew so did U.S. war activity on Okinawa. Not only did bombing raids originate there but the island also served as a missile base and a staging area for U.S. divisions deployed to Vietnam. In angry reaction the Diet passed a resolution calling for a halt to these activities:

The attacks from Okinawa against Vietnam are bringing uneasiness and terror to the . . . inhabitants and are dragging Okinawa into the war. This has become a serious question threatening not only the safety of Okinawa but that of the Japanese homeland.

The American response was unequivocal. "Okinawa is indispensable to our present posture in the Pacific," Admiral Ulysses Grant Sharp, the commander in chief of U.S. forces in the Pacific told reporters in late 1965. American accidents and crimes on Okinawa kept the issue on the front pages in Tokyo. A U.S. transport plane accidentally dropped a trailer and crushed a schoolgirl. As GIs poured onto the island the crime rate doubled. Okinawa schoolchildren on a beach discovered a hideous frog with eleven legs, a sure sign, the local paper reported, that the American military was contaminating the waters. The greatest resentment came from the farmers on the island whose land was taken for the ever-expanding military operations. By 1968 the Left opposition in Okinawa and Japan began to coordinate their efforts, for no issue better dramatized the nonreciprocal nature of the U.S.–Japanese alliance. Meanwhile in Washington the administration was secretly studying what it would mean to turn the government of Okinawa over to the Japanese, provided the bases could be kept. The Joint Chiefs of Staff argued that the unrest in Japan made the bases on Okinawa more important than ever. Fearing that a tough line on Okinawa would provoke a crisis in Japan in 1970 when the security treaty came up for renewal, the Johnson administration dropped hints that the island would revert to Japan in "a few" years.

The management of the alliance with America now required a political virtuoso. Eisaku Sato came close to being one. After the anti-American riots of 1960 and the rise of a strong leftist opposition had forced Nobusuke Kishi out of office, the business leaders and high-level bureaucrats who make up the Japanese establishment regrouped under Sato, his younger brother. (Kishi, following a common practice, dropped the Sato name when he was adopted by his wife's family.) *Time* found it fascinating that across the world there was a political dynasty to match the Kennedys. Smoother in appearance than his brother, Sato was considered by family members to be less gifted. But he was no less cunning. Upon graduation from Tokyo University he joined the railway bureaucracy, working his way up from ticket puncher to deputy minister. Sufficiently removed from wartime planning, Sato escaped the purge and became a protégé of Yoshida and eventually his political heir. Since Kishi belonged to a different party, the brothers were able to use their personal followings to put together the winning conservative coalition that had ruled Japan for almost thirty years. In 1954 Sato was accused of taking a large bribe from shipbuilding companies when he was in charge of raising money for the Liberal party. Yoshida rescued him by simply having the warrant for his arrest quashed. Later he was indicted on a lesser charge, but he escaped altogether when a general amnesty was proclaimed.

The incident actually helped him politically. He had demonstrated his loyalty to the party by refusing to save himself through the exposure of others, and since everyone believed that large sums had indeed changed hands, it showed that he was well connected. Indeed his reputation as a master schemer, but an utterly reliable one when it came to observing the feudal obligations of Japanese political life, served him well. A taciturn figure addicted to late-night games of solitaire, he held on as prime minister longer than any other postwar politician because for all the continuing unrest he seemed to know how to manage the strange new prosperity that had come to his country.

Japanese business leaders, the most powerful constituency of the ruling party, continued to be strong supporters of the alliance with the United States, especially since Japan was making so much money from the war. They had reason to be grateful to the Americans. Since the late 1940s U.S. officials had been doggedly pressing the Allies in Europe to admit Japan as a member of the new economic community. The Europeans, especially Britain, resisted welcoming Japan into the GATT (General Agreement on Tariffs and Trade), which would require them to lower tariff barriers against Japan and accord her most-favored-nation status. The potential trading partners remembered with bitterness the prewar Japanese export trade—"ruinous competition from inferior Japanese products dumped at a fraction of their cost," was a typical newspaper characterization. But in the 1940s and 1950s the Americans, pressing the cause of free trade with missionary zeal, acted as Japan's protector on the European market. If the Japanese could not break into the market in Paris and Frankfurt, their cheap shirts, radios, and bicycles would flood Chicago and San Francisco. Moreover, there would be no way to keep them from selling to the hated Chinese.

The Americans negotiated Japan's entry into GATT by purchasing European concessions to Japan with U.S. concessions to Europe. As a consequence of U.S. pressure, the OECD, the association of North American and West European industrialized nations, was expanded to include Japan. Worried about Japan's shaky economy in early postoccupation years and concerned that the Left might triumph if Japan did not recover, the Americans were also quite permissive concerning Japan's own discriminatory trading practices and tight controls. But, even as she was being initiated into the U.S.–designed free trade system for the capitalist world, Japan was developing the mercantilist approach that would bring her extraordinary returns. The state guided international trade, limiting imports to the barest essentials and subsidizing exports, just as in the prewar period. In technical negotiations the United States and the Europeans hammered away at Japanese trade barriers to their home market, including discrimination against the dollar. By the late 1950s U.S. textile manufacturers were complaining about Japanese competition and by the mid-1960s Japanese exports to the United States considerably outran U.S. exports to Japan. The Americans grumbled, the Europeans began retaliating against Japan, but few serious legal or diplomatic obstructions were put in Japan's way. In the highest reaches of the U.S. government, except when riots made the front pages, Japan was largely invisible. In Arthur Schlesinger's chronicle of John F. Kennedy's thousand days in the White House, Japan does not even appear in the index. Lyndon Johnson barely mentions Japan in his memoirs.

Johnson's interest in Japan centered almost entirely on her proximity to Vietnam. Official Japanese approval of the U.S. war effort was especially important to him since the defense of Japan was adduced as one of the main reasons for fighting the Vietcong. Sato's style was to pronounce words of encouragement in Washington so evanescent as to disappear by the time he returned to Tokyo. But the strategy infuriated the opposition in Japan who were greatly assisted by American clumsiness. Officials in Washington began to make public charges against Japan. In a speech Assistant Secretary of State William P. Bundy heaped scorn on Japanese conservatives for showing "virtually no interest" in the defense of the Pacific and displaying excessive "tolerance" for Chinese Communists and student radicals. Another assistant secretary of state, Douglas MacArthur II, charged that the two largest national newspapers in Japan had been "infiltrated" by Communists. George Ball, the under secretary of state, backed up the charge, which later had to be retracted, while Edwin Reischauer, the U.S. ambassador in Tokyo, trying to be diplomatic, merely suggested that Japanese journalists reporting on the war were naive and that the press was "biased." Reischauer, a Harvard specialist on Japan who had been born there and spoke the language fluently, had made a good impression, but defending the Vietnam War in Japan was beyond even his considerable talents. Shigeru Yoshida, in retirement, commented that supercilious attitudes based on feelings of race superiority were blinding the Americans to the realities of the Orient. Cables reporting this blunt statement of the most famous pro-American political figure in Japan produced dismay in Washington but nothing else.

7

As the year 1968 dawned it was becoming clearer that all the members of the alliance were being challenged by a cultural revolution that was sweeping the universities. Like 1848, 1968 would become a date to evoke heroic memories, dashed hopes, and deep-seated fears, a strange moment that confounded authorities everywhere before it receded like a spent wave. Within a twelve-month period police were engaged in pitched battles with students in New York, Paris, Tokyo, Berlin, and the violent confrontations with authority had

spilled over the frontiers of the liberal capitalist world into Mexico City and
Prague. The angry students appeared to be the vanguard of a much larger
movement against the established order. The West, as Acheson and the other
architects of the postwar alliance had put it, was much more than a military
arrangement. At heart it was the institutional expression of a common civilization, a vehicle to preserve a common set of values. Yet suddenly these
values were under simultaneous attack in every member country by the privileged beneficiaries of the extraordinary postwar prosperity.

The year began with a humbling event. The spectacular Tet offensive in
early February demonstrated that Vietcong guerrillas could even occupy the
basement of the U.S. embassy in Saigon. The Americans pronounced the
offensive a failure. The basement was recaptured. But neither the influential
American business and financial leaders who a few weeks later urged Johnson
to end the war nor the European public ever looked at the Indochina conflict
the same way again. The war was not only immoral, but futile. If the Americans could be so badly shown up by a fourth-rate military power, perhaps the
cause was hopeless. "Why doesn't he accept his defeat in Vietnam and make
the most of it—the way Kennedy did at the Bay of Pigs and Khrushchev did
in the Cuban missile crisis?" a solidly pro-American ambassador from West
Europe had quietly suggested to an American magazine editor more than a
year earlier. It was typical of much Old World advice of the time. You can't
run an empire, if you have to fight to hold it. You can't project power, if you
have to appear on television every night setting fire to women and children.
The more the United States appeared impotent in its rage, the more the crowd
smelled blood.

In the United States the Vietnam issue was the glue that joined a hundred
protest movements. By March, Senator Eugene McCarthy's presidential campaign to "dump Johnson" had gathered so much steam that LBJ announced
his retirement shortly after a humiliating showing in the New Hampshire primary. In August in Chicago a column of 5000 demonstrators set out to confront
Vice President Hubert Humphrey, now, with Johnson out of the running, the
hated symbol of American belligerence. Some jeered at the policemen lining
the route; a few threw cellophane bags of garbage and human waste. As the
crowd chanted, "The whole world is watching," the police suddenly let fly
with their clubs, aiming indiscriminately at young and old, bystanders, hippies,
and newsmen. "We wanted exactly what happened," Jerry Rubin, the organizer of the Yippie "Festival of Life," pointed out. "We wanted to create a
situation in which the Chicago police and the Daley administration and the
federal government and the United States would self-destruct. We wanted to
show that America wasn't a democracy, that the convention wasn't politics.
The message of the week was of an America ruled by force."

By late 1968 the protest movement appeared frighteningly international.
In Japan hundreds of snake-dancing, chanting students tried to close off the
Tokyo Airport to keep the prime minister from visiting Saigon and Washing-
ton. In West Berlin, the scene of John Kennedy's triumph five years earlier,

eggs and tomatoes were hurled at Hubert Humphrey. Clashes between middle-class students at elite universities and panicky police in riot gear were now commonplace in the key capitals of the West. In Paris the "May Movement," which culminated in a general strike, eventually toppled General de Gaulle. The most violent incident of all occurred in Mexico City where the future president of the Republic, Luis Echeverría, ordered the shooting of several hundred students in the square at Tlateloco. How did it happen that at the end of a decade of unprecedented prosperity the political institutions of the West seemed so weak? Why was it that the transnational forces of the anti-Establishment now seemed more in harmony than the harried leaders of the alliance?

Analyzing the protest movement became a growth industry in every Western country. Books and articles in the hundreds rolled off the presses. The "generation gap," the "crisis of affluence," and the "yearning for excitement" that prompted bored, middle-class youths in every industrial country to prefer brawls to books were solemnly explained to newspaper and magazine readers. Parents, teachers, and officials could take comfort from the fact that neither youth nor rebellion last forever and that student unrest had always come in waves. Depending on the political inclinations of the writers, the students were seen either as idealistic reformers betrayed into violence by the failures of their elders or as successors to the Nazi thugs who brought down the Weimar "system." Hustled by police through an angry throng into the Oxford Union to give a speech which most students boycotted, Richard Crossman was aghast. "In the 1960's the mass of the student Left is behaving in the way which we used to say the fascists behaved in the 1930's."

The analogy was misleading. Only a tiny minority of the hundreds of thousands of protesters resorted to violence, and these did so not to take over the system, but to destroy it so that something else could flower. The strategy was naive and in the end it was clearly counterproductive. The immediate effect of the protest movements was to isolate the students, alienate the middle class, and in the United States, elect a right-wing version of the very liberalism that was the object of attack. But the Nazis had used disorganization as a tactic in the service of a tightly disciplined counterorganization, while the New Left, as the loose collection of antiwar, antiracist, and anticapitalist protesters came to be called, was allergic to all organization, for at the root of its ideology was a rejection of the elitism and hierarchy of technocratic civilization.

The student movement of the 1960s was the unwanted child of reform and prosperity, a mark of the success of the West as much as its failure. Indeed the crisis it sparked was so profound exactly because it attacked the very meaning of success. The decade began with a burst of reform that challenged the comfortable values of the 1950s. In Rome, Pope John XXIII had vowed to "open wide the windows" and let in fresh air. The Vatican II Council, the antiwar encyclical *Pacem in Terris* and the anticapitalist encyclical of his successor, *Populorum Progressio* ("unchecked liberalism leads to dictatorship rightly denounced by Pius XI as producing the 'international imperialism of money' "), split the solid front that had made Christian Democracy flourish in Europe. It had its effect too on the comfortable civic religion in the United States in which Protestant preachers were expected to bless capitalist success as a sign of God's favor and a bulwark against Communism.

The American civil rights movement was a call to redeem the promises of America, just as the renewed concern for peace and justice in the church was a call for the faith to be true to its own teachings. The *Brown* decision of 1954 calling for the end of school segregation had dramatized the gap between promise and reality for the blacks in America at a moment when blacks around the world were emerging from colonialism. The sit-ins and mass marches to integrate schools, buses, and lunch counters in the face of police dogs, clubs, and tear gas not only radicalized a tiny minority of young, white, middle class Americans, some of whom took time out from school to join the black protest, but provided a well-publicized model for the whole world on the successful techniques of confrontation in a liberal democracy.

John F. Kennedy was no reformer, but he projected the image of reform, and in gestures like the Peace Corps he helped shape the consciousness of a generation. Public service, helping others, and building a nation offered far greater rewards than getting rich, fighting one's way up the bureaucratic ladder, or accumulating goods from department stores. By 1960 the West was on its way to spectacular economic success, but in the process family life was under increasing strain and the nature of industrial civilization was changing. Technocrats, engineers, and white-collar professionals were replacing the older blue-collar workers as the principal producers of wealth. There was more leisure to ask the urgent questions about the new industrial society: What is the meaning of life in a society of abundance? Is security all there is? Neither the flag nor the cross retained their old power. Surely the civilization of the West rested on something more than the dollar or the Mercedes or the television.

The official teaching of the 1950s was that it rested on humane liberal values, the civility and compassion that democracy and affluence made possible. This was the lesson of American magazines and it was taught to eager students in United States Information Agency (USIA) libraries across Europe. "My whole liberal education started in the Amerika Haus in Berlin where I studied the Declaration of Independence," one German student explained to an American reporter as he took up a token collection to buy weapons for the Vietcong. "What is happening now is an outright violation of such ideals." Students in the United States were becoming more radical as they put the liberal rhetoric next to the revelations of the day: the My Lai massacres, the manipulation of students by the CIA, and the brutality of police in reacting to peaceful protests. In Europe the growing disillusionment of bright, vocal Americans with their own system was like the disclosure of a dreadful family secret. The United States, the model of success, the cleanser of German Fascism, was secretly corrupt. The hypocritical reformers needed to be unmasked. Indeed the first major demonstration in Berlin was in front of Amerika Haus. The German SDS—Socialist Deutscher Studentenbund—with the coincidental initials of the leading U.S. radical student organization—adopted the slogan: "Vietnam is the Spain of our generation."

When crowds gathered in London, Paris, Berlin, Rome, Oslo, Amsterdam, and Tokyo on October 21, 1967, in support of the siege of the Pentagon, there was evident American influence everywhere. The European and Japanese demonstrators wore the same blue jeans, listened to the same rock music, and read the same denunciations of the war—most of them written by Americans—as the ten thousand camped on the Pentagon parking lot. The techniques of protest, even the gurus of the movement, came from America. Eckehard Krippendorff, a young political science instructor at the Free University in Berlin, had been a graduate student in Berkeley at the time of the Free Speech Movement. An outspoken left-winger, he returned to Berlin in 1965 and challenged the rector Berkeley-style, but soon found himself without a job. The Free University was famous as a center of Cold War scholarship, a university started after the war with substantial American aid as an "island of free inquiry" in the very midst of Marxist Germany. In the 1950s, one German sociologist reported sadly at the time, the students were uninterested in "deeper examination of political questions." The *Reader's Digest* was favorite reading matter. Political activity was encouraged, provided its focus was anti-Communist, and after the construction of The Wall, several students helped their fellow students from the East escape by guiding them through secret tunnels and furnishing forged passports. In the eyes of the Berlin public the students, who, most likely, were used as part of official intelligence operations, were heroes. But by the mid-1960s the temper had changed. The gap between promise and reality in German society and the shock of war in Vietnam were of greater concern than the Soviet menace. Intellectuals throughout Germany came to Krippendorff's defense and saved his job. He became one of the leaders of the protest movement.

American radicals, such as Tom Hayden, had a conscious strategy for "internationalizing" the student movement. At Bratislava, Czechoslovakia, in the fall of 1967, he met Vietnamese revolutionaries and student leaders from around the world and returned to the United States convinced that a new international was being formed "without a Comintern, without a bureaucracy, reaching outside and inside of parties, all the way around the world, students in France, West Germany, Cuba, Venezuela, Quebec. Vietnam was the internationalizing force and SDS was the inspiration." As if to prove his point, a Vietnam Congress was held a few months later in West Berlin against a backdrop of a three-hundred-foot-wide Vietcong flag. As two young Americans burned their draft cards, three thousand German students rose from their seats with clenched fists screaming, "Burn, baby, burn!"

Herbert Marcuse's theories of "repressive tolerance" and his critique of the "one-dimensional" character of the liberal consumer society helped give the protest movement even more of an international cast. The American professor, now in his late sixties, had with the sociologists Theodor Adorno and Max Hochheimer and the psychologist Erich Fromm been part of the Frankfurt

School in the 1920s. Fleeing from Hitler, the refugee scholars developed their theories in America—why in a society with guarantees of civic freedoms people did not feel free, how huge technocratic institutions manipulated men and women, and how true liberation had to transcend capitalist notions of "consumer choice." The theories were rooted in the German tradition of Hegel and Marx, but they had been elaborated in America and made concrete with American examples. The components were German but the assembly had been done in America. Embraced by German and American students alike, the theories were taken as validation for a strategy as the German SDS Chairman Karl Dietrich Wolff put it, of "agitation, disputes, and provocations in order to rip away the veil, unmask, and demystify the true workings of the capitalist system."

Governments in every major industrial country nourished the movements by behaving toward them precisely as the protesters' theory prescribed. On June 2, 1967, a West Berlin plainclothesman, standing a short distance from a crowd of students that had assembled in front of the Berlin Opera House to protest the evening's performance of *The Magic Flute* in honor of the visiting shah of Iran, fired a shot that killed Benno Ohnesorg, a twenty-six-year-old student. As the demonstrators who had come armed with eggs, smoke bombs, and tomatoes fled in panic, the police beat them mercilessly. "A systematic cold-blooded pogrom," the writer Sebastian Haffner pronounced the episode. The police had used the tactics of Storm Troopers. So panicked was the Berlin government by what was happening outside the opera house that orders were given for the orchestra to play unusually loud to drown out the disturbance. The dead student, it turned out, had come just to look. Quite unpolitical, he had never attended a demonstration before.

Fritz Teufel, a Maoist student, was thrown into jail for allegedly throwing a stone and kept there deprived of all legal rights. "Even the District Attorney no longer believes Teufel hit someone with a stone," *Die Welt,* a Springer paper quite hostile to student activism, reported. Ohnesorg and Teufel quickly became national symbols. A congress of four thousand students in Hannover held after Ohnesorg's funeral vowed to "politicize" the university and German society as well. About a third of the faculty at the Free University in Berlin, including the rector, sided with the students in condemning the police. Heinrich Albertz, the mayor of West Berlin who had "emphatically" endorsed the police conduct, was forced to resign. (Ten years later Albertz, a Protestant minister, would emerge as one of the leading figures of the peace movement.) The students became increasingly radical as officials panicked and lost the support of the press and law-abiding Germans. In *Konkret* magazine Ulrike Meinhof, who was writing patiently critical articles on Vietnam in 1965, began preaching rebellion by 1967, and by the end of the decade was a practiced terrorist. In Berlin the fiery orator Rudi Dutschke, a refugee from East Germany, became the leader of the radical student movement, and the tactics grew more daring and more violent. Fifteen thousand students marched on U.S. Army headquarters. A film on how to make Molotov cocktails was shown at the Free University, along with the suggested target, the building that housed the headquarters of Axel Springer's hated press empire. *Der Spiegel* reported that 67 percent of all young Germans liked what the students were doing. The government of Berlin quickly organized a counterdemonstration of 150,000 people in support of "law and order" and the American connection. A red flag was held aloft and burned.

The following month on Berlin's busiest thoroughfare, a young man fired three shots at Rudi Dutschke, wounding him severely in the head, neck, and chest. (Thirteen years later, when Dutschke drowned in his bath, it was said that he had died of these wounds.) The attack sparked demonstrations all over Germany. In Berlin more than 250 demonstrators and police were injured; almost 400 arrests were made. The Springer offices in major cities were damaged and bonfires of Springer papers lit the evening sky. In reaction the Bundestag passed Emergency Laws. It was a radical step to counter what was now increasingly accepted by Germans as a radical challenge, for the very term "emergency" evoked memories of the blank check the Reichstag had given Hitler in 1933 that legalized twelve years of totalitarian rule. The new legislation was sweeping. The government was now authorized "to use the armed forces for police functions, conscript all males 18 and over into civil defense units and all women between the ages of 18 and 55 into medical units, open mail, tap phones, restrict travel, suspend constitutional rights, and use the army against 'organized and militarily armed groups of insurgents.' "

Across the world in Japan, similar events were taking place. Hundreds of helmeted students brandishing thick square poles five feet long, chanting *"Funsai, funsai"* ("Pulverize! pulverize!) attacked the U.S. naval base at Sasebo in January 1968, screaming their determination to block the arrival of the nuclear-powered attack aircraft carrier, the U.S.S. *Enterprise.* The enraged students, members of Zengakuren, the National Federation of Student's Self-Governing Associations, had a few months earlier employed the same tactics at Tokyo Airport on two occasions, first to prevent Prime Minister Sato from visiting Vietnam and then to keep him from meeting Lyndon Johnson in Washington. One student had been killed and about a thousand persons had been injured, including hundreds of policemen. Behind the disturbances was the same student organization that had staged the riots in 1960. By 1968 the Japanese public was increasingly hostile to the militant students, but the brutal reaction of the Japanese police at the naval base won public sympathy for the demonstrators. About a thousand police suddenly surrounded the students and beat a good number of them senseless. The townspeople, who hated the violence but responded to the antinuclear cause, began collecting money for the students. All through 1968 student violence escalated, and by the end of the year forty-six universities throughout the country were paralyzed. More than 100,000 students were unable to attend classes.

The international protest movement had a disruptive effect on the American alliance. Eventually, it would help to stimulate a shift in American strategy. But even in the years in which the protest movements were greeted in

Washington by renewed acts of war, it forced a change of style. Alliances by tradition are private affairs. Kings would make agreements with one another, often secret ones, to come to one another's aid. Each monarch was the unquestioned keeper of the national interest. But from their inception NATO and the U.S.–Japanese security arrangement were presented to the public in each member nation as democratic alliances to be debated, understood, and supported by the public. In fact, except for the critical debate in Germany on rearmament in the early 1950s and in Japan around the ratification of the security treaty, the alliance was primarily the concern of a professional elite. Generals wrote plans for other generals. Professors analyzed for other professors. Politicians gave ritualistic speeches of support in every parliament. But for most citizens the alliance structure faded into the political landscape. Neither the commitments nor the costs were well understood in any member country, including the United States. With anti-American protest welling up all over the world, however, the management of the alliance could no longer be limited to private conversations, elite conferences, and the exchange of learned articles among the NATO establishment. The American connection, once an unalloyed asset for the ruling parties in every member nation, had become a burning political issue.

The worldwide crisis of the university reached its high point in the country that had gone the furthest to sever that connection. The "May Revolution" culminated in a violent clash between the students and the police in Paris and followed a paralyzing general strike. It all began in an old aviation depot which had become the campus for a new experimental university designed to attract a young and exciting faculty. Like Berkeley, Nanterre was a liberal university, one that encouraged new freedoms and new expectations, and like their counterparts at Berkeley, the authorities were unable to handle the consequences. When the students became aware of how little institutional change would actually be allowed, a strike was called. The authorities responded by calling in the police and closing the university.

The area of confrontation moved to Paris. On the night of May 24 students put up barricades. Thousands of demonstrators poured into the Place de la Republique. A fire was lit at the Stock Exchange. There was rioting in Bordeaux, Lyons, and Toulouse. By May 27 nearly ten million workers were on strike. Against the wishes of the Communist party which controlled the largest unions, workers and students briefly made common cause. Once more the brutal police sweeps had fanned an outpouring of rage against the state. De Gaulle flew secretly to Germany to enlist the help of the general in charge of French forces there.

The "May events" triggered a huge flight of capital. French reserves fell $300 million just in the month of May. By mid-June the Bank of France was forced to pay out $500 million in one week to support the franc. By the end of the month a billion had been taken out, much of it in valises and attaché cases after exchange controls were imposed. Since Germany was experiencing record prosperity and a huge surplus, speculators around the world rushed to convert their shaky francs into marks. For Lyndon Johnson, De Gaulle's plight was poetic justice, but the United States could not afford the collapse of the franc, for it could trigger all sorts of unpleasant consequences. Thus the United States made Federal Reserve credits available to shore up the franc and avoided snide comments.

The State Department believed that De Gaulle would have to sacrifice one of the props of his system of *grandeur* to the other. To maintain the franc, he would have to economize and that would mean cutting back on the *force de frappe*. In January 1968 the general had publicly endorsed the strategy of *"tous azimuths"*; henceforth French missiles would be targeted on all points of the compass, east and west. It was the most dramatic expression yet of French withdrawal from the East-West confrontation. But the May crisis and the Soviet invasion of Czechoslovakia three months later brought an abrupt change of tone. Within a year the new strategy was dropped and the defense minister announced that France would remain a signatory to the North Atlantic Treaty though it would continue to boycott the NATO bureaucracy.

The United States was both the inspiration and the target of the global protest movement. The influential 1966 pamphlet *De la misère en milieu étudiant* included rhetoric and analysis from the Berkeley Free Speech Movement. The spark at Nanterre was the activity of the Comité Vietnam, which broke windows and defaced the walls of the Paris offices of the Chase Manhattan Bank, American Express, and TWA. As in Germany and Japan, the student leaders, including the highly visible German immigrant Daniel Cohn-Bendit, who led the movement at Nanterre, came from social science disciplines, especially sociology. Although conditions varied greatly in the United States, Germany, Japan, and France, there was a common thread in the analysis of the militant students. Liberal capitalism was repressive. It would have to be unmasked by deeds, not words. "Extraparliamentary" political action was required because the political systems—parties, unions, and so forth—corrupted and crushed all decent impulses of reform.

As the new decade began, student activism began to decline despite brutal episodes like the killings at Kent State in May 1970. In the 1970s the campuses would be relatively quiet, and from the vantage point of the authorities, mercifully dull. When young people had moved from critics to revolutionaries and become more violent, public opinion had turned against them. Across the industrial world there was more support for "law and order." Just as the police clubbings provoked rebellion on the campus, the willingness of the state to sanction the killing of a number of students had a sobering effect on the movement, particularly as public support for the students waned. There was a new emphasis on "professional" police methods, more subtle ways of defending authority than clubs, tear gas, and attack helicopters, though all three were used with increasing public support. The prospect of students "trashing" the offices of university deans, brandishing Molotov cocktails, and forcing "confessions" from professors was terrifying to those Richard Nixon would dub "the silent majority." Police provocateurs helped to whip up the students to a self-destructive frenzy. Post-1968 elections in the United States, France, and Japan pushed all three societies to the right.

Yet the cultural revolution had lasting effects. Styles of dress, language, and social relations changed dramatically. The highly publicized student movement helped form different attitudes toward authority, sex, drugs, and the niceties of speech. Ironically, the internationalization of the counterculture produced a new global market for the multinational merchandisers of jeans, records, and camping equipment. The political parties in each society successfully co-opted many of the activists. In 1977 Sam Brown, the organizer of the biggest anti-Vietnam demonstration in the United States, received a presidential appointment from Jimmy Carter, and in 1981, Régis Debray, once imprisoned in Bolivia as a revolutionary firebrand, took over an elegant office in the French presidential palace as an adviser to François Mitterrand. In West Germany the SPD, coming to power in 1969, pledged itself to make the reforms that would attract the disaffected young people back into the mainstream. In the process of co-optation, the language of politics changed everywhere in the West. Some of the concerns of the student movements—racial and sexual inequality, the poisoning of the environment, the shoddiness of goods—were embraced by the major political parties. Even as they denounced the "rotten apples," as Richard Nixon called the student activists, politicians subtly borrowed the rhetoric of the protest movements. Even the imperious De Gaulle began to talk eloquently of "participation."

As the new decade began, the phenomenal economic growth and population explosion that had characterized the 1960s began to subside. In the United States, Japan, Germany, and France the university crisis had been heightened by the sudden appearance of the "baby boom" generation. In France there were almost twice as many persons under twenty-five at the end of the decade as in 1939, though the population as a whole increased by only 25 percent. But the universities and the fast-growing societies were out of phase. The "multiversity" was supposed to function as a conveyor belt, depositing technically trained students into the right slots, but for increasing numbers, particularly among the "soft" disciplines like sociology, there were no slots. And those that were available seemed meaningless in the light of the prevailing social criticism. In Japan and France the attack on the university was especially violent because the education system was the symbol of total frustration. The elite universities represented an exclusive avenue to power. It was almost impossible to rise to the top of the bureaucratic pyramid without a degree from the University of Tokyo or from one of the Grandes Ecoles in Paris. For growing numbers in the excluded majority, the humorless rationality of the system was infuriating and it seemed to call for an outrageous response. Since the politics of deliberation was restricted to the elite minority that counted, true democracy was possible only if politics turned into a "happening." To have a voice against the authorities, one must master the art of tantalizing the media and outraging ordinary citizens.

The United States had much less of a tradition of student protest than either West Europe or Japan, but the American movement exerted a global influence because the United States was at once a symbol of power and of idealism betrayed. It was also the place where the "happening" was developed to a fine art. The fiery rhetoric of Mao and Guevara and the theories of Marcuse ceased to be fashionable, but the protest movements continued to haunt the Establishment in every member of the American alliance. The decade that had begun in a burst of confidence born of economic success and a moral certitude ended in what Henry Kissinger would refer to as a "failure of nerve." Perhaps the most influential protest slogan of all was the one that appeared on bumper stickers in the United States: QUESTION AUTHORITY! By the early 1970s Establishment figures in every allied country had the experience of being picketed and denounced by their own children, and they were asking questions themselves.

PART III

UNRAVELING

SEVEN

THE DOUBLE DÉTENTE:

Mr. Nixon and Herr Brandt Look East

1

In 1969 two ambitious outsiders finally achieved supreme power. In January, Richard Nixon, a mercurial character whose disciplined mind never seemed quite in command of his awkward body, had arrived in the White House by turning personal weaknesses into political strength. Uncomfortable in human relationships save for one or two cronies, Nixon established successful contact with masses of voters because he knew their fantasies and could touch their fears. Few left the service of this strangely wounded personality without attempting some psychological theory to explain his constant craving for reassurance and his all too transparent guile. His intuitive brilliance he masked with a banality that dismayed intellectuals of all political persuasions, including the one he picked to be his principal adviser. He had made his reputation as an anti-Communist and hard-liner, but he campaigned for the highest office as a healer and peacemaker, and once in the White House promised "an era of negotiation." His political task, as he saw it, was to extricate the country from the disaster in Indochina, to calm the nation, and to put together what Henry Kissinger, his national security adviser, would call a "structure of peace." Kissinger, who had written his doctoral dissertation on the efforts of the great powers to put the world back together again after Europe had been rent by the French Revolution and the Napoleonic Wars, envisaged a world once again restored by the brilliance of diplomats.

Willy Brandt, who became Bundeskanzler later the same year, began as even more of an outsider than Nixon. But while the American president had been a dominant figure in American politics for more than twenty years without winning the trust of the press, certainly not the professors, not even important leaders of the East Coast banking and commercial world, the new German chancellor with the winning smile had been a respected international figure since his service as mayor of Berlin twelve years before. Given to fits of self-doubt no less than Nixon, he exhibited a heartiness that contrasted sharply with the president's evasive manner. Well to the left of the conservative West European politicians who made careers out of their Washington connections, Brandt had, nonetheless, been enthusiastically promoted with the U.S. Establishment for many years by John Foster Dulles' sister, who ran the Berlin desk in the State Department and shared her brother's politics.

Brandt was born in Lübeck, the city of *Buddenbrooks*. But his family was far removed from the high commercial culture depicted in the famous Thomas Mann novel. His mother was not married and he did not even know who his father was. As a young man he joined a revolutionary Socialist party that had broken away from the SPD when the party had lacked the moral courage to oppose the Nazis. Having made a reputation as a young rabble-rouser and pamphleteer, he feared for his safety when Hitler came to power and so, stuffing a few shirts into a briefcase along with the first volume of *Das Kapital,* he went into exile in Norway. He was sure that Hitler was only a passing fury, but he stayed twelve years, writing six books and numerous articles, marrying a Norwegian, and becoming one himself. When he decided to return to Germany after the war to reclaim his citizenship and to enter politics, his exile past continued to haunt him. In the 1960s he had to go to court on more than one occasion to defend himself against the calumny that was threatening his career—that he had put on a Norwegian uniform and fought against Germany in the war.

He became the SPD representative in Berlin shortly before the blockade and in 1957 became mayor. Privately a brooding, somewhat driven man, Brandt's human qualities, his smile, his love of jokes, friends, and music, and his easy manner made him an attractive figure in politics. Like his mentor Ernst Reuter, the mayor during the blockade, he personified the courageous struggle of Berlin, and this gave him a national political reputation. (During the blockade he would fly in and out of the city, and each time he returned he would bring in quantities of garden seeds in his briefcase.) In his years in Berlin, first as editor of the party newspaper, later as mayor, he hammered away at Adenauer's sterile approach to reunification. The helplessness of the NATO alliance in the face of the Berlin uprising of 1953 and the Hungarian revolution three years later convinced him, as he told a British audience in 1958, that the only possible course was "an unflinching, stubborn struggle for a peaceful solution by political action." He would speak of "normalization" of relations and "an open door policy in human and cultural contacts."

With Herbert Wehner, a former member of the Central Committee of the German Communist party with an unusually agile political mind, Brandt helped to move his party from "a sect with no political influence" as the party leader himself called it in 1959, to a Fabian reform party appealing to the middle class as well as workers. He led the party in the election of 1961, and while his personal popularity as a sort of German John F. Kennedy guaranteed large crowds—he too wrote books and projected the vigor of youth—the electorate was unwilling to vote against the Old Man who had managed to maintain such unprecedented prosperity. The SPD grew in strength but Adenauer stayed in office. Four years later Brandt tried again, and again he failed. The midpoint of the decade was a time of personal crisis for both Brandt and Nixon; both had been defeated twice in hard-fought electoral battles. After the succession of failures it seemed as though Brandt's chance for leadership was fading. He ate and drank too much and his own son was caught up in the revolutionary tide of the student movement. (Günter Grass, an enthusiastic if not always effective supporter of Brandt, had invited both his sons to play bit parts in a film of one of his novels which made fun of the *Ritterkreuz,* one of the highest German military decorations. Conservatives were outraged and SPD functionaries alarmed, but Brandt stood by his children.)

Nixon and Brandt, so different from each other as to be constitutionally incapable of serious communication, were both diplomatic innovators bent on changing history after a long debilitating freeze. Nixon relished the fact that as an American president elected as a centrist under the auspices of a conservative party that won only by attracting disaffected Democrats, he labored under few ideological restraints. He was free to dart, twist, and shock, and he would use these tactics in pursuit of a new world order which would assure the continuation of America's world supremacy. If to end the war without a humiliating defeat he had to convince the Vietnamese that he was capable of genocide—the "madman theory" it was called in the White House—he would do it. But he was equally capable of ignoring the ideological debris of a generation and literally sup with the same Chinese devil whom John Foster Dulles had refused even to greet almost twenty years before.

In 1966 Brandt became foreign minister in a Grand Coalition of the SPD and CDU. He was acutely conscious that—except for a brief moment in 1920 —he was the first Social Democrat in German history to be in charge of the nation's foreign policy. For his generation social democracy in its modern dress was the key to German revival and the maintenance of peace. Unlike France and Italy, in postwar Germany there was no Communist party; the Communist party was in the East and the intense anti-Communist feelings of most Germans could be projected onto Walter Ulbricht and his Stalinist apparat. But that meant that the SPD was the Left, that it had to play the role that the Left had failed to play in the pre-Hitler time: project a vision of a German progressive society in the middle of Europe that was neither resentful nor nationalist. For the Social Democrats the question that Adenauer refused to face was the all-important one: the question of German identity. Not that Brandt had the answer, but he was convinced that the question had to be taken from the back burner where Adenauer and his successors had left it, that it must be stripped of the hopeless propaganda of reunification; otherwise, the Federal Republic could never be a normal society.

German society twenty years after the war, like every Western society, was looking less and less normal. Brandt's years as foreign minister coincided with the cultural revolution that crested in 1968. At a party convention in Nuremberg young people swarmed into the hall tearing down SPD posters, throwing stones, and grabbing at Brandt's overcoat. One young man hit him with an umbrella. Brandt supported tough Emergency Laws in the face of mounting demonstrations. His son Peter drew a six-week suspended sentence for participating in one.

But Brandt was determined to reintegrate the student movement into the party.

In so far as these young people would accept a commitment to one of the parties of the Federal German "system", their interest centred mainly on the Social Democrats. It hit them all the harder that this very party should have entered into a coalition with a conservative bloc and subscribed to compromises which they found hard to understand. My friends and I were determined to integrate these youthful forces into our society, our state and party.

In his years as foreign minister, Brandt pressed forward with *Ostpolitik*. By the time he became chancellor he had already accomplished three important changes. He had made it clear that the Federal Republic would act for itself "instead of relying solely on others to speak for us. This meant that, while remaining in touch with our allies and retaining their confidence, we became the advocate of our own interests *vis-à-vis* the governments of Eastern Europe." Second, he had made it increasingly clear that the Federal Republic recognized the permanent loss of the territories now incorporated into Poland east of the Oder-Neisse Line. Although West Germans continued to refer to the German Democratic Republic as *Mittel-Deutschland,* the Federal Republic did not even control the area between the Elbe and the Oder. How could it ever reclaim the Eastern territories? To think that a generation of Poles would be uprooted to permit East Prussia to become German again was to indulge in dangerous fantasy. Third, with the active encouragement of the United States he had begun probing efforts to improve Germany's relations with Moscow and the nations of Eastern Europe, including East Germany itself.

Brandt understood that a détente of sorts had been in effect between the superpowers ever since the Cuban missile crisis, and as a result the map of Europe drawn by the victorious armies of World War II was acquiring a new legitimacy. Reduced tensions between the United States and the USSR offered stability on the continent, but they sealed its division. The brutal Soviet invasion of Czechoslovakia in August 1968 to end the Alexander Dubcek experiment in "socialism with a human face" dramatized the perverse nature of the new order that had settled on Europe. Détente was now more real than ever. The powerlessness of the West to do anything about the sickening events in Prague or even to suggest a strategy for the East other than long-term evolution simply restated the lesson of the Berlin Wall: West Germany had to give up the illusion of reunification through force. Michel Debré, De Gaulle's foreign minister, waved aside the Czech invasion as merely a "traffic accident" on the highway to détente, and the Americans indicated that once perfunctory denunciations were out of the way, arms negotiations with the Soviets would proceed. Embassy officials discouraged the hope a few Germans harbored of making an alliance with Mao to force the Russians to "disgorge" territory.

Despite Brandt's signals to East Germany in the late 1960s that the old hostility was abating—he stopped calling the GDR the "zone," and the chancellor even referred to the East German leader by his title, conceding thereby that he was running a state—Ulbricht was, nevertheless, deeply suspicious. West German approaches to Rumania, Hungary, and Yugoslavia threatened to outflank and isolate him, and indeed that was the intent of the Christian Democrats. Ulbricht insisted that the Russians stop the process, and the Soviets quickly agreed. Speaking at the United Nations, Gromyko charged Germany with a plan "to recarve the map of Europe."

Ostpolitik, which had been cautiously supported by the conservatives in the Grand Coalition, now became more controversial as the elections approached. Improving relations with Poland was a popular idea in Germany, not only because so many Germans and Poles had intermarried over the centuries, but because reaching out to Poland was like reaching out to Israel, an act of expiation. Yet when it became clear that there could be no peace with Eastern Europe without coming to terms with East Germany, the skepticism for *Ostpolitik* among the CDU grew once again. As the elections approached in October 1969 Brandt could show some rewards for his efforts. In 1968 about 1.5 million East Germans, almost all old-age pensioners, traveled to see family members in West Germany and 1.26 million West Germans visited the GDR. However, Brandt's coalition partners, especially Franz Josef Strauss, were determined to use *Ostpolitik* as ammunition against him. The CDU spread reports received from the Gehlen intelligence agency that Egon Bahr, Brandt's close associate, had for a number of years been secretly meeting with the East Germans. Cartoons suddenly appeared in newspapers depicting Brandt as a mouse about to be devoured by a Soviet cat.

Egon Bahr had indeed held a number of quiet talks with the authorities in East Germany while Brandt was mayor. The experience strengthened his conviction that the key to the German question was to concentrate less on the status of the two halves of Germany and more on human relations across the political divide. Starting as a radio commentator for RIAS, the radio station set up in the American sector of Berlin, Bahr had become the mayor's press secretary in 1960. When Brandt became foreign minister, Bahr accompanied him to Bonn, where he flaunted his gift for withering logic before the starched bureaucrats of the Foreign Office and revealed a talent for negotiation. Kissinger, himself a refugee from German prosecution, deeply distrusted this "unprepossessing . . . extremely agile . . . indefatigable" figure, for here was a Jew under Nazi law who had stayed and had even tried to become an officer in Hitler's army. A "reptilian" influence, a "pernicious" man, Kissinger would explode in private.

But having worked for years as the strategist of *Ostpolitik,* Bahr was now in a position to help bring it about. Years later Kissinger would call him "an old-fashioned nationalist," but the term had a different meaning for the Americans and the German Social Democrats. Kissinger, like Acheson and Dulles before him, was haunted by the prospect of Rapallo. There was little danger, Kissinger believed, that the Federal Republic would actually leave NATO, for no government would give up American protection. But if Germany refused to follow American policy outside of Europe, in Southeast Asia or in the Middle East, for example, that would adversely affect the balance of power on the Continent itself. Were Germany ever to spring loose ideologically from the Western alliance, it could become a pendulum swinging from side to side, eventually crashing like a wrecker's ball into the body of Europe.

The self-perception on the German side was quite different. Brandt and Bahr saw themselves as Atlanticists, veterans of many battles with the German "Gaullists." The Social Democrats had been the most ardent of cold warriors. In 1950 the party had set up *Ost Büro,* a clandestine intelligence operation to infiltrate propaganda into East Germany attached to balloons provided by the CIA, to help people escape, and to tweak Ulbricht's nose in a hundred ways. "We were the anti-Leninist Leninists," Stephan Thomas, the head of the organization put it, tough and experienced in fighting the Bolsheviks. Schumacher's generation of the SPD carried with it historical memories of which the Americans knew nothing, for their German contacts were principally the bankers and conservative politicians of the Rhineland, Ruhr, and Bavaria for whom the East was no more than a political symbol. But the SPD, the party of August Bebel and Rosa Luxemburg, saw itself as the *Mutterpartei* of all the Left parties of Eastern Europe which the Soviets had either co-opted or destroyed. In the eyes of the older Social Democrats it was the Soviets who were the revisionists and betrayers of the Socialist dream. The struggle over Berlin, which had brought Brandt and a new generation of SPD leadership to national prominence, was for them an ideological struggle as much as it was a struggle for power in central Europe, but while a few ideologues in the CIA understood the Social Democrats, the diplomats by and large did not.

In the years between the Berlin spy war and the October day in 1969 when Brandt moved his office into the chancellor's bungalow on the grounds of the Palais Schaumburg, the perception of the world held by German Social Democrats had changed. Stalin's hint in 1952 that he would liquidate the Ulbricht regime and permit a neutralized Germany to be reunited was taken by the SPD cold warriors as evidence that they had won. Stalin was ready to retreat from Germany. The summary rejection by the Allies of the Soviet proposal was a painful reminder of Germany's dependence. (Many of the older Social Democrats were convinced by Ulbricht's mutterings years later that Stalin was serious, and indeed the historical evidence supporting the conclusion that Stalin's successors were even readier to make a deal on Germany is impressive.) The other important memory for the Social Democrats was NATO's helplessness in the face of The Wall. But there were positive memories too. No sooner had Khrushchev and Kennedy absorbed the lessons of the missile crisis than the struggle over Berlin lost much of its force. By 1967 NATO had adopted the Harmel Report on the future tasks of the alliance which stated that "military security and a policy of detente are not contradictory but complementary." Détente was now not only a de facto reality but a respectable policy. The Atlanticists in Washington, fearing that the U.S. Senate was about to pass the Mansfield Amendment demanding the unilateral withdrawal of U.S. troops, quickly came up with a proposal to negotiate with the USSR for "mutual and balanced force reductions."

By 1969 Germany was still, as Brandt liked to say, an economic giant but a political pygmy. Thanks largely to the SPD economics minister Karl Schiller's program for stimulating and guiding investment, the Grand Coalition had restored prosperity. German economic power was now formidable. But the Federal Republic played virtually no role on the world stage. It was not even a member of the United Nations. Brandt and Bahr were not old-fashioned nationalists but new-fashioned ones who saw the necessity and the opportunity for Germany to reenter world politics. The key to Germany's becoming a significant world power was *Ostpolitik*, for the western remnant of Hitler's Reich could never act on the world stage until the fears of its neighbors and former victims in the East were allayed. The indispensable base from which a diplomatic thrust toward the East could be made was the Atlantic Alliance, for only with the Americans behind him could Brandt summon the strength to deal with the Russians.

2

Brandt and Nixon saw themselves, each in his own way, as a liberator and a restorer. When he became the first Bundeskanzler untouched by any Nazi participation or any Nazi associates, Brandt took advantage of the moment to declare that he was the leader not of a "conquered" but of a "liberated" Germany. His meaning, as his associate Horst Ehmke put it, was that he, unlike his predecessors, could not be "blackmailed" by holding up his country's Nazi past. Within the narrow bounds open to her, Germany would walk a more independent path and would redefine strictly German interests without being obsessed with having to remain so circumspect a power, for surely the man who had fought the Nazis for twelve years "did not need any lessons in anti-Nazism."

Nixon had his own burden of the past to remove. The Vietnam War was the project of a liberal establishment that had scorned the graceless, gutter-fighting California parvenu. The certitudes of Harvard, the Council on Foreign Relations, the boardrooms of the great industrial enterprises and Wall Street firms had come apart in the jungles of Indochina and the result was the greatest national disaster of the century. To pull the American war machine out of the mud and to put it once again on a track that would restore American power was, as Nixon saw it, the supreme challenge of statesmanship.

Nixon came into office with no Grand Design for a new world order. But he did bring a sense of priorities. The most urgent requirement was to create a political climate in which statesmen could maneuver. "We must lower our voices," he pleaded in his inaugural address. All he meant was that public pressure on the foreign policy establishment in the democratic societies should be relaxed so that leaders could protect the public interest as they saw fit. The first requirement of diplomacy was to soothe the forces in American society that were hamstringing his executive action abroad. But to quiet the country, commitments must be reduced and military burdens shared.

Nixon understood that none of this could be done without Soviet cooperation. The leaders in the Kremlin, Nixon believed, had three motives to help the United States in its hour of difficulty. First, they feared a wider war in Asia that might eventually suck them into a fateful confrontation. Second, they feared China more than America. Third, there would be economic benefits for them in legitimating and extending the détente with the United States—less money wasted on their own military and more money and technology from the West. But no one believed in the gospel of "negotiation from strength" more firmly than Nixon. He must not be too eager for agreement, and he must not negotiate in such a way as to erode the very basis of his strength by alienating the Allies in Europe. Above all, the alliance must present a common front to Moscow. But unlike the foreign policy elite of an earlier day, Nixon was hardly beguiled by dreams of Atlantica. Dean Acheson and John McCloy had moved so effortlessly across this mythical kingdom—settling into boardrooms, clubs, and country houses in England and on the Continent that resembled the ones they had just left on the Eastern seaboard, but this was not Nixon's world. Europe was neither a love, a protégé, nor a place in which he felt comfortable. Quite the contrary. Though he had traveled widely on the Continent in his Pepsi-Cola years and had been graciously received by heads of state, including De Gaulle, who was drawn to him as a "frank and steady personality," Nixon's awe at the self-assured ways of European statesmen reinforced his feelings of inferiority.

From his brief service as a consultant in the Kennedy administration Henry Kissinger was convinced that Washington should stop hectoring the Allies about a Grand Design for Europe. It was beyond American power to produce a design of its own making, he kept telling Nixon, and the world's greatest power was quite capable of adjusting to a variety of European developments, provided the process of change did not get out of control. In *The Troubled Partnership* he had written:

A united Europe is likely to insist on a specifically European view of world affairs —which is another way of saying that it will challenge American hegemony in Atlantic policy. This may well be a price worth paying for European unity; but American policy has suffered from an unwillingness to recognize that there is a price to be paid.

But since Kissinger was unwilling to pay any price for European unity at a moment when the United States was paying its dues for having been overextended in the rest of the world, the professor spent his time in office ignoring his own analysis.

Barely a month after taking the oath of office Nixon left for Europe, nervous about the hostile crowds he expected to meet but determined to launch his diplomatic offensive by repairing the strained relations with the Allies. His reputation as a cold warrior had preceded him, and he found Harold Wilson, among others, vigorously pressing détente. The "principal justification" of the alliance, Kissinger recalls Wilson arguing, was no longer defense but the relaxation of tension.

Having been accorded the unprecedented honor in London of attending a cabinet meeting, Nixon went on to Berlin fearing that his performance would be compared unfavorably with John F. Kennedy's triumph six years before. But his pale echo of the Kennedy rhetoric—"All the people of the world are truly Berliners"—and the efficient crowd management by the German authorities who shuttled people from one street to another to make the crowd look bigger produced a success. Nixon took the obligatory oath to defend Berlin in a speech in the Siemens factory. (Despite a propaganda campaign aimed at the upcoming presidential election to be held in Berlin, the Soviets already had indicated privately that they planned no confrontation over the divided city.) But the new president also hinted at negotiations. "[W]e do not mean that we consider the status quo to be satisfactory."

For Richard Nixon, Europe was a flank to be secured before daring diplomacy could be attempted elsewhere. In the campaign he had attacked the Democrats for allowing relationships with allies to deteriorate. It was time for "structural changes" in the alliance—more consultation, more concern for European interests, and a broader vision. NATO should now become concerned with the newly fashionable topic of environmental damage. More occasions for high NATO officials to get together were invented, more desultory discussion held, but this was not where Nixon's heart was, and the discussions bored him. By 1970 the new president had given a symbolic nod to Europe with his highly publicized journey to the Continent and had backed up his commitment with strong rhetoric. The United States could no more detach itself from Europe, the president told the Congress in his first State of the World message, than it could from Alaska. Yet competing priorities in Washington and Bonn began straining the alliance more than ever.

In April the new chancellor of Germany arrived in the United States. To smooth any feelings that may have been ruffled in Bonn by his premature congratulatory phone call to Chancellor Kiesinger whom Brandt had just narrowly defeated, Nixon extended imperial courtesies to his guest—the use of Camp David for three days to prepare for the White House meetings, complete with evening showings of recent Westerns on a wide screen. But Nixon and Brandt eyed each other warily from the start. Brandt thought of the Americans, especially Kissinger, as having "the disdain of the new Roman for Hellenic petty states," while the Americans worried that the new chancellor might be contemplating a Rapallo-like policy. Brandt had already initiated the frosty exchange with Willi Stoph, the chairman of the Council of Ministers of the German Democratic Republic. The bleak encounter had taken place less than a month before in Erfurt, the historic East German city where Brandt had reminded his host Germany had been united after the revolution of 1848.

Henry Kissinger regarded the prospect of a German diplomatic offensive as distinctly threatening. The new crowd in Bonn did not resemble the familiar CDU policians who had flocked to the summer seminar the professor had run for the up and coming of Europe and who so admired Kissinger's prose. The Brandt he had met in the 1950s seemed obsessed with the threat to Berlin, but the Brandt of the 1970s talked as if reunification could somehow be achieved through recognizing the division of Germany, and his chief adviser seemed especially interested in opening up Germany's room to maneuver, steering the same dangerous course that had led earlier German leaders to catastrophe. Brandt was a prisoner of his own mission, Kissinger worried, and these fears, widely shared by the Allies, became a major topic of conversation when Nixon met the British prime minister and the president of France. In place of Adenauer's ideological commitment to a capitalist West was a new, vague notion of a European restoration. There would be a gathering together of the sundered Continent through a process of slow convergence—more social democracy in the West eliciting more freedom in the East. Was this not a revival in new guise of the SPD ideas of Schumacher's time, a drift toward neutralism and revived German nationalism?

Even the process of negotiation disturbed Kissinger because it undermined his control over the global negotiations he contemplated with the Soviet Union. The aspiring architect of a new restored order worried that Brandt was too eager to prove *Ostpolitik* could work. His very zeal would hand the Soviets a diplomatic victory. Kissinger worried that a realistic détente, which he never saw as more than an antagonistic collaboration with the Soviet Union, was too complex a relationship for the public to understand and accept. Statesmen, he had written in *A World Restored,* "always have a difficult task in legitimizing their programmes domestically, . . . their greatness is usually apparent only in retrospect when their intuition has become experience." Too eager to tear down the barriers of a generation of Cold War, Brandt risked creating a new domestic political climate in the West in which a German chancellor could never again "afford the hostility of the Soviet Union." To sacrifice Western interests in Central Europe would obviously undermine the whole bargaining position of the new American administration. While publicly supporting *Ostpolitik,* Kissinger volunteered "background" comments that reflected the growing apprehension of those who, in Dean Acheson's phrase, had been "present at the creation" of the West, Lucius Clay, John McCloy and Acheson himself.

The American professor, who spoke English with a heavier German accent than Brandt, had managed a successful career on the fringes of power. A protégé of the richest politician on the national scene, Nelson Rockefeller, he had first come to the attention of important men by distilling the conventional wisdom of the 1950s into an influential book. Having laced Cold War ideology with just enough skepticism and a few novel ideas—the most notable was to defend the United States by being prepared to fight limited nuclear wars in Europe—Kissinger was widely accepted in the national security world as someone who was both orthodox and original. But to the outside world he was unknown. Once in the White House, principle no less than vanity propelled him in his prodigious efforts to change that reality.

Power, as Kissinger understood it, was built on a web of appearances. Without creating a public persona he would not have the credibility to take on the formidable antagonists to his subtle new diplomacy. By the time Brandt arrived in Washington three weeks before the Cambodian "incursion," Kissinger, still on leave as a Harvard professor, was already beginning to be touted as the "Merlin of diplomacy." Newsmen—unaware that he had ordered their telephones tapped—praised his candor. So skillful a self-packager was the man who would soon be dubbed by *Newsweek* as "the name that made foreign policy famous" that he could with impunity present himself as the president's supremely authoritative interpreter and yet titillate subordinates and courtiers of the press by referring to his boss as "my drunken friend." Such delicious tidbits of White House basement gossip, judicious flattery of friend and foe, the celebrated self-deprecating wit, and the flashing insight of a truly powerful mind all helped build the legend. Reaching for the image of a secret agent rather than a stuffy diplomat, Kissinger used his clandestine peregrinations with their spectacular denouement—dramatic scenes of reconciliation with the nation's enemies in Peking and Moscow—to legitimate deception, the critical instrument of his diplomacy. A brilliant flatterer, a savage taskmaster, a joyless swinger, he seemed to suffer some of the very ego problems he would describe so clinically in the man who made him famous. "Living as a Jew under the Nazis, then as a refugee in America and then as a private in the Army," he himself once observed, "isn't exactly an experience that builds confidence."

All through 1970 there was flurry of activity inside the State Department on Berlin, as second-level officials hammered out the technical details of an agreement guaranteeing Western access to Berlin. Only when it became clear by the end of the year that the Soviets were interested in the agreement did Kissinger mute his off-the-record skepticism and move from monitoring the negotiations to becoming the impresario. Decimating normal diplomatic channels through his consistent resort to so-called "back channels," the White House adviser was quite prepared to ignore what he calls in his memoirs "the not unreasonable" insistence of the secretary of state that the State Department conduct negotiations. Although the basic framework of the negotiations had been worked out with the British, French, and Germans, Kissinger's private talks with the Soviet ambassador Anatoly Dobrynin and Nixon's old law professor Kenneth Rush's secret conversations with Soviet officials in Germany were carried on without the knowledge of the Allies or the U.S. secretary of state. Besides infuriating the professionals in every foreign office, including the State Department, the secret superpower talks lent credence to the growing suspicion in Europe that a new Yalta was in the making. The national security adviser positively flaunted his secret diplomacy, as when he arranged to have Egon Bahr, upon leaving the White House by the front door, shake his State Department escort and reenter by the basement entrance to get down to serious business. State Department officials were of course quite aware of the whereabouts of their guest.

The pace and flurry of German diplomacy began to create pressure in Washington. In December 1970 Brandt flew to Warsaw, signed a treaty he had initiated for "full normalization" of relations, and sealed it by suddenly falling to his knees in tears before the memorial to the dead in the Warsaw Ghetto. The spontaneous gesture infuriated German nationalists, electrified the Poles, and worried the Americans. Events were moving too fast. This "sentimental" figure, perhaps the most negative epithet in the Kissinger political vocabulary, was a loose cannon entering into bilateral talks not only with Warsaw but with Moscow. His close adviser Horst Ehmke called at the White House to inform the Americans that Brandt now felt free to talk to the East Germans directly about Berlin access in the course of their discussions of normalizing relations. He urged the Americans to step up the pace of their own negotiations.

"As far as European-American relations were concerned," Brandt wrote in one of the more understated passages in his memoirs, "Nixon did not receive on the same wave length I was at pains to broadcast on." The suspicion about Bahr and Brandt in the Nixon White House now turned to alarm. The war-horses, as Brandt called them—Acheson, Clay, McCloy—were summoned, to the White House by Nixon, who expressed his outrage that Willy Brandt was writing the peace treaty "while the Allies are on the sidelines." After leaving the president, they publicly denounced the chancellor in a press conference and urged him to "cool off" what Acheson called his "mad race to Moscow." Falling back into line, Brandt now accepted the Kissinger concept of linkage. The ratification of the Warsaw Treaty, seen in Washington but not in Bonn as a major concession to the East, would be held up until the Soviets agreed to a Berlin settlement which the Allies could accept.

Henry Kissinger once told the former Israeli prime minister Yitzhak Rabin that he would never handle any "matter that he deemed hopeless." But by April 1971 the miraculous seemed possible: The Soviets might actually give up some of their leverage on Berlin which, thanks to the ambiguities of wartime agreements, permitted them to turn the screw on the United States and the Federal Republic whenever they liked. They even seemed ready to renounce rights they had by virtue of the UN Charter to "intervene" in the "former enemy state." The highly technical negotiations bogged down in trade-offs of legal nuances as the negotiators danced around the real issues. For the West these were a guarantee of access and the recognition of a delicate status that preserved the rights of the occupying powers but did not isolate the city from the Federal Republic to which it was spiritually but not legally connected. For Moscow the negotiations were part of a larger diplomatic mosaic for legitimizing the split of Europe and Soviet hegemony over the Eastern half. Since East

Germany was the linchpin of the Eastern bloc, the Soviets insisted on transferring the responsibility for access to Berlin to the East Germans, for the fiction
of German sovereignty could hardly be maintained if the GDR lacked the
normal prerogative of government to control the traffic across its borders.
Indeed, it was this issue that had sparked two major confrontations with the
West.

Old German hands in the State Department such as Martin Hillenbrand
greatly resented Kissinger's intrusion into the negotiations. They considered
his sudden interest as merely a sign that they were on the threshold of success
after much hard work and that he wished to take the credit. Kissinger, on the
other hand, saw the State Department as a foil against which to display the
speed, brilliance, and wit which were so notably lacking in that labyrinth of
paper. Accusing the Foreign Service of both immobilism and unseemly haste
in making concessions to the Soviets, Kissinger lost no occasion to pronounce
the professionals a formidable obstacle to getting anything done. As the negotiations matured it turned out that the German bureaucracy was also an adversary. The CDU-sympathizing bureaucrats in the Foreign Office who regarded
Bahr much as the State Department saw Kissinger, began leaking cables in
Axel Springer's *Quick* and other conservative German publications designed
to show that certain proposals Bahr was pushing originated in Moscow and
that he was, as one Bavarian newspaper charged, "selling out Berlin." The
negotiations ended with marathon sessions culminating in the signing of the
Quadripartite Agreement on September 3, 1971.

It is likely that the Soviets who had been involved in an actual border war
with China two years earlier felt some pressure to move toward détente with
the United States after Kissinger's trip to Peking was announced the previous
July. For the Kremlin, a German settlement was the culmination of years of
diplomatic effort to secure juridical recognition by the West of Soviet control
of the eastern half of Europe. Another factor influencing their decision was a
U.S. concession. Reversing a long-held position, the United States had agreed
in principle to participate in a Conference on European Security, something
which the Soviets had been relentlessly pushing for years. Kissinger insisted,
however, on making the convening of the conference conditional upon the
conclusion of acceptable agreements on Berlin and Germany. An essentially
meaningless gesture in Kissinger's view once the status quo in Europe had
been underwritten with the agreements on Berlin and Germany, the conference
was urged upon Nixon by Brandt as an instrument for developing a new relationship between the United States and Europe that would be based neither on
residual rights of conquest nor on America's role as chief guarantor of the
NATO alliance. The chancellor was worried about what he called "inordinate
U.S.-Soviet bilateralism" in the emerging détente. Moreover, the perennial
Mansfield Amendment for cutting the U.S. forces in Europe—this time by as
much as half—had been defeated in May 1971, but only after the entire stable
of NATO war-horses—Acheson, McCloy, and Generals Clay, Gruenther,
Norstad, and Lemnitzer—had been pressed into service as lobbyists, and the

Soviets had, much to Kissinger's amazement, suddenly taken the steam out of
the campaign for unilateral withdrawal by calling for mutual reductions. The
shifting tides of U.S. politics and the uncertain new relationship between
Washington and Moscow made a redefined U.S.–Europe connection a priority
for the Germans. But in American eyes the old relationships were positions of
strength based on unique advantages. They would not be exchanged lightly.

The Kremlin had replaced Ulbricht, the very symbol of intransigence on
the German question, and Brandt was deeply involved in the negotiations to
normalize relations with East Germany. Returning to the White House in December 1971 Brandt was perplexed by Nixon's remark that the United States
intended "to leave the Germans complete freedom of action, not tell them
what they should or shouldn't do." Since it was obvious that the Americans
were highly suspicious, the chancellor speculated that Nixon was disengaging
from the negotiations in anticipation of soon having a more congenial CDU
government as a partner.

During the three-month negotiation between the two Germanys on visits,
communications, and access in the divided city, Brandt was under increasing
pressure. The opposition kept repeating the charge that the Social Democrats
were selling out and demanded a new government. The negotiations on the
Basic Treaty between the Germanys drew even more fire. It called for a basic
renunciation of force, a recognition of the sovereignty of the two states, an
exchange of diplomatic missions, and the membership of both states in the
United Nations. It was the final recognition that the myth of reunification was
dead, that Germany, as Brandt wrote, could never again be a nineteenth-
century state. Its hope was "cultural nationhood," an idea which *realpolitikers*
in Washington and Paris viewed with suspicion, but which a large majority of
the German people instinctively understood and supported. After a wrenching
debate on ratification, Brandt called an election in November 1972 in which
the SPD gained significantly. As a result of strong popular support for *Ostpolitik,* the party emerged for the first time as the strongest in Germany.

Thus by 1972 a fragile détente was in place. In a diplomatic spectacular
unequaled since the end of the war, a product of three sleepless nights of
marathon negotiations, Nixon and Soviet President Leonid Brezhnev, in the
very midst of fighting a "proxy war" with one another in Indochina, signed a
battery of agreements—exchanges, scientific cooperation, principles of coexistence, and, most significantly, the SALT I arms limitation accord. Kissinger
had now caught up with Brandt. But from the start the German détente and
the American détente rested on completely different principles, priorities, and
assumptions, and for that reason the experience with détente would be evalu-
ated differently in Bonn and Washington ten years later.

For Kissinger détente was an essential instrument for achieving his overriding goals—stability and order. Too astute to believe that political change
could ever be frozen, Kissinger's idea of a stable order was one in which the
process of change was subjected to effective governance. As a naturalized
American *geopolitiker* the proposition that the United States should be the

gyroscope, if not the engine, of world politics was self-evident. Moreover, while the Americans might be neither more moral nor less naive than the Europeans, it was the Germans, French, British, and Russians, especially the Germans, who had allowed the world order to collapse in two world wars. Europe had not had "a legitimate government" since 1914, Kissinger told a group of State Department wives. Europe's misuse of power was the foundation of the American responsibility to keep the peace. Kissinger thus placed himself squarely in a line reaching from Dean Acheson who had encouraged him when he was a graduate student to Dean Rusk who once noted that America's global task was defined by the stubborn reality that at any one time more than half the people of the world are awake and making mischief.

But unlike men like Acheson, McCloy, and the other architects of Atlantica, Kissinger had no vision of how domestic structures in the United States or in Europe would or should evolve. The first postwar generation of American statesmen, politically conservative though they were, were sensitive to the connections between the expanding welfare state and foreign policy even if they did not always know how to make the connections work. For Kissinger, on the other hand, domestic structures were a given. Those who were in power were by definition more predictable, more reliable, and more orderly than those who were waiting to take power—unless they were perceived, like Salvador Allende in Chile, to be a subverter of order. In this sense only was Kissinger a conservative, for traditional conservative rallying cries like the evils of deficit spending and high taxes or the sanctity of the family meant nothing to him. He found economics boring and mystifying. He was quite content to serve, even genuinely admire, that quintessential American liberal, the free-spending economic interventionist Nelson Rockefeller. No wonder that Kissinger would become a hated symbol for American conservatives and that he would feel forced upon leaving office to reinterpret his own past in order to ingratiate himself with the right-wingers who would succeed him.

His was the world created by the Peace of Westphalia. One must keep "religious" differences out of politics. It was "sentimental" to think that the ideology or domestic structure of the Soviet Union could be changed by hectoring from abroad. The U.S. interest was not in reforming the Soviet Union but in making it a less dangerous adversary, avoiding wherever possible the "endless crises that led to the edge of confrontation," but not shrinking from confrontation when the status quo was being tested. Statesmen hedged their respective domestic orders with the shield of diplomacy backed by an unsentimental willingness to resort to force. The essence of an effective diplomacy was always to have more options than the adversary. The illusion of control was the very definition of power. Yet Kissinger understood that the American Century as articulated in the Truman Doctrine or by Lyndon Johnson's grandiloquence was over. The critical factor in America's decline as he saw it was not so much the changed economic relations of Europe, Japan, and America, or even the shifts in the balance of military power, but the fact that the domestic consensus that had supported American foreign policy had broken down.

Some level of Soviet cooperation was necessary to create a new American consensus and a new global policy that expressed it—a United States still number one in the world but less profligate in wasting its resources and more modest in its rhetoric. Kissinger still saw the Soviet Union as a "revolutionary power," just as he had in his first book, but now it was a tired one confronting a much more complex and puzzling world than Stalin ever faced. The tides of history had inevitably shifted against the United States. It was no longer a holder of that monopoly of world military and economic power that had been a unique American asset in the aftermath of victory. Détente could serve not only as a domestic slogan to re-create a consensus, but also as bait for the Soviets, an instrument for controlling Soviet behavior at a time when the United States was severely wounded by a war it could not win and dared not lose. In entering into the new relationship, Nixon and Brezhnev, as Kissinger later wrote, were each "betting on the future."

For Kissinger détente was the key to stability both within the U.S. political order and for the U.S. position in the world. His goal was the husbanding of power, the uses of which he could only dimly see. Brandt, on the other hand, saw détente as the necessary precondition for "normalizing" German society and for breaking out of Germany's crippling isolation. He was far more concerned with short-term results. What mattered most was to change the concrete conditions of life in the two Germanys and to moderate the human tragedy that kept fear alive and families apart. "A painful act of liberation," Brandt called *Ostpolitik,* that "released energies for the construction of the common Europe." Germany's economic growth would once again as in the past depend heavily upon expanded trade with the East. Brandt's détente was unequivocally successful in its own terms while Kissinger's was not, and the different experiences with the new relationship created a gap in U.S. and German perceptions of the world by the end of the decade. The consensus Kissinger prized broke down almost at the very moment of its creation because he was too secretive and Nixon too hungry for adulation to take the public into their confidence. The overselling of détente and the reaction it provoked, which Kissinger blamed unfairly on his employer, "destabilized" the very "structure" he tried to create.

3

Kissinger and Nixon were committed to a new "structure" of peace because the old one was now prohibitively expensive. For twenty-five years it had been possible to finance growth in the United States without inflation through an international monetary system that accorded unique privileges to the dollar. But that had begun to change dramatically when the U.S. economy heated up in the Vietnam War and the Europeans began to demand gold instead of dollars. Nixon remembered that it was the balance-of-payments crisis more than anything else that had prompted the business leaders to discourage Johnson from further escalation of the war. Monetary reality was now not only an economic limitation but a political one.

By 1970 the Vietnam War had already resulted in a dramatic decline in American power in Kissinger's own special meaning of the word. The United States now had fewer options than in the past for managing its own economy. The European powers were able to act more independently in managing theirs in ways that could damage U.S. interests. Cooperation with the other industrial nations in developing a new world monetary system was more urgent than ever, but each government responded to its own domestic political interests which made such cooperation difficult. The old identity between the American national interest and liberal internationalism had broken down. What was good for America and good for the international economy no longer coincided, for the decline of the dollar reflected the decline of the nation's economic dominance. In 1950 the U.S. share of world output was more than a third; by 1970 it was little more than a quarter.

In 1971 the United States experienced the first trade deficit in a century; a world market that had once been dominated by U.S. multinational corporations was now more and more the province of the challengers from West Europe and Japan. Their goods were cheaper because their production was more efficient and they did not have to contend with the inflationary burden of a huge jungle war. The Johnson reforms three years earlier had not proved effective. Time had run out on new gimmicks to make the international monetary system work for everyone's benefit.

The United States now moved toward an increasingly nationalistic strategy. As the economic interests of Europe, Japan, and the United States diverged, the Nixon administration resolved to take action to protect the U.S. economy and force the Allies to adjust to the new reality. The sense of international obligation that had caused John F. Kennedy to call the balance-of-payments deficit a problem second only to nuclear war was gone and in its place was an acceptance that imbalances were more or less permanent and normal. The economy should be run in response to domestic economic and political pressures. That meant higher tariffs in response to the demand of organized labor to protect jobs, tight money at home in response to increasing concern about inflation, and the further restriction of the U.S. commitment to exchange gold for dollars. Once the gold window was permanently closed, the flow of unwanted dollars would become the problem of the Europeans instead of the Americans. If they didn't want dollars flooding their countries, they could adjust their exchange rates and interest rates. By renouncing international obligations that interfered with domestic economic growth, the United States could assert its real power in the world. As long as the Allies were dependent upon America for their security, and as long as everyone measured his wealth in dollars, there were limits to what the Europeans and Japanese could do in retaliation. The internationalism of free trade and fixed exchange rates had been buttressed by the collective fears of the prewar generation: Beggar-thy-neighbor export wars of the 1920s had produced the shooting wars of the 1940s. But, as Nixon advisers, who urged "a passive balance-of-pay-ments strategy" or "benign neglect," now argued, the Europeans were so hooked to the dollar that extreme retaliatory measures would be suicidal.

In the early months of the new administration, the Federal Reserve adopted a tight money policy. The balance of payments improved but as the dollar strengthened and inflation mounted, the U.S. trade balance suffered. Responding to the president's plea at his swearing-in ceremony, "Dr. Burns, please give us some money," the new chairman of the Federal Reserve, Arthur Burns, obliged by raising the interest rates. Billions of dollars soon were slosh-ing across the Atlantic once more to the New York banks. In the autumn of 1970, in anticipation of the 1972 election, Nixon decided to deal with the mounting unemployment by stimulating investment with easy money. The low-ering of the rates caused a sudden reverse slosh and Germany soon acquired $13.5 billion in unwelcome Eurodollars, for the monetary flood undermined the tight money policy the German government was pursuing.

Richard Nixon blamed the "foreign speculators," but Susan Strange con-cludes in her study of the dollar crisis for the Royal Institute of International Affairs that the culprits were "either the American banks and companies op-erating in Europe and Japan," or foreigners provided by the Americans with "the wherewithal to speculate." U.S. policies now confronted the Germans with unpleasant choices. To maintain the present exchange rates required the central bank to keep purchasing huge amounts of dollars. To revalue the mark, an undisguised objective of U.S. policy, would hurt the Federal Republic's competitive trade position, the very foundation of its extraordinary prosperity. To let currencies "float" in a free market would disturb relations with the other members of the Common Market who had weaker currencies. Exchange controls were anathema to the German economics minister, who feared it would trigger an economic contraction that would jeopardize the new prosper-ity.

On May 5, 1971, the avalanche of dollars reached a peak. In the first hour of business $1 billion arrived at the Bundesbank. The Germans stopped sup-porting the dollar and the government soon announced that the mark would float in accordance with the law of supply and demand until the world was ready to set some new exchange rates. The French minister of finance Giscard d'Estaing refused German suggestions that the franc and the mark should float hand in hand; the French were not prepared to give up the benefits of an undervalued franc. Instead, Giscard suggested, why doesn't the United States recognize reality and devalue the dollar?

John Connally, the new secretary of the treasury who had assumed office three months earlier, had an answer. "We are not going to devalue. We are not going to change the price of gold." The three-time Democratic governor of Texas, the wounded survivor of the Kennedy assassination, a freewheeling lawyer, rancher, and oilman who had been an LBJ protégé was picked by Nixon in the hope that he could deliver Texas in 1972. It was a delicious moment for Nixon as he listened while Connally telephoned the depressed former president who had less than a year to live to tell him that he had switched sides. Nixon soon resolved that John Connally should be his successor. Not only did the tall, silver-haired Texan look like a president, as all the columnists wrote, but the multimillionaire son of a Texas dirt farmer symbolized the only money in the country Nixon really cared about. While conservatives in the East regarded him as no more savory than the man who had called him to Washington—"Can he add?" the Republican governor of Massachusetts snorted—the increasingly powerful economic interests of the Southwest liked the way Connally talked. "If we relinquish the leadership role our nation had thrust on it after World War II, the free world is going to be sunk. No structure yet exists to maintain order in the world without the U.S. playing its role." The open world economy championed for a generation no longer worked to America's advantage. "And to be perfectly frank," Connally told an audience in Munich, "no longer will the American people permit their government to engage in international actions in which the true long-run interests of the U.S. are not just as clearly recognized as those of the nations with which we deal." The political survival of the administration required a new economic policy that could not be fit within the rules of the international economy which the United States itself had devised almost thirty years before. The rules had to go.

On August 15, 1971, after meetings at Camp David from which Kissinger and the State Department were excluded, a "new economic policy" was announced. (So separate was strategy from economics in the Kissinger White House that of the 140 National Security Study Memoranda he ordered in his first three years in the White House only one dealt with international monetary policy.) The package included wage and price controls, federal employment cuts, tax cuts, and investment credits with a "Buy American" bias, in short something for everybody who would be voting in 1972. But the Europeans and Japanese would not be voting. They would now be expected to make their contribution to America's recovery. The United States announced that it was unilaterally suspending the convertibility of dollars into gold. An import surcharge increased tariffs 10 percent. "We had a problem and we're sharing it with the world—just like we shared our prosperity. That's what friends are for," John Connally grinned. As governor of Texas he knew the power of nationalist rhetoric. He had heartily approved the establishment of a "United States Day" as a counterweight to the traditional "United Nations Day." Now Connally saw the unilateral measures as a whip to force the Europeans and particularly the Japanese to lower their trade barriers, to revalue their currency, and to assume more of the "defense burden." Most Americans, he knew, would welcome a strong defense of the dollar and jobs.

The manner and style were deliberately brutal. The secretary of state telephoned the Japanese prime minister ten minutes before Nixon went on the air to announce the program. Mock gratitude for the courtesy was expressed in the Japanese press; an extra seven minutes' notice had been given beyond what the prime minister had received just a few months before when Nixon had gone on television to announce Kissinger's trip to China and the stunning transformation of Asian politics it portended.

The United States was no longer asking for cooperation in stabilizing its economy. It was acting and forcing the Allies to react. To be sure, there was nothing new about that. What was new was the rhetoric and the spirit of the new policy. In imposing a unilateral "surcharge" on imports, the Nixon administration was violating not only the spirit but the letter of the GATT, a cornerstone of the economic structure fashioned at the Bretton Woods Conference in 1944. For the first time since the war a U.S. administration felt forced to take radical action to change the rules of the international economy in order to deal with the protectionist pressures at home. The U.S. multinationals, though legally American corporations, were prospering from the European boom and were speculating successfully in the mushrooming Eurodollar market. But small businessmen and the newer businesses of the South and West, who were less dependent upon the world market, were beginning to echo the rising demands of organized labor for walling off the outside world, demanding tariffs, quotas, and regulations to keep dollars from sloshing back and forth across the Atlantic and to keep cheap foreign goods out. Even Henry Ford II, the most internationalist of the car makers, told Maurice Stans, the secretary of commerce in February 1971, "that America had become a service economy and could no longer compete internationally, and that the only way we could keep our industrial jobs was through tariffs and quotas."

As Nixon left the hastily convened conference at Camp David he was aware, as his chief economic adviser Herbert Stein put it, that the United States had made the most momentous decision in economic matters since the New Deal, but he worried about the reaction. "As I worked with Bill Safire on my speech that weekend," he later wrote, "I wondered how the headlines would read: Would it be *Nixon Acts Boldly*? Or would it be *Nixon Changes Mind*?" On the day following the announcement of the "new economic policy" the stock market rose thirty points. Except for some academic economists who warned that the Nixon shock treatment would bring the whole monetary system crashing down, there was wide support for the policy in the United States. The United States would show the world that it had the strength to force other countries to revalue their currency and render their goods more expensive. The dollar would stay where it was. Since other countries used the dollar as reserve, they could not afford to retaliate against the dollar without inflicting grievous harm on themselves. The United States had lost its unique economic position in the world but not its economic power, which was a holdover from that brief golden age when America was the world's banker.

The Connally strategy was to confront the Allies with a war of nerves until they were ready to meet U.S. terms for a new monetary order. "I knew they killed the wrong man in Dallas," British Prime Minister Edward Heath is said to have exploded privately. Kissinger worried that the arcane economic disputes he had been content to leave to others would undermine his global strategy. His primary goal was to press détente, which even in the best of circumstances would make West European leaders nervous that a superpower deal was being arranged behind their backs. Consultation with statesmen of Europe was therefore a precondition for the summit meetings with Brezhnev and Mao which would establish the "five power world" that excited Nixon. (The Nixon structure of peace was to be built on a constellation of the United States, Europe, Japan, China, and Russia.) The new pentagon of power to replace the bipolar world of the Cold War would be Nixon's crowning achievement, for the preeminence of the United States among the honorary "equals" would be clear. But Connally was aggressively threatening the whole strategy, which depended so critically on making the other powers feel important, for he kept reminding them that when economic self-interest was involved the United States would act on its own.

Connally had impressed Kissinger with the advice he offered him on arriving in Washington. "You will be measured in this town by the enemies you destroy. The bigger they are, the bigger you will be." The formidable Texan had indeed succeeded in relegating to the shadows the president's more timid and conventional advisers. Kissinger felt a sudden need to steep himself in the strange world of international money. He arranged to stop by evenings at Lord Cromer's, the British ambassador who had been governor of the Bank of England, for a crash course. He quizzed the economists who worked for him and was then ready, he suggests in his memoirs, to challenge Connally on negotiating tactics. As Connally later explained it: "I knew there had to be a deal soon—there is a momentum in these things, and if it went too long we would lose it." But the two men disagreed on how long to prolong the war of nerves. Kissinger saw the secretary as a politician who would play to nationalist sentiment at home even at the cost of losing that magic moment for settlement "when the other side is still suspended between conciliation and confrontation." Arthur Burns, who was a Kissinger ally, showed the national security adviser a "list of retaliatory measures planned by our major trading partners. . . ."

Edward Heath let it be known that he would not meet with Nixon until some progress on the monetary front had been achieved. The Germans hinted that the EEC, which Britain now finally was about to join, might well form a defensive monetary and trading bloc and that European terms for a monetary settlement would harden. Kissinger now persuaded the president to begin serious negotiations on the dollar.

The key, Kissinger argued, was Georges Pompidou, the imperious general's portly successor, who affected an equally regal bearing from a less commanding height. "Our preferred strategy was to permit Pompidou to establish a position of leadership in Europe by negotiating the terms of a settlement with us. We always had in reserve the threat to isolate him if he were totally intransigent." Scornful of the fine points of international finance, Kissinger brandished his ignorance, for he relished the idea of re-creating the monetary order on political intuition alone. For reasons of prestige Pompidou had an interest in being the European statesman to settle with the Americans and thereby set the tone for future transatlantic relationships.

The son of a shoeless peasant of the Auvergne, Pompidou was propelled to the pinnacle of Gaullist society by virtue of his financial cunning, longtime loyalty to the general, and elegant intuition. Within a little more than a decade he had held the principal levers of power of the Fifth Republic—director-general of the Rothschild Bank, premier, and now president. A discreet professional who got his start by managing the foundation De Gaulle had set up in memory of his daughter, a master of the economic details that bored the general, yet a man of sardonic wit and superior mind who enjoyed the company of successful novelists and artists, Pompidou had become De Gaulle's political executor, but he was no longer a disciple. In the midst of the student crisis of 1968, Pompidou had suggested that it was time for the general to step down, and when the crisis was over De Gaulle thanked him for his advice by dismissing him. Ever afterward the mere mention of his predecessor's name by foreign leaders would produce icy looks.

Nixon and Pompidou had gotten off to a bad start on the occasion of the French president's visit to the United States in 1970. In Chicago he and Madame Pompidou were besieged by Jewish demonstrators protesting France's refusal to sell Israel arms while supplying Mirage jets to the Libyans, who were suspected of shipping them to Egypt and Syria. "The French people were able to see on television their President and his wife getting out of the car in the midst of a screaming crowd, while the police looked on," Foreign Minister Michel Jobert remembers, "threats, screams, spitting, nothing was missing." Pompidou gave orders for an immediate departure from the United States, agreeing to stay only after a Nixon apology, but determined never again to set foot on American soil.

On December 14, 1971, Nixon, Connally, and Kissinger met Pompidou in the Azores to make their deal. Nixon, who had strongly admired De Gaulle, eagerly wished for a rapprochement with France, just like his two predecessors. The calculated aloofness of France was a continuing affront to the myth of American leadership. The era of active diplomacy with Moscow which Nixon envisaged would hold greater dangers if the French were once again to play an aggressively independent role in Europe. De Gaulle's anti-Americanism, State Department analysts argued, grew out of his personal wartime experiences with Roosevelt which Pompidou did not share. (The younger man had spent the war in occupied France teaching in a Paris lycée.)

Kissinger and Pompidou agreed that the United States would devalue the dollar by raising the price of gold $3 an ounce if France would revalue the franc. Giscard d'Estaing, Pompidou's finance minister, convinced the president that his predecessor's ideological commitment to gold was not shared anywhere in Europe and that France would be isolated if it did not promote a compromise with the United States. Too shrewd to believe that the Americans had really conceded much on the dollar, Pompidou warned Michel Jobert, "Try to keep the press from claiming this as a big victory. Appearances have changed but not reality." The dollar, weak or strong, was still an effective political instrument in America's hands.

Three days after the Azores meeting the major industrial nations of the

West met at the Smithsonian Institution in Washington and agreed to revalue their currencies, but not by as much as Connally had wanted and not, as it turned out, by enough to solve America's monetary problem. The Japanese revalued the yen by 16.9 percent. Connally claims that this strange figure was arrived at by setting it just below the 17 percent devaluation that had triggered the depression in Japan in 1932 that had prompted the finance minister to commit hara-kiri. Nixon proclaimed the Smithsonian Agreement "the most significant monetary agreement in the history of the world." But it is not even mentioned in his memoirs, for within eighteen months it had collapsed.

4

The unique hold of the United States on the world monetary system was the key to maintaining American power in the face of a radically transformed world economy. Despite the cries of alarm of the professional liberal economists that currency wars and nationalist banking practices would so weaken the dollar that the whole system would collapse into anarchy, such a disaster did not happen in the 1970s, which turned out to be a decade of permanent institutionalized crisis. The reasons Connally understood. For all the competing pressures on European and Japanese governments to expand exports, maintain employment, and control inflation, their destiny was too tied to the dollar to wish to see it destroyed. Thus between 1970 and 1974, a period of great German success in capturing the U.S. market for its exports, especially automobiles, the central bank lost the equivalent of one-third the value of its dollar holdings. This unpleasant reward for German industriousness happened because the millions of dollars received for Volkswagens, chemicals, and machinery fell in value by more than 50 percent against the deutsche mark, thanks principally to the enormous U.S. inflation rate. (In these four years the dollar lost more than a third of its domestic purchasing power.)

But if the monetary system was a citadel of U.S. strength where the United States could translate even its economic failures into political power, it was in the arena of world trade where American weakness showed. Here the Germans and Japanese were more than equal to the American challenge. Between 1965 and 1971 automobile exports from Germany to the United States increased by almost 250 percent. A huge increase in steel-making machinery, synthetic fibers, and other chemical products helped to create a significant trade imbalance. At the same time the United States share of the German market began to shrink as German firms looked elsewhere, chiefly to other EEC countries for more of their imported office machinery, electronic equipment, and computers.

As the 1970s opened, the neo-mercantilist battle cry "export or die" was heard in every major industrial country. In Germany the export sector grew faster than any other sector of the economy and was critically important in stabilizing the economy whenever the domestic market weakened, as in the

Erhard recession of the mid-1960s. Because German industrial capacity greatly exceeded domestic demand, exports were the key to stimulating ever-increasing capital investment and in maintaining full employment. Perhaps because of nightmare memories of the terrible inflation of the 1920s, German workers acquiesced more readily than British, French, or U.S. workers in the national goal of price stabilization and were modest in their wage demands. Erhard had predicted that the countries "that have lived beyond their means will put in the dock the one nation that has cared for stability and make it pay the penalty, in a revaluation, for their sins." By the middle of the decade Germany's trading partners were not only demanding revaluation but were also arguing that the Bonn government's frugal policies amounted to unfair competition. The work ethic could be carried too far!

The German miracle depended upon exporting between 15 and 20 percent of the gross national product. (Until the oil crisis of 1973 the United States never exported more than 5 percent of its GNP.) Two aspects of the German character increased the pressure to export. One was *Wanderlust*. Every year German families climbed into Volkswagens, Mercedes, and campers and roamed the Continent, piling up large payments deficits in the process that had to be balanced by an ever-greater flood of goods. In the years of prosperity Germany had an acute labor shortage. In some cities in the early 1960s the average worker had a choice of ten jobs. As German material expectations grew, the more menial jobs could not be filled at all. So the German export machine had to import "guest workers" by the millions. At one point one out of every seven manual workers in Germany was a foreigner. Three percent of the entire Greek labor force was at work in the Federal Republic. These workers sent billions of marks home to the villages to which they intended to return and in the process created additional incentive for the German government to stimulate exports even more.

The situation in Japan was similar. Here too was an economy that had achieved rapid growth, even faster than West Germany's—about 10 percent a year in the early 1960s—and had industrial capacity far beyond the needs of a domestic market. This was especially so since the government, contrary to the United States where consumer credit was fueling an enormous buying spree, encouraged its people to save. For the Japanese, like the Germans, the world trade competition, a deadly serious business, was also a morality play. Should not the followers of Benjamin Franklin's precepts benefit from their industry? Had not the United States during the occupation taught those values even if it had forgotten them?

The Japanese economy, less dependent on exports than West Germany, nevertheless was under much greater pressure to sell its goods abroad than was the United States and the pressure to export was increasing. By the time the Nixon administration took office, Japan had emerged as the number two capitalist power in the world, one whose phenomenal rate of growth based on high quality, technologically sophisticated consumer products, and industrial equipment now presented a serious economic challenge to the United States.

It was scarcely believable, as a senior State Department official observed, that this "chain of rocky islands only one-fifth arable, subject to typhoons and earthquakes, with no iron ore, no oil, little coking coal, little in the way of mineral resources for industry, and with a food and population problem of staggering proportions" had tripled its GNP in ten years, quadrupled its exports, and had achieved wage and per capita income levels comparable to those in Europe. As late as 1960 the United States had had a government program to teach the Japanese how to improve their industrial productivity. But in the years 1960–73 the growth in productivity in Japan was 8.9 percent, more than four times the U.S. rate.

It was a time of self-doubt for the Americans; the familiar underpinnings of a world that could be benevolently managed from Washington were crumbling. Now, in the midst of the Vietnam tragedy, the Japanese who had been part of the backdrop of world politics, suddenly became visible, and their appearance on center stage produced a certain panic in Washington. "The Japanese are still fighting the war," Secretary of Commerce Maurice Stans told *Time* in the spring of 1971, "only now instead of a shooting war it is an economic war. Their immediate intention is to try to dominate the Pacific and then perhaps the world."

The U.S. business press began running articles depicting "Japan, Inc." as an unstoppable "juggernaut" directed by the Japanese Ministry of International Trade and Industry (MITI) with secret plans for integrating the resources of government and business for ever greater commercial conquest. Government in Japan spends half its time helping business instead of harassing business as in the United States, so went a familiar refrain in the U.S. business press. Envy and fear of Japanese commercial success grew as a by-product of détente. The more Nixon held out the prospect of a multipolar world the less important Japan looked as an ally in the "obsolete" Cold War and the more important it looked as a commercial rival.

The most critical issue to threaten the U.S.–Japanese relationship when Nixon took office was the textile war. For thirty years Japan had been mounting a challenge to this U.S. pioneer industry, now perhaps the weakest link in the economy. In the occupation days American textile manufacturers had supplied the Japanese with technical expertise, including advice on export markets, and the U.S. government had provided financial assistance to help Japan earn foreign exchange. But by the mid-1950s Japanese cloth and women's blouses had invaded the American market. Even though the United States was still a net exporter of textiles, the domestic industry demanded quotas which the Eisenhower administration successfully resisted by arranging "voluntary" agreements with the Japanese to limit exports. John F. Kennedy came to office pledged to help the dying textile mills in his native Massachusetts and in the three critical Southern textile-producing states that had supported him in the close election. In the 1950s more than 300,000 jobs had been lost as textile mills closed. A multilateral agreement was negotiated in the Kennedy administration under which signatories agreed to limit exports. The agreement did not cover man-made fibers or wool fibers, but by the time Nixon came to office the U.S.–Japanese textile competition was now concentrated on these, and Nixon vowed in his campaign to do something about it. Bringing the Japanese to heel on the matter of textiles, he believed, was crucial to his "Southern strategy" for winning the election.

Maurice Stans, the secretary of commerce whose image of Japan was frozen somewhere in 1942, had launched a much publicized effort to force the Japanese to concede on the textile issue and had failed spectacularly. Kissinger now tried his hand in "back channel" negotiations with a secret agent of Prime Minister Sato, a "personal friend" as Kissinger describes him with no official position, who insisted upon using the nom de guerre "Mr. Yoshida" during extended, highly sensitive Tokyo–Washington telephone conversations conducted on open lines.

Kissinger and Nixon took Japan much more seriously than any of their postwar predecessors. The national security adviser on his first day at work ordered an interagency study of U.S.–Japanese relations. Responding to growing criticism, the Japanese had opened up their economy a bit further to U.S. investment and had permitted Chrysler to enter into a joint venture with a Japanese car manufacturer. But Nixon, despite his long history of free-trade rhetoric, was unimpressed. "This capital liberalization is not important to us politically," he scratched on a Kissinger memorandum. "We have to get something on textiles."

The computation of "trigger points" that would activate an export limitation on textiles was no more fascinating to Kissinger than the world of "dirty floats" and "currency snakes" he fleetingly mastered for his negotiations on monetary matters with Pompidou. But he knew that a breakthrough on textiles would be a political victory for which Nixon would be grateful. And in 1971 scoring points with the president was crucial to his survival in the bureaucratic jungle of the Nixon White House. Kissinger also knew that Sato, though under great pressure from the Japanese textile exporters, really cared about getting one thing from the United States: the reversion to Japan of sovereignty over Okinawa and the removal of all nuclear weapons from the island. Kissinger, who throughout his career celebrated "linkage" as the key to effective negotiation, expresses a certain uneasiness in his memoirs for his part in "blackmailing" the Japanese by linking "an issue of fundamental strategic importance with a transient domestic political problem." (It is not uncharacteristic that the geopolitician should rate a Pacific island ahead of an entire American industry.) But his retrospective regret undoubtedly had something to do with the fact that his secret diplomacy ended in a fiasco.

Nixon warmly welcomed Sato in Washington in November 1969. The Japanese prime minister and his brother, the former prime minister Kishi, had graciously received him in his wilderness years. The president was convinced, as he had written in *Foreign Affairs* the year before his election, that Japan must assume new "responsibilities" for its own defense and help to "secure the common safety of non-communist Asia." To induce Japan to play its role

as one of the regional peacekeepers under the "Nixon Doctrine"—a new
policy to rely more on "indigenous forces" rather than U.S. troops to combat
revolutionary nationalism—the reversion of Okinawa would be accepted provided a formula could be worked out for retaining the U.S. bases there. The
prickly point concerned nuclear weapons. The Joint Chiefs had agreed that
they did not need to be stored on the island in time of peace, but they insisted
upon some color of legality to support their reintroduction in the event of an
"emergency." But the verbal hook the Pentagon insisted upon had to be sufficiently unobtrusive as to arouse no suspicion in Japan, for Sato's political
future rested on producing a clean agreement. (The issue had, understandably,
become somewhat more heated in Japan after an American major had accidentally drilled holes in canisters of nerve gas stored on Okinawa, allowing some
of the deadly vapor to escape.) An ingenious formula was invented. Kissinger
describes the negotiations for getting it accepted, which he likened to a Kabuki
play:

"Yoshida" and I worked out a careful script in which we rehearsed our principals
several times so that the proper record would exist. "Yoshida" checked with Sato, who
thought this might work.
   Sato would open with the standard Japanese position opposing *any* introduction of
nuclear weapons. Nixon would counter by tabling a very tough formulation of our
maximum position. Sato upon a few minutes' reflection would then produce the previously agreed compromise. After pondering the matter for the benefit of officials (or at
least of the record), Nixon would accept Sato's "compromise." That way the formula
was a Japanese idea; it had not been imposed; the record would be pristine.

   At the summit, Sato, according to Kissinger, gave Nixon his word sealed
with a handshake "that textiles would be resolved as the President desired."
However, no mention of the delicate matter could be made in the communiqué
for fear of the domestic repercussions in Japan. It turned out that Sato was
unable to deliver on his pledge. The Japanese textile industry refused to make
the concessions demanded by the Americans and the Ministry of International
Trade and Industry supported the textile makers even after Sato, now embar-
rassed about appearing to renege on his word, had found a new minister. The
American trade bureaucracy, unaware that a charade had been prepared under
which the secret agreement would emerge from a gracious Japanese "compromise" of a U.S. tough line, displayed an excess of moderation, refusing, as
Kissinger ruefully recounts the story, to "hold to the hardline positions that
the scenario required." The negotiations dragged on for two years. Nixon's
former client and early backer, Donald Kendall, the Pepsi-Cola president,
almost succeeded in negotiating an agreement on his own, and Wilbur Mills,
the Democratic chairman of the House Ways and Means Committee, making
direct contact with Japanese industry leaders, scored a breakthrough of sorts.
He persuaded the Japanese industry leaders to make a unilateral declaration
limiting exports. But the U.S. textile interests were not satisfied. Moreover,
Mills's upstaging the administration infuriated the president. Even though most

of his advisers urged him to accept what Mills had negotiated, Nixon would have none of it. The White House denounced the agreement and threatened to invoke quotas under, of all things, the Trading with the Enemy Act. The two Nixon shocks—the China trip and the surprise announcement of the New Economic Policy on August 15, 1971, were thus administered with some pleasure. They had their desired effect. Within exactly sixty days the Japanese signed a textile agreement.

Nixon called it a "masterful job of negotiation," but Japanese-American relations plummeted to the lowest point since the war. "People here just won't forget how this was done," a senior Japanese official told *The New York Times*. In his memoirs Kissinger recounts the story as a comedy of errors. While in office he called it a "painful but transitory misunderstanding." Nixon, then already beginning to come apart under the pressure of Watergate, delivered a rambling toast to the health of Sato's successor, Prime Minister Kakuei Tanaka, when he visited the White House in July 1973: They had not "haggled over what is the textile quota going to be." They were not "a couple of desert rug merchants" but statesmen who avoided "the murky, small, unimportant, vicious little things" so that they could spend their time together "building a better world."

Ironically, the Japanese textile makers soon found themselves priced out of the American market by other Asian exporters of textiles. The prolonged negotiation which managed to tarnish the reputations of everyone connected with them in both countries made little substantive difference. Outside the industry the textile crisis passed almost unnoticed in the United States. But in Japan the "textile wrangle" was headline news, and America's Pyrrhic victory left a scar slow to heal.

5

While the Nixon nationalists, Connally and Stans, battled the Japanese, they also began to question the conventional State Department wisdom about the European Common Market. In 1971 it seemed as though Britain would now finally become a member. The new British prime minister, Edward Heath, had given his maiden speech in the House of Commons in 1950 on the urgency of joining Europe, and he had led the unsuccessful negotiations to that end in 1962. The son of a carpenter and a lady's maid, he arrived at Oxford on a scholarship to study the organ, but though he acquired a taste for Tory politics and manners, he never quite fit the conservative mold. When he turned Harold Wilson out of office in June 1970 in an upset election, he did it by calling for sacrifice and austerity, a radical new note that would soon become the dominant rhetoric of the decade. Tense, steely, and solitary—Crossman describes the glazed look that frequently came over him as producing a "lockjaw effect" —Heath was never quite forgiven by his Conservative colleagues for his erudition, his "mirthless smile," or his accent. "His vowels betray him," a Tory MP complained to *Time*.

Britain's ten-year battle to join Europe succeeded because the very logic of Gaullism now required that the Anglo-Saxon island be admitted. For De Gaulle's successor, Germany's new activist *Ostpolitik* was much more of a concern than the traditional Gaullist fear that Britain inside Europe would act as America's Trojan horse. Pompidou now preferred having Britain inside the camp as he told Nixon to balance and restrain a "resurgent Germany." He even seemed interested in "a London-Paris axis as a counterweight to uncontrolled German nationalism." De Gaulle himself in his last weeks in office had suggested to the British ambassador that Britain join a new concert of Europe free of "American domination and machinery." Attitudes toward the Common Market and European integration were changing fast, largely because the political and economic underpinnings of Jean Monnet's vision were collapsing.

Ironically, as the 1970s dawned it looked as though this might finally be Monnet's decade. In October 1972 the members of the European Community proclaimed their intention to achieve a form of European union by 1980. The next year Britain, Ireland, and Denmark joined the club. Not since the war had the idea of a limited Europe so caught the popular imagination. No longer economically dependent on America nor terrified by the American Challenge, Europe had escaped America's bloody war and the deep divisions that were tearing at American society. French and German political managers seemed better able to cope with the fallout of 1968 than the Americans by alternately intimidating, co-opting, and isolating the dissident elements in the society. The wave of terrorism in the Federal Republic in the early 1970s helped to rehabilitate the authority of the state and garner wide public support for authoritarian measures to control domestic "Communists." Indeed, the state in Germany used successfully some of the same techniques of data collection, surveillance, and disruption that led to the undoing of the Nixon administration. German political and legal tradition was more tolerant of state infringement of individual rights and the provocation in Germany was more real. On May 11, 1972, the "Red Army Faction" detonated three bombs at the headquarters of the Fifth U.S. Army Corps at Frankfurt, killing a U.S. officer and wounding thirteen other people. Ten days later the headquarters of the U.S. Army in Heidelberg was bombed and three U.S. servicemen were killed. Shortly thereafter Andreas Baader, Gundren Ensslen, Ulrike Meinhof, and others were apprehended, and all during the next two years while the United States was absorbed with the Watergate scandal, Germany by comparison seemed a model of stability, and so did most of the other European partners.

The dominant political force in Europe was social democracy, a modernized capitalism developed by traditional working-class parties that brought businessmen, professionals, and workers into a new consensus. In the late 1950s and 1960s the economic policies of the British Labour party and the German Social Democrats had become increasingly moderate as the traditional worker constituency became more prosperous. Social Democrats entered the

cabinet everywhere in Europe except France and Ireland. Keynesian economics, modest government intervention, and humane welfare policies were
the foundation of social stability and economic growth. In Italy the Communist
party, the largest in the country, seemed to share the prevailing political sentiment. "[T]he classical class struggle no longer made sense in Western Europe," Palmiro Togliatti, the head of the Italian Communist party wrote shortly
before his death.

Not only was there more ideological harmony in Europe but the "Atlanticist" vision no longer had its former power to keep Europe divided. De
Gaulle's concept of a Europe extending from the Atlantic to the Urals was less
quixotic than when he proclaimed it. The spiritual fusion of a slice of Europe
with the American eastern seaboard—that was as far as anyone's imagination
could take them—had always been an historically unsettling idea at best. It
had gained force in the early 1950s only as part of a defensive strategy to fight
the Cold War. If the continent was to be divided in a Manichaean struggle,
there was no alternative for those who believed in capitalism and liberal democracy but to line up behind the defender of "Western civilization." But now
with the American détente and the German *Ostpolitik,* the ideological battle
line seemed to be melting away. If the bipolar world was really coming to an
end, as Nixon announced, then it was time to think once more of a European
identity.

But while the idea of Europe grew stronger in the early 1970s as the Cold
War faded, its political incarnation in the European Community looked less
and less likely. In 1965 De Gaulle had delivered a decisive blow to the supranational pretensions of the Common Market. The commission, the governing
body of the burgeoning European bureaucracy, had proposed that duties on
agricultural imports be paid directly to itself rather than to member states. De
Gaulle would have none of this; giving international bureaucrats authority to
collect taxes in the billions threatened the sovereignty of France. When the
commission proposed to vote on the issue which would have put France in the
minority, De Gaulle ordered his representative to withdraw from Brussels, and
the French chair at the EEC remained empty until the member governments
agreed that but for exceptional cases, they would henceforth conduct their
business by unanimous vote. The Community was thereby converted from a
vehicle for supranational integration into one for facilitating international economic collaboration. It passed laws that promoted corporate mergers across
national boundaries and cleared the way for some of the transnational ventures
in technological collaboration such as the Concorde that were crucial to De
Gaulle's vision of a resurgent France. But efforts to achieve a common industrial policy failed.

Thus as the outward symbols of European integration, such as the European Parliament, were being put into place, the political force behind Monnet's
movement was losing steam for a number of reasons. Originally, the supranational vision was an answer to the internationalism of the Far Left, "the legitimation of liberal capitalism," as the British economist Stuart Holland puts it,

but by the 1970s that function was no longer necessary. No serious political alternative threatened the liberal capitalist consensus. The role the Community had played in the Marshall Plan days in attracting and marshaling capital for big business had been completed long before. The large enterprises now preferred a less activist role for the international bureaucrats. Efforts to clear away obstacles to private transnational operations were most welcome, but not public planning for the allocation of capital. The liberalizing of trade within Europe had produced the uneven development of which Paul-Henri Spaak had warned in 1956. Without government intervention, he had predicted, the market would operate to widen the gap between the poorer regions of the continent —such as southern Italy—and the most endowed, such as West Germany. Now poorer regions all over the continent—Wales, Ireland, Corsica, Britanny —were growing restive.

The Common Market was organized on the basis of a French-German bargain. France was willing to accept the advantages the Community would give its stronger industrial neighbor provided French farmers could have a protected European market and a system of price supports. The Common Agricultural Policy was designed to provide farmers with roughly the same standard of living as industrial workers. That required keeping the price of butter, for example, so high that consumption fell. (In 1972 the agricultural fund of the Community purchased excess butter which totaled 15 percent of all consumption and sold its "butter mountain" to the Soviets at about 10 percent of what European consumers were paying. Moscow then resold the butter at a profit to Chile.) Monnet's noble vision had lost its luster.

The U.S. attitude toward the Common Market had been slowly changing during the 1960s. The Kennedy Round of tariff reductions had been pronounced a success in the United States. Industrial tariffs had been cut some 25 percent after long, hard bargaining, but, as C. Fred Bergsten, a Kissinger aide on trade matters, pointed out, the United States began imposing so many quotas and "voluntary restraints" on industrial imports that the "restrictive impact is undoubtedly greater than the liberalizing effect of our tariff cuts in the Kennedy Round." The Europeans began establishing free-trade agreements with African and Mediterranean countries which hurt Florida citrus growers. A study prepared for Kissinger warned:

In the long run we could be confronted by an "expanded Europe" comprising a Common Market of at least ten full members, associated memberships for the EFTA [European Free Trade Area] neutrals, and preferential trade arrangements with at least the Mediterranean and most of Africa. This bloc will account for about half of world trade, compared with our 15%; it would hold monetary reserves approaching twice our own; and it will even be able to outvote us constantly in the international economic organizations.

Nixon's secretary of agriculture, Earl Butz, accused the Europeans of trying to "plunge the rest of the world into a trade jungle." Senator Hubert Humphrey released an internal government study showing that European agricul-

tural policies would mean a loss of at least $10 billion in U.S. farm exports in
the 1970s, no small matter, since agricultural products accounted for a fourth
of all U.S. exports. One Nixon administration trade official publicly demanded
that the United States bring home 20,000 troops from Europe for every Florida
and California citrus grower "put out of business by Common Market policies." Even as protectionist sentiment in the country grew, the Nixon administration reverted to the traditional rhetoric of free trade. "The situation we
face is of exceptional challenge," Peter G. Peterson, the U.S. trade representative, told a business group. The "drift" to a breakup of the postwar economic
order into trading blocs was dangerous. "Wars are rarely planned," he added
ominously.

Kissinger understood the dilemma. Once the dream of a U.S.–dominated
political community had faded, European economic integration was hardly a
promising development from the American standpoint. But it could not be too
strongly opposed, for "we could not risk wrecking European unity without
breaking the political influence of the very groups in Europe who had supported a strong Atlantic Alliance." As a matter of geopolitics, strong European
influence over the former colonial areas was indispensable to his structure of
peace, yet as an economic development a wider free-trade zone linking the
European Community with important Third World markets was a distinct
threat. A Europe united and independent was a serious economic rival, a
Europe divided a political liability in facing the Russians. How foolish the
United States had been, Kissinger later wrote, to emphasize economic integration rather than "a European community in the defense field," the area in
which the interests of the United States and its European Allies were most
likely to overlap. Yet a détente proclaimed as the end of the era of confrontation was hardly a propitious moment for pushing the military, the one sphere
in which the United States was clearly still the managing partner.

Pompidou, Brandt, and Heath, each in his own way, saw as the preeminent task of the 1970s the forging of a new political identity. For Pompidou the
problem was to establish a leadership role for France that conformed to reality
instead of Gaullist pretension. The reality was that Germany, not France, was
the leading economic and military power on the Continent. Brandt, having cut
free of the frozen policies of the past, was unsure how to shape the new
German identity in the face of the mounting suspicion of Germany's neighbors.
Heath believed that the way to stem Britain's decline was to draw strength
from a relationship with a resurgent Europe in preference to a largely honorary
"special relationship" with the United States. The "special relationship," as
Kissinger correctly understood, was more of a social club than a business
partnership. For a generation, American diplomats had extended special courtesies to their British counterparts with whom they could relax, reminisce, and
dream in ways they could never do with Germans, French, or Italians. But on
critical matters of British pride, notably the Suez affair of 1956, the "special
relationship" had proved to be as inconvertible as the dollar into gold. Heath,
who had been Chief Whip of the Conservative party at the time of Suez, would

bring up the sorry episode from time to time in his talks with the Americans. His coldness in Washington came naturally, but it was also calculated to establish credibility in Paris. Unlike his predecessors, he avoided the transatlantic telephone; he was determined, as Kissinger puts it, "to avoid any whiff of Anglo-American collusion."

The contradictory political and economic interests of the major European powers, the now general frustration with what De Gaulle had contemptuously called the Europe of bureaucrats, and the gathering mood of pessimism throughout the industrial world about the possibilities of sustained economic growth rendered any positive vision of Europe elusive. A European sense of identity, nevertheless, was in the making, a defensive alliance of the nation-states of West Europe against what Michel Jobert, the French foreign minister, would call the "condominium" of the superpowers.

The moment that détente with the Soviet Union became the most publicized and energetically pursued American policy, the partnership with Europe underwent a fundamental change. Never would the nations of Atlantica regard one another in the same way again. The acrimony of the 1980s had its roots in the confusions of the 1970s, the American inability to accept a diminished notion of what it meant to be number one in a postimperial world, and a European failure to muster the energy and imagination to create a common vision to replace the ones that had developed in the Cold War. If the United States was immobilized by illusions born of its brief Pax Americana, Europe was still, politically speaking, a victim of World War II. As much as the new generation of leaders longed to be independent of the United States, they did not dare to act together on these shared impulses because they had too little control over their own societies and too little trust in each other. Thus while it was a comforting cliché to note that the alliance had always been in "disarray" and that indeed the tempers of the partners had actually improved since Suez, this complacent view of American-European relations overlooked the essential difference between the fifties and the seventies. The conflicts in Dulles' time were over the vestiges of World War II, the last act of a drama already written. The conflicts that first became visible in Kissinger's time concerned the future, the establishment of new, uncertain roles for great nations with proud but traumatic histories.

Kissinger was hardly surprised that Heath, Pompidou, and Brandt should read into the intensive U.S.–Soviet negotiations the suggestion of an emerging U.S.–Soviet condominium. The bilateral agreement on the Prevention of Nuclear War, signed by Brezhnev and Nixon, despite some participation of Germans and British in the final drafting, disturbed all the Allies, especially the French. "How can Europe be absent from the negotiation when she is so profoundly affected?" Jobert wondered aloud in an angry speech before the French senate. To test his theory, the man Pompidou referred to as "*Mon Kissinger à moi*" made a point in a conversation with Brezhnev shortly after the U.S.–Soviet agreement was signed of referring over and over to "you and your American partner" and took the Soviet leader's failure to protest as complete confirmation. To be sure, superpower collusion to avoid war was preferable to superpower collision, but it too was unnerving, for it underscored the helplessness of the bystanders. As another French observer put it, elephants trample the grass, whether they fight or make love. The secrecy of Nixon-Kissinger diplomacy lent credence to European fears. Heath, for one, thought that he was entitled to more than an hour's notice of Nixon's China switch, especially since Britain for years had kept a consulate in Taiwan just to please the Americans. Kissinger, on the other hand, shared the traditional American impatience with the catch-22 spirit of European criticism. The United States could never escape withering looks from the Continent whatever it did. If the administration in Washington was not being blamed for courting war, then it was dividing up the world. Superpower cordiality seemed to be even more threatening to the Europeans than the belligerence of which they had so often complained and once again would denounce in the Reagan era.

At the heart of every alliance is the fear of betrayal that one member or another will make a secret accommodation with the adversary. By the early 1970s this classic concern had begun to surface in transatlantic discourse. The stated justification for the huge U.S. nuclear arsenal was to deter an attack on Europe no less than on the United States. The conventional armies on which the bulk of the U.S. military budget was expended were for the defense of Europe. Only skeletal forces remained on the American continent; Europe continued as it had ever since World War I to be America's forward defense. But the SALT I discussions with the Soviets on limiting long-range nuclear missiles were the first negotiations on a matter that touched European security in which Europeans did not participate. The more Nixon and Brezhnev toasted peace in private the more expendable it seemed Europe had become.

The strategists came up with the idea of "decoupling": Now that the Soviet Union had achieved "parity" with the United States, which meant that each side could destroy the other, the American guarantee to risk Detroit and San Francisco for Munich and Paris was no longer credible. Indeed the promise to destroy Moscow if the Russians menaced Western Europe had brought reassurance to the Allies in the 1950s and early 1960s only because the Americans remained relatively safe thanks to the small size and technological backwardness of the Soviet nuclear arsenal. Now two successive American administrations had signaled in not so subtle ways an intention to disengage from European defense. The United States had unilaterally pulled thousands of troops out of Europe to send them to fight a war most Europeans opposed. The increasingly strident nationalist rhetoric from across the Atlantic dispelled whatever was left of the magnificent myth on which the Atlantic Alliance was founded, that, spiritually speaking, all the territory it embraced was equally precious, Bavarian villages and Sun Belt cities, Edinburgh, Dallas, Florence, Mainz, Tallahassee, Lille, and Cleveland. The mirror image of the European fear of "decoupling"—the abandonment of Europe by an America no longer able nor especially interested in defending it—was the American fear of "Finlandization": In the face of the two contradictory developments of the new decade, lowering of tensions and the emergence of the Soviet Union as an equally formidable nuclear power, the nations of Europe could be expected to make their accommodation with Moscow. From the early 1970s on, under four different administrations, American policy toward Europe, especially Germany, was preoccupied with preserving the traditional Atlantic connection in the face of mounting evidence that the credo that had given the alliance its original vitality no longer compelled belief.

"Never have the Americans imposed egotistical decisions on their allies and partners with so much brutality and good conscience," the pro-American savant Raymond Aron wrote in *Le Figaro* in February 1973. "Worse still: I doubt if their egoism has the excuse of clear-sightedness." While the businessmen of Nixon's cabinet looked nervously at Europe's stumbling efforts to create economic union, the Pentagon generals followed Heath's explorations with Pompidou of an Anglo-French nuclear force with even less enthusiasm. Once again a transatlantic dance about defense had begun. The United States was spending about $10 billion directly on stationing U.S. troops in Europe, a billion of which had to be paid in expensive marks. The balance-of-payments consequences of the American troops in Europe were visible and politically disturbing. Europe, after all, now had a population as large as that of the Soviet Union and an economy that was considerably larger. What was unreasonable, Senator Mike Mansfield kept asking, about letting the Europeans look after their own defense?

Nothing, except politics. The American troops were crucial to all the partners for different reasons, most of which they were unwilling to state. The Seventh Army, now a somewhat diminished and ragged version of the proud force that had arrived in the 1950s to hold off the Soviet hordes, was plagued by drugs, poor discipline, and declining morale. No longer either occupiers nor liberators, the American soldiers felt themselves the objects of German indifference or contempt. The days of high living were long over, and some GIs had to live on handouts from German charities because they could not manage on their military pay. Now that a modern German army had been re-created, the Americans did not look quite so essential to the population. Yet in every foreign ministry of Europe their presence was critical. To replace them with local troops would require selling anew the Soviet threat, and no one wished to do that when both the Germans and Americans were pressing détente. The Americans understood that as long as a united Europe had no defense of its own, it would be tied indefinitely to the United States. As long as Europeans wanted the troops to remain, the Americans retained political leverage on the Continent, which according to Kissinger's "linkage" theory, would be used to America's political or economic advantage.

Pompidou wanted the American troops because, as he told Brandt privately, "France could not fail to be extremely alarmed by the neutralization of Central Europe." Pompidou had been instructed by Nixon to urge Brandt against unseemly haste in throwing German divisions into the pot in the troop reduction talks just beginning in Vienna. Although the French president had assured Brandt that he had no intention "of behaving towards Nixon like a vassal toward Caesar," this was a message he was glad to deliver. Neither the United States nor France wished to disturb present military relationships because their suspicion of Germany was at least as great as their concern about the Soviet Union. Radical new military relationships could trigger new political alignments. Moreover, Pompidou told Brandt, France had rearmed at great expense, especially the *force de frappe,* and she was not about to give it all up as part of a Russian-American neutralization scheme.

For the European partners military arrangements were far more important for defining the political relationship with the United States than with the Soviet Union. European wars, like those of the past, were no longer conceivable, Pompidou lectured Brandt. "The probability is that there will be peace in Europe while relations between the Soviet Union and China remain as they are." It could be taken as a "working hypothesis that political upheavals—in Yugoslavia, for example—or a communist takeover in Italy or even France might prompt a Soviet attempt to encroach on Western Europe . . . albeit not a very likely one." Détente, according to his view, did not affect the need for arms, since an attack had not been seriously expected anyway. European arms were instruments to balance Soviet power whatever the ideology, manners, or temperament displayed by the men in the Kremlin. The German Social Democrats, although they favored mutual reductions of NATO and Warsaw Pact forces, agreed that a strong national military focus on the Continent was especially needed in a time of détente in order not to have to accept neutralization at the hands of the superpowers. Thus Germany under Brandt and his successor, Helmut Schmidt, used the decade of détente to build up its formidable military forces, increasing its arms spending at a faster rate than any of the partners.

However, the Federal Republic and its continental neighbors were caught in a double bind of their own making. Their quest for national identity required their own European military forces, but these forces lacked credibility unless they were either independent of the Americans and sufficiently formidable to scare the Russians or, alternatively, were so linked with the Americans that a nuclear response from the United States appeared virtually automatic. Since the Americans opposed the first alternative and there was neither the political unity nor enthusiasm for conscription and huge defense budgets necessary to force it through over American objections, even the most nationalist leaders in Europe clung to the American "guarantee" to "defend" them with nuclear weapons.

But once having built their notions of national sovereignty on American nuclear weapons, leaders like Brandt and Pompidou became prisoners of American nuclear logic. Under the "flexible response" doctrine which the NATO partners reluctantly accepted in the mid-1960s, the brunt of an attack on Europe would be borne by conventional forces about three-quarters of which are made up of non-Americans. Since the Americans monopolize the control of tactical nuclear warheads, they would have the exclusive decision when or whether to escalate the conflict. American generals talked airily of a conventional war lasting weeks, but German generals knew that such a war would devastate their country almost as efficiently as a nuclear "defense." The decision to retaliate against the Soviet Union itself for a conventional attack on Europe remained and still remains an exclusively American decision, and one that becomes less credible with each new missile added to the Soviet arsenal. Neither the French nor the British would dare use their small nuclear force for anything other than to deter a Soviet nuclear attack on their own territory. Thus, as the British historian Michael Howard wrote in 1973, "At every level of NATO strategy, then, the American contribution is at present indispensable."

This then was Europe in 1973, "the Year of Europe," as Kissinger called it, much to his regret. In the spring of that year Nixon was already beginning to reel under the impact of the Watergate disclosures. Kissinger had survived the intrigue of the Nixon White House. Indeed, just a week after he proclaimed "the new Atlantic charter" in a speech before the editors of the Associated Press on April 23, 1973, his rivals and tormentors, John Ehrlichman and H. R. Haldeman, were dismissed, and Kissinger became politically indispensable to the collapsing administration. Here was the moment to secure his own reputation amid the rubble by returning to the issues on which he had first achieved prominence. But his proposal that the states of Europe accept American or "Atlantic" priorities and consult the United States in advance on all important decisions affecting the European Community just at a moment when European leaders were reaching for greater economic unity and seeking to compete more effectively with the United States was bound to antagonize the partners. Yet diplomats no less than generals have a fondness for replaying famous engagements of the past. Now that the Vietnam War had been "settled," Kissinger's idea was to launch a new diplomatic initiative toward Europe with a stirring address that would be reminiscent of George Marshall's Harvard speech launching the European recovery program. In January he had seen Jean Monnet, now eighty-four and enfeebled, but still afire with the vision that had been his life. "America should begin treating Europe as a political unit whether or not it had fully articulated its institutions," the old man told Kissinger.

Kissinger gave an outline of his text to Pompidou's closest adviser ten days before he delivered it. The British saw it in advance. The Japanese were to be swept up in the "Year of Europe" despite the accident of geography, but as usual they were not consulted at all. The ideas behind the speech had been the subject of one of Kissinger's fencing matches with Bahr. For all his vaunted skill as a media star, Kissinger's maiden speech as an administration official was a public relations disaster. To announce a "Year of Europe" from New York was naive and patronizing. To point out that the United States "has global interests and responsibilities" while "our European allies have regional interests" confirmed the worst fears of Pompidou, Heath, and Brandt. The Atlantic relationship still rested on the idea that Europe was very much a junior partner. The call for a new Atlantic Charter, a casual rhetorical flourish invented by someone with little historical sensitivity, fell harshly on German and French ears. The first Atlantic Charter announced at sea in 1941 by Roosevelt and Churchill was a wartime propaganda document aimed at Germany that proclaimed an Anglo-Saxon alliance.

Only the British greeted the speech positively. In Germany, Herbert Wehner, the deputy chairman of the SPD, called it "an outline for a monster." *Le Monde* accused Nixon of "making light of the existing European institutions." None of the governments of Europe rose to the bait. In part European politicians were reluctant to engage in a protracted negotiation with an American president who more and more looked mortally wounded. Kissinger's practiced eye immediately caught the subtle changes in the way foreign leaders treated the president. Brandt, for example, was now "a shade less deferential" and less likely to lapse into morose silence than in pre-Watergate days.

But even had Nixon been in full command, the American call for a new Atlantic Charter would hardly have been a strong seller. Suspicion of the superpower détente was too strong; no European nation was ready to allow any other to speak for it. Pompidou, Brandt, and now Heath, each presented himself to Washington as a European but without authority to speak for anyone else but himself. As one continental commentator put it, the Europeans had nothing to say to the Americans and so they decided to say it together.

In his memoirs Kissinger dwells for more than thirty pages on his duel over the year of Europe with Michel Jobert. The story as he tells it is a traditional account of American innocence traduced by Old World wiles. The French foreign minister "offered to help draft the new 'Atlantic Charter.' " France would carry the ball if the United States would in effect give her its proxy. Of course it could work only with a modicum of deception. "We should maintain the appearance of a difficult dialogue," Jobert told Kissinger. The brilliant, exasperating Frenchman knew his adversary. He was proposing precisely the sort of involuted negotiating drama that Kissinger had staged with the Japanese over Okinawa and textiles. But having become intoxicated with his role, Kissinger argues, Jobert turned the year of Europe into a wrestling match.

Ruthlessly exploiting our aloofness toward the European Community, which he had encouraged, he organized its ministers and officials—a touchy group in the best of circumstances—against us, and made himself their spokesman. An American initiative enabled Jobert to pursue the old Gaullist dream of building Europe on an anti-American basis.

By summer it was clear that the American initiative had in fact encouraged the rapid deterioration of U.S.–European relations. For the first time European politicians were exchanging drafts on Atlantic relations without showing them to the Americans. Nixon and Pompidou had had an especially frosty encounter at Reykjavik, Iceland, at the end of May where the French president treated the American president to heavy sarcasm—"For Europeans every year is the year of Europe"—and taunted him for being naive about the Soviet

Union as if "texts, agreements, treaties" could restrain the Russians. Nothing could wound Nixon more except perhaps the final insult communicated by the partners in the summer of 1973. The president, who was desperately looking for summit meetings to attend, was politely discouraged from having one with the Allies in Europe. He would be quite free to meet with foreign ministers but no other head of state would attend.

EIGHT

RESOURCE RIVALRY:

Dr. Kissinger Confronts the New Economic Order

1

In the early morning hours of October 25, 1973, almost exactly four months after the signing of the Agreement on the Prevention of Nuclear War—the new Yalta, Jobert had called it—Henry Kissinger ordered a worldwide alert of U.S. nuclear forces to keep the Russians out of the Middle East. There had not been a worldwide alert since the day almost ten years before when John F. Kennedy had been killed. B-52s loaded with 20-megaton nuclear bombs took off from Guam. The aircraft carriers *Franklin Delano Roosevelt* and *John F. Kennedy,* bristling with nuclear missiles, headed at full speed toward the eastern Mediterranean. In West Germany, U.S. anti-aircraft missiles were raised to firing position. Now secretary of state in a besieged administration, Kissinger spoke menacingly to the Soviet ambassador on the telephone. "This is a matter of great concern. Don't you pressure us. I want to repeat again, don't pressure us."

The event that had triggered the strong American reaction was the receipt of a letter from Chairman Brezhnev. A war in the Middle East that had started with Egypt's attack on Israel on Yom Kippur nineteen days earlier was now in a critical phase. The Israelis had turned the tide of battle, and the Egyptian Third Army faced destruction on the east bank of the Nile. In his letter Brezhnev proposed to dispatch Soviet and American military contingents to the Middle East to impose a superpower peace. "I will say it straight," Brezhnev declared, "that if you find it impossible to act jointly with us in this matter, we should be faced with the necessity urgently to consider the question of taking appropriate steps unilaterally." That was the sentence read against the background of sketchy intelligence reports of Soviet military preparations that prompted Kissinger to make a dramatic show of nuclear might.

The crisis subsided the next day. The Soviets made it clear that they had no intention of going into the Middle East alone with their military forces. But the political fallout was considerable. It did not take an especially malicious mind to conclude that the instant confrontation had been staged by the administration to divert attention from the gathering cries for the president's impeachment. Four days before, in a frenzy of self-pity, Nixon had fired Archibald Cox, the respected Harvard Law School professor he had appointed to investigate the Watergate scandal, and had at a single stroke created the very political coalition that would destroy him. "They are doing it because of their desire to kill the President. And they may succeed. I may physically die," Nixon cried out to Kissinger a few hours before the alert was ordered, "as agitated and emotional as I had ever heard him."

For Heath, Brandt, and Pompidou, Nixon's torment now projected into a Middle East war spelled enormous trouble. While the gossip of Watergate provided entertainment for newspaper readers and the television audience, the constitutional crisis in the United States was a black comedy of a dangerous sort. Too worldly wise to permit themselves the luxury of moral outrage over the famous "third-rate burglary," the wiretaps, the cover-up, much less the gutter language immortalized on the White House tapes, the statesmen of Europe worried that the United States was now rudderless. "After so many months of Watergate," the historian J. H. Plumb wrote in *The New York Times,* "the credibility of the Administration is at total risk. . . ." The alert of the nuclear forces, he suggested, belonged to the venerable tradition of absolutist monarchs who used foreign affairs to distract attention from domestic problems, but now, unfortunately, the rest of the world shared the risk. "What is wrecking America's image is not whether the President has technically broken or not broken the law," Plumb noted, "but that a man so self-confessed in misjudgment of other men and their actions should still be in control of the world's most powerful nation." After all, he noted for his American readers, James II broke no law, but the British chased him out of the kingdom nonetheless.

Watergate called into question two of the unstated premises of American leadership. Writhing in a constitutional crisis they seemed unable to terminate, the managers of the American political system could no longer be counted on as the rock of the alliance. Nor with the relentless exposure of their own political underbelly were the Americans any longer especially credible spokesmen for the "common values" inevitably celebrated in toasts, communiqués, and solemn speeches at NATO get-togethers. As the conservative British commentator Peregrine Worsthorne put it, commenting on Nixon's "enemies list," "This is not the language of civilization. It is the language of barbarism. . . ." Beyond a certain aesthetic revulsion European politicians had more practical concerns. The presidency and the NATO bureaucracy that served it were the only points in the American system with an abiding sympathy for the European connection. Now Nixon seemed to be destroying the presidency, and the free trader in the White House was losing control of the government to a Congress eager to show its power by curtailing the Chief Executive's ability to act abroad.

The October War had posed a dramatic test for the partners who were already feeling somewhat testy toward Washington even before the alert. Kissinger's strategy for maintaining the balance of power in the Middle East depended critically upon a massive airlift of supplies to the Israeli forces which had sustained heavy losses in absorbing the original Egyptian surprise attack. With the exception of the Netherlands and Portugal, one ally after another refused to allow their territory to be used as refueling stops for the American airlift. In Washington great bitterness was felt over Brandt's refusal to allow Israeli freighters to pick up U.S. arms at Bremerhaven (which would have been a clear violation of German neutrality) or to permit U.S. planes to overfly German territory on the way to the Middle East, which required American pilots to fly a two-thousand-mile detour. Henry Kissinger, according to one congressman present, completed his testimony before the House Foreign Affairs Committee with an unofficial aside. "I don't care what happens to NATO, I'm so disgusted."

The European politicians were equally furious about the mysterious alert. "The alliance," a German Foreign Office spokesman exploded, "is not just an instrument of American foreign policy." German officials who could observe U.S. troops on their soil moving to alert status had the benefit of "no prior consultation," as Kissinger admits. Yet U.S. unilateral decisions raised the risk of war, and since U.S. forces in Europe were used to convey the nuclear threat to the Soviets, the confrontation risked a Soviet attack on Europe. Heath told Brandt that he had not even been informed, much less consulted. Actually the British ambassador had been accorded the customary privilege of being English in an American security system and had been told some forty-three minutes after the alert message was dispatched from the Pentagon. Europe, Jobert declaimed in the Chamber of Deputies, had been "humiliated in its nonexistence." "The American decision not to consult was an outrage," Harold Wilson declared. "On an issue potentially lethal for the world it was a grave dereliction of duty owed by America to her allies." One European leader after another privately needled the architect of the "year of Europe": NATO was not involved in the Middle East, so how could they have failed their ally? Europe after all was merely a "regional power." The nation with "global responsibilities" should deal with the Middle East without endangering the interests of the Allies.

Since the founding of NATO the tangled politics of the region had periodically divided the Allies. Nowhere else in the world were differences in historical perception and in economic interest so evident. The subtle distinction between the European designation "Near East" and the American "Middle East" was a tip-off. The Arab world was geographically close and had been culturally intertwined with Europe since the Crusades. To the Americans the whole region was a mysterious piece of strategic real estate at the crossroads of world politics. The United States had virtually no ties there before the

Second World War, and from the earliest postwar days the overriding American objective was to keep the Soviets out. For the French, cities like Beirut and Damascus were part of their history, centers of important commercial and banking relations, and outposts of French culture. For the British, the bases east of Suez and the postcolonial concession arrangements with tiny sheikhdoms were toeholds of imperial power.

In May 1950, when NATO was a year old, the United States, Britain, and France had signed a Tripartite Declaration proclaiming themselves to be joint peacekeepers of the region and guarantors of the Arab-Israeli armistice of 1948. Eight years later the Eisenhower Doctrine coming on the heels of the Anglo-French Suez fiasco proclaimed the new reality that the United States was now the only great power that mattered in the region. Nonetheless, all the Allies, for quite different reasons, shared a common perspective on the Arab-Israeli conflict. Under the Fourth Republic, France saw Arab nationalism as much a threat as the United States did; a pro-Israeli stance was part of the strategy of fighting Arab revolutionaries in Algeria. For the Germans being pro-Israeli was dictated by the "burden of the past," but that morally inescapable position enabled the German Democratic Republic to secure recognition from a number of Arab states and to end its diplomatic isolation in the non-Communist world.

By the time of the Six-Day War in 1967 the common interests of the NATO Allies in the Middle East had begun to dissolve. The United States mired in one war in Asia was reluctant to get into another. Like his predecessors, Johnson was more inclined than the Europeans to see the Arab-Israeli conflict as a sideshow in the U.S.–Soviet global confrontation. Convinced by Nasser that the United States had conspired with Israel, most of the Arab states cut off relations with Washington. Soviet influence soared.

"Don't give up Gaza. It is essential to your security," De Gaulle had told the ultranationalist opposition leader Menachem Begin when he received him at Colombey shortly after the Suez fiasco in 1956. But once Algeria was settled, De Gaulle subtly changed the traditional French position on Israel. When the Israelis scored a stunning victory in the June 1967 war (largely with weapons he had supplied), the general became openly hostile. He refused to sell any more weapons, including fifty Mirages already paid for. The new French policy was to cultivate influence in the Mediterranean and in the Arab world, even to the point of diverting the Mirages to Colonel Muammar al-Qaddafi, the new radical nationalist ruler of Libya. De Gaulle saw that France's interest in the Middle East was to treat it not as an arena of the Cold War, for that would only benefit the superpowers, but as a target of opportunity. It was a time to innovate postimperial alliances with the new nationalist forces. His successors continued the policy and pressed the Germans to join in.

The Federal Republic, now a member of the United Nations, inched toward a more neutral stance in the Arab-Israeli conflict. Willy Brandt had visited Israel four months before the outbreak of the 1973 war, the first German chancellor to do so. For a German leader the visit to Yad Vashem, the memorial to the six million victims of Nazism, was a searing experience. (One member of the chancellor's official party still bore an Auschwitz number tattooed on her arm.) But, as Brandt explained to Prime Minister Golda Meir, Germany was a member of the European Community and the EC would continue to take common positions on the Middle East, and these were directly influenced by France. Pompidou had proposed to Brandt in 1970 that the two countries coordinate a policy for the Maghrib, the countries of Arab North Africa. Germany "could play a useful role in the Mediterranean area—preferably in concert with us—" Brandt reported on his conversation, "if only in preventing other powers from usurping our place there." As European statesmen grew more concerned about the danger of war in the Middle East, Israel was becoming more isolated. Only the United States, now Israel's arsenal, could be counted on as an unequivocal supporter.

2

The "year of Europe" had begun with a new sense on both sides of the Atlantic that a shift in the power relations of Europe and America had occurred. The year ended with a realization that power had shifted far more dramatically than anyone had anticipated—and in surprising ways. Not since the explosion of the atomic bomb over Hiroshima and Nagasaki had a single historical moment been perceived so immediately to have revolutionary implications for the whole world. This time the precipitating event was not a show of military power but a communiqué. On October 16, 1973, the ministers of the Organization of Petroleum Exporting Countries (OPEC) meeting in Vienna in the midst of the Middle East war, announced that they had decided to raise the price of oil 70 percent—from $3.01 a barrel to $5.12. The following day the Arab members of OPEC met in Kuwait and informed the world that they would cut their production 5 percent a month until Israel withdrew from the occupied territories. Saudi Arabia, America's biggest supplier, promised to cut back at twice that rate. On October 20 a complete embargo on oil shipments to the United States and the Netherlands, the most pro-Israeli country of West Europe, was announced by the Arab producers. In a little over six weeks the Arab oil producers had seized control of the most strategic resource of the industrial world. Within months they raised the price almost 400 percent. A pivotal event of the century, as Kissinger called it, had occurred.

It had been tried before. In 1948 the Arab oil producers had threatened to deny oil to any nation that had aided Israel and had resorted to the tactic again in the 1967 war. But in both instances the oil weapon had failed. Now the situation was quite different. In 1948 Western Europe depended upon oil for only 10 percent of its energy needs. By the late 1960s it had converted to a petroleum economy. Europe produced relatively little oil; most of it was imported from the Middle East. In 1973 Britain imported about 59 percent of its oil from the Arab world, France 72 percent, and Germany 75 percent. The

United States, still a major oil producer, imported only 16 percent of its total energy needs; Middle East oil accounted for only about 2 percent of America's total requirements.

Thus three revolutionary developments had quietly occurred before the "energy crisis" was discovered. (1) The industrial world had become hooked on oil. (2) The security of the most powerful industrial nations had become dependent on the decisions of militarily weak, feudal societies, but the resulting insecurity was far more serious for Europe and Japan than for the United States. (3) The end of cheap oil cast doubt on the basic political assumptions about growth and prosperity on which the politics of the postwar order had been based. These changes taken together transformed the industrial world.

Until the 1960s Europe was still primarily a coal economy. The European Coal and Steel Community, Monnet's original dream, maintained tight control over the coal market, guarding against the reemergence of the old prewar cartels and keeping prices artificially low. Depressed wages in the industry caused a mass exodus from the mines; the number of miners in the EEC countries declined by 60 percent. The international oil companies were under no comparable regulation and their flexibility and strategic pricing policy made it possible to convert Europe to a petroleum economy by the end of the decade. With a start from Marshall Plan money, the oil majors put refineries in Europe. Where they competed with coal, as in heating fuel, they underpriced their product. Where there was no competition, as in gasoline, they charged high prices.

Although warning signals were all around—sharply increased consumption of oil, nationalization, and a flurry of OPEC activism—no national leader on either side of the Atlantic saw the danger looming. Indeed, at the end of the 1960s the problem for governments and oil companies alike was still glut. In March 1969 the shah of Iran had come to Washington and offered to sell the United States a million barrels a day for ten years at the giveaway price of $1 a barrel, so worried was he about getting rid of his huge oil reserves. The oil companies failed to maintain a common front in the face of Qaddafi's historic bid the same year to take control of the oil production and pricing process, a move which set the precedent for OPEC diplomacy of the 1970s. However, they persuaded the Nixon administration that because of the impending oil crisis they should be free of antitrust constraints so that they could develop a common strategy. But they were reluctant to develop a common strategy with the U.S. government, for they feared government control if Washington became too heavily involved.

The shock effect in Europe of the sudden series of announcements that the price of oil had now quadrupled galvanized governments into emergency action, but not common action. Quite the contrary. The embargo of oil to the Netherlands and the United States in retaliation for their pro-Israeli positions threatened to close down the port of Rotterdam, a critical distribution point for all of West Europe. The European nations had previously established emergency allocation schemes, but they did not put them into effect for fear of

RESOURCE RIVALRY

further reprisals from the Arabs. Officials in London, Paris, Bonn, and Tokyo scrambled to make the best bilateral deals for their countries; private sympathy for the Netherlands would not be permitted to jeopardize their own nations' energy supply. No sympathy was wasted on the United States, for the world's largest national economy had many energy alternatives. If the United States lacked the power to protect Europe's energy supply, the Old World was much too vulnerable to help defend the new.

For Japan the "oil shock" was even more serious than for Europe. The Japanese refining industry predicted that crude oil arrivals for January 1974 would be 50 to 70 percent below normal. Many Japanese had vivid memories of the acute shortages right after the war. Panic and suspicion were in the air. Since Japan's supply depended so heavily on the oil majors, most of which were U.S. companies, the Japanese public was convinced that their precious petroleum allotment would be diverted to the Americans. Kissinger, it was widely believed, wished to see higher prices in order to drain off the foreign exchange reserves of America's commercial rivals, Germany and Japan. The Nixon administration, though it did not conspire to raise prices as many European critics later charged, had not worried unduly about the prospect until the October War. In a staff study prepared for Kissinger in 1971, C. Fred Bergsten and Harold Saunders had noted that a rise in the price of energy "would affect primarily Europe and Japan and probably improve America's competitive position."

The mythology of the energy crisis was as important as reality in shaping the new consciousness of the partners. Indeed, it was very hard to separate the two. Not only the Japanese but the French and others in Europe were convinced that the Americans welcomed the high prices. The shah of Iran had been a critical figure in pushing up energy costs, and he was an American client; he owed his throne to the Americans. With more oil revenues from Europe, the shah could buy billions in sophisticated armaments from the United States and solve America's balance-of-payments problem. In his memoirs, Kissinger dismisses the idea as "demagogic ignorance" and states that the United States government never saw the price rises as anything but a disaster. But the persistence of these unconfirmed rumors testified to the still strong belief in American power. How could such a revolution in the world economy take place against American wishes? Having spent two years worrying about the dangers of great power condominium, European statesmen had difficulty seeing that their plight was due less to superpower conspiracy than to the collapse of the bipolar world.

The most vulnerable of the partners, Japan, moved the most quickly to adopt a new energy strategy. By January 1974 the prime minister had announced a pro-Arab tilt sufficient to remove the country from the list of "unfriendly nations." It was the first open break with U.S. policy on a major world issue in the postwar period. A steady stream of envoys was dispatched to the Middle East to make bilateral deals, offer technical assistance, and economic aid. Japanese firms signed contracts to widen the Suez Canal, develop a petrochemical industry for Iran, and to borrow petrodollars from Saudi Arabia, Kuwait, and Abu Dhabi. The French signed a major oil deal with Saudi Arabia and the Germans with Iran. No industrial nation now could afford to be a purely "regional power."

From the start of the crisis Henry Kissinger saw the problem primarily as a political struggle. A producers cartel had been successfully formed because the consumers had let them do it. Weak nations had imposed "a dramatic change in the way of life" of the strong (along with everyone else) because the industrial democracies were too cowardly to present a "united front." The United States was in the best position to "go it alone," Kissinger pointed out in a speech in London in December 1973, while the embargo was still on, but "[w]e strongly prefer, and Europe requires, a common enterprise." If the producers had successfully organized a cartel to raise prices, the oil customers could resist with a cartel of their own.

The partners had a different view. Hugging the United States was not an advantage. The United States was so tied to Israel that it was hardly an effective advocate of European or Japanese interests in the Middle East. Indeed, U.S. intelligence picked up reports that the Allies were telling the Arabs that they deserved preferential treatment exactly because they had disavowed U.S. policy. The partners with an investment in pro-Arab policies were pressing the oil producers to be tough with the United States. They urged that "the embargo against us should be kept in force for several months," Kissinger remembers being told, "or else the European and Japanese dissociation from our policy would be seen to have been pointless."

In a conversation with Sir Burke Trend, secretary of the British cabinet, nine months before the outbreak of the war, Kissinger had anticipated the problem: ". . . how to prevent the producer nations from playing off the consumer nations against each other." By the end of the year the strategy had not been found. Secretary of Defense James Schlesinger hinted at military reprisals if the embargo were not lifted. Kissinger considered the warning "salutary," but the threat of military action was implausible because, as U.S. military experts had written publicly, paratroopers could seize oil fields but not keep a vulnerable oil system running. Pompidou, now desperately ill, was unusually irritable as he told Kissinger that a "consortium of consumers that would seek to impose a solution on the producers" was out of the question. "You only rely on the Arabs for about a tenth of your consumption. We are entirely dependent upon them. We can't afford the luxury of three or four years of worry and misery waiting for the Arabs to understand the problem."

For the next four months Kissinger and Jobert were locked in combat. Kissinger had two objectives. One was to organize a consumer organization to break OPEC. For the American nothing was more critical than to reverse the dramatic shift in power. His second objective was to establish peace in the Middle East without Russian participation and that required supporting Sadat and isolating him from the "radical" regimes of the region such as Iraq, Syria, and Libya. For the Europeans the critical issue was maintaining access to oil.

The Europeans feared that the American strategy would provoke the oil producers but not destroy them, and they saw no reason to avoid dealing with "radical" regimes with oil to sell. Jobert, who grew bolder as Pompidou faded, developed Kissinger-baiting into an art form, alternatively professing friendship, fury, trust, and outrage, and stirring up his European colleagues to plot the derailment of the secretary's elaborate plans. (How well Jobert succeeded in getting to Kissinger is indicated by the attention lavished on him in *Years of Upheaval* where the slight, excitable French foreign minister is described as "intransigent," "romantic," "absurd," "insinuating," "vitriolic," and "adamant.")

Jobert proposed that the partners collaborate on developing alternative energy—"a clever but too transparent" scheme to get American technology, Kissinger called it—but be free to deal bilaterally with the producers. At the same time the European Community would enter into a European-Arab dialogue to secure a reliable oil supply. The Kissinger solution was the Washington Energy Conference which, he told the British foreign secretary, would prepare common positions among the consumers. "They have a cartel. Why should they be able to order around the eight hundred million consumers?" Sitting down with the Arab radicals was a mistake. Iran and Saudi Arabia were the important countries in the region, "completely dependent on American political support."

Why shouldn't Europe want to use this American political power in the energy field? What we have here is an opportunity for a moral demonstration of what the West can do when it wants to get together and that it cannot be pushed around.

But meanwhile Jobert had been traveling to Syria and Iraq seeking barter deals for France, establishing his credentials as he went, by attacking Kissinger's "interim settlements" of the Middle East crisis and congratulating the Syrians on how well they were "consolidating your military position." He opposed Kissinger's Washington Conference as "a striking affirmation of American supremacy over the Western World." The symbolism of the Allies trooping to Washington to be organized by the Americans was wrong. Why, Jobert asked, should France be criticized for making bilateral arrangements when the United States had just signed an oil agreement with Saudi Arabia? The French government oil companies had been systematically excluded from Saudi Arabia when Aramco had been organized in 1946 by four U.S. majors, Exxon, Mobil, Texaco, and Socal. The memory rankled as Jobert sought to press a bilateral deal with the Saudis. But the Saudis pressed the French hard, more interested in being observed in Washington talking to Jobert than in making extensive deals. The French strategy, which included an $800 million sale of sophisticated weapons to the Saudis, produced some extremely expensive oil contracts from which Jobert's successor pulled back.

Meanwhile, Kissinger convened his Washington Energy Conference in February 1974. The European Community at its summit meeting in Copenhagen, to which Jobert had secretly invited several foreign ministers from Arab

countries, declared that there should be no "confrontation" with the producers. (The mysterious Arab diplomatic visitors, not surprisingly, echoed the
French demand that Europe speak with its "own voice.") At the Washington
Conference, Helmut Schmidt, Brandt's finance minister, whom Kissinger had
known for twenty years, supported the Americans and so in an artfully indirect
way did the Japanese. Nixon inadvertently handed Jobert some heavy ammunition in another of his rambling toasts. Reminding the partners once again of
isolationist sentiment in the United States, the growing sense "that the United
States unilaterally should withdraw forces from Europe, for that matter, withdraw its forces from all over the world and make our treaty commitments to
other nations in the Far East and in Europe meaningless," he made explicit
what Kissinger had urged be left unsaid: "Security and economic considerations are inevitably linked and energy cannot be separated from either."

In Washington, Kissinger achieved the semblance of success. The partners lined up with the United States and left Jobert essentially isolated. Kissinger's plans for an International Energy Agency were adopted over European
objections. The new organization was no consumer cartel but a vehicle for
emergency sharing and technical cooperation. It was a clear assertion of American power. The more energy a nation consumed, the more votes it had in the
organization. The role of the multinationals as energy allocators was essentially preserved, and American diplomacy vigorously defended their right to
withhold crucial data from governments. But it was a foregone conclusion that
energy would continue to divide the partners. The countries, like the United
States, with a variety of energy options had different interests from countries
whose survival depended upon imports. Within Europe, European Community
members, like Britain with the prospect of North Sea oil flowing within a few
years or the Netherlands with large deposits of natural gas, did not look at the
problem in the way France or Germany did. But the Germans had the capital
the British needed to turn their good luck into prosperity. None of the Europeans could tolerate the idea of being an American protectorate in the oil
struggle since they did not believe that American energy interests were the
same as theirs. The United States was also a major producer. It was the banker
for the billions of petrodollars extracted from their own economies. It was the
home base of a majority of the huge energy multinationals. "It would be a
mistake to approach the oil problem with illusion," Helmut Schmidt declared
in *Foreign Affairs* in early 1974, "with a swashbuckling rattle of the sword in
the manner of a past century's gunboat diplomacy or in an egotistical overbearing manner. . . . The hectic events of the past nine months appeared to
indicate that this point has by no means been fully grasped."

Yet Kissinger had made his major point. The great oil crisis had damaged
the whole industrial world but not equally so. The issues of the mid-1970s
promised to concern the sharing of what Helmut Schmidt called the "world
product," and on these issues the United States enjoyed impressive advantages. On the first anniversary of the oil shock in November 1974 at the World
Food Conference, Assistant Secretary of State Thomas O. Enders suggested

that the United States, the world's greatest grain exporter, would be using food as a weapon. "The food producers' monopoly exceeds the oil producers' monopoly . . . food will give us influence because decisions in other countries will depend upon what we do." (The United States was supplying about 70 percent of Japanese corn consumption, for example.) If resources now determined the world power structure, James P. Grant, president of the Overseas Development Council, observed, then "as part of this process resource-rich United States is returning to a position of political and economic preeminence comparable to that of fifteen years ago, when its leadership was indispensable for the success of any international effort." The United States was once again in a position to "formulate the rules of the game." A new deck had been dealt, and suddenly once again the Americans had the cards.

For Henry Kissinger the oil crisis was a political challenge. If underdeveloped countries could get away with unilateral changes in the world economic structure in one commodity why not others? To bargain over matters that had long been automatically set in the shadow of American power would be to admit a historic defeat; the very purpose of America's military might, its alliances, and its activist foreign policy was to preserve the existing international order. With another defeat hovering in the wings in Vietnam, this was hardly the time to be conciliatory.

Much of the European and Japanese resentment at the sudden resurgence of American power was focused on the oil companies. While the embargo was on, the oil majors, of which five out of seven were based in the United States, acted as allocators of oil. The companies, wishing to preserve the long-term stability of their markets, resisted political direction from governments, even their own. Exxon enforced the Arab boycott even to the point of refusing to sell to the U.S. Navy. As George Keller, vice-president of Socal, admitted, "the companies' stake in Saudi Arabia was such that they had become hostage to the Saudi Arabian Government." But captivity was not unprofitable. J. J. Johnston, vice-president of Aramco, in a telex to his superiors that came to the attention of the Senate Subcommittee on Multinational Corporations, suggested that the companies "could fuzz up the deal somehow" so that there would be no "lost financial position for current four owners" (Exxon, Texaco, Mobil, and Socal). When staggering oil profits were announced a few months later, the news fed the suspicion, particularly widespread in Europe and Japan, that the oil companies were conspiring with Kissinger. Actually, the oil companies, as Senator Frank Church concluded after his extensive hearings, "were not really susceptible to the direction of their home governments." Even the national oil companies in Europe refused on occasion to take direction from their owners. Thus CFP (Compagnie Française des Petroles), the French state oil company, according to its general manager, "ceased to deliver fuel to Air France within France because the prices the airlines offered were too low."

The suspicion that the majors were unfairly diverting oil to their home countries was unfounded. The companies whose primary interest was to keep control over a world market that was becoming harder to manage tried to allocate oil on a relatively equitable basis and responded to Kissinger's plea to "take care of the Dutch." Indeed, the companies were less than zealous in policing the embargo and extremely enterprising in circumventing the emergency controls imposed by the European governments. For all the dire warnings and austerity measures taken, it turned out that there was no real petroleum shortage in Europe. Reserves never fell below eighty days in the European Community, and in Italy reserves actually jumped 23 percent during the embargo. (But Pompidou sought to leave the impression that the foreign firms were strangling the country. Action would be taken; Frenchmen must not be made to shiver "to increase the profits of Royal Dutch-Shell.") In Germany, though more devoted to the free market in energy than anywhere else in Europe, the government demanded that the oil companies roll back their prices. "It is inadmissible," Hans Friderichs, the minister of commerce, declared, "that we should be kept in the dark about sales, policies, prices, and profits of the international petroleum companies which are operating in our territory and behaving like a state within a state."

3

Beginning in the spring and fall of 1974 the leaders of France, Germany, Britain, Japan, and the United States were swept from office within weeks of one another. Pompidou succumbed in March. With his death what was left of the Gaullist dynasty came to an end. The same month the Heath government suddenly called an election and was defeated, trapped by its failure to stimulate the sluggish industrial economy and its clumsy confrontation with the coal miners over pay increases. In Japan, Premier Kakuei Tanaka suddenly resigned in November after a team of reporters had discovered that he had received hundreds of millions of dollars in illegal contributions and had bought the premiership for about $15 million. In August, Richard Nixon was finally cornered and he resigned. Early in this global shake-up, on May 6, Willy Brandt announced his resignation as Bundeskanzler two weeks after learning that Günter Guillaume, a trusted subordinate with access to secret documents, was an East German spy.

The scandal was made to order for Brandt's enemies. Not only had the veteran intelligence officer of the East German army been able to read a private letter from Nixon, but he was in a position to collect precise information about the chancellor's long-rumored extramarital affairs. Just eighteen months before, Brandt had been triumphantly reelected under a slogan advertising Germany's new foreign policy: "Germans, we can be proud of our country!" He had won the Nobel Peace Prize, even a congratulatory telegram from a relative of Anne Frank. But within a year his political base had begun to unravel. Business leaders stepped up their attacks, worried that a stronger SPD would cut away their privileges. Special interests became more vocal; the government seemed hopelessly impotent in dealing with the demands of the air traffic controllers. The Young Socialists, about 250,000 strong, attacked the chancellor for betraying the traditions of social democracy with his appeal to the "new center." The spectacular foreign policy achievements had been completed, and the headlines were now filled with the energy crisis and the uncertainties of the new age of scarcity. Social Democratic party support plummeted in the public opinion polls, and the party suffered a stunning reverse in local elections in Hamburg.

Now sixty, Brandt was beset once more by bouts of despondency which impressive quantities of brandy did nothing to relieve. "I am finished," he told the wife of one of his cabinet ministers at his birthday party. Still able to give speeches that projected passion and idealistic vision, he was paralyzed as a leader and grew increasingly suspicious of his closest political associates. Helmut Schmidt, his finance minister who could scarcely mask his hunger for Brandt's office, nevertheless was also subject to the malaise. "I am tired of politics. There is no sense in going on," he confided to Kissinger one evening in February when they were alone in the secretary's enormous office. Urging his "cherished friend," the most unambiguously pro-American of all the leading German political figures, to stay the course, Kissinger also lapsed easily into the pessimism of the day. Indeed, he had become famous for a certain Spenglerian spin; the challenge to the West was historic and in the end diplomatic pyrotechnics could only serve as a holding action. Like the Greek city-states, he mused, the West had "dissipated its inspiration."

The uncertainties of the 1970s meant that it was no longer so much fun being a democratic leader. In the 1960s politicians in all the NATO countries had had a free ride. No matter what they did, the economy grew. Inflation was no great problem in the United States, Germany, or Japan. But this exasperating new decade defied all traditional politics and economics. Even before the oil crisis, commodity prices had suddenly shot up 65 percent from the end of 1971 to the spring of 1973. By the end of the 1970s, prices would jump 101 percent in the United States, 137 percent in Japan, 136 percent in France, 219 percent in Italy, and 236 percent in Britain. The decade began amid speculation that Europe was an emerging superpower. Scarcely three years later the Continent was reeling from mutually reinforcing shocks no one knew how to control: crop failures in the USSR, nationalization of minerals in Africa and Latin America, even the mysterious disappearance of Peruvian anchovies. (The anchovies had served as cattle fodder, and when grain was used instead, world food prices jumped.) No advanced industrial nation was impervious to these developments. No obvious common strategy to deal with the hazards of interdependence commended itself. It was politically tempting to blame the distress of the West on the sheiks and the oil companies, but while oil was certainly a major factor in the world inflation, it was hardly the exclusive cause. Indeed the inflation rate was much faster than the OPEC increases, and until the second oil shock of 1979, the real price of oil actually declined 25 percent.

Among the industrial nations Germany soon revealed an unusual capacity to adapt to the new conditions of economic life, a surprising showing since the Federal Republic was more dependent on exports than any of the other partners. The nation was also extremely dependent upon imported oil. Indeed, about 30 percent of it came from Libya, whose leader had threatened that "like Samson we shall destroy the temple; we shall ruin your industry, just as we shall ruin your trade with the Arab world. Europe should take heed of the catastrophe that faces it."

Anticipating the crisis, Brandt's government had introduced an energy program in September, and by the end of the year consumption had been cut 20 percent. Brandt imposed a Sunday-driving ban for a while, but his efforts to enforce a speed limit on the murderous autobahns aroused a wave of ideological opposition. The freedom to speed was a sacred right on which the state could not infringe. The Federal Republic made long-term oil agreements with Saudi Arabia and Iran. "Of all the friendly industrial nations," the head of a special economic mission from Saudi Arabia declared in Bonn, the Bundesrepublik is the one state which can fully assist in the industrial and technological development of Saudi Arabia. . . ." German sales to OPEC countries jumped more than 500 percent in four years. Alone among the industrial countries Germany had a strong payments surplus and by 1977 was the only major industrial country with a favorable trade balance in the Middle East. German goods were competitively priced, and thanks to a much more tranquil labor relations climate than in Britain and France, they were delivered on time. The Americans, who had the inside track in Saudi Arabia and Iran by virtue of a twenty-year history of being the regional protector and a well-advertised readiness to supply billions of dollars of sophisticated military hardware, nonetheless had one important disadvantage in competing with the Germans for Middle East contracts. The dollar was much more unstable than the deutsche mark. While the government in Bonn worried about inflation and imposed certain austerity measures, prices were far more stable than anywhere else in the industrial world.

Nonetheless, the mood in Germany was anything but euphoric, because the Germans—swept along with everyone else in the industrial world—could not escape the new sense of fragility. The decade had begun with two disturbing ideas even before the oil crisis sharpened the issues. One was the idea of ecological limits. In 1972 *Limits to Growth* was published. While the idea it advanced that the world was about to run out of minerals was easily discredited, the more profound point made by the growing ecological movement was not. Consumption had a long-term price, and not only in dollars or marks. Burn gasoline and cities choke in fumes. Burn coal, and the delicate ecological balance of the earth is jeopardized. Take the nuclear route, which Brandt's government decided to do, and you may be courting catastrophe. Issues of equitable distribution of resources, which had been largely ignored, had been forced onto the political agenda by vocal Third World countries like Algeria who demanded a "new international economic order," the new slogan for a more just distribution of power. At the beginning of his first administration

Richard Nixon had assured the American people that their appetite—for years they had been burning, bending, or melting more than a third of the world's nonrenewable resources—was a badge of greatness, but now staunch pro-Americans like Barbara Ward of the *Economist* wondered aloud why an American baby ought to claim five hundred times the resources of a Mongolian baby. The United States should stop expanding and "do a little disgorging as well."

A second development occurred in the mid-1970s that made governing industrial democracies an increasingly hazardous occupation. The boom years had yielded a harvest of enhanced expectations. In the United States, France, Germany, and Britain ever greater demands were placed upon the public treasury in behalf of the security, health, and comfort of citizens. Richard Nixon was, for all his conservative rhetoric, the last American celebrant of government spending. To buy social peace he advertised how he had reduced the proportion of the tax dollar spent on the military and increased the share spent on people. In a time of rampant inflation labor relations were smoothed with across-the-board wage increases. Everyone expected a salary increase as a right, from the million-dollar-a-year corporate president to the assembly-line worker. Under Nixon the United States increased the traditional entitlements of the social democratic state in the form of Medicare, food stamps, housing, job creation, and welfare programs. New pressure groups in behalf of pollution control, occupational safety, and better consumer protection were successful in creating new citizens' rights, each of which had a price tag. By 1978, according to M.I.T. economics professor Lester Thurow, "direct transfer payments accounted for $224 billion in annual spending. Over 10 percent of our GNP was devoted to taking income from one private individual and giving it to another private individual." In Germany where Bismarck had introduced health insurance in 1883, the idea that the first duty of the state was to provide economic security was well established. Almost one hundred years later the total payout for social security was DM 300 billion or about 30 percent of the GNP.

In 1974 Helmut Schmidt and Valéry Giscard d'Estaing took over the two nations that represented half of the wealth of Europe, each acutely aware that with the prospect of diminishing natural resources, slackening economic growth, and escalating popular demands, the times called for political magic. Schmidt, already celebrated for intimidating displays of self-confidence, had abandoned all talk of quitting and now seemed to relish the chance to be a world leader. Sensitive to the perils of the new age, he delighted in Germany's comparative strength. It was time to use its economic power to secure a stronger political role. When Harold Wilson, newly reinstalled as prime minister, joked at an EC summit meeting that Britain would soon have so much oil from the North Sea that she could join OPEC, Schmidt reminded him that he was utterly dependent on German loans. "Dear Harold, you still have two or three difficult years ahead of you. . . . Germany could survive without the community, but I am not sure any other country here could." He told Gerald Ford, the new president of the United States, that he had better not let New York default. It was an international financial center, and the "domino effect" would threaten other centers like Frankfurt and Zurich. He lectured François Mitterrand, the French Socialist leader, on the dangers of making political coalitions with the Communists.

Since the day in 1962 when a catastrophic flood in Hamburg destroyed thousands of homes and the young right-wing Social Democratic senator aggressively took charge of the rescue operation, elbowing the ineffectual mayor out of the way, he had been a well-known public figure. Confrontational in style, he was tagged in the press as *Schmidt-Schnauze* (Schmidt, the big mouth). Cooler, more disciplined than Brandt, more accomplished at striking a pose, he struggled no less with the anger and despair that periodically welled up within him. His socialism was learned at the officers' club, the SPD party whip Herbert Wehner once quipped. Though he could claim a grandfather who had worked the Hamburg docks and as chancellor would appear in the press in an Elbe bargeman's cap, Schmidt came from a solid middle-class suburb. His father, a schoolteacher in the Prussian mold, Schmidt once casually revealed in an interview, "did not tolerate talking back or crying or any show of feelings." Kissinger's judgment was that Schmidt's "somewhat overbearing manner was the defense mechanism of a gentle, even sentimental, man who had to stress his intellect and analytical power lest his emotions run away with him."

The new chancellor shared neither the early radicalism of his predecessor nor his anti-Nazi credentials. He had joined the Hitler Youth and even became a pack leader, but was "suspended," he explains, for being a "complainer." An antiaircraft lieutenant in the war, he served on the Russian front and in the Battle of the Bulge. In 1944 while still in uniform he attended the show trial following the plot to assassinate Hitler—against his will, he assured his British captors at the end of the war, and they believed him. He emerged from a British prisoner-of-war camp with an excellent working knowledge of English and a clean bill of health from the denazification authorities. His first love before the war had been drawing, and he had wanted to be an architect or a city planner, but now there was a whole society to redesign. He decided to study economics in Hamburg. At the university he became an SPD student leader, his socialism cool, theoretical, and moderate. Hamburg was the traditional center of Social Democratic politics, and the SPD the most promising vehicle for a political career in the city he loved. By age thirty-three he was in parliament and by the mid-1960s he was known among the international NATO establishment as Germany's leading "defense intellectual," for he had written two well-received works on military matters. Like Kissinger, he knew how to challenge the prevailing orthodoxy on the margins in such a way as to reinforce the impression of being completely reliable.

Impatient with Brandt's dreamy idealism, positively repelled by the young leftists of the party who called for nationalization—"Your preaching is emptying the church," he taunted—Schmidt cultivated the image of a pragmatic miracle worker. "I am not a visionary and I am skeptical of all the visionaries. Germans have an enormous capability for idealism and the perversion of it."

This was a sentiment long shared in Paris and Washington, and it was reassuring to hear a German chancellor express it. Germany's second Socialist Bundeskanzler was also disarmingly moderate in economic policy. Ernst Wolf Mommsen, the chairman of the executive board of Krupp steelworks, was a close friend. Schmidt proclaimed his support for the free market and his skepticism of the small steps toward bureaucratic planning that had characterized the Brandt era. He so squeezed the money supply in the renewed battle against inflation that the construction industry almost collapsed and had to be resuscitated with a modest government stimulus program in late 1975.

The entire industrial world was caught in a recession following the oil crisis, but the Federal Republic was in a position to weather it better than its neighbors. The mark was the strongest currency in the West. The years of budgetary austerity meant that while Schmidt's stimulus program would yield unprecedented government deficits, the inflation rate could still be kept to less than half of that of the other partners. In unemployment too West Germany had an advantage. Millions of "guest workers" would be "invited" to return to their villages in Turkey, Greece, or Yugoslavia before Germans themselves would feel the effects of the shrinking job market.

Schmidt saw the logic of *Ostpolitik* and strongly supported it, but his interest was *Westpolitik*. The challenge was to build a new relationship between West Europe and the United States that would allow Europe to play a more active role in world affairs without paralyzing conflict with the United States. He based his claim to be the leader of the new Europe on Germany's relative economic strength. Sharing none of the mystical notions of the German Gaullists about a common destiny of France and Germany, much less Adenauer's fleeting enthusiasm for merging the two nations, he held a view that the policies of the two economic giants of Europe needed to be harmonized before either could play the role on the world stage to which their industry and culture entitled them. Thus when Valéry Giscard d'Estaing was elected president of France, Schmidt promptly flew off to Paris to see him.

The new president, beating back challenges from Gaullists and from a shaky coalition on the Left headed by François Mitterrand, had managed to win a narrow victory under the slogan "change without risk." Tall, rich, first in his class at the Ecole Polytechnique, a cabinet officer at twenty-nine, Giscard presented himself to the electorate as a cross between Kennedy and De Gaulle. An aristocratic *arriviste* with a title appropriated from a defunct collateral line, as permitted under French law, the new president cultivated an image of informal elegance. He liked to be photographed in floppy sweaters, walking his dogs on his estate, playing the accordion, even receiving garbage men for breakfast at the Elysée Palace. But he was aloof, even imperious, and despite his elaborate efforts to ingratiate himself with the voters, he did not wear well.

Giscard was determined to create "an advanced liberal society," as he called it, a social democracy that would draw its strength from a new industrial revolution. Instead of the costly prestige projects that captivated De Gaulle, public money would be spent on the high-technology industries of the future.

The new president started the most ambitious nuclear energy program in the West, promising that by 1990 France would depend on imported oil for only 30 percent of its energy needs. The economy, expanding faster than any except Japan's, became increasingly enmeshed with the European Community. France was now the world's second leading exporter of agricultural products.

Giscard's forte was cultural reform. Within months he lowered the voting age, legalized abortion, eased divorce laws, and appointed prominent women to high office. But his efforts to overhaul the tax laws that perpetuated the most unequal income distribution of any Western industrial democracy collapsed because the liberal center eluded him. More tactician than ideologue, Giscard leavened his austerity program with new forms of government subsidies. But the experiment managed to produce 32,000 bankruptcies in his first two years. He forced firms to keep more than 300,000 unneeded workers on the payrolls, but unemployment among young people rose to 38 percent. Reconciling business and banking interests with the demands of a strong labor movement and the increasingly vocal farmers was especially difficult in France, for the country was a "halfway house" between a feudal past that still cast a long shadow and the coming postindustrial service economy.

A longtime member of Jean Monnet's Action Committee for the United States of Europe, Giscard was as relentless as his predecessors in attacking the vision of a supranational Europe. A modernized, less triumphal version of De Gaulle's *Europe des patries,* he believed, was now destined to play a crucial world role as America foundered. Harmless symbols of a European political culture, like the direct elections for a European Parliament, he could support. But not supranationalism. Europe could not federate itself and the United States had neither the legitimacy nor the power, and now not even the will to try. In France the Communist Left was every bit as nationalist as the Right.

Schmidt and Giscard, two self-proclaimed "pragmatists," had worked together for years as finance ministers. They played chess together and conversed easily in English. The two nations were now each other's biggest trading partners. To narrow the gap between the chronically feeble franc and the mark, Giscard promised to administer a strong dose of austerity, while Schmidt agreed to loosen up the German economy. Industrial cooperation made sense, for the two nations together had an economy bigger than that of the Soviet Union and about half the size of the United States. Whatever the rest of Europe did, France and Germany could become an economic superpower. But differences in national style and development made it difficult to cooperate. "The French complain that we do not invest in their provinces," a German official explained to an American reporter. "The truth is we don't because the phone service is so bad."

However, political relations between France and Germany improved considerably. The mutual suspicion that characterized the relationship of Pompidou and Brandt gave way to what Giscard now called the "Franco-German nucleus" of Europe. Giscard, another postwar French leader born in Germany, was determined to overtake the Federal Republic in economic power.

Why should France, with a higher birthrate, more natural resources, and a record of greater growth, resign itself to allowing its ancient enemy remain the dominant industrial nation on the Continent? But France could compete successfully only if the bourgeoisie became modern capitalists, shedding the shopkeeper mentality that kept families rich but the economy stalled. Perhaps the "growing symbiosis" of France and Germany, of which Helmut Schmidt spoke, might make France run as smoothly as its neighbor.

Giscard understood that France could never force Germany to choose between Paris and Washington. He removed the prickly Jobert and stopped making anti-NATO propaganda. French officers quietly joined a European group for planning NATO strategy, and Giscard altered the traditional Gaullist doctrine by hinting that in a war French troops would fight even if France herself were not directly threatened. United States Secretary of Defense James Schlesinger welcomed these conciliatory moves, declaring that there was "no need for France to be involved in the integrated command structure in order to participate fully in cooperation within the Alliance."

4

The United States had spent more than $2 trillion on the military between the end of the war and the nation's two hundredth birthday in 1976. But the mood of insecurity that prevailed on that day seemed to belie the enormous investment. The security problems were perceived as being more serious than they had been in at least twenty years—the threat of oil cutoff, the inflationary squeeze of the industrial system, the revolt of the poor resource-producing nations—but they were not military threats and they had no obvious military solutions.

Gerald Ford, the first appointed American president, a pleasant, dull, open-faced man, symbolized the New World management crisis. He promised an end to the "long nightmare" of Watergate, but was so trapped by it that he immediately proceeded to destroy himself by pardoning his shattered predecessor. Less impressive intellectually than Schmidt and Giscard, or indeed any other leader of the alliance, his task was far more formidable. The recovery of American hegemony was now theoretically possible because the nation enjoyed better access to energy than the other industrial nations and a controlling interest in world grain exports, but the reassertion of a new Pax Americana required a bravura performance: presidential leadership on every major front to reconstruct a new political, economic, and military order. The Nixon structure of peace had already begun to crumble. The famous wire photo of Americans being rescued by helicopter from the Saigon embassy roof as the North Vietnamese entered the city not only summed up the catastrophic loss of face, but it put into question the cornerstone of Kissinger's whole world strategy: the Nixon Doctrine. The United States could no longer afford to send its own forces everywhere, but neither could it count on local forces to preserve American interests as they had been so extravagantly defined ever since the Truman Doctrine of 1947.

Military power had been the glue of the NATO alliance from the start. More important than the "common values" and "common civilization" inevitably celebrated at gatherings of the alliance was a common faith in military power as an essential counterweight to Soviet expansionism. Whatever Kennan's original notion, that is what his idea of containment had become since the founding of NATO. Because no Western leader wished to fight a war in Europe nor believed that existing democratic societies could survive such a war, nuclear or conventional, the permanent alliance suffered from built-in contradictions from the start. Statesmen had to act as if they did not believe what their generals knew. The pretense of a defense free of suicidal consequences had to be maintained at all costs, for the whole idea of deterrence rested on that pretense.

By the mid-1970s the problem had become vastly more complicated. Since 1967 the alliance was charged with negotiating with the Russians and preparing for war against them simultaneously, a conventional enough idea in the world of strategic logic, but a difficult feat in the real world of political psychology. John Foster Dulles had worried fifteen years earlier about the hazards of coexistence. Reducing tensions would inevitably lead to "a lowering of our guard." Mobilizing a democracy to man a permanent battle line over a generation or more was hard enough, but opening up the lines periodically to send through food, money, and technology to the ideological enemy who was supposedly sworn to "bury" you exceeded the tolerable limits of political confusion. In the early 1970s Nixon and Brandt, each for his own reason, downgraded the "Soviet threat," and they did so at the very moment Soviet military power had become exceedingly formidable.

At the same time the U.S. military shield looked less impressive. "The 7th Army here in Europe is still suffering today as a result of Vietnam," General Michael S. Davidson, commander in chief of U.S. Army forces in Europe, had told the *Washington Post* in September 1971, "because we had to wreck the 7th Army in order to keep Vietnam going. . . ." Long before the final collapse of the long American effort in Indochina in 1975, many Europeans saw it as a historic betrayal. While Brandt and Schmidt resented the fact that the United States had crippled its ability to provide for the common defense in Europe to pursue a hopeless military adventure in Asia, ordinary German citizens could see the corrosive consequences in their midst. The unpopular war had alienated and demoralized the professional army. "Fragging" (shooting one's superior), heroin addiction, and other symptoms of the troubled military were imported from Vietnam to Germany. By 1973 the Vietnam War was so unpopular that the Nixon administration saw no alternative but to end the draft and accept the extra expense of a volunteer army that brought with it the sour mood, druggy habits, and racial bitterness of the American underclass from which it was heavily recruited. As an American infantry division commander put it, a sizable number of the Vietnam era draftees, as well as many who preceded them, "came out of the bowels of the big cities and they lived by fists and knives and bludgeons, etc. and they're trying to conduct their business here pretty much the same way."

The citizens of Kaiserslautern, Darmstadt, and Bamberg now increasingly felt the effects of America's racial tensions. Gang wars between white and black spilled over the barracks walls and turned into street brawls, even murders. "Sex is central to the racial issue in the Seventh Army," Harold Sims, an official of the National Urban League, concluded after an investigation in Germany. Thirty years after Hitler, Germans liked the idea of their own women consorting with the black soldiers about as much as the American white officers did.

About 46 percent of the army used drugs, according to official estimates, and 16 percent were habitual users. The drug culture of American ghettos was re-created in and around the American bases. In Kaiserslautern, GIs made up almost half the population, a highly visible half. With few exceptions the protectors of Germany spoke no German and were always astounded and frequently annoyed at the failure of the local population to understand their own mother tongue. At the level of national policy every GI withdrawn from Germany was a symbol of America's weakening resolve, but as far as local administrators were concerned their presence, even when they behaved themselves, was a mixed blessing. When the Americans moved into Kaiserslautern, Chief of Police Wilhelm Born recalled, "the prostitutes came from as far as England, like flies to a light."

By the mid-1970s the situation of the Seventh Army began slowly to improve. Cooperative efforts of German and U.S. Army officials calmed the racial tension somewhat. Discipline improved as more flexible policies were put into place. But run-down barracks and obsolete facilities were a constant reminder that the American balance-of-payments problem persisted. "These barracks are a disgrace to the American people. . . . If we repaired them 100 per cent they would be only half as good as they were when Hitler's troops lived in them," an American general complained. Funds for army housing, however, were scarce, and soldiers who tried living with their families "on the economy" discovered how little they could buy with a weak dollar.

"Tell Senator Mansfield that we only work two days a week here," a bored officer in an American base in Italy told an inquiring reporter. But the senator knew already and continued to demand that a large number of troops come home. The Ford administration was now pulled in two directions. With the establishment of the all-volunteer army—base pay for a private which had been $78 a month ten years earlier was now $384—and the urgent need to repair barracks, landing strips, and other support facilities for 310,000 American troops, the NATO commitment was becoming much more costly. The balance-of-payments consequences were becoming much more serious because troop costs were coming on top of huge oil imports. On the other hand, for the United States to withdraw from Europe at the very moment it was being expelled from the mainland of Asia would amount to knocking over one's own dominoes. Kissinger was determined to hold fast in Europe. The defense task, however, remained the insoluble dilemma it always was. The permanent preparations for a war no one believed was coming, except as a highly theoretical possibility, were designed to produce a "balance" which was hopelessly elusive. An unlikely attack was to be met by an incredible defense.

At the dawn of the nuclear age Albert Einstein had remarked that with the unleashing of the atom everything had changed but our way of thinking. But the notion that a balance of power could be achieved by the careful arrangement of military forces on two sides of a disputed line was an idea inherited from the Newtonian world of mechanics. The military task was like a physics problem—how to prevent an "imbalance" that would suck power from the stronger half of Europe into the weaker.

Political physics failed when anybody tried to quantify the balance. What did you count? NATO had more men under arms than the Warsaw Pact. On whose side in time of war did you count the Polish and Hungarian armies? Indeed, did not the very existence of the sullen satellite armies in their rear help to deter a Soviet attack on the West? The Soviets in 1975, according to the Defense Department, had 15,500 tanks deployed to 6000 in the NATO forces, but the attacker normally needs a greater superiority than that and the NATO forces had superior antitank weapons. And so the argument proceeded. The balance could be defined and characterized in many different ways, depending upon where one looked, what one counted, and what assumptions one made about what World War III would look like.

In 1967 the European Allies had accepted McNamara's notions of "flexible response"—the option to postpone the immediate resort to nuclear weapons in favor of a conventional defense lasting up to several weeks. They had had little choice. Increased American unhappiness with the endless strategic debate would have increased domestic pressures in the United States for bringing the troops home. That would have been even more of a diminution of American commitment than "flexible response" was perceived to be. Having banked so heavily on the notion of an automatic nuclear response to make deterrence "credible," European politicians had been doubly unhappy about downgrading nuclear weapons. If the Russians had reason to believe that the Americans might wriggle out of their commitment to drop the bomb, this might make the Kremlin more adventurous. The protracted conventional war across the German plain which the American planners offered as the alternative to reducing Germany to a radioactive wasteland on the first day of the war was regarded as an expensive fiction by most German politicians and generals. A conventional war was more likely to occur than a nuclear war, and it would be almost as destructive. It could never be won. After days or weeks of fighting, the decision would still be between accommodation and nuclear annihilation. To pretend that you were preparing for such a war cost considerable money. But despite the energy crisis, the European NATO partners increased their defense expenditures by 10 percent in real terms in the years 1972–75, while the United States reduced its military spending in 1973 to the lowest percentage of GNP since 1950. European politicians understood that if the United States troops were the "trip wire" for America's nuclear deterrent, their own forces were the adhesive to keep those troops in place. Despite the heated talk in the U.S. Congress about the failures of the Europeans to "share the burden of their own defense," there was more equality in military spending than was usually admitted. In 1973 the Allies spent 3.6 percent of their GNP on defense, while the U.S. government—if non-NATO-related expenditures were excluded—invested roughly 4.9 percent of the country's wealth in maintaining the European "balance."

By the mid-1970s the Bundeswehr was not only the largest army in Europe but the most modern. At the beginning of the decade, Helmut Schmidt, then defense minister, had drawn up a White Paper on the Security of the Federal Republic which the Social Democrats proposed as an integral part of their détente policy. The lessening of tensions with the East made possible measures to strengthen Germany's forces that before would have been greeted with great suspicion by her neighbors across the Elbe. But *Ostpolitik* was designed to provide reassurance in order to achieve a positive political purpose, opening up a greater role for the Federal Republic. That required a formidable capacity for self-defense, especially since the nation was forever bound by treaty from making or acquiring its own nuclear weapons. Moreover, a strong Bundeswehr could be an effective counter to Brandt's domestic political opponents who argued that *Ostpolitik* was a policy of capitulation. Two ideas were behind the new German defense policy. One was a stated assumption that the Soviet Union was now perceived as essentially "a conservative power defending the status quo." The other was that the modernized forces would be unmistakably defensive in character.

Throughout the 1970s the Federal Republic built up a highly mechanized 460,000-man armed force and a formidable military industry. Unlike the United States, conscription was retained. The German army shared many of the problems of the Americans. The draftees came from the urban working class, while university students managed to find exemptions. The antimilitary antibodies implanted in the society by the Hitler experience kept the level of conscientious objectors the highest in the world, and so strong was the concern over a revival of *militarismus* that German courts upheld the right of soldiers to wear their hair shoulder length and to be addressed by officers as "Herr." Officers complained about the lack of discipline in the new German army, but the problems were mild compared to those of the Seventh Army.

A much greater problem was defining the strategy that would allow the armed forces to fulfill their stated national purpose. Unlike the other NATO partners Germany kept all its troops on its own territory. Politics and strategy clashed. The Germans could not be part of an alliance whose strategy was to give up a third of German territory in order to pull back to more defensible positions. In 1977 the U.S. Presidential Review Memorandum Number 10 aroused a storm in Germany by proposing a "temporary retreat" from forward zones in the interests of military prudence. The Carter administration document was not the first expression of the perfectly logical preference of American generals for a more favorable battlefield. But no German politician could countenance such a retreat. Within one hundred kilometers of the border lie Hamburg, Hanover, Nuremberg, Frankfurt, 30 percent of the population, and a quarter of all German industry.

Another time-honored military strategy is to prepare to take the offensive if war is about to break out and try to fight the battle on the enemy's territory instead of your own. But here again political necessity interfered. The Federal Republic, having finally overcome a generation of Soviet propaganda about "German revanchism," could not base its defense on preemptive attack. Nor did it make military or economic sense for the NATO partners to treat the front like a giant subdivision in which each had its own tract to defend. Integrating support functions and using the same weapons would not only have avoided costly duplication and saved money but would have provided a more formidable defense. Yet the commanders of each nation's forces were reluctant to give up even that much independence. The sense of danger from the common enemy did not match the bureaucratic rivalries of the armed services nor the suspicion among the partners.

5

Nineteen seventy-four was the year the NATO alliance frayed at the edges. At the fringes of Europe, poorer, less developed nations like Ireland, Portugal, Spain, Greece, and Turkey resumed ancient quarrels as the reins of the Cold War slackened. Détente proved to be a time for subordinate nations on both sides of the ideological divide to rediscover their political past. As the fear of nuclear war with the Soviet Union receded, dramatic clashes occurred at each extremity of the American protectorate. A revolution in the West in Portugal and a war in the East involving Greece and Turkey over Cyprus imperiled American control over what the Pentagon liked to call NATO's "southern flank." The very idea that the North Atlantic Treaty should have a southern flank at all offended the original notion of the alliance, which was conceived in the State Department as a collection of like-minded Nordic peoples. But the strategic importance of the Mediterranean outweighed considerations of blood and common civilization. As early as 1946, the Sixth Fleet had arrived to convert the Mediterranean into an American lake from Gibraltar to Tel Aviv. As British power receded from the area, the American naval presence grew and with it the need for ports at strategic points along the shore. Greece and Turkey, which had been the original recipients of military and economic aid under the Truman Doctrine, became full-fledged NATO partners in 1952. By a decision taken in Washington, the political map of Europe was remade. Turkey was in and Russia was out.

Turkey became a precious asset in American global strategy, but also something of an embarrassment. More Asian than European, 99 percent Muslim, the modern Turkey of Atatürk was founded on nationalist antipathy to foreigners, Greeks in particular. With an authoritarian government operating fitfully under a democratic veneer, Turkey's membership in NATO always strained the argument that the alliance was the vanguard of "Western civilization." But by virtue of geography the nation had a military function no other ally could play. Turkey was indeed the only NATO nation actually to have experienced pressure from the Soviets at the end of World War II to hand over part of its territory, the region of Kars, which had been Russian from 1878 to 1920. The Soviets had also wanted to share control of the Dardanelles, but backed off both demands in the face of strong U.S. reaction. Between 1677 and 1946 there had been thirteen wars between Russia and Turkey over disputed territory. With the second largest army in NATO, the Turks pinned down twenty-four Soviet divisions just across the border. In 1950 Turkey cheerfully supplied troops to the U.S.–organized "police action" in Korea.

Information gathered by U.S. intelligence-gathering bases in Turkey about Soviet space activities, nuclear explosions, missile testing, and naval movements, according to the senior U.S. officials testifying before Congress, was "irreplaceable" and "critical." Turkey's control of the Dardanelles permits the U.S. Sixth Fleet to monitor Soviet submarines, which greatly increases their vulnerability. Most disturbing to the Soviets, several bases on Turkish territory house tactical aircraft capable of delivering nuclear weapons on cities and military installations far inside the Soviet Union. "I know dollar for dollar you are getting more in Turkey than you are any place in the world," a U.S. general testified in 1952.

In the Dulles era the wooing of Turkey reached its high point. A NATO-like treaty for the protection of the "nothern tier" of the Middle East was hastily devised as the British retreated from the region and Turkey took on an additional key defense role in American planning as a leader of the short-lived Central Treaty Organization (CENTO) alliance. The government in Ankara learned along with the rest of the world that a Turkish base had been used for the famous U-2 spy flight that was shot down over Sverdlovsk in May 1960, but there were no complaints, for the Turks continued to depend on their military aid subsidies from Washington to keep the government solvent. Yet the sense of military threat from the USSR that bound the two nations was beginning to weaken. The denouement of the Cuban missile crisis of 1962 forced a rethinking of Turkish priorities.

In the 1950s the United States had stationed a number of first-generation nuclear missiles, known as Jupiters, on Turkish soil. President Kennedy had considered taking these highly vulnerable and provocative weapons out of Turkey before the crisis, but the Turks objected. At the height of the crisis, Khrushchev publicly proposed a trade of Cuban for Turkish missiles, a deal which was vociferously rejected by the United States. Although Kennedy took the public position that he would risk nuclear war and the death of millions in order to avoid doing under pressure what he was already thinking about doing anyway, the trade-off became important in the private negotiations leading to an end of the crisis. Soon after the crisis subsided, the missiles were removed from Turkey. Not having been consulted during that fateful week, the Turks began to reassess their heavy dependence on an alliance over which they had so little control, and over the next few years repaired their relations with the Soviet Union.

Unlike Turkey, where Washington had only limited influence, the Greece that emerged from the Truman Doctrine aid program was effectively controlled by the Americans. The letter of the Greek government requesting American aid in 1947 was drafted in the State Department. Amid the intrigue of Athens politics, the CIA flourished. Allen Dulles, the director in the Eisenhower years, was a yachting companion of the queen and was delighted to make his agents available to the royal family for private briefings, travel information, and shopping. With the complete trust of the monarchy, the agency was able to set up a Greek intelligence organization, KYP, which spread cash to pro-American political parties. The U.S. ambassador, John Peurifoy, acted the part of "governor-general," as one Athens newspaper called him, publicly threatening to cut off aid if the Greeks did not adopt the U.S.–favored electoral system that would have effectively disenfranchised the Communists. The CIA station chief intervened with the king to assure the appointment of Constantine Karamanlis, the American candidate for prime minister. So pervasive was the CIA influence in Athens that when a military coup overturned the monarchy in April 1967, most Greeks automatically assumed that the United States was behind it.

Colonel George Papadopoulos, the leader of the coup, had indeed been the liaison officer between the CIA and Greek intelligence. The U.S. embassy was so worried about the election slated for July 1967 that the U.S. ambassador urged that $100,000 cash be made available through the CIA to buy the requisite number of votes. Otherwise, the CIA station chief believed, Andreas Papandreou, a naturalized American economics professor who had returned to his native Greece as leader of the Left, would triumph and "seriously damage vital U.S. interests in eastern Mediterranean area, weaken the southern flank of NATO and seriously destabilize . . . delicate Greek-Turkish relations. . . ."

But the Johnson administration embroiled in the Dominican Republic as well as Vietnam could not bring itself to act quickly in Greece. While the CIA bureaucracy was sifting lists of suitable plotters within the Greek army to support, a group of colonels surprised the Americans by moving to take over the government. At the moment the colonels were seizing power, the CIA station chief John Maury was caught at one of their military roadblocks. But since the Americans had run things in Greece for so long, it was inconceivable to Greeks of all political persuasions that the United States had not signaled its approval in advance. The Americans were now in the unenviable position of being held responsible by most Greeks for a NATO dictatorship whose rule by torture had become an international scandal, when in fact the United States, having set the parameters of Greek politics for so long, no longer exercised control over internal events in Greece. The Johnson administration cut off some military aid to the Greek junta but took care to preserve the U.S. military bases, including the storage facilities for nuclear weapons that had sparked considerable controversy in the 1950s. By supporting the junta, the United States aroused more anger in Europe, for America's Greek connection was a powerful symbol for the 1968 generation of the reactionary cast of American foreign policy. The NATO Allies condemned the coup and West Germany cut off all military aid.

When the Nixon administration took office in 1969, it immediately moved toward the resumption of military aid to Greece. Vice President Spiro Agnew and Thomas A. Pappas, an important Nixon backer with a $200-million investment in Greece, formed a formidable Greek lobby. Elmo Zumwalt, the chief of naval operations, who wanted to use the port of Athens as the home port for a new Mediterranean carrier task force, provided added weight for backing the junta. While the Nixon administration defended its decisions on the ground that the junta was moving toward restoration of democracy, Colonel Papadopoulos reneged on his promise to hold elections. The Council of Europe heard extended testimony on the use of torture by the junta and, despite U.S. efforts to stop it, issued a strong condemnation of Greece.

The Nixon administration strategy for preserving American influence in the eastern Mediterranean collapsed in the summer of 1974 when Greece and Turkey went to war with each other over Cyprus. The island had had a long history of being in the way. It had been occupied in turn by Richard the Lion-Hearted, the Templars, the Franks, the Venetians, and the Turks, most recently by the British who had held it until 1959 when a terror campaign forced the granting of independence. Perversely located forty miles off the Turkish coast and about five hundred miles from the Hellenic peninsula, the island is more than 80 percent Greek. Since the 1950s the Greek Cypriots had been fighting for *enosis,* political fusion with the mother country. The Turkish minority, on the other hand, demanded partition, and under the treaty granting independence Turkey had a right to intervene to protect its nationals on the island.

In 1964 the Turks had been about to invade, stopped only by what Under Secretary of State George Ball called "the most brutal diplomatic note I have ever seen." The NATO Allies, Lyndon Johnson wrote the Turkish president, might well reconsider "whether they have an obligation to protect Turkey from the Soviet Union if Turkey takes a step which results in Soviet intervention, without the full consent and understanding of its NATO allies." The Turks acceded to the warning but never forgot it.

The Cypriot president, Archbishop Makarios—that "pious looking replica of Jesus Christ," as Adlai Stevenson called him—enjoyed a reputation in the State Department as the Castro of the Mediterranean, for although he was a nationalist, not a revolutionary, and certainly no Communist, he was quite ready to accept arms from the Russians. His wiliness and fierce independence in the face of such obvious weakness infuriated all the Americans who dealt with him. Ball once screamed at Makarios in the midst of a negotiation, he recalls, "For Christ's sake, Your Beatitude. You can't do that!"

At the heart of the Cyprus problem was the recrudescence of three warring nationalist movements—Greek, Turkish, and Cypriot—an indigestible and explosive mixture that defied the efforts of the virtuosos of American diplomacy. Dean Acheson had invented for President Johnson a lawyerly solution, a "double *enosis*" that would buy stability by uniting the people with Greece and the strategic bases with Turkey, but Makarios, who built his support on leftwing trade unions and Moscow aid, now insisted upon independence from both mother countries. Ironically, the patriarch's obstructionism was the fruit of an earlier U.S. diplomatic success. Ten years before, the United States had secretly pressed Makarios to drop his demand for immediate *enosis*. After the Greek colonels took over in 1967, they proceeded with CIA encouragement to try to pacify Cyprus, break the power of Makarios and his left-wing support, indeed to make something like Acheson's deal with Turkey once Makarios was out of the way. Assassins working for a variety of interested parties proceeded with the latter task, but the archbishop, like Rasputin, that political holy man of an earlier day, seemed mysteriously invulnerable.

As the 1970s dawned, both Greece and Turkey were being turned with U.S. encouragement and support into military dictatorships. Under Suleyman Demirel, the right-wing Turkish leader who had previously represented a U.S. company in Turkey, martial law was declared in March 1971, and the army was carrying out search-and-destroy missions against trade unionists and Kurdish nationalists with one hand and keeping parliament in tow with the other. The Turkish military had carried out, as Social Democractic leader Bulent Ecevit noted, a coup similar to the Greek model, "except that ours is more refined and skillful." In Greece, "the greatest government since Pericles," as an American general enthusiastically greeted the colonels of Athens, was taken over by the police chief, Brigadier Dimitrios Ionnides, in the spring of 1974. A practiced torturer who had never set foot out of Greece except to Cyprus, Ionnides proceeded to shore up the unraveling dictatorship by trying to arrange a foreign policy triumph, the long-awaited *enosis* of Cyprus. The Greek military encouraged the former head of the Greek Cypriot terrorist execution squad, Nikos G. Sampson, to kill Makarios, take over in Cyprus, and arrange the fusion with Greece. Makarios managed, however, to escape in a British helicopter.

For the Turkish government, Sampson was not merely "unsavory," as Kissinger calls him in his memoirs, but a genocidal threat to the Turkish minority. By 1974 the shaky coalition in Turkey was headed by Ecevit, the Westernized Social Democrat who had translated T. S. Eliot and attended Kissinger's Harvard seminar. The new Turkish premier knew that he was on trial as far as the military were concerned, for public anger against Greek repression of Cypriot Turks ran high and he saw no alternative but to invade the island. In July and August the Turks landed 40,000 men and occupied 40 percent of Cyprus in the face of stout resistance. Ninety percent of the weapons Greeks and Turks fired at each other were supplied by the Americans.

The misfiring of the Cyprus coup was enough to topple the Greek colonels. The veteran pro-American politician Karamanlis returned to power, but anti-Americanism was so strong after seven years of the American-backed police state that although Karamanlis was conservative and bore no little responsibility himself for the unraveling of Greek democracy, he was forced to distance himself from the United States. Greece withdrew from the formal NATO structure, becoming in effect the France of the eastern Mediterranean.

For Britain, Germany, and the other NATO countries, the political composition of the two warring Allies on the fringe of Europe was important, for long-term plans called for their becoming an integral part of the new Europe. Ridding the birthplace of democracy of the murderous colonels was widely celebrated as a human rights victory. But for the United States, less obliged and less prepared to live with a distant political muddle, NATO's "southeastern flank" was little more than a piece of strategic real estate. So naked was Kissinger's *realpolitik* in the Cyprus crisis that his reward was the fierce hostility of both Greece and Turkey. George Ball's charge that the virtuoso diplomat had "absentmindedly let the Greek junta mount a coup in Cyprus" is a bit unfair, as if somehow the intricacies of Aegean politics were no more than an American management problem. But Kissinger's posture of tilting toward Greece while the junta was in power and toward Turkey once the colonels were overthrown did nothing for his reputation anywhere. James Schlesinger, the secretary of defense, had wanted to withdraw nuclear weapons from Greece as a sign of displeasure over the Cyprus coup that provoked the crisis, but Kissinger, arguing that the junta would not survive, insisted that strategic interests rather than human rights considerations should dictate. That meant choosing the landlords of America's military anchor on Asia Minor over the lesser landlords who happened also to be the heirs of Pericles. Greek Americans, who exercised considerable influence in both Republican and Democratic parties, now succeeded over Kissinger's strenuous objections in pushing through a congressional embargo on military aid to Turkey.

Within a year Turkey abrogated most of its military arrangements with the United States in retaliation for the cutoff of U.S. weapons. The access to intelligence data about Soviet military movements on which the Pentagon depended was severely cut. The hobbling of the president's discretion to spread military largesse robbed the executive of the very instrument of secret diplomacy Kissinger believed was most needed to stem the decline of American power.

At Europe's other extremity, Portugal was convulsed by a military coup with a revolutionary cast. On April 25, 1974, the Fascist dictatorship organized by Antonio de Oliveira Salazar, and ruled by him for almost fifty years, was overthrown in a remarkably peaceful takeover by General Antonio de Spinola, the Portuguese military commander in the African colonies. Portuguese Fascism, like Turkish militarism, had always been something of an ideological embarrassment to the Western alliance. Yet on meeting Salazar in 1952, Dean Acheson "felt drawn to him as rarely on first meeting," struck by the beauty of his hands and his relaxed manner. The former economics professor from Columbia University, Acheson decided, was "not a dictator in his own right but a dictator-manager [who] did not depend . . . on the harsh suppression of individual liberties." Perhaps "convinced libertarians" might disapprove of him, but Acheson doubted that Plato would have done so. Now twenty-two years later soldiers marched in Lisbon with their rifles festooned with carnations, proclaiming liberation.

Like Turkey and Greece, the western sliver of the Iberian peninsula had failed to participate in the 1960s boom that had brought prosperity to Italy, France, and Germany. The coup was prompted by the collapse of Portuguese control over their centuries-old colonies in Africa. The officers behind it knew that the sacrifice of Portuguese blood and treasure to hold onto Angola, Mozambique, and Guinea-Bissau would not succeed and would destroy Portugal in the process. But once started, the revolutionary process assumed a chaotic life of its own. Anarchists, homosexuals, stoned militants of the international youth culture, and members of every leftist sect imaginable burst forth from the stagnant repressive culture and turned Portugal for a time into a revolutionary festival. The officers' movement that was nominally in charge moved rapidly to the left in its economic analysis and prescription. For Henry Kissinger the most ominous aspect was the existence of a large Communist party disciplined by almost fifty years of repression and led by a classic hard-line militant, Alvaro Cunhal, who remained fanatically loyal to Moscow.

Portugal had never been very important to the American alliance. It was a gateway to Europe whose membership in NATO was useful because European objections to Franco kept Spain out of the formal alliance. (The Spanish bases, especially the nuclear submarine base at Rota, leased under a bilateral arrangement with the Americans, were more important to the U.S. military than the Portuguese facilities.) It was a traditional retirement post for aging CIA operatives and obstreperous right-wingers like Admiral George W. Anderson, Jr., whom John Kennedy had dismissed as chief of naval operations and sent to Lisbon as ambassador. The CIA worked closely with PIDE/DGS, Salazar's pervasive secret police. Documents that came to light after the revolution revealed that one in every four hundred Portuguese citizens was a paid informer and that the hated PIDE officials had regularly come to the United States for four-month training courses on interrogation methods and related skills. Allen Dulles' letter from the 1950s pronouncing the students to be "of high caliber, diligent and gracious visitors" was published in revolutionary Portugal and fed the universal suspicion that the CIA was still meddling in the country.

For the first time since 1947 there were Communist ministers in a West European cabinet. With the Communists able to garner more than 12 percent of the vote and the officers' movement lurching more and more to the Left, it looked to Kissinger as though the Western anchor of NATO-Europe was about to join the East. Indeed the secretary, more pessimistic than the State Department professionals, believed that it was virtually inevitable. This was consistent with Kissinger's belief that the whole world was sliding out from under effective American influence. "I don't see how you can have a Communist element significant in an organization that was put together and formed for the purpose of meeting a challenge by Communist elements from the East," Gerald Ford, the new American president, puzzled aloud for reporters, suggesting that perhaps Portugal ought to be expelled from NATO. Much was made of the fact that the Communists in the Lisbon government would have access to NATO secrets, but that was not the real problem. The channels for controlling sensitive information inside NATO had been long perfected by the Americans.

The more serious problem posed by the revolution in Portugal was its ruinous impact on Kissinger's Africa policy. Impatient with what he considered to be the ineffectual moralizing of the liberals with respect to Portuguese colonial exploitation, Kissinger had in 1970 recommended moving closer to Portugal as well as South Africa itself. "[T]he whites are here to stay," an interdepartmental group on Africa had reported to the National Security Council a year earlier, "and the only way that constructive change can come about is through them." Export-Import Bank loans were extended to the Portuguese colonies. The largesse of the CIA, which had been covertly spread for some years to Holden Roberto's black resistance group in Angola, was curtailed and the secret subsidization of factions within Mozambique's Nationalist Movement (FRELIMO), considered to be pro-American, was stopped. Reversing a policy dating from the Kennedy administration, which had registered its disapproval of Portugal's colonial wars, the United States now moved to support them. The U.S. Navy stepped up its use of Portuguese facilities in Mozambique and Angola. Portuguese jet fighter pilots used U.S. Air Force facilities in Germany for training. Portuguese officers attended the U.S. Army's Jungle Warfare School in Panama for counterinsurgency training. United States commercial jetliners were made available to Salazar and converted into troop carriers. The NATO Defense Planning Committee began drawing up contingency plans for the air and naval defense of South Africa in the event of war. But no sooner had Portugal assumed new importance in the Kissinger grand design as a strategic link between Europe and the Dark Continent than Portuguese power in Africa collapsed and with it stability in Portugal as well.

Not only was the Portuguese revolution an embarrassment because of its impact on Africa, but, as Kissinger saw it, it posed a mortal threat to the status quo in Europe. The Franco regime was about to come to an end, for plainly it could not survive the aging dictator. There too another large and battered Communist party had managed to survive years of repression. In Italy the new leader of the Communist party, Enrico Berlinguer, had just proposed a "historic compromise," a plea to end the isolation of Italy's largest party by shedding its doctrinaire rhetoric and by appealing to a broader constituency of professionals, shopkeepers, and even smaller entrepreneurs. In France,

Georges Marchais became the new Communist boss and moved to make an ideological alliance with Berlinguer and a political alliance with François Mitterrand, leader of the French Socialists, under a strange new slogan for what had been the most Stalinist of the Communist parties of the West: "The surest road to socialism is the broadening of democracy." The new generation of functionaries sought occasions to demonstrate their independence from the Soviet Union. All these developments in 1974 increased the prospect of Communist participation in a variety of European governments. If Communists came to power in Portugal by a peaceful revolution, the domino effect would be disastrous, Kissinger believed.

When Mario Soares, the Portuguese Socialist leader who was foreign minister, came to the State Department for lunch in October 1974, Kissinger called him naive, "a Kerensky" who would pave the way for the Communists. "I certainly don't want to be a Kerensky," Soares replied. "Neither did Kerensky," Kissinger snapped. Portugal presented the same challenge as Allende's Chile. A part of the ideological West was moving toward Marxist Socialism not by bloody revolution or Soviet subversion but by legitimate internal processes. The more legitimate the revolution, the more of a magnet it was likely to be for other countries. Yet the riposte that had been used so successfully to topple Allende, a CIA campaign of destabilization in support of the strong resistance inside Chile to radical change, was not obviously available for use in Portugal in 1975. Indeed, the agency was under considerable public pressure because of the disclosures of the CIA activities in Chile five years earlier. Several congressional committees and a commission headed by Vice President Nelson Rockefeller were investigating covert operations of the past. It was politically dangerous to risk new ones.

Nonetheless, Kissinger secured approval of the 40 Committee, the high-level group in the executive branch that must pass on covert operations, for a low-level effort in Portugal. According to an investigation by the former *New York Times* reporter Tad Szulc, money was passed to conservative parties, and CIA operatives "infiltrated some conservative organizations . . . working directly through elements of the Roman Catholic Church." General Vernon Walters, the CIA deputy director who had assisted the Brazilian military with their coup in 1964, visited Portugal in August 1974 and confirmed Kissinger's fears. The country was headed for a Communist dictatorship. The secretary wanted to take a tough position in Portugal to force the Communists out of government and to isolate the country until the Communist danger had passed. Neither the American ambassador, Frank Carlucci, nor most European leaders favored such a course. They believed that the outcome in Portugal was by no means foreclosed and that the emphasis should be placed on defeating the Communists in the elections. Ultimately this view was vindicated. In March 1975, after the failure of a right-wing coup of which the United States had advance notice but did not arrange, the leftward march of the revolution quickened. But Cunhal, the Communist leader, overplayed his hand. Though urged by Santiago Carillo, the Spanish Communist leader and Gian Carlo Pajetta, the foreign policy theorist of the Italian Communist party, to slow down, Cunhal made a clumsy bid to take power and failed. The moderate Socialists, with overt and clandestine help from the European Socialist parties, won the elections and eventually broke the power of the revolutionary officers' movement. The Soviets who, according to the U.S. embassy in Lisbon, were passing about $2 million to $3 million a month to Cunhal to buy printing presses and a new headquarters building for the party, made it clear to Kissinger that Portugal was not worth a confrontation with the United States or doing damage to détente. With gathering problems in Poland, Brezhnev had mixed feelings about doing anything to accelerate the breakup of the blocs. Portuguese Communists should be supported, of course, but Portugal should stay with the West.

Henry Kissinger had once made a joke about the unimportance of Allende's Chile in order to mask his intense interest in the electoral experiment with Socialism in that country. But Portugal was clearly no "dagger pointed at the heart of Antarctica." It was dangerously close to Italy, in American eyes a perennial political volcano with a government more subject to American direction than any other in Europe and the biggest Communist party in the West. By the mid-1970s the Christian Democrats, who had with considerable American help ruled the country since 1948, were showing signs of wear. For almost thirty years they had dominated the cabinet, the parliament, and the civil service with a "civic indulgence," as historian H. Stuart Hughes calls it, that expressed itself in an excess of Christian charity to unregenerate but rehabilitated Fascists, wealthy tax cheats, petty censors of public morals, and small-minded officials with a weakness for dipping fingers into the public treasury. By reforming the economy at the margin, and maintaining the swollen bureaucracies of Italy's Fascist party, the Christian Democrats, for a time, managed to stimulate faster economic growth than elsewhere in Europe. The United States government kept urging modest reform and in the Marshall Plan era helped to redraft the country's porous tax system. But from the early postwar times the major American preoccupation was to keep leftists out of the government.

Almost a year before the extraordinary public involvement of American officials in the 1948 election, the U.S. ambassador in Rome, James Dunn, had counseled that "aid to Italy perhaps should be based upon a *quid pro quo* of necessary changes in political orientation and policies." Whereupon six days later Premier Alcide de Gasperi obediently dissolved his cabinet and excluded the Socialists and Communists. By 1953, however, De Gasperi's coalition was breaking up and he was voted out of office. His successors held the ruling coalition together but at a price. Governments fell with dizzying regularity. The economy grew impressively but unevenly, and political life was approaching paralysis. Parties split on both the Left and the Right. Most significantly, the Socialists, who under Pietro Nenni had if anything been more militant and orthodox than the Communists, broke with Moscow over the invasion of Hungary and offered themselves as a nonrevolutionary leftist leaven for the frustrated Christian Democrats. The emerging liberal faction of the Christian Democrats favored accepting their offer. Italy's only hope, they believed, was a center-left government. Under Pope John XXIII the Vatican moderated its intense hostility to the Socialists.

By 1961 the Kennedy administration was in office and was casting about for places in the world to demonstrate its new spirit of progressive anti-Communism. Arthur Schlesinger, Jr., Averell Harriman, and parts of the CIA believed that Socialists in office would be the best bulwark against the dread possibility of having to deal with Communist ministers. It would, as Schlesinger put it, make Italy "a more effective supporter of the foreign policy of the Kennedy administration in Europe and elsewhere. . . ." But the U.S. government was bitterly divided. For Outerbridge Horsey, deputy chief of mission in Rome, the New Frontiersmen who dared to meet with Italian politicians long anathema to the State Department and to write them letters on white House stationery were amateurish and unprincipled. The ubiquitous Vernon Walters, then military attaché in Rome, strongly urged at an embassy meeting that American troops be used to keep the Socialists out of the government. But the Kennedy advisers convinced the Italian politicians that they really had changed their minds about the Socialists, and under the shrewd leader Aldo Moro, the Christian Democrats were emboldened to try putting together "an opening to the Left."

The economic miracle that had increased production 85 percent between 1953 and 1960 continued. Cars, office machines, and typewriters poured out of Italy's factories. Two million peasants flocked to the cities. The Fascist laws designed to keep poor southern Italians in their place were removed and huge migrations north occurred. The strong unions, the source of Communist party strength, pushed wages up. But by the mid-1970s Italy's frenetic, disorderly prosperity had left it one of the world's most indebted nations, with an annual inflation rate of 25 percent. If the discontents—of women, workers, peasants —were not of revolutionary proportions as in the immediate postwar period, they ran deep indeed.

When it came into office the Nixon administration resolved to reverse the Kennedy and Johnson policy toward Italy, since the opening to the Left had failed in its purpose. Nixon appointed Graham Martin, a true believer in the worldwide Communist conspiracy, to be ambassador to Rome. (Martin, a Foreign Service officer who had shrewdly treated Nixon like a chief of state when the former vice president called at the embassy in Bangkok in his wilderness years, was later made America's last ambassador in Saigon as his final reward.) Ambassador Martin proceeded to spend $10 million of CIA clandestine funds on the 1972 parliamentary election. There was nothing new about under-the-table generosity in Italy. According to the House Select Committee on Intelligence, $65 million had been spent in the previous two decades. But normally the funds went to centrist parties. This time, however, funds went to "Italian political groups and individuals on the far right of the political spectrum (that is to forces close to the neo-Fascist Italian Socialist Movement MSI)." In addition to these political contributions, $800,000, the House Select Committee on Intelligence discovered, went to Vito Miceli, head of Italy's Defense Intelligence Service, to conduct a propaganda campaign against the Left. Miceli was so notorious a right-winger that the CIA station chief complained to Washington that the ambassador was recklessly endangering the agency's reputation. Admitting that he did not care "a helluva lot" about the campaign, Martin advised the CIA station chief that the generous subvention was really "to demonstrate solidarity for the long pull." But he was sufficiently annoyed with what he regarded as CIA timidity that he threatened to have the marine guards bar the station chief from the embassy.

Despite his efforts the Communist party of Italy grew in strength, established control of municipalities throughout Italy, often in collaboration with the Socialists who were supposed to be the instrument of their demise. The government once again turned into a revolving door for a familiar cast of increasingly harried Christian Democratic politicians. In the midst of mounting corruption, terrorism, and economic woe, the Italian Communists, who ran free streetcars and other municipal services in the big industrial Italian cities with businesslike dispatch and financial probity, began looking to more and more Italians as a rock of stability. This was especially so since the new leader, Enrico Berlinguer, a Sardinian aristocrat who had denounced the invasion of Czechoslovakia, the "Brezhnev Doctrine" that blessed it, and other indigestible tenets of "Soviet internationalism," proclaimed an independent, nonrevolutionary path to Italian Socialism. Communist rhetoric became increasingly moderate. One by one the words of the credo—"dictatorship of the proletariat," even "class struggle"—were jettisoned in a successful appeal to those Italian moderates who could not bear the prospect of another reshuffled Christian Democratic government. Looking about the world in his seventh year in office, Henry Kissinger saw the Left on the march everywhere—Vietnam, Angola, Portugal, Spain, and Italy. If there was one country where the Communists must be stopped, it was Italy, for if the United States lacked the power to do that in a country where it had molded and sustained the government for so many years, it had indeed become a pitiful, helpless giant.

NINE

THE FAILURES OF TRILATERALISM:

Mr. Carter Honors and Confuses the Partners

1

The slender peanut farmer with sandy hair and gleaming teeth had "run against Washington," the political commentators agreed, promising a government as good as the people, in which the president would keep his office door open and never lie. But Jimmy Carter, a one-term Georgia governor, a political unknown, had, for all his populist rhetoric, captured the presidency in the autumn of 1976 by appealing to the traditional constituents of the Democratic party and by promising a restoration. Remove the hardhearted, secretive, corrupt Republicans, and the country could relive the proud days of its past under a government of well-intentioned, efficient managers.

The Ford interregnum presented a satisfying target. The unelected president radiated mediocrity, and the man who made foreign policy famous no longer seemed to be able to make foreign policy. Some of the ideas behind the "conceptual framework" with which Kissinger dazzled diplomats and the press had been either disproved by experience or rejected. "Linkage" plainly did not work either as a description of reality or as a policy. The Spenglerian curse had also failed to materialize. As the 1976 U.S. election approached, Portugal, thanks to the low U.S. profile maintained by the U.S. ambassador who ignored Kissinger's insistence on greater CIA meddling, emerged from free elections with a moderate government headed rightward. In Spain the new king legalized the Communist party against American advice and the result was much the same. In Italy the election that Kissinger feared would shake Western civilization instead maintained the pattern of a generation. The Communist party came in second, though now with a third of the vote instead of a quarter. United States influence in southern Europe was at an ebb, but the catastrophic consequences which Kissinger predicted were nowhere in evidence. For better or worse European nations had their own stabilizers. "Peace and prosperity are impossible without a major American role," Nixon had declared a few years earlier. Now southern Europe seemed to be moving in the direction of moderate liberal democracy and northern Europe was moving perceptibly to the right—and it was happening without American involvement.

Détente had crumbled to such an extent that the word, a campaign slogan four years earlier, was banished from the Republican vocabulary. From the very start the new U.S.–Soviet relationship was shaky because important expectations on both sides were quickly disappointed. The Jackson and Stevenson amendments passed by the Congress in 1974 prevented "most-favored nation" status from being granted to the USSR and severely limited the extension of credit unless the Soviets agreed to the emigration of Jews on a scale satisfactory to the United States. The Kremlin was unwilling to accord a role for Senator Henry Jackson in setting Soviet emigration policy, but this predictable show of pride cost the USSR the principal advantages it hoped to derive from its new relationship with the United States.

For its part, the Nixon administration had hinted in many ways in its 1972 electoral bid that its brilliant diplomacy had caused a basic modification of Soviet strategy and behavior. Soviet leaders, however, had stated privately and publicly that the "ideological struggle" would go on, and that struggle, they made clear, included continuing military and economic support for revolutionary or "progressive" regimes. In late 1975 and early 1976 Cuban troops airlifted to Angola with Soviet support played the decisive role in the victory of the Popular Movement for the Liberation of Angola (MPLA), a Marxist-Leninist guerrilla group long opposed by the United States. Because of the huge expense of the Vietnam War and congressional disenchantment with the military in the wake of that catastrophe, the United States had launched no new major weapons system in the 1970s, although it continued development of the cruise missile and fitted existing missiles with far more accurate and destructive warheads. At the end of the Ford administration, U.S. satellites began to detect deployment of a number of new Soviet missile types: The steady military buildup which began after the Cuban missile crisis was exceeding the predictions of U.S. intelligence analysts. By the 1976 election a number of military officers and defense contractors were grumbling to influential columnists that the Soviets had put one over on the United States. Why if the two sides were negotiating a SALT agreement in good faith, should the Soviet continue its nuclear buildup when the United States had, broadly speaking, stopped? Like most of his predecessors, Jimmy Carter knew little about foreign policy. But his political antennae were remarkably sensitive. In the shock of Vietnam and Watergate the public worried about secret, unwieldy, unfeeling government so out of touch with citizens that officials could comfortably confuse their own financial dreams and political ambitions with the national interest. But the nation's leading businessmen and bankers, and the "opinion leaders" from the press and university worlds, having watched their own dinner parties, families, and organizations being torn apart by the war, worried instead about the collapse of the foreign policy consensus. To win, Carter knew that he would have to reassure the membership of the Metropolitan and the Knickerbocker clubs while he was reaching out to the people.

Meanwhile U.S. foreign policy appeared stalled, and as a consequence Henry Kissinger, a world hero just a few short months before, was now a vulnerable political target. The secretary, Carter charged, using a famous indiscretion the brilliant interrogator Oriana Fallaci had extracted from Kissinger a few years before, was the self-described Lone Ranger of international politics. Moreover, he had violated the most hallowed principles of the bipartisan foreign policy. The secretary, who in private called the Europeans "craven, contemptible, pernicious, and jackal-like" for doubting the necessity or wisdom of his 1973 nuclear alert, engaged in "one-man diplomacy" and "unilateral dealing with the Soviet Union," Carter charged in a speech to the Foreign Policy Association, and this confused and outraged the Allies. Instead of such dangerous unilateralism there must be a "partnership of North America, Western Europe and Japan."

The reassertion of the American commitment to the alliance echoed the mainstream views held for almost two generations by the very Eastern Establishment against which Carter leveled his carefully programmed populist attacks. Even the trilateral note was hardly new. In his 1953 Godkin lectures at Harvard, John J. McCloy had predicted the need for a genuine partnership with both Germany and Japan once they had recovered. But since 1972 "trilateralism" had become a fashionable concept among what its members liked to call the "foreign policy community." In that year David Rockefeller, worried that the liberal internationalists of the Wall Street and Washington law firms who had managed U.S. foreign policy under Republican and Democratic administrations alike had been discredited by Vietnam and replaced by dangerous Nixonian nationalists like Connally, put up the seed money and supplied his personal prestige for the Trilateral Commission, which was launched the following year. This private organization, composed of the "best brains" of the industrial world, as its executive director regularly explained to reporters, was a collection of leading bankers, senior corporate executives, former high government officials, and well-connected academics. The U.S. contingent represented an acceptable list of the rich, influential, and famous such as any enterprising Democratic or Republic fundraiser would like to assemble. The European and Japanese representatives seemed almost as impressive. Into this company Jimmy Carter, about to finish his term as governor, was inducted in the summer of 1973. "We were a little light on people from the South," George Franklin, an old Rockefeller hand who organized the group, later explained. Hedley Donovan, the publisher of *Time,* had come up with his name.

The Trilateral Commission was barely mentioned in the 1976 campaign. When the Carter cabinet was announced, a few columnists noted the coincidence that so many of them belonged to Mr. Rockefeller's new organization.

By the time Jimmy Carter ran for a second term, however, the Trilateral Commission was a major campaign issue, suddenly attacked from the Far Right for being a collection of crypto-Communists and one-worlders and from the fringe Left for being a Rockefeller conspiracy to turn the Third World over to the multinational corporations. Though the view of the Left was somewhat more plausible than that of the Right, both characterizations were excessively respectful of the Trilateral Commission's cohesiveness, influence, and drive.

But neither was it just an elegant seminar. The commission was important not for what it achieved, which was very little, but for its pretensions. The Trilateral Commission did not mastermind the Carter presidency as some breathless accounts of the time contended. On the contrary, it articulated the needs and goals which the administration failed to meet and gave up trying to meet. High officials like Secretary of State Cyrus Vance, Secretary of Defense Harold Brown, and Secretary of the Treasury Michael Blumenthal were not picked for the cabinet because they were trilateralists; they were trilateralists because they were already part of the select pool of eligible national security managers. (A number of younger members of the commission, however, such as Richard Holbrooke and C. Fred Bergsten, did manage to turn their trilateral contacts into assistant secretaryships.) The commission had as its purpose nothing less modest than the creation of a transnational elite with a shared consciousness. The coordinated management of the increasingly interdependent market economies of North America, Europe, and Japan had become urgent at the very moment when internationalist leaders were becoming hard to find.

It was not the first such effort. At the end of the war prodigious energy had gone into the creation of an Atlantic consciousness. Various private groups organized by well-connected individuals sprang up in the Marshall Plan days to strengthen the transatlantic bonds among the elite of Europe and America. A key figure was Dr. Joseph H. Retinger, whom George Ball, an enthusiastic collaborator, describes as a "political adventurer in the pattern of a Casanova, Cellini or Tom Paine." A friend of André Gide and Joseph Conrad, Retinger had lived in Mexico before the war where he counseled the government on expropriating the oil properties of American companies. Later he became a top aide to General Wladyslaw Sikorski, leader of the Polish government-in-exile, and parachuted into Poland in 1944 at age fifty-seven to make contact with the underground. During the war he pushed for regular consultations of foreign ministers, something then unknown, out of which had come the creation of the Benelux customs union. More brash than Jean Monnet, whose activities he paralleled, Retinger was a master organizer of the powerful—magnates, intellectuals, prime ministers, kings, and those poised to join their number. Like Monnet he believed strongly in European unity. In 1947 he organized the European Movement, a group of organizations to propagate the importance of U.S.–European collaboration. The funds came ostensibly from American philanthropic sources but about five-sixths of the money was supplied by U.S. intelligence agencies.

Retinger was worried about rampant anti-Americanism in Europe after the war, not just on the Left but among conservative circles who looked on the reorganizers of Europe from across the sea as clumsy, naive, and uncultured. The decisions needed to remake Europe, he believed, were not understood by the public, which was still mired in old-fashioned nationalism. Public opinion, he was convinced, "follows the lead of influential individuals." As his longtime secretary John Pomian put it, "He much preferred working through a few carefully selected people to publicity on a massive scale."

Building on his wartime associations with men like Averell Harriman, he came to know the most powerful men in the United States and proceeded to enlist them in his cause. One of Retinger's ideas for breaking down transatlantic barriers was to have influential Europeans confront influential Americans in a congenial, utterly private setting concerning McCarthyism and other aspects of America that disturbed Europeans and then let the Americans have "an opportunity to answer the indictment." Men like John S. Coleman, president of Burroughs, Harry Bullis, president of General Mills, John J. McCloy, and George Ball were already trying to organize public opinion in the United States against the anti-European protectionist impulse that was once again making itself felt. They liked the idea of institutionalizing old wartime friendships into regular get-togethers. The participants would all belong to that special breed of citizen who feels the weight of public responsibility whether in office or out.

Thus the Bilderberg meetings were launched soon after Eisenhower arrived in the White House. Prince Bernhard of the Netherlands, Paul Van Zeeland, the former Belgian prime minister, and Paul Rykens, chairman of the board of Unilever, were recruited by Retinger as the European leadership, and in the United States, Coleman and Ball handled the recruiting in close collaboration with C. D. Jackson, Eisenhower's assistant for psychological warfare, and Walter Bedell Smith, another close wartime associate of the new president who had been head of the CIA. The group had been carefully selected for balance within the accepted political limits of the day. The former Socialist premier of France, Guy Mollet, was brought into the planning, along with the former conservative premier, Antoine Pinay. C. D. Jackson established a certain rapport by talking frankly about Senator Joseph McCarthy, whose rampages were coming to a climax. "We are bound to get this kind of supercharged emotional freak from time to time," he explained. Hinting that the senator might well be assassinated, Jackson promised the Bilderbergers that by next year "he will be gone from the American scene."

The cast of notables met under heavy guard at the Hotel Bilderberg at Oosterbeek, Holland, in late May 1954. Held year after year in similar elegant settings around the world, the Bilderberg meetings discussed matters of great weight such as "the role and control of nuclear weapons within NATO" (1958), "elements of instability in Western society" (1969), and "the possibility of a change of the American role in the world and its consequences" (1971) with greater frankness and more leisure than was available to the participants

when they met under more official circumstances. Informal seminars on nuclear weapons, De Gaulle's obstructionism, and what to do about the restive
students were held in what Sir Eric Roll, a former senior British civil servant
and investment banker, calls "the intimacy of the senior common room." To
be eligible a participant had to be a powerful or prestigious figure from a
capitalist industrialized country of Western Europe or North America and fall
comfortably within the centrist orthodoxy of his society. One of the few exceptions was the right-wing British MP Enoch Powell, who attended once and
pronounced the proceedings "largely futile but perfectly harmless." Another
was Marshall McLuhan who, in a daring opening to the new intellectual currents of the late 1960s, was invited one time, but as one veteran Bilderberger
told *The Times* (London), "he used so many four-letter words that we learnt
our lesson."

David Rockefeller tried out his idea of a Trilateral Commission at a Bilderberg meeting. "David thought things were falling apart," George Franklin,
an old Rockefeller associate, recalls, and many shared his concern. Bringing
Japan into regular international elite discussions seemed like a good idea. "If
we are going to move effectively," Franklin put it, "the industrialized democracies must not work at cross purposes." The commission was formed in
October 1973. Columbia University professor Zbigniew Brzezinski, a Polish
émigré who grew up in Canada and had impressed Rockefeller with a cascade
of ideas that ran easily from orthodox Cold War liberalism of the 1950s to
"world order" concerns of the 1970s, was made director. Jimmy Carter became an eager participant. Having determined to run for president in 1976, he
saw the Trilateral Commission as a convenient gathering place of the very men
he must impress. "The Democratic candidate in 1976," Brzezinksi predicted
in an interview in late 1973, "will have to emphasize work, the family, religion,
and, increasingly, patriotism if he has any desire to be elected." On this Jimmy
Carter agreed. As far as "world order" was concerned, the energetic, ambitious, but rather colorless politician was eager to learn what he could from the
professor's rapid-fire presentations.

Like many members of the "foreign policy community," Brzezinski was
convinced that the Vietnam War, "the Waterloo of the elite," was lost only
because the elite lost its nerve. Kissinger, he told *Los Angeles Times* reporter
Robert Scheer in January 1977 a few days later after settling into his office in
the White House as national security adviser, was "perhaps the last spokesman for the fading elite." Without a new elite riding a new world view, the
foreign policy consensus could not be put back together again and U.S. foreign
policy would remain paralyzed. Trilateralism was an effort to modernize U.S.
foreign policy thinking to enable the nation to continue exercising leadership
in a world where allies were no longer clients but competitors.

In broad strokes trilateralism sounded eminently sensible. Instead of unilateralism, cooperation. Instead of obsession with the East-West struggle, a
balanced concern for relations with the Third World. Instead of an "inordinate
fear of communism," as Carter later put it in a speech at Notre Dame, a more

subtle and flexible approach to the diversity of world politics. The world views of the industrial states had to be harmonized if conflict were to be kept to manageable limits.

But the actual output of the commission was less a tonic for the "biological fatigue" that, Brzezinski claimed, had overtaken the elite than a symptom. Most of the studies received little attention. The one that did, *The Crisis of Democracy,* became an embarrassment. It was a warning that the "democratic distemper" of the time was making the modern industrial state ungovernable. The "excess of democracy" could be treated by more controls on the press, more secrecy, and more concentration of power.

These ideas were hardly new. A consistent theme running through Bilderberg meetings, the deliberations of the Atlantic Council, and the numerous other organizations that sprang up to reinforce Atlanticist consciousness is that "the public" is a problem. Such organizations have traditionally celebrated the transnational bonds of class and ideology as a counterweight to those popular pressures within each nation that threaten the orderly management of international relations. Participants are in a sense allies of one another against the unenlightened nationalists of their own countries. No wonder that so many conspiracy theories sprang up. In an age of egalitarian rhetoric and expectations, the NATO establishment had organized another rich man's club and made the rich Japanese honorary members of the West.

Thus the Trilateral Commission was indeed a conspiracy of a sort, not to take over the world or to give away the Panama Canal, but to create a transnational lobby to shape elite opinion in each of the industrial countries. The World War II generation—Harriman, McCloy, Acheson, and their British and French counterparts—who felt closer to one another than to most of their own countrymen were no longer in power. The unique personal relationships forged in wartime London, the heady days of the Strategic Bombing Survey and the Marshall Plan could not be easily duplicated in the 1970s. The position of elites in each NATO country was shakier, their pictures of the good society fuzzier and more contradictory than in the past. It was hard to recapture the spirit of Atlanticism, much less extend it to the Pacific. In the strange new economic climate of the 1970s the forces of competitive nationalism in each country were gaining the ascendancy.

2

"Sometimes I think people look too hard. They're looking for something that isn't there," Jimmy Carter suggested to a journalist who was probing the president-elect's character on the eve of his taking office. But no recent president's character had been so puzzling. The individual traits became familiar political lore: the flinty determination and merciless will that propelled him through grueling, seemingly hopeless months of campaigning. ("I told you I didn't intend to lose," he exulted before an early-hour television audience as the final votes were counted.) The pride in attention to detail. (As a Georgia state senator he had kept his promise to read every one of the 2300 bills introduced, and as president his appetite for trivia was equally voracious— "the best deputy assistant secretary in town," exasperated party leaders called him.) The gift for preaching without passion. (His born-again Baptism meant more to him than the presidency, but he recoiled from the emotional impact of the revivalist thunder he had heard in his youth, and projected a cerebral piety that irritated voters who did not share his roots and world leaders who felt the reproach in his icy blue eyes.)

The persona of any American president, thanks to television and global wire services, was now a staple of journalism around the world. But Carter's appearance at the summit of power was such a surprise that there was more than the usual interest in the man. American presidents since John Kennedy had struck Europeans as flawed characters or, like Ford, a limited man, and since the inhabitant of the White House had considerable power over their own lives, this added to the general frustration at being part of the American protectorate. So high hopes rested on the new president who promised to make "partnership" so central to his policy. Americans were optimistic too. For Norman Mailer, who had spent several days with him at his home in Plains during the campaign, Carter "had that silvery reserve only the most confident astronauts ever showed."

Jimmy Carter turned out to be a man who abounded in good qualities he could neither discipline nor integrate. A decent, genuinely moral man, his success in translating his morality into politics was limited. Though chilly in personal relations with subordinates and political figures, he was compassionate as a matter of principle. He drove himself as much as he drove others— "Why not the best," the words of Admiral Hyman Rickover, his boss in his nuclear submarine days, weighed heavily upon him, he tells us in his biography, as did the memories of his father's whippings and a preacher's reproach for being a part-time Christian. But he never learned to hold himself together, much less master his own government or the alliance by which he set so much store. Though he had shown some courage in battling the race prejudice of the old South, once in the White House he temporized and retreated before the gathering attacks on the most enlightened aspects of his foreign policy. By the end of his term the image of steely determination and managerial competence had given way to one of vacillation and confusion. Jimmy Carter had had the bad luck to have his wishes granted at the wrong historical moment. A long legacy of mistakes and complacency reaching back to the Kennedy era had created the need for a miracle worker in the White House, and not even he had promised that.

The new administration was scarcely a year old before the private views of European leaders about Jimmy Carter began making their way into print. Helmut Schmidt, who took an instant dislike to him, let it be known that he considered the nuclear engineer a bit *"schwach"* in the head, and one of his ministers told an American reporter that "we are not sure your president knows what he's doing." Even before important issues arose to irritate U.S.-

European relations—the neutron bomb, the sale of nuclear reactors, sanctions against the Soviet Union after its invasion of Afghanistan—leading magazines and newspapers in Germany and France were ridiculing or patronizing the new president for his self-righteousness and inconsistency.

The foreign policy mirrored the man. Admirable goals, like his own admirable character traits, collided with one another. Carter needed to establish a reputation as a man with a new vision of America's role in the world if he were to restore a foreign policy consensus. That was a tall order for a one-term Georgia governor. But within four months the contours of the policy were announced in a remarkable speech he delivered at Notre Dame. Not for thirty years had there been so much new music in a presidential pronouncement on foreign policy—talk of the "intellectual and moral poverty" of our "failure" in Vietnam, of responding to "the new reality of a politically awakening world," avoiding "manipulation" through power, rising above "narrow national interests" to solve the global problems of "nuclear war, racial hatred, the arms race, environmental damage, hunger, and disease." Zbigniew Brzezinski told *U.S. News & World Report* that the United States now had a chance to set the direction of international politics, just as it did at the end of World War II.

The new president attempted to gather into a bipartisan consensus the two groups that had broken with Kissinger, the liberals who were revolted by his cynicism and double-dealing, and the hard-liners who thought he had given away too much to the Soviets. To the liberals Carter offered a return to morality in foreign policy, a concern with human rights, a promise to scold dictators who ruled by torture, and an acknowledgment that the United States was the leading merchant of death in the Third World. To the hard liners he vowed that he would make détente a two-way street and be a tougher bargainer than Kissinger.

Commitment to high principle would produce a foreign policy that would once again make Americans "feel good" about their country. Brzezinski, the new national security adviser, argued that stressing human rights violations in the Soviet Union would allow the United States once again to occupy the ideological high ground it had lost in the Vietnam War. The Soviets, he told an interviewer in the spring of 1977, had "gotten away with murder" just because they hadn't been in Vietnam, for the Vietnam era was a time for exposing America's moral weakness. Now was the time to put the shoe on the other foot and expose the Soviets at their point of vulnerability—the gulag, the Orwellian uses of mental hospitals, the obscene trials of dissidents. Imbued with a mysterious optimism as striking as his predecessor's pessimism, Brzezinski argued that there was a "trend" in the world toward "dramatic worldwide advances in the protection of the individual from the power of the state." When the president intoned these words at Notre Dame, the national security adviser exclaimed that the United States had finally taken up the challenge of the "ideological struggle" and was now prepared to beat the Soviets at their own game.

Since the United States had regularly been attacked in Europe for its excessive tolerance of murderous dictators in Greece, Vietnam, and Latin America, the new administration did not anticipate the negative reaction from the Allies. Indeed, public opinion polls in Europe showed high approval for Carter's human rights stand—79 percent in West Germany, 68 percent in France. But the leaders had a different view. When Leonid Brezhnev denounced Carter for receiving Soviet dissidents in the White House and carrying on "psychological warfare" against his regime, the president publicly expressed "surprise" that his moral concerns should be taken in Moscow as a threat to U.S.-Soviet relations. For Helmut Schmidt that merely confirmed the fact that the new president was hopelessly naive. Carter was acting "like a faith healer" not a leader. Tweaking Brezhnev's nose might win votes in the United States, but, as Giscard put it publicly, it "compromised the process of détente." A critical diplomatic achievement on which Europeans, especially Germans, had come to depend was now at the mercy of American amateurs. Schmidt and Giscard would laugh at the new American president at their get-togethers, and they resolved to develop a common strategy for dealing with the misguided enthusiasms of Washington.

As if to institutionalize his own ambivalence, Carter's principal foreign policy appointments made it certain that he would receive irreconcilable advice. Cyrus Vance, the new secretary of state, was a calm, gentlemanly Wall Street lawyer who had gone to the right schools, joined the right clubs, become a partner in a prestigious firm, and for twenty years had been in and out of Democratic administrations negotiating the most sensitive issues such as the future of Vietnam and Cyprus and what to do about riots in the Panama Canal and in Detroit.

His style was deliberately colorless and his instincts moderate. He had been involved in the planning of the Vietnam War, but like many members of the foreign policy leadership in the Democratic party, he had learned enough from the experience to understand the practical limits on the use of force. It was in the U.S. interest, he believed, and in the Soviet interest "to manage the relationship in a way that seeks to reduce tension and to find broader areas of common understanding." The Strategic Arms Limitation Talks (SALT) agreement was a matter of "life or death" and would "set the tone for the rest of the relationship." Vance was the quintessential trilateralist. The problem of peace was infinitely more complex than keeping the Russians off balance. The economic threats facing the United States—energy crises, the failure of the monetary order, growing conflicts with the resource-producing nations—were at least as serious as the Soviet threat. Good relations with the Soviet Union were a precondition for dealing with these problems, but the Soviet Union was not the key to their solution. The so-called "North-South issues," he believed, had been neglected because of the preoccupation with the East-West struggle. Vance had been part of a United Nations Association panel a year before taking office that discounted a growing Soviet military threat and expressed confidence in reaching mutually advantageous arms control arrangements with the Soviet Union. The new secretary of state believed that America's great advantage lay in its economic power. If barriers could be lowered and trade expanded, there could come into being a world order based on enlightened self-interest, the multinationals acting, in economist Marina Whitman's phrase, as "the primary vehicles of interdependence." Military confrontation was a dead end and the escalating arms race financially ruinous.

Zbigniew Brzezinski could scarcely have been more of a contrast. As boyish and playful in manner as Vance was grave and deliberate, Brzezinski had made his reputation with intriguing ideas as Vance had made his with steady counsel. Most of the trilateralist message the professor had written himself. Indeed, his writings in the early 1970s had influenced Rockefeller. But he had also written books on "the permanent purge" that supposedly characterized the Soviet Union and the "technetronic society" where robots would produce "an increasingly cultivated and programmed" life for Americans and other inhabitants of the advanced industrial world. In short, he seemed to have a flair for capturing fashionable intellectual currents of the moment in catchy phrases and surrounding them with brilliant, contradictory, at times flamboyantly wrong-headed observations. His pixieish charm, which could suddenly dissolve into an arrogant look or peremptory dismissal, won him few admirers in the press, which presented him more often than not as an awkward, impulsive, and somewhat immature figure. Brzezinski's image helped to build the administration's reputation for unsteadiness.

Although he commended himself to Carter as a global thinker, Brzezinski was no less transfixed than Kissinger by the "deep-seated" U.S.–Soviet competition. He saw no inconsistency between fighting the Cold War with the Soviet Union and "managing interdependence." The world had "entered a phase of political awakening and some disorder," he told *New Yorker* writer Elizabeth Drew in early 1978. "So that the real danger is not Soviet domination but anarchy. The United States has to play an active world role because if it doesn't, I think, there is a high danger the world will fragment in a way that is chaotic." These views were not essentially different from Kissinger's, but the German-American was a master at impressing politicians and columnists and the Polish-American was not. (The German chancellor, Brzezinski noted with surprise, "visibly recoiled when I responded to his 'Zbig' with 'Helmut.' ") It was easy to attribute the anti-Soviet edge to his geopolitical thinking to his being the son of a Polish diplomat of the *ancien régime*. But the professor seemed more concerned with becoming accepted into the American elite than in fighting Old World battles. (He was a "very close" friend to David Rockefeller, he once explained to a reporter, whereas Kissinger had merely worked closely "for" Nelson Rockefeller.) Some German officials considered him insufficiently assimilated, however, believing that his Polish origin made him as congenitally anti-German as anti-Russian.

Perhaps the issue that divided him the most from Vance was his attitude toward the use of force. He did not seem to share the secretary's growing belief that the effective use of military power was far more limited than American leadership had once assumed. Indeed, Brzezinski, while in the university, had been rather free with recommendations to resort to military action. At the height of the Cuban missile crisis he had written McGeorge Bundy a letter urging the immediate bombardment of the missile sites in Cuba. In 1968, writing on the revolutionary turmoil at Columbia University and elsewhere in the industrial world, he wrote, "Force must be designed not only to eliminate the surface revolutionary challenge, but to make certain that the revolutionary forces cannot later rally under the same leadership. If that leadership cannot be physically liquidated, it can at least be expelled from the country." Once in the White House he was more open to military confrontation than Vance or Harold Brown, the secretary of defense. He favored sending a naval task force to the Horn of Africa to impress the Soviets in Ethiopia, though the secretary of defense could not think of what the force would do when it got there. In order to "help stiffen the back of the Administration," he told an interviewer, he drafted a tough speech which the president gave at Wake Forest University, hinting at a military buildup. Brzezinski considered Vance overly concerned about achieving a strategic-arms accord and unwilling to press the Russians hard enough about their military involvement in the Horn of Africa.

3

In the four years of the Carter administration, American and European views on the most critical issues affecting the alliance—what to do about the arms race, how to handle the Soviet Union, how to manage the economies of the industrial world—diverged more deeply than ever. In contrast to Henry Kissinger, who angered the Allies on more than one occasion by ignoring them, Carter infuriated them by his confused attentions. "With Nixon and Kissinger," one British cabinet official put it, "you felt you were in the presence of people who enjoyed governing and were in command. In this administration you never know who is in charge."

Ambivalence in Washington was matched by uncertainty in Europe. Not only were the appropriate policy choices unclear in virtually every field, from the setting of interest rates to the conduct of arms negotiations, there was no common understanding of objective reality. Differing perceptions were particularly striking on the matter of the European military balance and what to do about it. By the end of the decade they would strain the alliance almost to the breaking point.

Since the beginning of the alliance there had always been a gap between the political consensus of national leaders and the daily working assumptions of their military planners. The task of the latter was to prepare for the war which the former assumed could not and would not happen. In the 1970s this gap widened. Political relations between West Europe and the Soviet Union improved dramatically as a consequence of *Ostpolitik* and détente. But the "Soviet threat" defined in purely military terms loomed larger than ever. As the politicians in the United States and Europe warily extended the hand of friendship to the Soviets, along with technology, credit, and expanded contacts of all sorts, generals pored over intelligence reports and maps of the battlefield they were supposed to defend and became increasingly disturbed about what they saw.

In February 1974 and then again at the end of 1976, Senator Sam Nunn of Georgia, a Democratic member of the Senate Armed Services Committee, made an inspection tour of NATO facilities. Four days after Carter's inauguration Nunn and Senator Dewey F. Bartlett, Republican from Oklahoma, issued a report called *NATO and the New Soviet Threat*. The Soviets together with the rest of the Warsaw Pact were "moving toward a decisive conventional military superiority over NATO" as a consequence of a series of changes in the military balance. After the Czechoslovak invasion, the Soviets had increased their forces in the center of Europe by five divisions. They modernized their tanks and brought in more of them. Their tactical aircraft were improved to the point where they were no longer limited to defending the territory embraced by the Warsaw Pact but now represented "a powerful offensive force." All these developments, the senators contended, added up to an entirely new threat: "Soviet forces deployed in Eastern Europe now possess the ability to launch a potentially devastating conventional attack in Central Europe with little warning." Since the planning of the Department of Defense assumed three weeks warning time, strategy must be revised and forces must be "modernized."

From time to time in his 1976 campaign for the presidency, Jimmy Carter had advertised his plans to cut the U.S. military budget by $5 to $7 billion. But within six months of taking office he was making increased military spending the centerpiece of his national security policy. The alliance was already spending $100 billion a year to keep the Soviets out of Western Europe and the United States was paying 45 percent of this bill.

At U.S. urging the NATO governments agreed at a meeting in May 1977 to make annual real increases in defense spending "in the region of 3 percent." In the previous year only Denmark and Belgium had achieved such a growth rate in military spending; the Germans had hardly increased theirs at all. Unless the Europeans were prepared to sacrifice more for defense, Pentagon officials warned, the Kremlin would conclude that NATO did not take the Russian threat seriously and that would weaken the whole deterrent purpose of the very expensive army that had been manning battle stations for a generation and a half.

But while U.S. military planners were worrying about the conventional military balance, German politicians were becoming concerned about nuclear weapons. Here again the anxiety was prompted by a combination of political and military considerations. There had never been such a thing as a European nuclear balance. Since the late 1950s the Soviets had targeted all the large cities of West Europe with their intermediate-range missiles. In Soviet strategy Europe was a hostage; not yet having developed a nuclear force capable of destroying the United States, their threat to Europe was designed to deter a

United States attack on Russia. With the exception of the small French and
British forces, the Europeans had no means of their own to carry out nuclear
retaliation on the Soviet Union. The Americans, it will be recalled, had tried
out various ideas for enhancing the European sense of security, including the
installation of some intermediate-range missiles on the Continent and the prolonged negotiation for a Multilateral Force with European fingers on, or more
accurately, near the button. These innovations served to exacerbate rather
than assuage Allied tensions. Either they were bad weapons in a technical
sense, such as the first-generation "Euromissiles," which took so long to
launch that the Soviets were virtually certain to stage a preemptive attack on
them should the attempt ever be made to fire them, or they were political
monstrosities like the Multilateral Force. In the end a bookkeeping solution
had been adopted. Five nuclear submarines were "assigned" to NATO. They
carried out their missions as before. The missiles could be fired only by the
Americans, but the paper rearrangement was a symbol of America's restated
commitment to put its nuclear arsenal at the defense of Europe.

As the steady Soviet buildup of its nuclear forces proceeded, it was increasingly evident to European leaders that the American "nuclear umbrella"
was becoming less credible. What had seemed shockingly disloyal when De
Gaulle said it in the early 1960s suddenly appeared self-evident: now that the
United States could be annihilated by Soviet hydrogen bombs, a U.S. president
was unlikely to respond to Soviet aggression in Europe with a nuclear strike
on the Soviet homeland. No matter how sincerely suicidal the Americans
sounded, it was not a good bet that they would sacrifice New York and Washington for Munich and Paris.

European military planners wrestled with the gaping hole in deterrence
theory. The answer had been to place large numbers of so-called "tactical"
nuclear weapons in Germany. Since 1962 the United States had maintained
about 7000 nuclear warheads in Europe with another 10,000 that could be
brought in quickly, all at a cost of about $2 billion a year. The weapons were
designed to be fired from artillery, airplanes, and short-range rockets, and their
yield ranged from 1 to 100 kilotons. (The Hiroshima bomb was 13 kilotons.)
As far as the U.S. Army was concerned, such weapons as the Lance missile
first deployed in 1974 were war-fighting instruments. They were to be targeted
on mobile command posts, ammunition supply points, and troop assembly
areas. Special commando units were assigned the task of emplacing some 300
nuclear land mines, including small ones that a single soldier can carry, on
bridges, dams, and tunnels or at airfields and command posts behind enemy
lines. But the growing realization that their use would destroy that which was
to be defended undercut their deterrent effect. Yet the sheer numbers of these
weapons and their wide dispersal throughout the NATO forces were designed
to create the impression that they would be used in a war, despite their implau-
sibility as a weapon of defense in the classic sense of the word. The use of the
nuclear weapons would produce an automatic chain reaction leading rapidly to
the explosion of nuclear weapons on the Soviet Union itself. Thus the physical

presence of vast numbers of nuclear weapons on European soil was an essential part of the "madman theory" on which deterrence now rested.

Weapons systems designed to cement the alliance had from time to time had the opposite effect. In the late 1970s even sharper controversies arose over three new systems, the cruise missile, the Pershing II intermediate-range rocket, and the neutron bomb. European military planners were fascinated with the cruise missile. Invented by the Germans in the Second World War, various versions of the slow, air-breathing guided missile had been in the arsenals of the major military powers for a long time. But in the 1970s technologies that had been successfully applied in civilian life—kitchen blenders, for example—and pursued in the military with less happy results—small flying machines for use by individual soldiers—were combined with the latest advances in radar technology to produce a much longer range, highly accurate, significantly less vulnerable cruise missile that best of all from the European standpoint, looked cheap.

Every weapons system emerges from the drawing boards with a built-in political coalition behind it. The cruise missile engendered more enthusiasm than most because it was a classic application of what Robert Oppenheimer once called "sweet" technology. In January 1977 the director of defense research and engineering, Malcolm C. Currie, called it "perhaps the most significant weapon development of the decade." The cruise missile was at the frontier of lethal science, a virtuoso technological mix that seemed to fit marvelously. Because it was supposedly cheap in that it required no expensive launching pads, it appealed not only to finance ministers but also to the new breed of strategists who regarded the arms race not so much a competition in destructive power—there was more than enough of that—as a competition to make destruction ever more cost-effective. If, in the eerie game that the arms race had become, you could force the adversary to overspend merely to keep up, perhaps someday he might give up.

In the SALT negotiations the Soviets expressed concern about these weapons which could cause great damage to their territory should they be placed in considerable numbers in Europe. Kissinger had proposed putting limits on the range of the cruise missile as an element of his bargain with the Russians. Helmut Schmidt and his advisers, already concerned that the superpowers were deciding the question of European security behind the backs of the Europeans as a by-product of détente, were especially concerned that the cruise missile negotiations infringed on European prerogatives. After all, the weapons were of concern to the Soviets only if they were located within striking distance in Europe. For the Soviets, on the other hand, the distinction between "strategic" and "intermediate range" meant nothing, since both were equally capable of devastating Soviet cities and incinerating Russians.

The Carter administration had come to the conclusion that the enthusiasm of NATO generals and finance ministers for the cruise missile was misplaced. It was not as cheap as it first appeared. It would complicate arms negotiations because the weapon was so small and portable that it was hard to verify its presence, or more important, its absence. Leslie H. Gelb, a third-level State Department official, visited NATO officials in the summer of 1977 with a paper on cruise missiles that Schmidt took as a dash of cold water. Since his advisers had been telling him that the cruise missile was the top priority weapon of the decade, he was annoyed. Another visitor in the autumn of 1977, Paul Warnke, the chief negotiator for SALT, confirmed Schmidt's fears that the United States intended to negotiate limits on the range of the cruise missile. The weapon was to be bargained away by the Americans without participation by the nations for whose sake the European "military balance" presumably existed. The new administration had already given grounds for concern by adopting a top-secret but well-leaked memorandum, PRM-10, which proposed to abandon large areas of Germany in the event of war in order to execute a better conventional defense of the rest.

On October 28, 1977, Helmut Schmidt vented his annoyance with the Americans in a speech to the International Institute for Strategic Studies in London. "Strategic arms limitation confined to the United States and the Soviet Union will inevitably impair the security of the West European members of the Alliance vis-a-vis Soviet military superiority in Europe," the chancellor declared. The main purpose of the chancellor's speech, as Simon Lunn, director of the Military Committee, North Atlantic Assembly, has pointed out, "was to make public his concern that under the bilateralism of the SALT process, certain aspects of European security were being ignored." Schmidt did not mention the need to build up "theatre nuclear forces." Taken literally, the speech was a criticism of U.S. negotiating policy and, seemingly, a bid to participate in some way in the negotiations.

Such blunt criticism was not uncommon for Schmidt; the chancellor had made his career as a defense expert. As early as 1970 he had pointed out that "Soviet superiority in the Central Sector [NATO jargon for Germany] is further reinforced by about 750 medium-range ballistic missiles that have no NATO counterpart." Schmidt had warned the North Atlantic Council, the political directorate of NATO, in June 1977 that "the SALT process may lead to a paralyzation of the Soviet and American central strategic forces and that the strategic nuclear component will become increasingly regarded as an instrument of last resort, to serve the national interest and protect the survival of those who possess these weapons of last resort." America and Europe's strategic interests were now in the process of being "decoupled"; SALT symbolized a balance of terror at the level of intercontinental missiles, but the mutual immunity enjoyed by the superpowers now made the imbalance in Europe all the more serious.

Normally speeches by NATO government leaders are restatements of prevailing strategic orthodoxy or ritualistic expression of enthusiasm for the alliance. Schmidt's was neither. His London speech, which he came to regret, turned out to be the most important of his career. Like Winston Churchill's speech at Fulton, Missouri, in 1946, which proclaimed the existence of the "Iron Curtain," or George Marshall's speech at Harvard a year later on Eu-

ropean recovery, the Schmidt speech had momentous unforeseen consequences. The chain of circumstances Schmidt seemingly triggered in a few
sentences included serious new strains in the alliance, the rise of a huge peace
movement, and the mortal wounding of his own government.

The speech was immediately used by bureaucratic interests in Washington
and in Europe with an interest in developing new "theatre-range" nuclear
missiles. True, the top officials of the Carter administration were cool to the
idea of a buildup in Europe to balance the Soviets. Brzezinski pointed out that
there never had been such a thing as a "Euro-strategic balance." If Europe
had survived years of massive Soviet superiority in middle-range rockets in the
years of the Cold War, why worry about it now in the context of détente,
shaky though it may be? To put easily targeted land-based ballistic missiles in
Europe would give the Europeans no new options, for the control buttons
would still be in American hands. The Soviets would be more nervous because
the flight times would be considerably shorter than the missiles fired from the
"NATO-assigned" submarines in the North Sea, and the new generation of
missiles were far more accurate.

But while Brzezinski and Brown concluded that there was no military
necessity, a rising chorus of weapons experts took a different view. In 1974
the Soviets deployed the Backfire bomber and two years later the SS-20
missile. "The spectre of such weapons grows like a towering cloud over
Europe and Asia," Fred Iklé, the director of the U.S. Arms Control and Disarmament Agency, declared in the closing months of the Ford administration.
The Backfire was supposed to be able to reach the United States with refueling and thus became a thorny issue in the SALT negotiations because the
Soviets refused to count it as a "strategic" weapon. The SS-20, a mobile,
more accurate missile than the earlier SS-4 and SS-5 missiles, was being deployed at the rate of one a week. By the end of the Carter presidency, 180
had been deployed inside the USSR, all but 23 of which were aimed at Western
Europe.

Thus more than the usual coalition of contractors and Pentagon weaponeers were bent on promoting the cruise missile and the deployment of new
intermediate-range missiles in Europe. There had not been a new generation
of nuclear weapons capable of hitting the Soviet Union since the 1960s. Deployment had been thwarted by the Vietnam War, but development continued.
Joining the coalition was General Alexander Haig, the supreme allied commander. The Pershing missile first deployed in 1962 to provide "battlefield
support" (with some warheads thirty times the strength of the Hiroshima
bomb) had been modernized in the years 1969–71. Now, Haig believed, the
missile should be replaced altogether with a Pershing II, but unlike the earlier
generation, which had a maximum range of 400 miles, the new one should have
a range of 1000 miles. Very fast, very accurate, the new generation missile
could hit deep into western Russia.

Because of the European concern about the Soviet missile buildup, the
United States had agreed in May 1977 to the formation of a "High Level

Group." It had its first meeting two weeks before Schmidt's speech. With that impetus it developed a program for European theater nuclear weapons. By the spring of 1979 it had come up with its recommendations, 572 U.S. produced nuclear missiles for Europe: 108 Pershing II missiles and 96 cruise missiles in the Federal Republic, 160 cruise missiles in the United Kingdom, 112 in Italy, and, as befitting their size and anticipated ambivalence about the weapons, 48 each in the Netherlands and Belgium.

As with all weapons systems the number was more of a political estimate of what could be deployed than a scientific calculation of what would produce a "balance." No agency of the U.S. government supported the idea of putting 572 new missiles into Europe with the exception of the Department of Defense, which initially wanted a higher number. Brzezinski, who chaired the Special Coordinating Committee of the National Security Council looking into the matter, declared that there was no military argument for the missiles at all. But putting them in would solve two political problems. It would reassure the Germans that the United States was not compromising their security and thus would elicit more German enthusiasm for SALT. This in turn was essential to head off the hawks in the Senate like Senator Henry Jackson who would use their devotion to NATO as the excuse to reject the arms control treaty with the Soviets, which they deeply distrusted anyway. Brzezinski argued that since the weapons were for political purposes only, one might as well opt for the largest number, for that would give the largest number to bargain away. From the start it was envisioned within the U.S. government that there would be a "two-track" policy, but the emphasis was on the stick, not the carrot. The weapons would be developed; complex political arrangements for their deployment would be undertaken simultaneously with complex negotiations for their abandonment.

For Helmut Schmidt the missiles were important to his political survival. The "two-track" approach seemed to offer a device to keep the ruling coalition together. The Free Democrats were strongly for "modernization" because, as their leader, Foreign Minister Hans-Dietrich Genscher, put it, "the Soviet arms lead with regard to medium range arms is endangering the balance." Pressing the issue appeared to be the road to greater power for the FDP within the coalition. On the other hand, Schmidt's professed concern about the military balance placed him at odds with a substantial number in his own party who were against rearmament and strongly for arms negotiations with the Soviets. All during 1979 Schmidt played to both audiences. Before the SPD Bundestag faction in November 1979 he claimed that the NATO proposal to remove a thousand tactical nuclear warheads from Europe as a unilateral initiative was his idea. But he strongly opposed delaying the deployment of new missiles until negotiations with the Soviets were tried. "In private conversations," Jimmy Carter later noted, "he was very tough in dealing with the Soviet threat, often the leader among Europeans in proposing strong action. But in German political debates he employed the opposite facet of the same question and seemed reluctant to do anything which might be interpreted as

anti-Soviet.'' At the party congress, Helmut Schmidt was overwhelmingly reelected as party leader with the biggest vote ever.

The personal relations between the American president and the Bundeskanzler worsened steadily from their first meeting. Schmidt found it distinctly
unsettling to have the American leader suddenly suggest that ''you and I have
to get the Russians out of Berlin.'' Here is a man, he told his friend Theo
Sommer, the editor of *Die Zeit,* ''who knows everything and understands
nothing.'' Brzezinski assured the president that Schmidt's unconcealed hostility was a simple product of jealousy. After all, the London *Times* had just
called Carter the first real leader of the West since Kennedy. German leaders
tended to be unstable psychologically, Brzezinski explained to the president.
Like Willy Brandt, Schmidt showed signs of being a bit of a manic-depressive.
Perhaps the Chancellor was angry at being rebuffed by Carter when in the
early weeks of the new administration he had offered to act as an intermediary
with Brezhnev. In his private assessment for his diary written in June 1979,
Carter complained ''Helmut is strong, somewhat unstable . . . postures, and
drones on, giving economic lessons when others are well aware of what he is
saying . . .'' When the leaders of the alliance met in Venice a year later,
Schmidt fumed at Carter for having sent a letter he considered insulting which
warned the chancellor not to make any commitment on the missiles in his
private meetings with Brezhnev. Brzezinski attacked Schmidt for publicly
venting his contempt for the president, and the German responded hotly,
''Well, I don't mind a fight. If necessary, one has to criticize.''

Into this nettled relationship had come crashing the neutron bomb. The
enhanced radiation weapon, as it is officially known, had been a favored project of a few enthusiastic weaponeers at Livermore Laboratory since the late
1950s, but was ignored by political leaders and was unknown to the public. A
small hydrogen bomb designed so as to reduce blast effect, the minibomb was
advertised as an ideal antitank weapon because its lethal power was concentrated. It could be safely used in populated areas near the frontier without
causing undue damage to buildings and the surrounding population. Apparently
unknown to either President Carter or Secretary of Defense Brown, $43 million
for the deployment of the neutron warhead had been inserted in the last Ford
military budget, and this item which appeared only in disguised form survived
the change of administration. In mid-1977 a *Washington Post* reporter uncov-
ered the story and the weapon quickly became a public issue. Under pressure
from the new Committee on the Present Danger for being ''soft'' on defense,
President Carter in July 1977 decided that a modest sum for neutron bomb
development was a good political investment.

The neutron bomb soon became the perfect symbol of the bankruptcy of
the arms race. The proponents exaggerated its military advantages. While it
would indeed reduce collateral property damage, it was by no means clear that
its lethal effects could be limited to the battlefield. Moreover, as George Kistiakowsky, who was chief of explosives division at Los Alamos at the time of
the Manhattan Project and a leading adviser on nuclear weapons for twenty-

five years thereafter, put it, tank drivers exposed to radiation would not die immediately but "would know that they are walking dead" and might be expected to fight all the more fiercely for hours and even days before they dropped. The opponents noted that the neutron bomb was another weapon that made nuclear war seem fightable and winnable, that blurred the distinction between conventional and nuclear armaments, and hence made nuclear war more likely. Besides, the Soviets had "dirty" tactical nuclear weapons, too, and would use them in retaliation. But beyond these rational objections was a powerful aesthetic revulsion against a weapon designed to kill people and spare property. Egon Bahr, now executive secretary of the SPD, pronounced the weapon a "symbol of mental perversion." A weapon that destroyed people but left property intact was the ultimate capitalist weapon, Soviet propagandists charged, sensing the unease with which the European public greeted news of the neutron bomb. In Holland a million signatures against its deployment were quickly collected.

The Pentagon now argued that it was all the more essential to deploy the neutron bomb. Soviet propagandists must not be allowed to dictate NATO weapons decisions. Helmut Schmidt had never been enthusiastic about tactical nuclear weapons but he was prepared to lobby the left wing of the SPD in favor of the bomb if Carter wanted it. He told the president, however, that he would deploy the controversial weapon in Germany only in the unlikely event that another European ally would take it too. As the public clamor over the weapon mounted, Carter became increasingly uncomfortable. He told his top advisers, as Brzezinski noted in his diary in mid-August 1977, that "he did not wish the world to think of him as an ogre and we agreed that we will press the Europeans to show greater interest in having the bomb and therefore willingness to absorb some of the political flack or we will use European disinterest as a basis for a negative decision."

After the chancellor had expended considerable political capital in obtaining German acquiescence under these conditions, and an elaborate "scenario" had been begun to defend production of the weapon as a "bargaining chip" in arms control negotiations with the Soviets, Carter suddenly changed his mind. In late March 1978, much to the surprise of his closest advisers, he decided not to produce the bomb. He had a "queasy" feeling, he told Brzezinski, that "his administration would be stamped forever as the administration which introduced bombs that kill people but leave buildings intact" and he wanted a "graceful" way out. But none existed, for the political drama was in its second act and Schmidt and the other principal performers had already delivered their lines. Carter compounded the confusion by delaying his public pronouncement for almost two weeks after he had decided to bring down the curtain on the affair. As Secretary of Vance later wrote, "Politically, the costs were extremely high. The President's standing in the alliance received a strong blow." The fiasco made it essential, as Vance put it, for the Americans to redouble their efforts to restore the unity of the alliance by dealing "firmly" with the issue of theater nuclear forces.

At the Guadalupe summit meeting in January 1979, Giscard was strongly for deploying the new Pershing II and cruise missiles before negotiating with the Russians; otherwise they would not take the West seriously when it came time to talk. Prime Minister James Callaghan of Great Britain, on the other hand, favored talking before spending the money. The reconciliation was the "two-track" notion that the U.S. government had favored from the beginning. Schmidt made it clear that Germany would not take the missiles unless at least one other continental country took them too. Germany could not afford to be singled out as more anti-Soviet than its neighbors. Brzezinski, present as the notetaker for the meeting, expressed his annoyance at Schmidt in his diary. The chancellor was indulging in "melancholy whining" about U.S. nuclear strategy, at once throwing his weight around and expressing West Germany's utter impotence in looking after its own security interests. All during the remainder of the year, NATO bureaucracies churned; memos, studies, and visits followed one another in a rising crescendo. Meanwhile a new Soviet SS-20 was put into position in western and central Russia every few days.

At the NATO meetings in Ottawa on December 12, 1979, the "two-track" decision was officially adopted. All NATO countries agreed to the modernization program if accompanied by arms control negotiations. Norway and Denmark, which had an explicit national policy of refusing nuclear weapons on their own soil, acquiesced in the decision, as did Belgium and Holland, though their representatives made clear at the meeting that domestic opposition to emplacing cruise missiles in the Low Countries was strong. A Soviet campaign to derail the decision had been under way for several months. Beginning with warnings that the new missiles would jeopardize European economic relations with the Soviet Union and Eastern Europe, by October 1979 Brezhnev was offering to stop the further deployment of SS-20s and to negotiate a reduction in its Europe-threatening arsenal if NATO abandoned its plans to "modernize" its forces. He announced a unilateral withdrawal of 20,000 troops and 1000 tanks, but the Soviet defense minister threatened "appropriate retaliatory measures" if the West went ahead with its plans.

As he stepped down from his post as supreme commander at the end of 1979 to survey his presidential possibilities, General Alexander Haig pronounced the NATO modernization decision as "only political expediency and tokenism" and argued that much more rearmament was needed. Other hawkish defense experts, including William Van Cleave and Charles Burton Marshall, thought that the numbers were totally inadequate to provide a serious threat to the Soviets. The idea that they would trade their SS-20s for the new missiles was a little like "a high school football coach hoping to make a player deal with the Dallas Cowboys." Critics in Europe, on the other hand, asked why an American president would be more likely to release missiles in Europe than from a submarine off the coast of Europe. Indeed, did not the whole idea of an "escalation ladder" in which the lower-rung missiles in Europe are fired first suggest a strategy of limiting the nuclear war to Europe?

4

The Trilateral Commission had devoted more attention to energy in its publications than to anything else because the shock to the world oil system was clearly transforming economic relations throughout the industrial world. Jimmy Carter took office convinced that America's oil dependence and its consequences threatened the nation's security more than the Soviet missile buildup or anything else. The energy crisis, he declared in a televised sermon to the nation, was the "moral equivalent of war." But by the time Jimmy Carter succeeded to the presidency, energy had become the most divisive issue in the alliance. The gas lines had disappeared and there seemed to be enough fuel to go around, but the absence of a reliable, affordable energy supply remained the overarching management problem of the world economy. To restore a stable economic order that permitted real growth without horrendous inflation required unprecedented cooperation among the industrial nations on energy matters. But Henry Kissinger had never succeeded while in office in breaking OPEC, and the NATO Allies and Japan were still pitted against one another as consumer nations. By successfully isolating the French and scuttling their efforts to develop an independent European approach to the oil producers, the United States had demonstrated that in confrontations with members of the alliance it still knew how to get its way.

Yet the United States was powerless to bring its vast military might to bear on the Middle East to prevent the damage caused by uncertain oil prices. Nor did it seem able to stop consuming ever greater quantities of imported oil. In the five years since the OPEC revolution, the nine members of the European Community had succeeded in reducing their energy import dependence by 4 percent, but the United States in the same period increased its dependence on imported oil by 32 percent. The one strategy that promised to improve the bargaining position of the West—reducing American imports of Middle East oil—the Carter administration lacked the domestic power to adopt.

The energy crisis was the quintessential trilateral problem and the one that most clearly cried out for a trilateralist solution. But it demonstrated more clearly than any other the reasons for the failure of coordinated technocratic planning for nation-states that compete with one another to stay alive as functioning economies. The problem, as some members of the Trilateral Commission had pointed out, was compounded by domestic politics in every country. The more leaders tried to cooperate with one another, the more each faced opposition at home. In the United States, the Carter energy program was immediately stalemated. Americans continued to use more than twice as much oil per capita as the members of the European Community and to pay about one-third the price. The Chicago Council on Foreign Relations conducted a poll in late 1978 and found that while "opinion leaders" favored raising the price to discourage consumption, an overwhelming margin of Americans opposed even a 25 percent increase.

But political expediency was not exclusively an American problem. The French subsidized the squandering of electricity by keeping it artificially cheap and the British and Germans discouraged use of a plentiful resource by permitting their mining companies to charge twice as much for a ton of coal as the world market price. Yet it was West Germany, though it imported virtually 100 percent of its oil at world market prices, that seemed most adaptable to the eerie new economic order of the 1970s. With few natural resources but its own tightly run export machine—85 percent of its manufactured goods were shipped abroad—the Federal Republic managed to amass the largest monetary reserves in the world, and in the year in which oil prices quadrupled ran a $22 billion balance-of-payments surplus. At the same time Germany was increasing its military forces, developing an armaments industry to lure Arab oil revenues, making more of a show of foreign aid as the United States cut back, and financing its exports with huge loans.

During his first three years in office Helmut Schmidt's natural cockiness was reinforced by Germany's unique record of economic performance. Even before he took the measure of Jimmy Carter, Schmidt had been openly challenging the Americans on economic issues. The Bundeskanzler opposed Kissinger's ideas for economic warfare and political isolation for Portugal and rallied European support against his confrontational tactics against OPEC. Having been reelected in triumph in 1976 and hailed by much of the press as the senior statesman of the Western world, Schmidt had no compunctions about lecturing the new American president on critical energy matters. Action was now particularly urgent as the Carter years began, since Germany's remarkable respite from the winds of recession was coming to an end. The high price of oil had shrunk the volume of world trade and Germany was beginning to feel the effects, for one out of every five jobs depended upon the export market. Inflation, still small by the standards of most countries, was creeping up, triggering that peculiar German panic among finance officials, bankers, and businessmen that baffled their counterparts in the rest of the inflation-riddled capitalist world.

No aspect of the energy problem was more entangled in domestic politics than nuclear power. In the early 1970s the nuclear reactor appeared to be the vehicle for restoring America's unquestioned dominance in the energy field. In announcing Project Independence which called for a major inrease in nuclear reactors, Richard Nixon predicted that nuclear energy would be supplying half of the nation's electricity by the end of the century. Not only would the atom be the key to energy self-sufficiency, it would also provide a major export market. General Electric and Westinghouse, the principal manufacturers of reactors, expected to sell $40 billion a year in nuclear fuel and equipment in Europe. The OECD predicted that Europe would supply half of its total energy needs with nuclear energy by the turn of the century. Japan too was going nuclear. More than fifty new nuclear plants were to be put into operation by the mid-1980s. The government opened negotiations with GE and Exxon for the building of an enrichment plant in Japan. American companies had a com-

manding lead in nuclear technology and the United States was the principal
source of enriched uranium. Unlike the "seven sisters" of oil who were increasingly independent of their home governments, the suppliers of nuclear
energy, handsomely subsidized, to be sure, were subject to considerable direction and control by the U.S. government, for the industry was the child of the
weapons program.

Until 1974, the program that had been launched twenty years before by
Dwight Eisenhower as "Atoms for Peace" was the very symbol of progress.
A clean efficient fuel developed by cracking the mystery of matter instead of
despoiling mountaintops and fouling beaches offered seemingly limitless
amounts of energy. If it was no longer "too cheap to meter," as its enthusiasts
had insisted, it was cheap enough. Every social-democratic government in
Europe was committed to a nuclear future. But by the end of the Nixon administration the outlook for nuclear power in the United States changed radically.
Environmental groups had begun to assemble a long bill of particulars, charging the nuclear industry and the Atomic Energy Commission (AEC) with designing dangerous facilities, minimizing the nuclear waste problem, and
concealing vital information from the public. A number of leading scientists
began raising questions about safety. As delays developed in constructing
plants and orders were canceled by utilities because of the decline in electricity
consumption in the 1975–76 recession, bankers and investors began to worry
about the cost of nuclear energy.

By the mid-1970s the antinuclear movement had become an international
political force. On Washington's birthday in 1974, Sam Lovejoy, a local activist, knocked down a weather-monitoring tower belonging to Northeast Utilities
in Massachusetts to dramatize the point that the nuclear plant about to be built
on the spot was unsafe. Exactly a year later in the little village of Wyhl nestled
among the vineyards of Kaiserstuhl, 28,000 people from all over Germany
appeared about a week after ground was broken for the building of a nuclear
plant. A remnant refused to go home after the demonstration and stayed for
more than a year occupying the site and preventing the plant from being con-
structed. (The successful tactic became the model for the U.S. antinuclear
demonstration at Seabrook, New Hampshire.) Before long there were confrontations between demonstrators and police in the German towns of Brokdorf,
Grohnde, and Kalkar, where tens of thousands gathered to prevent the building
of nuclear plants. The issue split the SPD and gave impetus to a new political
force in Germany that came to be known as "the Greens." No issue since the
Vietnam War had such power to radicalize. Daniel Cohn-Bendit, the veteran
of the May 1968 strike in Paris, now ran for office in Frankfurt on an ecology
ticket. Ten years later, he was no longer Danny the Red, he said, but Danny
the Green:

For me, the ecology movement is an attempt to reformulate all the critiques of society
that have been put forward since the sixties. . . . For me, being an ecologist is not a
reconversion. . . . Ecology comes before the economy. It questions economic industrial
growth, no matter what the type of society, capitalist or socialist. Ideas about revolution, socialism, have to be seen again through the (sun) glasses of ecology. . . .

Throughout Europe ambitious plans for solving the energy crisis with nuclear fuel were revised as organized opposition spread. France, which had the most far-reaching program for nuclear energy of any country in Western Europe, also had the earliest opposition. De Gaulle had tried to develop a purely French gas-cooled reactor as an alternative to the American water-cooled system that would free the country from dependence upon the U.S. multinationals, but his successors abandoned the effort and U.S.–style reactors built under license to Westinghouse and General Electric were now France's long-term answer to the energy problem. The very first antinuclear demonstrations had taken place in France. In 1971 at Fessenheim on the German border, a crowd gathered to try to stop a nuclear plant from going up, and when it was built a few years later it was bombed. The opposition in France appeared to crest in 1977 when more than 60,000 people from all over France and Germany came to Malville, a small village in the Rhone Valley where a fast-breeder reactor was about to be built. This time the government declared martial law and called out the national guard in strength. A thirty-one-year-old high-school physics teacher was killed by a grenade when the soldiers launched an attack on the demonstrators.

The nuclear issue defined the boundaries of the counterculture. Protesters in Europe and America were attacking not only the dangers of radiation, but also government secrecy, high-handedness, deception, and the loss of freedom threatened by a plutonium economy. But in France the Socialist and Communist parties, trying to maintain an uneasy alliance for the 1978 elections, kept their eyes on the traditional economic issues of growth and employment and, with few exceptions, remained equally pronuclear. As François Mitterrand gained in popular support, the Socialists cut into the ranks of the antinuclear movement and it began to fade rapidly. But the opposition had already forced the government to the realization that going nuclear was not as easy as it was once thought to be. Once again "the public" had complicated technocratic plans to solve the trilateralist dilemma.

Because the home market for nuclear reactors had shrunk below expectations, the French and German nuclear industries could not break even without substantial extra revenue from sales of reactors abroad. Thus the state-controlled nuclear monopolies in France and Germany that manufactured nuclear plants under license to the American companies looked increasingly to the Third World as customers. With the price of petroleum spiraling upward, nuclear reactors looked like the answer to the energy needs of poor countries without oil. The chief problem for the recipients of U.S.–style nuclear reactors, however, was dependence upon the Americans for enriched uranium, the fuel needed to turn the reactors into generators of electricity. In 1974, Richard Nixon, in an attempt to force up the world price of uranium, had restricted the amount available to other countries and indicated that the supply might indeed be cut off. The AEC could not fill its extensive back orders for enriched uranium in Europe and the Third World.

Despite the domestic opposition, nuclear energy was more important than ever to their long-term plans, and so Schmidt and Giscard worried about their increasing dependence upon the Americans for uranium. They had seen how the U.S. government had used its monopoly on fuel to influence nuclear programs in other countries. While American business interests were eager to proliferate reactors, the national security establishment worried about the proliferation of bombs. With the right technology reactors could produce weapons-grade fissionable material. The United States, not surprisingly, used its controlling role in the production of energy for peaceful purposes to discourage weapons programs. On this sensitive issue its technological lead carried with it a recognized right to meddle. In the late 1960s the French and Germans had started construction of enrichment facilities of their own, but these would not be ready before the late 1970s. But when they were, France and Germany could become alternative suppliers of nuclear fuel to the Third World. With the Americans looking less and less reliable as a source of enriched uranium, Kraftwerk Union, the German nuclear monopoly, began taking orders in the Third World which the U.S. companies had always assumed were theirs. In 1974, to the dismay of GE and Westinghouse, Iran ordered two reactors from Germany and two from France.

On February 12, 1975, the Federal Republic and Brazil concluded negotiations for the sale of eight reactors at a cost of $5 billion. Not only had the Germans broken into what had been one of Westinghouse's most promising markets—Brazil is a fast industrializing giant of a country with virtually no oil —but to sweeten the deal the Germans were offering two sensitive technologies that would permit the Brazilians eventually to enrich and reprocess their own fuel. Bechtel had sought the order and lost, not only because the U.S. supply of fuel was uncertain but also because the State Department had refused to let Bechtel build the Brazilians their own enrichment plant.

When the terms of the agreement were announced in June, *The New York Times* pronounced the arrangement "nuclear madness." Senator John O. Pastore, Democrat from Rhode Island, took the floor to condemn Schmidt's government for "creating a likely peril in our backyard, while we are heavily engaged in Germany's backyard to defend them against likely peril." The Brazilian military immediately responded that they were not in anyone's backyard, that they had a right to advanced technology if they could pay for it, and the general response in Germany was that the United States was being unsportsmanlike about losing a juicy contract.

Jimmy Carter came to the White House with more ambivalence about nuclear energy than any of his predecessors. This was hardly surprising, for he knew more about it. In the campaign he had made a bid of support from the growing antinuclear movement. Though he would build more of them, he saw the hydrogen bomb as a morally questionable weapon. The goal of "ridding the earth of nuclear weapons," as he expressed in his inaugural address, was a real yearning. The preaching of the environmentalists also struck a responsive chord. He disagreed strongly about the wisdom of a "zero-growth" economy; economic expansion was the key to progress. But conservation and renewable energy sources were better bets than nuclear technology whose

serious hazards he understood from his own experience in the navy with nuclear reactors.

Within three days of taking office, the new president sent Vice President
Walter Mondale to see Schmidt to tell the chancellor that he was "unalterably
opposed" to the Brazilian agreement. The following April Carter announced
his nonproliferation program. "We will defer indefinitely the commercial reprocessing and recycling of the plutonium produced in the U.S. nuclear power
programs." Carter explained that he was not "trying to impose our will on
those nations like Japan and France and Britain and Germany which already
have reprocessing plants in operation." The new measure did not mean that
the Europeans had no access to enriched uranium. For a number of years
France, Germany, and other nations in West Europe had been buying up to
two thirds of their requirements from the Soviet Union! But the Americans
had continuing control of the fuel which they had already supplied, and if they
refused to reprocess it, the huge nuclear expansion planned in Europe would
be jeopardized. Since much of the expansion depended upon increasing use of
the fast breeder reactor, a technology which the administration did not favor
because it is peculiarly dangerous from the point of view of weapons proliferation, it seemed clear that the Americans were trying to restrict the nuclear
programs of its allies. United States policy embodied in the Nuclear Non-
Proliferation Act of 1978 was, as Gunter Hildenbrand, a high official of Kraftwerk Union put it, "designed to maintain the dependence of the importing
countries on the United States through a combined strategy of denying technology and increasing influence on the importing countries' nuclear fuel procurement and waste management programs."

The Germans and Japanese who had large fast-breeder programs ready
were furious. "The Americans sit on 30 percent of the world's coal, and say
there is no economic necessity for Japan to recycle plutonium, and develop
fast breeders," one Japanese official fumed. "We call that hypocrisy." The
suspicion ran high that commercial considerations were behind U.S. policy no
less than national security; in 1978 U.S. firms secured only two out of twenty-
nine foreign orders for nuclear reactors.

France announced it was going ahead with the fast breeder and the European Community denounced Carter's "political embargo." Within a month the
Carter Administration drew back. It could not stop the Brazilian deal. The
most it could do was to press for more "international safeguards" of dubious
value and to secure a conditional pledge from Schmidt and Giscard that they
would suspend further exports of reprocessing technology. Schmidt reacted
angrily against Carter's pressure on the nuclear issue, for he felt Carter's heavy
moral disapproval. There was an insulting suggestion in the American attitude,
German officials felt, that somehow by entering into partnerships to produce
nuclear power, Germany was evading its treaty obligations not to acquire
nuclear weapons.

As far as the alliance was concerned, the energy crisis was not the moral
equivalent of war. Though governments indulged in much rhetoric to the con-

trary, the historic transformation of the world economy was viewed neither in Washington nor Paris nor Bonn nor Tokyo as a common threat against which to take common action. It was rather regarded as a series of crises which each individual government should address by pressing its own comparative advantage, making as few concessions as possible to any other. The energy issue touched people's lives more directly than most and mobilized their fears and anger at a deeper level. Thus in theory it was the perfect issue for trilateral action, but in practice the politicians of the industrial democracies who were severely pressed by their domestic constituencies were unwilling to act on the statesmanlike rhetoric which graced every occasion on which they met.

What was true of the energy crisis was also true of the broader economic crisis that had been left in its wake. Every industrial country was showing symptoms of the new disease of industrial civilization, "stagflation," a condition that defied the wisdom of economists who had built whole theories on the proposition that inflation and unemployment never occurred together. But every industrial country was experiencing disturbing rates of inflation and mounting unemployment. To complicate matters, the timing and the rates differed from country to country. While the rest of the industrial world was battling inflation in the midst of a recession, Germany from 1974 to 1976 was in the midst of an orderly boom. Eighteen months later, the United States was recovering from the recession as its allies began to encounter new economic difficulties. Each was trying to reconcile its ambitious domestic policy goals with the realities of its ever-changing position in the world economy.

The most fundamental message of trilateralism was "interdependence." The industrial nations had to cooperate because their economies were inextricably linked. Though some like Germany and Japan depended more than others on exports, even the United States could no longer isolate itself from the vicissitudes of the international market. Through the operation of multinationals, "the vehicles of interdependence," the U.S. economy was now really a branch of the world economy. Its workers were, like it or not, part of a global labor pool competing with Taiwanese computer assemblers and Japanese autobody welders. The temptation for politicians in the new unsettling world economy was to take all necessary measures to export their inflation and unemployment. Since the early 1960s a neo-mercantilist trend was discernible everywhere. The Japanese, of course, had a reputation for being notoriously protectionist, but the United States, the bastion of economic liberalism, was also applying trade restrictions. Indeed, this very trend, symbolized in the imposing person of John Connally, had sparked much of the original interest in the Trilateral Commission.

If the Carter administration was committed to anything on taking office, it was to the proposition, as Secretary of the Treasury Michael Blumenthal put it ten days after the inauguration, that in solving the problems of unemployment and economic growth "all countries must work together."

The Carter Administration believes strongly in such collaboration and will strive to foster it. Today, for example, it is important that those stronger countries, like the United States, Germany, and Japan, work together to expand as rapidly as is consistent with sustained growth and the control of inflation.

But as a Democratic president, Carter, who had made much of the high unemployment rates, was also committed to economic expansion. He had narrowly defeated an incumbent by attacking Ford's slow recovery from the recession of 1974. Though the Republican administration had left a huge deficit of $66.4 billion, the unemployment rate was still hovering close to 8 percent. The new administration brought the traditional Democratic remedies: a bigger federal budget, tax reduction, and their inevitable consequences, big deficits and rising inflation. In order that the United States should not be the only country to court inflation, thereby pricing its goods out of the world export market, the administration encouraged the Allies to stimulate their economies too. With economic growth in Germany and Japan, there would be money to buy U.S. goods and so reduce the large trade deficits the United States main- tained with its protectorates. Thus when Vice President Mondale went to see Helmut Schmidt a few days after the inauguration, he strongly pushed what the new administration liked to call "the locomotive theory." The way to pull the world out of recession was for the world's three strongest economies to get a new head of steam, and like a supercharged troika, drag the faltering econo- mies of the West and the Third World into prosperity. Since the learning of economists did not provide much guidance any longer, the metaphor of the little engine that could was something to pin one's hopes on. Besides, the theory had respectable lineage. It could be traced to the recommendation of the OECD Secretariat in the summer of 1976 that the United States, West Germany, and Japan simultaneously adopt expansionary fiscal and monetary policies.

Helmut Schmidt was considerably annoyed. He had lectured Ford about running the U.S. economy, but he did not appreciate advice in return. He especially did not like the recommendation that the Federal Republic reflate the economy. In Germany, recommending a little inflation as a cure for any- thing was like recommending cancer. The memory of million-mark loaves of bread sold in the 1920s had made price stability almost a national religion. The Bundeskanzler's press aide explained that Herr Schmidt had been speaking only "theoretically" when he suggested that American economists who pro- pose reflation "should please shut their mouths," and that he certainly meant no criticism when he told *The New York Times* that Carter's inaugural address "was lacking in clear direction." At the London summit meeting in May 1977, the United States scored a paper victory. Germany promised to attain a 5 percent growth rate and Japan a rate of 6.7 percent.

But the Coordinated Reflation Action Program to which the Japanese and Germans reluctantly agreed—its acronym was as well conceived as the rest of the program—was a complete failure. The Federal Republic adopted just enough expansionary measures to serve Schmidt as a convenient explanation for the German recession three years later. The German growth rates fell during 1977 and so did the Japanese. Germany was continuing to run a trade surplus with the United States and Japan a much larger one.

The American attempt to educate the Germans and to interfere in their economy in order to rescue the United States from the consequences of its own past mistakes was bitterly resented. The German message was delivered repeatedly by Schmidt and his colleagues. The problems of the American economy were of its own making; they were neither caused by nor could they be cured by changes in the German economy. The United States was living beyond its means. It had a trade deficit because U.S. companies were no longer competitive. It was continuing to finance the Great Society by printing money. The uncontrolled inflation courted by the new administration set the United States apart from the other industrial nations that knew better than to follow such a course. The United States had no discipline. It could not come up with an energy program that would obviate the need to finance a staggering $45 billion a year in oil imports. Hard work and thrift were the answers to America's problems. It was time for the United States to adjust to the realities of the world economy rather than to continue cajoling other countries to make the world safe for American profligacy.

There was much in the lecture to elicit the agreement of important elements of the U.S. business press, of bankers, and high corporate managers who also worried about the effects of courting a new round of inflationary growth. Not surprisingly, however, Schmidt left out one crucial point: the huge size of the U.S. military budget, a significant portion of which went to maintain over 200,000 troops and 200,000 civilians in Germany.

When the "locomotive theory" failed, the Carter administration adopted a policy of "benign neglect" for the dollar. It was not appropriate, the 1978 Report of the Council of Economic Advisers stated, "to maintain any particular value for the dollar." The Treasury regarded the precipitous drop of U.S. currency on world financial markets with such equanimity that American bankers accused Secretary Blumenthal of deliberately "talking the dollar down" for the depreciation had the effect of making U.S. goods cheaper and more competitive in the export market. But it also accelerated inflation and brought high interest rates, all of which angered the Germans and Japanese. While the leading firms of these countries took advantage of the cheap dollar to buy up or set up factories in the United States, the overall effect of the sinking dollar was disastrous since the price of oil was set in dollars. Beginning in December 1978 the dollar price of oil jumped 120 percent in eighteen months, a process that began well before and was later accelerated by the sharp drop in Iranian oil production in 1980.

The Carter administration shifted gears several times. It roared into office with an expansionary program that harked back to the big-spending years of earlier Democratic rule. When Jimmy Carter left the White House, however, with an annual inflation rate of 17 percent, his off-again, on-again experiments with tight money policy had brought the prime rate to an unprecedented 20 percent. The wild gyrations in U.S. economic policy made it difficult for the other industrial nations to manage their own economies. Confidence in the dollar was so shaken that the price of gold rose from $431 an ounce on December 10, 1979, to $850 on January 21, 1980.

Instead of exerting pressure on its allies to modify their domestic economic policies, the United States now found itself submitting to foreign pressures backed up, to be sure, by conservatives at home. The angry complaints of central bankers and finance ministers were important in helping to decide the Carter administration to adopt anti-inflationary, tight money policies at home and with the help of foreign credits to stabilize the dollar. In no small measure did the pressure from America's principal protectorates transform Jimmy Carter into the most conservative Democrat in the White House since Grover Cleveland.

It was easy to make fun of Carter's impressionistic, unpredictable approach to the gathering economic storm, but the truth was that no one quite knew what to do. Within months Germany's own situation would look so precarious that lectures from the economics professor in the chancellor's bungalow could be safely ignored. It was a bitter and expensive irony that an administration so committed to trilateral cooperation should prove such an unsteady partner, but the managers of every industrial society were so preoccupied with taming their own unpredictable economies that the spirit of cooperation was lacking everywhere. More obviously than in earlier economic crises, this one seemed bigger than the sum of its parts, for the world economy was now operating by rules no one understood.

5

With the failure of the "locomotive" and "benign neglect" strategies to solve the U.S. trade deficit, the Carter administration turned toward protectionism. This was no small irony, considering that many of the trilateralists now in power had made their reputations on the evils of protectionism. Richard N. Cooper, the Yale economics professor whom Carter selected as under secretary of state for economic affairs on the strength of having written a number of studies for the Trilateral Commission, expressed the standard liberal view upon taking office. "Imports are a natural scapegoat for what is basically deficient total demand," he told a Senate subcommittee in March 1977. "Import restrictions, however, will never work collectively—unemployment will only be exported." Early in his term Carter rejected the recommendations of the International Tariff Commission to set import quotas for color television sets and shoes. But domestic pressures mounted. Thousands of layoffs occurred in the steel industry; 5000 workers in just one plant in Youngstown, Ohio, received notices on a Friday afternoon not to come in the following Monday. U.S. Steel charged that the entire Japanese steel industry was engaged in "dumping," selling below cost in the United States to steal the market. George Meany, the president of the AFL-CIO, cried, "Free trade is a joke and a myth. And a government trade policy predicated on old ideas of free trade is worse than a joke—it is a prescription for disaster."

Ever since the EEC was established in 1958, the United States had managed to maintain a favorable balance of trade with the Community every year but one; this continued into the first year of the Carter administration when, despite the strong protectionist stance of the EC Common Agricultural Policy, 28 percent of the U.S. agricultural exports ended up in Europe. But Germany by itself maintained a substantial trade surplus of $3 billion even as the mark grew stronger and the dollar weakened. The Federal Republic spent an equivalent sum between 1974 and 1977 on U.S. arms which helped to prevent a much larger trade imbalance, for as German officials complained, the United States did not reciprocate. Despite declarations of intent at NATO meetings to internationalize weapons procurement, the United States bought virtually no German arms at all. The Pentagon rejected the Leopard tank, the pride of the German arms industry, on the grounds that it did not meet American standards, but the Germans believed with some justice that the real problem was its failure to meet the needs of the powerful U.S. weaponsmakers' lobby.

For the Federal Republic the United States was an important but not overwhelmingly important trading partner; it did more business with Belgium than with the United States. In 1976 Volkswagen put up a large factory in Westmoreland County, Pennsylvania, and by the late 1970s German multinationals were investing more in the United States than American firms were investing in Germany. The German economic threat was seen by some Carter administration officials as involving much more than the trade deficit. Schmidt was playing an increasingly independent role in organizing a European Monetary System and in providing leadership for the European Community's efforts to develop a system of trade preferences with vast areas of the Third World. All this threatened to shut out U.S. firms in the future. When the Carter administration had proposed a kind of "special relationship" for the United States and Germany to coordinate the management of the world capitalist economy, Schmidt politely refused.

The trade problem with Japan was of an entirely different order. In 1978, the U.S. trade deficit with the island economy, now the world's second largest, was almost $12 billion. More than 40 percent of this staggering figure was represented by Japan's recent dramatic capture of a large segment of the U.S. automobile market. Similar Japanese successes in capturing a big share of the steel market, in becoming a major supplier of color televisions for American families, and in threatening the U.S. giants in the semiconductor and computer business at the very frontier of technology put the trade issue on the front pages of American newspapers. The new challenge, coming at a time of mounting unemployment, threatened the U.S. economy at a number of its weak points simultaneously, and thus made the flurry over textiles that had so excited the Nixon administration look inconsequential by comparison.

Japanese economic success began to touch a raw nerve in the late 1970s, and by the end of the Carter era the new economic superpower of the East was stirring up panic. "People are starting to slit tires and throw rocks through dealer's windows," a Republican congressman representing the Mahoning Valley of Ohio reported his constituents' feelings about Japanese cars. "I can feel the anger, I know these people." His district had been devastated by the consequences of Japanese industriousness and American neglect. The steel industry in the valley once employed 68,000 workers, now only 10,000. The workers' credit union at one plant refused to finance Japanese cars. At the Teledyne plant in Milwaukee, workers tore down a Japanese flag hung in honor of a visiting Japanese businessman. Cartoons of buck-toothed Japanese pilots "bombing" the United States with cars, TVs, and cameras appeared in a couple of nationally circulated magazines. With more than 200,000 auto workers lining up each week for unemployment relief or on welfare, Congressman John Dingell of Michigan laid the blame on "those little yellow people" who seemed to know how to make better cars than they made in Detroit.

Other politicians evoked the latent anti-Japanese feelings of the Second World War generation more subtly. Running for president in 1976, John Connally had threatened to shut the Japanese out of the U.S. market, whipping up the crowds by picturing the Asians "sitting on their docks in Yokohama in their Toyotas, watching their Sonys. . . ." Unlike Europe where most of the U.S. elite that had managed the bipartisan foreign policy since the war felt at home, Japan was either a blank page or an unpleasant wartime memory. He had been shot down twice in the war by the Japs, one corporation president snapped at a *New York Times* reporter, and he didn't intend to be shot down in peacetime by predatory competition. A Yale professor of Japanese studies, Hugh Patrick, called on by the Carter administration for advice was shocked that U.S. officials seemed to share these feelings. "I heard things that I thought were behind us—the notion that the Japanese were somehow not to be trusted, that the Japanese weren't really important to us, and the only thing they understood was force." Despite the thirty-five-year-old alliance, U.S. experts on Japan were few in number, and none of them held top positions in the government or in the leading banks and corporations.

Japan's emergence as a serious economic challenge to its protector was particularly traumatic largely because the Americans were not paying attention to what was happening to this distant ally. As late as 1956 Japan was an agricultural country; 40 percent of the population were farmers. The island chain was an economic as well as military protégé. The U.S. government had helped the Japanese to enter the European market. United States corporations had licensed advanced technology in hundreds of fields. Neither action, to be sure, was motivated by altruism, but both reflected the comfortable assessment that Japan was a pupil, not a teacher, a nation to be helped, not feared. But each year between 1950 and 1977 Japan's economy grew at a rate double that of the United States and by 1978 its output, by some estimates, surpassed that of the Soviet Union. The following year Professor Ezra Vogel of Harvard wrote a book *Japan as Number One,* making the case that the Asiatic power was headed for the hegemonic position in the world economy, one of a welter of books purporting to teach the lessons of Japanese success. Several became best-sellers. The sudden awareness of the new superpower bred a new interest in Japanese culture. United States publishers made arrangements to introduce Japanese authors to an American audience. Japanese film festivals and film criticism became fashionable. Classic Kabuki theater, of interest to a few aficionados only a few years earlier, was a sellout at the Kennedy Center in Washington.

The Japanese were more worried than flattered by the new attention. The American export market was absolutely "vital to our survival," Prime Minister Masayoshi Ohira told a European visitor with obvious feeling and concern. If the Americans ever did make good on the threats of demagogic politicians to close off the U.S. market, it would spell ruin. You do not understand the precariousness of Japanese prosperity, officials and academics would tell visiting businessmen and correspondents from the United States. Japan must export or die. Because of dietary changes associated with affluence—meat and dairy products consumption had tripled in twenty years—the country imported half of its food. Virtually all of its oil, about 75 percent of its coal and natural gas, 90 to 100 percent of its nickel, iron, tin, bauxite, zinc, all its cotton and wool, more than 60 percent of its lumber—in short all but a fraction of its natural resources—were imported. To pay for it the country had to export on a grand scale.

Much of the rancor felt in the United States at the Japanese takeover of major segments of the American market sprang from a sense of failure. In the auto and steel industries the Japanese scored successfully by filling needs which American entrepreneurs were unwilling or unable to meet. The motorcar was the quintessential American product. The mass-produced automobile was invented and improved in the factories of Ford, GM, Chrysler, and by companies long defunct like Studebaker and Hudson that once were household words. At the end of World War II the big U.S. automakers set out to conquer a great slice of the world market. As the 1980s began, despite the huge rise in auto use across the planet, the U.S. home market still had 40 percent of the world's registered automobiles. Postwar America was a country designed for the automobile like no other. Seventy percent of American workers drove alone to work and back. (The car poolers, the walkers, and the users of mass transit made up just under a quarter of the work force, according to the Bureau of Census.) The government subsidized the automobile economy by keeping gas cheap, taxes on cars low, and providing an unparalleled network of interstate highways the use of which was mostly free.

In 1928 Shōtaro Kamiya, the man who forty years later would engineer Toyota's hugely successful sales campaign in the United States went to work for GM. In that year the number of cars in Japan barely exceeded the number of rickshaws. By the end of the Second World War the Japanese auto industry, which had been producing mostly military vehicles, was in ruins; in 1946 Japan manufactured 110 passenger cars. Contrary to the prevailing American myth, the Japanese government did not launch the postwar car industry. A handful of imaginative entrepreneurs and engineers started making cars over official opposition. "It is enough for Japan to manufacture trucks only," the governor of the Bank of Japan declared. "Stop manufacturing passenger cars in Japan." In 1951 MITI (Ministry of International Trade and Industry) did take a hand in protecting, rationalizing, and financing the industry. The import of foreign auto technology was made easy, the import of competing cars from abroad difficult, and foreign investment in Japan's growing auto industry was made impossible. MITI, never bullish on the industry, tried to induce Japan's eleven automakers to consolidate themselves into three giants. But Japanese carmakers refused, and unlike the rest of the world where increasing concentration in the industry seemed inexorable, the biggest automotive producers in Japan lost some of their share of the market to newcomers.

In the United States, on the other hand, about the only cars imported before World War II were a few Rolls-Royces and Ferraris. In the postwar years, when Americans began to buy imports in greater numbers, Volkswagen dominated the imported car market. But in 1975 Toyota, which ten years earlier had sold a mere 3000 cars in the United States, pushed ahead of Volkswagen and became the number one seller of foreign cars in the United States. In 1975, 800,000 Japanese cars were sold. Four years later the number had increased by a million. Japanese imports now accounted for more than 20 percent of the U.S. market.

The Japanese had gambled that the era of cheap oil would not last forever and that even Americans would have to outgrow the gas guzzler. United States firms had stuck too long to the position once expressed by Henry Ford that "mini-cars make mini-profits." The second energy crisis of 1979 was the moment when millions of Americans first came to believe that gas prices would keep going up and that small cars were a necessity. The Japanese knew how to make them well and they were available. Just as the crisis began there were 850,000 unsold Japanese cars piled up on U.S. docks.

How did it happen that the world giants of the industry had been so damaged in their own home markets? They had clearly made mistakes in underestimating the good sense of the American consumer. It was tempting to blame the disaster on Japan's special advantages, government subsidies and cheap labor. But the auto industry was not subsidized and as a 1979 article in *World Motors* reported, "Labour costs per head in Japanese car firms have been higher than most European (except West German) firms and almost as high as American manufacturers for at least (the last) three years." (Nonwage costs in Japan, such as subsidized lunches, recreation, and so forth, are much higher than in the United States.) Japanese companies had seen a need which American carmakers had not seen until it was too late. Honda had done the same thing in developing light recreational motorcycles, a market which the lone U.S. maker, Harley-Davidson, had ignored.

In other fields such as steel the Japanese, like the Germans, were the unintended beneficiaries of U.S. Air Force bombs dropped in World War II.

Stodgy U.S. companies with a near monopoly hold on the market, like U.S. Steel, did not modernize their plants. Starting from scratch the Japanese installed the most modern and productive facilities with American help. Of the world's twenty largest blast furnaces, fourteen were in Japan. In color TV, the decisive factor behind Japanese success was quality. According to an industry expert writing in the December 1978 issue of *Quality Progress,* "During the middle 1970's the first Western color TV sets were failing in service at a rate of about five times that prevailing in Japanese sets." Matsushita bought out Motorola's color television. Sanyo took over Whirlpool's television operation. By 1977 only 30 percent of the value of color television sets sold in the United States represented work done by U.S. labor.

Beleaguered U.S. industries, like the steelmakers and the color TV manufacturers, charged that the Japanese were conquering the market by "dumping" their goods in the United States below cost. The business consultant Peter F. Drucker called it "conducting a gigantic clearance sale abroad." No doubt there was some truth to the charge, but dumping was hard to prove and even harder to police. The industries took their Japanese competitors to court for a protracted battle with more than $1 billion in damages at stake.

The official position of the Carter administration, like that of its predecessors, was that the Japanese trade imbalance was due to unfair competition at home as well as abroad; U.S. firms were being unfairly excluded from the Japanese market. Yet in the 1970s Japan had sharply reduced its high tariffs; at the end of the decade the average rate on dutiable goods was 6.9 percent, a little less than the levels in the United States and the European Community. The number of import products subject to quotas had been reduced from 500 to 136 as far back as 1964. By 1979 only 27 quotas remained at a time when the United States had quotas on 23 products. Yet three of the Japanese quotas were on products of great concern to domestic U.S. industry: oranges, beef, and manufactured leather goods. (Import quotas for oranges are treated in Japan as rewards for contributions to the ruling Liberal Democratic party. There are clearly local profits to be made. A box of Sunkist oranges that yields $4 to the California grower is sold retail in Japan for $88.) For the Japanese government the hardest American charge to rebut is that relating to the unfair use of nontariff barriers. Certain products have to be tested in Japan, a requirement considered onerous by U.S. companies. Health and safety regulations have been used to keep products out. Americans even argued at one point that the Japanese language constituted a trade barrier!

In dealing with the mounting American rage, Japanese officials were torn between making soothing promises and offering rebuttals that wounded American pride. One reason, according to MITI, the Japanese were more successful in the U.S. market than the Americans were in the Japanese market is that they tried harder. There were in 1979, 20,844 Japanese salesmen in the United States and a U.S. sales force in Japan of fewer than 2000. The Japanese studied the U.S. market as if it were a military objective. Until the late 1960s most U.S. firms dismissed the Japanese market. The people were too poor to make promising consumers. In the early 1960s, an article in *Fortune* conceded, U.S. color TVs were superior to the Japanese and could undersell Japanese TVs by $150 a set. There was no import quota and the tariff was not onerous. But the U.S. companies failed to invest and lost a potential market. There were many businessmen in Japan who had spent their lives studying the U.S. market. United States companies had few who knew enough of the language to understand Japan, although, as one Japanese official acidly remarked, one does not have to be a linguist to know that it would help to sell American cars in Japan (which follows Britain's rule of the road) if they came equipped with right-hand drive.

For Jimmy Carter, Japanese trade was a no-win issue. His supporters were bitterly divided on what to do. The multinationals already safely ensconced behind tariff walls around the world clung to the true religion of the free traders. The failing industries which felt the heat of Japanese competition, including the auto companies and their allies, the backbone of the U.S. economy, were becoming almost as protectionist as organized labor. The president entrusted the negotiations with the Japanese to Robert Strauss, the former Democratic party chairman, a Lyndon Johnson protégé with a reputation for being tough. Secretary of Defense Harold Brown, who had already decided to remove U.S. troops from South Korea, was reported to have told visiting Japanese that the United States might withdraw from the whole area, a punishment, as the Japanese saw it, for their trade practices. Richard Rivers, a third-level official with a low-key manner, was sent to Tokyo to lobby for a bigger Japanese growth rate and other concessions. The hapless bureaucrat became a pawn in a complex domestic drama:

Japanese bureaucrats leaked a stream of reports of the meetings in order to influence their internal policy debate. Those in the Ministry of Finance who opposed greater deficit spending portrayed Rivers as absolutely outrageous, hoping perhaps to generate a nationalist backlash. But MITI and Gaimusho officials sympathetic to some of the proposals also painted Rivers as a "bad guy": they wanted to intensify the sense of U.S. pressure, and thus its power in generating policy change. And the Japanese dailies, themselves interested in shaking up the government on economic policy, further amplified the reports.

For some parts of the Japanese establishment the rougher the American pressure the better it facilitated their own domestic objectives. Appearing to bow to the United States, Prime Minister Fukuda reshuffled his cabinet to give more power to individuals who reputedly favored the expansionist and liberal economic policies demanded by the Americans. Having made such an extraordinary "concession," he could then afford to take a tougher position on the trade issues.

In July 1977 Strauss had succeeded in negotiating an Orderly Market Agreement by which Japan "voluntarily" limited its export of color television sets to the United States. It amounted to a negotiated quota, a device used later for automobiles and other products. In January 1978 after tough bargaining, the Japanese signed an agreement with a promise to reflate the economy, so that Japanese consumers could buy more American products, but the goal of a 7 percent growth rate was not reached and a pledge "to achieve basic equity in . . . trading relations by affording . . . substantially equivalent competitive opportunities . . ." was a paper victory that guaranteed American business almost nothing. A few tariffs were reduced. Ten thousand tons of Texas beef were elbowed into Japanese hotels. The trade issue receded from the headlines for a few months but the anger in America did not. William Safire, a *New York Times* columnist in a scurrilous aside, compared the Japanese handshake that sealed Strauss's agreement with the smiles and assurances of the emperor's envoys who visited Secretary of State Cordell Hull on the day before Pearl Harbor.

Japanese competition undeniably hurt and it hurt more because it was so unexpected. But the anger was compounded of something more than racism and wounded pride. The Japanese success dramatized the crisis of American values. The success of Japan's carmakers, steelmakers, and computer salesmen in Japan was felt in America not only as an economic loss but as a cultural defeat. The achievements, against great odds of the economic superpower, were attributable, the rush of books, reports, and TV documentaries confirmed, to the celebration of precisely those Benjamin Franklin values now honored in the breach in the United States. The Japanese, for all the feudal aura that still hung over the society, were magnificent capitalists who understood the mysteries of accumulation. One-third of the nation's output went to fuel the accumulation process, while in the United States only one-sixth went for investment. Individual Japanese saved at a rate three times that of the Americans who had been feeding their prosperity on bank loans and credit cards.

The emphasis on education and information as the key to success harked back to American attitudes of an earlier time. The Japanese record of higher productivity, higher motivation among workers, and efficiency represented an appropriation of what once were thought to be peculiarly American virtues. It was humiliating that the Japanese could buy coking coal in West Virginia, ship it 12,000 miles to Japan, and use it to manufacture steel that could "undersell steel made 75 miles from West Virginia with the same raw material."

The more Japanese cars appeared on U.S. highways, the more it became fashionable not only to attack but to idolize Japan. Japanese workers, many observers noted, seemed to care about the corporation for which they worked and to take pride in the product they made. Rosy descriptions of Japan as a workers' paradise now appeared in U.S. business magazines. But less than 40 percent of Japanese employees had a guarantee of "lifetime employment"; for most life was hard and no more secure than in the United States. Yet Japan seemed to be a real community with a sense of national purpose that had been lost in the United States. "Personal freedom, autonomy, and independence are the highest values for Americans," American sociologist Robert Bellah has noted, confirming with a team of interviewers what de Tocqueville observed

150 years ago. "We place a high value on being left alone, on not being interfered with. The most important thing is to be able to take care of yourself." The Japanese, on the other hand, had built a society in which individuals to a much greater extent identified their personal welfare with the success of their corporation and the prosperity of the nation.

In the process they seemed to have perfected what economist David Gordon calls "the social structure of accumulation" by developing an incentive system rooted in an understanding of deep human need. Business school researchers in the United States discovered that far more employee suggestions were offered in large Japanese companies and a much higher percentage are adopted than in U.S. corporations. The Japanese were less entangled in corporate bureaucracy. "There are five layers between the first line workers and the chairman at Toyota, and there are 17 at Ford," Stanford Business School professor Thomas J. Peters noted. The Japanese had designed the corporation of the future with "Honda workers racing around straightening out windshield wipers in their spare time while General Motors workers sit silently watching a piece of junk go by," and it seemed the ultimate assault on American self-esteem.

As the 1970s ended Ronald Reagan was bringing audiences to their feet across America by holding up the vision of a future copied from the nation's past. His was a picture of a small-town America in which the rugged individualists who ran GM or IBM or worked for them—the differences were unimportant because we were all Americans—enriched the country by looking after themselves. But in the nation's leading universities and business research organizations a different note was being struck: If the United States were to avoid being outclassed by Japan, it must imitate Japan, for it was in Japan that the contours of twenty-first-century capitalism were being designed. The "lessons" were more government involvement with business, not less, better welfare and education, not less, more harmonization of class interests instead of government of, for, and by the rich.

6

One important purpose of the Trilateral Commission was to develop a common strategy of the industrialized powers toward the Third World, the vast regions of the planet that once were colonies where the wretched of the earth made their home. Here rather than in Europe was the likely theater of war between the superpowers. The regions had witnessed continuous warfare since the Europeans had stopped fighting one another; there had been more than 25 million casualties since 1945. Here were billions of people and most of the world's natural resources. Somehow it all had to be integrated into the world capitalist system if that system were to grow. Population had stabilized throughout the industrialized world. The big new potential markets were in Asia, Africa, and Latin America.

Beginning in the 1950s the United States committed itself to the goal of developing the underdeveloped world not only for national security purposes —keeping a lid on violence and keeping the Soviets out—but also in the interests of capitalist expansion. The American strategy was based on the success of the Marshall Plan. Massive amounts of economic aid would be transferred in such a way as to trigger economic development in poor countries. However, the results were disappointing. Growth rates were slow and the process of development uneven; as countries grew richer according to the measurements of economists, hundreds of millions of people remained mired in poverty which was now more of a political problem than ever because the gaps between rich and poor were widening. The United States assumed a policeman's role for a large beat that had once been the responsibility of European empires, but despite some conspicuous short-term successes in places like Iran (1953) and Lebanon (1958) could neither keep order nor set the terms of domestic development.

In the 1950s and 1960s Britain and France lacked the resources to emulate the United States in state philanthropy. Their efforts were concentrated on repairing and strengthening economic relations with their former colonies. The United States watched while the European Community adopted the Lomé Convention, a trading agreement with more generous terms for the Third World than the United States was normally willing to accept; but while some in the U.S. government worried about the creation of trading blocs from which the United States might well be excluded, it was not a "front-burner" issue. The NATO commitment, as everyone interpreted it in practice, did not require cooperation outside of Europe.

In the 1970s the Third World assumed dramatic new importance in the capitals of every industrialized nation. The rise of OPEC heralded the possibility for an even larger shift of economic power. Other resource-rich nations might well imitate what the Arabs had done. Inspired by OPEC's success and the realization that the conventional development strategies of the West would never solve their problems, the poor nations became a vocal force. In November 1974 the United Nations in which poor countries now held a large majority, adopted a Charter of Economic Rights and Duties of States which cut into the traditional prerogatives of the industrialized countries. Though the charter had no binding legal effect, the poor nations demanded "a new international economic order" in which the industrialized world would negotiate concessions on a wide variety of economic issues. In order to reverse the unfavorable economic trends that had kept so much of the Third World poor, the rich nations should agree to stabilize higher prices for natural resources, to provide easier credit, and to give preferences to goods produced by their infant industries, to use the term American protectionists coined in the last century for Massachusetts shoe factories and Carolina textile mills.

Under Kissinger the United States initially took an unrelenting hard line on these demands. Daniel P. Moynihan and John Scali, the U.S. ambassadors to the UN, heaped scorn on the "tyranny of the majority" that would assault the fundamental notions of private property. The poor nations were insisting on something for nothing. They lacked the military and political clout to take it and their moral position to demand it was weak.

The leaders of the European Community shared these views by and large, but their dependence upon the Third World for raw materials was much greater. Moreover most of France's and Britain's overseas investment was in their former colonies. Most of the French multinational subsidiaries were in French-speaking Africa and the British were heavily invested in the Commonwealth nations. All this investment was at risk if the newly independent nations should choose to exercise their sovereign right to expropriate it. Being more vulnerable to Third World pressures than the United States, Schmidt and Giscard counseled a more subtle policy than confrontation. The United States managed to isolate itself by its harsh rhetoric. At a meeting of the UN Industrial Development Organization, the United States cast the sole negative vote against such principles demanded by the developing nations as improved terms for the transfer of technology.

In a series of fruitless conferences between the industrialized states and the developing nations, the rich countries diverged somewhat in rhetoric, but the basic stance was the same. The substance of the Third World demands were opposed. West Germany no more than the United States was prepared to meet what Minister of Economics Hans Friderichs termed "these extremely far-reaching demands," such as revising the International Monetary Fund to give poor countries more credit or introducing notions such as indexing into international trade. (The poor countries argued that since the price of primary agricultural products declined even as the price of the imported machines needed to cultivate them rose, the two should henceforth be tied by agreement.) The German economics minister, echoing American arguments, contended that such innovations "would imply a dismantling of the market-based international economic system and its replacement by a largely dirigistic structure." Japan was a bit more forthcoming in the matter of commodities and agreed to make a contribution to a common fund to stabilize the market if such could be agreed upon, all the while reasserting its strong belief in the market system as the most efficient allocator of resources.

The UN had voted that the industrialized countries should agree to the goal of giving 0.7 percent of their GNP in the form of "overseas development aid." The United States refused to accept such a goal, although it came closer to meeting it in practice than did most of its alliance partners who did accept it. France, which consistently adopted the most accommodating rhetoric of the industrialized nations, also showed the best aid record of the big countries, but this was somewhat deceptive. Almost half went to technical and financial support (salaries for French teachers and engineers). Over half the goods transferred to poor countries under the program had to be procured in France.

On no cluster of issues was the perceived common interest of the rich countries clearer. The international order was already in crisis. To be sure Denmark and the Netherlands, the latter particularly under the influence of the church, had adopted a generous development program. A minority in every developed country had been touched by watching TV reports of the horrendous famines in the Sahel and elsewhere. Some of the charges of Third World oratory had rubbed off on middle-class Europeans and Americans and elicited a certain amount of guilt. But every industrial country faced severe financial problems and unemployment. To talk about transferring wealth to the poor countries when the populations of Europe and America were hardly in a philanthropic mood seemed utterly utopian to the politicians in virtually every rich country.

Willy Brandt, Edward Heath, and other prominent Europeans and Americans developed the Brandt Report, a document which argued that the long-term interests of capitalist expansion required more generous terms for the Third World. The customers of the future were in the Third World, and they could not play that role unless their incomes rose. That could not happen without some change in the world economic arrangements that kept them poor. Indeed, some development economists argued a "locomotive theory" in reverse. The only places on earth where rapid economic growth could be expected were in a few dynamic economies of the Third World. Everything should be done to encourage this growth so that the South Koreas and Taiwans might pull the world economy out of its rut. A Marshall Plan for the potential winners in the Third World could usher in the next stage of capitalist growth.

The Trilateral Commission had taken the view that in the sweep of history "North-South" issues were more important than East-West issues. As far as the alliance was concerned, they were certainly less divisive. The unstated assumption behind the Trilateral Commission that the industrialized nations had a strong common interest in facing down the demands of the Third World had proved correct. At the level of global negotiations the partners would stick together. However, as the world moved closer to regional trading blocs which cut across the political relations represented by the alliance, the day-to-day strategies of the partners diverged. The West Europeans, particularly concerned about access to minerals, sought to draw such countries as Zaire and Zambia into the European Community, not only to drive a wedge between them and CIPEC, an OPEC-like organization of world copper producers, but also to compete with U.S. influence in the region.

Increasingly, arms became the instrument for carrying on the competition. Beginning in the early 1970s the French started selling Mirage fighters to Peru, Brazil, and Argentina. Latin America had long been an exclusive captive market for U.S. cast-off weapons. The Carter administration tried to stem the tide of advanced military technology that was pouring into the Third World in the late 1970s by making agreements with its partners who were major weapons suppliers, chiefly France and Britain, not to introduce new lethal technologies into such regions, but France, Germany, and Britain considered it essential to establish influence through arms. By selling AWACS and the advanced F-15 fighters to Iran and Saudi Arabia, the United States, they argued, had violated its own precepts. Beyond the powerful urge to secure some influence over the oil market with arms, Britain and France, and increasingly the Federal Republic, were becoming dependent upon arms sales to put idle factories to work, particularly in the aerospace industry and in the shipyards. France stepped up its sales to Latin America, and the Federal Republic, which had been circumspect about selling arms in "areas of tension," sold five submarines to Chile.

By the end of the 1970s it was becoming clearer that the EC and the United States had increasingly competitive interests in the Third World. The European nations exported 60 percent more to the poor nations and imported 73 percent more than did the United States. European investment in the Third World manufacturing sector, according to one study, "matched, if not surpassed," that of the United States. Even in Latin America, a study by the economist Constantine Vaitsos concluded, "West European–controlled firms in the mid-1970's were closely rivaling those of US firms."

The non-American multinationals were more open to taking minority positions in local subsidiaries and to sacrificing short-term return in the hope of developing long-term stable relationships in the local economy. While these private corporations sought to be less obtrusive overseas than U.S. companies, they also counted more on help from their own governments. The Japanese and French governments embarked on a worldwide campaign to acquire ownership of foreign uranium and copper reserves. Some of these foreign mines were government-owned. Others were privately developed with large government loans. In a feverish effort to develop the small mineral base in the home island, Japan conducted a comprehensive national exploration program and then subsidized development by domestic companies. Schmidt's government subsidized West German companies up to two-thirds of the cost for overseas uranium exploration. Thus while they talked a common language of capitalism as they faced the developing countries side by side in the "North-South dialogue," the alliance partners had quite different notions in practice of how to act in a world market economy.

7

As the 1970s came to an end, it was becoming clearer that, with respect to the Third World, the alliance partners had common interests but divergent strategies. But when it came to taking action against the common enemy that had summoned the alliance into existence, the interests of the partners now more and more diverged. Of course all were agreed that a balance of power was needed to discourage the Soviet Union from making war. All considered Soviet expansionism a potential threat. All viewed the capitalist system, representative democracy, and the other common institutions of "the West," with all their problems, as the hallmark of a morally superior civilization and certainly more effective vehicles for producing wealth than the bureaucratic Socialism of the Soviet Union.

But a credo and a strategy are not the same. These shared beliefs in the United States, Europe, and Japan were never stronger than in 1979, but there were profound differences on how to achieve a balance of power, or for that matter what constituted power. Above all, there were differences about what sort of challenge the Soviet Union represented and what should be done about it. Scarcely three years earlier the worry in Bonn had been the embrace of the superpowers. But so quickly had the infatuation cooled that the growing chill between Moscow and Washington raised anxieties in Europe. Helmut Schmidt worried about Carter's inability to conclude an arms agreement with the Soviet Union for the same reason he had worried about Kissinger's idiosyncratic view of détente. A reversion to the Cold War confrontation dismembered Europe as much as a superpower deal that ignored the interests of the continental partners. East Europe and Russia were part of Europe by virtue of history and geography. For a few years after World War II geopolitics had proved stronger than both. Russia herself and the ancient states of Eastern Europe were cut off from the rest by an Iron Curtain which gave the Americans the opening to make a protectorate of Europe's richer half and to tie it to themselves. Maintaining the new independence that had come to the states of West Europe, Germany especially, in the 1970s, depended upon keeping the Iron Curtain from falling again. In Washington hard-liners talked increasingly of a "Finlandized" Europe too afraid of Soviet bombs and tanks to contemplate détente on anything but Soviet terms, but in Bonn and Paris the fear was that promising avenues to the solution of national problems, such as energy vulnerability and economic slowdown, would be lost if the Cold War were declared anew.

When 1979 began, the United States appeared to the Allies more than ever like a giant that could not make up its mind. Just before the turn of the year Paul Volcker took over the chairmanship of the Federal Reserve and proceeded to put the nation into recession with a series of drastic deflationary measures. After long urging by the Allies, Carter had committed himself to end the "benign neglect" of the dollar. "The dollar's recovery in foreign exchange markets," the British economist Andrew Shonfield pointed out, depended upon convincing foreign bankers that the economy would be wrung dry of double-digit inflation. "[W]hatever good domestic economic reasons there may have been for curbing the pace of an already flagging economy . . . the form of the final deflationary squeeze and the degree of its severity were imposed by external forces." At the same time no progress whatever had been made on reducing U.S. dependence on imported oil. In the fall of 1978 Congressman David Stockman dismissed the need for a national energy policy with the suggestion that Carter's energy sermons were the rantings of a Chicken Little. Most Americans were equally skeptical of the energy crisis. When the CIA had published an alarmist study of the world oil market the year before, it had been largely dismissed as propaganda for the administration's energy bill.

Events seemed to conspire to dramatize American impotence. In January 1979 the shah of Iran was forced to leave the country as millions thronged the streets inspired by a fundamentalist Islamic revolution led by Ayatollah Ruhollah Khomeini which the United States failed to predict and was powerless to resist. Perhaps nothing illustrated its decline of power as the American inability to rescue the shah a second time. Unlike 1953, when the CIA coup opened the territory to dominant American influence, Iran in the 1970s had for many years been the linchpin of U.S. policy in the Middle East and Persian Gulf. This was no Vietnam of dubious strategic importance but the most critical area of the world for the West. Billions of dollars of sophisticated U.S. military equipment had flowed into the country for the purpose of securing the ancient Persian kingdom as a reliable source of oil. The weapons were supposed to establish the shah as the stabilizer of the whole region, who with Saudi Arabia, another beneficiary of American military largesse, would fend off the "radical" Arab states considered in Washington to be the principal threat to U.S. interests.

The Iranian revolution had begun with strikes in the oil fields. While these disruptions were in progress, OPEC agreed to a 14.5 percent increase in the price of oil. But as the crisis deepened with more and more Iranian oil off the market, the price jumped again and again. OPEC collapsed as a vehicle for disciplining prices, but this meant higher, not lower prices, as had often been predicted. In the "free-for-all" that now existed, to use the Saudi Arabian oil minister Yamani's term, producers broke ranks and competed with one another to raise prices. Since America's Allies, faced with a sudden new crisis, also competed with one another to buy the oil—even more fiercely than they had in the first oil crisis—the price increase in 1978–79 in absolute terms was greater than in 1973–74.

Europe and Japan depended much more on Iranian oil than did the United States. Thus American loss of leverage over Iran posed a serious problem. Overnight Iran had gone from client to enemy, but the United States could not assure access to Persian Gulf oil with its military power. In the eyes of the revolutionaries the United States was a "satanic" power for having put the shah on the throne and kept him there for almost thirty years.

On November 4, 1979, Iranian students swarmed into the U.S. embassy compound in Tehran and took sixty-three American hostages. Schmidt, Giscard, and Ohira were horrified. Diplomacy was dangerous enough work already; dodging bullets and negotiating with kidnappers were enlivening ambassadorial tours in a number of posts around the world. So the impulse was very great in every capital of the industrial world to punish such a brazen challenge to the conduct of international relations. But the Japanese especially were worried that the United States would do something rash that would interfere with their access to Persian Gulf oil and give the Soviets some opening to move into the area. Just before the embassy takeover, Japanese officials had approached the revolutionary government in Tehran with a proposal to complete a huge petrochemical plant then about 85 percent finished which represented Japan's largest single overseas investment, some $2 billion. Prime Minister Mehdi Bazargan was eager to have the Iran-Japan Petrochemical Company project completed. Japan desperately wanted to go forward as well because the negotiations were linked to an increased allotment for Japan of Iranian oil. (In the 1979 crisis the oil majors that supplied two-thirds of Japan's needs had cut back by one million barrels a day.) As one vice-minister of finance put it, the petrochemical project was "our hostage."

Good relations with Iran were also deemed essential in Tokyo since 70 percent of Japan's total oil imports passed through the Strait of Hormuz between Iran and Iraq. The Japanese prime minister worried that the Russians might try to move in and that the Americans would respond with an act of war. "If World War III occurs," he remarked to a close adviser, "it will surely start in the Middle East." Thus when the hostages were taken, the Japanese government was silent for one month; in early December, Japan's ambassador at the UN delivered what U.S. officials considered a maddeningly tepid statement deploring what was happening in Tehran.

Eight days after the hostages were taken, the United States called for a boycott of Iranian oil. But in Japan memories of past oil boycotts did not elicit enthusiasm for this one. "Our first oil shock was in 1940," a high official of the Finance Ministry explained to a visiting academic from the United States while the U.S. embassy was still under siege. "At that time, America stopped shipments of heavy oil because of what we had done in Manchuria and Shanghai. The U.S. boycott turned around the Navy that had opposed war with America, and forced it to move for Indonesia. From that lesson, we learned an oil cut-off may have unforeseen political consequences. . . ." But the Japanese government did not want to anger the Americans by buying the boycotted oil that was now showing up on the spot market. The Foreign Ministry urged Japanese companies to look elsewhere for fuel, but, despite the directive, according to a report of a leading Japanese newspaper, *Asahi Shimbun,* "Japanese firms purchased over half the petroleum bound for America at a figure nearly double the posted Iranian price."

When he met Foreign Minister Saburo Okita in Paris on December 10, Cyrus Vance dropped his usual mild manner. Much to the annoyance of Japanese officials an accurate account of the secretary's tongue lashing was reported on Paris television: "On a scale of one to fourteen the Secretary of State gave Japan a one rating for its concern over the Americans in Tehran." Japan was being used as a whipping boy to bring the other Allies into line, the Foreign Ministry concluded. Vance scolded the Japanese not only for buying up the boycotted oil but for evading the freeze on Iranian assets which the United States had imposed the month before. When Deputy Secretary of the Treasury Robert Carswell met Finance Vice-Minister Takehiro Sagami, however, the American refused to give the evidence because, the Japanese official assumed, he did not want to reveal the names of U.S. banks making charges against Japan. "We all know that the German and especially the Swiss banks are up to funny business on the matter of an assets freeze evasion," the official noted. It was infuriating that Japan be singled out for condemnation. The government announced that Japan's cooperation in the Iranian sanctions would match the performance of the other Allies.

Germany intended to be an "absolutely trustworthy ally and friend," Helmut Schmidt promised in parliament shortly after the embassy takeover. But the Federal Republic, along with the others in Europe, had no intention of cutting off their remaining trickle of trade with Iran, nor of denying themselves Iranian oil, nor, indeed, of interfering with their own bankers. Privately Schmidt worried about Carter's unsteadiness, fearing that he might be driven by domestic pressures to take some ill-considered military measure that could provoke a war with the Soviets. The hostage taking had been provoked by an invitation to the exiled shah, now dying of cancer, to come to the United States for medical treatment. Privately, Schmidt, Giscard, and others in Europe wondered whether Henry Kissinger's and David Rockefeller's debt of friendship to the shah—they had supplied the principal political pressure to extend the invitation over the strenuous objections of the U.S. embassy in Tehran—should cost Europe so dear, for at stake was not only oil but possibly peace itself.

The humiliation of the Carter administration and its understandable obsession with the issue made the United States look even less like a confident leader. It was all "distressingly like amateur night at the Palace," the *Manchester Guardian,* a paper usually friendly to Democratic administrations, noted with sadness. "Those (like this paper) who feel keen anger at the plight of the hostages wait dolefully for the next rush of measures. . . ." The wait was short. Within two weeks the administration had made a public statement in response to Allied concerns that it was delaying military action until mid-May, and that the most likely action would be a naval blockade. This assurance was itself a cover story for a disastrous rescue mission in the desert undertaken two days later. The need for extraordinary secrecy was a fatal flaw in the operation which, as an official Pentagon inquiry later concluded, was so secret as to confuse the military itself. Secretary of State Vance, convinced that the helicopter raid on Tehran would be as catastrophic as it turned out to be—eight U.S. commandos died in the attempt—had resigned once the final go-ahead was given. Schmidt, Giscard, and all the Allies were horrified. Their hearts went out to the severely damaged American president who had now lost whatever chance he might have had to obtain the release of the hostages before the November election. But the disaster took the pressure off the Europeans and Japanese. At a Western leaders' summit meeting in Venice later in June, the final communiqué did not even mention Iran.

The U.S. embassy in Tehran had been under siege for a little less than two months when a far more serious crisis arose to test the partnership. In late December 1979 five mechanized infantry divisions made up largely of reservists from the Central Asian provinces of the Soviet Union crossed the border into Afghanistan. Soviet armored units rolled across the stark winter terrain, setting fire to villages and strafing and bombing the population. The head of state, Hafizullah Amin, was summarily executed and Babrak Karmal installed in his place. The Soviets, echoing the arguments of the Americans in Vietnam, claimed to have come to the aid of a sovereign government, but there is evidence to suggest that they shot the man who invited them. As the resistance escalated, the Soviets sent more than 80,000 men into Afghanistan. Despite much heavier censorship and control than existed in Vietnam, the Soviet's brutal counterinsurgency war was publicized and condemned around the world. The official Soviet explanation that they were rescuing the revolution from foreign enemies instead of from itself was believed by no one—not even by Georges Marchais, the French Communist leader who, having broken with the Socialists, reverted once again to a passionate defender of the most indefensible aspects of Moscow's foreign policy.

For Jimmy Carter, the invasion, coming on the heels of the Iranian crisis and a string of victories for revolutionary forces in Ethiopia, Nicaragua, and elsewhere, represented a political disaster. A hawkish group known as the Committee on the Present Danger had already been so successful in convincing newspaper editors and other influential leaders that the softness of the Carter administration was giving a "green light" to Soviet expansionism that the ratification of the SALT II agreement appeared increasingly problematical. Zbigniew Brzezinski had articulated an updated dominoes theory: the Horn of Africa, the Middle East, and the Persian Gulf constituted an "arc of crisis" which because of its strategic position in the oil economy and political instability was an irresistible target of Soviet meddling. The very turmoil of this vast and important region suggested a new pattern of Soviet expansionism. To stop this process firm action had to be taken.

The Soviet invasion of Afghanistan in December 1979 shocked Jimmy Carter because on five separate occasions, having received reports of the continuing Soviet buildup on the border, he had warned the Soviets against attempting so blatant a challenge to the status quo. With the SALT II agreement still pending, the president could not believe that the Soviets would take an action that would destroy what little support for détente now remained in the United States. Eager to show firmness in the face of crisis, Carter succeeded only in projecting anger, naïveté, and confusion. The Soviet move, he exclaimed, was "the greatest threat to peace since the Second World War." In Bonn, Helmut Schmidt remarked that perhaps "from an American point of view" this might be so, but personally, "the Berlin crisis comes to mind." In an interview, Carter remarked that after hearing Brezhnev's defense via the "hot line," he experienced "a more dramatic change in my own opinion of what the Soviet Union's ultimate goals are than anything they have done since I have been in office." Afghanistan, Carter told the nation on January 4, was "a stepping stone to possible control over much of the world's oil supplies."

From the first there was a profound difference between the American and European assessments of what the Soviets were up to, and this had a great deal to do with their divergent attitudes as to what should be done about it. Beginning in the early postwar years each of the partners had periodically revised their assessments of Soviet intentions and motives, often tailoring them to fit the policy preferences of the moment. A specific Soviet threat, the intimidation of Western Europe with a possible invasion, had summoned the alliance into being. The hard evidence of any such intention was conspicuously absent in 1948, but it served convergent interests in Washington and in the capitals of Western Europe to assume the threat. In the 1970s when the alliance had long been built and America's commitment was as solid as it was ever likely to be, though Soviet military capabilities were much greater than before, their intentions were assumed to be more pacific and their goals more moderate. No other assessment was consistent with a policy of détente, and in both Washington and Bonn détente was needed.

Inside the United States government Sovietologists carried on a behind-the-scenes debate about Kremlin intentions all during the détente era. The dominant view was consistent with Richard Nixon's: Soviet leaders were opportunistic; the Kremlin would seek to fill "power vacuums" in the Third World where the possibilities presented themselves, but there was no timetable for world conquest. It was possible to keep Soviet expansionism in check with a judicious mix of carrots and sticks. Brzezinski preferred to look upon Soviet Russia as a continuation of Czarist Russia. The men in the Kremlin had the same designs on the Persian Gulf as Catherine the Great. Had not Molotov tipped his hand in the secret protocol he drew up with Von Ribbentrop in 1940? (". . . the area south of Batum and Baku in the general direction of the Persian Gulf is recognized as the center of the aspirations of the Soviet Union.") The CIA now reported a powerful new motive for Russian expansion into the area. It lacked oil itself and its situation might become desperate. Morever, it could break up the Western alliance if it controlled the routes through which 50 to 75 percent of Europe's and Japan's oil flowed. Russia's military buildup in the 1970s, particularly its increase in naval power, was designed to neutralize American capabilities to protect the interests of the West in this vital region.

The rising chorus of foreign policy critics on the right, the Committee on the Present Danger, neoconservative publicists such as Norman Podhoretz, and nervous politicians sensing a change in the political winds had been warning for more than two years that the Soviets were on the march. Carter's political advisers reported that the president was extremely vulnerable to the charge of having encouraged Soviet aggression by canceling weapons programs such as the B-1 bomber and by his talk of "inordinate fear of Communism." Two groups, the American Security Council and the American Conservative Union, had just spent $4.8 million dramatizing the Soviet menace in a media blitz to defeat the SALT II treaty. Although the president had already shifted course before the Afghanistan invasion by pressing the Europeans to go forward with the Pershing II and the cruise missile and by promising in a speech to the Business Council that he would increase defense spending 5 percent a year, he was urged to seize upon the Afghan crisis to outflank his critics.

The most alarming aspect of the Russian move was that it represented an escalation in the use of force. Never before in the postwar period had the Soviet Union sent its armed forces outside the vast region in Eastern Europe actually occupied by the Red Army at the end of the war. The tacit code of the Cold War had been asymmetrical—the Soviet Union could intervene with military power only in Eastern Europe without provoking a military showdown while the United States could intervene with impunity anywhere else—but the code had been scrupulously observed, except for the Cuban missile crisis, and in that case it had been enforced. If the Soviets were now prepared to sweep aside the unspoken restraints of the Cold War, no one could say where they would stop. Jimmy Carter's political advisers and his geopolitician in residence, Zbigniew Brzezinski, convinced the president that Afghanistan itself should be treated as a "prelude" to something more sinister.

The leading adviser on Soviet matters in the administration, Marshall Shulman, the former head of the Russ n Institute at Columbia University, had another view. Evidence was marshaled in the State Department that suggested a very different explanation of Soviet behavior. Some pointed out what George Kennan stated publicly, that Afghanistan, which contains "some of the most inhospitable territory of southern Asia" and a tradition among its mountain tribesmen of fierce resistance, was an odd stepping-stone to take toward the Persian Gulf. The evidence rather suggested that Soviet moves in Afghanistan were motivated by events in that country itself and represented a response to a rapidly deteriorating situation.

Afghanistan had been the classic Finlandized country, a feudal monarchy, which defined its foreign policy as not displeasing the Russians. From all indications, having a stable reactionary government on its borders suited the Soviet government. The non-Communist government of Mohammed Daud Khan imported 95 percent of its weapons from the USSR, and from 1974 to 1976 had Soviet military advisers down to the company level. In the late 1970s under the increasing influence of the shah of Iran and his secret police, Daud moved perceptibly toward the West in foreign policy and against the left wing at home. In April 1978 he was overthrown by a group of left-wing army officers. No evidence has come to light implicating the Soviets in the coup, but the self-styled Marxist officers immediately looked to the Soviets for aid in turning the country into a Socialist society. The people of Afghanistan, one of the most traditional, Islamic, and anti-Communist countries in the world, fiercely resisted the "revolution." The clumsy, brutal tactics of the regime in the pursuit of such policies as land reform and increased freedom for women aroused the whole country to arms. Increasingly the Soviets found themselves playing a role reminiscent of that played by the United States in Vietnam, supplying a shaky regime with the guns to stay in power, all the while urging it to moderation—to be less radical in its reforms, to make peace with the trading class, and to be gentler with the people. These efforts failed, and the Soviets, as Henry Kissinger later wrote, "calculated the Communist Government in Kabul could not maintain itself without Soviet forces."

In Europe this so-called "defensive" theory of Soviet behavior made more sense than the "stepping-stone" theory. For one thing, the interpretation seemed to fit better with the facts. The Soviet operation showed many signs of improvisation. The Russians were clearly surprised by the intensity of the resistance and the sharpness of the American response. But most important, the more alarmist interpretation would have required the NATO Allies to take action that would have hurt their own political and economic relations with the Soviet Union.

On January 4, 1980, the American president had announced a series of sanctions. There would be a ban on licensing technology to the Soviet Union, a partial embargo on grain, and a severe curtailment of the Soviet right to fish in American waters. United States citizens, the president hinted, might well boycott the summer Olympic Games in Moscow. Most significantly, he would request the Senate to defer consideration of the SALT II treaty.

"This means we must do more to cement our links with Third World countries in the area," Schmidt reportedly exclaimed on hearing the news that Soviet troops had poured across the Afghan border. While condemning the Soviet interference in Afghanistan, the chancellor quickly emphasized that it should not mean the end of détente. "Punishing" the Soviet Union, he told James Reston, "was unproductive and could be dangerous." Like many Europeans, Schmidt believed that Carter had exaggerated the crisis to serve his electoral interests.

Germany promised more aid for Pakistan and Turkey. Foreign Minister Genscher toured the Gulf states, proposing an agreement to strengthen economic ties between the EC and the countries of the region. Pointedly, he emphasized the willingness of the European Community members to promise that they would never freeze assets of the oil-producing countries as the United States had done with Iran. All these measures seemed to make much more sense than dismantling détente or engaging in economic warfare against the Soviet Union.

Schmidt was under the mounting pressure of an election; in October he would face Franz Josef Strauss at the polls. In defending ten years of *Ostpolitik* he could not afford to be maneuvered by the strongly pro-American rhetoric of his opponent into appearing lukewarm about cooperating with the United States. At the same time, acceding to the American insistence that the Federal Republic cut contacts and trade with the East would anger large segments of the population. As Schmidt would point out to visiting Americans, détente had made it possible for a quarter million Germans to resettle in the Federal Republic between 1975 and 1980. "All this could come to a standstill." With more than 16 million Germans still living under Communist rule, Germany was "not in a position to act as a spearhead or as a forerunner in a conflict between the superpowers." Thirty years before, the superpower rivalry had been critical to Germany's passage from defeated enemy to ally, but today Germany's interest was to do everything to contain and moderate the rivalry, not exacerbate it.

The volume of trade between the Federal Republic and the Soviet Union and Eastern Europe now roughly equaled its trade with the United States. Eighteen percent of its natural gas came from the Soviet Union; Deputy Minister of Trade Yuri Krasnov noted that the USSR "could turn off the natural gas tap" if the Germans joined the United States in a campaign of economic warfare. But the threat was scarcely necessary. Whole communities, particularly in the Ruhr, now depended critically upon trade with the East. One West German steel company contracted to sell the Soviets 700,000 tons of pipe. Less than a month after the Soviet move into Afghanistan, representatives of Deutschebank began discussions with the Soviets for a $13 billion deal for a natural gas pipeline.

Giscard followed Schmidt's line. He would condemn the Soviet action, and call for the Russians to withdraw, but he would not buy the "stepping stone" theory either. The French foreign minister, François Poncet, declared that the oil of the Middle East was not endangered by the Soviet invasion. Giscard noted immediately after the event that it "was not necessarily programmed. One cannot say it was premeditated. Perhaps it was determined by the internal situation in Afghanistan." In the next nine months French trade with the Soviet Union jumped 33 percent over the previous year. Later in the year the French signed a ten-year contract to supply an estimated $6–$8 billion worth of agricultural products, oil rigs, a steel mill, and other pieces of French technology in return for oil and other raw materials. A month after the Afghanistan intervention France began importing its first Russian gas. The only concession to Carter was to cancel the elaborate ceremonies that were to take place when the first French village was hooked up to the Soviet pipeline.

But the Afghanistan crisis split the alliance at a level deeper even than the trade issue. For Schmidt and Giscard the sudden tough talk from Washington, far from dispelling doubts about the forcefulness of American leadership, confirmed them. Yes, the Soviets should be condemned. Yes, the Kremlin had ventured beyond the territory conceded to it by the West, but not all that far beyond, for Afghanistan had been under Soviet influence in foreign affairs for a long time. If the United States was so upset about Afghanistan, why didn't it move in 1978 when the leftist coup occurred? No, Carter was using the Afghanistan crisis, Schmidt and Giscard concluded, to face down hawks at home and to build political support for a military buildup he had already decided upon. That was fine, but he must not be allowed to destroy détente in the process. The president's statements were rather extreme. He would "punish" the Soviets by suspending virtually every important aspect of the U.S.–Soviet détente and call upon the Allies to do the same. In the so-called Carter Doctrine he sought to deter further moves against the Persian Gulf with an explicit threat of military action which, Pentagon briefers went to some pains to emphasize, included the possible use of nuclear weapons.

Carter was now involving Europe in a "deadly game," Schmidt exploded, but his goals were obscure and his strategy dubious. Yes, the Federal Republic, unlike France, would probably boycott the Olympic Games. After all, the German ambassador to NATO who remembered the boost Hitler received when athletes around the world thronged to Berlin in 1936 may well have been the first to think of the gesture. But fanning the flames of war would not get the Soviets out of Afghanistan. Rather it would produce a war scare in Europe that would greatly complicate the task of every political leader. Schmidt had already brooded publicly about the similarities of the current situation to 1914 and how easily the world could slide into a war no one wanted.

It was unclear how the United States could use its military power to contain the Soviet threat to the Persian Gulf, if indeed there was one. The $9 billion Rapid Deployment Force announced three weeks after the Afghanistan intervention was an expensive but inadequate response to a Soviet drive for Middle East oil. The United States was having difficulty finding any nation in the region willing to offer bases for the forces which, if it were ever activated, would draw troops from Europe. The Federal Republic had no interest in being drawn into a military confrontation with the Soviet Union over Afghanistan.

Instead, Schmidt proposed a "division of labor" in the alliance. The Europeans should take advantage of the severe political vulnerability of the Soviet Union in the wake of Afghanistan to shore up political and economic relations with Pakistan, Turkey, and other nations of the region, a "positive" use of economic power, as a German official explained to American reporters, instead of the "negative" use which President Carter was urging. Giscard and Schmidt would also be willing to serve as "interpreters" of the superpowers to one another. Both leaders had private talks with Brezhnev in the months after the crisis broke, which angered Carter considerably. In a radio interview in Paris, Henry Kissinger, though hardly an admirer of the president, effectively conveyed his feelings: "I do not believe in divisible détente in the sense that one side does the defense and the other side does the negotiating . . . that Europe should have a monopoly on détente and America a monopoly on defense."

Surprisingly, the strongest support for Carter's strategy, apart from British Prime Minister Margaret Thatcher, who seemed to relish a fight with the Russians on principle, came from Japan. Masayoshi Ohira, a slow-moving, heavyset technocrat who had held cabinet posts for almost twenty years, had become prime minister the year before in an upset victory. His pedigree was unusual for a Japanese politician. A convert to Christianity, he had even preached the gospel on street corners. A Japanese politician who did not drink, it was even more astonishing that he had managed to rise to the top without having gone to the elite Tokyo University. But he shared the prevailing sentiment within the Liberal Democratic party about rearmament. Despite increasing U.S. pressure to step up military spending, he was against it.

The Japanese Foreign Ministry, however, unlike its counterparts in Europe, was quite prepared to accept the Brzezinski theory that the Soviet move into Afghanistan fitted into a wider pattern of aggression. Japanese officials worried about the recent buildup of conventional forces in what they called the "northern territories," the group of small islands off the northeastern coast of Hokkaidō which the Soviets had occupied since the end of World War II. They worried also about the Soviet naval buildup in the Pacific. Japanese-Soviet relations had deteriorated recently over fisheries negotiations and other irritants.

The principal concern, however, that prompted the Japanese to an unusual level of cooperation with the Americans, including a freeze on credits to Russia, a delay of meetings and visits between the two countries, and the suspension of a major joint Siberian development project, was the instability of the Middle East. With the U.S. geopolitical strategy overturned by the revolution in Iran, the nations of the Persian Gulf on which Japan depended for oil seemed vulnerable. The United States needed support in "punishing" the Russians exactly because the Americans were now seriously weakened. Washington had no political strategy and its military options were limited. Therefore, the Foreign Ministry agreed with Schmidt and Giscard that "Japan and other Western Allies would have to ensure the stability of individual nations in the region." Ohira ordered the Japanese Sports Federation to boycott the Moscow games, threatening to withhold $7 million from the federation if any Japanese athletes participated.

The Japanese now became more open to economic sanctions against Iran and more eager to cooperate fully with the European Community. Ohira had become so worried about American nerves that he looked to the Europeans for support in developing a strategy to protect Japan's access to oil. Carter and his aides seemed "psychologically abnormal," a high-ranking Japanese official confided to a visiting academic from America. The Americans seemed so uncertain of what to do that the Japanese government, as another senior official put it, "feared that Washington might give Iran to Moscow on a silver platter." When Ambassador Mike Mansfield raised the possibility in Tokyo of the government's breaking off diplomatic ties with Iran, the Japanese response was "a polite but firm no." In Washington, Jimmy Carter fumed at the partners who seemed ready to attack him whatever he did and to desert America in a dark time.

TEN

DRIFTING APART:

Mr. Reagan Celebrates
and Confronts the New Nationalism

1

It was a measure of how low expectations of American leadership had fallen that the election of Ronald Reagan in November 1980 was greeted in the foreign offices of Europe with equanimity. The new leader of the West had prepared for his "rendez-vous with destiny" (the famous Rooseveltian flourish was a Reagan standby) by a route that confirmed the worst suspicions about the American political process. In Europe politicians usually rose on their wiles, their family, their erudition, their money, occasionally their sword, but this "cowboy," as disdainful professionals called him, seemed to have ascended on the strength of his resonant voice, twinkling eyes, and splendid torso. (He was dubbed "Twentieth Century Adonis" by the Division of Fine Arts of the University of Southern California in 1940 for having "the most nearly perfect male figure.") In the midst of the Great Depression his breathless play-by-play description on a Des Moines radio station of baseball games he did not attend won him a reputation that led to a screen test and a Hollywood career. After making fifty-one forgettable movies, eight of them in a single eleven-month stretch, his film career sagged, and he turned to politics.

Switching from a New Deal Democrat to a Goldwater Republican, he barnstormed the country on behalf of the General Electric Company and conservative candidates for public office. His new views coincided with a rightward shift in the country. Though distrusted by the Washington and New York Establishment and rarely taken seriously by the leading newspapers, the enthusiastic support of some of the new millionaires of the West helped win him the governorship of California, which he immediately proceeded to use as a stepping-stone to the presidency. Unlike his predecessor or, for that matter, the moody German chancellor, Reagan seemed remarkably adept at living life on the surface, projecting an easy affability, sincerity, and absence of pomposity that contrasted strikingly with the baffling personalities who had recently preceded him in the White House.

Helmut Schmidt was prepared to believe that the new president, the hope of the extreme right-wing in America, who regularly read their publications and contributed to them, echoing their primitive nationalism and bloodcurdling militarism in radio commentaries five days a week, could well turn out to be an improvement on Jimmy Carter. But the record of his public positions on foreign policy was hardly reassuring. In the campaign he had at various points suggested a blockade of Cuba to get the Russians out of Afghanistan, a mining of Iranian harbors to secure release of the hostages, and while he opposed Carter's grain embargo in speeches to the farmers of the Midwest, he once advocated a suspension of *all* trade. His casual approach to the use of force went back a long time. In October 1965, just as Johnson was pouring troops into Vietnam, he observed: "We could pave the whole country and put parking stripes on it and still be home by Christmas." "Let us not delude ourselves," he told *The Wall Street Journal*, "the Soviet Union underlies all the unrest that is going on. If they weren't engaged in the game of dominoes, there wouldn't be any hot spots in the world."

The Bundeskanzler was determined to avoid the prickly relations with the White House that developed under Carter. It was better to ignore the naive and disquieting statements—after all, wasn't every public statement by the Californian a campaign statement—and assume that irrespective of his ideological preferences, he would have to moderate them in order to govern.

Ronald Reagan took office on a note of triumph and nostalgia. The release of the hostages had been arranged by the outgoing administration but the homecoming of the captives coincided with his inauguration. The new president promised to restore the strength and confidence of small-town America. Doing battle with the Russians and inflation at the same time required a radical increase in military spending and a radical cut in government spending which would somehow be undertaken together. This mystifying policy did not inspire confidence in Europe. It was difficult to see how spending more than $1.5 trillion in four years while slashing government revenues with a tax cut would restore health to the American economy, the essential prerequisite, the Europeans believed, to the reestablishment of America as a dependable senior partner.

From the first the Reagan administration was enveloped in a fog of wishful thinking about Europe. Just as Schmidt and Giscard preferred to believe that the new president's views could not possibly be as antagonistic to European interests as they sounded, so the hard-liners recruited by the new administration from the ranks of the Committee on the Present Danger chose to assume that the Europeans, thoroughly disenchanted with Jimmy Carter's "appeasement" policy, would welcome tough talk and firm action from Washington. It was a costly misunderstanding. There was little awareness in Washington of the rising war jitters in Europe caused by the collapse of détente. Six months before Reagan's accession one poll reported that 89 percent of the French believed that a grave international crisis was imminent and six out of ten Germans thought that World War III was a distinct possibility.

Administration spokesmen seemed bent on inducing panic in Europe. Eugene Rostow, the president's nominee for chief arms control planner, was on record as believing, "We are living in a pre-war and not a post-war world." At his first White House press conference Ronald Reagan showed no sign of moderating his campaign rhetoric. The Russian leaders, he said, reserved "the right to commit any crime, to lie, to cheat." Every foreign office in Europe was appalled. The new crowd in Washington was even more amateurish than their predecessors. More serious, they all had a taste for confrontation and some seemed to want a war. Richard Pipes, a Harvard history professor called to service in the White House, volunteered to a Reuters correspondent his view that the Soviets would have to choose between changing their system "or going to war." The professorial ultimatum was delivered with disquieting insouciance: "There is no alternative—and it could go either way." Pipes also suggested that Foreign Minister Genscher's advice would be ignored in Washington because he was too susceptible to Soviet pressure. While his views were angrily disavowed by more senior officials—"it isn't helpful to say that détente is dead or war is inevitable"—confusing and belligerent statements continued to stream out of Washington. Richard Allen, the national security adviser, dismissed the "contemptible better red than dead" attitudes of Europeans as the product of a wave of "pacifism" that had swept over their countries. The secretaries of state and defense regularly contradicted one another in public on what the administration believed or was planning to do.

But of even greater concern in Europe than the war whoops and public displays of internecine warfare in Washington were the policies that emerged. Secretary of State Alexander Haig, who quickly earned a reputation as the advocate of Europe's interests within the administration on the strength of his prior service as NATO commander, managed to precipitate an immediate conflict with the partners over El Salvador. The new secretary came into office believing that the tiny Central American country offered the best possible place to overcome the "Vietnam syndrome" and to demonstrate at last the effective use of U.S. military power. Here was a war that could be won, a war in America's traditional sphere of influence that would be supported by the American people and America's friends, a war that involved no real risk of wider confrontation. None of it proved to be true.

The call to do battle with the "Russian threat" by killing peasants in El Salvador whipped up a flurry of opposition in the United States. To the surprise of the administration, the Roman Catholic Church, which reported that the Salvadorian government had killed 30,000 people and turned 13 percent of the population into refugees, took a strong stand against U.S. intervention. The brutality of the "authoritarian" regime, as the administration called the junta to distinguish it from the infinitely more evil "totalitarian" regimes of the

Communist world, aroused sympathy for the rebels in Europe. Thus when State Department officials flew to Bonn and Paris in March 1981 to secure support for the administration's line with "captured documents" allegedly showing the Kremlin was backing the rebellion, they were not only politely rebuffed but told that there was considerable sentiment among the moderate Left governments on the Continent for a political settlement with the very forces whose extermination the United States was now underwriting. Months later Under Secretary of Defense Fred C. Iklé told members of the Senate Foreign Relations Committee that some European allies were "deceived by totalitarian propaganda or some may be outright mischievous."

By the summer of 1981 the contours of the Reagan defense policy had emerged: Every effort would be made to delay arms control negotiations with the Soviets until a massive buildup in U.S. nuclear weapons was under way. Administration spokesmen hammered away at the theme that the Soviet Union was far ahead in nuclear and conventional weapons. Although a major general on the National Security Council was transferred for giving a speech to the effect that Soviet "strategic superiority" had produced a "drift to war," a year later the president himself publicly worried about the "definite margin of superiority" enjoyed by the Soviets that rendered U.S. missiles vulnerable to a first strike. United States war plans called for producing every available nuclear weapons system, including the B-1 bomber, rejected by Carter on cost-effectiveness grounds, the MX missile, for which a basing system had yet to be found, the neutron bomb, and about 37,000 new nuclear warheads of all types.

Defense ministries in Europe were puzzled. It did nothing for deterrence to have high American officials say the United States was vulnerable to a Soviet attack even if it were true, which, emphatically, it was not. Despite the impressive Soviet buildup of the 1970s, no U.S. military leader would elect to trade military establishments with the Kremlin. Reagan's nominee as chairman of the Joint Chiefs of Staff, General John Vessey, dismissed the suggestion at his confirmation hearings as if it were absurd. It was revealing that in drumming up public support for increased military spending, the new administration usually talked as if the alliance did not exist. Caspar Weinberger, the secretary of defense, warned about being "outspent" by the Soviet Union on the military. But the United States and NATO allies together outspent the Soviet Union and its allies by more than $300 billion in the 1970s. While the whole discussion was quixotic—the Soviet defense budget was reconstructed in the CIA by pretending that they paid their conscripts on the same scale as the U.S. volunteer army and that they procured their tanks from Chrysler—it was significant that in calculating its own security requirements, the United States did not include Europe's contribution. Thus the Pentagon talked of the serious "imbalance" in conventional forces in Europe, but taken together U.S. and NATO forces virtually balanced (and by some counts exceeded) the Soviet and Warsaw Pact forces arrayed against them.

It was ironical that the ostensible beneficiaries of the projected American buildup became increasingly nervous. The theory of the Reagan defense advisers, which had been expressed at length in the publications of the Committee on the Present Danger, was that the loss of U.S. nuclear superiority would lead to the intimidation of Europe by the Soviet Union and the eventual neutralization of the continent. In fact, the prestige of the Soviet Union was at an all-time low in West Europe, even among the intellectuals who had been traditionally sympathetic. But the United States, not the Soviet Union, was now the principal source of fear. Helmut Schmidt, who threatened to resign if his party adopted a neutralist stance, knew that the Reagan rhetoric would boomerang. It was impossible to follow the lead of the United States in the 1980s if the United States appeared to be courting war.

The hopes of the new administration for avoiding war or an unending arms race rested on a belief that the Soviet Union, despite its great arsenal, was vulnerable. So serious were its economic difficulties, so fundamental its ideological crisis, and so advanced was the dissolution of its political institutions that the Kremlin could not and would not match a serious move by the United States to escalate the arms race. As the president had said many times in the campaign, the way to make the Soviets negotiate seriously was to confront them with a massive buildup. This the leaders of the SPD considered utterly naive. Even Margaret Thatcher, who shared Ronald Reagan's world view to a remarkable extent, was nervous about postponing arms negotiations with the Russians.

Throughout the first eighteen months of the administration one provocative decision after another, each seemingly calculated to elicit fear and fury on the Continent, emanated from Washington. Weinberger called a press conference to announce that the United States would produce the neutron bomb whether the Europeans liked it or not. No decision had been made to deploy it in Europe, but a Pentagon general volunteered that "hundreds" might be used in Europe in the event of a war. As if to reassure the million or so Belgians, Dutch, and Germans who had already signed petitions or marched against the bomb, it was pointed out that it wasn't an immoral weapon that "kills people and leaves buildings undamaged"; within twenty-five acres of the blast all the buildings would go too.

A few months later the president suggested in an offhand comment to a group of editors that he "could see where you could have the exchange of tactical weapons against troops in the field without it bringing either one of the major powers to pushing the button," thus confirming suspicions in Europe that the United States regarded Europe as a battlefield for a "limited nuclear war" with Russia. The Reagan gaffe provided a magnificent propaganda opening for Brezhnev, who took advantage of it by reiterating the hopelessness of "winning" a nuclear war, and promising never to start one.

In its first year in office the administration seemed more interested in projecting a determination to fight and "win" nuclear wars than in allaying European fears. The Republican platform had called specifically for a restoration of U.S. nuclear "superiority," and the numbers of weapons ordered by the new administration suggested a belief that this goal was attainable. The annual Defense Department "defense guidance statement" leaked to *The New York Times* stated that "protracted nuclear war is possible"—up to six months, Pentagon briefers explained—and that "American nuclear forces must prevail and be able to force the Soviet Union to seek earliest termination of hostilities on terms favorable to the United States."

A National Security Council directive approved by the president asked the Pentagon to come up with a strategic plan for victory in a "protracted" nuclear conflict. Eighteen billion dollars was budgeted to improve command, control, and communication so that U.S. generals in deep underground bunkers or aloft in airplanes or spacecraft could continue to order the nuclear destruction of the enemy even after the devastation of the United States. But the suspicion grew in Europe that the United States was counting on the destruction being mostly limited to the Old World. T. K. Jones, the deputy under secretary of defense for Strategic Theatre Nuclear Forces, suggested that in the coming war Americans could save themselves by digging a hole and climbing in. "If there are enough shovels to go around everybody's going to make it," he advised. The term "theatre" now assumed a sinister connotation. Were the superpowers to be the producers of war and the audience while the people of Europe were the players in the lethal drama? The word went out from the White House that "theatre" nuclear weapons would henceforth be called "intermediate-range" weapons.

2

"It's like Harry Truman used to say about public opinion," a former senior NATO commander exploded. "If you tell them nothing, they go fishing and if you tell them something, they go crazy." By 1981 every politician in Europe worried about the peace movement. Even before Reagan took office more than 250,000 had marched in Bonn in the fall of 1980 to protest the 1979 decision to deploy the cruise missile and the Pershing II in Germany. In the early months of the Reagan era officials in Washington dismissed the movement as a collection of malcontents "bought and paid for" by Moscow, but politicians in Germany, Holland, Britain, Belgium, and Italy, though they detected Moscow's hand at some points in the protest activities, knew better. The fear of war was widespread among the people of Europe, and it was growing. The United States, not the Soviet Union, was seen now as the principal danger to peace.

In Europe, it was evident, the strategy of the Carter and Reagan administrations of reasserting American leadership by dramatizing and exaggerating the Russian threat had backfired. By the end of 1981 more than two million people across West Europe were marching in the streets of London, Bonn, Hamburg, Amsterdam, Brussels, Rome, and Madrid. Holding aloft such banners as: WE ARE NOT AMERICA'S GUINEA PIGS, and REAGAN'S PEACE IS OUR

DEATH, the European peace marchers took Margaret Thatcher, Helmut Schmidt, and Ronald Reagan by surprise.

The demonstrators were too numerous, too disparate in age, and politics, too broadly based geographically, to dismiss as fringe. The immediate impulse in Washington was to attribute the disturbing phenomenon to the KGB. But, Dutch Minister of Interior Ed van Thijn reported, there was "not even a scrap of evidence" that the InterChurch Peace Council, the leading Dutch peace organization and perhaps the most influential in Europe, which had avoided local Communists, was taking money or direction from Moscow. Assistant Secretary of Defense Richard Perle attributed the new wave of pacifism and neutralism in Germany to "Protest *Angst*" though, he admitted, the Catholic Church was beginning to exhibit some of the same symptoms. Other worried Reagan officials, embracing the term invented by one conservative intellectual, thought that all Europe was succumbing to an attack of "Hollanditis," the historic pacifism of trading nations too comfortable to afford red-blooded patriotism. It was a measure of the growing isolationist mood in America that high officials preferred to trivialize the extraordinary events in Europe than to understand them. But then European leaders were no less puzzled. The peace movement drew its militants from all ages but in the pictures of the crowds that flashed across the world's TV screens blue jeans, zipper jackets, and youthful beards stood out. It was a young crowd, and for those in power, as in 1968, youth rather than politics offered a convenient explanation of an unpleasant challenge. Helmut Schmidt mused about youth that seemed to last forever, a generation "informed, disinformed, deformed" by the mass media that lived "in great material well-being" but showed only contempt for what they claimed as their due. There was a hopelessness that had overtaken young people in Germany and elsewhere, the chairman of the SPD youth organization noted, that expressed itself in mass protest. Perhaps it had to do with not having a job and not really wanting one. In the outpouring of instant analysis of the peace movement that had been ignored until it became a force powerful enough to make governments tremble, everything seemed to be grist except history. Yet the new generation of marchers calling for an end to the nuclear arms race and a new relationship to the superpowers had a long, largely forgotten lineage.

The peace demonstrators were the heirs of powerful political losers of the past. In Britain a "ban the bomb" movement had burst forth intermittently since 1945, gaining visibility whenever the danger of war appeared to increase. In 1950 the British Peace Committee, organized by prominent scientists and academics such as V. Gordon Childe and J. D. Bernal, that included Hewlett Johnson, the dean of Canterbury Cathedral, collected almost one million signatures in support of the Moscow-organized Stockholm Peace Appeal. The left wing of the Labour party led by Aneurin Bevan had a strong antinuclear and neutralist bent, but went down to defeat after bitter struggles. "The petition now being canvassed," a Labour party statement declared was "a fraudulent attempt to shift the responsibility" of the arms race from Russia to America;

membership in the Peace Committee was declared to be "incompatible with membership in the Labour Party."

In the 1950s in Britain as in the United States, the word "peace" was suspect as a Communist slogan, for in the West the watchword was rearmament. But by 1958 in reaction to the Sputnik panic, nuclear tests in the atmosphere, and the mounting threat of war over Berlin, another peace movement had been organized. The Campaign for Nuclear Disarmament carried out well-publicized four-day marches to the atomic weapons research establishment outside of London at Aldermaston. Bertrand Russell, who had once proposed dropping the bomb on the Russians if they did not disarm, was chairman, and its membership included Michael Foot, the leader of the Labour party in the 1980s. This time it was not so easy to dismiss the group as pro-Russian, for Soviet nuclear tests were denounced as well as those of the United States. A strong theme was unilateralism: Britain, for its own safety, should opt out of the mad nuclear arms race of the superpowers. With the passing of the Berlin crisis and the beginning of détente, the movement receded.

In West Germany the peace movement had stronger roots. The SPD under Schumacher was avowedly neutralist; reunification, it was widely believed, could be achieved in no other way. There was also a profound antimilitarist reaction to the years of bloody Nazi rule. As Willy Brandt observed, "There have been worse things in Germany than young people demonstrating for peace and disarmament." Prominent political figures such as Gustav Heinemann, the president of Germany, had built their reputation by opposing German rearmament. Hans Apel, Schmidt's minister of defense, had once joined the clenched-fisted marches against "atomic death." Heinrich Albertz, the mayor of West Berlin in 1968 who had been driven from office for having condoned the use of excessive force against the students, was now a Protestant pastor and a leader of the peace movement. All through the 1950s and into the 1960s each of the German political parties had its dissidents who favored various schemes for disengagement, "thinning out" of the forces of the superpowers on German soil, East and West, and nuclear-free zones. The dissidents had been crushed, but to a new generation of Germans these opponents of militarism took on a heroic cast. Their struggle suggested that history could have been different and, that more important, an alternative future to the arms race and a superpower war in Europe was possible even now.

The peace movement of the 1980s erupted in reaction to the alarming breakdown of détente and the ever insistent calls for rearmament. As one German professor tried to explain to *Time* magazine, young people in Germany "feel like passengers in a car racing toward an abyss. They have a desire to grab the wheel." The seemingly endless, and in the end fruitless, SALT II negotiations, during which the arms race leaped ahead, suggested that the superpowers neither knew how to end the arms race nor wished to do so. "Talking to the superpowers about disarmament," Volkmar Deile, secretary of Action for Reconciliation, a church-based peace group, perhaps the most influential in Germany, explained, "is like talking to drug dealers about stopping drug deliveries." The emphasis of the new peace movement was unilateralism—not unilateral abandonment of defense as U.S. officials charged, for only a small traditionally pacifist minority favored such a course—but unilateral action by the Europeans to opt out of a nuclear arms race no one could win. What gave the movement its unexpected force was the conjunction of two fears, one of the weapons of extermination themselves and the other of what Ulrich Albrecht, an influential professor in the German peace movement, called "the American grip." Significantly, the peace movement did not catch fire unless both elements were present. In traditionally prodisarmament Sweden, a center of anti–Vietnam War protest, the crowds were small; Sweden was already neutral and there was no American grip. In Paris the peace movement was pathetically weak and what there was of it was, unlike most of Europe, heavily influenced by the Communist party. French nuclear weapons, though less numerous, were just as lethal as American bombs, but in France they were symbols of nationalism, while everywhere else in Europe the bomb symbolized an irretrievable loss of independence and sovereignty. In France pacifism was tinged with the shame of collaborationism, for the antimilitarists of the prewar days, Left and Right, were perceived as having unwittingly delivered France to the Nazi yoke without a struggle. On the myth of the Resistance against the Nazi occupation rested the national consensus embracing all the major political parties that France's security depended upon her own atomic bomb.

Elsewhere in Europe the peace movement reflected both nationalism and internationalism. In Britain, Holland, and Germany the strongest impulse behind the movement was a long repressed feeling that democracy was meaningless if Americans and Russians made the decisions whether the nations would live or die. In Britain the crucial decision to deploy the cruise missile had been made by the Labour government without public discussion. Local governments did not even know the location of nuclear weapons, and the decision when or where to use them, which would determine Soviet retaliation, was exclusively in American hands.

In Germany, especially, the nuclear weapons stimulated nationalist feelings, for in a war the missiles of the two outside powers would explode on German soil. The opposing nuclear-armed forces confronting each other at the Elbe dramatized the dilemma of German identity. Yet the movement was not nationalist in the classic sense. The crowds marching in London, Bonn, and Amsterdam were not calling for a Fortress Britain or a Fortress Germany, much less a Fortress Holland, but a nuclear-disarmed Europe united in peace. The German movement for the most part stressed the reunification of Europe "from Portugal to Poland," in the alliterative slogan of the European Disarmament Campaign, rather than the reunification of Germany, which had been the concern of the peace and neutrality activists of the preceding generation.

The peace movement grew as established political leaders found themselves increasingly blocked and frustrated. In Britain, Margaret Thatcher, the militantly middle-class, Oxford-educated grocer's daughter who had become prime minister in the spring of 1979, anticipating Reagan's own policies, called for a return to solid nineteenth-century values, "sound money," an end to a tax system that "penalized success," and a cut in public spending save the military. She pursued these policies so relentlessly—"It's as if she had taken holy orders," an admirer put it—that as the economy careened toward catastrophe, her political fortunes plummeted until by a stroke of good luck Argentine generals ten thousand miles away presented her with a winnable war in the Falkland Islands.

In France, François Mitterrand, the veteran of eleven cabinets in the Fourth Republic, a former fighter in the Resistance after brief service in the Vichy government, an eloquent loner with a philosophical bent, masterminded a brilliant and surprising victory of the Left in May 1981 by outwitting and emasculating the French Communist party. He promised a new brand of Socialism based on high technology, decentralized political structures, and a strong measure of social justice, but within a year he was stalled on all fronts. The franc had fallen, unemployment had risen, and the trade deficit had worsened. Turning the country to the left while all about him were turning to the right amidst a world economic crisis was beyond even his considerable political skills. Far more anti-Soviet than the Gaullists who preceded him, he quickly proclaimed his loyalty to the Atlantic Alliance which, he told *Time,* "is the basis of our foreign policy." When it came to military matters the French Socialist sounded much like Ronald Reagan: The Soviets had "upset the military equilibrium in Europe. I will not accept this and I agree that we must arm to restore the balance." The calls within Germany to loosen its ties with the United States worried him. After thirty years of German rearmament, the traditional French fear of German militarism had been replaced by a fear of German pacifism. Indeed, Mitterrand for a time established himself as Reagan's most reliable public supporter on military matters. Not only was the Soviet threat a club to use against the still formidable French Communists, but espousing Reagan's views on these matters would help blunt the ideological antagonism to be expected from the American conservative president. Besides, it was easy to endorse controversial missiles that were never to be deployed in France. But for all her sudden new enthusiasm for the alliance, France refused to disclose the location of her submarines to the U.S. Navy, thus making the tracking of Soviet submarines significantly more difficult.

Against the backdrop of governmental weakness—by the end of 1981 all European incumbents seemed vulnerable—the new breed of peace activists received more than the usual attention, for they were the only source of new ideas on how to prevent the war more and more people believed was coming. Edward P. Thompson, a historian who had written the classic study of the English working class, was a man of the Left who had broken with the British Communist party after the invasion of Hungary. In response to the Thatcher government's effort to revive interest in civil defense, he wrote a pamphlet *Protest and Survive,* which spoke directly to the growing fear of nuclear war in Europe. The cruise missile and the Pershing II were the latest products of an irrational system of "defense" that was now out of control. Once the weapons were emplaced in 1983, targets in the Soviet Union would be only five minutes away from nuclear destruction at the hands of the Americans, a reality that made the Germans, British, Dutch, and Italians extremely vulnerable to a Soviet preemptive attack. New, highly accurate, "counterforce" technology on both sides—weapons targeted against weapons—significantly increased the danger of war without adding a measure of security to either side.

The organizers of the great marches took pains to dispel the impression that the movement was anti-American by inviting well-known Americans like Coretta King to speak to the crowds, and some traveled up and down the United States trying to explain what was happening. But Reagan administration officials demanded to know why the crowds in Europe were marching against American missiles still on the drawing boards when hundreds of SS-20s were already targeted on their cities, deployed by a regime that had just invaded Afghanistan, and was conducting threatening maneuvers on the Polish border. Didn't that prove that the movement was anti-American?

It was a good question with a complicated answer. Some of the leaders of the European peace movement had studied and taught in America and identified with many things in the United States. But the United States, not the Soviet Union, was the ally; the Americans, as Erhard Eppler, a former SPD cabinet minister and a leader in the church-based peace movement put it, had the ability to determine in the last instance "when and if Europeans are to die," because the Americans were the ones who would push the button. The United States was to be held accountable as a democracy presumably subject to popular pressure. The Soviet Union was equally responsible for the arms race but it scarcely pretended to be accountable—to its own people, much less to anyone else. For the sophisticates in the movement, the danger of war came from America, not Russia, because of the likely way it would start. No one believed in an attack from the blue by Russia. Much more probable was a superpower confrontation in, say, the Persian Gulf in which the Americans would compensate for their geographical and military disadvantages by escalating the conflict. That was precisely what the Carter Doctrine had implied. In an interview with *Der Spiegel* a few months after leaving office, Zbigniew Brzezinski admitted that the Democrats no less than the Republicans were seeking to use nuclear weapons in a "non-suicidal way" for political purposes. "If necessary, that includes limited nuclear war. . . . It could escalate, would probably escalate. . . ."

The Reagan rhetoric, the huge increases in the U.S. arms budget, the growing realization that the United States, not the Soviet Union, had consistently been the technological pacesetter in the arms race, achieving a variety of lethal breakthroughs five to seven years before the Soviets, all helped to focus European fears on the United States. The Soviet government was dangerous to its own people and to Afghans and Poles; the American government was dangerous to the people of West Europe. The Soviets talked peace while they continued to prepare for war, even to make war in Afghanistan, but the

Americans talked about starting a nuclear war and winning it. A West German official who worked for NATO headquarters was asked by his mother, a conservative *Hausfrau* who voted consistently for the CDU, why he could work for an American organization like NATO. "The Americans are not civilized."

Hundreds of peace organizations sprang up in the Federal Republic, but the two most powerful forces were the Greens, originally an extra-parliamentary action group organized to oppose nuclear power and other assaults on the environment, and the Protestant Church. The environmental movement had been strongly influenced by political forces within the United States. Petra Kelly, a young woman who had gone from a German convent to attend a university in the United States, became convinced that nuclear radiation from power plants posed a mortal danger and that if this were so, nuclear weapons posed a far greater danger. Ralph Nader, the consumer activist, and the U.S. environmental movement were strong influences and so were a group of American women who demonstrated at the Pentagon in November 1980. The death of her younger sister from cancer helped to turn her from a full-time bureaucrat into a tireless activist. As chairperson for the Greens, she was determined to show that concern for the earth required confronting the danger of nuclear war. The Greens declared themselves to be "beyond" Left and Right, and indeed attracted adherents across the political spectrum. The movement struggled to define a new political philosophy that defied the traditional ideological categories of the past.

The Greens dramatized the immediacy of the nuclear danger by procuring a map of all the nuclear installations in Germany and arranging to have it published in *Der Stern*. The map with dozens of dots each representing at a minimum the destructive power of a Hiroshima made West Germany look like a child with measles, as *Stern* put it. As the Social Democrats split over the nuclear issue—Schmidt continuing to insist that the "Euromissiles" be deployed—more and more young people were attracted to the Greens.

The other powerful antinuclear voice was the church. Schmidt himself disclaimed a world leadership role for the Federal Republic because, as he would say privately, "we are the Nation of Auschwitz." The Protestant Church, deeply conscious of having in the main failed to oppose the monstrous evil of the century, was moved to resist the weapons that threatened to make an Auschwitz of the whole earth. The Reagan nuclear threats were a form of blasphemy. "In April of the year of our Lord 1981," the theologian Uta Ranke-Heinemann, daughter of the former German president, Gustav Heinemann, cried at the huge demonstration, "another lord pronounced the order to build the neutron bomb." Some of the moving spirits were themselves veterans of the struggle against Hitler, septuagenarian members of the Confessing Church which in May 1934 called on Christians to oppose the state because the Nazis had gone "beyond the limits of God's commandments." The antinuclear strain in the church went back many years. In 1958 the influential theologian Karl Barth had declared, "Not just the use of these weapons, but also to threaten to use these weapons is inadmissable." Pastor Martin Niemöller, the World

War I U-boat commander who was imprisoned seven years under the Nazis, now over ninety, denounced the Americans in terms once reserved for Hitler. The United States, he said, was using the arms race to ruin the European and Japanese economies. "Then there will be no obstacles, to extending their empire across the whole world." Although German Protestants were not churchgoers by and large, the message concerning the irrationality, danger, and immorality of the bomb began to break through the psychological resistance to confronting the weapon that could theoretically bring the death of everything.

After more than one hundred years the insistent questions that had provoked two world wars still remained. What is Germany? What are its true borders? In ordinary conversations Germans talked of themselves as "the Germans" instead of "we." (In Moscow visiting professors were surprised to hear Soviet officials speak of the German Democratic Republic as "our Germans" and the Federal Republic as "the Germans.") World War II had compounded the historic identity problem. For almost forty years the division of Germany had served as punishment, but also for some German conservatives a perverse sort of absolution for the Nazi past. Since the Russians were responsible for the permanent frustration of German nationhood, Germans need not feel guilty for Hitler's assault on the Soviet Union. The Cold War was proof that Hitler was more right than wrong. The Education and Science Ministry recommended that textbooks and maps restore the former German names to cities such as Gdańsk (Danzig) and Kaliningrad (Königsberg) and was dissuaded only by a sharp Soviet protest. Reporting on Germany, U.S. newspapers emphasized the revival of German assertiveness. American soldiers reported being forced off the road or finding themselves the target of angry or obscene gestures. Egon Bahr, *The New York Times* reported, now liked to refer to the United States as "the former occupying power."

Public opinion polls throughout Europe, U.S. embassies confidently reported to Washington, showed large majorities still in favor of NATO, the American connection, and the prevailing military strategy. But the Reagan administration knew that the peace movement, large in itself, reflected much wider anxieties. All during the 1960s the major political parties of West Germany had been united in their strong support of NATO and the American connection. The Socialists had been, if anything, more Atlanticist than their opponents, for they saw Atlanticism and *Ostpolitik* as two sides of the same coin. But by 1981 a radical shift seemed under way. "Stop behaving as if the Americans were your enemies and the Soviets your friends," Schmidt shouted at the growing numbers within his own party who feared that the U.S. pressure on Germany to take the new missiles in the midst of a redoubled arms race would lead to war. Schmidt had badly miscalculated on the "Euromissiles" decision, but he had staked the prestige of the government and he could not back down. His only avenue of escape was a successful negotiation between the United States and the Soviet Union. In the spring of 1982, Ronald Reagan bowed to the pressure of the Atlanticists in the State Department and the entreaties of every Allied politician. He proposed his own version of the "zero option" advocated in Europe: The new missiles would not be deployed if the Soviets agreed to remove all their SS-20s and other missiles threatening West Europe. The measure was designed to deflate the European peace movement, but it had the opposite effect. So unlikely was it that the Soviets would give up hundreds of missiles already deployed in exchange for a promise, so far apart were the superpowers altogether, that to many it seemed all the more necessary that Europeans take their fate into their own hands.

The fear of war and growing uneasiness with the American relationship extended not only to Social Democrats but to a growing number within the CDU and FDP. An Allensbach Institute poll in the summer of 1981 showed as usual a majority of Germans favoring NATO, but it included another figure that astounded German watchers in the State Department: 45 percent of young Germans (below thirty) favored what many on the Left called "emancipation" from the alliance with America. Thirty-five years of the American alliance had not solved the "German Question." For almost twenty years Adenauer's answer to the question, "What will become of us?" was accepted: The more powerful and united the West became, the sooner the Soviet grip on the Germans across the Elbe would be loosened. With *Ostpolitik* a completely different strategy was envisaged: Eventually the systems would converge and through expanded human contacts a common German identity would once again be shared by all Germans. "I will not live to see it," Helmut Schmidt assured the viewers of *60 Minutes*. The U.S. government, which had gone to war twice in the century to combat German nationalism, was in no hurry. NATO itself had been sold and resold within the United States and West European foreign policy establishments as a leash for the Germans.

3

Visiting the White House in May 1981, Zenko Suzuki, the new prime minister of Japan, smiled as he signed a communiqué celebrating the "alliance" with the United States. The conservative ruling party, recovering from the scandals and factional fights, had scored impressive electoral gains. Like much of the rest of the world the nation appeared headed rightward. Opposition to increasing the military budget was waning. The state of the world economy had brought the usual problems to Japan, but the country was doing better in most respects than the other industrial economies—huge trade surpluses, lower inflation, less unemployment. First elected to the Diet as a Socialist after a brief career as a labor organizer, Suzuki had switched parties so that he could represent the fishing industry where his family had made its money. Having worked both sides, the prime minister was practiced in the art of calming troubled waters.

In Japan his acceptance of the word "alliance" created a furor. The foreign minister angrily told reporters that the communiqué was "not binding."

The American connection embodied in the Security Treaty was much less controversial than twenty years before, but the military connotation of the word "alliance" hit a raw nerve. The Reagan administration on taking office had immediately stepped up the pressure on Japan to rearm. U.S. senators denounced Japan in ever stronger terms for "sticking American taxpayers with the bill" for its defense. Spending less than 1 percent instead of 7 percent of the national wealth each year on the military, as in the United States, added up to a considerable competitive advantage. Military expenditures were peculiarly inflationary, created relatively fewer jobs than other government expenditures, and the payoffs from military research and development in the civilian market were rare. American pressure to remilitarize Japan was motivated less by the need for reinforcements in the East than by the desire to see Japan share the pain of military expenditures. The linkage between economic and defense issues, expressed in clumsy and tentative language in the Nixon and Carter eras, was now made precise. Secretary of Defense Caspar Weinberger told the Japanese, according to *The New York Times,* that "unless Japanese military abilities were substantially and swiftly increased, Congressional pressure might lead to more American restrictions on Japanese imports or to the withdrawal of American military forces. . . ."

Organized opposition to raising the military budget had fallen, but the nuclear "allergy," as the Americans called it, was still present. Edwin Reischauer, the former ambassador, casually noted that U.S. ships had for years been bringing nuclear arms into Japanese ports with the tacit agreement of the government and the revelation created a sensation. The foreign minister reported to the Diet on Reischauer's remarks which he termed "uncalled-for meddling by an American with big-power arrogance." But the Japanese government did agree to increase the defense budget by a little over 7 percent and to consider undertaking the defense of Pacific sea lanes as far as a thousand miles from the home islands.

As the 1980s began, a debate was shaping up in Japan over its long-range security strategy and the U.S. defense connection. The Soviet buildup in the Pacific and the strong U.S. pressure to increase military spending strengthened the Japanese military. In the 1970s the military budget increased sixfold, and by the end of the decade Japan had the seventh-largest military establishment in the world. Former Prime Minister Fukuda had already noted that the antiwar provision of the constitution did not preclude Japan's acquiring nuclear weapons for "self-defense." Another cabinet minister had publicly called for getting rid of the "MacArthur" war prohibition. Japanese naval forces conducted large-scale maneuvers with the U.S. Pacific Fleet.

Yet despite these signs of change the prevailing security strategy laid out in the Japanese government's 1980 *Report on Comprehensive National Security* contrasted strikingly with U.S. thinking. The emphasis was far more political. The Soviet Union was identified as the only military threat to Japan and to be sure, a self-defense force to deter an attack on the home islands was specified. But the likelihood of such attack was rated low, and particularly so as long as China and the Soviet Union remained enemies instead of allies. Thus the Japanese worried more about the cooling of relations between Washington and Peking than about Soviet submarines. The critical security need for Japan was the maintenance of access to food and energy. Access could not be assured, the report pointed out, by military force but by what one commentator characterized as "an infinitely complex range of economic, technical, financial, moral, scientific, political and diplomatic responses." Japan must not allow its relations with its Asiatic neighbors to deteriorate. Further dramatic increases in the Japanese military could evoke memories of World War II and destroy the Asian coprosperity sphere Japan had developed since the war.

Japanese politicians well understood that the "nuclear umbrella" was an Orwellian term. America's nuclear bombs could not "defend" Japan in the literal sense, and no one believed that the United States was going to court its own nuclear destruction just because Japan was threatened. If the "umbrella" no longer reached London, Paris, and Munich, surely it was not much use in Yokohama. Some believed that America's global nuclear strategy was more like a spider web than an umbrella; Japan was integrated into U.S. nuclear war plans and thus risked being a target in a nuclear war initiated elsewhere having nothing to do with Japan. Japanese officials and commentators resented the nuclear missionaries in Washington who, as one paper put it, propose to cure the Japanese people's aversion to nuclear weapons as if it were merely an "emotional" hangover from Hiroshima and Nagasaki. The leading newspaper, *Asahi,* warned, "The Japanese hate nuclear weapons because we are aware of the danger of involvement in the nuclear strategy of a superstate" and it added ominously: "We cannot rule out the possibility Japan can become a military power to threaten its Asian neighbors and the United States." As the United States approach to security became increasingly militarized in the Reagan administration, the Japanese, though continuing to rearm, were even more conscious of how little they could do with military power. Despite the calls for more arms there remained a broad consensus on a global security strategy for Japan based on a view of the world and how to influence it that clashed with that of the White House and the Pentagon.

But if America no longer played its old roles as teacher, model, sponsor, and protector of postwar Japan, its importance remained undiminished. The United States was the crucial market, the site of increasingly large Japanese industrial development, an essential source of food, the most formidable commercial rival for the rest of the century, and for the moment the only ally in sight. America had supplied the inspiration and the driving force behind the postwar technological revolution and still had a crucial role in Japan's technological development. The answer to every Japanese problem, it seemed, was high technology. In defense, former Foreign Minister Saburo Okita had suggested that the nation's extreme vulnerability could be reduced through highly sophisticated defensive technology in the fields of information gathering, communications, and command and control. The answer to the energy crisis was to develop new technologies to improve energy efficiency and productivity.

Aware that the self-inflicted wound of the U.S. carmakers would eventually heal and that Detroit would someday make efficient, energy-saving vehicles, Japanese industrial planners sought to outflank its competitors once again by developing markets for new high-technology products.

Less than forty years before, Douglas MacArthur had thought America's Japanese problem was Nippon's legacy of heroic feudalism, but the problem had turned out to be Japan's extraordinary rush to embrace and to master the culture of materialism. In a futuristic factory at the foot of Mount Fuji industrial robots were at work twenty-four hours a day making more robots; more than fourteen thousand were already relentlessly welding, painting, lifting, even slicing sushi all across Japan. Japanese businessmen seemed more in tune with the age, more modern, in a way, than their competitors in the New World. In 1955 Sony had intuitively understood that the peculiar isolation of contemporary men and women made them ideal customers for a simple artificial connector like the mass-market transistor radio. In 1980 Masaya Nakamura, sensing perhaps that people, having lost control over their lives, would want to indulge their fantasies and do battle with the machines, invented Pac-Man, the world's most successful video game. From MITI's project for a self-programming computer to video recorders—90 percent of which were now made in Japan despite labels like RCA or Zenith—to the preemptive marketing of the fabulous 64K random access memory chip, the "Japanese challenge" seemed to be at the frontier of technology everywhere. Although still far behind IBM in computers, the Japanese set a goal of capturing 30 percent of global sales by 1990.

Thus there was a tinge of relief to the anger at news of the arrest in June 1982 of thirteen Hitachi employees as they were about to purchase stolen IBM secrets. The Justice Department had caught them in a "sting" setup which did nothing for the reputation in Japan of American sportsmanship. But the incident confirmed old American prejudices. If the United States was being outcompeted, someone was doing something underhanded. As for the Japanese, they only knew how to copy technology, not "innovate" it.

For a generation of American managers who had long been used to setting the pace of technological development all over the world, it was hard to believe anything else. After all, the United States still produced Nobel Prize winners almost as if it had a corner on scientific ideas. But the new generation of technology was a product of painstaking, well-financed "copying," called "development" in polite circles, rather than brilliant flashes of "pure" research. Japanese firms were committing huge funds to this effort, mostly from their own savings. Japanese executives sacrificed for the firm by taking far greater pay cuts in bad times than their American counterparts, and the salaries were much smaller to begin with. The workers were more productive because they were more secure. Because of the high ratio of debt to equity shareholders were relatively unimportant and the managers were not under the pressure of U.S. publicly traded companies to return quick profits.

As Japan entered the 1980s, however, enormous problems loomed. As the economy slowed, the island superpower was exhibiting the familiar strains of prosperity. The costs of the welfare state were rising steeply. Affluence was changing traditional attitudes toward hard work. While the Japanese work ethic was being celebrated in America, it was already beginning to disappear in Japan. Japanese multinationals were moving more and more of the nation's production to the factories of East Asia where a work force that resembled Japan's a generation before awaited, and the consequence was mounting unemployment. As the internationalization of the Japanese economy proceeded, the importance of exports grew and with it the potential for even greater economic conflict with the United States. The composition of Japanese-American trade helped to explain the new tension. From the industrial giant of the world the protectorate in the far Pacific was buying primarily melons, logs, corn, wheat, and coal while managing to dominate 70 percent of the superpower's home market in advanced computer memory chips. "Whoever controls memory chips in the coming decade," a high Reagan administration trade official warned, "will be a little like the oil exporters of today. The stakes involve not only world economic leadership, but national security."

4

"Your isolationism is feeding our own," a succession of American diplomats warned German Foreign Office officials in the aftermath of the great peace demonstrations. It was meant as a threat and it was not an idle one. "The American people may not wish to bear the burden of necessary defense expenditures if they think some are doing less as we do more," Secretary of Defense Weinberger goaded the Europeans. The style of the new administration was unilateralist. Americans would be looking after their own interests. The Europeans and Japanese, with a combined GNP of about 90 percent of that of the United States, spent far less on defense—1 percent of GNP for Japan, 3.5 percent for the NATO countries compared with 5.8 percent for the United States—and with the onset in 1981 of the worst economic crisis since World War II, there was no chance whatever that they would keep their promises to raise spending 3 percent a year. Indeed the Germans planned to reduce the military budget. If Europeans did not wish to be protected, if they saw the Soviet Union more as a customer than as an adversary, more and more Americans argued, perhaps the alliance was over. A senior Reagan adviser early in the administration gave his private prediction that NATO would not last three years.

Much of the isolationist rhetoric from America was familiar posturing. Since the days of the Mansfield Amendment, threatening to bring the troops home had been used as a bludgeon to secure European cooperation on a whole series of issues. Just as Adenauer had once evoked the specter of German nationalism and Rapallo in bargaining with the allies, thirty years later the Americans evoked their own isolationist history. (A new Rapallo was now a

sufficiently plausible possibility that the German government devoted its efforts to minimizing the threat, not evoking it.) But in 1982 the Americans were
no longer merely posturing. The domestic consensus in support of NATO was
beginning to erode. Neoconservatives like Irving Kristol, once the most enthusiastic supporter of the network of military alliances, now concluded that
"NATO ceased to be a living reality some years ago. . . ." In *The Wall Street
Journal,* one of the regular conservative contributors to the editorial page
declared, "The time has come for the U.S. to sever its ties with NATO."

Historically, isolationism had meant not retreat from all parts of the world
but rather rejection of Europe and increased engagement elsewhere, and now
Pentagon plans themselves suggested a revival of this impulse. The huge increase in military spending was going primarily to purchase new nuclear weapons systems to be used by the United States alone, a much expanded navy, a
Rapid Deployment Force and new bases for the projection of U.S. military
power in the Third World, and a space race, none of which promised an increase in European security. At the same time U.S. defense officials dropped
hints that the United States might not renew the treaty restricting the antiballistic missile, more evidence, along with the administration's enthusiasm for
civil defense, that Americans believed that they could survive a nuclear war—
fought somewhere else. Pentagon documents exploring possible new alliances
with Middle East partners or with the nations of the "Pacific Rim," were
periodically leaked in the newspapers. All these signs of American restiveness
in response to the political turmoil of Europe reinforced the credibility of the
neutralists on the Continent who argued that the United States wanted only
clients, not allies.

The cost of building a Fortress America would in quite direct ways be
borne by Europeans as well as the American taxpayers. To spend $1.6 trillion
in four years, a 14 percent increase over the Carter budget projections, guaranteed a federal deficit of well over $100 billion a year. Since the Treasury (on
behalf of the Pentagon, to a great extent) was the nation's number one bor-
rower, its formidable credit requirements drove interest rates up even more
than the tight money enthusiasts at the Federal Reserve had planned. The
result was that investment in Europe stagnated as the dollar grew stronger.
European central banks did not dare to match the American interest rates for
fear of courting a depression, and with the flow of capital out of Europe, the
dollar value of major European currencies declined 40 percent in less than two
years. All this had devastating effects on trade and investment. "How can we
defend our alliance with the United States," French Finance Minister Jacques
Delors snapped, "when critics say American policy is making us bankrupt?"

The world was now in a depression. The word, of course, was no longer
fashionable, but no other did justice to the reality: thirty million unemployed
in the twenty-four industrialized nations of the OECD, excess industrial capacity, lagging productivity, and major business failures. (Braniff, Telefunken, and
others.) As world demand shrank, the major industrial countries put increasing
emphasis on exports as a solution to their flagging economic growth and

mounting unemployment. In the 1970s both the United States and Japan doubled the share of their gross national product devoted to exports. Thus the
preconditions for an intensified trade war were set. As Japan felt the rising
protectionist reflex in the United States, it stepped up its export offensive in
Europe, but this led the vice-president of the European Commission to predict
the possibility of "a total ban on Japanese imports." The island superpower
was actually the "most vulnerable" to trade barriers. Parts of the Ruhr, Lorraine, and Wallonia now looked like Youngstown—idle mills, bankruptcies,
dejected faces of the unemployed—for the world steel industry was operating
between 60 and 80 percent of capacity.

Reagan administration officials charged the Europeans with dumping steel
in the United States. Congressman John D. Dingell called it a form of "economic warfare" by the European Allies that had "pushed 80,000 steelworkers
in[to] the unemployment lines." Even in the principal source of America's
export power, the agricultural economy, the Europeans were resisting U.S.
grain, corn gluten, soybeans, and other products from the great food belt on
which the nation so heavily depended for foreign exchange. Not only were the
Europeans importing less food but they were exporting more in traditional
U.S. markets in the Middle East and Latin America, an "unfriendly action,"
Secretary of Agriculture John R. Block declared. "We are clearly on a collision
course," Deputy Secretary of Agriculture Raymond E. Lyng predicted. The
European Community, now twenty-five years old, was beset by internal squab-
bles—diplomats in mirrored halls haggling over the price of a leg of lamb, as
the British negotiator put it—and becoming increasingly protectionist-minded.
German beer was not quite "pure" enough to enter Alsace-Lorraine; Italian
wine was not quite right for France, and so on. The Monnet dream was gone.
The fight for markets within Europe made it improbable that the Common
Market would back down in the face of American threats.

Against the backdrop of these structural changes in the world economy,
the Polish crisis of 1982 precipitated an acrimonious split in the alliance.
Though rooted deep in her own history, including age-old antipathy to Russia,
Poland's crisis was a product of détente. Edward Gierek had come to power at
the beginning of the 1970s determined to deal with the public anger that had
periodically exploded in strikes and riots by putting more food on the table,
more goods in the shops, and more money in people's pockets. In the new
political climate this could be done by integrating Poland into the world economy. By the mid-1970s Poland was the third-fastest growing country in the
world, its new prosperity fueled by exports financed through enormous loans
by West European and American banks. But by the time the loans came due
at the end of the 1970s the prosperity was over. The export market had shrunk
thanks to the energy crisis and the world recession. Poland had tied its fate to
the world economy at the wrong time. Now the government could no longer
subsidize food and other essentials to the same extent. But even modest steps
toward austerity provoked strikes which coalesced into an independent workers' movement known as Solidarity. By late 1981 the movement, which had

elicited admiration from trade unionists, Catholics, Democratic Socialists, and anti-Communists, as well as mounting anxiety from the bankers waiting to have their loans repaid, had made a bid to share political power with the Communist party. The Soviets issued periodic warnings that this would not be tolerated and punctuated them with threatening military maneuvers. For a year politicians in the West openly speculated about a Soviet armed intervention.

On the night of December 13, 1981, Polish General Wojciech Jaruzelski executed a lightning-swift military coup. The entire leadership of Solidarity was arrested. Martial law was declared. Communications with the outside world were cut. At least seven miners were killed near Katowice. As Neal Ascherson puts it in his study *The Polish August,* "Soviet instigation of the coup remains unproved." It may have been a purely Polish initiative to forestall a Soviet intervention. But Soviet responsibility for the national tragedy was clear; adhering to his own dominoes theory, Brezhnev was determined to preserve the authority of the Polish Communist party.

All across West Europe there was shock at the speed with which Solidarity was suppressed, relief that the Soviets had not marched, and compassion for the people of Poland. Millions of food parcels were shipped to Poland in an outpouring of spontaneous humanitarian sentiment. At the same time there were mixed feelings about the victims who had precipitated the crisis. Solidarity had gone too fast, tried too much. Now perhaps the Poles would go back to work and pay off the staggering debts to German, French, and Italian banks, some of which faced bankruptcy in the event of a Polish default.

Ronald Reagan was interrupted while watching a movie at Camp David with the first reports of the coup and he immediately issued orders to prepare a range of punishments to administer to the Soviets. Helmut Schmidt was sleeping in a hunting lodge in East Germany, the guest of Erich Honecker, the head of the Communist Party. He continued his talks the next day as if the brutal events in Poland had not occurred. From the first hours of the Polish crisis it was evident that the leaders in Europe and the United States saw it differently. Reagan spoke of what the Soviets had done, but Schmidt, Mitterrand, and the rest preferred to act on appearances; the Soviets had not done anything that anyone could see, and what they had done in fact no one knew for sure. The president, who had just finished smashing the air controllers' union, found himself in the unusual role of championing workers' rights, but the White House rhetoric was dismissed widely in Europe as a pretext for squeezing the Soviets economically. Not only had the administration advertised a hard-boiled attitude on human rights violations everywhere outside the Soviet bloc, but more than once it had volunteered its view that the Soviet Union was in deep economic trouble and that concerted pressure from the West would pay big dividends.

Schmidt took a cautious view of the Polish affair from the start. It was an internal matter. It would surely not be permitted to disrupt détente. When a high State Department official flew to Bonn in the aftermath of the coup with a list of possible sanctions, Foreign Minister Genscher would not even discuss them. After a meeting with Reagan in early January, Schmidt delivered a mild public rebuke of the repression in Poland. In his private conversations, a White House aide briefed the press, "he did his usual sermon. It seemed a clear effort to stave off awkward exchanges on Poland." Returning to Bonn the Bundes-kanzler ordered a reduction of diplomatic attendance at Soviet and Polish cocktail parties and a few other traditional gestures for registering sovereign displeasure, but to join the United States in its own program of denying tech-nology sales, suspending air service, and all further government credits for Poland was out of the question—especially since the sanctions were an-nounced without consultation on three hours' notice. The U.S. attitude summed up by a German diplomat—"We'll tell you what we are going to do, we do it, and we expect you to follow suit"—was offensive. The Germans were determined to prove to the Americans that it "just doesn't work."

Ironically, the Europeans who came closest to echoing the outrage of Ronald Reagan over Poland were peace movement activists for whom the coup made the dream of a united, denuclearized Europe seem all the more attractive and all the more unlikely. Admiring of Solidarity's brave effort, sensitive to the charges of "appeasement" of the Russian colossus, the Greens, many on the left wing of the Social Democratic party, and church activists denounced the Soviets even as they intensified their efforts for disarmament. The putsch posed a moral dilemma for the peace movement no less than for the govern-ment. Fear had brought millions to the streets but fear alone was not enough to sustain the movement. Acquiescence in the *fait accompli* in Poland sug-gested not only a certain degree of intimidation but also the one-sided critique of the superpowers which the movement had struggled to avoid. The moral vision that the peace activists held out as the alternative to a "Europe of the superpowers" clashed with the emerging political reality: It was not wholly implausible that the American troops might one day soon be called home, but when would the Soviet troops leave Eastern Europe? Official peace move-ments financed by the governments were vocal throughout the East, but when an independent peace movement openly supported by Protestant church lead-ers suddenly appeared in East Germany and organized marches with several thousand people, East German officials clamped down harshly.

When the Polish coup was a little over two weeks old, the United States announced an embargo on shipments of all technology to the USSR relating to the production or transportation of oil and gas. From the first it was evident that West Germany and France would not follow suit. As a philosophical matter neither believed in economic warfare of this sort. With an estimated 450,000 German jobs depending upon trade with the East amidst the worst unemployment crisis in more than a generation and more than 700 firms en-gaged in various production arrangements in Eastern Europe, economic sanc-tions made no sense for the Federal Republic. The jobs, the $1.5 billion trade surplus with the East, and above all the Germans living under Soviet control were hostages to the continuation of normal relations. The issue of sanctions that increasingly brought the United States into conflict with its Allies centered on a $15 billion pipeline project to carry natural gas from the Yamal Peninsula east of the Urals far above the Arctic Circle to West Germany, France, Italy, the Low Countries, and Scandinavia. In the summer of 1982 the dispute over the Soviet pipeline erupted, producing an atmosphere of crisis as serious as any in the history of the alliance.

United States officials had long been worried about Europe's growing dependence upon gas and oil from the East since the Kennedy administration when the issue of building oil pipelines connecting the two halves of Europe had first been proposed. In July 1980 the West German government had approved the pipeline deal and agreed to lend the Soviets $4.75 billion. The Reagan administration had two reasons for wanting to break up the arrangements. The Federal Republic, U.S. officials believed, would be even less willing to resist disturbing moves by the U.S.S.R. if it were more dependent upon Soviet gas. Moreover, the Soviets would earn billions in foreign exchange which would ease their economic difficulties and make them more formidable military competitors.

The strategic planners in Washington seemed in the grip of ideological passion, not logic. No one believed that the sanctions would cause the Russians to order the end of martial law in Poland. The dependency argument was exaggerated. When the Soviet gas deliveries reached their peak, Count Otto Lambsdorff, the West German minister of economics, pointed out, they would represent about 30 percent of gas consumption or about 5 to 6 percent of total energy needs. "We have a flexible West European gas pipeline network which would allow us to switch to other resources. . . ."

The minister denied the American charge that the Germans were giving the Soviets "foreign aid" by granting loans to Moscow with below market interest rates. The concessions on loans were balanced by commercial concessions. Besides, the OECD countries had agreed to raise the interest rates. The most telling rejoinder to the administration was to point out that to stop the deal would hurt the West far more than the Soviet Union. The USSR depended little on trade. It was simply not credible that a few billion dollars in foreign exchange would cause the Soviets to change their military priorities, especially since most of the raw materials for military production were procured within the USSR. There were chinks in the moral arguments of the Americans. Turkey had been under a particularly brutal martial law without it even being publicly noticed in Washington. Moreover, it seemed hypocritical that even as he pressed the Allies not to sell technology to the Russians, President Reagan promised "record" Soviet wheat deals for the Kansas farmers.

In early June, Reagan set out on a European tour advertised as a major effort to repair the alliance. A few days before, the Düsseldorf offices of IBM and Control Data Corporation had been bombed, along with the headquarters building of the Fifth Corps in Frankfurt and officers clubs at three other military bases. The ten-day swing through Europe was produced as a pageant—horseback riding with the queen of England with "photo opportunities" for all, a glittering dinner at Buckingham Palace (a request to have White House stewards observe the preparation of food was politely refused), speeches to the British Parliament and the Bundestag. Beneath the veneer of pomp, the atmosphere was prickly. The Secret Service insisted on inspecting the carbines of the honor guard welcoming the president to Bonn to ensure that the weapons were not loaded. The climax was a summit meeting in the magnificent Salle du Sacre at Versailles, during which Ronald Reagan occasionally dozed off. The president struck the leaders of Europe as gracious, ignorant, and stubborn.

The allies disagreed as usual about many things. On none was more heat generated than the matter of the Soviet pipeline. The president alone argued for dropping the project but no one agreed, and every leader left the meeting with the belief that the Americans would reluctantly bow to the inevitable. Thus the shock was considerable exactly two weeks later when the president announced without prior warning that the sanctions against selling energy-related technology to the Soviets enacted six months earlier would now be extended to overseas subsidiaries of U.S. companies and to non-American companies producing such technology under a license from U.S. firms. Any foreign firm that violated the ban could be denied access to U.S. goods and information and was subject to a fine. British companies like John Brown Engineering, Ltd., the venerable builder of the *Lusitania* and the *Queen Elizabeth,* was now threatened with the loss of a $182 million contract to supply turbines. The Italian company Nuovo Pignone now faced the loss of a $650 million contract to sell compressor stations. AEG Telefunken, recently the object of an unusual rescue operation by the German government to stave off collapse, would lose $270 million by complying with the president's order.

From the start it was evident that the Europeans would not comply. More than considerable amounts of money was involved. The United States was invoking the principle of extraterritoriality, purporting to control the economic activity of other countries to serve its own policy objectives which those countries did not share. "For all practical purposes," Schmidt declared, "U.S. policy . . . has taken on a form that suggests an end to friendship and partnership." Margaret Thatcher was "deeply wounded." François Mitterrand could not believe that his loyalty to Reagan on the missiles would be rewarded with a challenge to French sovereignty. The Europeans ordered the projects to continue and the Reagan administration began proceedings to blacklist the leading firms of its allies. The sanction decision provided the clearest evidence yet of the isolationist turn American policy had taken.

5

By 1982 relations among the Allies deteriorated further. French Foreign Minister Claude Cheysson warned of the "creeping divorce" that was taking place between America and Europe. "We no longer speak the same language." A joint report on the state of the alliance by the Council on Foreign Relations and the most influential foreign policy institutes in London, Bonn, and Paris solemnly concluded: "The days of the old 'Atlantic' system, based on U.S. predominance and its corollary, European reluctance to take wider responsibilities are over." When the U.S. under secretary of state, Lawrence Eagleburger, declared that his goal was to "create an identity of interests [with West Germany] based on the visions of the 1980's which is equally as strong as that which was based on the visions of the 1940's and 1950's" he dramatized the problem. Common interests remained in the 1980s but the view from Washington, Bonn, Rome, Paris, and Tokyo increasingly diverged. The military, economic, and political underpinnings of America's Atlantic and Pacific alliances had come loose.

The military reality had changed and the public perception of that reality had changed even more. The American protection against the theoretical but unlikely prospect of Soviet military aggression was no longer a relatively cost-free insurance policy. Whatever credibility the American promise to sacrifice New York for Frankfurt had ever had since the end of America's own brief period of invulnerability rested on Soviet fear of American irrationality. The Americans just might proceed step by step into the war that would destroy their own two-hundred-year experiment and perhaps the whole world. But increasingly the nuclear strategy for keeping Europe free appeared to be based on absurdity and gamble—the absurdity that the American president would precipitate the destruction of the United States to "save" Europe and the gamble that the solemn pledge to commit suicide would never be tested. As long as the arms race was relatively stable, Europeans and Japanese simply repressed the danger. But the very process of deterrence seemed to require periodic escalation in the development of lethal technology, and the selling of astronomical military appropriations seemed to demand periodic campaigns to scare the public. America's belligerence and frustration, so it appeared to growing numbers in Europe and Japan, endangered their ancient civilizations with no real promise of defending them. With all its emphasis on military power as the basis of its leadership, the United States managed to demonstrate the limits of military power by its defeat in Vietnam and its show of impotence in Iran.

Junior membership in an American alliance struck the moderate or conservative politicians of Europe and Japan in the 1950s and 1960s as a price well worth paying to secure the benefits of American power in dealing with the Soviet Union. Identification with America's global objectives proved to be an important source of domestic political support because of the widespread fear of Communism and the Soviet Union among the voters. But while distrust of the Soviet Union remained in Europe and even grew somewhat in Japan in the 1980s, the analysis of the Soviet colossus had changed. Local left-wing forces no longer appeared as Soviet agents. The theoretical danger of a Soviet military attack remained, but it was more dubious than ever. Winston Churchill's famous assertion that but for the American bomb the Red Army would have been at the English Channel looked in retrospect rather implausible. Though it was impossible to prove one way or another, the lack of any historical evidence

of such intentions and the devastation under which the Soviets labored at the
end of the war made this essential myth undergirding NATO less and less
compelling. Unable to stabilize its hegemony over Eastern Europe with large
occupation forces, the Russians could hardly look forward to a comfortable
time in West Europe, assuming that there was much left to control or to steal
once they got there. The unreliable armies of their Polish, Czech, and Hungarian allies in their rear were more a deterrent to marching west than a military
asset.

The Americans lacked a winning military strategy to deal with the crude
threat to which their preparations were addressed; neither the nuclear arsenals
nor the rapid deployment force deterred the Soviets in Afghanistan and nothing
suggested that an American military establishment twice as big would have
been more successful. In Tokyo as well as in the European capitals, the Soviet
Union was perceived as a nation for which a strategy of coexistence had to be
devised, not as a power to be defeated or a pariah to be quarantined. To the
extent that the Americans looked at the Soviet threat in apocalyptical or ideological terms, the more attractive it became for Europeans and Japanese to
reclaim responsibility for their own defense. What the Americans asked of
them was something quite different: Not independent defense planning but
greater contributions to a common defense strategy orchestrated in Washington. But the more the Americans seemed fixed on a hopeless military competition with the Soviet Union, the less effective they seemed as managers of the
common cause that had brought the alliance into being.

The pioneer revolutionary power of the modern era had become less a
cause and more a troubled country. But the United States, now beset by
unprecedented economic problems and political uncertainty, was not a particularly inspiring model either. Indeed, for the 90 percent of the earth's population who were neither Russians nor Americans the Cold War was a
monstrously expensive irrelevance which diverted resources and energy from
attacking the chronic poverty and institutional violence that threatened billions
of men and women in Asia, Africa and Latin America. The American alliance
was incapable of dealing with these issues. Indeed the partners were already
vying with one another for positions of influence in the Third World as they
cut separate deals with developing countries.

Economic relationships among the allies had changed as radically as the
foundations of the military alliance. By the 1980s the U.S. share of world
manufactured exports had fallen precipitously, and though the dollar was
strong once again, Washington no longer controlled the world monetary system. With the U.S. economy more dependent than ever on exports, U.S.
manufacturers were increasingly challenged in world markets—including their
own home market. Thirty-five years after the MacArthur occupation, Japan
was offering a line of credit to the state of Michigan, home of the stricken car
industry. In its moment of supremacy, the United States had been forced to
diffuse its extraordinary power in the hope of securing long-term stability, but
in the process it built competitors and undermined its own hegemonic concep-

tion of a Western alliance run from Washington. The United States was still the world's largest economy, better able to take the shocks of deep recession than its junior partners. Yet all through the 1970s, by almost any measure —that is, productivity, rate of savings, energy conservation, and product innovation—the protectorates had done better economically than the protector.

The revival of the neutralist impulse in Europe evidenced by the publication in 1981 of books such as Peter Bender's *The End of the Ideological Age* reflected the loss of America's ideological as well as economic hegemony. By the 1980s the Vietnam generation had come to positions of prominence in politics and in television, magazines, and newspapers throughout Europe and Japan and they did not regard the U.S. government in the same positive light that prevailed in their parents' generation. (Symbols of wounded pride or moral outrage stick in the national memory; occasions for gratitude are easily forgotten.) High-technology culture was now international: America was no longer its unique source. Other industrial countries (once unwanted "guests" were deported) looked after their workers and the poor and helpless with greater compassion than the United States did. In no other industrial country were the centers of major cities such wastelands. With a homicide rate eight times that of West Germany, the United States looked less and less like the moral arbiter of the Free World.

The history of diplomacy is a story of shifting alliances. George Washington and De Gaulle understood better than most contemporary politicians who missed the great surprises of our age such as the Sino-Soviet dispute or the Iranian revolution that nations do not, cannot, have permanent attachments. The present anarchic international system is always in motion. Times change, and so do allies. The postwar alliance of victors and vanquished was itself proof of that.

By the early 1980s both the United States and the Soviet Union were seeking to reassert greater control over their respective allies and clients and in the process tensions within both blocs increased. The arms race, the lethal game that absorbed both superpowers, struck their respective allies as suicidal. Increasing numbers in West Europe and in the Soviet client states of the East found themselves more absorbed with the problems posed by their protector than by their adversary. Détente nourished a spirit of independence and diversity in both halves of Europe, which made it more difficult to revive Cold War confrontation or to reestablish superpower discipline over the junior partners of the West and the satellites of the East.

The domestic political consensus behind the alliance was eroding on both sides of the Atlantic and in Japan. What Europeans complained of as "hegemony," Americans considered unappreciated sacrifice. Support for the security arrangements with the United States remained strong in Japan, but privately politicians and diplomats raised once unthinkable questions about what Japan's relations with its protector should be in a world where the risks of ever fiercer trade wars and arms races were mounting. The restiveness of allies elicited impatience and resentment in America for the costs of alliance mounted even as the benefits became harder to define.

Since the age of empires was over, and vainglorious rhetoric was no longer in fashion, presidents had built domestic support for the alliance by talking about responsibilities, burdens, and sacrifice. President Reagan put it most starkly. America is great. America is good. The economic and political rationale that had impelled the original architects of the alliance—that the United States must play the hegemonic power in Europe or face a continent dominated by either Russia or Germany—had scarcely ever been mentioned in public discourse. Most Americans understood NATO in purely military terms, a modern-day Maginot Line to keep Russian tanks out of Berlin, Frankfurt, and Paris. Why then, more and more of them now asked, should they devote hundreds of billions of dollars to defend Europeans who did not appreciate the sacrifice? In Europe and Japan, on the other hand, America's faltering leadership raised new doubts about the wisdom of entrusting their defense to a distant superpower in evident confusion over its very identity as a world actor. Yet the fear of the Soviet Union and the lingering suspicion of a Germany cut off from the American alliance kept the partnership from unraveling altogether. The industrial nations of North America and Europe needed one another no less than before, and for the Japanese, reversion to isolationism was not an option. But the extraordinary alliance of the industrial nations had, over 30 years, helped to create a new world in which the common security required a new burst of innovation no less than that which occurred almost two generations ago.

NOTES

These notes are provided for the reader who wishes to further document or explore in greater detail the events described in the text. Abbreviated citations are provided for books; for a full citation see the Bibliography. Articles and government documents are cited in full.

Chapter 1

Page
15 Adenauer's visit to Arlington cemetery recorded in Charles Wighton, *Adenauer: A Critical Biography,* p. 181. For another biography of Adenauer's life and political career see Terence Prittie, *Konrad Adenauer: 1876–1967.*
16 "We wish to know, sir . . .": Wighton, p. 72.
17 "as a constant reminder . . .": Konrad Adenauer, *Memoirs,* vol. I, p. 20.
17 Lucius D. Clay's reaction to JCS 1067 found in his *Decision in Germany,* p. 17.
17 Clay's meeting with Roosevelt, ibid. p. 5.
18 Robert Murphy's opinion of JCS 1067 in his memoirs, *Diplomat Among Warriors,* p. 283.
18 Allied objectives on Germany stated at Yalta recorded in Joyce and Gabriel Kolko, *The Limits of Power,* p. 113. Primary data on the Yalta Conference found in the U.S. Department of State, *Foreign Relations of the United States: The Conference at Malta and Yalta, 1945.*
18 For statistics on war damage in Germany see Edwin Hartrich, *The Fourth and Richest Reich,* pp. 32, 33.
19 Speer quoted in ibid., p. 31.
19 Statistics on malnutrition and disease in postwar Germany cited in Alfred Grosser, *Germany in Our Time,* p. 52.
19 "I slept in an unheated room . . .": Adenauer, p. 56.
20 "state of intoxication": Golo Mann quoted in Hartrich, p. 63.

20   German jokes about occupation in ibid.

20   For examples of "German contempt," see "Die Sauhund' hau'n Wir Wieder 'Naus" in *Der Spiegel,* no. 47, 1980.

20   Zuckmayer quoted in Grosser, *The Western Alliance,* p. 49.

21   Enzensberger quoted from personal interview with author.

21   "No steps . . . would be taken . . .": Hartrich, p. 46.

21   Statements of resentful Germans drawn from Drew Middleton, "Germans Today: Doleful and Angry," in *The New York Times Magazine,* September 16, 1945, pp. 10, 11.

21   For Coser's article see "Germany 1948: Incidents Taken From the German Press and Letters," *Commonweal,* June 11, 1948, pp. 208, 210, 211.

22   "Whatever secret cynicisms . . .": Murphy's cable to Washington cited in Jean Edward Smith, "The View from USFET: General Clay's and Washington's Interpretation of Soviet Intentions in Germany, 1945–1948," in Hans A. Schmitt, ed., *U.S. Occupation in Europe after World War II,* p. 68.

22   "eastern Germany is now experiencing . . .": Kolko, p. 134.

22   Statistics on industrial output in ibid.

23   "The entire records of . . .": Clay quoted in Smith, p. 70.

23   "The French Government . . .": Murphy quoted in ibid., p. 68.

23   "without American help . . .": Grosser, *Alliance,* p. 26.

23   "What an injustice if now . . .": ibid., p. 6.

24   "The United States brings . . .": Charles de Gaulle, *War Memoirs,* vol I, p. 209.

24   Account of De Gaulle's speech before the Normandy invasion in Grosser, *Alliance,* p. 26.

24   See Arthur Conte, *Yalta ou le Partage du Monde.*

25   See Grosser, *Western Alliance,* pp. 23, 27, for De Gaulle's wartime conflicts with Eisenhower.

26   Adenauer's treatment at the hands of the British described in his *Memoirs,* p. 32; see also Wighton, p. 77.

27   Statistics on German war prisoners in Grosser, *Germany,* p. 59.

27   "middle course between the requirements . . .": Hartrich p. 279.

27   "We're going to have to fight . . .": Patton quoted in E. H. Cookridge, *Gehlen, Spy of the Century,* p. 127.

27   "With a gleam in his eye . . .": Murphy, p. 294.

29   For more on Reinhard Gehlen see his autobiography, *The Service: The Memoirs of General Reinhard Gehlen,* and Heinz Hoehne and Herman Zolling, *The General Was a Spy: The Truth About General Gehlen and His Spy Ring.*

29   For a full account of how the White Russian Nazi collaborators were brought to the United States by U.S. intelligence agencies, see John Loftus, *The Belarus Secret.*

29   "We French take the point . . .": Perrin-Pelletier quoted in Hartrich, p. 65.

29   Statistics on Nazi trials in British Zone cited in ibid., p. 66.

29   "As we Russians are . . .": ibid., p. 64.

30   For American denazification policy, see John Gimbel, *The American Occupation of Germany: Politics and the Military, 1945–1949,* p. 103.

30   "a Nazi torture camp . . .": Murphy, p. 294.

30   "We are sorely disappointed . . .": Gimbel, p. 106.

30   "I cannot operate these banks . . .": Hartrich p. 282.

31   For Lewis H. Brown's denunciation of denazification, see his *A Report on Germany,* pp. 37, 38.

31 "Denazification is a failure . . .": see Joseph Napoli, "Denazification from an American's Viewpoint." *The Annals of the American Academy,* vol. 264, 1950, p. 121.

31 "the evidence of bones . . .": ibid., p. 116.

32 "Can't you think of something . . .": Hartrich, p. 71.

33 United States efforts to rebuild German unions described in Kolko, p. 125. See also Hartrich, pp. 90–99, on U.S. and German redemocratization.

33 "best thing we ever did . . .": Howley quoted in Kolko, p. 130.

33 "In any event, political education . . .": Hartrich p. 98.

34 Deindustrialization discussed in Hartrich, pp. 75–90.

34 See ibid., p. 83, for statistics on decartelization.

34 "could see no purpose . . .": Stimson quoted in ibid., p. 78.

34 "To keep the German people . . .": Henry Morgenthau, *The Morgenthau Diary,* p. 74. *See under* Government Documents.

35 "see in central agencies . . .": Kennan quoted in Kolko, p. 136.

35 "If economic unity proves . . .": Clay's cable cited in Hartrich, p. 85.

35 "We saw more than a scattering . . .": James Stewart Martin, *All Honorable Men,* p. 219.

36 "You know that we have got . . .": ibid., p. 11

36 Francis Biddle's testimony cited in ibid., p. 14.

36 For Joseph Borkin's study of I. G. Farben, see *The Crime and Punishment of I. G. Farben.*

37 General Clay's opinion of the decartelization group and characterization of Martin in Clay, p. 331.

37 Bentley's testimony cited in Morgenthau, p. 10.

38 "represented economic principles . . .": quoted in Martin, p. 232.

39 The case of Alfried Krupp discussed in William Manchester, *The Arms of Krupp: 1587–1968.* John McCloy quoted, p. 762.

39 "We got back on our feet . . .": ibid., p. 746.

40 The use of Lucky Strikes as currency described by Hartrich, pp. 39, 40.

40 "inevitable alternative of treating . . .": Clay quoted in Kolko, p. 141.

41 "one of the harshest acts . . .": Crawley quoted in Hartrich, p. 128.

41 [it] transformed the German scene . . .": Henry Wallich quoted in ibid., p. 132.

42 Erhard and his policies are described in Grosser, *Germany,* and in Hartrich, pp. 135–50.

42 "Various liberalizing measures . . .": quoted in Grosser, *Germany,* p. 178.

42 "Everywhere, in France, Denmark, . . .": Grosser, *Alliance,* p. 52.

43 "It seems to me . . .": Clay quoted in Jean Edward Smith, ed., *The Papers of General Lucius D. Clay,* vol. III, p. 376.

43 Clay's efforts to counter Socialism, see Gimbel, pp. 117, 118.

44 See William Harlan Hale, Germany's "deformed conscience," *Harper's,* January 1946.

44 For articles on "the German mind," see Eduard C. Lindeman, "Inside the German Mind," *Saturday Review of Literature,* December 15, 1945; and Shepard Stone, "Report on the Mood in Germany," *The New York Times Magazine,* January 26, 1947.

44 Statistics on unemployment and inflation in Germany cited in Hartrich, pp. 140, 141.

45 German economic recovery described in ibid., pp. 142–49.

45 "ignoring the prescriptions . . .": *The Wall Street Journal* quoted in ibid., p. 285.

46   The Berlin Blockade and subsequent Allied airlift described in Clay, pp. 358–92.

47   For more on drafting of the Basic Law, see Gimbel, Chaps. 12, 13.

47   The best biography of Kurt Schumacher in English is by Lewis J. Edinger, *Kurt Schumacher: A Study in Personality and Political Behavior.*

48   German public opinion surveys cited in ibid., pp. 76, 77.

49   "This sad beggar's role . . .": Schumacher's quoted in ibid., p. 92.

49   "[F]riends and pathmakers . . .": ibid., p. 151.

49   "[T]he world is very well able . . .": ibid., p. 153.

49   "We cannot regard . . .": ibid.

49   For Schumacher's views on the United States see Edinger, pp. 181–86.

49   Acheson recalls his first meeting with Adenauer and Schumacher in his book, *Sketches from Life of Men I Have Known,* pp. 171, 172.

51   "Only a great party . . .": Adenauer, p. 45.

51   "National Socialism was simply . . .": ibid., p. 39.

51   "By force of his quiet . . .": quoted in Wighton, p. 84.

53   "We had to oppose . . .": Adenauer, p. 174.

54   "He relished his brushes . . .": Kirkpatrick quoted in Prittie, p. 151.

54   "it is no longer France . . .": Wighton, p. 104.

55   "It is always difficult . . ." Poncet quoted in ibid., p. 114.

56   "Rearmament might be the way . . .": Adenauer, p. 270.

56   For a description of East Germany's "Peoples Police," see Prittie, pp. 159, 160.

56   Pleven Plan described in ibid., p. 163.

57   "God has twice dashed . . .": ibid., p. 162.

57   "to bear arms once again . . .": Schumacher quoted in William Henry Chamberlin, *The German Phoenix,* p. 204.

57   For Adenauer's demands for a new German military, see Wighton, p. 146.

57   Adenauer's memorandum to McCloy cited in Kolko, p. 658; McCloy's reaction cited in Wighton, p. 145.

57   McCloy's letter to Stimson cited in Kolko, p. 657.

Chapter 2

Page

59   MacArthur describes his meeting with Emperor Hirohito in Douglas MacArthur, *Reminiscences,* pp. 287, 288.

60   "I come to you, General . . .": Hirohito quoted in ibid., p. 288.

60   Statistics on war deaths and damage in Japan in William Manchester, *American Caesar: Douglas MacArthur, 1880–1964,* p. 520.

60   "The Emperor is to Japan . . .": Harry Emerson Wildes, *Typhoon in Tokyo: The Occupation and Its Aftermath,* pp. 66, 67.

60   "I cannot bear . . .": quoted in Manchester, p. 533.

61   "the Japanese people will never . . .": Atcheson's cable reprinted in the U.S. Department of State, *Foreign Relations of the United States, 1945: The Far East,* p. 827.

61   "The ties between us . . .": Hirohito quoted in MacArthur, p. 311.

62   For a description of MacArthur's occupation of Japan see Manchester, *American Caesar,* pp. 536–645. Insider's accounts of the occupation include: Mark J. Gayn, *Japan Diary;* William Sebald with Russell Brines, *With MacArthur in Japan;* Courtney Whitney, *MacArthur: His Rendezvous with History;* and Charles A. Willoughby, *MacArthur: 1941–1951.*

63 "a spiritual recrudescence . . . he pleads for freedom . . .": MacArthur quoted in Manchester, pp. 529, 530.
63 "the wizardry of MacArthur . . .": Sebald, p. 103.
64 "And why, as a sovereign . . .": Manchester, p. 552.
64 "Give me bread . . .": ibid., p. 544.
64 "Sometimes my whole staff . . .": ibid., p. 562.
64 "We look to MacArthur . . .": cited in John D. Montgomery, *Forced to Be Free: The Artificial Revolution in Germany and Japan,* p. 17.
65 Statistics on purges cited in ibid., p. 26.
65 "nothing more than a rewording . . .": MacArthur, p. 300.
65 "That committee is not catching . . .": Manchester, p. 587. The "constituent assembly" discussed, p. 588.
66 Whitney's exchange with Yoshida's aide cited in Whitney, pp. 251, 252.
66 "sense of deep satisfaction . . .": MacArthur, pp. 251, 252.
67 "assume any responsibility . . .": Whitney, p. 267.
67 "The only thing that will . . .": Whitney quoted in Manchester, p. 549.
67 "many of the so-called liberal . . .": MacArthur, p. 309.
67 Statistics on war damage cited in Manchester, p. 543.
68 "Certainly Whitney was no . . .": Wildes, p. 54.
68 "MacArthur's aides were Communists . . .": quoted in ibid., p. 30.
69 The attacks on MacArthur's "socialistic economic policies," cited in Manchester, p. 582. See Sebald, pp. 47–51, for his opinions of the "communist danger" in Japan.
70 Homma's and Yamashita's trials and executions are discussed in Manchester, pp. 568–74.
70 For statistics on political purges in Japan, see Hans H. Baerwald, *The Purge of Japanese Leaders Under the Occupation,* pp. 78–90.
71 "The purge as a political . . .": Montgomery, p. 33.
71 *The New Republic* and Kennan quoted in Manchester, p. 581.
71 "The Japanese police problems . . .": Whitney, p. 288.
71 "After all, my section . . .": see Mark J. Gayn, "Interview with a Tokko Official," in Jon Livingston et al., *Postwar Japan: 1945 to the Present,* p. 36.
72 Police reforms discussed in John W. Dower, *Empire and Aftermath: Yoshida Shigeru and the Japanese Experience, 1878–1954,* p. 348.
72 "The Japanese women were . . .": Whitney, p. 291.
72 For MacArthur's efforts to bring Christianity to Japan, see William P. Woodward, *The Allied Occupation of Japan: 1945–1952 and Japanese Religions.* Quotations from pp. 241–45.
74 "The *Mombusho* . . .": Hall quoted in Dower, p. 356.
74 Goals of SCAP's land reform program cited in Tadashi Fukutake, "Land Reform Laws," in Livingston et al., p. 188.
75 "When I heard the news . . .": Tekehide quoted in Kolko, p. 318.
75 On peasant unions and land reform see R. P. Dore, "Execution of Land Reform," "The Hamlet: Status, Dependence, and Class," and "The Japanese Land Reform in Retrospect," in Livingston et al.
76 For a discussion of the first postwar Japanese elections, see Thomas A. Bisson, "April 1946 Elections," in ibid., pp. 56–67.
76 Dower offers the most extensive study in English of Shigeru Yoshida's life and political career.
76 "I am not behind others . . .": Konoye quoted in ibid., p. 34.

77   "crude army intrigues . . .": ibid., p. 92.

77   "You should go to an insane asylum . . .": ibid., p. 103.

77   "Recently, as the war enters . . .": quoted in ibid., p. 263.

78   "The present economic . . .": Acheson quoted in ibid., p. 277.

78   "Hundreds of thousands . . .": Dower, p. 310.

79   MacArthur's opinion of Yoshida, cited in ibid., p. 311.

79   "I thought this very true . . .": quoted in ibid., p. 312.

80   Hakamada's boasts of Communist control of the unions cited in Wildes, p. 270.

80   "While the labor division . . .": Gayn, pp. 331, 332.

80   "I will not permit the use . . .": MacArthur, p. 308.

81   For documentation of SCAP's "reverse course," see Livingston et al., pp. 107–39.

81   Statistics on purge of leftists, see Dower, p. 316.

82   "Their faces suggest . . .": Yoshida quoted in ibid., p. 363.

82   "It is the intention of . . .": MacArthur quoted in Bisson, "The Yasuda Plan," in Livingston et al., p. 82.

83   The Edwards Report is the unofficial title of the State-War Mission on Deconcentration, *Report of the Mission on Japanese Combines*, Department of State, pub. no. 2628. ". . . the low wages . . .": p. vii.

83   Statistics on the extent of *zaibatsu* control over the Japanese economy cited in "Antitrust Fizzles in Japan," *Business Week*, April 29, 1950.

83   "A comparable business organization . . .": see Eleanor H. Hadley, "Trustbusting in Japan," *Harvard Business Review*, July 1948, p. 429. See also Hadley's longer study, *Antitrust in Japan*.

83   "Managers are those persons . . .": Thomas A. Bisson, *Zaibatsu Dissolution in Japan*. See pp. 17–21 for further discussion on Mitsui company.

84   Pledge of Mitsubishi employees cited in Hadley, "Combine Dissolution: Severing Personal Ties" in Livingston et al., p. 88.

84   "It is a great mistake . . .": Yoshida quoted in Dower, p. 297.

85   "I am far from . . .": Ginjiro Fujihara, *The Spirit of Japanese Industry*, pp. 131–34.

86   "the expression of a desire . . .": Yoshida quoted in Hadley, *Antitrust*, p. 11.

86   Kauffman's attack on plans to dismantle *zaibatsu* industries in *Newsweek*, December 1, 1947, pp. 36–38.

86   Senator Knowland's attack on MacArthur's "shocking economic policies" cited in *Newsweek*, December 22, 1947, p. 31. See also Hadley, *Antitrust*, chap. 7.

88   The Army Air Force planning document cited in Perry McCoy Smith, *The Air Force Plans for Peace, 1943–1945*.

88   For a complete examination of the remilitarization of Japan, see Dower, "The Eye of the Beholder: Background Notes on the U.S.–Japan Military Relationship," in the *Bulletin of Concerned Asian Scholars*, October 1969.

89   "It might not be beyond . . .": Kern quoted in ibid., p. 18.

90   "to erase the image of . . .": Dower, *Empire and Aftermath*, p. 397.

90   "for centuries the Japanese . . .": ibid., p. 398.

90   the idea of rearmament . . .": Shigeru Yoshida, *The Yoshida Memoirs: The Story of Japan in Crisis*, pp. 191, 192.

91   "Why don't you give someone . . .": Dulles quoted in John R. Beal, "Bull's Eye for Dulles," *Harper's*, November 30, 1951, p. 90.

91   Tokutaro's proposal for a secret army cited in Dower, *Empire and Aftermath*, p. 395.

91 "in the new Japan . . .": Allison quoted in ibid.

92 "As far as Japanese skies . . .": Yoshida, cited in ibid., pp. 390, 391.

92 "The son of a bitch . . .": Truman quoted in Manchester, p. 770.

92 For Yoshida's reaction to MacArthur's firing, see MacArthur, p. 396.

92 The political battle in the United States over Japan and the People's Republic of China described in Dower, pp. 400, 401.

92 For a discussion of Japan's economic crisis and the "Dodge Line," see M. Bronfenbrenner, "Four Positions on Japanese Finance," in *The Journal of Political Economy,* August 1950; and Jerome C. Cohen, "Economic Recovery in Japan," *Current History,* October 1950. See also Dower, chap. 11.

94 "There should be no fear . . .": Dodge quoted in Kolko, p. 522.

94 "Under the drastic methods . . .": quoted in Dower, p. 423.

94 "Japan can be independent . . .": ibid., p. 420.

94 "the first step to . . .": Hayoto quoted in ibid., p. 416.

Chapter 3

Page

95 "At this time . . .": De Gaulle quoted in Grosser, *Alliance,* p. 39.

95 "One thing I am sure . . .": Churchill quoted in ibid., p. 41.

96 For a biography of Monnet, see Merry and Serge Bromberger, *Jean Monnet and the United States of Europe.*

97 "Our greatest strength . . .": Uri quoted in ibid., p. 47.

98 "I was one of Monnet's . . .": George Ball, quoted in Grosser, p. 103.

99 Churchill's famous phrase, "the United States of Europe," cited in Bromberger, p. 56.

100 "Aren't you at least . . .": cited in Richard Hofstadter, *The American Political Tradition,* p. 348.

101 See *Problems of a Regional Security Organization,* cited in Max Beloff, *The United States and the Unity of Europe,* p. 5.

101 "Free trade is itself . . .": the *Economist* quoted in David P. Calleo and Benjamin M. Rowland, *America and the World Political Economy,* p. 23.

102 "promised the elimination . . .": see *The Memoirs of Cordell Hull,* vol. II, p. 976.

102 "Will you allow me . . .": Winston S. Churchill, *Closing the Ring,* p. 698. Churchill's instructions to Eden, p. 713.

103 "A modern form of mercantilism . . .": Calleo and Rowland, p. 39. See pages 37–42 for their discussion of the economic conflict between Britain and the United States during the war.

104 "because their principal competition . . .": Morgenthau quoted in John M. Blum, *From the Morgenthau Diaries: Years of War, 1941–1945,* p. 353.

104 "The world looks to the U.S. . . .": McCloy quoted in Daniel Yergin, *Shattered Peace,* p. 197.

104 "we face a world . . .": Forrestal quoted in ibid., p. 199.

104 Walter Lippmann's experience with Senator Vandenberg recorded in Ronald Steel's biography, *Walter Lippmann and the American Century,* p. 419.

105 "The failure to form . . .": Lippmann quoted in ibid., p. 405.

105 "I would minimize . . .": FDR's last cable cited in Yergin, p. 68.

105 "As long as Stalin . . .": Churchill quoted in ibid., p. 65.

106 "He was a changed man . . .": ibid., p. 119.

106 "Russian plans for establishing . . .": Harriman quoted in ibid., p. 77. Harriman's

conversation with Forrestal cited in Walter Millis, ed., *The Forrestal Diaries*, p. 47.

107 Truman's April 23 meeting with Molotov described in Yergin, pp. 82. 83.

107 "What frightens me . . .": Harriman quoted in ibid., p. 198.

107 Stimson's exchange with McCloy cited in ibid., p. 80.

107 "We must make the Russians . . .": Kennan in ibid., p. 198.

108 Forrestal on the Russians, see Millis, pp. 95, 96.

108 "The objectionable feature . . .": Dulles quoted in Yergin, p. 221.

108 Admiral Mahan quoted in Calleo and Rowland, p. 49; Henry Adams quoted ibid., p. 51.

109 "Our planet today . . .": De Gaulle quoted in Grosser, *Alliance*, p. 62.

109 "The issue in the world . . .": Marshall's memo to Truman on Sweden cited in U.S. Department of State, *Foreign Relations of the United States, Western Europe, 1948*, vol III, pp. 134, 135.

110 "minimize repercussions and avoid . . .": Grosser, p. 70.

110 "Great Britain had within . . .": see Joseph M. Jones *Fifteen Weeks: February 21–June 1, 1947*, p. 7.

111 "Greek-Turkey-Iran barrier . . .": cited in ibid., p. 133.

111 "In the past eighteen months . . .": see Dean Acheson *Present at the Creation*, p. 219. See also Jones's account of this meeting, pp. 140–45.

112 "If FDR were alive . . .": Acheson quoted in ibid., p. 159.

112 For Kindleberger's memo on the Marshall Plan, see "Origins of the Marshall Plan," dated July 22, 1948, in *Foreign Relations of the United States, the British Commonwealth, Europe*, vol. III (1947), pp. 241–47.

113 For Kennan's recommendations on containment, see his "Mr. X" article, "The Sources of Soviet Conduct," *Foreign Affairs*, July 1947.

113 "The Policy Planning Staff . . .": Kennan's memo to Acheson found in *Foreign Relations of the United States, 1947*, vol. III, pp. 224, 225.

113 For Kennan's notes on the Marshall Plan, see ibid., p. 335.

114 ". . . our foreign loans . . .": Dulles quoted in Kolko, p. 359.

114 Statistics on French dependency on U.S. aid cited in Grosser, *Alliance*, p. 66. "There's the German pig . . .": ibid., p. 68.

115 "Our Uncle which art . . .": in ibid., p. 72.

115 For Bevin's remarks on "Britain's example" see *Foreign Relations of the United States, 1947*, vol. III, p. 255.

116 Council of Economic Advisers report cited in Kolko, p. 375.

116 "It is idle . . .": Marshall quoted in ibid., p. 376.

116 "One of Bissell's great . . .": Harlan Cleveland quoted in Kolko, p. 381.

116 "We now have in our hands . . .": Wilcox letter cited in ibid., p. 366.

117 "The symbols of nationalism . . .": Kindleberger's memorandum cited in Beloff, p. 16.

117 "We all know that . . ." Senator Smith quoted in Beloff, p. 127.

118 "France is the gainer . . .": Monnet in Bromberger, p. 68. Schuman and Auriol quoted in ibid.

118 "I believe that only . . .": Jean Monnet, *Memoirs*, p. 272.

118 "a profound, real, immediate . . .": Monnet quoted in Ball, p. 88.

119 "The general opinion . . .": see Janet Flanner, p. 44.

119 Statistics on European industrial production cited in William A. Brown and Opie Redvers, *American Foreign Assistance*, p. 244.

119 "The average Frenchman . . .": Flanner, p. 82.
119 Kolko cites statistics on consumption and income of French workers, pp. 440, 465.
120 Statistics on Belgium and Italian unemployment in ibid., p. 463.
120 "For five years . . .": Emmanuel quoted in Flanner, p. 110.
121 De Gaulle's "grand design" cited in Bromberger, p. 75.
121 The exchange between De Gaulle and Robert Murphy recorded by Steel, p. 400. See ibid. for Lippmann's feelings on the French general.
122 "The French could not become . . .": Monnet, p. 277; see pp. 277–82 for discussion of French-British merger.
123 "to invent new political methods . . .": ibid., p. 282.
123 "a German ally that is strong . . .": Acheson quoted in Bromberger, p. 83.
123 "It would be such a good thing . . .": Churchill quoted in Bromberger, p. 89; Monnet on Bidault, see his *Memoirs,* p. 275.
123 Schuman's background described in Bromberger, pp. 84–86; his meeting with Adenauer described p. 91.
124 "If one were not . . .": De Gaulle quoted in Monnet, p. 287.
124 "Coal and steel . . .": ibid., p. 293.
124 "to make a breach . .": Monnet, ibid., p. 296.
124 "The arrangement could become . . .": Acheson, *Sketches From Life,* p. 37. See p. 39 for Acheson's account of his meeting with Bevin.
125 In every respect . . .": Monnet cites the British Labour party report, "European Unity," p. 315.
125 "advantages of a huge unified . . .": interview with Monnet in *The United Nations World,* February 1953, p. 20.
125 For the *Newsweek* interview, see "Jean Monnet: Farewell to the Past," *Newsweek,* February 16, 1953, p. 44.
126 "Above all . . .": see Monnet, p. 380.
126 "I love France . . .": Churchill's exchange with Moran in Grosser, *Alliance,* p. 121.
127 "Those goddam Americans . . .": Ripka quoted in Yergin, pp. 345, 346.
128 "We are faced . . .": Truman's letter quoted in Margaret Truman, *Harry S. Truman,* pp. 358–60.
128 Clay's March 5 cable reproduced in Smith, *The Papers of General Lucius D. Clay,* pp. 568, 569.
128 "The tragic death . . .": for Truman's speech and his advisers' reactions, see Yergin, pp. 353, 354.
129 "A general stiffening . . .": John Hickerson quoted in Yergin, p. 363.
129 "Political and indeed spiritual . . .": Sargent quoted in Yergin, p. 362.
130 "I do not know of any . . .": Dulles quoted in Kolko, p. 499.
130 "that only . . .": CIA assessment cited in Gregg Herken, *The Winning Weapon: The Atomic Bomb in the Cold War, 1945–1950,* p. 325.
130 Clifford's memorandum, "American Relations with the Soviet Union," is reprinted in Arthur Krock, *Memoirs: Sixty Years on the Firing Line,* Appendix A.
130 For an account of Soviet military developments and strategic thought during these years see Raymond Garthoff, *Soviet Strategy in the Nuclear Age,* and David Holloway, *The Soviet Union and the Arms Race.*
131 For a useful biography on Acheson see Gaddis Smith, *Dean Acheson.*
132 "There is no intention . . .": Acheson quoted in Smith, p. 238.

132 "Are we going . . .": quoted from Richard J. Barnet and Marcus G. Raskin, *After 20 Years*, p. 24.

132 "We have decided . . .": See A. G. Sims memorandum, "Our Policies in Europe," November 14, 1950; *The Declassified Documents Reference System*, Carrollton Press, 1977.

134 See NSC 100 *Recommended Policies* and *Actions in Light of the Grave World Situation*," January 11, 1951, pp. 2, 4. NSC Box, United States Joint Chiefs of Staff Records, Modern Military Section, National Archives, Washington, D.C.

134 "There is no question . . .": cited in Monnet, p. 342. Monnet describes the origins of the "Pleven Plan," pp. 336–50.

135 Smith describes the meeting between Acheson and Eisenhower, pp. 249–51.

135 "hair-raising description . . .": see Dean G. Acheson, *Present at the Creation*, p. 590.

136 "To sum it up . . .": Eisenhower quoted in Edward Fursdon, "A History of The European Defense Community Experience, 1950–1954," January 1978, p. 137.

137 "We seemed to have . . .": quoted in ibid., p. 260.

137 "In one telling sentence . . .": Eden quoted in Acheson, p. 626.

139 "It is the belief of . . .": Ambassador Dunn's cable to Acheson, see *Foreign Relations of the United States, 1948*, vol. III, p. 739. Dunn warned that a Communist-led "attempt at general revolt will probably occur any time between now and March."

139 Cardinals Montini and Tardini quoted in ibid., p. 745.

139 "a major effort to take over . . .": the National Security Council Report, "The Position of the United States with Respect to Italy," in ibid., pp. 765–69.

139 For Kennan's memorandum on inviting an Italian civil war, see ibid., pp. 848, 849.

140 Clandestine political, cultural, and economic activities to influence the Italian election listed in a June 16, 1948, cable from Ambassador Dunn to the secretary of state. See ibid., pp. 879–82.

140 "At least we're getting . . .": Allen Dulles quoted in Thomas Powers, *The Man Who Kept the Secrets: Richard Helms and the CIA*, p. 55.

141 The AFL-CIO liaison with the CIA in Europe cited in Joseph C. Goulden, *Meany*, pp. 128, 129. "[w]e played a major part . . .": Meany quoted in ibid., p. 128; "[i]t was my idea . . .": Braden quoted in ibid., p. 130.

142 CIA funding of the National Student Association was revealed by Sol Stern, "NSA: A Short Account of International Student Politics & the Cold War with Particular Reference to the NSA, CIA etc.," *Ramparts*, February 1967. See also *The New York Times*, February 24, 1967.

142 For an account of the CIA's cultural operations, see Christopher Lasch, "The Cultural Cold War," *The Nation*, September 11, 1967.

142 "a legal lynching . . .": Sartre quoted in Grosser, *Alliance*, p. 117.

143 See *The New York Times* three-part series, "CIA: Secret Shaper of Public Opinion," December 25, 26, 27, 1977.

Chapter 4

Page

147 "a kind of dream boy . . .": Lippmann and Stevenson on Eisenhower quoted in Ronald Steel, *Walter Lippmann and the American Century*, pp. 481, 482.

147 "You don't suppose . . .": Eisenhower quoted in ibid., p. 481.

147 "We think too much . . .": quoted in Blanche Wiesen Cook, *The Declassified Eisenhower*, p. 79.

148   "These are not . . .": Eisenhower's conversation with Warren recorded in ibid.,
      p. 173.
148   "Atlantic Union defense forces . . .": ibid., p. 87.
148   "Western Europe . . .": quoted in ibid., p. 117.
148   "I wish I could . . .": ibid., p. 91.
148   "understand that our foreign . . .": quoted in Donald Neff, *Warriors at Suez*,
      p. 38.
149   "[W]e are rapidly . . .": quoted in Cook, p. 166. "People are frightened . . .":
      p. 42.
149   ". . . an ecclesiastical type . . .": Richard Crossman on Dulles in Janet Morgan,
      ed., *The Backbench Diaries of Richard Crossman*, p. 62.
149   Dulles' *Life* magazine article described in Townsend Hoopes, *The Devil and John
      Foster Dulles*, pp. 126–28.
150   "We sense with . . .": Eisenhower's speech quoted in Peter Lyon, *Eisenhower:
      Portrait of the Hero*, p. 478.
150   "never made a serious . . .": Cook, pp. 151, 152.
150   "just as provincial . . .": Alsop's description cited in Crossman, p. 485.
150   "Finally, cut off . . .": quoted from David P. Calleo, *The Atlantic Fantasy: The
      U.S., NATO and Europe*, p. 39.
151   "just about the only . . .": C. D. Jackson on psychological warfare and his Cold
      War strategy cited in Cook, pp. 177, 178.
151   "It would be unsafe . . .": CIA report cited in ibid., p. 179.
151   "we ought to be . . .": Dulles quoted in Hoopes, p. 180.
151   "The stability of . . .": the Basic National Security Policy cited in Cook,
      p. 181.
151   CIA's invasion plan for Albania cited in Powers, pp. 57, 58.
152   "a backward civilization . . .": Eisenhower quoted in Lyon, p. 486.
152   "there is no longer . . .": quoted in ibid., p. 627.
153   "I would say . . .": O'Donnell quoted from *Military Situation in the Far East*,
      hearings before the Senate Committee on Armed Services and the Committee on
      Foreign Relations, Part 4, 82d Cong., 1st sess. Washington, D.C., Government
      Printing Office, 1951, p. 3075.
153   Allen W. Dulles is described in Powers, p. 104.
154   ". . . we cannot safely limit . . .": Allen W. Dulles quoted from his *The Craft of
      Intelligence*, pp. 235, 236.
154   "His Majesty's Government . . .": Eden from his *Full Circle: The Memoirs of
      Anthony Eden*, pp. 216, 217.
155   Eden describes his meeting with Eisenhower on Iran, ibid., pp. 235, 236.
155   Kermit Roosevelt describes how he accomplished the overthrow of Mossadegh in
      his book, *Countercoup*.
155   "[t]he guns that they had . . .": Stewart's testimony cited in Lyon, p. 551; Lyon
      cites Roosevelt's cable on the shah, p. 552.
156   "What they give . . .": Auriol quoted in Grosser, *Alliance*, pp. 129, 130.
157   "a solid though unavowable . . .": ibid., p. 132.
157   "The loss of . . .": NSC report cited in Lyon, p. 580.
157   "Our general tendency . . .": Makinsky quoted in Cook, p. 159.
157   "We have engaged . . .": Eisenhower in Lyon, p. 580.
158   "would mean a general war . . .": Eisenhower quoted in "When Ike was Asked
      to Nuke Vietnam," the *Washington Post*, August 22, 1982.
158   Eisenhower's April 4 letter to Churchill found in Eisenhower, pp. 346, 347.

159 "He had never . . .": Radford's remarks described by Eden, p. 115; "to move armed forces . . .": Eden, p. 116.

159 Mendès-France described and quoted in Flanner, pp. 229, 240.

160 "Mr. Dulles thought it . . .": quoted in Richard J. Barnet, *Intervention and Revolution*, p. 228.

160 "the only case of a bull . . .": Churchill quoted in Hoopes, p. 221.

160 The exchange between Lippmann and Dulles, see Steel, p. 504.

162 "My own view . . .": ibid., p. 505; see Flanner, pp. 242, 243, for French debate over the EDC.

163 "These considerations . . .": Eden, p. 284.

164 "Conclusions on Trip": Dulles memo cited in Lyon, p. 547.

164 "I cannot tell you . . .": quoted in Neff, p. 74.

165 "Anthony seems to me . . .": Churchill quoted in Neff, p. 185.

165 See ibid., p. 143 for description of Dulles' lunch with Eden and Cadogan.

165 On Britain and the H-bomb see Grosser, *Alliance*, p. 170.

166 Copeland's and Roosevelt's relations with Nasser described in Neff, pp. 87, 88.

166 "We have a lot of cards . . .": Dulles quoted in ibid., pp. 92, 93.

167 "we have the Russian offer . . .": Ambassador Ahmed Hussein's meeting with Dulles described in Hoopes, p. 340.

168 "But what's all this . . .": Eden quoted in Neff, p. 182.

168 For a description of the secret meeting in Sèvres, see ibid., pp. 342–46.

169 "You will not get a dime . . .": Humphrey quoted in Grosser, *Alliance*, p. 144.

169 "I would not have been . . .": see Harold Macmillan, *Riding the Storm, 1956–1959*, p. 164.

169 "I am afraid, Anthony, . . .": Eisenhower quoted in Hugh Thomas, *The Suez Affair*, p. 70.

170 "Why did you stop . . .": Ibid., p. 149.

171 The assassination attempt on Adenauer described in Prittie, p. 206.

172 "Without the presence of . . .": see Acheson "The Illusion of Disengagement," *Foreign Affairs*, April 1958, p. 377.

173 Adenauer describes his meetings with Khrushchev in *Memoirs*, pp. 474, 481.

173 Kennan's recommendations for European disengagement and Adenauer's concerns cited in Prittie, p. 253.

174 Allen Dulles' visit with Adenauer cited in ibid., p. 254.

175 "I believe that it is . . .": Brentano quoted in Arnulf Baring, ed., *Sehr verehrter Herr Bundeskanzler!; Heinrich von Brentano im Briefwechsel mit Konrad Adenauer, 1949–1964*, p. 206.

176 For the effects of rearmament on the European Allies, see Robert Osgood, *NATO, The Entangling Alliance*, pp. 64–101.

176 "Carte Blanche" discussed in ibid., p. 126.

178 "I want to make it . . .": Montgomery quoted in ibid., p. 110, Gruenther's study cited p. 109.

179 "conceive of any president . . .": Herter quoted in Barnet and Raskin, p. 5.

179 "I would not recommend . . .": Brown quoted in Osgood, p. 142.

179 Adenauer's and Strauss's demands for control over nuclear weapons cited in Roger Morgan, *The United States and West Germany, 1945–1973*, p. 66.

180 "this fantastic new dominance . . .": Crossman from his *Diaries*, p. 624.

181 "England is like a rich man . . .": Adenauer, p. 85.

183 "You Americans forced us . . .": Kodaki Akira quoted in Douglas H. Mendel, *The Japanese People and Foreign Policy: A Study of Public Opinion in Post-Treaty Japan,* p. 61.

183 See ibid., p. 159, for Mendel's discussion of the *Lucky Dragon* incident.

183 "with the neighboring Red areas . . .": Eisenhower's opinions on Japanese trade with China cited in Dower, p. 581.

184 Japanese production of materials for the Korean War cited in Kolko, p. 643, and Chitoshi Yanaga, *Big Business in Japanese Politics,* p. 255.

184 "a forward bastion . . .": Allison quoted in Dower, p. 434.

184 For a biography on Kishi, see Dan Kurzman, *Kishi and Japan: The Search for the Sun.* Kishi is also profiled in *Time,* January 25, 1960, pp. 24–30.

185 "The Germans say they have . . .": Kishi quoted in Kurzman, p. 273.

187 The public protest in Japan over the Security Treaty is described in George R. Packard III, *Protest in Tokyo: The Security Treaty Crisis of 1960.*

187 "if a government friendly . . .": Herter quoted in Yanaga, p. 291; Hagerty's experience in Tokyo described in *Newsweek,* June 20, 1960, pp. 46, 49, and Packard, pp. 288–91.

188 "Foster Dulles . . .": Macmillan, *Riding the Storm,* p. 320.

189 "have not understood . . .": Mitterrand quoted in Grosser, p. 149; "by taking sides . . .": Thierry Maulnier quoted in ibid.

190 ". . . French policemen . . .": quoted in Flanner, p. 363.

190 Flanner describes the 1958 Algerian coup, pp. 364–69.

191 "the promoters of the EEC . . .": see Lawrence B. Krause, *European Economic Integration and the United States,* p. 12.

192 French attempts to block Britain's entrance in the EEC described by Macmillan, *Pointing the Way, 1959–1961,* p. 442.

193 "I am an expansionist . . .": ibid., p. 47.

193 "The Germans and French . . .": ibid., p. 48.

Chapter 5

Page

194 "He is quick . . .": Macmillan, *Pointing the Way, 1959–1961,* p. 359.

195 "if a single . . . soldier . . .": quoted from Arthur Schlesinger, *A Thousand Days: John F. Kennedy in the White House,* p. 309; Kennedy on "Sputnik diplomacy," p. 311; " 'The greater our variety . . .' ": p. 318.

196 "The man of action . . .": see W. W. Kulski, *De Gaulle and the World,* p. 10.

197 "like the princess . . .": ibid., p. 3.

197 "As you know . . .": quoted in ibid., p. 8.

197 "This was what we were . . .": see Charles de Gaulle, *Memoirs of Hope: Renewal and Endeavor,* p. 171.

198 "My aim, then . . .": ibid., p. 202.

198 "As I expected . . .": ibid., p. 203.

198 "In everything that constitutes . . .": De Gaulle quoted in Grosser, *Alliance,* p. 184.

198 Macmillan describes his meeting with De Gaulle, *Pointing,* p. 180.

199 "the 'Anglo-Saxons' cry . . .": quoted from Grosser, *Alliance,* p. 186.

199 "Whatever happens . . .": cited in ibid., p. 185.

199 "somewhat fumbling . . .": See De Gaulle's *Memoirs,* p. 254.

199 "What really matters . . .": Kennedy quoted in Schlesinger, p. 654.
200 Statistics on U.S. gold stocks in Michael Hudson, *Global Fracture: The New International Economic Order*, pp. 12, 13.
200 "The United States should . . .": Dillon quoted in Robert Solomon, *The International Monetary System: 1945–1976*, p. 39.
201 "When a banker . . .": *Fortune* cited in ibid., p. 36.
201 "the orthodox business reverence . . .": Schlesinger, p. 623.
201 "The United States must . . .": Kennedy quoted in Solomon, p. 39.
201 "by occasional withdrawals . . .": Tobin quoted in Schlesinger, p. 653.
201 "Of the $8.5 billion . . .": Solomon, p. 31.
202 "impact of United States rearmament . . .": commission's report cited in Fred L. Block, *The Origins of International Economic Disorder*, p. 243.
202 For statistics on European investment in the United States, see Christopher Tugendhat, *The Multinationals*, p. 39; for U.S. investment in Europe, see Jack N. Behrman, *National Interests and the Multinational Enterprise*, p. 15.
203 The Atlantic Institute study, cited in Tugendhat, p. 32.
203 "Faced with a deteriorating . . .": see Robert Gilpin, *U.S. Power and the Multinational Corporation*, p. 14.
204 "When we think of Nazis . . .": see J. C. Louis and Harvey Yazijian, *The Cola Wars*, p. 78; see p. 76 for attacks against Coke in Belgium and Austria.
204 James A. Farley's role with the Coca-Cola company detailed in ibid., pp. 61–67.
205 "You can't spread . . .": quoted in ibid., p. 78.
205 For turn-of-the-century books on U.S. investment in Europe, see Fred A. McKenzie, *The American Invaders; Their Plans, Tactics and Progress*, and William Thomas Stead, *The Americanization of the World, or The Trend of the Twentieth Century*.
205 For a history of Thomas Watson and his company, IBM, see William Rodgers, *Think: A Biography of the Watsons and IBM*.
206 "International trade and good will . . .": Behn quoted in Anthony Sampson, *The Sovereign State of ITT*, p. 27; see p. 43 for assistance given ITT by Allen Dulles.
207 "The tides of U.S. prestige . . .": Geneen's memo cited in ibid., p. 75.
207 "Between your products . . .": quoted in Behrman, p. 30; *Der Stern* cited p. 33.
207 "There, Mr. President, is our . . .": Dreyfus quoted in *Atlas*, November 1967, p. 19.
208 "We, my dear Crossman . . .": Macmillan quoted in Sampson's biography, *Macmillan*, p. 62.
209 "People often don't realize . . .": ibid., p. 160.
209 "Britain can knock down . . .": Randolph Churchill quoted in Grosser, *Alliance*, p. 171.
210 Schlesinger describes Kennedy's lunch with Amery, p. 858: "Kennedy wondered aloud . . . whether Skybolt would ever work. Amery, much upset, responded that it was the basis of British nuclear defense; if anything happened, it could have far-reaching effects on Anglo-American relations."
210 "relatively weak national . . .": McNamara quoted in ibid., pp. 848, 849.
210 "was the first time . . .": Lord Thorneycroft quoted from a recorded interview with David Nunnerly, June 18, 1969, p. 16, John F. Kennedy Library Oral History Program.
211 "resentment and suspicion . . .": London *Sunday Times* reporter Henry Brandon quoted in Schlesinger, p. 864.

211 "Great Britain has lost . . .": Acheson's speech cited in Grosser, *Alliance*, p. 205.
212 "somewhat in the same light . . .": in Theodore Sorensen, *Kennedy*, p. 563.
212 "had led us to think . . .": ibid., pp. 562, 563.
212 "that any agreement . . .": Tyler quoted in John Newhouse, *De Gaulle and the Anglo-Saxons*, p. 216.
212 "happily joined by policies . . .": Schlesinger, p. 842.
212 "He simply felt . . .": ibid., p. 855.
213 "the history of any . . .": Sorensen, p. 563.
214 Adenauer's view of British treatment of the continental countries cited in Prittie, p. 268.
214 Macmillan describes his first meeting with Adenauer in his *Tides of Fortune*, p. 479.
214 "Our people are not . . .": Macmillan quoted in Nora Beloff, *The General Says No*, pp. 58, 59.
214 Harriman's lunch with Cripps described in ibid., p. 53.
214 "in a rather detached way . . .": Macmillan, *Pointing*, p. 351.
214 Kennedy's "Declaration of Interdependence" cited in Grosser, *Alliance*, p. 201.
215 For the disagreement among the Allies over a "United Europe," see ibid., pp. 203, 204.
215 "The tragedy of it all . . .": Macmillan, *Pointing*, p. 428.
216 "It was calculated . . .": Eisenhower's diary entry recorded in *Declassified Documents Reference System*, Carrollton Press, 1977.
217 "wish France to remain . . .": For a variety of French views on U.S. policy with respect to French colonialism see Grosser, *Alliance*, chap. 5.
218 "Who can say . . .": De Gaulle quoted in Robert Osgood, *NATO, The Entangling Alliance*, p. 258.
219 "with equal vigour . . .": Macmillan, *End of the Day*, p. 334.
219 "McNamara's foolish speech . . .": ibid., p. 335.
220 For a detailed history of the MLF, see John D. Steinbruner, *The Cybernetic Theory of Decision*, chaps. 8, 9.
220 "something of a fake": Kennedy's opinion of the MLF cited in Schlesinger, p. 872.
220 "The whole debate . . .": Kennedy quoted in ibid.
220 "[I]n answer to the specific questions . . .": De Gaulle describes his meeting with Kennedy, pp. 257, 258.
221 "to tie Germany more firmly . . .": quoted in Schlesinger, p. 871.
221 Public opinion in West Germany on nuclear missiles cited in Karl W. Deutsch and Lewis J. Edinger, *Germany Rejoins the Powers*, p. 27.
221 "I can guarantee . . .": Straus quoted in Newhouse, p. 59. Khrushchev's *aide memoire* cited in Jack M. Schick, *The Berlin Crisis, 1958–1962*, p. 140.
223 "loaded with nuclear bombs . . .": cited in Steinbruner, p. 182.
223 For an account of Kennedy and Berlin see Sorensen, chap. 11.
223 "a cross between a . . .": Adenauer's opinion of Kennedy cited in Prittie, p. 283.
223 "The real trouble is . . .": ibid.; "I sense I'm talking . . .": quoted in Sorensen, p. 559; "a greater man than . . .": Schlesinger, p. 404.
224 Acheson's memorandum on Berlin described in Schlesinger, pp. 380–82.
224 "Many Americans are in the grip . . .": Acheson to Kennedy, Box, 82, John F. Kennedy Library.

225 "I go as the leader . . .": Schlesinger, p. 349.
225 "The European view . . .": Acheson quoted from a recorded interview with Lucius D. Battle, April 27, 1964, p. 14, The John F. Kennedy Oral History Program.
225 For Kennedy's Vienna meetings with Khrushchev, see Schlesinger, pp. 358–74, and Sorensen, pp. 584–86.
225 "prospects for nuclear war . . .": quoted in Sorensen, p. 549.
226 "air safety service . . .": Ulbricht quoted in Schick, p. 147.
226 "That son of a bitch . . .": quoted in Schlesinger, p. 391.
227 "a really serious non-nuclear . . .": Nitze quoted in Schick, p. 152.
227 "[y]ou do not wish . . .": De Gaulle, p. 223.
227 "[W]hen Khrushchev summons you . . .": ibid., p. 258.
227 "The three Western powers . . .": ibid., p. 229.
227 McCloy's meeting with Khrushchev described in Schlesinger, p. 392.
229 The case of Erwin Shabe is recorded in Martin J. Hillenbrand, *The Future of Berlin,* p. 45.
229 "nuclear exchange . . .": Schlesinger, p. 395.
229 The mounting tension over Berlin described in Curtis Cate, *The Ides of August,* pt. 5; "Tell me, are you nervous? . . .": Kennedy and Clay quoted in ibid., pp. 485, 486.
230 . . . "confirmed that they still . . .": Willy Brandt quoted from his *People and Politics,* p. 35.
230 "Why not in this summer . . .": quoted from an undated, unsigned memorandum, Box 82, NSF German/Berlin file, The John F. Kennedy Library.
230 For Robert Kennedy's August 17, 1961, memo, see Box 82, NSF collection General German series, The John F. Kennedy Library.
230 "Well goddammit . . .": Johnson quoted in Cate, p. 410.
231 "the western powers were . . .": Khrushchev cited in Schlesinger, p. 400.
231 Brandt recalls his chat with his son in Brandt, *People and Politics,* p. 38.
231 Sorensen details the Cuban Missile Crisis, pp. 667–718.
231 "somewhere between one out of . . .": Sorensen, p. 705.
231 "[W]e had to be aware . . .": Robert Kennedy, *Thirteen Days,* p. 77.
232 "If there is a . . .": De Gaulle quoted in Schlesinger, p. 815. Acheson also described his meeting with De Gaulle in a recorded interview with Lucius Battle, April 27, 1964, The John F. Kennedy Library Oral History Program, pp. 26–28.
232 For British reaction to crisis, see Schlesinger, pp. 816, 817.
233 Kennedy's Berlin Wall speech and European tour described in ibid., p. 885.
233 "In the summer of 1963 . . .": ibid., p. 888.

Chapter 6

Page
234 "I think he likes me . . .": quoted in Rowland Evans and Robert Novak, *Lyndon B. Johnson: The Exercise of Power,* p. 385.
235 "The President comes into a room . . .": See Michael Davie, *LBJ: A Foreign Observer's Viewpoint,* p. 3.
235 "Johnson personally directed . . .": see Robert Caro, "The Years of Lyndon Johnson," *Atlantic Monthly,* October 1981, p. 43.
235 "I realized that if . . .": Doris Kearns, *Lyndon Johnson and the American Dream,* p. 194.
236 "Every time I came into . . .": ibid., p. 164.

236 "If you let a bully . . .": ibid., p. 258.
236 "break out again . . .": Philip Geyelin, *Lyndon B. Johnson and the World*, p. 28.
237 "not only peaceful but apathetic . . .": Kearns, p. 142 "Coward! Traitor! . . .": ibid., p. 253.
237 "[P]urely and aggressively . . .": Geyelin, p. 122.
237 "I was still illegitimate . . .": Kearns, p. 170.
239 "browbeating a group . . .": Caro, *Atlantic Monthly*, p. 43.
240 "I love President Johnson . . .": Erhard quoted in R. Morgan, p. 146.
240 "We support the establishment . . .": Geyelin, p. 160.
241 "Though enormously intelligent . . .": Crossman in J. Morgan, p. 972.
241 Wilson describes his White house meeting with Johnson in Harold Wilson, *The Labour Government, 1964–1970*, pp. 47–49.
242 "I made it clear . . .": ibid., p. 4.
242 "foothold in Hong Kong . . .": Healey quoted in Richard Crossman, *The Diaries of a Cabinet Minister, 1964–1966*, vol. 1, p. 95.
242 "in such a way . . .": see Steinbruner, p. 304.
245 "Treaties are like . . .": De Gaulle quoted in Wolfram F. Hanrieder, *West German Foreign Policy, 1949–1979*.
245 Bahr's "change through contact" program cited in R. Morgan, p. 157.
245 "We must improve . . .": Johnson's speech in ibid., p. 155; "Put yourself in . . .": p. 154.
246 "There is a growing . . .": Schröder quoted in Hanrieder, *The Stable Crisis: Two Decades of German Foreign Policy*, p. 104. See chap. 3., for discussion of early rapprochement between West Germany and Eastern Europe.
248 For analysis of Germany's economic problems, see Hanrieder, p. 79.
248 "When a man . . .": see Lyndon B. Johnson, *The Vantage Point*, p. 305.
248 "began whispering on the . . .": ibid., p. 306.
249 "[N]ever before have . . .": Ambassador Alphand quoted in Grosser, *Alliance*, p. 209.
250 "Truly it is hard . . .": Solomon, p. 55.
250 "is a forceful but . . .": Rueff quoted in Gordon L. Weil and Ian Davidson, *The Gold War: A Story of the World's Monetary Crisis*, p. 94.
251 Growth in Europe's industrialized countries and the slump in Britain manufacturing is described in Andrew Gamble, *Britain in Decline*, pp. 19, 20.
252 "None of us . . .": Wilson, p. 403.
252 "The greatest absurdity . . .": De Gaulle's opinion of the United States in Vietnam cited in ibid., pp. 405, 406.
253 "The pound served as . . .": Block, p. 185.
253 "We agreed to continue . . .": Johnson, p. 319.
254 "French money . . .": Servan-Schreiber quoted from "U.S. and Europe: Pointed Questions, Candid Answers," *Atlas*, March 1968, p. 24. See also *The American Challenge*.
254 "woodcutters and water carriers . . .": Wilson quoted in Grosser, *Alliance*, p. 224.
255 "three-fourths of the European . . .": see Hoyt Gimlin, "American Investments in European Industry," in *Editorial Research Reports*, January 26, 1968, p. 72; statistics on U.S. corporate investment and control of German industries cited in William Gerber, "West German Prosperity," *Editorial Research Reports*, January 29, 1969, p. 69.

255 Statistics on West German and U.S. shares of world trade cited in ibid., p. 68.

255 See Stephen Hymer and Robert Rowthorn, "Multinational Corporations and International Oligopoly," in Charles Kindleberger, ed., *The International Corporation*, pp. 70, 71.

257 The activities of Hans Gunther Sohl cited in Hartrich, pp. 213–17.

257 For Shonfield's discussion of Germany's industrial system, see p. 247.

258 "Two of the largest steel companies . . .": ibid., p. 256.

260 "a conspiracy in the public interest . . .": ibid., pp. 130–31.

261 On Japan restrictions on U.S. investment see "Japan Opens Wider for Capital from West," *Business Week*, June 10, 1967, pp. 143, 144. See also Robert Guillain, *The Japanese Challenge*, p. 132.

262 The Zaikai is described in Chitoshi Yanaga, "What Is a Zaikai?" in Livingston et al., pp. 396–400.

263 Debt financing statistics cited in Pacific Basin Reports, "The Reaches of Zaibatsu Power," in ibid., p. 401.

263 Study on MNCs done by National War College Strategic Research Group cited in Richard J. Barnet and Ronald E. Müller, *Global Reach*, pp. 101–2.

264 "is against what the U.S. . . .": quoted from "Europe's Opposition to War in Asia Chills Its Relations with US," *The Wall Street Journal*, May 9, 1967.

265 De Gaulle's speech in Cambodia quoted in *Newsweek*, September 12, 1966, p. 30.

265 "If you want to help . . .": Johnson quoted in Wilson, p. 80.

265 On Allied "presence" in Vietnam, see "What the U.S. Can Expect from Allies in Vietnam," *U.S. News & World Report*, March 14, 1966, pp. 31–33.

265 "That I could still be . . .": Wilson, p. 247.

266 "The communists do not . . .": Brown quoted in Crossman, *The Diaries of a Cabint Minister, 1964–1966*, vol. I, p. 619; "I don't like . . .": p. 564.

266 "We should tell Washington . . .": *Bild Zeitung* cited in Grosser, *Alliance*, p. 238.

267 Polling figures on Japanese opposition to war cited in William Dickinson, Jr., "Rising Japanese Nationalism," *Editorial Research Reports*, January 5, 1966, p. 5.

268 "Okinawa is indispensable . . .": Sharp quoted in Akio Watanabe, *The Okinawa Problem*, p. 65. For more on the conflict over Okinawa, see Stephen Salaff, "Shadow of the Bomb," *Far Eastern Economic Review*, October 10, 1968.

268 For biographical information on Sato, see Takashi Oka, "As the Japanese Say: Premier Sato Would Tap His Way Across a Stone Bridge to Be Sure It Was Safe," *The New York Times Magazine*, November 16, 1969.

270 Bundy's and MacArthur's verbal attacks on the Japanese cited in Dickerson, pp. 4, 5.

271 "Why doesn't he . . .": quoted in "Europe's New Mood—Its Meaning for U.S." *U.S. News & World Report*, June 20, 1966, p. 41.

271 "We wanted exactly . . .": Rubin quoted in Milton Viorst, *Fire in the Streets: America in the 1960s*, p. 459.

272 "In the 1960s . . .": Crossman, vol. II, p. 566.

273 "My whole liberal education . . .": quoted in "Letter from Berlin," *The New Yorker*, November 18, 1967, p. 177.

274 "without a Comintern . . .": Hayden quoted in Viorst, p. 445. The Vietnam congress and student unrest in West Berlin are described in Robert Greenstein, "Revolution and Reaction: The Student Revolt in West Germany," *The New Republic*, June 8, 1968.

275 "agitation, disputes, and provocations . . .": Dietrich quoted in ibid., p. 19.

275 The death of Benno Ohnesorg is described in Christel Koppel and Dagmar
     Schultz, "Young Rebels, Old Fears," *The Nation,* May 6, 1968.
276 The Dutschke shooting is described in Richard L. Merritt, "The Student Protest
     Movement in West Berlin," *Comparative Politics,* July 1969, p. 516.
276 For an overview of Japanese student protest, see Fukashiro Junro, "Student
     Thought and Feeling," *Japan Quarterly,* April/June 1969.
277 For a study of the May Revolution in France, see Alain Touraine, *The May Move-
     ment: Revolt and Reform.*

Chapter 7

Page
283 Biographies on Richard M. Nixon include: Rowland Evans and Robert Novak,
     Nixon in the White House: The Frustration of Power; William Safire, *Before the
     Fall: An Inside View of the Pre-Watergate White House;* and Garry Wills, *Nixon
     Agonistes: The Crisis of the Self-Made Man.*
284 Biographies on Willy Brandt include: Terence C. Prittie, *Willy Brandt: Portrait of
     a Statesman,* and David Binder, *The Other German: Willy Brandt's Life and
     Times.*
284 "an unflinching, stubborn struggle . . .": quoted in Prittie, p. 118.
286 "In so far as . . .": see Willy Brandt, *People and Politics,* p. 205.
286 "instead of relying . . .": ibid., p. 168.
286 Debré's and the U.S. position on the Czech invasion cited in R. Morgan, p. 187.
287 "unprepossessing . . . extremely agile . . .": Egon Bahr described by Kissinger
     in his *Years of Upheaval,* p. 146; and in Binder, p. 266.
289 The Harmel Report, named after Belgian Foreign Minister Pierre Harmel, is cited
     in R. Morgan, p. 180.
289 "did not need any . . .": quoted in Binder, p. 261.
290 "A united Europe . . .": Kissinger, *The Troubled Partnership: A Re-appraisal of
     the Atlantic Alliance,* p. 40.
291 "principal justification . . .": Henry Kissinger, *White House Years,* p. 89.
291 [W]e do not mean . . .": Nixon quoted in Honoré M. Catudal, Jr., *The Diplomacy
     of the Quadripartite Agreement on Berlin: A New Era in East-West Relations,*
     p. 14.
292 "always have a difficult . . .": Kissinger, *A World Restored,* p. 329.
293 "the name that made . . .": *Newsweek* quote cited in Roger Morris, *Uncertain
     Greatness,* p. 196.
293 "Living as a Jew . . .": Kissinger quoted in Joseph Kraft, "In Search of Kiss-
     inger," *Harper's,* January 1971, p. 57.
294 "As far as European . . .": Brandt quoted in Catudal, p. 143.
294 Acheson's, McCloy's, and Clay's description of Brandt cited in Catudal, p. 142.
295 For an account of the negotiations on Berlin, see ibid., chaps. 4, 5, 6.
296 "leave the Germans . . .": Nixon quoted in Brandt, p. 302.
296 Brandt describes "cultural nationhood," p. 397.
297 "endless crisis that . . .": For a critical analysis of Kissinger's world objectives,
     see D. C. Watt, "Henry Kissinger: An Interim Judgment," *Political Quarterly,*
     vol. 48, 1977.
298 "A painful act . . .": Brandt quoted in his Op-Ed article "The Old World, the
     New Strength," *The New York Times,* April 29, 1973.
299 For statistics on changes in U.S. share of world output, see Wolfe, p. 164.

300 "either the American banks . . .": see Susan Strange, "The Dollar Crisis 1971," *International Affairs,* April 1972, p. 199.

300 "We are not going . . .": Connally quoted in Solomon, p. 181.

301 "If we relinquish . . .": Connally quoted in Richard J. Whelan, "The Nixon-Connally Arrangement," *Harper's,* August 1971, p. 41.

301 "And to be perfectly . . .": quoted in Kissinger, p. 953.

301 "We had a problem . . .": Strange, p. 205.

301 For Japanese reaction see "10 Minute Advance Notification This Time; Secretary of State Telephones Prime Minister on U.S. Dollar Defense Measures," *Asahi,* August 17, 1971.

302 "that American had become . . .": Ford quoted in Martin Mayer, *The Fate of the Dollar,* p. 182.

302 "As I worked . . .": Nixon quoted in ibid., p. 189.

302 "I knew they killed . . .": Heath quoted in Andrew Roth, *Heath and the Heathmen,* p. 224.

303 "You will be measured . . .": Connally quoted in Kissinger, p. 951.

303 "I knew there had to be . . .": Connally quoted in Mayer, p. 198.

303 "when the other side . . .": Kissinger, p. 957.

303 "Our preferred strategy . . .": ibid., p. 958.

304 "The French people . . .": Michel Jobert quoted in his *Memoires d'Avenir,* p. 169.

304 Kissinger describes the Azores meeting with Pompidou, pp. 959–64.

304 "Try to keep the press . . .": Pompidou quoted in Jobert, p. 194.

305 Statistics on German auto exports to the United States cited in *Commerce Today,* November 1972.

306 "that have lived . . .": Erhard quoted in William Gerber, "West German Prosperity," *Editorial Research Reports,* January 29, 1969, vol. 1, p. 67.

306 Exports as percentage of GNP cited in Gerhard Hirseland, "West German Miracle Revisited," *Challenge,* May 1975, p. 53.

307 "chain of rocky islands . . .": See Philip H. Trezise, "US–Japan Economic Relations" in The Commission on International Trade and Investment Policy, *United States International Economic Policy in an Interdependent World,* vol. II, p. 183.

307 Comparative productivity statistics cited in Scott Davidson, "The Sources of Decline in U.S. Productivity Growth," ibid., p. 137.

307 "The Japanese are still fighting . . .": Stans quoted in I. M. Destler et al., *The Textile Wrangle,* p. 270. Destler documents the history of the textile conflict between the United States and Japan.

308 Kissinger describes his back channel negotiations on textiles, pp. 330–40; "This capital liberalization . . .": Kissinger quotes Nixon, p. 330.

309 " 'Yoshida' and I worked out . . .": ibid., p. 335; "that textiles would be . . .": p. 336.

310 "People here just won't forget . . .": quoted in Destler, p. 315; see p. 332 for Nixon's toast to Tanaka.

311 "His vowels betray . . .": quoted in *Time,* June 28, 1970.

311 "a London-Paris axis . . .": Pompidou's concerns about Germany recorded in Kissinger, p. 422.

312 "The classical class struggle . . .": Togliatti quoted in Mary Kaldor, *The Disintegrating West,* p. 188.

312   "the legitimation of . . .": Stuart Holland, *The Uncommon Market*, p. 15.
313   Statistics on EEC purchases and sales of butter to USSR cited in Kaldor, p. 180.
313   "restrictive impact is . . .": Bergsten quoted in Kaldor, p. 97.
313   "In the long run . . .": unidentified economic study cited in Kissinger, p. 426.
314   "The situation we face . . .": Peterson quoted in Kaldor, pp. 104, 105.
314   "we could not risk . . .": Kissinger, p. 427.
315   "to avoid any whiff . . .": ibid., p. 143.
315   "How can Europe . . .": Jobert quoted in James O. Goldsborough, "France, the European Crisis and the Alliance," *Foreign Affairs*, April 1974, p. 538; Jobert's conversation with Brezhnev cited on p. 548.
317   "Never have the Americans . . .": Aron quoted in Anthony Hartley, "Transatlantic Frivolity: The USA v. Europe," *Encounter*, April 1973, p. 58.
317   "France could not fail . . .": Pompidou quoted in Brandt, p. 270.
318   "The probability is . . .": ibid., p. 271.
319   "America should begin . . .": Monnet quoted in Kissinger, *The Years of Upheaval*, p. 139.
319   For Kissinger's own treatment of the conflict over the "Year of Europe" see *Upheaval*, chap. 5.
320   "We should maintain . . .": Jobert quoted in ibid., p. 174.
320   "Ruthlessly exploiting our . . .": ibid., p. 165.

Chapter 8

Page
322   "This is a matter . . .": Kissinger cites his call to Dobrynin, *Upheaval*, p. 585.
322   "I will say it . . .": Brezhnev's letter cited, ibid., p. 583.
323   "They are doing it . . .": Nixon quoted, ibid., p. 581.
323   "After so many months . . .": see J. H. Plumb, "Letter from London," *The New York Times Magazine*, December 16, 1973, p. 55.
323   "This is not . . .": Worsthorne quoted in "The World Looks at Watergate," *Atlas*, May 1974, p. 36.
324   "I don't care . . .": Kissinger quoted from "Kissinger Said to Express Disgust at Allies' Position," *The New York Times*, October 31, 1973.
324   "The alliance is . . .": quoted in "US-NATO Dispute Still Unresolved," *the New York Times*, November 11, 1973.
324   "The American decision . . .": Wilson quoted in "New Strains on the U.S.–Europe Alliance," *U.S. News & World Report*, November 1973.
325   "Don't give up . . .": De Gaulle quoted in Eric Roleau, "French Policy in the Middle East," *The World Today*, May 1968, p. 209.
326   "could play a useful . . .": quoted in Brandt, p. 465.
326   Statistics on oil imports by European nations cited in the U.S. Central Intelligence Agency, Foreign Assessment Center, *International Energy Statistical Review*, February 2, 1983, pp. 5, 6.
328   "would affect primarily . . .": quoted in Kissinger, *Upheaval*, p. 863.
328   For more on Japan and the oil crisis, see Koji Taira, "Japan After the 'Oil Shock': An International Resource Pauper," *Current History*, April 1975; and Yeshi Tsurumi, "Japan," in Raymond Vernon, *The Oil Crisis*.
329   "The embargo against us . . .": Kissinger, *Upheaval*, p. 875.
329   ". . . how to prevent . . .": ibid., p. 870.

329 "consortium of consumers . . .": Pompidou quoted in ibid., p. 897.

330 "They have a cartel . . .": Kissinger in ibid., p. 902. For Jobert's reaction see his *Memoires*, pp. 284, 285.

330 Kissinger describes the Washington Energy Conference in *Upheaval*, pp. 905–25.

331 "that the United States . . .": Nixon quoted in ibid., pp. 915, 916.

331 "It would be a mistake . . .": see Helmut Schmidt, "The Struggle for the World Product," *Foreign Affairs*, April 1974, p. 443.

332 "The food producers' . . .": Enders quoted in Geoffrey Barraclough, "Wealth and Power: The Politics of Food and Oil," *The New York Review of Books*, August 7, 1975, p. 25.

332 Keller and Johnston quoted in Frank Church, "The Impotence of Oil Companies," *Foreign Policy*, Summer 1977, p. 40; "were not really . . .": see p. 41.

333 On European reserves during the oil crisis, see Romano Prodi and Alberto Cio, "Europe," in Vernon, p. 101.

333 "It is inadmissible . . .": Friderichs quoted in ibid., p. 104.

334 "I am finished . . .": Brandt quoted in Binder, p. 327.

334 "like Sampson we shall . . .": Qadaffi quoted in Hartrich, p. 250.

335 "Of all the friendly . . .": Hassen ben Said quoted in ibid., p. 253.

336 "direct transfer payments . . .": see Lester Thurow, *The Zero-Sum Society*, p. 155.

336 For statistics on German social security payments, see Hartrich, p. 245.

336 "Dear Harold . . .": Brandt quoted in Clyde H. Farnsworth, "Schmidt the Lip," *The New York Times Magazine*, May 2, 1976, p. 14.

337 "somewhat overbearing manner . . .": Kissinger on Schmidt in *Upheaval*, pp. 908, 909. For more biographical information on Schmidt and his political career, see John Vinocur, "The Schmidt Factor," *The New York Times Magazine*, September 21, 1980.

337 "I am not visionary . . .": ibid., p. 113.

338 On Giscard, see James O. Goldsborough, "The Plight of Giscard d'Estang," *The New York Times Magazine*, September 11, 1977; Simon Serfaty, "The Fifth Republic Under Giscard d'Estaing: Steadfast or Changing?" *The World Today*, March 1976; and "Relaxed President for a Tense New Era," *Time*, June 3, 1974.

339 Giscard's austerity program described in John Ardagh, *The New France: A Society in Transition, 1945–1977*, p. 92.

339 "The French complain . . .": quoted in James O. Goldsborough, "The Franco-German Entente," *Foreign Affairs*, April 1, 1976, p. 501.

340 "no need for France . . .": Schlesinger quoted in ibid., p. 503.

341 "The 7th Army here . . .": General Davidson quoted in "The U.S. Army: A Battle for Survival," the *Washington Post*, September 12, 1971.

342 "came out of the bowels . . .": Major General Marshal B. Garth quoted in ibid.

342 "Sex is central to . . .": Sims quoted in William L. Hansen, *America's Army in Crisis*, p. 81. See also "Ending Army Racism: Strategy for Europe," *Christian Science Monitor*, November 18, 1971.

342 For the problems of U.S. GIs in Kaiserslautern, see "G.I.'s Change the Character of a West German Town," *The New York Times*, November 29, 1971.

343 Statistics on Allied defense expenditures cited in Alain C. Enthoven, "U.S. Forces in Europe: "How Many? Doing What?" *Foreign Affairs*, April 1975, pp. 518, 519.

343 For a review of West Germany's defense White Paper, see Stuart Drummond,

"The West German Defense White Paper of 1970," *The Army Quarterly and Defense Journal,* January 1971.

344 For more on the German military see Earl F. Ziemke, "West Germany's Security Policy," *Current History,* May 1972.

346 On the importance of Turkey to the United States see *Turkey's Problems and Prospects: Implications for U.S. Interests,"* report prepared for the House Sub-committee on Europe and the Middle East, Committee on Foreign Affairs, 96th Cong. 2d sess, May 3, 1980.

346 "I know dollar for dollar . . .": quoted in Dankwart A. Rustow, "Turkey's Tra-vails," in *Foreign Affairs,* Fall 1979, p. 85.

347 Central Intelligence Agency involvement in the 1967 Greek coup and the history of U.S. policy toward Greece, Turkey, and Cyprus are documented in Lawrence Stern, *The Wrong Horse;* "seriously damage vital . . .": see p. 37.

348 "the most brutal . . .": Ball, p. 350; to Johnson letter quoted on p. 351.

349 "For Christ's sake . . .": ibid., p. 346.

349 "except that ours . . .": Bulent Ecevit quoted in Christopher Hitchens, "Détente and Destabilization: Report from Cyprus," *New Left Review,* November/Decem-ber 1975, p. 68.

351 "felt drawn to him . . .": Acheson, *Creation,* pp. 627, 628.

351 The CIA-PIDE connection cited in Kenneth Maxwell, "Portugal Under Pres-sure," *The New York Review of Books,* May 29, 1975, p. 20.

352 "I don't see how . . .": Ford quoted in Tad Szulc, "Lisbon and Washington: Behind the Portuguese Revolution," *Foreign Policy,* Winter 1975/76.

352 "[T]he whites are here . . .": quoted in ibid., p. 21.

353 Soares' lunch with Kissinger described in ibid., p. 3.

353 "infiltrated some conservative . . .": ibid., p. 11.

354 "aid to Italy . . .": James Dunn's cable cited in Alan A. Platt and Robert Leo-nardi, "American Foreign Policy and the Postwar Italian Left," *Political Science Quarterly,* Summer 1978, p. 199.

355 "a more effective supporter . . .": Schlesinger quoted in ibid., p. 206.

356 Covert funding of Miceli cited in ibid., p. 212; see also "U.S. Paid 800,000 to Italian General; CIA Fought Move," *The New York Times,* January 30, 1976.

Chapter 9

Page
359 "craven, contemptible . . .": Kissinger quoted in James Chace, "American Jin-goism," *Harper's,* May 1976, p. 43.

359 "We were a little light . . .": Franklin quoted in Jerry Flint, "What's a Trilateral Commission?" *Forbes,* November 24, 1980, p. 46. For a critical study of the Trilateral Commission see Holly Sklar, ed., *Trilateralism: The Trilateral Commis-sion and Elite Planning for World Management.*

360 "political adventurer . . .": Retinger quoted in Ball, p. 104.

360 On the European Movement's secret U.S. funding see Sklar, pp. 184, 185.

361 "He much preferred . . .": Pomian quoted in ibid., p. 163.

361 "We are bound . . .": C. D. Jackson quoted in ibid., p. 167; for more on the background of the Bilderberg Group, see Caroline Moorehead, "An Exclusive Club, Perhaps Without Power, but Certainly with Influence," *The Times* (Lon-don), April 18, 1977.

362 "David thought things . . .": Franklin quoted in Flint, p. 46.

362 "If we are going to move . . .": ibid.

362 "The Democratic candidate . . .": Brzezinski quoted in Robert Scheer, "Brzezinski—Activist Seeker of World Order," *Los Angeles Times,* January 24, 1977.

363 *The Crisis of Democracy* was written by Michel Crozier, Samuel P. Huntington, and Joji Watanuki.

363 "Sometimes I think . . .": see "Man of the Year," *Time,* January 3, 1977.

364 For Norman Mailer's article on Carter, see "The Search for Carter," *The New York Times Magazine,* September 26, 1976.

364 "we are not sure . . .": European opinion on Carter recorded in Andrew Kopkind, "Why Not the Best? Europe's View of Carter," *Working Papers for a New Society,* May/June 1978, p. 6.

365 For the text of Carter's famous Notre Dame speech, "America's Goal: A Foreign Policy Based on Moral Values," see *The New York Times,* August 23, 1977.

366 Schmidt's and Giscard's opinions of Carter's human rights policy cited in "Carter Spins the World," *Time,* August 8, 1977.

366 "to manage the relationship . . .": Vance quoted in Elizabeth Drew, "A Reporter at Large: Brezezinski," *The New Yorker,* May 1, 1978, p. 118.

367 "entered a phase . . .": Brzezinski quoted in ibid., p. 108.

367 "visibly recoiled when I . . .": quoted in Zbigniew Brzezinski, *Power and Principle: Memoirs of the National Security Adviser, 1977–1981,* p. 293.

368 "Force must be designed . . .": see Zbigniew Brzezinski, "Revolution—Counterrevolution (but Not Necessarily About Columbia!)," *The New Republic,* June 1, 1968, p. 24.

369 "moving toward a decisive . . .": quoted in Sam Nunn and Dewey F. Bartlett, *NATO and the New Soviet Threat,* Report to the Senate Committee on Armed Services, 95th Cong., 1st sess., January 24, 1977, p. 1.

369 "Soviet forces deployed . . .": ibid., p. 6.

369 On the debate over the 3 percent defense spending commitment, see Les Aspin, "The Three Percent Solution: NATO and the U.S. Defense Budget," *Challenge,* May/June, 1979.

370 For data on the U.S. nuclear arsenal deployed in Europe see William Arkin, "Nuclear Weapons in Europe," in Mary Kaldor and Dan Smith, eds. *Disarming Europe,* pp. 35–63.

371 "perhaps the most significant . . .": Currie quoted in Simon Lunn, *The Modernization of NATO's Long-Range Theater Nuclear Forces,* report prepared for the House Subcommittee on Europe and the Middle East, 96th Cong. 2d sess., December 31, 1980, p. 17.

372 "Strategic arms limitation . . .": Schmidt's speech quoted in Walter Pincus, "Arms Decision Stirred Storm Around NATO," *The Washington Post,* November 18, 1981; "was to make public . . .": see Lunn, p. 16.

373 "The spectre of such weapons . . .": Iklé quoted in ibid., p. 16.

374 The "High Level Group's" recommendation cited in ibid., p. 23.

374 "the Soviet arms lead . . .": Genscher quoted in ibid., p. 56.

374 "In private conversations . . .": see Jimmy Carter, *Keeping Faith,* p. 537.

375 "Helmut is strong . . .": Carter, p. 113.

375 "Well, I don't mind . . .": Schmidt quoted in Brzezinski, p. 310.

375 On the neutron bomb debate see: George B. Kistiakowsky, "Enhanced Radiation Warheads, Alias the Neutron Bomb," *Technology Review,* May 1978; William Sweet, "The Neutron Bomb and European Defense," *Editorial Research Reports,*

NOTES   463

August 15, 1980; and Wayne Biddle, "Neutron Bomb: An Explosive Issue," *The New York Times Magazine,* November 15, 1981.

376 "he did not wish . . .": Brzezinski, p. 302.

376 "his administration would be . . .": ibid., p. 304.

376 "Politically, the costs . . .": See Cyrus R. Vance, *Hard Choices: Four Critical Years in Managing America's Foreign Policy,* p. 96.

377 "only political expediency . . .": Haig quoted in Lunn, p. 34; "a high school football coach . . .": Marshall quoted p. 35.

378 Statistics on U.S.oil companies and price as compared to Europe see Robert J. Lieber, "Europe and America in the World Energy Crisis," *International Affairs* (London), October 1979, pp. 542, 543.

379 The West German economy described in Robert Gerald Livingston, "Germany Steps Up," *Foreign Policy,* Spring 1976.

380 On the international expansion of the nuclear industry, see Mark Hertsgaard, *Nuclear Inc: The Men and the Money Behind the Nuclear Industry in America,* chap. 4.

380 Cohn-Bendit quoted in Anna Gyorgy, ed., *No Nukes: Everyone's Guide to Nuclear Power,* pp. 352, 353.

381 For an account of antinuclear demonstrations throughout Europe in the 1970s, see ibid., sec. 4.

382 "creating a likely peril . . .": Senator Pastore quoted in William W. Lowrance, "Nuclear Futures for Sale: To Brazil from West Germany, 1975," *International Security,* Fall 1976, p. 147.

383 Mondale's meeting with Schmidt cited in "Schmidt May Modify Rio Atom Pact," *The New York Times,* January 27, 1977.

383 "designed to maintain . . .": see Gunter Hildenbrand, "A German Reaction to U.S. Nonproliferation Policy," *International Security,* Fall 1978, p. 54.

384 "all countries must work . . .": Blumenthal quoted in Robert O. Keohane, "American Policy and the Trade-Growth Struggle," *International Security,* Fall 1978, p. 27.

385 For an economic analysis of the locomotive theory, see Diana Winkler and Mathias Lefeldt, "Locomotive Theory: The Basic Ideas and Prospects," *Intereconomics,* May/June 1978. For a Japanese perspective, see Leon Hollerman, "Locomotive Strategy and United States Protectionism: A Japanese View," *Pacific Affairs,* Summer 1979.

385 "should please shut . . .": quoted in "Mondale Asks Bonn to Spur Its Economy," *The New York Times,* January 26, 1977.

386 Carter's economic policy toward the dollar described in Calleo, p. 146.

387 "Imports are a natural . . .": Cooper quoted in Keohane, p. 35.

388 "Free trade is a joke . . .": Meany quoted in ibid., p. 38.

388 Statistics on U.S. trade with EEC countries cited in Werner J. Feld, "Trade with West Europe and Japan," *Current History,* May/June 1979.

389 "People are starting . . .": Congressman Lyle Williams quoted in "In Ohio, the Enemy Is Japan," *The New York Times,* April 25, 1972.

389 "those little yellow . . .": Dingell quoted in ibid.

389 "sitting on their docks . . .": Connally quoted in "U.S., Japan Find Old Relationships Have Unraveled," *National Journal,* June 30, 1970, p. 1068.

389 "I heard things . . .": Patrick quoted in Michael Berger, "Hidden Dimension in U.S.–Japan Trade," *Pacific Community,* April 1978, p. 329.

389 Besides Vogel's book, see William Ouchi, *Theory Z: How American Business Can*

Meet the Japanese Challenge, and Richard T. Pascale, and Anthony G. Athos, *The Art of Japanese Management.*

390 Statistics on Japanese imports cited in *National Journal,* p. 1075.
390 Statistics on American usage of the automobile cited in *Auto Situation: 1980,* Report of the House Subcommittee on Trade, 96th Cong., 2d sess., June 6, 1980.
390 For a history of Toyota, see Shōtaro Kamiya, *My Life with Toyota.*
391 "It is enough . . .": quoted in *Auto Situation,* p. 33.
391 Statistics on Toyota and Japanese auto imports cited in ibid., pp. 28–31.
391 "Labour costs per head . . .": quoted in ibid., p. 41.
392 Japan's successes in steel and televisions described in *National Journal,* pp. 1074–77.
392 Japanese tariffs and quotas described in ibid., p. 1072.
393 Trade conflict with Japan during the Carter Administration described in I. M. Destler, "U.S.–Japanese Relations and the American Trade Initiative of 1977: Was This 'Trip' Necessary?" in William J. Barnds ed., *Japan and the United States: Challenges and Opportunities.*
393 "Japanese bureaucrats leaked . . .": ibid., p. 210.
394 "to achieve basic equity . . .": cited in ibid., p. 214.
394 Statistics on Japanese accumulation cited in *National Journal,* p. 1077.
394 "undersell steel made . . .": from a *Washington Post* column by Nicholas Von Hoffman cited in Berger, p. 332.
394 "Personal Freedom, autonomy . . .": Bellah quoted in Louise Bernikow, "Alone: Yearning for Companionship in America," *The New York Times Magazine,* August 15, 1982, pp. 26, 27.
395 "There are five layers . . .": ibid., p. 29.
397 "would imply a dismantling . . .": see Hans Friderichs, "Basic Problems of the World Economy," in Karl P. Sauvant and Hago Hasenpflug, eds., *The New International Economic Order: Confrontation or Cooperation Between North and South?* p. 87.
397 Details on French aid programs cited in Adrian Hewitt, "European Aid Donors," in Jacques de Bandt et al., *European Studies in Development: New Trends in European Development Studies.*
399 "West European–controlled firms . . .": for European investment in the Third World and imports and exports from that region, see Constantine V. Vaitsos, "The Role of Europe in North-South Relations," in De Bandt, p. 45.
400 "The dollar's recovery . . .": see Shonfield, "The World Economy, 1979," in *Foreign Affairs, America and the World, 1979,* p. 596.
400 For Stockman's opinions of Carter's energy policy, see David Stockman, "The Wrong War? The Case Against National Energy Policy," *Public Interest,* Fall 1978, pp. 3–44.
401 On the 1979 oil crisis and the aftereffects of Iran's revolution, see Robert Stobaugh and Daniel Yergin, "Energy: An Emergency Telescope," *Foreign Affairs: America and the World, 1979.*
402 "If World War III occurs . . .": Ohira quoted in Michael M. Yoshitsu, "Iran and Afghanistan in Japanese Perspective," *Asian Survey,* May 1981, p. 503.
402 "Our first oil shock . . .": ibid., p. 502.
402 "Japanese firms purchased . . .": ibid., p. 504.
402 "On a scale of one . . .": quoted in ibid., p. 506.
402 "We all know . . .": ibid.

402 Schmidt's early response to the hostage crisis and the position of other Allied countries cited in "Allies Plan Limits to Their Support of U.S. Sanctions," *Washington Post*, January 19, 1980.

403 "distressingly like amateur night . . .": the *Guardian* quoted in "America's Reluctant Allies: Europe Resists Carter's Pleas," *The New York Times*, April 14, 1980.

403 For the official inquiry into the rescue mission debacle, see The Special Operations Review Group of the Joint Chiefs of Staff, *Rescue Mission Report*, August 1980.

404 "the greatest threat . . .": Carter's reaction to the invasion cited in *An Assessment of the Afghanistan Sanctions: Implications for Trade and Diplomacy in the 1980s*, Report prepared for the House Subcommittee on Europe and the Middle East, 97th Cong., 1st sess., April 1981, p. 19. For Schmidt's response, see p. 99.

404 "a more dramatic change . . .": Carter quoted in Richard S. Newell, "International Responses to the Afghanistan Crisis," *The World Today*, May 1981, p. 174.

405 "the area south . . .": Molotov's memorandum cited in *Afghanistan Sanctions*, p. 12.

406 "calculated the Communist Government . . .": Kissinger quoted in ibid., p. 18.

407 "This means we must . . .": Schmidt quoted in Stephen Milligan, "Such Good Friends? Afghan Crisis Tests Atlantic Alliance," *Europe*, March/April 1980, p. 10.

407 "All this could come . . .": Schmidt's position on sanctions recorded in "An Interview with Helmut Schmidt," *The Wall Street Journal*, March 10, 1980.

408 "was not necessarily . . .": Giscard's position quoted in Newell, p. 180.
Statistics on the increase in French trade with the USSR cited in *Afghanistan Sanctions*, pp. 104, 105.

409 "I do not believe in . . .": Kissinger quoted in "Paris-Bonn Summit Seeks Joint Position on Carter's Policy," *Washington Post*, February 4, 1980.

410 "Japan and other . . .": quoted in Yoshitsu, p. 507.

410 "feared that Washington might . . .": ibid., p. 511.

Chapter 10

Page

411 "Twentieth Century Adonis . . .": see Hedrick Smith et al., *Reagan the Man, the President*. pp. 58 ff.

412 "We could pave . . .": Reagan quoted in Ronnie Dugger, "Ronald Reagan and the Imperial Presidency," *The Nation*, November 1, 1980, p. 431.

412 "Let us not delude . . .": quoted in Hedrick Smith, "Reagan: "What Kind of World Leader, *The New York Times Magazine*, November 16, 1980, p. 172.

413 Polls on German and French opinion reported in "Why They Distrust the U.S.," *Newsweek*, June 23, 1980. p. 33.

413 "or going to war . . .": Pipes quoted in "A Strategy of Tough Talk," *Newsweek*, March 30, 1981, p. 20; Pipes's reference to Genscher cited in "Discordant Voices," *The New York Times*, March 20, 1981.

414 On European reactions to U.S. lobbying on El Salvador see "U.S. Allies Cool to El Salvador Drive," *Washington Post*, February 27, 1981, and "U.S. and Its Allies at Odds on Central American Policy," February 20, 1982. Iklé quoted in "Pentagon Calls Soviet Arms a Threat to Central America," *The New York Times*, March 15, 1983.

414 When asked whether he would "swap U.S. military capability overall for that of

the Soviets," General Vessey replied: ". . . overall would I trade with Marshall Ogarkov? Not on your life, not to live there or have his job or his responsibilities or to have his forces in comparison to ours." See *Nomination of John W. Vessey Jr. to be Chairman of the Joint Chiefs of Staff.* Hearing before the Senate Committee on Armed Services, 97th Cong., 2d sess., May 11, 1982.

414 NATO–Warsaw pact comparisons cited in "Questions and Answers on the Military Balance in Europe," *The New York Times,* April 12, 1982.

415 "kills people and leaves . . .": see Biddle, pp. 46, 60.

415 "could see where . . .": Reagan quoted in "Brezhnev and Reagan on Atom War," *The New York Times,* October 21, 1981.

416 "protracted nuclear war . . .": quoted in *Los Angeles Times,* August 15, 1982. See also Robert Scheer, *With Enough Shovels.*

416 T. K. Jones quoted in ibid., p. 18.

416 "It's like Harry Truman . . .": quoted in "Questions and Answers," *The New York Times,* April 11, 1982.

417 For coverage of European peace movement demonstrations, see "Disarming Threat to Stability," *Time,* November 30, 1981.

417 "not even a scrap . . .": Ed van Thijn quoted in ibid., p. 40.

418 For a history of the British Peace Movement and the Campaign for Nuclear Disarmament (CND), see John Cox, *Over Kill: The Story of Modern Weapons,* chap. 12.

418 "There have been worse . . .": Brandt quoted in "Disarming Threat," *Time,* November 30, 1981, p. 42.

418 "feel like passengers . . .": Horst Eberhard Richter quoted in ibid., p. 43; "Talking to the superpowers . . .": Deile quoted p. 39.

419 For background information on Thatcher see R. W. Apple, Jr., "Margaret Thatcher: A Choice, Not an Echo," *The New York Times Magazine,* April 29, 1979.

420 "upset the military equilibrium . . .": Mitterrand quoted in Samuel F. Wells, Jr., "The Mitterrand Challenge," *Foreign Policy,* Fall, 1981, p. 59.

421 "when and if . . .": Eppler quoted in Andrew Arato and Jean Cohen, "The Peace Movement and Western European Sovereignty," *Telos,* Spring 1982, p. 167.

421 "If necessary, that includes . . .": Brzezinski quoted in ibid., p. 57.

422 On the development of the Greens party, see James M. Markham, "Germany's Volatile Greens," *The New York Times Magazine,* February 13, 1983.

422 The maps of the nuclear installations reproduced in *Der Stern,* February 19, 1981.

422 "we are the Nation . . .": Schmidt quoted from an interview on *60 Minutes,* Vol. XIII, Number 7, p. 18. Broadcast November 2, 1980.

422 "In April of the year . . .": Ranke-Heinemann quoted in Russell Berman, "Opposition to Rearmament and West German Culture," *Telos,* p. 145.

422 "Not just the use . . .": Barth quoted in Signs of Reconciliation, "Germany's Peace Movement Gains Strength," mimeographed. "Then there will be no . . .": Niemöller quoted in "This Movement Won't Go Away," *In These Times,* November 4–10, 1981.

423 "the former occupying . . .": Bahr quoted in John Vinocur, "The German Malaise," *The New York Times Magazine,* November 15, 1981, p. 123.

423 "Stop behaving as if . . .": Schmidt quoted in ibid., p. 117.

424 The Allensbach poll cited in ibid., pp. 116, 117.

424 Japanese outcry over the Suzuki-Reagan communiqué described in "Tokyo Aides'

Straight Talk Raises Eyebrows," *Washington Post,* July 4, 1981; see "Defense Efforts of Japan, Europe Flayed in Senate," *Washington Post,* March 27, 1982, for criticism of Japanese military spending. For a broader discussion of Japanese defense strategy in the 1970's see Nasu Kiyoshi, "Dilemmas of Japanese Defense," *Asian Affairs,* November/December 1978.

425 "unless Japanese military abilities . . .": quoted in "Weinberger Cautions Japanese on Arms," *The New York Times,* March 28, 1982.

425 "uncalled-for meddling . . .": Sunao Sonoda quoted in "Tokyo Aides," *Washington Post,* July 4, 1981.

426 "an infinitely complex range . . .": The *Report on Comprehensive National Security* is analyzed by Robert Barnett, "Japan as No. 1—in Defense?" *Far Eastern Economic Review,* September 25, 1981.

426 "The Japanese hate . . .": *Asahi* quoted in "Nuclear 'Facts of Life' Intrude into Japanese Defense Furor," *Christian Science Monitor,* June 3, 1981.

427 On the Japanese technological challenge see "Japan's High Tech Challenge," *Newsweek,* August 9, 1982; see also "Japan's Strategy for the 80's: A Changing Nation," *Business Week,* December 14, 1981.

428 "Whoever controls memory . . .": quoted in "Chip Challenge from Japan," *New York Times,* February 1, 1982.

428 "The American people may not . . .": Weinberger quoted in James Chase, "Europe and America: Double Isolation?" *SAIS Review,* Summer 1982, p. 2.

428 Defense spending statistics cited in "Japanese Upset by Criticism in U.S. Trade Imbalance," *The New York Times,* April 12, 1982.

429 "NATO ceased to be . . .": quoted in Chase, p. 9.

429 "How can we defend . . .": Delors quoted in "Allies Rebuking Reagan Sharply on Big Deficits," *The New York Times,* February 13, 1982.

429 On the world depression, see "Gloomy View from Versailles," *The New York Times,* June 8, .1982.

430 "economic warfare . . .": Dingell quoted in "U.S. Warns Illegal Steel Faces Retroactive Duties," *Washington Post,* May 13, 1982.

431 For books on the rise of Solidarity and the Polish military coup see Neil Ascherson, *The Polish August* and Daniel Singer, *The Road to Gdansk.*

431 On the different views of the Allied leaders on Poland, see "The West's Mixed Chorus," *Newsweek,* January 18, 1982, and "An Oversupply of Voices," *Time,* January 18, 1982.

432 "he did his usual . . .": quoted in ibid., p. 11.

432 "We'll tell you . . .": ibid.

433 For an overview of the pipeline conflict, see George W. Ball, "The Case Against Sanctions," *The New York Times Magazine,* September 12, 1982.

433 "We have a flexible . . .": see Otto Graf Lambsdorff, "The German Case for the Pipeline," *Washington Post,* July 28, 1982.

434 For the threatened losses to foreign firms involved in building the Siberian pipeline, see "Firms Are in a Bind over Pipeline," *Washington Post,* August 9, 1982.

434 "For all practical purposes . . .": Schmidt's reaction to Reagan's pipeline sanctions cited in "Europeans See U.S. Insensitive in Extension of Pipeline Ban," *Washington Post,* June 25, 1982; Thatcher's reaction cited in "Mrs. Thatcher Critical," *The New York Times,* August 2, 1982.

434 "We no longer speak . . .": Cheysson quoted in "Divorce, Alliance Style," *Newsweek,* August 2, 1982, p. 37.

435   "The days of the old . . .": The Council on Foreign Relations Report see Karl
      Kaiser et al. *Western Security: What Has Changed? What Should be done?* p. 17.
435   "create an identity . . .": quoted from Lawrence Eagleburger, "U.S.–German
      Contacts," *Das Parlament,* Spring 1982.

BIBLIOGRAPHY

Books

Acheson, Dean G. *The Pattern of Responsibility*. Edited by McGeorge Bundy. Boston: Houghton Mifflin, 1952.
―――. *Present at the Creation: My Years in the State Department*. New York: Norton, 1969.
―――. *Sketches from Life of Men I Have Known*. New York: Harper, 1961.
Adenauer, Konrad. *Erinnerungen Fragmente, 1959–1963*. Stuttgart: Deutsche-Verlags-Anstalt, 1968.
―――. *Memoirs, 1945–1953*. Translated by Beats Ruhm von Oppen. London: Weidenfeld and Nicholson, 1966.
Alexandre, Philippe. *The Duel: De Gaulle and Pompidou*. Boston: Houghton Mifflin, 1972.
Ardagh, John. *The New France: A Society in Transition, 1945–1977*. Harmondsworth: Penguin, 1977.
Aron, Raymond. *The Great Debate: Theories of Nuclear Strategy*. Translated by Ernst Pawel. Garden City, N.Y.: Doubleday, 1965.
Aron, Raymond, and Lerner, Daniel, eds. *France Defeats EDC*. New York: Praeger, 1957.
Ascherson, Neil. *The Polish August*. New York: Viking Press, 1982.
Baerwald, Hans H. *The Purge of Japanese Leaders Under the Occupation*. Berkeley: University of California Press, 1959.
Ball, George W. *The Past Has Another Pattern: Memoirs*. New York: W. W. Norton, 1982.
Bandt, Jacques de; Mándi, Péter; and Seers, Dudley, eds. *European Studies in Development: New Trends in European Development Studies*. New York: St. Martin's Press, 1980.
Baring, Arnulf. *Sehr verehrter Herr Bundeskanzler!: Heinrich von Brentano im Briefwechsel mit Konrad Adenauer, 1949–1964*. Hamburg: Hoffman und Campe, 1974.

Bark, Dennis L. *Agreement on Berlin: A Study of the 1970–1972 Quadripartite Negotiations*. Washington: American Enterprise Institute for Public Policy Research, 1974.

Barnds, William S., ed. *Japan and the United States: Challenge and Opportunities*. New York: New York University Press, 1979.

Barnet, Richard J. *Intervention and Revolution*. New York: New American Library, 1972.

———, and Müller, Ronald E. *Global Reach: The Power of the Multinational Corporations*. New York: Simon and Schuster, 1974.

Beaufre, André. *NATO, and Europe*. New York: Knopf, 1968.

Behrman, Jack N. *National Interests and the Multinational Enterprise: Tensions Among the North Atlantic Countries*. Englewood Cliffs, N.J.: Prentice-Hall, 1970.

Bell, Coral. *The Debatable Alliance*. New York: Oxford University Press, 1964.

———. *The Diplomacy of Detente: The Kissinger Era*. New York: St. Martin's Press, 1977.

Beloff, Max. *The United States and the Unity of Europe*. Washington: Brookings Institution, 1963.

Beloff, Nora. *The General Says No: Britain's Exclusion from Europe*. Baltimore: Penguin, 1963.

Bergsten, C. Fred. *The Dilemmas of the Dollar: The Economics and Politics of the United States International Monetary Policy*. New York: New York University.

Bigsby, C. W. E., ed. *Superculture: American Popular Culture and Europe*. Bowling Green, Ohio: Bowling Green University Popular Press, 1975.

Binder, David. *The Other German: Willy Brandt's Life and Times*. Washington: New Republic Book Co., 1975.

Bisson, Thomas A. *Zaibatsu Dissolution in Japan*. Berkeley: University of California Press, 1954.

Block, Fred L. *The Origins of International Economic Disorder*. Berkeley: University of California Press, 1977.

Blum, John M. *From the Morgenthau Diaries: Years of War, 1941–1945*. Boston: Houghton Mifflin, 1959–67.

Bohlen, Charles E. *Witness to History, 1929–1969*. New York: Norton, 1973.

Borkin, Joseph. *The Crime and Punishment of I. G. Farben*. New York: Free Press, 1978.

Brandt, Willy. *In Exile: Essays, Reflections and Letters, 1933–1947*. Translated by R. W. Last. London: Wolff, 1971.

———. *The Ordeal of Coexistence*. Cambridge, Mass.: Harvard University Press, 1962.

———. *People and Politics: The Years 1960–1975*. Translated by J. Maxwell Brownjohn. Boston: Little, Brown, 1978.

Brickman, William W., and Lehrer, Stanley, eds. *Conflict and Change on the Campus: The Response to Student Hyperactivism*. New York: School and Society Books, 1970.

Bromberger, Merry, and Bromberger, Serge. *Jean Monnet and the United States of Europe*. Translated by Elaine P. Halperin. New York: Coward-McCann, 1969.

Brown, Lewis H. *A Report on Germany*. New York: Farrar, Straus, 1947.

Brown, William A., and Redvers, Opie. *American Foreign Assistance*. Washington: Brookings Institution, 1953.

Brzezinski, Zbigniew K. *The Fragile Blossom: Crisis and Change in Japan*. New York: Harper and Row, 1972.

————. *Power and Principle: Memoirs of the National Security Adviser, 1973–1981.* Farrar, Straus and Giroux, 1983.

Calleo, David P. *The Atlantic Fantasy: The U.S., NATO, and Europe.* Baltimore: Johns Hopkins University Press, 1970.

————. *The Imperious Economy.* Cambridge, Mass.: Harvard University Press, 1982.

————, and Rowland, Benjamin M. *America and the World Political Economy: Atlantic Dreams and National Realities.* Bloomington: Indiana University Press, 1973.

Campbell, John C., and Caruso, Helen. *The West and the Middle East.* New York: Council on Foreign Relations, 1977.

Camps, Miriam. *European Unification in the Sixties: From Veto to the Crisis.* New York: McGraw-Hill, 1966. Published for the Council on Foreign Relations.

Carter, Jimmy. *Keeping Faith: Memoirs of a President.* New York: Bantam, 1982.

Casserly, John J. *The Ford White House: The Diary of a Speech Writer.* Boulder, Colo.: Colorado Associated University Press, 1977.

Cate, Curtis. *The Ides of August: The Berlin Wall Crisis—1961.* New York: M. Evans, 1978.

Catudal, Honoré M., Jr. *The Diplomacy of the Quadripartite Agreement on Berlin: A New Era in East–West Relations.* Berlin: Berlin-Verlag, 1978.

Cerny, Philip G. *The Politics of Grandeur: Ideological Aspects of De Gaulle's Foreign Policy.* Cambridge and New York: Cambridge University Press, 1980.

Chamberlin, William Henry. *The German Phoenix.* New York: Duell, Sloan and Pearce, 1963.

Churchill, Winston S. *Closing the Ring.* Boston: Houghton Mifflin, 1951.

Clay, Lucius D. *Decision in Germany.* Garden City, N.Y.: Doubleday, 1950.

————. *The Papers of General Lucius D. Clay: Germany, 1945–1949.* Edited by Jean Edward Smith, Bloomington: Indiana University Press, 1974.

Cohen, Stephen D. *International Monetary Reform, 1964–1969.* New York: Praeger, 1970.

Conte, Arthur. *Yalta ou le Partage du Monde.* Paris: Laffont, 1964.

Cook, Blanche Wiesen. *The Declassified Eisenhower.* Garden City, N.Y.: Doubleday, 1981.

Cookridge, E. H. *Gehlen, Spy of the Century.* New York: Random House, 1972.

Cooper, Chester L. *The Lion's Last Roar: Suez, 1956.* New York: Harper and Row, 1978.

Cormier, Frank. *LBJ the Way He Was.* Garden City, N.Y.: Doubleday, 1977.

Cox, John. *Over Kill: The Story of Modern Weapons.* Middlesex, England: Pelican Books, 1981.

Crossman, Richard. *The Diaries of a Cabinet Minister, 1964–1966.* Vol. I. New York: Holt, Rinehart and Winston, 1975.

————. *The Diaries of a Cabinet Minister, 1966–1968.* Vol. II. New York: Holt, Rinehart and Winston, 1976.

Crozier, Michel; Huntington, Samuel P.; and Watanuki, Joji. *The Crisis of Democracy: Report on the Governability of Democracies to the Trilateral Commission.* New York: New York University Press, 1975.

Davidson, Eugene. *The Death and Life of Germany: An Account of the American Occupation.* New York: Knopf, 1959.

Davie, Michael. *LBJ: A Foreign Observer's Viewpoint.* New York: Duell, Sloan and Pearce, 1966.

Dean, Vera. *Europe and the United States.* New York: Knopf, 1950.

de Gaulle, Charles. *Memoirs of Hope: Renewal and Endeavor.* Translated by Terence Kilmartin. New York: Simon and Schuster, 1971.

———. *War Memoirs.* New York: Simon and Schuster, 1955–60.

De Porte, Anton W. *Europe Between the Superpowers: The Enduring Balance.* New Haven, Conn.: Yale University Press, 1979.

Destler, I. M., ed. *Managing an Alliance: The Politics of U.S.–Japanese Relations.* Washington: Brookings Institution, 1976.

———; Fukui, Haruhiro; and Sato, Hideo. *The Textile Wrangle: Conflict in Japanese and American Relations, 1969–1971.* Ithaca, N.Y.: Cornell University Press, 1979.

Deutsch, Karl W., and Edinger, Lewis J. *Germany Rejoins the Powers.* Stanford: Stanford University Press, 1959.

Dobney, Frederick E., ed. *Selected Papers of Will Clayton.* Baltimore: Johns Hopkins Press, 1971.

Dower, John W. *Empire and Aftermath: Yoshida Shigeru and the Japanese Experience, 1878–1954.* Cambridge, Mass.: Harvard University Press, 1979.

Drummond, R., and Coblentz, G. *Duel at the Brink: John Foster Dulles' Command of American Power.* Garden City, N.Y.: Doubleday, 1960.

Dulles, Allen W. *The Craft of Intelligence.* New York: Harper and Row, 1963.

Eden, Anthony. *Full Circle: The Memoirs of Anthony Eden.* Boston: Houghton Mifflin, 1960.

———. *The Reckoning: The Eden Memoirs.* London: Cassell, 1965.

Edinger, Lewis J. *Kurt Schumacher: A Study in Personality and Political Behavior.* Stanford, Calif.: Stanford University Press, 1965.

Eisenhower, Dwight D. *The White House Years: Mandate for Change, 1953–1956.* New York: A Signet Book, 1963.

———. *The White House Years: Waging Peace, 1956–1961.* Garden City, N.Y.: Doubleday, 1965.

Evans, Douglas. *Western Energy Policy: The Case for Competition.* New York: St. Martin's Press, 1979.

Evans, Rowland, and Novak, Robert. *Lyndon B. Johnson: The Exercise of Power: A Political Biography.* New York: New American Library, 1966.

———. *Nixon in the White House: The Frustration of Power.* New York: Random House, 1971.

Fields, Rona M. *The Portuguese Revolution and the Armed Forces Movement.* New York: Praeger, 1976.

Finer, Herman. *Dulles over Suez.* Chicago: Quadrangle Press, 1974.

FitzGerald, Frances. *Fire in the Lake: The Vietnamese and the Americans in Vietnam.* Boston: Little, Brown, 1972.

Fitzgibbon, Constantine. *Denazification.* London: Michael Joseph, 1969.

Flanner, Janet [Genet]. *Paris Journal, 1944–1965.* Edited by William Shawn. New York: Atheneum, 1965.

Ford, Gerald. *A Time to Heal.* New York: Harper and Row, 1979.

Free, Lloyd A. *Six Allies and a Neutral: A Study of the International Outlooks of Political Leaders in the United States, Britain, France, West Germany, Italy, Japan, and India.* Glencoe, Ill.: Free Press, 1959.

Fujihara, Ginjiro. *The Spirit of Japanese Industry.* Tokyo: The Hokuseido Press, 1936.

Fukuda, Haruko. *Japan and World Trade: The Years Ahead.* Lexington, Mass.: Saxen House/Lexington Books, 1973.

Furniss, Edgar S., Jr., ed. *The Western Alliance: Its Status and Prospects.* Columbus: Ohio State University Press, 1965.

Gamble, Andrew. *Britain in Decline*. Boston: Beacon Press, 1981.

Garthoff, Raymond L. *Soviet Strategy in the Nuclear Age*. New York: Praeger, 1958.

Gatzke, Hans Wilhelm. *Germany and the United States: A "Special Relationship"?* Cambridge, Mass.: Harvard University Press, 1980.

Gayn, Mark J. *Japan Diary*. New York: W. Sloane Associates, 1948.

Gehlen, Reinhard. *The Service: The Memoirs of General Reinhard Gehlen*. New York: World Publishers, 1972.

Geyelin, Philip L. *Lyndon B. Johnson and the World*. New York: Praeger, 1966.

Gibney, Frank. *Japan: The Fragile Superpower*. New York: Norton, 1975.

Gilpin, Robert G., Jr. *U.S. Power and the Multinational Corporation*. New York: Basic Books, 1975.

Gimbel, John. *The American Occupation of Germany: Politics and the Military, 1945–1949*. Stanford, Calif.: Stanford University Press, 1968.

———. *The Origins of the Marshall Plan*. Stanford, Calif.: Stanford University Press, 1976.

Goldman, Eric Frederick. *The Tragedy of Lyndon Johnson*. New York: Knopf, 1969.

Goldsborough, James O. *Rebel Europe*. New York: Macmillan London, Collier Macmillan, 1982.

Goulden, Joseph C. *Meany: The Unchallenged Strong Man of American Labor*. New York: Atheneum, 1972.

Graff, Henry Franklin. *The Tuesday Cabinet: Deliberation and Decision on Peace and War Under Lyndon B. Johnson*. Englewood Cliffs, N.J.: Prentice-Hall, 1970.

Grosser, Alfred. *The Federal Republic of Germany: A Concise History*. Translated by Nelson Aldrich. New York: Praeger, 1964.

———. *French Foreign Policy Under De Gaulle*. Translated by Lois Ames Pattison. Boston: Little, Brown, 1967.

———. *Germany in Our Time: A Political History of the Postwar Years*. Translated by Paul Stephenson. New York: Praeger, 1971.

———. *The Western Alliance: European-American Relations Since 1945*. Translated by Michael Shaw. New York: Continuum, 1980.

Guillain, Robert. *The Japanese Challenge*. Translated by Patrick O'Brian. Philadelphia: Lippincott, 1970.

Gunther, John. *The Riddle of MacArthur: Japan, Korea, and the Far East*. New York: Harper, 1951.

Gyorgy, Anna, ed. *No Nukes: Everyone's Guide to Nuclear Power*. Boston: South End Press, 1979.

Hadley, Eleanor H. *Antitrust in Japan*. Princeton, N.J.: Princeton University Press, 1970.

Halliday, Jon. *A Political History of Japanese Capitalism*. New York: Pantheon Books, 1975.

Hanrieder, Wolfram F. *The Stable Crisis: Two Decades of German Foreign Policy*. New York: Harper and Row, 1970.

———, ed. *The United States and Western Europe: Political, Economic, and Strategic Perspectives*. Cambridge, Mass.: Winthrop Publishers, 1974.

———. *West German Foreign Policy, 1944–1963*. Stanford, Calif.: Stanford University Press, 1967.

———, ed. *West German Foreign Policy, 1949–1979*. Boulder, Colo.: Westview Press, 1980.

Hardley, Arkes. *Bureaucracy, the Marshall Plan, and the National Interest*. Princeton, N.J.: Princeton University Press, 1972.

Harriman, W. Averell. *America and Russia in a Changing World: A Half Century of Personal Observation,* Garden City, N.Y.: Doubleday, 1971.

Hartrich, Edwin. *The Fourth and Richest Reich.* New York: Macmillan, 1980.

Hauser, William L. *America's Army in Crisis.* Baltimore: Johns Hopkins University Press, 1973.

Haviland, H. Field, Jr., ed. *The United States and the Western Community.* Haverford, Pa.: Haverford College Press, 1957.

Heller, Deane, and Heller, David. *The Berlin Wall.* New York: Walker, 1962.

Hellmann, Rainier. *Weltunternehmen nur amerikanisch?* Baden-Baden: Nomos, 1970.

Herken, Gregg. *The Winning Weapon: The Atomic Bomb in the Cold War, 1945–1950.* New York: Knopf, 1980.

Hersh, Seymour M. *The Price of Power: Kissinger in the Nixon White House.* New York: Summit Books, 1983.

Hertsgaard, Mark. *Nuclear Inc.: The Men and the Money Behind the Nuclear Industry in America.* New York: Pantheon, 1983.

Hervé, Alphand. *L'etonnement d'être.* Paris: Fayard, 1977.

Hillenbrand, Martin J. *The Future of Berlin.* Montclair, N.J.: Allenfeld, Osmun, 1980.

Hilsman, Roger. *To Move a Nation: The Politics of Foreign Policy in the Administration of John F. Kennedy.* New York: Doubleday, 1967.

Hiscocks, Richard. *The Adenauer Era.* Philadelphia: Lippincott, 1966.

Hoffman, Stanley. *Gulliver's Troubles.* New York: McGraw-Hill, 1968.

Hofstadter, Richard. *The American Political Tradition and the Men Who Made It.* New York: Vintage Books, 1974.

Holborn, Hajo. *American Military Government: Its Organization and Policies.* Westport, Conn.: Greenwood Press, 1977.

Holland, Stuart. *The Uncommon Market: Capital, Class and Power in the European Community.* London: Macmillan, 1980.

Hollander, A. N. J. den, ed. *Contagious Conflict: The Impact of American Dissent on European Life.* Leiden, Brill: European Association for American Studies, 1973.

Holloway, David. *The Soviet Union and the Arms Race.* New Haven and London: Yale University Press, 1983.

Hoopes, Townsend. *The Devil and John Foster Dulles.* Boston: Little, Brown, 1973.

Howard, Anthony, and West, Richard. *The Road to Number 10.* New York: Macmillan, 1965.

Hudson, Michael. *Global Fracture: The New International Economic Order.* New York: Harper and Row, 1977.

Hughes, H. Stuart. *The United States and Italy.* Cambridge, Mass.: Harvard University Press, 1979.

Hull, Cordell. *The Memoirs of Cordell Hull.* New York: Macmillan, 1948.

Hunsberger, Warren S. *Japan and the United States in World Trade.* New York: Harper and Row, 1964. Published for the Council on Foreign Relations.

Jobert, Michel. *Memoires d'Avenir.* Paris: Edition Grasset et Fasquelle, 1974.

Johnson, Chalmers. *MITI and the Japanese Miracle.* Stanford, Calif.: Stanford University Press, 1982.

Johnson, Lyndon B. *The Vantage Point: Perspectives of the Presidency, 1963–1969.* New York: Holt, Rinehart and Winston, 1971.

Jones, Joseph M. *Fifteen Weeks: February 21–June 1, 1947.* New York: Harcourt, Brace and World, 1964.

Jordan, Robert S. *The NATO International Staff/Secretariat, 1952–1957.* London: Oxford University Press, 1967.

Kahn, Herman. *The Emerging Japanese Superstate: Challenge and Response.* New York: Prentice-Hall, 1970.

Kaiser, Karl. *German Foreign Policy in Transition.* London: Oxford University Press, 1968.

Kaiser, Karl, and Morgan, Roger. *Britain and West Germany, Changing Societies and the Future of Foreign Policy.* London: Oxford University Press for the Royal Institute of International Affairs, 1971.

Kaiser, Karl, et al. *Western Security: What Has Changed? What Should Be Done?* New York: The Council on Foreign Relations, 1981.

Kalb, Marvin L., and Kalb, Bernard. *Kissinger.* Boston: Little, Brown, 1974.

Kaldor, Mary. *The Baroque Arsenal.* New York: Hill and Wang, 1981.

———. *The Disintegrating West.* New York: Hill and Wang, 1978.

Kaldor, Mary, and Smith, Dan, eds. *Disarming Europe.* London: Merlin, 1982.

Kamiya, Shōtaro. *My Life with Toyota.* Translated by Thomas I. Elliot. s.l.: Toyota Motor Sales Company, 1976.

Kearns, Doris. *Lyndon Johnson and the American Dream.* New York: Harper and Row, 1976.

Keller, John W. *Germany, the Wall and Berlin: Internal Politics During an International Crisis.* New York: Vantage Press, 1964.

Kennan, George. *Memoirs, 1950–1963.* Boston: Atlantic-Little, Brown, 1972.

Kennedy, Robert F. *Thirteen Days.* New York: Norton, 1971.

Khrushchev, Nikita S. *Khrushchev Remembers.* Boston: Little, Brown, 1970.

Kimball, Warren F. *Swords or Plowshares?* Philadelphia: Lippincott, 1976.

Kindleberger, Charles P., ed. *The International Corporation.* Cambridge: The Massachusetts Institute of Technology Press, 1970.

Kissinger, Henry A. *The Troubled Partnership: A Re-appraisal of the Atlantic Alliance.* Garden City, N.Y.: Doubleday, 1966.

———. *White House Years.* Boston: Little, Brown, 1979.

———. *A World Restored: Metternich, Castlereagh, and the Problems of Peace, 1812–22.* Boston: Houghton Mifflin, 1973.

———. *Years of Upheaval.* Boston: Little, Brown, 1982.

Kolko, Gabriel. *The Roots of American Foreign Policy.* Boston: Beacon Press, 1969.

Kolko, Gabriel, and Kolko, Joyce. *The Limits of Power: The World and United States Foreign Policy, 1945–1954.* New York: Harper and Row, 1972.

Krause, Lawrence B. *European Economic Integration and the United States.* Washington: Brookings Institution, 1968.

Krock, Arthur. *Memoirs: Sixty Years on the Firing Line.* New York: Popular Library Eagle Books edition, 1968.

Kuklick, Bruce. *American Policy and the Division of Germany.* Ithaca, N.Y.: Cornell University Press, 1972.

Kulski, W. W. *De Gaulle and the World: The Foreign Policy of the Fifth French Republic.* Syracuse, N.Y.: Syracuse University Press, 1966.

Kurtzman, Joel, and Laszlo, Ervin, eds. *Western Europe and the New International Economic Order.* New York: Pergamon Press, 1980.

Kurzman, Dan. *Kishi and Japan: The Search for the Sun.* New York: I. Obelensky, 1960.

Laing, Margaret I. *Edward Heath, Prime Minister.* New York: Third Press, 1973.

Landau, David. *Kissinger: The Uses of Power.* New York: Crowell, 1974.

Landes, David S., ed. *Western Europe: The Trials of Partnership.* Lexington, Mass.: D. C. Heath, 1977.

Livingston, Jon, et al. *Postwar Japan: 1945 to the Present*. New York: Pantheon Books, 1974.

Lockwood, William W. *The Economic Development of Japan: Growth and Structural Changes*. Princeton, N.J.: Princeton University Press, 1954.

————, ed. *The State of Economic Enterprise in Japan*. Princeton, N.J.: Princeton University Press, 1965.

Loftus, John. *The Belarus Secret*. New York: Alfred A. Knopf, 1982.

Louis, J. C., and Yazijian, Harvey Z. *The Cola Wars*. New York: Everest House, 1980.

Lyon, Peter. *Eisenhower: Portrait of the Hero*. Boston: Little, Brown, 1974.

MacArthur, Douglas. *Reminiscences*. New York: McGraw-Hill, 1964.

McCreary, Edward A. *The Americanization of Europe: The Impact of Americans and the American Business on the Uncommon Market*. Garden City, N.Y.: Doubleday, 1964.

McKenzie, Fred A. *The American Invaders; Their Plans, Tactics and Progress*. London: H. W. Bell, 1901.

Macmillan, Harold. *At the End of the Day, 1961–1963*. New York: Harper and Row, 1973.

————. *Pointing the Way, 1959–1961*. London: Macmillan, 1972.

————. *Riding the Storm, 1956–1959*. London: Macmillan, 1971.

————. *Tides of Fortune: 1945–1955*. New York: Harper and Row, 1969.

Mally, Gerhard. *The New Europe and the United States: Partners or Rivals*. Lexington, Mass.: Lexington Books, 1974.

Manchester, William R. *American Caesar: Douglas MacArthur, 1880–1964*. Boston: Little, Brown, 1978.

————. *The Arms of Krupp: 1587–1968*. New York: Bantam, 1970.

Martin, James Stewart. *All Honorable Men*. Boston: Little, Brown, 1950.

Mayer, Martin. *The Fate of the Dollar*. New York: New York Times Books, 1980.

Meadows, Donella H. *The Limits to Growth: A Report for the Club of Rome's Project on the Predicament of Mankind*. New York: University Books, 1974.

Mendel, Douglas H., Jr. *The Japanese People and Foreign Policy: A Study of Public Opinion in Post-Treaty Japan*. Berkeley: University of California Press, 1961.

Mendershausen, Horst. *Coping with the Oil Crisis: French and German Experiences*. Baltimore: Published for Resources for the Future. Incorporated by Johns Hopkins Press, 1976.

Merritt, Anna J., and Merritt, Richard L. *Public Opinion in Occupied Germany: The OMGUS Surveys, 1945–1949*. Urbana: University of Illinois Press, 1970.

Miller, Merle. *Lyndon: An Oral Biography*. New York: Putnam, 1980.

Millis, Walter, ed. *The Forrestal Diaries*. New York: Viking Press, 1951.

Moffitt, Michael. *The World's Money*. New York: Simon and Schuster, 1983.

Monnet, Jean. *Memoirs*. Garden City, N.Y.: Doubleday, 1978.

Montgomery, John D. *Forced to Be Free: The Artificial Revolution in Germany and Japan*. Chicago: University of Chicago Press, 1957.

Morgan, Janet, ed. *The Backbench Diaries of Richard Crossman*. New York: Holmes and Meier, 1981.

Morgan, Roger. *The United States and West Germany, 1945–1973: A Study in Alliance Politics*. London: Published for the Royal Institute of International Affairs and the Howard Center for International Affairs by Oxford University Press, 1974.

Morris, Roger. *Uncertain Greatness: Henry Kissinger and American Foreign Policy*. New York: Harper and Row, 1977.

Murphy, Robert D. *Diplomat Among Warriors*. Garden City, N.Y.: Doubleday, 1964.

Myrdal, Alva, ed. *Dynamics of Nuclear Disarmament*. Nottingham, England: Spokesman Books, 1981.

——. *The Game of Disarmament: How the United States and Russia Run the Arms Race*. New York: Pantheon Books, 1976.

Neff, Donald. *Warriors at Suez*. New York: Linden Press/Simon and Schuster, 1981.

New Left Review, ed. *Exterminism and Cold War*. London: Verso, 1982.

Neustadt, Richard E. *Alliance Politics*. New York: Columbia University Press, 1970.

Newhouse, John. *De Gaulle and the Anglo-Saxons*. New York: Viking Press, 1970.

Nixon, Richard M. *RN: The Memoirs of Richard Nixon*. Vol 1. New York: Warner Books, 1978.

——. *U.S. Foreign Policy for the 1970's: A Report of President Richard Nixon to the Congress, February 25, 1971*. New York: Harper and Row, 1971.

Nutter, G. Warren. *Kissinger's Grand Design*. Washington: American Enterprise Institute for Public Policy Research, 1975.

Odell, Peter R. *Oil and World Power*. Harmondsworth, England: Penguin, 1979.

Osgood, Robert E. *Alliances and American Foreign Policy*. Baltimore: The Johns Hopkins University Press, 1968.

——. *NATO, The Entangling Alliance*. Chicago: University of Chicago Press, 1962.

——, et al. *Retreat From Empire? The First Nixon Administration*. Vol. II. Baltimore: The Johns Hopkins University Press, 1973.

Ouchi, William. *Theory Z: How American Business Can Meet the Japanese Challenge*. Reading, Mass: Addison-Wesley, 1981.

Owen, David. *The Politics of Defense*. New York: Taplinger, 1972.

Paarlberg, R., ed. *Diplomatic Dispute: U.S. Conflict with Iran, Japan and Mexico*. Cambridge, Mass.: Harvard University Press, 1978.

Packard, George R., III. *Protest in Tokyo: The Security Treaty Crisis of 1960*. Princeton, N.J.: Princeton University Press, 1966.

Pascale, Richard T., and Athos, Anthony G. *The Art of Japanese Management*. New York: Simon and Schuster, 1981.

Peterson, Edward N. *The American Occupation of Germany, Retreat to Victory*. Detroit: Wayne State University Press, 1977.

Pfaltzgraff, Robert L., Jr. *Energy Issues and Alliance Relationships: The U.S., Western Europe and Japan*. Cambridge, Mass.: Institute for Foreign Policy Analysis Inc., 1980.

Pierre, Andrew J. *Nuclear Politics: The British Experience with an Independent Strategic Force, 1939–1970*. Oxford, England: Oxford University Press, 1972.

Pinder, John. *Europe Against De Gaulle*. New York: Praeger, 1963.

Powers, Thomas. *The Man Who Kept the Secrets: Richard Helms and the CIA*. New York: Knopf, 1979.

Prittie, Terence C. *Konrad Adenauer: 1876–1967*. Chicago: Cowles Book Co., 1971.

——. *The Velvet Chancellors: A History of Post-War Germany*. London: Muller, 1979.

——. *Willy Brandt: Portrait of a Statesman*. New York: Schocken Books, 1974.

Quandt, William B. *Decade of Decisions: American Policy Toward the Arab-Israeli Conflict, 1967–1976*. Berkeley: University of California Press, 1977.

Radosh, Ronald. *American Labor and United States Foreign Policy*. New York: Random House, 1969.

Reischauer, Edwin O. *The United States and Japan*. Cambridge, Mass.: Harvard University Press, 1965.

Richardson, James L. *Germany and the Atlantic Alliance: The Interaction of Strategy and Politics*. Cambridge, Mass.: Harvard University Press, 1966.

Rodgers, William. *Think: A Biography of the Watsons and IBM*. New York: Stein and Day, 1969.

Roosevelt, Kermit. *Countercoup*. New York: McGraw-Hill, 1974.

Rose, François de. *La France et la Défense de l'Europe*. Paris: Editions du Seuil, 1976.

Rostow, W. W. *The Diffusion of Power*. New York: Macmillan, 1972.

Roth, Andrew. *Heath and the Heathmen*. London: Routledge and Kegan Paul, 1972.

Safire, William. *Before the Fall: An Inside View of the Pre-Watergate White House*. Garden City, N.Y.: Doubleday, 1975.

Sampson, Anthony. *The Arms Bazaar: From Lebanon to Lockheed*. New York: Viking Press, 1977.

———. *Macmillan: A Study in Ambiguity*. New York: Simon and Schuster, 1967.

———. *The Sovereign State of ITT*. New York: Stein and Day, 1973.

Sauvant, Karl P., and Hasenpflug, Hajo, eds. *The New International Economic Order: Confrontation or Cooperation Between North and South?* Boulder, Colo.: Westview Press, 1977.

Scalopino, Robert. *American-Japanese Relations in a Changing Era*. New York: Library Press, 1972.

Schaetzel, Robert. *The Unhinged Alliance: America and the European Continent*. New York: Harper and Row, 1975. A Council on Foreign Relations Book.

Scheer, Robert. *With Enough Shovels: Reagan, Bush and Nuclear War*. New York: Random House, 1982.

Schick, Jack M. *The Berlin Crisis, 1958–1962*. Philadelphia: University of Pennsylvania Press, 1971.

Schlesinger, Arthur M., Jr. *A Thousand Days: John F. Kennedy in the White House*. Boston: Houghton Mifflin, 1965.

Schmidt, Helmut. *The Balance of Power: Germany's Peace Policy and the Superpowers*. Translated by Edward Thomas. London: Kimber, 1971.

Schmitt, Hans A. *The Path to European Union: From the Marshall Plan to the Common Market*. Baton Rouge: Louisiana State University Press, 1962.

———, ed. *U.S. Occupation in Europe After World War II*. Lawrence: Regents press of Kansas, 1978.

Schoenbrun, David. *The Three Lives of Charles de Gaulle*. New York: Atheneum, 1966.

Schwarz, Hans-Peter. *Von Reich zur Bundesrepublik*. Neuwied, Germany: Luchterhand, 1966.

Sebald, William J., with Brines, Russell. *With MacArthur in Japan: A Personal History of the Occupation*. New York: Norton, 1965.

Servan-Schreiber, J. J. *The American Challenge*. New York: Atheneum, 1968.

Sharp, Tony. *The Wartime Alliance and the Zonal Division of Germany*. Oxford, England, Clarendon Press, 1975.

Sheehan, Edward. *The Arabs, Israelis, and Kissinger: a Secret History of America's Diplomacy in the Middle East*. New York: Reader's Digest Press, 1976.

Sherwin, Martin J. *A World Destroyed: The Atomic Bomb and the Great Alliance*. New York: Knopf, 1975.

Shiels, Frederick L. *Tokyo and Washington*. Lexington, Mass.: Lexington Books, 1980.

Shonfield, Andrew. *International Economic Relations of the Western World, 1959–1971*. Vol 2.

————. *Modern Capitalism: The Changing Balance of Public and Private Power*. London: Oxford University Press, 1965.

Shoup, Laurence H. *The Carter Presidency and Beyond: Power and Politics in the 1980's*. Palo Alto, Calif.: Ramparts Press, 1980.

Shrimsley, Anthony. *The First Hundred Days of Harold Wilson*. New York: Praeger, 1965.

Singer, Daniel. *The Road to Gdansk*. New York: Monthly Review Press, 1981.

Sklar, Holly, ed. *Trilateralism: The Trilateral Commission and Elite Planning for World Management*. Boston: South End Press, 1980.

Smith, Gaddis. *Dean Acheson*. The American Secretaries of State and Their Diplomacy Series, edited by Robert H. Ferrel, vol. 16. New York: Cooper Square Publishers, 1972.

Smith, Gerard. *Double Talk: The Story of the First Strategic Arms Limitation Talks*. Garden City, N.Y.: Doubleday, 1980.

Smith, Hedrick, et al. *Reagan the Man, the President*. New York: Macmillan, 1980.

Smith, Jean Edward. *The Defense of Berlin*. Baltimore: Johns Hopkins University Press, 1963.

Smith, Perry McCoy. *The Air Force Plans for Peace, 1943–1945*. Baltimore: Johns Hopkins University Press, 1970.

Solomon, Robert. *The International Monetary System: 1945–1976*. New York: Harper and Row, 1977.

Sorensen, Theodore C. *Kennedy*. New York: Harper and Row, 1965.

Speier, Hans. *German Rearmament and Atomic War: The Views of German Military and Political Leaders*. Evanston, Ill.: Row, Peterson, 1957.

Starr, Joseph R. *Denazification, Occupation and Control of Germany, March–July 1945*. Salisbury, N.C.: Documentary Publications, 1977.

Stead, William Thomas. *The Americanization of the World, or the Trend of the Twentieth Century,* New York: H. Markley, 1901.

Steel, Ronald. *Walter Lippmann and the American Century*. Boston: Little, Brown, 1980.

Steinbruner, John D. *The Cybernetic Theory of Decision*. Princeton, N.J.: Princeton University Press, 1974.

Stern, Lawrence. *The Wrong Horse: The Politics of Intervention and the Failure of American Diplomacy*. New York: New York Times Books, 1977.

Stimson, Henry L., and Bundy, McGeorge. *On Active Service in Peace and War*. New York: Harper, 1948.

Strange, Susan. *International Monetary Relations*. London: Oxford University Press. Published for the Royal Institute of International Affairs, 1976.

————. *Sterling and British Policy: A Political Study of an International Currency in Decline*. London: Oxford University Press, 1971.

Szulc, Tad. *The Illusion of Peace: A Diplomatic History of Foreign Policy in the Nixon Years*. New York: Viking Press, 1978.

terHorst, Jerald F. *Gerald Ford and the Future of the Presidency*. New York: The Third Press, 1974.

Textor, Robert B. *Failure in Japan*. Westport, Conn.: Greenwood Press, 1951.

Thomas, Hugh. *The Suez Affair*. Harmondsworth: Penguin, 1970.

Thompson, E. P. *Beyond the Cold War: A New Approach to the Arms Race and Nuclear Annihilation*. New York: Pantheon Books, 1982.

Thorne, Christopher G. *Allies of a Kind: The United States, Britain and the War Against Japan, 1941–1945*. London: Hamilton, 1978.

Thurow, Lester C. *The Zero-Sum Society*. New York: Basic Books, 1980.

Tökés, Rudolf L., ed. *Eurocommunism and Detente*. New York: New York University Press, 1978.

Touraine, Alain. *The May Movement: Revolt and Reform*. New York: Random House, 1971.

Treverton, Gregory F. *The Dollar Drain and American Forces in Germany: Managing the Political Economics of Alliance*. Athens: Ohio University Press, 1978.

Trewhitt, Henry L. *McNamara*. New York: Harper and Row, 1971.

Triffin, Robert. *Europe and the Money Muddle: From Bilateralism to Near-Convertability, 1947–1956*. New Haven, Conn.: Yale University Press, 1957.

Truman, Margaret. *Harry S. Truman*. New York: Morrow, 1973.

Tugendhat, Christopher. *The Multinationals*. London: Eyre and Spottiswode, 1971.

Van Der Beugel, Ernst H. *From Marshall Aid to Atlantic Partnership*. Amsterdam: Elsevier, 1966.

Vance, Cyrus R. *Hard Choices: Four Critical Years in Managing American Foreign Policy*. New York: Simon and Schuster, 1983.

Vernon, Raymond, ed. *The Oil Crisis*. New York: Norton, 1976.

Viorst, Milton. *Fire in the Streets: America in the 1960s*. New York: Simon and Schuster, 1979.

Vogel, Ezra F. Japan as Number One: Lesson for America. Cambridge, Mass.: Harvard University Press, 1979.

Watanabe, Akio. *The Okinawa Problem: A Chapter in Japan–U.S. Relations*. Melbourne, Australia: Melbourne University Press, 1970.

Weil, Gordon L., and Davidson, Ian. *The Gold War: A Story of the World's Monetary Crisis*. New York: Holt, Rinehart and Winston, 1970.

Weinstein, Martin E. *Japan's Postwar Defense Policy, 1947–1968*. New York: Columbia University Press, 1971.

Werth, Alexander. *De Gaulle: A Political Biography*. New York: Simon and Schuster, 1966.

———. *The De Gaulle Revolution*. London: R. Hale, 1960.

Whetten, Lawrence L. *Germany's Ostpolitik: Relations Between the Federal Republic and the Warsaw Pact Countries*. London: Oxford University Press for the Royal Institute of International Affairs, 1971.

Whitney, Courtney. *MacArthur: His Rendezvous with History*. New York: Knopf, 1956.

Wighton, Charles. *Adenauer: A Critical Biography*. New York: Coward-McCann, 1963.

Wildes, Harry Emerson. *Typhoon in Tokyo: The Occupation and Its Aftermath*. New York: Octagon Books, 1978.

Willoughby, Charles A. *MacArthur: 1941–1951; Victory in the Pacific*. London: Heinemann, 1956.

Wills, Garry. *Nixon Agonistes: The Crisis of the Self-Made Man*. Boston: Houghton Mifflin, 1970.

Wilson, Harold. *Final Term: The Labour Government, 1974–1976*. London: Weidenfeld and Nicolson, 1979.

———. *The Labour Government, 1964–1970: A Personal Record*. London: Weidenfeld and Nicolson, 1971.

Woodhouse, C. M. *Something Ventured: The Autobiography of C. M. Woodhouse*. London: Granada Publishing, 1982.

Woodward, William P. *The Allied Occupation of Japan: 1945–1952, and Japanese Religions.* Leiden: E. J. Brill, 1972.
Wooten, James. *Dasher: The Roots and the Rising of Jimmy Carter.* New York: Summit Books, 1978.
Yanaga, Chitoshi. *Big Business in Japanese Politics.* New Haven, Conn.: Yale University Press, 1968.
Yergin, Daniel. *Shattered Peace: The Origins of the Cold War and the National Security State.* Boston: Houghton Mifflin, 1977.
Yoshida, Shigeru. *The Yoshida Memoirs: The Story of Japan in Crisis.* Translated by Kenishi Yoshida. Boston: Houghton Mifflin, 1962.
Zurcher, Arnold J. *The Struggle to Unite Europe, 1940–1958.* New York: New York University Press, 1958.

Selected Articles

Ball, George W. "The Case Against Sanctions." *The New York Times Magazine*, September 12, 1982.
Barnet, Richard J. "Carter's Patchwork Doctrine." *Harper's*, August 1977.
Barraclough, Geoffrey. "Wealth and Power: The Politics of Food and Oil." *The New York Review of Books*, August 7, 1975.
Berger, Michael. "Hidden Dimensions in U.S.–Japan Trade." *Pacific Community*, April 1978.
Callender, Harold. "A Prophet of a United Europe." *The New York Times Magazine*, February 8, 1953.
"A Changing Nation: Japan Inc. Goes International." *Business Week*, December 14, 1981.
Dickinson, William, Jr. "Rising Japanese Nationalism." *Editorial Research Reports*, January 5, 1966.
Dower, John. "The Eye of the Beholder: Background Notes on the U.S.–Japan Military Relationship." *Bulletin of Concerned Asian Scholars*, October 1969.
Drew, Elizabeth. "A Reporter at Large: Brzezinski." *The New Yorker*, May 1, 1978.
Dulles, John Foster. "Security in the Pacific." *Foreign Affairs*, January 1952.
Feld, Werner J. "Trade with West Europe and Japan." *Current History*, May/June 1979.
Flint, Jerry. "What's a Trilateral Commission?" *Forbes*, November 24, 1980.
Garthoff, Raymond L. "Brezhnev's Opening: The TNF Tangle." *Foreign Policy*, Winter 1980–81.
Gimlin, Hoyt. "American Investments in European Industry." *Editorial Research Reports*, January 26, 1968.
Goldsborough, James O. "France, the European Crisis and the Alliance." *Foreign Affairs*, April 1974.
———. "The Franco-German Entente." *Foreign Affairs*, April 1976.
———. "The Roots of Western Disunity." *The New York Times Magazine*, May 9, 1982.
Heilperin, Michael A. " 'Little Europe' or Atlantic Community?" *Fortune*, December 1953.
Hitchens, Christopher. "Détente and Destabilization: Report from Cyprus." *New Left Review*, November/December 1975.
Howard, Michael. "NATO and the Year of Europe." *Survival*, January/February 1974.

Kaplan, Fred. "Warring Over New Missiles for NATO." *The New York Times Magazine*, December 9, 1979.

Kennan, George F. "Japanese Security and American Policy." *Foreign Affairs*, October 1964.

Kreile, Michael. "West Germany: The Dynamics of Expansion." *International Organization*, Autumn 1977.

Lasch, Christopher. "The Cultural Cold War." *The Nation*, September 11, 1967.

Lieber, Robert J. "Europe and America in the World Energy Crisis." *International Affairs* (London), October 1979.

Maxwell, Kenneth. "The Hidden Revolution in Portugal." *The New York Review of Books*, April 17, 1975.

———. "Portugal Under Pressure." *The New York Review of Books*, May 29. 1975.

Middleton, Drew. "Germans Today: Doleful and Angry." *The New York Times Magazine*, September 16, 1945.

———. "NATO Changes Directions." *Foreign Affairs*, April 1953.

Motoo, Gotō. "Crisis in Japan–U.S. Relations." *Japan Quarterly*, October–December 1968.

Philip, André. "The U.S. Vs. Europe." *Atlas*, February 1964.

Pincus, Walter. "Arms Decisions Stirred Storm Around NATO." *Washington Post*, November 18, 1981.

Platt, Alan A., and Leonardi, Robert. "American Foreign Policy and the Postwar Italian Order." *Political Science Quarterly*, Summer 1978.

Samuelson, Robert J. "U.S., Japan Find Old Relationships Have Unraveled." *National Journal*, June 30, 1979.

Schoenbaum, David. "Dateline Bonn: Uneasy Super-Ally." *Foreign Policy*, Winter 1979–80.

Smart, Ian. "The New Atlantic Charter." *The World Today*, June 1973.

Strange, Susan. "The Dollar Crisis 1971." *International Affairs*, April 1972.

Vardamis, Alex A. "German-American Military Fissures." *Foreign Policy*. Spring 1979.

Watt, D. C. "Henry Kissinger: An Interim Judgment." *Political Quarterly*, vol. 48, 1977.

Government Documents

Federal Republic of Germany. Presse und Informationsamt der Bundesregierung. *White Paper 1970 on the Security of the Federal Republic of Germany and on the State of the German Armed Services*, May 1970.

Kormann, John G. *U.S. Denazification Policy in Germany, 1944–50*. Historical Division; Office of the Executive Secretary, Office of the U.S. High Commissioner for Germany, 1952.

U.S. Senate, *Morgenthau Diary (Germany)*, prepared by the Subcommittee to Investigate the Administration of the Internal Security Act and other Internal Security Laws of the Committee on the Judiciary. (Washington, D.C.: Government Printing Office, 1967).

U.S. General Accounting Office, report by the comptroller general of the United States, *United States–Japan Trade: Issues and Problems* (Washington, D.C.: General Accounting Office, September 21, 1979).

United States International Economic Policy in an Interdependent World, papers submitted to The Commission on International Trade and Investment Policy and published in conjunction with the commissioner's report to the president. Compendium of Papers: vol. II, July 1971, Washington, D.C.

U.S. Congress, House, Committee on Foreign Affairs, Subcommittee on Europe and the Middle East, *An Assessment of the Afghanistan Sanctions: Implications for Trade and Diplomacy in the 1980s,* 97th Cong. 1st sess., April 1981 (Washington, D.C., Government Printing Office, 1981).

U.S. Congress, House, Committee on Foreign Affairs, Subcommittee on Europe and the Middle East, *The Modernization of NATO's Long-Range Theater Nuclear Forces,* 96th Cong. 2d sess., December 31, 1980 (Washington, D.C., Government Printing Office, 1981).

U.S. Congress, House, Committee on Foreign Affairs, Subcommitte on Europe and the Middle East, *NATO After Afghanistan,* 96th Cong., 2d sess., October 27, 1980. (Washington, D.C.: Government Printing Office, 1980).

U.S. Congress, House, Committee on Foreign Affairs, Subcommittee on Europe and the Middle East, *Turkey's Problems and Prospects: Implications for U.S. Interests,* 96th Cong., 2d sess., May 3, 1980 (Washington,.D.C., Government Printing Office, 1980).

U.S. Congress, House, Committee on Foreign Affairs, Subcommittee on Europe and on the Near East and South Asia, *United States–Europe Relations and the 1973 Middle East War,* 93d Cong., 1st and 2d sess., hearings November 1, 1973, and February 19, 1974 (Washington, D.C.: Government Printing Office, 1974).

U.S. Congress, House, Select Committee on Foreign Aid (the Herter Commission), *Final Report on Foreign Aid,* 80th Cong., 2d sess., H. Rept. 1845, May 1, 1948 (Washington, D.C.: Government Printing Office, 1948).

U.S. Congress, Senate, Select Committee to Study Government Operations with Respect to Intelligence Activities. *Supplement, Detailed Staff Reports on Foreign and Military Intelligence,* Book I, 94th Cong. 2d sess. (Washington, D.C.: Government Printing Office, 1976).

U.S. Congress, House, Select Committee on Intelligence, *CIA* (Nottingham, England: Spokesman Books for the Bertrand Russell Peace Foundation, 1977).

U.S. Congress, House, Committee on Ways and Means, Subcommittee on Trade, *Auto Situation: 1980,* 96th Cong., 2d sess., June 6, 1980 (Washington, D.C.: Government Printing Office, 1980).

U.S. Office of Military Government for Germany, *Ownership and Control of the Ruhr Industries,* special report of the military government, November 1948.

U.S. Congress, Senate, Committee on Armed Services, *NATO and the New Soviet Threat,* a report by Senator Sam Nunn and Senator Dewey F. Bartlett, 95th Cong., 1st sess., January 24, 1977 (Washington, D.C.: Government Printing Office, 1977).

U.S. Congress, Senate, Committee on Foreign Relations, *Crisis in the Atlantic Alliance: Origins and Implications,* 97th Cong. 2d sess. March 1982 (Washington, D.C.: Government Printing Office, 1982).

U.S. Congress, Senate, Committee on Foreign Relations, *NATO Today: The Alliance in Evolution,* 97th Cong. 2d sess., April 1982 (Washington, D.C.: Government Printing Office, 1982).

U.S. Congress, Senate, Committee on Foreign Relations, *Nomination of Eugene V. Rostow,* hearings, June 22 and 23, 1981. 97th Cong., 1st sess., (Washington, D.C.: Government Printing Office, 1981).

U.S. Congress, Senate, Special Senate Committee Investigating the National Defense

Program, *Confidential Report on the Preliminary Investigation of Military Govern-ment in the Occupied Areas of Europe,* November 22, 1946.

U.S. Department of Defense, *Report on Allied Contributions to the Common Defense: A Report to the United States Congress by Caspar Weinberger, Secretary of De-fense,* March 1982.

U.S. Library of Congress, Congressional Research Service, *The Mansfield Proposals to Reduce U.S. Troops in Western Europe, 1967–1977,* by Charles R. Gellner (Wash-ington D.C.: Congressional Research Service, June 25, 1980).

U.S. Library of Congress, Congressional Research Service. *NATO Theater Nuclear Forces: Modernization and Arms Control,* by Stanley R. Sloan. (Washington, D.C.: Congressional Research Service, August 4, 1981).

U.S. Department of State Bulletin, Various issues.

U.S. Department of State, *Cartels and Combines in the Occupied Areas. American Policy Concerning German Monopolies,* by Isaiah Frank, and *Dissolution of Ja-pan's Feudal Combines,* by Raymond Vernon and Caroline Wachenheimer (Wash-ington, D.C.: Government Printing Office, 1947).

U.S. Department of State, Foreign Broadcast Information Service.

U.S. Department of State, *Foreign Relations of the United States:* Various volumes, 1945–1950.

U.S. Department of State and the War Department, *Report of the Mission on Japanese Combines, Part I.* Washington, D.C., March 1946.

War Department Pamphlet, *Dissolution of the Nazi Party and Its Affiliated Organiza-tions, Civil Affairs Guide,* vol. 31–110, July 22, 1944.

U.S. War Department, Civil Affairs Division, *U.S. Policy Toward German Cartels* (unapproved draft report, n.d.).

Oral Histories/The Kennedy Library

Dean G. Acheson   Lucius D. Clay
Foy D. Kohler   McGeorge Bundy
Thomas Finletter   William Fulbright
Lord Peter Thorneycroft   Charles E. Bohlen
Couve de Murville

INDEX